War and Gender

Gender roles are nowhere more prominent than in war. Yet contentious debates, and the scattering of scholarship across academic disciplines, have obscured understanding of how gender affects war and vice versa. In this authoritative and lively review of our state of knowledge, Joshua Goldstein assesses the possible explanations for the near-total exclusion of women from combat forces, through history and across cultures. Topics covered include the history of women who did fight and fought well, the complex role of testosterone in men's social behaviors, and the construction of masculinity and femininity in the shadow of war. Goldstein concludes that killing in war does not come naturally for either gender, and that gender norms often shape men, women, and children to the needs of the war system. Illustrated with photographs, drawings, and graphics, and drawing from scholarship spanning six academic disciplines, this book provides a unique study of a fascinating issue.

JOSHUA S. GOLDSTEIN is Professor of International Relations at American University, Washington, DC. He is the author of a broad range of research works on international conflict, cooperation, and political economy, with a central focus on great-power relations and world order.

War and Gender

How Gender Shapes the War System and Vice Versa

Joshua S. Goldstein

CAMBRIDGE UNIVERSITY PRESS

CAMBRIDGE UNIVERSITY PRESS
Cambridge, New York, Melbourne, Madrid, Cape Town, Singapore, São Paulo, Delhi

Cambridge University Press
The Edinburgh Building, Cambridge CB2 8RU, UK

Published in the United States of America by Cambridge University Press, New York

www.cambridge.org
Information on this title: www.cambridge.org/9780521001809

First published 2001
First paperback edition 2003
Second edition 2004
Third printing 2006

A catalogue record for this publication is available from the British Library

ISBN 978-0-521-80716-6 hardback
ISBN 978-0-521-00180-9 paperback

Transferred to digital printing 2009

For my parents
Professor Emerita Dora B. Goldstein, scientist and feminist
Professor Emeritus Avram Goldstein, scientist's scientist

Contents

Figures

Tables

Preface

Recently, I discovered a list of unfinished research projects, which I had made fifteen years ago at the end of graduate school. About ten lines down is "gender and war," with the notation "most interesting of all; will ruin career – wait until tenure." Fortunately, other political scientists in those years – almost all of them women – were not so timid in developing feminist scholarship on war. These pioneers laid the intellectual foundations for this project, and were often kind enough to teach me and encourage my gender interests. I am indebted to Carol Cohn, Francine D'Amico, Jean Bethke Elshtain, Cynthia Enloe, V. Spike Peterson, Simona Sharoni, Christine Sylvester, J. Ann Tickner, and others. (And, fortunately, I did get tenure.)

A second debt I owe to the John D. and Catherine T. MacArthur Foundation, which funded a research leave based on my vague idea of writing an interdisciplinary book about war. When it proved slow a-borning, the foundation staff said simply that they would leave a space on their library's shelf of "MacArthur books." Here it is, only seven years late.

The roots of this project – and a third debt – go back further. I grew up on the Stanford campus, with two molecular biologists for parents. I worked occasionally in my father's lab, and picked up a feeling for the world of natural science. Only in retrospect do I appreciate what an extraordinary privilege it was to grow up inside Stanford when it was still a small town and, for me, an interdisciplinary incubator.

Science and scholarship are never entirely unbiased, since knowledge-production occurs within social and political contexts. Scientists occupy positions in social hierarchies. Arguments serve purposes and reflect political agendas. Personally, I write from a position of privilege and security, as a white, male, North American, tenured social scientist. I have never been in a war or served in the military, though I was born in the shadow of World War II and turned 18 during Vietnam – as a peace activist. My political agenda today is anti-war and pro-feminist, tempered over several decades by an appreciation of the enormous complexity and difficulty of these important changes in human society. All these perspectives, no doubt, affect the character of my book, but I would single out especially that of being a man. Men *should* pay more attention to gender. We learn about ourselves by doing so. I have, at least.

This book summarizes a large and complex body of evidence drawn from different research communities in a variety of academic disciplines. Bringing this material together requires some translation, but I try not to over-translate others' voices, nor to massage the mass of sometimes contradictory material to fit a single theory or dogma. The result is a longer book, but a richer one. I have tried hard to be careful, fair, and above all honest – about where the empirical evidence leads, and about how poorly simplistic models and theories describe our complex world.

The research literatures covered here are growing exponentially. My review, with some exceptions, ends in early 1999, although new and interesting works continue to appear (notably Kurtz ed. 1999 and Bourke 1999). Many others will follow. For updates and discussions, see this book's website, www.warandgender.com.

Exchanging ideas with scholars from other disciplines has been a special pleasure of this project. For their suggestions on a previous draft and on the project, I thank in particular John Archer, Frans de Waal, Mel and Carol Ember, Seymour and Norma Feshbach, Walter Goldschmidt, Jane Goodall, Sir Michael Howard, Paul Kennedy, Melvin Konner, Charles Lawrence, Eleanor Maccoby, Mari Matsuda, Richard Wrangham, and the late Carl Sagan.

In my own discipline I especially thank – in addition to the feminist theorists mentioned earlier – Hayward Alker, Neta Crawford, Randy Forsberg, Peter Haas, Ruth Jacobson, Sarah Johnson, Adam Jones, Stephen Krasner, Nanette Levinson, Jack Levy, Lory Manning, Jane Mansbridge, Craig Murphy, Shoon Murray, Robert North, Jim Rosenau, Bruce Russett, Cathy Schneider, Shibley Telhami, and others. Thanks also to participants in seminars and conversations at Yale, Stanford, Cornell, University of Massachusetts, American University, the University of Maryland, Rutgers, and the Peace Science Society and International Studies Association conferences. For research assistance and support, I thank the incomparable Elizabeth Kittrell, Wendy Hunter, Brook Demmerle, Briana Saunders, Teruo Iwai, Maryanne Yerkes, American University, University of Southern California, University of Massachusetts, Yale, and Harvard. For seeing the potential of this book, I thank my editor at Cambridge University Press, John Haslam. Thanks to Reena Bernards, Cynthia Schrager, Elena Stone, and Allan Lefcowitz for writing help. For long-distance spiritual support during this long, difficult project, I appreciate Joyce Galaski, Ericka Huggins, and Reena Kling. Finally, thanks to Andra, Solomon, and Ruth for companionship and humor.

About the footnotes

The footnotes, grouped by paragraph of text, provide work and page citations for quotes and specific claims, indicated by an identifier word before the page number. A subject word followed by a colon applies to subsequent citations until the next colon. A citation without identifier or subject word refers to a discussion relevant to the paragraph but not to any particular claim or quote in it. Some authors cited for a paragraph may be dissenting arguments from the paragraph's point. Some of the footnotes encapsulate running conversations, which the interested reader can reconstruct from the sequence of page citations given.

About the website

Discussions and updates regarding the topics raised in this book may be found at its site on the World Wide Web, www.warandgender.com. Scholarly resources include a searchable list of the References. Join an interdisciplinary conversation, check for errata (sigh), or read the first chapter.

1 A puzzle: the cross-cultural consistency of gender roles in war

INTRODUCTION

Recently, the roles of women in war have received increased attention in both scholarship and political debate. US moms went off to battle in the 1991 Gulf War, to a global audience. Since then, women have crept slowly closer to combat roles in Western militaries. Meanwhile, women were primary targets of massacres in wars in Rwanda, Burundi, Algeria, Bosnia, southern Mexico, and elsewhere. The systematic use of rape in warfare was defined as a war crime for the first time by the international tribunal for the former Yugoslavia.

Despite this growing attention to *women* in war, however, and a surge of recent scholarship in relevant fields, no comprehensive account has yet emerged on the role of *gender* in war – a topic that includes both men and women but ultimately revolves around men somewhat more than women. This book brings together knowledge from a half dozen academic disciplines to trace the main ways in which gender shapes war and war shapes gender.

The evidence presented here is complex and detailed, forming more of a mosaic than an abstract painting. A single case rarely makes or breaks a hypothesis, but many together often can. Only by assembling large bodies of empirical evidence from multiple disciplines can we assess the meaning of a single event or result in the context of the overall picture. A central challenge to bringing together relevant knowledge about war and gender in this comprehensive way is that the topic spans multiple *levels of analysis*. That is, relevant processes operate in a range of contexts varying in size, scope, and speed – from physiology to individual behavior, social institutions, states, the international system, and global trends. As a result, understanding war and gender requires operating across such disciplines as biochemistry, anthropology, psychology, sociology, political science, and history. One aspect of this challenge is that different research communities use terminology differently. I try to clarify, without over-translating, disciplinary languages.

"Sex" and "gender"   Many scholars use the terms "sex" and "gender" in a way that I find unworkable: "sex" refers to what is biological, and "gender" to what is cultural. We *are* a certain sex but we *learn* or *perform* certain gender roles which are not predetermined or tied rigidly to biological sex. Thus, sex is fixed and based in nature; gender is arbitrary, flexible, and based in culture. This usage helps to detach gender inequalities from any putative inherent or natural basis. The problem, however, is that this sex–gender discourse constructs a false dichotomy between biology and culture, which are in fact highly interdependent.[1]

More concretely, the conception of biology as fixed and culture as flexible is wrong (see pp. 251–52). Biology provides diverse potentials, and cultures limit, select, and channel them. Furthermore, culture directly influences the expression of genes and hence the biology of our bodies. No universal biological essence of "sex" exists, but rather a complex system of potentials that are activated by various internal *and* external influences. I see no useful border separating "sex" and "gender" as conventionally used.

I therefore use "gender" to cover masculine and feminine roles and bodies alike, in all their aspects, including the (biological and cultural) structures, dynamics, roles, and scripts associated with each gender group. I reserve the word "sex" for sexual behaviors (recognizing that there is no precise dividing line here either). However, I retain the term "sexism" which is in common usage, and retain original terms such as "sex role" when quoting.

By *patriarchy* (literally, rule by fathers), I mean social organization based on men's control of power. *Masculinism(ist)* refers to an ideology justifying, promoting, or advocating male dominanation. *Feminism –* my own ideological preference – opposes male superiority, and promotes women's interests and gender equality.

"War"   "War" and the "war system" also need clarification. According to some scholars' definitions of war, it is impossible for small-scale simple societies – such as prehistoric or modern gathering-hunting cultures – to have war. Some military historians argue that only organized, large-scale pitched battles are *real* war. A common definition used in political science counts only wars producing 1,000 battle fatalities. Obviously, only an agricultural, complex society can muster such a large-scale force. Yet many anthropologists (not all) consider warfare to exist in smaller and less complex societies, including gathering-hunting societies. (The term "gathering-hunting" is preferable to the familiar "hunting-gathering"

---

[1] Tuana 1983, 625; James 1997, 214; Oudshoorn 1994; Laqueur 1990, 8.

since gathering typically provides the majority of nutrition in these societies.)

I define war broadly, as *lethal intergroup violence*. If members of a small gathering-hunting society go out in an organized group to kill members of another community, I call that war. Indeed, warfare worldwide in recent years seldom has taken the form of pitched battles between state armies. A very broad definition such as "organized violence" has advantages, and still excludes individual acts of violence that are not socially sanctioned and organized. However, "organized violence" is not quite specific enough, since it would include, for example, the death penalty. The difference is that wars occur between groups (communities, ethnic groups, societies, states). Wars also cross an important threshold by killing people. Not all intergroup violence has this lethal quality. By my definition, some urban gang violence (sustained, territorial, lethal) is a form of war, though on a scale closer to gathering-hunting societies than to modern states.[2]

I define the *war system* as the interrelated ways that societies organize themselves to participate in potential and actual wars. In this perspective, war is less a series of events than a system with continuity through time. This system includes, for example, military spending and attitudes about war, in addition to standing military forces and actual fighting.

In understanding gendered war roles, the *potential* for war matters more than the outbreak of particular wars. As Hobbes put it, war "consisteth not in actuall fighting; but in the known disposition thereto during all the time there is no assurance to the contrary." Kant similarly distinguished between peace as it had been known in modern Europe through the eighteenth century – merely a lull or cease-fire – and what he called "permanent peace." From 1815 to 1914, great-power wars largely disappeared, and some people thought warfare itself was withering away. But when conditions changed, the latent potential for warfare in the great-power system emerged again, with a vengeance, in the twentieth century. Thus, like a patient with cancer in remission, a society that is only temporarily peaceful still lives under the shadow of war.[3]

Plan of the book

Chapter 1 describes a puzzle: despite the diversity of gender and of war separately, gender roles in war are very consistent across all known human societies. Furthermore, virtually all human cultures to date have faced the possibility, and frequently the actual experience, of war (although

[2] Forsberg 1997a, 17; Carneiro 1994, 6; Reyna 1994, 30; Ferguson 1984, 5.
[3] Hobbes in Taylor 1976, 131; Kant 1795; Forsberg 1997b.

Table 1.1 *Summary of hypotheses*

The consistency of gendered war roles across cultures might be explained by:

1. Gender-linked war roles are not in fact cross-culturally consistent
2. Sexist discrimination despite women's historical success as combatants:
   (A) In female combat units
   (B) In mixed-gender units
   (C) As individual women fighters
   (D) As women military leaders
3. Gender differences in anatomy and physiology
   (A) Genetics
   (B) Testosterone levels
   (C) Size and strength
   (D) Brains and cognition
   (E) Female sex hormones
4. Innate gender differences in group dynamics
   (A) Male bonding
   (B) Ability to work in hierarchies
   (C) In-group/out-group psychology
   (D) Childhood gender segregation
5. Cultural construction of tough men and tender women
   (A) Test of manhood as a motivation to fight
   (B) Feminine reinforcement of soldiers' masculinity
   (C) Women's peace activism
6. Men's sexual and economic domination of women
   (A) Male sexuality as a cause of aggression
   (B) Feminization of enemies as symbolic domination
   (C) Dependence on exploiting women's labor

Note: Hypothesis numbers match chapter numbers in this book. Summary assessment of evidence is in Table 7.1 (pp. 404–5).

I do not think this generalization will last far into the future). In every known case, past and present, cultures have met this challenge in a gender-based way, by assembling groups of fighters who were primarily, and usually exclusively, male. The empirical evidence for these generalizations, reviewed in the chapter, shows the scope and depth of the puzzle. The chapter then reviews three strands of feminist theory that offer a variety of possible answers to the puzzle. From these approaches, I extract 20 hypotheses amenable to assessment based on empirical evidence (see Table 1.1). The results fill chapters 2–6. All three feminist approaches turn out to contribute in different ways to understanding the puzzle of gendered war roles.

Chapter 2 considers the numerous historical cases in which women for various reasons participated in military operations including combat. This historical record shows that women are capable of performing successfully in war. Thus, the near-total exclusion of women from combat roles does not seem to be explained by women's inherent lack of ability. This evidence deepens the puzzle of gendered war roles. Many societies have lived by war or perished by war, but very few have mobilized women to fight. Why?

Chapter 3 tests five explanations for the gendering of war based on gender differences in individual biology: (1) men's genes program them for violence; (2) testosterone makes men more aggressive than women; (3) men are bigger and stronger than women; (4) men's brains are adapted for long-distance mobility and for aggression; and (5) women are biologically adapted for caregiving roles that preclude participation in war. Each of these hypotheses except genetics finds *some* support from empirical evidence, but only in terms of average differences between genders, not the categorical divisions that mark gendered war roles.

Chapter 4 explores dynamics within and between groups, drawing on animal behavior and human psychology. Several potential explanations come from this perspective: (1) "male bonding" is important to the conduct of war; (2) men operate better than women in hierarchies, including armies; (3) men see intergroup relations, as between the two sides in a war, differently from women; and (4) childhood gender segregation leads to later segregation in combat forces. The strongest empirical evidence emerges for childhood segregation, but that segregation does not explain the nearly total exclusion of women as combatants.

Chapter 5 discusses how constructions of masculinity motivate soldiers to fight, across a variety of cultures and belief systems. Norms of masculinity contribute to men's exclusive status as warriors, and preparation for war is frequently a central component of masculinity. I explore several aspects: (1) war becomes a "test of manhood," helping overcome men's natural aversion to participating in combat, and cultures mold hardened men suitable for this test by toughening up young boys; (2) masculine war roles depend on feminine roles in the war system, including mothers, wives, and sweethearts; and (3) women actively oppose wars. The last two of these contradict each other, but I argue that even women peace activists can reinforce masculine war roles (by feminizing peace and thus masculinizing war), creating a dilemma for the women's peace movement. Overall, masculinity does contribute to motivating soldiers' participation in war, and might do so less effectively with women present in the ranks.

Chapter 6 asks whether, beyond their identities as tough men who can endure hardship, soldiers are also motivated by less heroic qualities. Misogyny and domination of women, according to some feminists, underlie male soldiers' participation in war (thus explaining women's rare participation as combatants). The chapter explores several diverse possibilities: (1) men's sexual energies play a role in aggression; (2) women symbolize for male soldiers a dominated group and thus cannot be included in the armed ranks of dominators; and (3) women's labor is exploited more in wartime than in peace, so patriarchal societies keep women in civilian positions. Chapter 6 explores both the men's roles in these dynamics, and the corresponding women's roles as prostitutes, victims, war support workers, and replacement labor for men at war.

Chapter 7 concludes that the gendering of war appears to result from a combination of factors, with two main causes finding robust empirical support: (1) small, innate biological gender differences in *average* size, strength, and roughness; and (2) cultural molding of tough, brave men, who feminize enemies in dominating them. The gendering of war thus results from the combination of culturally constructed gender roles with real but modest biological differences. Neither alone would solve the puzzle.

Causality runs both ways between war and gender. Gender roles adapt individuals for war roles, and war roles provide the context within which individuals are socialized into gender roles. For the war system to change fundamentally, or for war to end, might require profound changes in gender relations. But the transformation of gender roles may depend on deep changes in the war system. Multiple pathways of causality and feedback loops are common in biology, acting as stabilizing mechanisms in a dynamic system, and come to the fore at several points in this book. Although I focus mainly on gender's effects on war, the reverse causality proves surprisingly strong. The socialization of children into gender roles helps reproduce the war system. War shadows every gendered relationship, and affects families, couples, and individuals in surprising ways.

The diversity of war and of gender

The cross-cultural consistency of gendered war roles, which this chapter will explore, is set against a backdrop of great diversity of cultural forms of both war and gender roles considered separately.

Apart from war and a few biological necessities (gestation and lactation), gender roles show great diversity across cultures and through history. Human beings have created many forms of marriage, sexuality, and division of labor in household work and child care. Marriage patterns differ widely across cultures. Some societies practice monogamy and some polygamy (and some preach monogamy but practice nonmonogamy). Of the polygamous cultures, most are predominantly polygynous (one man, several wives) but some are predominantly polyandrous (one woman, several husbands). Regarding ownership of property and lines of descent, a majority of societies are patrilocal; women move to their husbands' households. A substantial number are matrilocal, however, with husbands moving to their wives' households. Most societies are patrilineal – tracing descent (and passing property) on the father's side – but more than a few are matrilineal. Norms regarding sexuality also vary greatly across cultures. Some societies are puritanical, others open about sex. Some work hard to enforce fidelity – for example, by condoning killings of adulterers – whereas others accept multiple sexual relationships as normal. Attitudes towards homosexuality also differ across time and place, from relative acceptance to intolerance. Today, some countries officially prohibit discrimination against gay men and lesbians, while other countries officially punish homosexuality with death.

Gender roles also vary across cultures when it comes to household and child care responsibilities. Different societies divide economic work differently by gender (except hunting). Political leadership, while never dominated by women and often dominated by men, shows a range of possibilities in different cultures, from near-exclusion to near-equality for women. Even child care (except pregnancy and nursing) shows considerable variation in the roles assigned to men and women. The areas where gender roles tend to be most constant across societies – political leadership, hunting, and certain coming-of-age rituals – are those most closely connected with war. Thus, overall, gender roles *outside* war vary greatly.

Similarly, forms of war vary greatly, except for their gendered character. Different cultures fight in very different ways. The Aztecs overpowered and captured warriors from neighboring societies, then used them for torture, human sacrifice, and food. A central rack contained over 100,000 skulls of their victims. The Dahomey also warred for captives, but to sell into slavery to European traders. The Yanomamö declare that their wars are about the capture of women. The ancient Chinese states of the warring-states period sought to conquer their neighbors' territories and populations intact in order to augment their own power.

For the Mundurucú of Brazil, the word for enemy referred to any non-Mundurucú group, and war had no apparent instrumental purpose beyond being an "unquestioned part of their way of life." The civil war in Lebanon had "no clear causes, no stable enemy ... The chaos penetrated every aspect of daily life so that everyone participated always."[4]

Some wars more than pay for themselves; others are economic disasters. The economic benefit of cheap oil was arguably greater than the cost of the Gulf War, for Western powers that chipped in to pay for the war. Similarly, the nomadic peoples of the Eurasian steppes who invented warfare on horseback found profit in raiding. But the Vietnam War bankrupted the "Great Society" in the United States, and incessant wars between France and Spain drove both into bankruptcy in 1557. The Thirty Years War so devastated central Europe's economy that the mercenary soldier was described as "a man who had to die so as to have something to live on."[5]

Some wars seem almost symbolic because they absorb great effort but produce few casualties. Among the Dani of New Guinea, formalistic battles across set front lines – fought with spears, sticks, and bow and arrows – lasted from midmorning until nightfall or rain, with a rest period at midday, and with noncombatants watching from the sidelines. A different form of ritualistic war occupied the two superpowers of the Cold War era, whose nuclear weapons were built, deployed, and maintained on alert, but never used. Other wars, such as the Napoleonic Wars, the US Civil War, and the World Wars, were all-too-real spectacles of pain and misery that defy comprehension. A quarter of the Aztecs' central skull rack could be filled by a single day's deaths, 26,000 people, at the battle of Antietam.[6]

Some wars take place far from home, when armies travel on expeditions to distant lands. In the Crusades, European armies pillaged Muslim and Jewish communities for the glory of a Christian God. Later, European armies occupied colonies worldwide. Americans fought in the World Wars "over there" (Europe). Cuban soldiers in the 1980s fought in Angola. For traveling soldiers, home was a long way away, and for their home societies, war was distant. For most European peasants of the sixteenth century, war seldom impinged on daily life except through taxation. Other wars, however, hit extremely close to home. In recent decades, civil wars often

---

[4] Aztecs: Hassig 1988; Keegan 1993, 108–14; Harris 1977, skulls 159; women: Chagnon 1996; Durbin and Bowlby 1939, 114; Chinese: Sun Tzu 1963; Brazil: Murphy 1957, 1025; Lebanon: Cooke 1987, 164.

[5] Howard 1976, mercenary 37.

[6] Dani: Ember and Ember 1990, 406; cf. Maring: Harris 1974, 64; Civil: Keegan and Holmes 1985, 141–43.

have put civilians and everyday life right in the firing line. The World Wars made entire societies into war machines and therefore into targets. In such cases the "home front" and the "war front" become intimately connected.

Sometimes soldiers kill enemies that they have never met, who look different from them and speak languages they do not understand. The Incas of Peru assumed the incomprehensible Spanish invaders to be gods. By contrast, in some wars neighbors kill neighbors, as in the 1992 Serbian campaign of terror in Bosnia. Soldiers sometimes kill at great distances, as with over-the-horizon air and ship missiles. At other times, they kill at close quarters, as with bayonets. Some, like the soldiers who planted land mines in Cambodia and Angola in the 1980s, have no idea whom they killed. Others, such as snipers in any war, can see exactly whom they kill.

Combatants react in many different ways. Many soldiers in battle lose the ability to function, because of psychological trauma. But some soldiers feel energized in battle, and some look back to their military service as the best time of their lives. They found meaning, community, and the thrill of surviving danger. In many societies, veterans of battle receive special status and privilege afterwards. Sometimes, however, returning soldiers are treated as pariahs. Some soldiers fight with dogged determination, and willingly die and kill when they could have run away. In other cases, entire armies simply crumble because they lack a will to fight, as happened to the well-armed government forces in Africa's third largest country, Zaire (Democratic Congo), in 1997.

The puzzle   War, then, is a tremendously diverse enterprise, operating in many contexts with many purposes, rules, and meanings. Gender norms outside war show similar diversity. The puzzle, which this chapter fleshes out and the remaining chapters try to answer, is why this diversity disappears when it comes to the *connection* of war with gender. That connection is more stable, across cultures and through time, than are either gender roles outside of war or the forms and frequency of war itself.

The answer in a nutshell is that killing in war does not come naturally for either gender, yet the potential for war has been universal in human societies. To help overcome soldiers' reluctance to fight, cultures develop gender roles that equate "manhood" with toughness under fire. Across cultures and through time, the selection of men as potential combatants (and of women for feminine war support roles) has helped shape the war system. In turn, the pervasiveness of war in history has influenced gender profoundly – especially gender norms in child-rearing.

> **Hypothesis 1.** Gender-linked war roles are not in fact cross-culturally consistent.

The cross-cultural consistency of gendered war roles could be explained by various hypotheses, but the first task is to establish whether this consistency actually exists, and if so how strong it is. Is it contradicted by supposed counter-examples, such as ancient Amazons or matriarchal gathering-hunting societies? Universal generalizations often silence the voices of those whose experiences do not fit. To seek out those voices, to look at the outliers, can reveal important information. Thus, I tried to track down any report of a human society in which gender roles in war were significantly equalized or reversed, or where war was absent altogether (and therefore gender-linked war roles could not exist). Very few held up under scrutiny.

A. THE UNIVERSAL GENDERING OF WAR

In war, the fighters are usually all male. Exceptions to this rule are numerous and quite informative (see pp. 59–127), but these exceptions together amount to far fewer than 1 percent of all warriors in history. As interesting as that fragment of the picture may be – and it is – the uniformity of gender in war-fighters is still striking.[7]

Within this uniformity, some diversity occurs. For one thing, women's war roles vary considerably from culture to culture, including roles as support troops, psychological war-boosters, peacemakers, and so forth. Although men's war roles show less cross-cultural diversity, societies do construct norms of masculinity around war in a variety of ways (see pp. 251–380). Nonetheless, these variations occur within a uniform pattern that links men with war-fighting in every society that fights wars.

In the present interstate system, the gendering of war is stark. About 23 million soldiers serve in today's uniformed standing armies, of whom about 97 percent are male (somewhat over 500,000 are women). In only six of the world's nearly 200 states do women make up more than 5 percent of the armed forces. And most of these women in military forces worldwide occupy traditional women's roles such as typists and nurses (see pp. 83–87; 102–5). Designated *combat* forces in the world's state armies today include several million soldiers (the exact number depending on definitions of combat), of whom 99.9 percent are male. In 1993, 168 women belonged to the ground combat units of Canada, Netherlands, Denmark, and Norway combined, with none in Russia, Britain,

---

[7] Ehrenreich 1997a, 125; Tiger 1969, 104; Van Creveld 1993, 5.

Germany, France, and Israel. Change since 1993, although not trivial, has been incremental. In UN peacekeeping forces, women (mostly nurses) made up less than 0.1 percent in 1957–89 and still less than 2 percent when UN peacekeeping peaked in the early 1990s.[8]

These data reflect a time period in which women had reached their highest social and political power to date, and in which the world's predominant military force (the United States) was carrying out the largest-scale military gender integration in history (see pp. 93–105). Despite these momentous changes, combat forces today almost totally exclude women, and the entire global military system has so few women and such limited roles for them as to make many of its most important settings all-male.

Did these rigid gender divisions in today's state military forces occur in other times and places, or are they by-products of specific contexts and processes embodied in today's states? I will show, in this section, that war is gendered across virtually all human societies and therefore did not "acquire" gender, so to speak, as a result of state formation, capitalism, Western civilization, or other such influences.

Myths of Amazon matriarchies

The strongest evidence against universalizing today's gender divisions in war would be to show counter-examples from other times and places, especially female armies (Amazons). What would happen if an entire army were organized primarily using women? How would a society fare if its fighters were mostly, or entirely, female? We do not know, because no evidence shows that anyone has ever tried it. Ancient historians reported that Amazons had once existed, but no longer did. A few modern historians agreed, but despite much effort, no hard evidence has emerged showing that anything close to the mythical Amazon society ever existed.[9]

The Amazons of Greek myth not only participated in fighting and controlled politics, but exclusively made up both the population and the fighting force. They supposedly lived in the area north of the Black Sea about 700 years before the fifth century BC when the historian Herodotus reports hearing stories about them. According to myth, the Amazons were an all-female society of fierce warriors who got pregnant by neighboring societies' men and then practiced male infanticide (or sent male babies away). Supposedly they cut off one breast to make shooting a bow and arrow easier, although most artistic renditions do not show this. (The

---

[8] United Nations Women 1995; Segal and Segal 1993; Presidential Commission 1993, ground C31.
[9] Eller 2000; few: Anderson 1967, 75; De Pauw 1998, 43–48; Kanter 1926, 32; Boulding 1992/I, 218–19; Alpern 1998, 7.

Figure 1.1 Battle of Greeks and Amazons (sarcophagus). [Alinari/Art Resource, NY.]

word "Amazon" is no longer thought to derive from "without breast" although the word may have some connection with breasts.) Amazons are an important theme in Greek art, and – in various forms – in subsequent cultural currents throughout history. Greek, Hellenistic, and Roman art incorporated battles with Amazons on a regular basis (see Figure 1.1), including a scene engraved on the west side of the Parthenon.

The mythical Amazons had their capital in Themiscyra, and were ruled by a series of queens. The Greek hero Heracles, as one of a series of quests, had to capture the sacred girdle of the Amazon queen, Antiope. His army defeated the Amazons and captured the queen's sister, Hippolyta, whom the Athenian king Theseus married. Later, the Amazons retaliated by attacking Athens with a large army, possibly including allied Scythians (who also lived north of the Black Sea). The months-long battle caused high casualties on both sides, but ultimately the Greeks prevailed. In some accounts, the Amazons also fought against the Greeks in the Trojan War. Some ancient manuscripts added a verse to *The Iliad* saying that the Amazons under Queen Penthesilea arrived to support the Trojans.[10]

Herodotus reports that after the Greek victory at Themiscyra, the Greeks took three ships full of captured Amazons back towards Athens, but the Amazons overpowered the Greeks and (not knowing navigation)

---

[10] Seymour 1965, Trojan 628.

drifted ashore in Scythian territory. Finding some wild horses inland, they began riding off in search of loot and found themselves battling the Scythians, who were amazed to find afterwards that the Amazons had been women. The Scythians then courted the Amazons, to produce children by such amazing women. (As fellow hunters and plunderers the Scythians were a good match for the Amazons.) This interbreeding succeeded, but the Amazons refused to settle down (relatively speaking) with the Scythians, where women "stay at home in their wagons occupied with feminine tasks" (Herodotus). Instead they invited their new husbands to go off with them to a new place, and that is how the Sauromatian people are supposed to have originated. For Herodotus, this account explained why Sauromatian women go "riding to the hunt on horseback sometimes with, sometimes without their menfolk, taking part in war, and wearing the same sort of clothes as men" and why they "have a marriage law which forbids a girl to marry until she has killed an enemy in battle."[11]

The stories Herodotus heard about the Sauromatians may have been exaggerated, but some archaeological evidence from the early Iron Age indicates that nomadic women in the region of the Eurasian steppes – especially near modern-day northern Kazakhstan – rode horses, may have used weapons, and may even have had some degree of political influence, though probably not dominance, in their society. Jeannine Davis-Kimball recently reported that excavations at a Sauromatian site (fourth century BC to second century AD) near the Russia–Kazakhstan border "suggest that Greek tales of Amazon warriors may have had some basis in fact." Actually, as Davis-Kimball notes, archaeologists in the 1950s had already discovered "that many graves of females contained swords, spears, daggers, arrowheads, and armor" in fourth-century BC graves of nomads in southern Ukraine. These sites would have been much closer to the supposed Amazons that fascinated the Greeks (though still to the east of them). Davis-Kimball's site is 1,000 miles to the east, so her Sauromatians "cannot have been the same people" as the Amazons.[12]

In Davis-Kimball's sites, seven graves of females were found with "iron swords or daggers, bronze arrowheads, and whetstones to sharpen the weapons, suggesting that these seven females were warriors." One young girl's bowed legs "attest to a life on horseback" and "she wore a bronze arrowhead in a leather pouch around her neck." Another woman's body contained a bent arrowhead, "suggesting that she had been killed in battle." (I would note that women killed in war might not be combatants.) Since females generally "were buried with a wider variety and larger quantity of artifacts than males," Davis-Kimball concludes that "females ...

[11] In Kleinbaum 1983, 7–8.
[12] Davis-Kimball 1997, suggest 45, armor 8, same 48.

seem to have controlled much of the wealth." This seems doubtful, however. Using a variety of objects hardly implies control of wealth.[13]

Despite the hype about Amazons, Davis-Kimball never suggests that women were the main warriors in this society, but merely that they may have taken to arms to defend their relatives and animals when attacked. Indeed, 40 of the 44 males buried at the site appeared to be warriors, while four males appeared to be other than warriors. But only seven females may have been warriors compared to 28 female graves containing "artifacts typically associated with femininity and domesticity," and five females who may have been priestesses (graves with altars and ritual objects). If these graves represent a fair sample, something like 90 percent of the men, but only 15–20 percent of the women, took part in war. It is an important case since these percentages of women participation are high, but it is not a case of the majority of women being warriors, or the majority of warriors being women, by far. Furthermore, women buried with horses and spears may indicate that some women fought, at least at times, but does not show that women predominated either in military or political life. The fact that Amazons have not been dug up does not *disprove* their existence, of course. But absent any real empirical evidence of a matriarchal society of women warriors, the burden of proof is on showing it did exist, not that it could never have existed.[14]

The puzzling question of horses   The nomadic equestrian warriors of the steppes helped shape warfare along its historical lines. Horses later provided the decisive military advantage in various historical contexts including ancient Eurasian civilizations, the rise of West African kingdoms, and the conquest of the New World. "[T]he most important new weapon of the Bronze Age, the war chariot," appeared in Mesopotamia after 3000 BC and a thousand years later in Egypt. After 2000 BC "the horse-drawn, spoked, war chariot was the elite striking arm of ancient armies." Domesticated horses quickly spread through the Middle East and Europe. The horses were "not ridden but harnessed to chariots." The invention of the composite bow made of wood, gut, and bone – which could reach 250 yards – made the war chariot a powerful weapon. But chariots remained "extremely expensive to establish and maintain" owing to "complex logistics" of horse-breeding, chariot-building, metal smiths, support teams, and riders. The chariot was thus available only to rich kingdoms – suitable for a "heroic mode" of fighting by kings, or by high-priced mercenary charioteers. It was typically used

---

[13] Davis-Kimball 1997, 47–48; Kleinbaum 1983, 8.
[14] Hype: Wilford 1997a; Perlman 1997; Sawyer 1997; Davis-Kimball 1997, artifacts 47; Taylor 1996, 199–205; Fraser 1989, furthermore 18–19.

Figure 1.2 Ramses on war chariot, *c.* 1285 BC. [© Thames & Hudson Ltd, London. From *The Origins of War* by Arther Ferrill, published by Thames & Hudson Inc, New York.]

at the critical moment of a battle, to break enemy infantry ranks, and then for "turning defeat to rout."[15]

Women ride horses as well as men do. This is clear from the Olympic Games' gender integration of equestrian events, in contrast to the other events. The Iron Age steppes women warriors and the mythical Amazons share the element of raiding on horseback. If women participated in war in ancient nomadic steppe societies, they were in some sense present at the creation of civilizational war, yet they disappeared from cavalry as larger-scale military units formed and empires arose. This seems puzzling. For example, Ramses II in his war chariot at the thirteenth-century BC battle of Kadesh (Figure 1.2) cuts a rather femme figure by today's norms of manly warriorhood. Yet his army was equal to the best in its time, and successfully expanded Egypt's territorial borders. The successful deployment of such a chariot would seem to depend on (1) skill in controlling the horse and (2) accuracy, more than sheer strength, in shooting arrows. It is hard to see why all women would be unqualified in such skills. Given the limited number of war chariots (an expensive item), an empire would presumably succeed best by allocating chariots to the very best, most skilled individuals regardless of gender. Down through

[15] Keegan 1993, 136; Barfield 1994; Diamond 1997, 74–77, 91, 164, 358; Sanday 1981, 146; Ferrill 1985, most–arm 40; Watkins 1989, heroic 28, rout 31.

Figure 1.3 South American Amazon cannibals, from Hulsius, *Voyages*. [Rare Books Division, New York Public Library; Astor, Lenox, and Tilden Foundations.]

history, one might have expected cavalry to be a point of entry for women into fighting forces, but this did not occur. The question of horses is an intriguing but unanswered aspect of the puzzle of gendered war roles.

South American Amazons   As with ancient Greece, little evidence exists for Amazons in South America, although European explorers believed that such societies existed (see Figure 1.3). Friar Gaspar de Carvajal in 1542 claimed to have witnessed and participated in fighting with women warriors (leading the men), at one point on the Orellana expedition down the Amazon river. Contemporary skeptics in Europe called Carvajal's account either a fabrication or a fever-induced mirage.[16]

Spanish conquerors in the northern Andes and eastern Venezuela alluded frequently to women who accompanied warriors and sometimes also fought. These reports, however, reflect an uncertain mix of actual observations, inferences based on native women's transvestitism, and local legends passed along. Reports of women fighters rest on Ecuador, Colombia, Venezuela, and the Inca culture. Unfortunately, all these cases

[16] Henderson and Henderson 1978, mirage xiii.

come from Spanish conquerors' centuries-old accounts of cultures they conquered (cultures the Spaniards wanted to portray as barbaric), and are thus hard to evaluate. In any event, except for Carvajal's account, these reports claimed only that women participated in fighting, not that they were the main fighters.[17]

Some specific claims about South American Amazons are easy to refute. For example, the *Encyclopedia of Amazons* states: "The anthropologists Yolanda and Robert Murphy found that even today Brazilian tribal women live apart from men 'in convivial sisterhood.' Their authority exceeds that of men in all practical matters." What Murphy and Murphy actually describe is a highly sexist society in which women's sisterhood arises from their common terrorization by the men. "The superior status of the male is manifest in the rituals of everyday life." Women until menopause "sit in the rear, walk in the rear of a file, and eat after the men do." Women who are considered sexually "loose" are punished by gang rape by twenty or more men, as are women who peek at the men's sacred musical instruments. "[T]he men consciously state that they use the penis to dominate their women."[18]

Purposes of Amazon myths   The Greek Amazons – always imagined as somewhere outside the civilizing sphere of Greek conquest – represented a symbolic place for Greek heroes to subdue the barbarians on their periphery. So did the South American Amazons for Spain. Similarly, Virgil marked the establishment of the Roman empire with a story about the defeat of the Italian man-killing warrior Camilla, of great beauty and nearly supernatural power. These mythical women warrior societies represent a foreign, topsy-turvy world. Representing women in this way reinforced men's construction of their own patriarchal societies as orderly and natural.[19]

Although some feminists embrace Amazon myths, the various representations of Amazons through history have carried a mixed message because men use those myths to reinforce their own masculinity. Abby Kleinbaum writes: "As surely as no spider's web was built for the glorification of flies, the Amazon idea was not designed to enhance women." For example, Katharine Hepburn's first major role, as Antiope in the 1931 Broadway play *The Warrior's Husband* (see Figure 1.4), was remembered by reviewers as the play in which she "first bared her lovely legs." Television's "Xena: Warrior Princess" is sometimes invoked as a

---

[17] Steward and Faron 1959, 190, 209, 223, 245; Dransart 1987, 62, 65; Shoumatoff 1986, 13, 36, 44.

[18] Salmonson 1991, 96–97; Murphy and Murphy 1985, 130–33.

[19] Fraser 1989, 19–22; Enloe 1983, 117–18; Kleinbaum 1983; Kanter 1926; Bennett 1967; DuBois 1982; Tyrrell 1984; Salmonson 1991; Wilford 1997a; Alpern 1998, 8; Macdonald 1987a, 8; Macdonald 1987b; Kirk 1987; Dransart 1987.

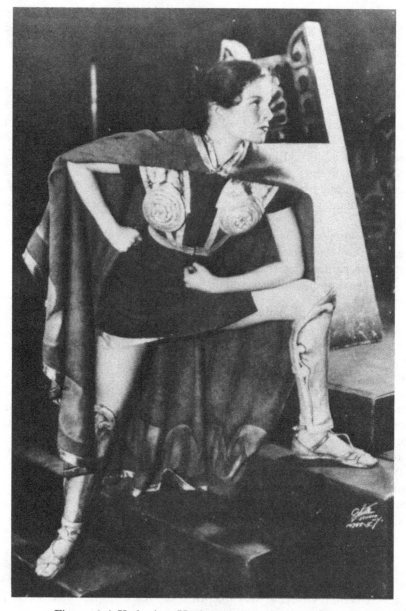

Figure 1.4 Katherine Hepburn as Antiope in *The Warrior's Husband*, 1932. [Billy Rose Theatre Collection, the New York Public Library for the Performing Arts; Astor, Lenox and Tilden Foundations. Photograph: White Studio.]

pro-feminist symbol of power – Madeleine Albright jokingly called her "one of my role models" in 1998 – but also contains an anti-feminist undertow. A male interviewer of Xena actress Lucy Lawless (who describes herself as "a woman's woman") writes, "As Xena, the tall, strong, athletic beauty with gloriously blue eyes is togged out in boots, a leather miniskirt and metal breastplates that do her breathtaking body no harm at all." This mix of sex-object and power figure recurs in the Amazon genre.[20]

Most recently, the gunslinging British digital-character "Lara Croft" on Sony's Playstation continues this ambiguous tradition. Of the 25,000 World Wide Web sites that mention Croft (as of 1999), over half also contained the term "nude." Croft's corporate spokesperson said, "A lot of people who play video games fantasize about her. She's not overtly sexual. OK, she is physically sexual, but she has a personality." The design of Croft's cyberbody, like the costumes worn by actresses such as Hepburn and Lawless with their bare legs and accentuated breasts, seems geared more to male viewers than feminists.[21]

In summary, Amazons provide interesting material for the analysis of culture and myth in sexist societies, but little historical evidence for the participation of women in war. As far as available evidence goes, no society exclusively populated or controlled by women, nor one in which women were the primary fighters, has ever existed.

Gendered war roles in preindustrial societies

In present-day gathering-hunting and agrarian societies, it is common to have special gender taboos regarding weapons, and special cultural practices focused on men's roles as warriors. In many gathering-hunting cultures, gender roles in war connect with gender roles in hunting. Sometimes war and hunting are the only two spheres of social life that exclude women, or the two spheres where that exclusion is most formalized. Taboos govern whether, and if so when and how, women may touch weapons used in hunting as well as those for war.[22]

The gendering of war is similar across war-prone and more peaceful societies, as well as across very sexist and relatively gender-equal societies. Consider two societies that occupy extreme positions regarding both war and gender equality – the Sambia of New Guinea and the inhabitants of Vanatinai island in the South Pacific.

---

[20] Kleinbaum 1983, flies 1, 202, 206–7; *Washington Post*, August 3, 1998, Albright D3; Brady 1997.
[21] www.tombraider.com; Alta Vista search engine, June 23, 1999; Goodfellow 1998; personality: in Barboza 1998.
[22] Lee 1979, 388.

The Sambia are among the most warlike cultures ever studied, and also among the most sexist. Women are not only disenfranchised and subject to abuse, but villages are laid out with different paths for men and women. Male Sambia warriors are taken from their mothers at 7 to 10 years old to be trained and raised in a rigid all-male environment. Younger boys sexually "service" older ones, eventually reversing roles as they grow into warriors. This homosexual phase is supposed to build masculinity in the warrior. After marrying, these young men adopt heterosexuality but treat their wives very harshly. Sambia society is marked by extreme male dominance and the suppression of the feminine in the male's world. Not surprisingly, warfare among the Sambia is strictly a male occupation. Nor are the Sambia exceptional in this regard. Of the most warlike societies known, none requires women to participate in combat, and in all of them cultural concepts of masculinity motivate men to fight.[23]

Vanatinai island, by contrast, is one of the most gender-egalitarian societies ever studied. In this culture, men and women are virtually equal in power and move fluidly across gendered roles. One exception to this gender equality (mentioned late in a newspaper article that declared the "sexes equal" on Vanatinai) was that "[i]n earlier times, warfare was the one important activity reserved exclusively for men." Although long pacified by colonial rule, the culture still retains this asymmetry: when a 6-year-old girl joined some boys in throwing mock spears, her mother "came out of the house . . . and said, irritably, 'Are you a man that you throw spears?' The girl burst into tears and ran into the house." So although gender relations on Vanatinai are radically different from those among the Sambia, one commonality is war-fighting – a male occupation.[24]

The pattern of Vanatinai repeats in five other relatively peaceful and gender-equal societies – the Semai of Malaya, the Siriono of Bolivia, the Mbuti of central Africa, the !Kung of southern Africa, and the Copper Eskimo of Canada. All are gatherer-hunters and the first two also engage in some slash-and-burn agriculture. All have in common "open and basically egalitarian decision making and social control processes." Long-term material inequality between individuals cannot exist because these societies "produce little or no surplus." In these five societies, relative gender egalitarianism prevails in most areas of life (compared with agricultural and industrial societies). Both genders (and sometimes children) participate in food gathering in four of the five societies (!Kung food gathering is mainly a female occupation). Both genders likewise participate in fishing (the Semai), and in horticulture (in both slash-and-burn societies). In some instances only females perform "domestic" tasks

[23] Herdt 1987; Herdt 1981, 209; Huyghe 1986, 35; none: Goldschmidt 1989.
[24] Lepowsky 1993; Wilford 1994.

(the Eskimo). Among the Semai, women engage in basket weaving, carrying water, and harvesting rice, but both genders cook. Among the Mbuti, both genders help with camp tasks from age 6 and with net hunting from age 9. The gender division in child-rearing is unclear, except among the Siriono, where women are the primary caretakers but both parents spend a lot of time playing with their children. This appears to be true of the !Kung as well, among whom gender participation in child-rearing is relatively egalitarian. This gender equality largely disappears, however, in war. (Gender division also characterizes specialized hunting.) Among the Semai, Siriono, and !Kung, only males hunt, although !Kung women help locate prey. Among the Mbuti, only males hunt with bows and arrows, although both genders, and children, hunt with nets. Among the Eskimo, males and some younger women hunt. Among the Siriono, from age 8 boys accompany their fathers in hunting, and girls help with household work.[25]

Thus, among contemporary preindustrial societies, both the very war-prone and the relatively peaceful ones share a gender division in war with men as the primary (and usually exclusive) fighters. This commonality contrasts with the diversity of these societies' gender divisions outside war.

Cases of female participation in combat

In several cases, women have participated in combat more than occasionally, although still as a minority in a mostly male army. This is the level of participation found in Davis-Kimball's excavations of early Iron Age Eurasian steppes sites discussed earlier. In recorded history, however, these cases turn out to be extremely rare. The two documented historical cases of substantial organized female participation in combat by state armies are the Dahomey Kingdom of West Africa in the eighteenth and nineteenth centuries and the Soviet Union in World War II. In Chapter 2, I describe these unusual cases, and the many cases where a few women are scattered individually among combatants.

Only in the Dahomey Kingdom did substantial female combat participation last for longer than a short crisis period. Women made up one wing of the standing army, the so-called "Amazon corps," and sometimes constituted as many as a third of all soldiers. They lived in the palace, followed special rules, and were excellent soldiers whose presence substantially increased the kingdom's military power. Dahomey is an important case since it shows the possibility of an effective, permanent, standing women's combat unit making up a substantial minority of the army. However, it is the only case of its kind, and the context is very

[25] Fabbro 1978, open 138, surplus 138; Ross 1993b, 38; Shostak, 1981, !Kung 239-46.

unusual. Society revolved around war totally. The economy was based on conquering neighboring peoples to sell as slaves to European traders (who, in turn, completed the cycle by selling guns and other military supplies to Dahomey). The kingdom lasted from 1670 to 1892, coinciding with the slave-trading era.

In the Soviet Union during World War II – absolutely desperate times – women were mobilized into combat units but on a smaller and shorter-term basis than for Dahomey. At the peak of this effort, reportedly, some 800,000 soldiers or about 8 percent of the total Soviet forces were women. Most were medical workers but a few thousand were combatants. A problem with this case is sorting out how many of the available accounts were war propaganda – cheering on a devastated society with the glorious exploits of women fighters, who symbolized the mobilization of the whole population for the war effort (and shamed men into fighting harder). Overall, the evidence indicates that the women fought about as well as the men – both were to some extent just "cannon fodder" in a war of attrition and starvation. Nonetheless, as soon as circumstances permitted, the women's units were disbanded, and the Red Army returned to all-male combat units. Even if official estimates do not exaggerate, the women combatants at their peak would have made up fewer than 1 percent of Soviet combat forces.

War consumed Soviet society during World War II as it did the Dahomey Kingdom and the early Iron Age steppes societies discussed earlier. In all these cases, warfare reached an extreme level and overshadowed the productive economy (agriculture, industry, etc.). However, even at similar extremes of desperation, most societies (such as Germany and Japan at the end of World War II) still have not mobilized women in large numbers as fighters. Thus, history and prehistory contain only a handful of known cases in which women have participated in combat in substantial numbers.

B. THE UNIVERSAL POTENTIAL FOR WAR

These consistent gender roles *in* war apply to all societies because of the pervasiveness *of* war across cultures. Evidence in this section will show that in virtually every human culture, war exists in some form, as an ever-present potential that is realized at least occasionally (and in many cultures, incessantly). The universal potential for war in human society suggests that the gendering of war may matter even in relatively peaceful times and places, because even a society that is not at war may someday go to war.

The near-universality of the potential for war applies, certainly, to the present-day interstate system. Except for a few small states (notably Costa

Rica and Mauritius), all of today's nearly 200 states have standing armies. The large states of the world maintain massive military machines, and periodically engage in war. In today's world, active warfare is not occurring in most places, but war lurks in the background as a possibility even when it is remote. In several dozen places around the world, active wars are continuing (though fewer and smaller than a decade ago).

The myth of peaceful origins

Marxist (and other) scholarship has long portrayed both sexism and war as products of a certain stage in human history – that of private property and the state system following the invention of agriculture over 10,000 years ago. Originally, it is claimed, humans lived in matriarchal societies (women held political power) which did not have war. Evidence comes from the supposedly peaceful and gender-equal character of modern-day gathering-hunting societies. Thus, both patriarchy and war are products of economic class relations which changed with the rise of the state, in this view.

Marx's collaborator Friedrich Engels links the beginning of war to the rise of the state – and thus the end of war to the anticipated post-state era of communism. Engels argues that societies before the invention of agriculture were matriarchies and that when, with agriculture, private property came into being, gender relations were transformed and men seized power. The rise of the state and the beginning of war were products of that same transformation. Gender and war are here linked, but only indirectly, both being effects of the transformation of economic class relations after property came into being. The solution to war, therefore, is to move beyond private property to a classless society, by means of a revolution against the current phase of private property, namely capitalism.[26]

Several decades ago, the evidence seemed to imply that early humans were peaceful and egalitarian. Modern gatherer-hunters were reputedly peaceful, and the fossil record contained no compelling evidence of war. Thus, war appeared to be characteristic of a phase in human history, a mere 1 percent of the time we have been around as a species (and thus decoupled from any biological basis). In the event of a future transformation of the state system, or of the class divisions first sparked by agriculture (which made surplus possible), war itself might end as abruptly as it began. The end of war would be *natural* since we would need only to fall back on our deep human nature – 3 million years of peaceful prehistory – to rediscover ourselves as creatures of peace. The idea that human beings

[26] Engels 1884.

are naturally peaceful and war is an aberration makes this story appealing. (A related myth held that humans are the only animal that kills its own species, again showing social violence as a deviation from nature. In fact, however, over a hundred other species kill their own kind.)[27]

Thus, this perspective urges us to fall back on our true selves, go back to nature, change oppressive class relations, and/or do away with the state system, in order to achieve real peace. Incidentally, gender relations are not very important in this story. (Many Marxists see class relations as more important than gender relations.)[28]

Present-day gathering-hunting societies

The story does not hold up, however. The evidence from modern-day gathering-hunting societies, whose supposed peaceful nature was assumed to reflect peaceful human origins, in fact shows the opposite: modern gathering-hunting societies are *not* generally peaceful. Of 31 gathering-hunting societies surveyed in one study, 20 typically had warfare more than once every two years, and only three had "no or rare warfare." I will get to those "rare" cases, but the point for now is that if typical gathering-hunting societies found today represent the typical societies found before the rise of the state – as advocates of peaceful origins have claimed – then those original societies were warlike.[29]

In theory, the absence of war altogether among gatherer-hunters is not essential for the idea of peaceful human origins. As a fall-back position, one could argue that gathering-hunting societies were *relatively* more peaceful than the chiefdom and state societies which followed. Even that argument, however, fails in light of empirical evidence. According to cross-cultural anthropological studies, nonstate societies have as much warfare as states do. Furthermore, overall per capita levels of violence (i.e., among individuals) may actually be higher in simpler gathering-hunting societies than in complex agrarian or industrialized societies, although this is hard to measure.[30]

Clearly, cross-cultural anthropological data do not support the idea that humans started out more peaceful in simple societies and became more warlike in complex societies, culminating in modern states.

---

[27] Species: Lorenz 1963; Itani 1982, 361, 367; Eibl-Eibesfeldt 1979, 231; Shaw and Wong 1989, 7; Van Der Dennen and Falger eds. 1990, 14.

[28] Leacock 1981; 1982; Casey and Tobach 1991; Casey 1991, 17–18; Dyer 1985, 5–11, 5; Eisler 1987; De Pauw 1998, 26–33, 14; Benderly 1987, 69.

[29] Ember 1978, rare 444; Eibl-Eibesfeldt 1974; Knauft 1991, 418; Van Der Dennen 1990b, 257–69; Kelly 2000; Robarchek 1990.

[30] Ember and Ember 1994, 189–91; Meggitt 1977, 201; Cohen 1986; measure: Knauft 1987; Lee 1979, 398–99; Keeley 1996, 29–30.

Admittedly, the evidence is not conclusive regarding human origins, because generalizations about today's gathering-hunting societies – most of which have been altered in both subtle and obvious ways by contact with the industrialized world – may not tell us much about the gathering-hunting societies that existed before the invention of agriculture. Usually, by the time the first anthropologists arrived on a scene the culture was far from "pristine." Even if the society itself had no regular contact with European colonizers, the process of colonization had often pushed it into a fraction of its former territory and severely reduced its population, as appears to have happened with some Canadian Eskimo peoples. In the case of Australian desert Aborigines, metal knives and tools had filtered in from surrounding areas that had contact with Europeans long before any white person arrived to meet or observe the Aborigines. In these contexts, it is quite plausible that depopulation and territorial contraction could have caused an upswing in conflict and war due to resource scarcity. Alternatively, the encroachments of Western colonizers could have caused a warlike society to cut off warring, and band together for survival. Furthermore, as colonizers actually overran and took control of local cultures, they often engaged in "pacification" of local conflicts.[31]

The point is that a society in the midst of such a radical transformation may not reflect the nature of early human societies. Consider one prominent example of this problem. The extremely warlike Yanomamö Indians of Brazil and Venezuela were studied intensively by anthropologist Napoleon Chagnon, who wrote them up as "the Fierce People." Among the Yanomamö, all female babies are killed until the first son is born. This creates a shortage of women for wives, and competition for this scarce resource is a major object of wars. The Yanomamö say their wars have the purpose of capturing women, although some anthropologists propose other underlying reasons. Non-anthropologists often refer to the Yanomamö when discussing gathering-hunting societies, or even call them "pristine." In fact, however, decades before anthropologists first arrived, the Yanomamö had already acquired steel tools (machetes, metal cooking pots, and axes) from the outside, allowing more efficient production of bananas and plantains, as well as axe fights. Thus, "pristine is *passé*." Overall, however, colonial effects mainly suppress war and thus do not explain the presence of war in simple societies.[32]

[31] Eibl-Eibesfeldt 1974, Canadian 136; Keeley 1996, Australian 30; Ember and Ember, 1997, pacification 4–5; Ferguson 1997, 331; Ferguson and Whitehead eds. 1992; Ferguson 1990, 51–54; Harding 1986, 96; Knauft 1993.

[32] Yanomamö: Chagnon 1996; Chagnon 1967; Chagnon 1990; Harris 1984; M. Harris 1989, 311; Walton 1981; Keegan 1993, 104, pristine 94; Harris 1977, steel 67–78; Chagnon 1992, machetes 110, 105–9; passé: Reyna and Downs 1994, xiii; suppress: Ember and Ember, 1997, 4–5.

Hundreds of cultures, both preagricultural and agrarian, are documented in the Human Resources Area Files (HRAF) – "the only worldwide, systematic collection of information concerning societies." Anthropologists Melvin and Carol Ember, who run HRAF, analyze a sample of 90 societies. They note that "we cannot compare societies with and without war" because "the vast majority . . . had at least occasional wars when they were first described, unless they had been pacified." The Embers find only eight societies where wars occur less frequently than once in ten years on average. Over half of the 90 societies were in a constant state of war or readiness for war, and half of the remaining cases fought every year during a particular season. They conclude that "war is almost ubiquitous in the ethnographic record, *in the absence of external powers that imposed pacification*, and the frequency distribution is skewed sharply toward the high end."[33]

Prehistoric evidence   In theory, the best evidence about whether humans were peaceful before the invention of agriculture would be the direct record of those times as studied by archaeologists and paleontologists. This record is very spotty, however, and not compelling for either war or peace. To summarize, the evidence is consistent with (but not proof of) the presence of warfare at least sporadically throughout all periods of prehistory. It is doubtful that war followed along after (and hence possibly as a result of) the Neolithic Revolution (the beginning of agriculture, herding, and proto-urban settlements about 10,000 years ago), since strong evidence points to war's presence early in the Neolithic era. It is even possible that war played a central role in *creating* the Neolithic Revolution. A new and growing, though still limited, body of tangible evidence – ranging from discernible fortifications around settlements to remnants of weapons and the residue of injuries on bodies – suggests the presence of war before agriculture. One paleontologist writes that only after many years of excavating "skeletons with embedded projectile points" did he question his "acceptance of the traditional view that the native peoples of California had been exceptionally peaceful."[34]

The rise of states   No one disputes that war played a central role in the rise of states and civilizations after the Neolithic Revolution. In 12,000 to 8000 BC "there was a revolution in weapons technology . . . Four staggeringly powerful new weapons make their

---

[33] Reyna and Downs 1994, only xvii; Ember and Ember 1994, compare 188–89; Ember and Ember, 1997, ubiquitous 5.
[34] Martin and Frayer eds. 1997; Keeley 1996, skeletons viii, 65–69, 174, 32–35, 89, 110; Leakey and Lewin 1992.

first appearance...: the bow, the sling, the dagger... and the mace, [and] ... produced true warfare." The bow and arrow were inexpensive and reached 100 yards versus 50 for spears, and an individual could carry more arrows than spears. It "spread rapidly around the Mediterranean. Neolithic cave paintings clearly reveal their use against men as well as animals." The sling had double the range of the bow and arrow (200 yards), and was also extensively used in Neolithic times. Along with the new weapons came the invention of military tactics, especially the organization of soldiers in columns and lines. With these changes in the offensive power of armies, the fortification of settlements began, which then spread around the eastern Mediterranean from 8000 to 4000 BC. Jericho – one of the earliest fortified sites with 13-foot-high stone walls and a tower – may have started as a hunting site (around an oasis), with the walls coming next as defense against armed enemies (thereby committing the inhabitants to a sedentary life), and agriculture following. Evidence from the earliest historical societies shows warfare well ensconced. War played a central role in the rise of the early Middle Eastern civilizations, and was already strongly gendered.[35]

To summarize in reverse chronological order, war played a central role in the rise of the first states and civilizations (and thereafter). It may have driven rather than resulted from the Neolithic Revolution. Evidence indicates war in the period just before the start of recorded history. Although the earlier prehistoric period does not provide adequate evidence for or against the presence of war, we do know that those societies had both the social organization and the weapons necessary for organized intergroup violence. War may plausibly have played a role in the rapid expansion of modern humans starting 150,000 years ago, which led to the extinction of other early humans including the Neanderthals – although we have no hard evidence of this. We cannot say whether early humans, dating back several million years, engaged in lethal intergroup violence, but at least one other primate species (chimpanzees) does so in its natural habitats (see pp. 187–88). Finally, present-day gathering-hunting societies worldwide virtually all have war, and violence in these simple societies appears to be at least as prevalent as in agrarian and industrialized societies.

Thus, the myth of peaceful origins finds no empirical support. Again, this does not mean that any group of people at a particular time and place are forced to have war. It does mean that war, like gender, has deep roots. It is not overlaid on our "true" selves, but runs deep in us.

[35] Ferrill 1985, 18–19, 38–44; Watkins 1989, 16, 22; O'Connell 1995; Ghiglieri 1999, 161.

Specific peaceful societies

Even if humans did not experience a peaceful phase, *individual* peaceful societies might still exist at various times in history, or at present. Again, by peaceful society I mean one where war is truly absent rather than merely latent. However, there appear to be virtually no such peaceful societies. Some societies are far more (or less) warlike than others, in terms of the frequency of war, its effect on mortality rates, and its place in the culture. But these are all differences of degree. In virtually no society is war unknown.

Several present-day societies in which war is relatively infrequent have been described as "peaceful" by various writers. One favorite is the !Kung San (the "!" indicates a clicking sound). They are southwest African bush people who were widely studied in the 1950s and 1960s by English-speaking anthropologists. They were observed to behave very peacefully, and with relative egalitarianism and gender equality – "the harmless people" as one observer called them. They seemed to enjoy abundant resources relative to their population, and to go to war rarely. However, "[f]ierce competition and warfare characterized much of San relations with their Bantu-speaking neighbors prior to the arrival of the Dutch in South Africa in 1652." The Dutch carried out a "near-total extermination" of 200,000 San (bush people) in nearby South Africa.[36]

A hundred years ago, German-speaking anthropologists described the !Kung as very warlike, with frequent raids and battles. A 1916 report states that the !Kung warred frequently with neighboring peoples until the European colonialists arrived, only then becoming more peaceful. The report recounts a !Kung raid early in the century: "Women frantically seized their children and tried to flee, but were slaughtered without compunction. Here a mother nearly managed to escape with her baby, but . . . a few blows with a kiri smashed the child's skull and finished off the mother too. Only a few lucky ones managed to get away . . . The victors . . . started looting. Everything useful was taken away. Clay pots were smashed and the huts set on fire."[37]

If this is a peaceful society, perhaps Bosnia in 1992 would fit that category as well! Indeed, Bosnian society – somewhat parallel to !Kung society – was considered by some observers to be an exemplary case of peaceful, tolerant intergroup relations (interrupted several times in history by the incursion of great-power wars into the region). In the Tito era, many Bosnian marriages were between the "ethnic" (actually

[36] Thomas 1959 harmless; M. Harris 1989, 288, 302; Shostak 1981, fierce–near 345; Lee 1979, 32.
[37] Eibl-Eibesfeldt 1979, 171, from Wilhelm 1953, 155, from Weule 1916.

religious) groups – a far cry from the "ancient ethnic hatreds" to which
the Bosnia war was sometimes attributed. Yet that tolerant society fell victim to extreme hatred and brutality. Like Bosnia, the case of the !Kung
shows how a superficial peace can disguise the latent potential for war.[38]

After the war-prone !Kung of the 1920s became the harmless !Kung
of the 1960s, the pendulum swung back again in the 1970s and 1980s,
when the !Kung became caught up in warfare in Namibia and Angola.
Also around that time, many of the !Kung switched from hunting and
gathering to larger sedentary settlements engaged in agriculture and wage
work. There was a new wave of violence among the !Kung in this period,
triggered by their rapidly changing conditions. Within communities, "the
!Kung do fight and not infrequently with fatal results . . . [H]omicide is not
rare."[39]

Despite the evidence that the !Kung were not peaceful, and that most
of the gathering-hunting societies studied by ethnographers have known
war, many scholars outside anthropology continue to get the story wrong.
The fine *historian* John Keegan, for instance, writes: "Ethnographers
who have devoted themselves to the study of some still-existent groups
are champions of the view that hunting-gathering is compatible with an
admirably pacific social code, and that the former may indeed foster
the latter. The San (Bushmen) . . . are commonly held up as models of
unassertive gentleness."[40]

Another reputedly peaceful case is that of the Semai of Malaysia. The
ethnographer of the Semai portrays the Semai as "nonviolent" – referring
to "the horror that physical violence inspires in Semai." They almost
never hit their children or each other, and they "are not great warriors . . .
[T]hey have consistently fled rather than fight." But he continues:

Many people who knew the Semai insisted that such an unwarlike people could
never make good soldiers. Interestingly enough, they were wrong. Communist
terrorists had killed the kinsmen of some of the Semai counterinsurgency troops.
Taken out of their nonviolent society and ordered to kill, they seem to have been
swept up in a sort of insanity which they call "blood drunkenness."

After the episode, the Semai were "unable to account for their behavior"
and "shut the experience off in a separate compartment." They returned
to their gentle, nonviolent lives.[41]

Marvin Harris's "favorite list" of "peoples who are reported never to
wage war" consists of the Andaman Islanders, the Shoshoni and Mission

---

[38] Malcolm 1994.
[39] Thomas 1959, 10–11; Lee 1979, rare 370; Eibl-Eibesfeldt 1979, 88, 153–61.
[40] Keegan 1993, 120.
[41] Dentan 1979, 58, compartment 59; Keegan 1993, 120; Wrangham and Peterson 1996,
81; Wilson 1978, 100.

Indians (California), Yahgan (Patagonia), the Semai, and "the recently contacted Tasaday of the Philippines." Several of these, however, "consist of refugees who have been driven into remote areas by more warlike neighbors." Thus, "most of the evidence no longer supports" the view that "organized intergroup homicide" was absent in Stone Age cultures.[42]

Ashley Montagu in the 1970s used the Tasaday case to argue that aggression is not innate or instinctual in humans. The Stone Age Tasaday, he says, are "closest to our prehistoric ancestors" of any people, and they are "undoubtedly among the gentlest and most unaggressive people on this earth.... From infancy the Tasaday has learned to be cooperative and unaggressive." This shows, according to Montagu, not only that individuals can learn to control aggression but that an entire society can never learn to behave aggressively in the first place.[43]

The Tasaday, however, turned out not to be a Stone Age culture representing our innocent human past. After Ferdinand Marcos lost power in the Philippines, anthropologists could get more information than when a Marcos crony controlled access to the Tasaday, and the whole thing was declared by some to be a hoax. The American Anthropological Association launched a review in 1989, and sponsored a volume assessing the evidence. Although controversy continues, most anthropologists think that the Tasaday exist as a distinct people but one that resembles other peoples of the region and was formerly agricultural. Montagu's prime example of the non-necessity of aggression, therefore, turns out to be a false report.[44]

Other reports of peaceful societies also reveal, upon examination, a latent tendency for war. For example, the Gilbert Islands appear to be quite peaceful. Yet war played an important role in Gilbertese culture before colonization and pacification by the British (at the point of a gun, after which the "peaceful" society emerged). The Gilbertese origin myth says that long ago the Gilbertese *were* a peaceful society that did not know how to make war. But then came fierce warriors from Samoa to make war on them (which included eating the losers). One of the Samoan warriors thought he was being treated unfairly by the Samoan war leadership (he was not getting high-prestige body parts to eat). So he defected and taught the Gilbertese how to make war. They went on their own warring expedition, defeated the Samoans, and received their present-day islands as a home where they settled down.[45]

[42] Harris 1977, 47.
[43] Montagu 1976, 182–83.
[44] Sun 1989; Headland ed. 1992.
[45] Grimble 1953; 1972, 251–53.

The Gilbertese origin myth is reminiscent of Rianne Eisler's argument about Bronze Age Minoan civilization on the island of Crete. Like the Gilbertese of myth, the goddess-worshiping Minoans were supposedly peaceful until conquered by warlike neighbors (the mainland Greeks). Eisler argues that on Crete "there are no signs of war." (Eisler claims the Minoan double-sided axes, sometimes used today as feminist symbols, are not battle-axes but agricultural tools.) Notably, the elaborate Minoan palaces did not include fortifications, in contrast to those on the mainland. But did the Minoans not know war? The evidence suggests otherwise. They had weapons and "probably...fought sea battles." An island with a strong fleet perhaps does not need to fortify its palaces. In the middle of the second millennium BC the Minoans dominated the Aegean area. Greek legends tell of mainland cities paying over tribute to the legendary King Minos (seven lads and seven maidens to feed the Minotaur on Crete; at least they were gender-balanced in that regard). Even for a rich trading island-state, to dominate neighbors and exact tribute means using war. The written language of the Minoans of this period has not been deciphered so we have a hard time knowing the actual role of war in the culture.[46]

Other prehistoric "peaceful societies" reinforce the lesson of latent wars as well. On Easter Island, Polynesian culture apparently flourished for centuries without (much?) war, then fell into disastrous "endemic warfare." Mayan society, which flourished more than a thousand years ago, was thought until recently to exemplify a peaceful society. Recent archaeological discoveries, however – especially the deciphering of the language – indicate that the Mayans were very warlike, especially in their last decades when they may have driven their civilization into rapid decline through devastating wars. "[W]ar was already a part of Maya life at the beginning of their written history, some 2,000 years ago." The Mardudjara Aborigines of the Australian desert have been called a peaceful society, but that society does fight wars, with shields, clubs, spears, and boomerangs. Granted, its wars are highly ritualistic and did not actually kill anyone while the anthropologists were watching.[47]

The Copper Eskimo are one of those few societies that rarely make war, according to the cross-cultural surveys mentioned earlier. However, they "experienced a high level of feuding and homicide before the Royal Canadian Mounted Police suppressed it," and they carried out at

---

[46] Eisler 1987, signs 31, axes 36, battles 35–36; Boulding 1992/I, 214–17.
[47] Easter: Keegan 1993, 24–28; Maya: Keeley 1996, ix; Demarest 1993, 111; Schele 1991, 6; Aborigines: Keeley 1996, 30; Tonkinson 1978, 32, 118–19.

least one massacre of Indians with whom they were trading. An early observer of the Copper Eskimo wrote: "They at first with us carried their knives ... in readiness for immediate use; but notwithstanding the dread of our firearms may have kept them quiet, I am inclined to think they are an inoffensive race" – not a ringing endorsement of peacefulness. Other studies of Copper Eskimo society do not mention either an especially peaceful or warlike tendency. A similar situation seems to prevail among the Eskimos of eastern Greenland, who do not seem to fight wars. A 1937 report refers to an "attitude of suspicion and slander" between groups, but actual behavior of hospitality towards both enemies and friends. However, "murder is of frequent occurrence."[48]

Another *relatively* peaceful society, the Mbuti, has known plenty of war in the last few centuries, facing successive invasions by non-Mbuti tribes, the explorer Stanley, slave traders, villagers encroaching on the Mbuti's forest, and Belgian colonizers. (They are currently again in a war zone in northeastern Democratic Congo.) The Mbuti live in dense forest and apparently do not fight back much, preferring to run and hide. However, when caught between warring tribes of villagers invading the forest in the past, the Mbuti sided with one or another of them. In territorial disputes between groups, the culture includes the "possibility of a resort to fighting with wooden clubs," although this was not observed by the ethnographer.[49]

Regarding the Shoshone, one group was "sufficiently isolated in the deserts to have escaped the warfare to the east. They had no regalia and no interest in war. And when hostile war parties happened to enter their country they simply ran away to the mountains." But another Shoshone group "were sufficiently exposed to raiding parties ... and sufficiently in contact with warring Shoshoni and Ute to have acquired some interest in warfare ... [and] have war regalia."[50]

Actual peaceful societies   Despite these cases where peaceful societies turn out to hold the latent potential for war, a handful of exceptions – in all the world and all history – qualify as truly peaceful societies (i.e., cultures where war is absent). These cases are why I say "virtually all" rather than "all" societies know war. These societies all exist at the fringes of ecological viability, in circumstances where small communities

---

[48] Keeley 1996, feuding 29; Jean Briggs, personal communication 2000; Jenness 1970, knives 235; Stefansson 1921; McGhee 1972; Condon *et al.* 1996; Thalbitzer 1941; Mirsky 1937, slander 62, frequent 70.

[49] Mosko 1987; Turnbull 1983, 20, 22; Turnbull 1961, 245, 275; Turnbull 1965, clubs 220; Schebesta 1933, 214.

[50] Steward 1938, 176, 179.

are scattered in a harsh environment with little contact with each other. These cases demonstrate the extremes to which one must go to find a society where war is absent.[51]

The Eskimos of western Greenland present such a case. They lived in small communities, distant from each other, on a sheet of ice at the edge of a frigid sea. Many of the men of what might elsewhere be "warrior age" died while hunting in treacherous conditions. To make war on a neighboring group would have required several days' arduous journey just to get there, and would have brought no tangible benefits. The territory could not be used and a larger territorial unit could not be administered. Stealing women would have been worthless (in a material sense) since population was limited by scarce resources. Nor did groups compete over those resources, being so spread out. Standing wealth was restricted to a few tools and shelters which each group already had. Thus, in these extreme conditions, war did not occur. Peace in this case certainly resulted from the environment and not the culture itself. These Eskimos were fully capable of lethal violence against individuals. And even a remote, harsh environment does not preclude war, as shown by the warlike Eskimos in Alaska where conditions resembled Greenland.[52]

The Semang use bows for hunting, but do not know about shields or armor, so the bow probably is not used as a weapon. Semang culture makes a few references to past times of fighting with neighboring tribes, but relations with neighbors are now "fairly amicable," and ethnographies do not refer to war. The diminutive Semang (who average less than 5 feet in height) appear to be a refugee people, driven into inaccessible "least favored corners" of the Malayan islands where they live a "poor and insecure" life.[53]

The Xinguano of Brazil are another rare example of a society with "no tradition of violence." They "do not conform to the profile of the typical peaceful society," particularly because tribes in the Xingu basin are not isolated from each other but interact closely. However, the entire basin is "geographically isolated" and apparently long "served as a refuge for peoples menaced by more aggressive tribes."[54]

One survey of 50 societies finds four – the Copper Eskimo, Dorobo, Tikopia, and Toda – that did not have military organizations or warfare. The common factor was their isolation from their neighbors.

---

[51] Fringes: Gregor 1990, 107; Eibl-Eibesfeldt 1979, 162.

[52] Mirsky 1937; Nuttall 1992; Thalbitzer 1941; Jean Briggs, personal communication 2001.

[53] Schebesta 1973, 197, past 216; Evans 1937, amicable 39; Skeat and Blagden 1906; Lisitzky 1956, insecure 33–34.

[54] Gregor 1990, 106–7.

Nonetheless, "individuals from all four groups did fight and kill outsiders when the occasion demanded."[55]

Thus, the potential for war is universal in human society, except for a handful of cases in which unusual circumstances make war impractical. The actual practice of war is not necessary or preordained. The frequency of war varies greatly. War is more important in some cultures than others. Nonetheless, war *exists* in virtually all cultures, and the potential for war can suddenly come to the fore even in a relatively peaceful society. This generalization applies across cultures, across today's national states, and throughout history and, arguably, prehistory. This finding extends the scope of gendered war roles to virtually all societies.

C. FEMINIST THEORIES OF WAR AND PEACE

Given the strength and scope of gendered war roles, what possible explanations might solve the puzzle of their consistency? I explore 20 possible answers, drawn primarily from feminist theories of war and peace. Feminist theorists disagree in basic ways about how gender relates to war, but they have long treated the question as important. Many of their male colleagues do not seem to share this interest, however.

Seeing gender

In North American political science and history, male war scholars' interest in the puzzle of gendered war roles has been minimal. The topic has not attracted the funding or publications among male scholars as, for example, the similarly intriguing regularity known as the "democratic peace" (democracies rarely fight each other). *Feminist* political scientists and historians – nearly all women – pay attention to gender in war, but others relegate gender to the dark margins beyond their (various) theoretical frameworks for studying war. Feminist literatures about war and peace of the last 15 years have made little impact as yet on the discussions and empirical research taking place in the predominantly male mainstream of political science or military history. This omission is measurable by counting the number of headings and subheadings in a book's index on topics relating to gender. The typical political science and history books about war – the "big" books about war's origins and history – score zero.[56]

---

[55] Otterbein 1989, 20–21; Wrangham and Peterson 1996, demanded 81; Keeley 1996, 30.

[56] [Number of index entries for women, men, female, male, feminine, feminist, masculine, gender, sex, rape, or prostitution – total is zero unless listed after year.] Historians: Howard 1976; Tuchman 1984; Ferrill 1985; Van Creveld 1985; Keegan and Holmes

Doyle's recent and comprehensive survey of scholarship on war and peace contains six gender-related index entries but devotes only about one-tenth of 1 percent of its space to gender. All the gender references concern women; men still do not have gender. Similarly, when gender occasionally shows up in other mainstream war studies, it does so gratuitously, as a passing note – something that could be interesting, but plays no substantive role in *any* of the main competing theories about war. (This pattern is less true in recent years than previously, however, and less true in Britain and Australia than in the United States. Men there are more often both subjects and authors in gender studies.)[57]

By contrast, anthropology – in North America and since decades ago – gives serious attention to gender-related subjects in studying war. Margaret Mead's conclusion in the first major anthropological symposium on war (1967) called for paying "particular attention . . . to the need of young males to validate their strength and courage, and to . . . the conspicuous unwillingness of most human societies to arm women." Anthropological thinking that connects war and gender is not limited to one ideological perspective, nor just to female scholars. Also, anthropology engages gender even though women are poorly represented among anthropologists studying war. Similarly, independent scholars outside of anthropology, political science, or history – such as Gwynne Dyer (a man) and Barbara Ehrenreich – have engaged both the mainstream war studies literatures and feminist theories of gender in war. And in 1929, sociologist Maurice Davie devoted two whole chapters of his book on war to gender.[58]

The gender blinders in mainstream war studies carry over to the foreign policy establishment. For example, a recent mainstream foreign policy book about "contending paradigms in international relations" – which

1985; Kennedy 1987; Keegan 1993; Kagan 1995; political scientists: Aron 1954; Waltz 1959 (1); Waltz 1979; Beer 1981 (1); Levy 1983; Keohane ed. 1986; Goldstein 1988; North 1990; Vasquez 1993; Brown 1994; Porter 1994 (2); Doyle 1997 (6); Vasquez ed. 2000; cf. anthropologists: Fried, Harris, and Murphy eds. 1967 (2); Nettleship, Givens, and Nettleship eds. 1975; Ferguson ed. 1984 (4); Foster and Rubinstein eds. 1986 (13); Turner and Pitt eds. 1989; Haas ed. 1990 (8); Ferguson and Whitehead eds. 1992 (2); Reyna and Downs eds. 1994; other disciplines: Keeley 1996 (2); Dyer 1985 (2); Ehrenreich 1997a (31).

[57] Doyle 1997; Van Creveld 1991, 222; Waltz 1959, 46; Beer 1981, 172; Porter 1994, 177–78; Katzenstein ed. 1996, 16, 47; Keohane ed. 1986; Rotberg and Rabb eds. 1988; Doyle and Ikenberry eds. 1997; Holsti 1985.

[58] Foster and Rubinstein 1986, xii; Mead 1967a, 1967b; Fried, Harris, and Murphy eds. 1967; Nettleship, Givens, and Nettleship eds. 1975; Ferguson ed. 1984; Foster and Rubinstein eds. 1986; Rubinstein and Foster eds. 1988; Turner and Pitt eds. 1989; Haas ed. 1990; Ferguson and Whitehead eds. 1992; M. Harris 1989; Harris 1974, 83–107; Divale and Harris 1976; Casey 1991; Mead 1967b, 236; Di Leonardo ed. 1991; Shaw and Wong 1989, 181–82; Dyer 1985, 122–25; Ehrenreich 1997a, 125; Ehrenreich 1997b; Davie 1929, 23–45, 96–102.

Table 1.2 *Author's gender and attention to gender in 45 postmodern international relations chapters*

	Includes gender	Omits gender
Author is . . .		
Male	1	31
Female	9	4

$p < .001$ by Fisher's Exact Test (see Blalock 1972, 287). Included chapters are those of Beer and Hariman eds. 1996, MacMillan and Linklater eds. 1995, and Shapiro and Alker eds. 1996.

sounds promising for the inclusion of gender – lacks any reference to gender in its 19 chapters, all written by men. The influential monthly *Foreign Affairs* did not carry a single article about gender issues in 1990–96. In 1998, an article on gender appeared, written by a man and arguing that biological gender differences make women more peaceful, so the "feminization of world politics" over the last century (since the suffrage movement) has created today's "democratic zone of peace." *Foreign Affairs* treated the article as a novelty, retitling it "What if Women Ran the World?" on the cover and illustrating it with bizarre century-old cartoons and photos of women in poses dominating men (e.g., with boxing gloves).[59]

The gender blinders also extend to male postmodern international relations scholars. Each of several recent edited volumes in postmodern international relations contains a requisite chapter about gender, written by a woman, and typically no mention of gender at all in the chapters written by men. In fact, the author's gender is a highly significant predictor of whether the chapter includes or omits gender (see Table 1.2). Thus, even in postmodern international relations, gender is ghettoized.[60]

Feminist scholarship on war   Given so many men's low interest level, most political science studies of gender roles in war come from a feminist perspective and most are written by women. In the International Studies Association, women scholars are seven times more likely than men to belong to the gender studies section, and this disparity is

[59] Foreign Affairs 1997, paradigms; Steuernagel and Quinn 1986, 6; Hunt 1997; Fukuyama 1998, 34–40; Ehrenreich *et al.* 1999.
[60] Whitworth 1994b, 50–55; Beer and Hariman eds. 1996; MacMillan and Linklater eds. 1995; Krause 1995; O'Brien and Parsons 1995; Shapiro and Alker eds. 1996; Pettman 1996b; Patton 1996; Sánchez-Eppler 1996; Ferguson 1996.

Table 1.3 *Major works of feminist political science scholarship on war, 1982–98*

Judith Hicks Stiehm, ed. *Women and Men's Wars.* [1982 journal issue] 1983.
Cynthia Enloe. *Does Khaki Become You? The Militarization of Women's Lives.* 1983.
Betty Reardon. *Sexism and the War System.* 1985.
Birgit Brock-Utne. *Educating for Peace: A Feminist Perspective.* 1985.
Jean Bethke Elshtain. *Women and War.* 1987.
Ruth Roach Pierson, ed. *Women and Peace: Theoretical, Historical and Practical Perspectives.* 1987.
Cynthia Enloe. *Bananas, Beaches and Bases: Making Feminist Sense of International Politics.* 1989.
Judith Hicks Stiehm. *Arms and the Enlisted Woman.* 1989.
Adrienne Harris and Ynestra King, eds. *Rocking the Ship of State: Toward a Feminist Peace Politics.* 1989.
Birgit Brock-Utne. *Feminist Perspective on Peace and Peace Education.* 1989.
Sara Ruddick. *Maternal Thinking: Towards a Politics of Peace.* 1989.
Jean Bethke Elshtain and Sheila Tobias, eds. *Women, Militarism, and War: Essays in History, Politics, and Social Theory.* 1990.
Rebecca Grant and Kathleen Newland, eds. *Gender and International Relations.* [1989 journal issue] 1991.
V. Spike Peterson, ed. *Gendered States: Feminist (Re) Visions of International Relations Theory.* 1992.
Ann Tickner. *Gender in International Relations: Feminist Perspectives on Achieving Global Security.* 1992.
Cynthia Enloe. *The Morning After: Sexual Politics at the End of the Cold War.* 1993.
V. Spike Peterson and Anne Sisson Runyan. *Global Gender Issues: Dilemma in World Politics.* 1993.
Betty Reardon. *Women and Peace: Feminist Visions of Global Security.* 1993.
Christine Sylvester. *Feminist Theory and International Relations in a Postmodern Era.* 1994.
Sandra Whitworth. *Feminism and International Relations.* 1994.
Peter Beckman and Francine D'Amico, eds. *Women, Gender, and World Politics.* 1994.
Francine D'Amico and Peter Beckman, eds. *Women in World Politics.* 1995.
Jan Pettman. *Worlding Women: A Feminist International Politics.* 1996.
Judith Hicks Stiehm, ed. *It's Our Military, Too!* 1996.
Jill Steans. *Gender and International Relations: An Introduction.* 1998.
Lois Ann Lorentzen and Jennifer Turpin, eds. *The Women and War Reader.* 1998.

greater at the leadership level, even though the section welcomes men and has done organized outreach to them. The authors and editors of 25 international relations books that address war and peace from explicitly feminist perspectives consist of 21 women and one man (see Table 1.3). Nearly all the individual contributors to the edited volumes on this list are also female. Of course, many women scholars are not feminists, and a *few* male scholars do study gender. Yet, as Ann Tickner puts it, "there is something about this field [international relations] that renders it particularly inhospitable and unattractive to women." Many recent signs suggest change in the discipline, and gender articles now appear occasionally in mainstream journals, but gender is still segregated conceptually from the subjects that most scholars of war study.[61]

Feminist scholarship on war, building on a long tradition, has grown rapidly since the late 1980s. As in other fields, feminist research often tries to bring out the role of gender, and of women, in social relationships. In doing so, however, feminist theorists follow several schools of thought, with different and sometimes incompatible assumptions and analyses about war. I will try – within the limits of this cursory review – to give a sense of how feminist theorists of different schools think about war and peace.

Strands of feminist theory   "The feminist theory" of war does not exist. Rather, a number of feminist arguments provide sometimes contradictory explanations and prescriptions. Feminist political theorist Jean Elshtain describes a "polyphonic chorus of female voices...At the moment [1987], feminists are not only at war with war but with one another." This chorus is not simple to categorize, and to cover a range of approaches I will need to oversimplify.[62]

Most feminist approaches share a belief that gender matters in understanding war. They also share a concern with changing "masculinism" in both scholarship and political-military practice, where masculinism is defined as an ideology justifying male domination. They see women as a disadvantaged class, unjustly dominated and exploited by men. (According to 1981 data, women worldwide are half the population and a third of the paid labor force. They work two-thirds of the hours, but receive only a tenth of the income and own a hundredth of the property.)[63]

Beyond these points of agreement, different feminist schools diverge. Various authors describe feminist theories in terms of three perspectives or schools of thought. (Similar categorizations of theories into three schools have been applied to economics, history, and international relations.) I sort feminist theories of war into three main strands, though most feminists combine elements of these approaches in various ways. They explain gendered war roles in different ways.[64]

[61] ISA headquarters, personal communication, June 13, 1997; Sylvester 1994; Pettman 1996a; Peterson 1997b; Alexandre 1989; Grant and Newland 1991; Sylvester ed. 1993; Murphy 1996; Stiehm 1982; Steans 1998; Steuernagel and Quinn 1986; Elshtain 1985; Tickner 1991, something 28; Whitworth 1994a, ix–1; Meyer and Prügl eds. 1999; Kelson and Hall 1998; Kelson 1999; cf. Ehrenreich 1997b, 21; signs: Keohane 1989; Tickner 1997; Keohane 1998; Marchand 1998; Tickner 1998; Murphy 1998, 93.
[62] Elshtain 1987, 232–33; Flax 1990, 188; Cock 1991, 188.
[63] Masculinism: Brittan 1989, 4; data: Tickner 1992, 75.
[64] Harding 1986; Sylvester 1994; Whitworth 1994a, 11–23; Whitworth 1994b, 75–86;

Liberal feminism: sexist discrimination – women can be capable warriors.

Difference feminism: deep-rooted and partly biological gender differences.

Postmodern feminism: arbitrary cultural constructions favoring those men in power.

These strands roughly organize my hypotheses and thus my presentation of empirical evidence. Chapter 2 tests liberal feminism against the record of women's participation in combat. Chapters 3 and 4 test difference feminism against evidence from biology and psychology. Chapters 5 and (in part) 6 test theories about the construction of gendered war roles, against historical and cross-cultural evidence.

Liberal feminism

Liberal feminists argue that women equal men in ability, and that the gendering of war reflects male discrimination against women (i.e., sexism). Liberal feminism often frames gender inequalities in terms of a classical liberal emphasis on individual rights. Women have the right to participate in all social and political roles (including war roles) without facing discrimination. The exclusion of women from positions of power in international relations both is unfair to women *and* prevents half the population from making its best contribution to the society. Liberal feminists do not believe women's inclusion would fundamentally change the international system, nor a given country's foreign policy, nor war itself. Liberal feminist scholars often include women as subjects of study – women state leaders, women soldiers, and other women operating outside the traditional gender roles in international relations. This strand of work pays homage to women who succeeded in nontraditional positions, despite the obstacles they faced in a sexist society.

Liberal feminism does not treat war very differently from other aspects of social life in which men dominate the high-paying, advantaged roles. Soldiering as a job holds potential for future high-paying political and military leadership positions. Ten US Presidents were generals, and combat experience helped others such as George Bush and John Kennedy to win election. From a liberal feminist perspective, women's exclusion as soldiers resembles their exclusion through history as doctors, lawyers, politicians, and other high-status professionals. Calls for the inclusion of

Burguieres 1990, 3, 9; Goldstein 2001, 124–39; variants: Carroll and Hall 1993; Pettman 1994; Jaggar 1983; economics: Ward 1979; history: Nelson and Olin 1979; international: Doyle 1997; Viotti and Kauppi eds. 1999; Goldstein 2001, 8–9.

Figure 1.5 US Army nurses arrive in Britain, 1944. [US National Archives, NWDNS-111-SC-192605-S.]

women and the end of gender discrimination are not radical challenges to the status quo, according to liberal feminists.[65]

Liberal feminists argue that women have performed well when, under military necessity, they have been allowed to participate in military operations – such as the WACs shown in Figure 1.5 – but have faced persistent discrimination, including dismissal from such positions once a war ends. When the US military shifted from conscription to an all-volunteer force, after Vietnam, it became expedient to integrate more women into the military, especially since social pressures for women's equality were rising and since the military itself was shifting towards more support troops relative to "combat" troops. Starting in the late 1970s, liberal US feminists supported extension of the military draft to include women: "Liberal feminists . . . [argue that] the best way to insure women's equal treatment with men is to render them equally vulnerable with men to the political will of the state." Liberal feminists reject the idea that women are any more peaceful than men by nature. Eleanor Smeal, as President

[65] Boulding 1992/I, 23; Huntington 1957, political 157–58; Tobias 1990, 164, 181–82; Addis, Russo, and Sebesta eds. 1994; Lorber 1994, 3; Howes and Stevenson eds. 1993; Schneider and Schneider 1991; Stiehm 1989; Stiehm ed. 1983; Isaksson ed. 1988.

of the National Organization for Women, once declared that "Peace is not a feminist issue."[66]

US helicopter pilot Rhonda Cornum, who was captured by Iraq in the Gulf War, exemplifies liberal arguments regarding women soldiers. She writes that while housed in a parking garage in Saudi Arabia, "my being female seemed to make no difference to most people," and she was aghast at the idea of separating the ten women there from their units to live together. The lack of privacy "didn't seem to bother anyone." "Being a girl just didn't matter."

I think women are just like men; women who are motivated to be in the military have the same range of reasons as men. In terms of performance, there's also that same range. I think some women will be terrific, some will be brainless, and the vast majority will simply do their job and do it well... [W]omen behave the same when they are captured as men do.[67]

Feminist critiques of liberal feminism   The major criticism of liberal feminism from other feminists has been that it "ask[s] women to exchange major aspects of their gender identity for the masculine version – without prescribing a similar 'degendering' project for men." By integrating into existing power structures including military forces and the war system without changing them, women merely prop up a male-dominated world instead of transforming it.[68]

Difference feminism

Difference feminists believe that women's experiences are fundamentally different from men's. In this view, the problem is not that men and women are different but that sexist cultures devalue "feminine" qualities instead of valuing, celebrating, and promoting them. Regarding war, difference feminists argue that women, because of their greater experience with nurturing and human relations, are generally more effective than men in conflict resolution and group decision-making, and less effective than men in combat. Some difference feminists see such gender differences as biologically based, whereas others see them as entirely cultural, but they agree that gender differences are real, and not all bad.

Variants and related approaches to difference feminism include "standpoint feminism" (women's experiences provide a shared perspective or

---

[66] Stiehm 1981; Stiehm 1988; Enloe 1983; Weinstein and White 1997; Jones 1990, state 125, 125–38; Elshtain and Tobias 1990, issue xi.

[67] Cornum 1996, 9–12, 20.

[68] Harding 1986, asks 53; D'Amico 1996, 380; D'Amico forthcoming.

standpoint on the world), and "essentialist feminism," meaning that gender has a core essence (used as an accusation these days). "Radical feminism" sees women's oppression worldwide as rooted in patriarchy – male dominance of social life from the family to the economy, the state, and international relations – and sees reforms and integration into men's spaces as inadequate. Some difference feminists favor gender separatism, in order to create a space for women that is not dominated by men.[69]

Difference feminists advance two theoretical claims relevant to war: first, men are relatively violent and women relatively peaceable. Second, men are more autonomous and women more connected in their social relationships.[70]

Violent men, peaceful women   In this view, women's caregiving roles and potential for motherhood best suit them to give life, not take it. Women are more likely than men to oppose war, and more likely to find alternatives to violence in resolving conflicts. (Hillary Clinton in 1996, for example, told a radio audience that her husband finds "action" movies "relaxing" but she does not like them, explaining that "I think that's kind of a male thing.") Thus, according to difference feminism, women have unique abilities as peacemakers. Even Secretary of State Madeleine Albright – an exemplary case for liberal feminism by virtue of her success as a "hawk" in the male-dominated establishment – holds some difference-feminist views. She argues that correcting the gender imbalance in foreign affairs is "not simply about fairness. Today's world needs the unique set of skills and experiences that women bring to diplomacy. I am convinced, for example, that greater numbers of women both as ambassadors and as managers at the UN would lead to a greater emphasis on practical solutions." She told refugee girls from Afghanistan that women around the world "are all the same, and we have the same feelings." The idea of integrating women into mainstream politics in order to change war has male advocates as well, dating back to World War I.[71]

---

[69] Dinnerstein 1976; Fuss 1989; Ferguson 1993, 81–84; Hartsock 1983, 231; Peterson and Runyan 1993, radical 117–18; Runyan 1994, 201; Tickner 1992, 16; Sylvester 1994, 49–52; Pettman 1994, 197–98; A. Johnson 1997; Walby 1990; O'Brien 1981, 87–88, 91–92, 191–94; Mies 1986, 27; French 1994, 26; Cock 1991, 26, 28–29; Goldberg 1993, 14–15, 2.

[70] Ruddick 1989, 141–59.

[71] Ruddick 1989, 148; Di Leonardo 1985; Segal 1990, 261–71; *Washington Post*, October 22, 1996, Clinton D3; Erlanger 1997, feelings; Albright 1997; cf. Waisbrooker 1894, 6; dating: Fukuyama 1998; Cohen 1950, 108–9; Colby 1926; Hansbrough 1915, 40, 89.

Some feminist scholars see an unprecedented political empowerment of women now underway, which could soon reach a "critical mass" that would transform world politics as countries adopted less warlike policies and reduced their military spending. Of 32 women presidents or prime ministers in the twentieth century, 24 held power in the 1990s.

The data on women in politics worldwide, however, make me wonder how close we are to a critical mass. In the 1980s, women made up about 5 percent of heads of state, cabinet ministers, and senior policy makers worldwide, and about 10 percent of members of national legislatures and senior officials in intergovernmental organizations. In the United States, fewer than 10 percent of legislators were women. Norway had the highest percentage of women legislators in the world, but over 98 percent of chairpersons of the powerful municipal councils were men, as were nearly 90 percent of Norwegian judges. (The ten countries with most women in legislatures were all either communist or Nordic countries, where legislatures held little real power.) In Sweden, men made up 90 percent of senior government officials. In China, 67 ministries were headed by men and the other five were vacant. Among the top 4,000 executives of *Fortune* 500 companies, fewer than half of one percent were women. From the early 1980s to the late 1990s, these data changed only incrementally. By 1997, women still held only 15 percent of seats in national legislatures in developed countries and about 10 percent in developing countries. As of 2000, women's seats in legislatures worldwide stand at 14 percent (and only in six small Northern European countries do they exceed 33 percent). In 1995, the world's UN delegation heads were 97 percent male.[72]

Many difference feminists have long believed that women cannot change masculine institutions by joining them, and are better off remaining apart from them (thus preserving valued feminine qualities). In 1792, Mary Wollstonecraft argued that women deserved equal rights with men, but should not participate in war. Wollstonecraft did not see women's maternal experience as making them opposed to war, but rather saw gender equality as compatible with a division of labor in which men served in the military and women served as mothers.[73]

Virginia Woolf's 1938 *Three Guineas* answers a male friend who has asked what feminists might contribute to preventing war (as fascist aggression escalated in Europe and Japan). Woolf links the participation

[72] Goldberg 1993, data 23–26; 1980s: Peterson and Runyan 1993, 6, 46–57; Jaquette 1997, developing 26; stands: International Parliamentary Union website (www.ipu.org), May 2000; UN: Seager 1997, 83.
[73] Cock 1991, 187; Pierson 1987, 207.

of men in war to the male-dominated power structures within Britain, notably the military, the university, government, and business. Woolf argues that "the public and the private worlds are inseparably connected," and teases liberal Englishmen, who benefited from the oppression of women, for their fear of being oppressed by fascism (which she finds similar to patriarchy). Woolf tells men: "Obviously there is for you some glory, some necessity, some satisfaction in fighting which we [women] have never felt or enjoyed." She rejects men's patriotism: "[A]s a woman, I have no country. As a woman I want no country. As a woman my country is the whole world." The international bonds among women create a transnational community not tied to the state system. Woolf's approach – strategic disengagement of women from the war system – contrasts with the suffragists' move to integrate women into the war system (via the vote) in order to change it.[74]

Women's peace activism has a long history (see pp. 322–31). Peace was an important plank of the suffrage program, and pacifist women during World War I organized the Women's Peace Party. Women's peace groups helped win the test ban treaty in the early 1960s and US disengagement from the Vietnam War in the 1970s. During the 1980s, women played a leading role in the movement against nuclear war, and several peace actions or organizations (notably the Greenham Common protests in Britain) developed specifically feminine modes of politics to work for peace (see Figure 1.6).

The prototypical figure of a woman peacemaker is, ironically, the product of a man's imagination. The Athenian playwright Aristophanes wrote a political comedy, *Lysistrata*, critical of the costly and unpopular Peloponnesian War. In the play, a young woman named Lysistrata organizes the Athenian and Spartan women to withhold sex from the men until the men stop the war. The women also raid the Acropolis to make off with the treasury that is financing the war. The men soon come to their senses and make peace. Spartans and Athenians become friends at a banquet and everyone lives happily ever after.[75]

Some feminists link men's violent nature with male sexuality (see pp. 333–56). Observers have noted the phallic quality of many weapons, from spears to guns to missiles. Other writers see in war not so much an extension of men's sexuality but an attempt to compensate for men's innate inability to bear children (and, hence, the meaninglessness of their lives). Militaristic discourses play on men's fears of meaninglessness, as when Mussolini said, "War is to man what maternity is to women." Male

[74] Woolf 1938, public 217, teases 156, glory 9, country 166, 219, 163, 165; Ruddick 1989, 148; Pierson 1987, 220; Yudkin 1982; Andrew 1996, 120–21; Bourke 1999, 303.
[75] Aristophanes 411 BC.

Figure 1.6 Women peace activists circle the Pentagon joined by scarves, 1980. [Photo © by Dorothy Marder.]

insecurity is a source of male violence, according to some difference feminists.[76]

Autonomous men, connected women   A second difference-feminist argument holds that men and women think differently about their separateness or connection with other people. A large literature in this area grows out of "object relations theory" in psychology (an offshoot of psychoanalytic theory). The argument in a nutshell is that boys differentiate themselves from their female caregivers whereas girls identify with their female caregivers. Therefore boys construct social relationships in terms of autonomous individuals, interacting according to formal rules, whereas girls construct social relationships as networks of connection. This gender difference might adapt men to kill in war. Although somewhat grounded in biology (via mothers' nursing), the outcome is driven by childcare arrangements, which cultures can change.[77]

Carol Gilligan's 1982 *In a Different Voice* popularized the separation-versus-connection theme, and stimulated much research on girls (and, recently, on boys). Gilligan argues that girls and boys develop different moral systems – based on individual rights and group responsibilities respectively – although empirical evidence has tended not to support this idea. Gilligan also connects separation-versus-connection to different patterns of play among boys and among girls, including girls' more stable friendships (see pp. 234–35). She argues that men tend to fear connection and women tend to fear competition, and she sees aggression and violence as responses to these fears. She proposes images of hierarchy and web as alternative models of social relationships for men and women respectively. Men seek to be alone at the top of a hierarchy, fearing that others will come too close. Women seek to be at the center of a web, fearing the isolation of the periphery. Others applied these ideas directly to war, arguing that women have a distinctive perspective on war based on "maternal thinking" (a perspective rooted more in culture than biology, but still shared by women only).[78]

[76] Cohn 1987; Gubar 1987; inability: Hartsock 1989, 139, 145; Kinney 1991, 47; Mussolini: Schoenewolf 1989, 86; Broyles 1984, 62.

[77] Winnicott 1965; Dinnerstein 1976, 3–8, 37, 28–31, 93, 161, 176–77; Chodorow 1978, 141–70, 3, 8–10, 15–31, 83; Harding 1986, 131–34; Sayers 1986, 64–78; Elliot 1991, 99–146; Hartsock 1983, 237–39; Elshtain 1982, 345, 347; Elshtain 1987; Ruddick 1989; Brown 1988; Coole 1988; Brittan 1989, 133–38; Hirschmann 1989, 1230–31; Hirschmann 1992, 1, 11–13, 21; Held 1990, 297–302; Stevens and Gardner 1994, 65–82, 71–72, 113; Mansfield 1982.

[78] Gilligan 1982, 8, 10, 31–38, 42, 45, 62, 63, 74, 173; Piaget 1932, 13–16, 76–83; Kohlberg 1976; Huston 1983, 397; Batson 1998, empirical 293–94; Turiel 1998, 883, 881–89; Lever 1978; Pollak and Gilligan 1982, 159; Tannen 1990; war: Reardon 1985, 88–92; Ruddick 1989, 143–57.

One problem with Gilligan's work and the genre it epitomizes, say critics, is that it universalizes the experience of white American women at a particular time and place in history. All women are not the same. Gilligan herself is careful on this point. She does not think the "ethic of care" is necessarily a feminine one, although it has been associated with females in "the advantaged populations that have been studied." Anti-feminist critics also find Gilligan's work empirically flawed.[79]

An important aspect of men's disconnectedness, according to some difference feminists, is men's and women's different views of social relationships within groups. In this view, men tend to see their position relative to others in the group – especially other males – in terms of a competitive hierarchy. Women tend to see their position within a group in terms of mutual support. Hierarchical organization is widespread – and generally male dominated – in the military, business, religion, and other spheres of social life. In this situation, men are especially attuned to how they look in the eyes of their fellow men. Avoiding humiliation and maintaining face become especially important. By contrast, women are seen as more practical, less concerned with rank or honor, and thus better able to cooperate within a group without letting intragroup tensions undermine the group's work. Difference feminists would rather value women's cooperative abilities than encourage women to become more competitive, as liberal feminism sometimes does.[80]

Ecofeminism   I place *ecofeminism* with difference feminism because it begins from radical connectedness. Ecofeminism fuses various practices and theories of feminism, environmentalism, and movements for social justice and equality. Ecofeminists argue that all forms of oppression are deeply connected, with the two most fundamental forms being gender oppression and "man's" exploitation of nature. War is an extension of the aggressive and exploitative relationships embodied in sexism, racism, and the "rape" of the environment. This whole package should be addressed in a holistic way in order to get at the problem of war. Ecofeminism influenced the character of women's peace movements in the 1980s and 1990s, and of the Greens political parties in Europe. For instance, the women pictured in Figure 1.6 above said, "We understand all is connectedness. The earth nourishes us..."[81]

---

[79] Hartsock 1989, 133; Hartsock 1982, 283; Benton *et al.* 1983; Weiner *et al.* 1983; Scheper-Hughes 1996, 353–57; York 1996, 325; Sampson 1988; Brittan 1989, 142; Harter 1998, 596; careful: Tronto 1987, 445, 239; flawed: Summers 2000, 124–32.

[80] Brittan 1989, 77–107; Tannen 1990, 24–25, 75–76, 188–215; Gray 1992, 10–11, 19; Barry 1984.

[81] Diamond and Orenstein eds. 1990; Diamond 1994, ix, Greens 48, 146, 29–30; Shiva 1993, 12–15; Boulding 1992/II, 332; Warren and Cady 1996, 12; Adams 1996, 83;

One line of ecofeminist thinking focuses on the supposed overthrow of peaceful goddess-worshiping nature-based religions around 4500 BC. Rianne Eisler claims that a "partnership model" was prevalent in ancient times (notably in Crete) but was displaced by the now-prevalent "dominator model." In the partnership model, which Eisler seeks to resurrect, gender differences are not "equated with inferiority or superiority." Eisler's account of peaceful prehistory, however, is empirically wrong (see p. 31).[82]

Ecofeminist Susan Griffin sees the separation of war from women's daily lives as a form of denial (which cannot work because the mind knows everything on a deep level). She connects combat trauma with family traumas through the concept of secrets. Secrets have an "erotic edge," she writes, because they move us "closer to a sequestered sexual body at the core of being." Although war occurs in public, and child abuse in private, they lead to similar forms of denial.[83]

Irene Diamond traces war to an "ideology of control" that gives rise to various forms of oppression (and is even reflected in liberal feminism's demand for birth control so that women can control their bodies). She suggests that seekers of control should instead open themselves to the possibilities of mystery, wonder, and spirituality. Thus, ecofeminism sees the problem of war in very broad terms, connecting peace to a deep restructuring of society.[84]

Feminist critiques of difference feminism   Liberal and postmodern feminists question both women's peace movements and linkages among gender, ecology, and social oppressions. Some contest the idea that women in the military can change the military (making it reflect feminine values). Others criticize theories about women's peaceful nature, for adopting a strict male–female dualism that reinforces patriarchy, and for supposedly validating caretaking while obscuring the role of caretakers in supporting war and warriors. Elshtain seeks to "disenthrall" difference feminists of the opposite images of "just warrior" and "beautiful soul." Contrary to the notion of "men's wars," she finds women complicit in the construction of gendered war identities. Other critics argue that "the traditional women's peace movement is based on constricting stereotypes and rigid sex roles." However, difference feminists respond that the ideals of femininity and motherhood can be rehabilitated to serve

King 1990; Harding 1986, 17; Elshtain 1987, 169–70; McAllister ed. 1982, nourishes 415; McBride 1995, v.

[82] Eisler 1987, 42–58, xvii; Eisler 1990; Spretnak 1990, 9–11; Montouri and Conti 1993.

[83] Griffin 1992, 4, 11, 16, 32–33, 38.

[84] Diamond 1994, 5, 3, 13, 21, 47.

peace, and that women's peace movements today do so better than in the past.[85]

The positions of difference and liberal feminists regarding war can be somewhat reconciled by acknowledging their different levels of analysis – the individual for liberal feminism and the gender group for difference feminism. The abilities of an individual are not determined by her or his group, so liberal and difference feminisms are not incompatible. The two genders may show different propensities on average, yet individuals in both genders may span roughly the same range of abilities. (Chapter 3 shows how this concept maps onto men's and women's bell-curve distributions for various measures.)

Postmodern feminism

A third strand, *postmodern feminism*, questions the assumptions about gender made by both liberal and difference feminists. Rather than take gender as two categories of people that really exist (whether they are very different or hardly different), postmodern feminists see gender itself, and gender roles in war, as fairly fluid, contextual, and arbitrary. Gender shapes how both men and women understand their experiences and actions in regard to war. Therefore gender is everywhere, and some scholars reveal and deconstruct the implicitly gender-laden conceptual frameworks of both theorists and practitioners of war. Some postmodern feminists analyze the uses of binary oppositions, which readily map onto gender, to structure models or theories:[86]

Masculine/subject	*Feminine/object*
Knower/self/autonomy/agency	Known/other/dependence/ passivity
Objective/rational/fact/logical/ hard	Subjective/emotional/value/ illogical/soft
Order/certainty/predictability	Anarchy/uncertainty/ unpredictability
Mind/abstract	Body/concrete
Culture/civilized/production/ public	Nature/primitive/ reproduction/private

[85] Question: Elshtain 1987, 243; Cornum 1996, 21, 4, 11, 12, 18; dualism: Wheelwright 1989, 16; Kaplan 1996, 165; Beckman and D'Amico 1994, 4; D'Amico and Beckman 1994, 3; Young 1990, 305–7; complicit: Elshtain 1987, 14–43, 164–66, 341–43; Cooper, Munich, and Squier 1989, xiii; critics: Carter 1996; Peterson and Runyan 1993, 123–29; Richards 1990, 213–18; Cameron 1991; Harris and King 1989, roles 1–3; A. Harris 1989.

[86] Binary: Wilden 1987, 3–4; Flax 1990, 209–11; Peterson and Runyan 1993, 22–25, map 25.

Figure 1.7 Gunners in dresses, World War I. [© Topham/The Image Works.]

Postmodernism generally rejects the idea of a single, objective reality. This makes postmodernism itself difficult to describe. Various writers describe themselves as poststructuralist, postpositivist, postbehavioral, or sometimes "constructivist." All share a general skepticism about established categories and methods of knowledge, and all emphasize the role of culture in shaping experience. The idea of a coherent category, "postmodern feminism," may not be viable, although I use it to simplify this brief overview.

For postmodern feminists interested in war and peace, women play many roles in war, some of them even seemingly contradictory, and masculinity too differs from place to place. For example, the World War I male artillery crew in Figure 1.7 was rehearsing a Christmas play when the alert sounded. Their ability to fight war in drag symbolizes the great flexibility and diversity with which war participants enact gender roles. Because they see this diversity as important, postmodern feminists also delve into the connections among gender, race, ethnicity, nation, class, and other aspects of identity. Postmodern feminism embodies a tension, however, between the postmodern emphasis on the diversity of women's experience and the feminist assumption that women constitute a meaningful category.[87]

Some postmodern feminists have analyzed the place of gender – not just women – in *literary* representations of war from both contemporary and historical times, and from a variety of non-European locales. Other feminists (using postmodern and more traditional methods) analyze the gendered construction of states and wars in various times and places.[88]

A strong version of postmodern feminist analysis – claiming that all gender roles are arbitrary and pliable – runs into some trouble with war. In such a view, "[w]hat is considered masculine in some societies is considered feminine or gender-neutral in others and vice versa; the only constant appears to be the importance of the dichotomy." Yet this chapter has identified another cross-cultural constant – primary gender roles in war.[89]

Feminism and biology

For decades, feminists of all schools have fought anti-feminists regarding biology. In its crudest version, the argument is whether or not male superiority is biologically ordained. Many feminists are alarmed by arguments that lead in the direction of biological necessity as an explanation of present-day gender relations.

The basic argument that many feminists challenge states that gender roles in general, and those concerning violence and aggression in particular, are genetically determined, natural, difficult to change, and adaptive in an evolutionary sense. These accounts portray modern life – sexist

---

[87] Pettman 1996a, ix–x; Scott 1988, 48; J. Butler 1990a, 25, 2–4, 13; J. Butler 1990b; Butler and Scott eds. 1992; Ferguson 1993; Mohanty, Russo, and Torres eds. 1991; Trinh 1989; Darby ed. 1997; Walker 1988, 47–48, 57, 68, 100, 135–36, 162; Di Stefano 1990, 74; Jabri and O'Gorman eds. 1999; Flax 1990, 107–32, 18, 19, 110, 174–76; Harrington 1992; Bordo 1990, 136; Sedghi 1994.

[88] Literary: Jeffords 1996; Huston 1982; Bowen and Weigl eds. 1997; Cooke and Rustomji-Kerns eds. 1994; Cooke 1996a, 3, 4, 16; Cooke 1996b; Cooke 1987; De Pauw 1998, 17; Cooper, Munich, and Squier eds. 1989; Cooke and Woollacott eds. 1993; Lynch and Maddern eds. 1995; Hanley 1991; Hobbs 1987; Gilman 1915; A. Harris 1989; Runyan 1994, 204–14; states: Pettman 1996a, 3–24; MacKinnon 1989; Brown 1988; Peterson 1992a, 33–44; Peterson 1997a, 185; Elshtain 1990, 256–58; others: Peterson and Runyan 1993, 17–44; Bem 1992, 1–3; Cohn 1987, 690–95; Cohn 1989; Cohn 1993; Elshtain 1982; Elshtain 1987; Enloe 2000; Enloe 1989, 4, 16; Enloe 1983, 207–10; Walker 1988, 97; Goodman 1984; Saywell 1985; tension: Peterson ed. 1992; Sylvester 1994, 52–63, 95; Alcoff 1988, 406; Harding 1986, 29; Hirschmann 1992, 33; other: Vansant 1988; Kitch 1991; Isaksson 1988; Inglis 1987; Moghadam ed. 1994, 5.

[89] Harding 1986, what 29.

and warlike – as a reflection of unchanging biological wiring since pre-historic times. Desmond Morris's 1967 *The Naked Ape* exemplifies this tendency: "for 'hunting' read 'working', for 'hunting grounds' read 'place of business', for 'home base' read 'house,' for 'pair-bond' read 'marriage', for 'mate' read 'wife', and so on." Note that he did not say "for 'mate' read 'husband.'" The account revolves around males. Females, be they primates or modern wives, are treated as passive.[90]

Leading sociobiologist E. O. Wilson argues that in the majority of animal species, "[m]ales are characteristically aggressive, especially toward one another." Wilson argues that "temperamental differences between the human sexes are . . . consistent with the generalities of mammalian biology. Women as a group are less assertive and physically aggressive." The degree of difference varies by culture, he says, but this is much less important than the consistency of the qualitative difference. The difference in behavior is "genetic[:] . . . girls are predisposed to be more intimately sociable and less physically venturesome." Wilson and other sociobiologists see war as innate and (at one time) adaptive in human evolution. The soldier risks his life to protect or better the lives of other members of his family group, increasing his genes' reproductive success, in this view.[91]

In addition to their substantive objections to these arguments, some feminists challenge methods of knowledge generation that they see as based on masculine qualities – such as objectivity, control, and theoretical parsimony (especially binary dualisms) at the expense of detailed knowledge about complex social relationships. As Simone de Beauvoir wrote, men describe the world "from their own point of view, which they confuse with absolute truth." The seventeenth-century philosopher of science Francis Bacon cast nature as female and "used quite explicit sexual metaphors to demonstrate the requisite relations of domination and seduction that were to replace an earlier attitude of wonder and contemplation." Feminists particularly object to "determinism" – the idea that our biology determines our destiny as genes simply play out their programs (see pp. 128–32).[92]

[90] Morris 1967, 84; Wright 1994; Masters 1989a; Fausto-Sterling 1997; Fausto-Sterling 1985, 156–58; Tuana 1983, 624; Harding 1986, 93, 98–100; Oudshoorn 1994; Harris 1974, 77; Taylor 1996, 44–45; Di Leonardo 1991, 7; Chesser 1997; Strange 1997; Hunter ed. 1991, ix, xii; Oyama 1991, 64; Chodorow 1978, 18–23; Maccoby 1998, 291.

[91] Wilson 1978, another 125, physically 128, genetic 129, 99, 116, 119–20; Wilson 1975, 254; Goodall 1999, 141–43; Dart 1953; Ardrey 1966; Barash 1977; Barash 1979, 187–88, 170–98; Konner 1982; Dawkins 1976; Axelrod and Hamilton 1981; Ridley 1997; Ghiglieri 1999, 238–40; Van Der Dennen and Falger eds. 1990; Shaw and Wong 1989, 182, 21, 179; Van Hooff 1990, 49–53; Peres and Hopp 1990, 123; Goldstein 1987.

[92] Tickner 1992, truth 1; Coole 1988, contemplation 269; Harding ed. 1987; Peterson

Table 1.4 *D'Amico's comparison of approaches to international relations theory*

	Realist	Pluralist	Critical	Feminist
Actors	States	States, IOs, MNCs	Classes, social movements	People
System	Anarchy	Community	Hierarchy	Multiple hierarchies or patriarchy
Character	Independence	Interdependence	Dependence	Multiple relations

Source: D'Amico 1994, 57.

Feminism and international relations theory

In political science, feminist scholarship forms a theoretical perspective distinct from all the traditional approaches to war and peace (see Table 1.4). Beyond the obvious point that mainstream approaches omit both gender and women, some feminist political scientists argue that traditional theories of war reflect deep masculinist biases – their models of the world (like Bacon's above) assume male superiority.[93]

Realism   Realism, the dominant theoretical school in international relations theory, is a particular subject of feminist rethinking. Realists conceptualize war and peace in terms of (1) territorial states operating as autonomous actors, (2) states rationally pursuing their own interests, and (3) an "anarchic" system of sovereign states (lacking a central government to enforce rules). Feminist theorists criticize each of these three assumptions. They note that the focus on the interstate level of analysis largely blinds realists to gender effects, since gender relations operate mainly at the group and individual levels. Some feminists argue that realists emphasize autonomy and separation because men find separation less threatening than connection. The assumptions of state sovereignty, then, reflect the ways in which *males* tend to interact and to see the world. These

1992a, 11–15; Peterson 1992b; Harding 1986, 23–26, 134–35; Keller 1983; Keller 1985, 158–76; Keller 1984, 47; Belenky *et al.* 1986; Goldberger *et al.* 1996, 7; Schiebinger 1993; Myers 1996, 106; Peterson and Runyan 1993, 25, 22–23; Tuana 1983, 631; Angier 1994b; Rosoff 1991; Sunday 1991; Hrdy 1981, 14; Oudshoorn 1994, x, 1–9.

[93] Nelson and Olin 1979, 5–6; Beckman 1994; D'Amico 1994, table 57, 71; Elshtain 1987, 86–91; Peterson ed. 1992; Peterson 1996a; Krause 1995; Tickner 1992; Morgenthau 1948; Tickner 1991, 29; Grant and Newland 1991, 5; Reardon 1996, 317; Keller 1984, 46.

constructions date from the classical masculine-dominated states, notably in ancient Greece, which were models for modern Western states.[94]

The realist conception of rationality – formal, mechanistic, and selfish – has also been criticized by many feminists as a radically incomplete view of human nature. It is not that emotional females lack rationality – though some difference feminists find male rationality unnecessarily purged of emotion – but rather that rationality need not be defined so individualistically and myopically. "The nation is often called up in familial language . . . that is strangely different from the Realist representations of power politics and rational self-national interest." Some feminists – like traditional liberals in nonfeminist international relations theory – see the alternative to realists' anarchy as community. (The international community can be readily cast as familial: the director of a Gallup poll of Eastern European countries characterized the motivations of those wanting to join NATO as resembling what a "child does when it cuddles a mother, for no particular reason but to generally feel safer.")[95]

Gender in classical realism   Gender themes weave through several of the classical works favored by modern realists. Sun Tzu instructed Chinese state rulers 2,500 years ago on using power to advance their interests and protect their survival. (His book became required reading for US Marine officers in the 1980s.) In the most famous episode in Sun Tzu's book, a king was thinking of hiring Sun Tzu as an advisor. As a test, he asked Sun Tzu if he could turn the king's harem of 200 concubines into troops. Sun Tzu divided the women into two units, and put them under the command of the king's two favorite concubines respectively. To show he meant business, he brought in the equipment used for executing people. Then he explained to the harem the signals to face forward, backward, right, and left. When he gave the signals, the women just laughed. Sun Tzu explained the signals again, but again the women just laughed. Finally, Sun Tzu found the "officers" (the two favorite concubines) at fault, had them both executed on the spot, and replaced them with the next most high-ranking concubines. Now when Sun Tzu gave the

---

[94] Waltz 1979, 19; Waltz 1959; Keohane ed. 1986; Nye 1988; Buzan, Jones, and Little 1993; Holsti 1985; Enloe 1989, 4; Jones 1996, 408–17; Keohane 1986, 2–6; territorial: Diehl ed. 1999; Goertz and Diehl 1992; Vasquez 1993, 123–52; Ruggie 1993; Huth 1996; Duchacek 1970; level: Levy 1985; Levy 1989; feminist: Tickner 1994; Tickner 1992, 74; Beckman 1994, 21; Burguieres 1990, 2; Sylvester 1992; Walker 1992; Peterson 1988; Grant 1991, 11–14.

[95] Howard 1983, 22; Morgenthau 1948; Reynolds 1989; Tickner 1991, purged 30, defined 37; Tickner 1992, 73; Pettman 1996a: strangely 49; Ruddick 1990, 232; Brittan 1989, 198–204; Di Stefano 1990, 67–73; Hartsock 1983, 38–39; Keohane 1984, 120–32; anarchy: Bull 1977; Taylor 1976; familial: Perlez 1997, A14; Cohn 1990, 38.

signals, the harem obeyed flawlessly. Sun Tzu declared that the troops were in good order and could be deployed as the king desired. In this story, as with the Greek Amazon myths discussed earlier, feminine and masculine seem to represent undisciplined nature and controlled domination respectively. The development of power begins by bringing the feminine under control by violence.[96]

Another favorite realist classic, Thucydides' account of the Peloponnesian War, declares that "the strong do what they have the power to do and the weak accept what they have to accept." What the strong have the power to do in the incident he describes – and in fact do – is to kill all the adult male Melians and take the women and children as slaves (as was typical in Greek warfare). Central to this key realist text is the division of males as people, who must be killed, from females as property, which can be taken.[97]

Machiavelli wrote: "Fortune is a woman, and it is necessary if you wish to master her, to conquer her by force." In his short chapter on "How a State is Ruined Because of Women," two men representing different factions of a polity competed for marriage to a rich woman whose father was dead. The two factions came to arms, each sought outside allies, and one side's allies conquered the city leaving the winning faction dependent on an outside power. Machiavelli draws the lesson that "women have been causes of much ruin, and have done great harm to those who govern a city, and have caused many divisions in them." Machiavelli lists rape and violation, along with the breaking of marriage promises, as the types of injury (i.e., to men, of course) that could make enemies unnecessarily. In his chapter on conspiracies, Machiavelli gives a half dozen examples in which women's presence disrupts plans or creates an information leak leading to disaster. He endorses Aristotle's warning that "the insolence of women has ruined many tyrannies," and that quarrels concerning women can spark major political problems. Thus, the theme of gender domination runs through several classics of realism.[98]

Liberalism and peace studies   Traditionally, liberals in international relations (including "idealists") dispute the three main assumptions of realism, as feminists do. They pay attention to individuals, groups, and societies below the state level. They find in the psychology of individual and group decision making – including misperception, emotion,

---

[96] Sun Tzu 1963; Trainor 1989.
[97] Thucydides, 400 BC, 402.
[98] Tickner 1992, force 39; Machiavelli 1996, 272–73; Machiavelli 1983, 398–424; Aristotle 1943, 251, 217–18; Pitkin 1984; Sylvester 1994, 80; Elshtain 1981, 92–99; Elshtain 1987, 169; Ferguson 1993, 73–75; cf. Hobbes: Coole 1988, 79–83.

fatigue, bias, self-delusion, personal and bureaucratic rivalry, and group-think – deep challenges to the idea of rational statecraft. Liberals also see international interactions as structured not by anarchic power relations but by norms and institutions based on reciprocity and even law. Liberals focus not on power over others but on power to accomplish desirable ends, which may require capitalizing on common interests. (Some feminists treat "power over" as a masculinist concept.)[99]

Traditional liberalism, then, would seem to have great potential for the inclusion of gender in studying war and peace. In fact, however, traditional liberalism has paid little attention to gender. Kant's feminist critics say he exhibits gender bias. He downgrades human emotions and other qualities associated historically with women, giving them little moral weight because they lie outside the realm of reason. The idea of reason, central to Western liberal values, has a long history on the masculine side of a gendered dichotomy. The early idealist emphasis on international law, and the ongoing liberal emphasis on individual human rights, may reflect masculinist tendencies to see human interactions in terms of autonomous individuals governed by formal rules. Liberalism depends deeply on the idea of autonomous individuals, and the "notion of community in liberal theory is fragile and instrumental." Liberals once explicitly excluded women from their theories, but recently have assumed that all humanity behaves in the same way.[100]

Liberal international relations scholarship in recent years has focused on the war propensities of democratic versus authoritarian states, seeking to explain the "democratic peace" – democracies fight, but almost never against each other. Some feminists argue that the enfranchisement and empowerment of women is a crucial aspect of democratization worldwide. (Early suffragettes thought women would vote against war more often than men, but this materialized as only a modest tendency.) The possible gendered aspects of democratic peace deserve systematic study.[101]

Neoliberalism, which emerged in international relations theory in the 1980s, abandons the traditional liberals' critiques on all three realist assumptions, and argues that even so, realists' pessimism about peace and cooperation do not follow. From feminist perspectives, neoliberalism

---

[99] Kant 1795; Angell 1914; Jervis 1976; Peterson and Runyan 1993, masculinist 45; power: Whitworth 1994b, 78; Beckman 1994, 26.

[100] Elshtain 1990, Kant 261–65; Tickner 1992, instrumental–excluded 74; Tickner 1991, 37; Whitworth 1994a, 39–63, 45–47; Halliday 1991, 162; Harrington 1992, 65; Feste 1994, 41, 45; rules: Walzer 1977; Elshtain 1987, 154–55; Elshtain 1983, 343–44; Ruddick 1989, 150.

[101] Russett 1990; Doyle 1986; D'Amico forthcoming; Regan and Barnello 1998; Kerber 1990, 90; Tickner 1992, 38; Hartsock 1983, 283; Phillips 1991.

moves backward from traditional liberalism by granting realists the very assumptions that feminists criticize. Ironically, though, a leading neoliberal theorist, Robert Keohane, is the rare high-status male international relations theorist who has engaged gender issues.[102]

Scholars of peace studies, like many feminists and traditional liberals, view war in the context of multiple levels of analysis rather than just the interstate level, see oppression as a cause of war, and support peace movements. Peace studies has been more accepting of the assumptions behind difference feminism – that gender differences are real, that women are more peaceful – than have most scholars in women's or gender studies. Some feminists in peace studies worry that criticizing these "essentialist assumptions" would open rifts that could weaken peace studies. Despite these connections of feminism with peace studies, feminist theory has had a limited impact to date on peace studies overall, and again most of the relevant work is by women.[103]

CONCLUSION

The evidence presented in this chapter establishes that war is deeply rooted in the human experience, and that gendered war roles are permanent – a part of a society's readiness for the possibility of war. Males occupy the ongoing role of potential fighters, even in relatively peaceful societies. Amazon myths aside, in only one documented case (Dahomey) did women make up a substantial fraction of combat forces in a regular standing army over many years. This regularity in gender roles in war contrasts with the much greater diversity found both in war itself and in gender roles outside war.

Although most male scholars of war bypass questions of gender, feminist theorists have elaborated a number of ways that gender affects war. In some areas, such as paying attention to gender and to women, the various feminist approaches overlap. In other areas, such as whether men are innately violent, the approaches often diverge or contradict each other.

---

[102] Baldwin ed. 1993; Oye ed. 1986; Waltz 1959, 167–70; Tickner 1992, 31, 63; Grant 1991, 14–16; Keohane 1989; Keohane 1998; Murphy 1996, 529–30.
[103] Turpin and Kurtz eds. 1997; Forsberg 1997a; Goldstein 2001, 146–58; Lorentzen and Turpin eds. 1998; Alonso and Chambers eds. 1995; Reardon 1985, 58, 39–106, 4, 25, 40; Reardon 1989, 20, 17; Reardon 1996, 315; Krogh and Wasmuht 1984; Brock-Utne 1985; Brock-Utne 1989; Burguieres 1990; Forcey 1989, 10; Forcey 1991, 341–42; Forcey 1993; Forcey 1995, rifts 11–12; Pierson ed. 1987; McAllister ed. 1982; Feminism and Nonviolence Study Group 1983; Carroll 1987; Ås 1982, 355; Vickers 1993; limited: Boulding 1984, 2; Klare and Chandrani eds. 1998; Woehrle 1996, 417, 420.

From theory to evidence   I hope to survey the "state of knowledge" – a zone of shared understandings among experts in various fields of study, based on robust empirical evidence. In any research community, this consensus is roughly demarcated, with contested zones around the borders (and sometimes closer to the core). For any science, furthermore, the state of knowledge is *always* provisional, pending new evidence that may emerge. Nonetheless, for a given, specific, little question, in many cases some body of reliable empirical evidence can adequately answer it. The evidence may be complex and even contradictory in places, but it is not arbitrary. The evidence presented in this book is my attempt to synthesize the state of knowledge on the relationship of war with gender.[104]

The foregoing discussion gives complex theoretical debates short shrift, because this book is a dossier of evidence, not a theoretical contribution. As the theoretician Freud wrote, when asked by Einstein about ending war, "little good comes of consulting a theoretician ... on practical and urgent problems!" With apologies to theorists, then, I will follow that famous deductivist, Sherlock Holmes, and turn to empirical investigation to sort out an array of theories: "'Data! Data! Data!' he cried impatiently. 'I can't make bricks without clay.'"[105]

[104] Kuhn 1970, 5.
[105] Freud 1933; Hacking 1983; Doyle 1892, 120.

2   Women warriors: the historical record of female combatants

Hypothesis 2. Sexist discrimination despite women's historical success as combatants:

A. In female combat units
B. In mixed-gender units
C. As individual women fighters
D. As women military leaders

INTRODUCTION

After the evidence in chapter 1 about the rarity of women's participation in combat, one might expect this to be a short chapter indeed. However, even a fraction of a percent of combat participants adds up to many cases, given the hundreds of millions of soldiers who have fought in wars in the twentieth century alone.

The question of women combatants has generated substantial historical research in recent years, sparked by feminist scholarship's interest in uncovering the previously ignored roles of women in social and political history. Several accounts chronicle the role of individual women soldiers in a variety of societies and time periods. Historian Linda Grant De Pauw writes, "Women have always and everywhere been inextricably involved in war, [but] hidden from history... During wars, women are ubiquitous and highly visible; when wars are over and the war songs are sung, women disappear."[1]

Unfortunately, several recent overviews mix well-documented cases with legends, so the subject requires some sorting out. In particular, John Laffin's 1967 *Women in Battle* contains almost no documentation, and the caveat that the stories therein were "difficult to acquire and even more difficult to verify." (Laffin's own opinion is that a "woman's place

[1] De Pauw 1998, disappear xiii; Pennington ed. n.d.

59

should be in the bed and not the battlefield.") Yet Laffin's stories turn up as fact in Jessica Amanda Salmonson's 1991 *Encyclopedia of Amazons* – a confusing mix of historical and mythical cases – and David Jones's 1997 *Women Warriors*, among others. Linda Grant De Pauw is more reliable and provides good documentation on US and European history, despite accepting too uncritically some unsupported claims concerning prehistory, anthropology, and non-Western countries. De Pauw groups women's roles in war into four categories: (1) the classic roles of victim and of instigator; (2) combat support roles; (3) "virago" roles that perform masculine functions without changing feminine appearance (such as warrior queens, women members of home militias, or all-female combat units); and (4) warrior roles in which women become like men, often changing clothing and other gender markers.[2]

The evidence on women soldiers and that on women political leaders in wartime seems to support liberal feminists; women *can* perform these roles effectively. I review women's participation in each of several settings in turn – female combat units, mixed-gender units, individual women in groups of men, and women military leaders of male armies.

A. FEMALE COMBAT UNITS

Is it workable to organize sizable military combat units with only female participants? The answer is a qualified yes – it has been tried only a handful of times in all of history, but the results show the possibility of success, defined as strengthening the military's effectiveness in war. These cases, although few, demonstrate the *possibility* of effective women combatants.

Dahomey in the slave-trading era

The eighteenth- and nineteenth-century Dahomey Kingdom of West Africa (present-day Benin) is the only documented case of a large-scale female combat unit that functioned over a long period as part of a standing army. The Dahomey Kingdom arose in the late sixteenth century when an aggressive clan conquered its neighbors and expanded its territory. The economy of Dahomey was fundamentally based on the slave trade – go to war against neighboring societies to capture slaves; trade the slaves to Europeans for guns; use the guns to go to war. Interwoven with these wars were extreme acts of large-scale human sacrifice, torture, and cannibalism, practiced on prisoners captured in war. Dahomey was one of the

---

[2] Laffin 1967, verify 186, bed 185; Salmonson 1991; Jones 1997; De Pauw 1998, 17–25.

most successful military organizations ever in its region, and was rightly feared by its neighbors. It grew up with the slave trade – which expanded after 1670 and eventually exported 2 million people from the area – and ended when France conquered it in 1892, at the end of the slaving era. The kings of Dahomey enjoyed showing off the Amazon corps to visiting Europeans (Dahomey's slave-export customers) who were always interested in the phenomenon, and thus we have direct reports from English visitors in 1793, 1847, and 1851. Stanley Alpern has documented the case well.[3]

The "Amazon corps" appears to have originated in 1727 when Dahomey faced a grave military situation. King Agadja armed a regiment of females at the rear, apparently just to make his forces appear larger, and discovered that they actually fought well. Subsequently, the king organized the Amazon corps as a kind of palace guard. The corps' size, which varied over time and is in some dispute, apparently ranged from about 800 women early in the nineteenth century to over 5,000 at the mid-century peak, several thousand being combat forces. Women comprised a substantial minority of the Dahomean army, varying from under one-tenth to over one-third of the total. Some of the women were native-born, while others were captured in war and showed surprising loyalty. In one instance, a girl who had been captured young and raised in Dahomey was recaptured while fighting in the Amazon corps but refused to go back to her parents, insisting on returning to Dahomey instead.[4]

The women soldiers were armed with muskets and swords. They drilled regularly and resembled the men in dress and activities (see Figure 2.1). They stayed in top physical condition and were fast and strong. In the field, the Amazon corps carried mats and bedding on their heads, along with powder, shot, and food for a week or two. Some writers describe the women as rather large and strong. However, this physique is common to the other countries of West Africa, none of which used women as soldiers.[5]

The women showed at least as much courage as the men – more, by several accounts – and had a reputation for cruelty. There was no known case of women warriors fleeing combat, although men often did so. One

---

[3] Polanyi 1966, 3, 26–27; Manning 1982, 9–11; Duncan 1847, visiting 233–38; Alpern 1998; Dalzel 1967.

[4] Polanyi 1966, 28; Snelgrave 1734, 125–26; Wrangham and Peterson 1996, 109–10; size: Alpern 1998, 72–75; Forbes 1851/I, 14–15, Forbes 1851/II, 55–56; Obichere 1971, 67; loyalty: Ajayi and Smith 1971, 52.

[5] Duncan 1847, muskets 224–27, 231–35; Forbes 1851/I, resembled 23; Smith 1989, mats 59; physique: Herskovits 1938, 46; Burton in Alpern 1998, 36; Smith 1989, none 43, 47; Turney-High 1971, 155, 159–60.

Figure 2.1 Dahomean Amazon, as drawn by English visitor, 1850. [Forbes 1851, plate 2. Smithsonian Institution Libraries. © Frank Cass & Co.]

European observer concluded that, "if undertaking a campaign, I should prefer the females to the male soldiers."[6]

The women of the Amazon corps said: "We are men, not women!... Our nature is changed." They dressed, ate, and behaved as the men did. The Amazon corps members were technically married to the King (but did not have sex with him), were extremely loyal to him, and were forbidden to have sex with men (at the risk of death for both, although some observers thought the rule was frequently broken anyway). Several thousand lived in the palace, along with civilian wives (perhaps 2,000 of them) and female slaves. According to one report, female prostitutes were employed in the palace to serve the Amazon corps, although this is unclear. The Amazon corps was totally segregated from men. Outside the palace, its approach was announced by a ringing bell. Everyone had to turn their backs, and males had to move away.[7]

The Dahomean army was not primarily female. Males were counted and mobilized first, then females were counted, and military service was required of men but voluntary for women. A village could send women in place of men who did not want to serve. The army was divided into two parts, the left and the right, and each was in turn divided into a male and female component – a division which somewhat reflected the organization of Dahomey political administration.[8]

Although not in the majority, the women soldiers played a key role in the Dahomey army, and performed admirably in combat. In a battle in 1840, an enemy force routed the male Dahomean soldiers and only a rally of the Amazon corps prevented disaster. Using female soldiers had some drawbacks, however. In 1851, 10,000 males and 6,000 females faced 15,000 defenders in a neighboring society. The defenders were "infuriated" by the discovery – as they were preparing to castrate a prisoner of war – that some of the Dahomean soldiers were women. They redoubled their efforts, with their own women acting as supply troops, and repulsed the Dahomey attack with 2,000 to 3,000 Dahomey killed. In 1890–92, France conquered Dahomey, but it required several bloody attempts (showing that Dahomey was the strongest military power in West Africa at the time). In the first major battle, in 1890, Dahomey women soldiers took part and several were found dead on the battlefield, to the surprise of the French soldiers. In a later battle, the French commander noted that the Amazon corps, about 2,000 strong, led the

---

[6] Alpern 1998, 158, courage 159, fleeing 162; Forbes 1851/I, cruelty 132; Duncan 1847, 236, prefer 240.

[7] Forbes 1851/I, we 23, 134; Alpern 1998, 44–47; Herskovits 1938, broken 46, segregated 48; Duncan 1847, bell 257–58.

[8] Polanyi 1966, mobilized 42–43; Herskovits 1938, send 76, administration 85.

attack in the presence of the king and showed remarkable speed and boldness.[9]

Dahomey probably turned to women soldiers in part because, unlike its neighbors, it faced a severe military manpower shortage for three reasons. It was exceptionally warlike and lost men in war. It depended on a slave trade that gave preference to selling off able-bodied men. And it faced a hostile neighbor ten times larger than itself. Firearms had only recently been introduced to the region, but this does not explain the Amazons (by equalizing men's and women's strength) as Marvin Harris claims. Although muskets were basic weapons, they were crude and often ineffective. A machete-like sword was decisive. Women effectively used this and a variety of weapons including daggers, bayonets, battle-axes, bows and arrows, clubs, and a giant folding razor (with a blade over 2 feet long) apparently used mainly for decapitation but possibly for castrating enemies as well.[10]

Dahomey is a critical case because it shows that women can be physically and emotionally capable of participating in war on a large-scale, long-term, and well-organized basis. Far from being weakened by the participation of women, the army of Dahomey was clearly strengthened. Women soldiers helped make Dahomey the preeminent regional military power that it became in the nineteenth century. Yet Dahomey is virtually the only case of its kind. The puzzle is why this successful case was not emulated elsewhere.[11]

The Soviet Union in World War II

Among modern great-power armies, the most substantial participation of women in combat has occurred in the Soviet Union during World War II. Following a rapid, forced industrialization of the Soviet economy in the 1930s under Stalin, in which women were drawn into nontraditional labor roles, the Soviet Union faced a dire emergency when it was invaded by Nazi Germany in 1941. Over the next three years, the Soviets would count tens of millions of war dead, and large parts of their country would be left in ruins. In this extreme situation, the Soviet Union mobilized every possible resource for the war effort, eventually including women for combat duty. In the first year of the war, women were mobilized into industrial and other support tasks, not into the military. These

[9] 1840: Forbes 1851/I, 14–15; infuriated: Ajayi and Smith 1971, 37–39, 50–51; France: Obichere 1971, 67–75, commander 75, 107; Alpern 1998, 104.

[10] Alpern 1998, manpower 36–37, weapons 61, 65–68; firearms: Smith 1989, 51, 81; M. Harris 1989, 285.

[11] Obichere 1971, preeminent 120–21.

tasks included those women were already doing – they were already 40 percent of the industrial labor force at the outset – as well as new occupations that had been all male, such as mining. Women also dug trenches and built fortifications for the Soviet military.[12]

Beginning in 1942, faced with manpower shortages, the Soviet Union drafted into the military childless women not already employed in war work. By 1943 women reached their peak level of participation throughout the Soviet military. Their main areas of involvement were in medical specialties (especially nursing) – these were often front-line positions – and antiaircraft units which "became virtually a feminized military specialty."[13]

Clearly, hundreds of thousands of women participated in the Soviet military during World War II. However, sources "are distressingly vague" on the actual number. The official figures state that about 800,000 women participated in the Red Army and about another 200,000 in partisan (irregular) forces. These figures put women at about 8 percent of overall forces (with 12 million men). Of the total of 800,000, about 500,000 reportedly served at the front, and about 250,000 received military training in Komsomol schools. Most were in their late teens.[14]

All the information regarding Soviet women's participation in World War II comes to us through "a mass of hyperbolic and patriotic press accounts and memoirs." Playing up the contributions of women helped the formidable Soviet propaganda machine to raise morale in a dispirited population, and spur greater sacrifices by the male soldiers. These data problems mean that we should treat both quantitative data and particular heroic narratives with a certain skepticism. The "majority of women did not serve in direct combat."[15]

Despite all that, clearly women participated on a substantial scale – hundreds of thousands of individuals, a nontrivial minority of the total forces. Even if we reduce the extent and heroism of female participation from the official version, we are left with an important historic case of large-scale women's participation in combat – probably the largest such case in modern history.

The overriding impression left by the case is that women performed a very wide range of combat tasks and "proved themselves" in those tasks, eventually gaining the "acceptance and even admiration" of Soviet military men who had been "initially skeptical or hostile." I will summarize

[12] Griesse and Stites 1982, labor 68–69.

[13] Griesse and Stites 1982, drafted 31, specialty 69.

[14] Griesse and Stites 1982, vague–Komsomol 73, teens 31; De Pauw 1998, 239–45; D. Jones 1997, 137–45.

[15] Griesse and Stites 1982, memoirs–combat 75, 71–75; Presidential Commission 1993, C28.

each of the main areas in which women took part, in rough order of the importance of female participation to that area – front-line medical support, antiaircraft, combat aviation, partisan forces, infantry, and armor.[16]

Medical support tasks in the Soviet military were integrated with combat to an unusual degree. Doctors and nurses served at the front lines under intense fire. All nurses and over 40 percent of doctors in the Soviet military were women. Many of the heroic stories about these women – some of which appear to be true even if some are exaggerated – revolve around their actions in dragging and carrying wounded male soldiers to safety on the battlefield, sometimes by the dozen. In other cases, women medical soldiers joined and even commanded infantry units when the male ranks were decimated. Reportedly, Vera Krylova enlisted as a student nurse in 1941, was sent to the front, and dragged hundreds of wounded comrades to safety under fire. When her isolated unit was ambushed and its leaders killed, in the chaos of the German advance of August 1941, the wounded Krylova jumped on a horse, took command of the company, and led a two-week battle through encircling enemy forces to rejoin Russian forces. The next year, fighting with a different unit which was retreating from a tank battle, Krylova moved forward to collect hand grenades from wounded comrades being left behind, then single-handedly charged the German tanks with grenades, slowing the advance enough for the Russians to evacuate their wounded. Such tales, although not verifiable in particular cases, reflect an overall reality – that many thousands of Soviet women served as front-line medical workers and some also participated directly (and effectively) in combat.[17]

Antiaircraft units were staffed and commanded entirely by women – apparently hundreds of thousands in all. (British forces in World War II included women in antiaircraft units but had men fire the guns. US home-territory antiaircraft defense, though not needed in the end, also relied on women.) One German pilot is quoted as saying that he would rather fly ten times over hostile Libya than "pass once through the fire of Russian flak sent up by female gunners." One reason cited for the women's success was that, in these all-female military units, a "military female subculture" emerged which did its work in a warmer and more casual way than in men's units.[18]

In the Soviet air force, three women's regiments were formed – a small fraction of the total force but a useful test of all-female combat units. The women pilots were organized by Marina Raskova, a kind of Amelia Earhart celebrity in the Soviet Union in the 1930s, who was flooded

[16] Griesse and Stites 1982, hostile 72.
[17] Griesse and Stites 1982, 71; Krylova: Jones 1997, 137–40.
[18] Griesse and Stites 1982, pass 69, subculture 72; British: Quester 1977, 81–82.

Figure 2.2 Soviet night-bomber flown by women pilots, World War II. [Photo by Yevgeny Khaldei, courtesy of Anne Noggle.]

with offers by women pilots to volunteer in World War II. She convinced Stalin of their potential value in the war effort, and went on to organize the regiments and lead one of them until her death (at age 31) in a crash *en route* to their first deployment in 1943.[19]

The most famous was the 588th Night Bomber Air Regiment (46th Guards Bomber Regiment), sometimes called the "night witches." It had over 4,000 members, and at its peak carried out hundreds of sorties per night (officially, 24,000 missions in all). These pilots flew cheap, combustible biplanes (see Figure 2.2) – often unarmed, sometimes armed with a light machine-gun in back, to drop bombs on German positions at night (they could not have survived in daytime). They suffered substantial losses. Although the plane could land almost anywhere, the crew did not have parachutes, so a fire was often fatal. At dusk the women would fly from a rear base to a temporary airfield near the front, then send one plane every three minutes out to and back from the target all night long, with each plane completing up to three missions in one night. The system provided the Germans with no rest at night, but also let them

---

[19] Cottam 1983; Noggle 1994, 15–17, 99–101; White 1994, 7–11; Griesse and Stites 1982, 70; Pennington 1993; [less reliable: Myles 1981; Jones 1997, 140–45].

anticipate the arrival of a plane and catch it in spotlights, making it an easy target. The pilots learned to slip-slide out of the spotlights and make their bombing runs with engines turned off until after they had dropped their six to eight bombs. Especially in winter, when nights were longest, "[t]he women – pilots and ground crews alike – lived on the verge of physical collapse, managing a bit of sleep or a meal whenever they could."[20]

The unit was the only truly all-female one – not only pilots and navigators but also most of the ground crew (e.g., mechanics and bomb-loaders) were women. (The other two regiments were commanded by males who replaced the original women leaders, when Raskova died and another commander was recalled for ill health. The appointment of male commanders seems to have been an expedient measure under time pressure to get the regiments into service.) The night bomber regiment was famous during the war, receiving extensive domestic and international press.

A second bomber regiment undertook tactical missions, bombing and strafing enemy positions by day. Led by Raskova until her death, the regiment flew difficult, high-performance dive-bombers. Some of the ground crew, and some tail-gunners, were men, but all the pilots and navigators were women. Unlike the night bombers, this regiment received very little publicity during the war and operated under virtually the same conditions as the equivalent male bomber regiments. The commander said: "During the war there was no difference between this regiment and any male regiments. We lived in dugouts, as did the other regiments, and flew on the same missions, not more or less dangerous."[21]

The third regiment was an interceptor unit (the 586th). Also commanded by a man, it eventually incorporated a male squadron (ten planes) to join the two female squadrons. Some of the ground crew were men, mainly because the sophisticated aircraft required skills beyond the rudimentary training of most women mechanics at that time. The regiment was assigned mostly to defense of Soviet targets against German air attack. Its role was to drive away attacking planes rather than pursue them. Therefore it recorded relatively few "kills." In one episode recounted first-hand, two women pilots of this regiment (in two planes) boldly attacked straight into the middle of 42 German bombers defended with machine guns, shooting down four and turning back the rest before being forced down. Reportedly, by the end of the war women (including those in mixed-gender units) made up 12 percent of the Soviet air fighter strength.[22]

---

[20] White 1994, 9–11, verge 10; Noggle 1994, 18–98.
[21] Noggle 1994, 99–156, dangerous 105; White 1994, 9.
[22] Noggle 1994, 157–219, attacked 160–61; White 1994, 8; Cottam 1983, strength 7.

Some individual women pilots also served in mostly male units. Raskova's attempt to gather women aviators together did not entirely succeed. In 1942, eight women from the interceptor regiment were detached and assigned to male interceptor regiments to help in the Battle of Stalingrad. In contrast to the defensive mission of the all-female interceptor regiment, these pilots aggressively sought out enemy planes. Two of these women became "aces," each credited with about a dozen kills. One of them, Lilya Litvyak, was known as the "White Rose of Stalingrad." In her perhaps-too-perfect story, the heroine starts as the "wingman" (supporting plane) to a male pilot, falls in love with him, is filled with fervor after his death, gets shot down multiple times, and is ultimately ambushed by eight German fighters at once, with her wreckage lost (it was reported found in 1989).[23]

In the partisan forces – irregular guerrillas who operated in and around areas under German occupation – women played an important role, though not in all-female units. By one estimate, about 27,000 women participated, making up over 8 percent of the total partisan forces (and 16 percent in the partisan stronghold of the Belorussian forests). The women performed various tasks, mostly "medical, communications, and domestic chores; but all were armed, and many fought." The extent of women's participation, and the degree of ("clearly romanticized") gender equality within the partisans, seem to have varied from place to place. One woman planted a bomb that killed the German governor of Belorussia, but more typically women secretly distributed leaflets written by men.[24]

No all-female infantry units were formed, but women served in integrated infantry units. Several hundred thousand received training in firing mortars, machine-guns, and rifles. A special school was established in 1943 which trained hundreds of women snipers. They "performed well" (except in throwing hand grenades and climbing trees). One woman killed off an entire German company over 25 days, and another was decorated for killing over 300 German soldiers. Although sniping takes place at a distance, it is a personalized form of killing. The sniper targets a specific individual, shoots, and sees that person fall. Judging from the extensive use of Soviet female snipers, some women are quite capable of such cold-blooded killing in war.[25]

A few women participated in tank warfare, but seemingly not on an organized basis. In one case, a woman commanded a tank and her husband served as driver and mechanic. In another famous case, a woman

---

[23] Noggle 1994, 157–58; White 1994, 8–9; Jones 1997, 142–43.
[24] Griesse and Stites 1982, 71–72.
[25] Griesse and Stites 1982, integrated–snipers 69–72; Jones 1997, 45; cf. Randall 1981, grenades 145–46.

whose husband was killed in action bought her own tank, named it the "Front-line Female Comrade," and was killed in a tank battle.[26]

Overall, in Soviet forces during World War II, "women proved of equal competence in those few moments when a fluid situation and the force of circumstances threw them into a central role." They performed a wide variety of combat tasks effectively. It is difficult to discern the overall picture amidst the romantic propaganda, and the record is complex. For example, German sources sometimes were contemptuous of Soviet women's ability and willingness to fight, while at other times they gave grudging respect to Soviet women fighters they had faced. The Soviet Union, faced with a dire emergency, mobilized women extensively into military tasks for which the culture had afforded them little experience and few scripts to follow. Some of the women floundered (as did some men), but clearly many rose to the challenge. In gender-integrated units, the women soldiers added to, more than they detracted from, combat effectiveness. This is why women kept being sent to those units. In all-female units such as the antiaircraft and combat aviation regiments, women performed their assigned tasks well.[27]

The Soviet case, thus, underscores the lesson of the Dahomey Kingdom, that women can be organized into effective large-scale military units. In neither case were women the majority, but in both cases the mobilization of a substantial minority of women soldiers increased the state's military power.

However, the Soviet case also underscores how extreme the threat to a society must be before it will use women in combat (see pp. 10–22). The Soviet Union of World War II – invaded, occupied, its cities decimated and besieged, its people starving – still mobilized over 90 percent men. Its women soldiers were rarely assigned to ground combat roles and, like today's American women soldiers, fought mainly when circumstances thrust them into the line of fire. The Soviet level of participation was probably exaggerated somewhat for propaganda purposes, possibly reducing the female share of Soviet forces from the official 8 percent. Even that level of participation occurred only in the Soviet Union, of all World War II belligerents – a society that preached (albeit, hardly practiced) gender equality, and which had already integrated women into many traditionally male industrial jobs. None of that takes away from the main conclusion of the case, however: women participated in combat in large numbers, and their participation added to the Soviet Union's military strength. Hundreds of thousands of women made good soldiers.

[26] Griesse and Stites 1982, 72.
[27] Griesse and Stites 1982, proved 73, German 75.

Contrast with Nazi Germany   Despite the cases of Dahomey and the Soviet Union, not every society obsessed with war, or even desperately fighting for its survival, allows women into combat. For example, Germany in World War II contrasts with the Soviet Union. Germany's position in both World Wars would seem to favor reliance on women, since Germany faced chronic shortages of "manpower" (lacking, among other things, the colonial populations of Britain and France). In World War I, when the expected quick victory turned to protracted war, German women entered industrial jobs (about 700,000 in munitions industries by the end of the war), and served as civilian employees in military jobs in rear areas (medical, clerical, and manual labor; women trained for jobs in the signal corps late in the war but never deployed). German women won the vote after World War I, and some kept their jobs in industry.[28]

However, the Nazi ideology promoted a gender division, with women assigned to the home and the production of German children, while the men engaged in politics and war. Therefore Germany went into World War II with a different gender ideology than the Soviet Union, one much less conducive to the participation of women in war. Given a labor shortage, which became more severe during the war, Nazi Germany did draw on the work of women, but in ways that kept them away from combat, at least until the final collapse. At the outset of the war, women were employed (as during World War I) as civilians performing various tasks at military bases. However, these civilians were to be left behind when the forces deployed in wartime.[29]

The labor needs created by the war, especially as Germany found itself administering a large territory that it had rapidly conquered, led to the creation of a women's Signal Auxiliary of radio and telephone operators (picking up from the underused World War I signal corps women). It had about 8,000 members in the second half of the war. A Staff Auxiliary allowed about 12,000 women to carry out about one-third of the higher-level clerical jobs in rear areas throughout occupied Europe. The air force made most extensive use of women in an Auxiliary role – 100,000 by the end of the war. Most performed clerical, communications, and weather-related tasks, but many worked in antiaircraft units – not working with guns but staffing searchlight batteries (15,000 women running 350 batteries) and similar functions.[30]

All these uses of women by the Nazi military aimed to free men soldiers for combat while rigidly separating women from combat. Even the women's auxiliaries – who served in uniform, with rank, and under

[28] Tuten 1982, 48–49.
[29] Tuten 1982, 51.
[30] Tuten 1982, 54–55.

military discipline – "were neither trained in the use of arms nor were they allowed, under any conditions, to use them," even as a last resort to prevent capture. (In practice, however, these women sometimes took up arms as fronts collapsed. Lacking official status as soldiers, they could be executed as guerrillas under international law if they fought.) German military leaders were "horrified" at the Soviets' use of women soldiers, and resisted arming women even late in the war as manpower demands became extreme. In the last months of the war, Hitler reluctantly authorized creation of an experimental women's combat battalion, and later a mixed-gender guerrilla organization, but neither unit was deployed before the end of the war.[31]

The key factors that apparently opened the door for Soviet women in combat were desperation, total militarization of society, and an ideology that promoted women's participation outside of traditional feminine roles. Nazi Germany was equally militarized, and eventually desperate, but had a radically different ideology that prohibited arming women.

Other cases

Several other historical cases show the potential to use women's units in combat. These cases generally are smaller scale and of shorter duration than the Dahomey and Soviet cases.

Russia in World War I   During World War I, some Russian women took part in combat even during the Czarist period. These women, motivated by a combination of patriotism and a desire to escape a drab existence, mostly joined up dressed as men. A few, however, served openly as women. "The [Czarist] government had no consistent policy on female combatants." Russia's first woman aviator was turned down as a military pilot, and settled for driving and nursing. Another pilot was assigned to active duty, however.[32]

The most famous women soldiers were the "Battalion of Death." Its leader, Maria Botchkareva, a 25-year-old peasant girl (with a history of abuse by men), began as an individual soldier in the Russian army. She managed (with the support of an amused local commander) to get permission from the Czar to enlist as a regular soldier. After fighting off the frequent sexual advances and ridicule of her male comrades, she eventually won their respect – especially after serving with them in battle. Botchkareva's autobiography describes several horrendous battle scenes

[31] Tuten 1982, 55–56; De Pauw 1998, 245–47; Jones 1997, 200; Seifert 1995; practice: Ruth Seifert, personal communication 2000.
[32] De Pauw 1998, 214–16, 207–30; Hirschfeld 1934, 110–23; Stites 1978, policy 280.

in which most of her fellow soldiers were killed running towards German machine-gun positions, and one in which she bayoneted a German soldier to death. After two different failed attacks, she spent many hours crawling under German fire to drag her wounded comrades back to safety, evidently saving hundreds of lives in the course of her service at the front. She was seriously wounded several times but always returned to her unit at the front after recuperating. Clearly a strong bond of comradery existed between her and the male soldiers of her unit.[33]

After the February 1917 revolution, Alexander Kerensky as Minister of War in the provisional government allowed Botchkareva to organize a "Battalion of Death" composed of several hundred women. The history of this battalion is a bit murky because both anti- and pro-Bolshevik writers used it to make political points. (By contrast, the earlier phase of Botchkareva's military career is more credible.) Botchkareva's own 1919 account was "set down" by a leading anti-Bolshevik exile in the United States, who says he listened to her stories in Russian over several weeks and wrote them out simultaneously in English. The narrative is just a bit too politically correct (for an anti-Bolshevik); the stories of her heroic deeds are a bit too consistently dramatic. The language and analysis at times do not sound like the words of an illiterate peasant and soldier, and the book explicitly appeals for foreign help for Russian anti-Bolsheviks. (Louise Bryant's *pro*-Bolshevik account is equally unconvincing.)[34]

Botchkareva was aligned with Kornilov's faction, which wanted to restore discipline in the army and resume the war against Germany, contrary to the Bolshevik program of ending the war and carrying out immediate land reform and seizure of factories at home. During mid-1917, army units elected "committees" to discuss and decide on the unit's actions. Botchkareva insisted on traditional military rule from above in her battalion, and got away with it (though with only 300 of the original 2,000 women) because the unit was unique in the whole army. This endeared Botchkareva to many army officers and anti-Bolsheviks. It also put her battalion at the center of the June 1917 offensive – she says that it was the only unit capable of taking offensive action.

The battalion was formed in extraordinary circumstances, in response to a breakdown of morale and discipline in the Russian army after three horrible years of war and the fall of the Czarist government. By her own account, Botchkareva conceived of the battalion as a way to shame the men into fighting (since nothing else was getting them to fight). She argued that "numbers were immaterial, that what was important was

[33] Botchkareva 1919, 71–136; Stites 1978, 280.
[34] Botchkareva 1919, 154–71; Stites 1978, 280; White 1994, 4–5, 13; Bryant 1918, 212, 216–18.

to shame the men and that a few women at one place could serve as an example to the entire front . . . [T]he purpose of the plan would be to shame the men in the trenches by having the women go over the top first." The battalion was thus exceptional and was essentially a propaganda tool. As such it was heavily publicized: "Before I had time to realize it I was already in a photographer's studio . . . The following day this picture topped big posters pasted all over the city." Bryant wrote in 1918: "No other feature of the great war ever caught the public fancy like the Death Battalion, composed of Russian women. I heard so much about them before I left America . . ."[35]

The battalion began with about 2,000 women volunteers and was given equipment, a headquarters, and several dozen male officers as instructors. Botchkareva did not emphasize fighting strength but discipline (the purpose of the women soldiers was sacrificial). Physical standards for enlistment were lower than for men. She told the women, "We are physically weak, but if we be strong morally and spiritually we will accomplish more than a large force." She was preoccupied with upholding the moral standards and upright behavior of her "girls." Mostly, she emphasized that the soldiers in her battalion would have to follow traditional military discipline, not elect committees to rule as the rest of the army was doing. "I did not organize this Battalion to be like the rest of the army. We were to serve as an example, and not merely to add a few *babas* [women] to the ineffective millions of soldiers now swarming over Russia." When most of the women rebelled against her harsh rule, Botchkareva stubbornly rejected pleas from Kerensky and others – including direct orders from military superiors – to allow formation of a committee. Instead she reorganized the remaining 300 women who stayed loyal to her, and brought them to the front, fighting off repeated attacks by Bolsheviks along the way. The battalion had new uniforms, a full array of war equipment, and 18 men to serve them (two instructors, eight cooks, six drivers, and two shoemakers).[36]

The battalion was to open the offensive which Kerensky ordered in June 1917. (Since the February revolution, there had been little fighting and growing fraternization on the Russian–German front.) The Bolsheviks opposed the offensive, and the tired, demoralized soldiers were not motivated to participate in it. By sending 300 women over the top first, Botchkareva envisioned triggering an advance along the entire front – 14 million Russian soldiers – propelled by the men's shame at seeing "their sisters going into battle," thus overcoming the men's cowardice.

[35] Shame: Botchkareva 1919, 157, 207, 211, studio 161; Bryant 1918, 10.
[36] Botchkareva 1919, began 163–64, swarming 173, 172–83, 202–5, uniforms 189, 192, 197.

When the appointed time for the attack came, however, the men on either side of the women's battalion refused to move. The next day, about 100 male officers and 300 male soldiers who favored the offensive joined the ranks of the women's battalion, and it was this mixed force of 700 that went over the top that night, hoping to goad the men on either side into advancing too. Locally, the tactic worked, and the entire corps advanced and captured three German lines (the men stopping at the second, however, to make immediate use of alcohol found there). As the Russian line spread thin, however, another corps which was supposed to move forward to relieve them refused to advance. A costly retreat to the original lines ensued. The shame tactic had failed, except for a local effect, which anyway may have been caused as much by seeing comrades under fire as by feeling shame about women going first. Ultimately, Botchkareva concludes about the Russian army, "the men knew no shame."[37]

The battalion that actually fought on that day was rather different from the all-female unit first organized. The battalion arrived at the front with 300 women and two male instructors. Before battle, it received 19 more male officers and instructors, and a male "battle adjutant" was selected. During final preparations, a "detachment of eight machine guns and a [male] crew to man them" were added. Lined up in the trenches for the first night's offensive that did not materialize, six male officers were inserted at equal intervals, with Botchkareva herself at one end and her male adjutant in the center. In the force that actually went over the top the next night with 400 male soldiers and officers added, the "line was so arranged that men and women alternated, a girl being flanked by two men." Botchkareva notes that in advancing under withering fire, "my brave girls [were] encouraged by the presence of men on their sides." Although the women fighters clearly were brave, and one-third of them were killed or wounded, their effect (and indeed their purpose) lay not in their military value – 300 soldiers could hardly make a difference among millions – but in their propaganda value. However, this latter effect did not materialize as hoped.[38]

Other women's battalions were formed in several other cities – apparently less than 1,000 women in all – but they suffered from a variety of problems, ranging from poor discipline to a lack of shoes and uniforms. These other units never saw combat. There was not another offensive before the Bolsheviks took power in October and sent most of the women soldiers home, telling them "to put on female attire."[39]

[37] Botchkareva 1919, sisters 207, knew 262.
[38] Botchkareva 1919, adjutant 205, 208–12.
[39] Bryant 1918, 212–13.

The Battalion of Death, then, never tested an all-female unit's effectiveness in combat. Nonetheless, on one day in 1917, 300 women did go over the top side by side with 400 male comrades, advanced, and overran German trenches. The women apparently were able to keep functioning in the heat of battle, and were able to adhere to military discipline. These women were, of course, an elite sample of the most war-capable women in all of Russia. Nonetheless, they did it – advanced under fire, retreated under fire, and helped provide that crucial element of leadership by which other nearby units were spurred into action, overcoming the inertia of fatigue and committee rule. The Battalion of Death did this not as scattered individual women but as a coherent military unit of 300 women – instructed by Botchkareva that "they were no longer women, but soldiers."[40]

Taiping Rebellion and other cases   Very occasionally, all-female military units have cropped up elsewhere in the world for short periods of time. In the nineteenth-century Taiping Rebellion in China, the rebels formed and then later disbanded female units in their army. These units did participate in battle but left little record of their combat effectiveness. The rebellion – a massive uprising led by a Christian cult leader, with roots in the Hakka ethnic group of southern China – became perhaps the bloodiest civil war in history (tens of millions killed). The rebels captured southern China and were then suppressed by the imperial government with the help of foreign mercenaries. The Taipings' puritanical religious doctrine called for rigid gender separation, with men's and women's quarters in cities, and even married couples faced execution if found together. This segregation was abandoned after several years owing to its bad effect on morale (especially since it had never been followed by top leaders).[41]

Rumors of female armies in ancient China are murky. I have been unable to find any historically documented cases. In times of siege, units of women, of children, and of old men were formed to help with defense, but in support rather than combat roles. The *Cambridge History of China* makes a passing reference to China's frontier region in the second century AD where "even Chinese women had been transformed into fierce warriors under the influence of the Ch'iang" ethnic group. The book's description of the Ch'iang does not mention women fighters, however. The war participation of women in second-century China, whatever its extent, appears to reflect the Wild West character of the

[40] Botchkareva 1919, soldiers 165.
[41] Spence 1996; Fairbank ed. 1978, 276–77; Michael 1966, 43–45; Jen 1973.

region rather than the incorporation of women *en masse* in a regular army.[42]

Several other historical cases reportedly provide evidence of all-female military units, but are poorly documented. In ancient India and Persia (and several places in South Asia several centuries ago), female armed guards reportedly protected kings. A Chinese art historian states that the Hsi-hsia army – in a non-Chinese state northwest of the Song dynasty in the eleventh to thirteenth centuries – used female shock troops and had a tradition of female warriors going back hundreds of years. Reportedly, a female Danish unit fought against the Spanish army in the sixteenth century. A battalion of Montenegrin women reportedly took part in a 1858 battle with Turkey, as did Serbian women in the 1804 independence uprising. In the Congo in 1640, the Monomotapa confederacy supposedly had standing armies of women. The first army in postcolonial Malawi in 1964 reportedly included an elite unit of 5,000 women to guard the Tanganyikan border. (Shaka Zulu's army by one erroneous account had an all-female front-line regiment. Scholarship on Shaka's military tactics makes clear that all the soldiers were men.)[43]

B. MIXED-GENDER UNITS

In addition to the extremely rare cases of all-female military units, evidence of women's combat potentials appears in cases where mixed-gender military units have engaged in combat. Although main combat-designated units are nearly always all-male, some units not designated primarily for combat have included women, in a variety of cultures and time periods. These units, trained in the use of arms, sometimes find themselves engaged in combat, with the women participating. We have evidence from guerrilla organizations, from the few NATO countries that currently allow women into combat positions, and from the present-day US experience with gender integration.

Guerrilla armies

Guerrilla warfare provides a rich source of data on mixed-gender combat units. Women fighters are not uncommon in guerrilla armies (see Figure 2.3). From the Cold War and post-Cold War eras alone, scholars

---

[42] Boulding 1992/I, 237; David Graff, personal communication 1998; Peter Lorge, personal communication 1998; De Pauw 1998, 204–5, 332–33; Li 1995; Twitchett and Loewe 1986, Ch'iang 433, 422–23.

[43] Ancient: Alpern 1998, 2–3; Chinese: Yu forthcoming; Danish: Francke 1997, 243; Montenegrin–Serbian: Jancar 1982, 87; Congo–Malawi: Brown 1998; Shaka: Brown 1998; Edgerton 1988, 38–39, 107; Thompson 1969, 344.

Figure 2.3 Kurdish women guerrillas, 1991. [AP/Wide World Photos.]

have illuminated women's crucial roles in a variety of wars, including in Vietnam, South Africa, Argentina, Cyprus, Iran, Northern Ireland, Lebanon, Israel, Nicaragua, and others.[44]

In World War II, in addition to the Soviet partisans (see pp. 000–000), women participated in the partisan forces of other occupied countries as well – countries that did not allow women into regular military forces – including Italy, Greece, France, Poland, and Denmark. They took part in street fighting, carried out assassinations, and performed intelligence missions. In Italy, reportedly 35,000 women were partisans, of whom 650 were killed. In the French Resistance, women were much more excluded from combat roles (although they played many dangerous support roles). Only a few women were "full-time, gun-carrying women fighters." Because of prejudice in France against women fighters, one of the few

[44] Pettman 1996a, 126–53; Isaksson 1988; Ruddick 1990, 231; Elshtain 1987, 184–85; Zur 1989, 315–20; Zur and Morrison 1989; Vietnam: D. Butler 1990; Jason ed. 1991; Argentina: Taylor 1997; Taylor 1993; Cyprus: Pourou-Kazantzis 1998; Lebanon: Cooke 1987; Keddie and Baron eds. 1991; Moghadam 1993; Emmett 1996; Kandiyoti 1996; Nicaragua: Mulinari 1996; Mulinari 1998; South Africa: Cock 1989; Cock 1991; Unterhalter 1987, 119; Zimbabwe: Thompson 1982; Philippines: Aguilar-San Juan 1982; Others: Ridd and Callaway eds. 1986; Matthews 1993; S. Carter 1992; Noakes 1998, 103–63; Mora 1998; Beilstein 1998; Collett 1996; Peterson and Runyan 1993, 129–35.

women who had a leadership position in combat often pretended to be a representative of a male leader when organizing the Resistance. Another was excluded from participating in armed attacks because the uniformed army of de Gaulle opposed giving guns to women, even though local Resistance men considered her an equal comrade.[45]

Most notable among the World War II women partisans were those of Yugoslavia, a country where centuries of tradition allowed some role for women as fighters, and where conditions were nearly as desperate as in the Soviet Union. Most women's work in the mass resistance to Nazi occupation was in traditionally feminine support roles. Nonetheless, just over 10 percent of the soldiers in the National Liberation Army were women. They received the same kinds of minimal basic training as men (but first aid or medical training more often than men), and the official communist ideology declared them equivalent. In practice, women tended to remain at low ranks and to be concentrated in medical tasks. In one set of units studied, 42 percent of the women were "fighters" and 46 percent medics. "Clearly, the role of medic became 'feminized' . . . [I]f there was a single woman in the [unit], she would be designated the medic." Nonetheless, in guerrilla war even medics are usually fighters too. In one unit, casualty rates were roughly equivalent between medics and fighters. "Women partisans led the same life as men – they slept in the same quarters, ate the same food, and wore the same clothes." The partisan force "severely discouraged" sexual relations in the ranks, although arrangements were made for married couples.[46]

Accounts of the effectiveness of the women soldiers, even taken in the same cautious vein as the Soviet case (with allowance for propaganda distortion), suggest that women made an important contribution overall. By official count, 100,000 women were in the National Liberation Army and partisan units so thousands must have been fighters. Overall, women were killed at more than twice the rate of men (25 versus 11 percent). Despite the limits on their participation, the women of the Yugoslavian resistance acquitted themselves well in combat, showing above-average bravery and stamina. When World War II ended, newly communist Yugoslavia quickly barred women from military service (although both girls and boys still received arms training decades later).[47]

The Vietnamese communists' war against the French and Americans shares several features with the World War II Yugoslavia case – a

[45] Wilhelm 1988, Italy 119; Weitz 1995, 147–70, fighters 148, 150, comrade 155; Jones 1997, 199–203.

[46] Jancar 1982, roles 85, 100, NLA 90, 99, training 93–94, medic 97–98; Jancar-Webster 1990, clothes–married 89.

[47] Jancar-Webster 1990, 88; Jancar 1982, 93.

communist-led "people's war" in a country with some tradition of women warriors (see the Trung sisters, p. 121). This tradition was updated, in the "war of liberation" (1946–75), to the picture of a Vietcong woman with a baby in one arm and a rifle in the other. As in Yugoslavia and the Soviet Union, the image of women fighters symbolized the mobilization of the entire society for the cause. Behind the image, propaganda aside, was a hard reality of women's participation. One Vietnamese military historian estimates that 60,000 women were in the regular forces, over 100,000 in the volunteer youth corps, and over 1 million in militias and other local forces. In the People's Liberation Armed Forces (PLAF) in the 1960s, a woman veteran of local uprisings was appointed deputy commander, and by one estimate 40 percent of all regimental commanders were women. The women soldiers served in both all-female and mixed-gender units. Reportedly, the latter experienced some problems regarding male attitudes, and the men often considered the women inferior in combat. Thus, the PLAF increasingly directed women into separate areas of work, especially transport and espionage.[48]

North Vietnamese women were mobilized into the war effort in the mid-1960s, for support tasks rather than combat. Even those within the army itself mainly worked on medical, liaison, antiaircraft, or bomb-defusing tasks. "It was general policy to discourage active combat for women." Women did serve in local militia units in the North – working in the fields with rifles slung over their shoulders – but these areas were far from the "front." Nonetheless women in the North played an important part in shooting down US airplanes and capturing pilots. In the South, meanwhile, more women were recruited by the communist army, but mainly for support functions. Women did apparently participate in combat during the 1968 Tet offensive. But as guerrilla war gave way to conventional war, women were separated more from combat. "In the end, the role of women in the Vietnamese revolution was a significant but somewhat restricted one." (In the South Vietnamese government army, some women also fought.)[49]

Ideals of motherhood and feminine duty supported participation in the North Vietnamese war effort. Women participants in the war effort experienced it not in terms of glorious exploits but as a huge added burden on an already full basket of "women's work." Women carried most of the loads along the Ho Chi Minh trail to sustain the war effort. Although they might take part in fighting, especially in antiaircraft defense of their home communities, women's main function in the war was to provide cheap labor. Women's combat participation, although glorified during the war

[48] Duiker 1982, 114–15; Turner 1998, estimates 20–21; De Pauw 1998, 269–72.
[49] Duiker 1982, policy–one 117–19; south: Francke 1997, 244.

as a model of self-sacrifice for the nation, was downplayed and largely forgotten after the war, as in other countries.[50]

The image of the woman holding a rifle and a baby is found in liberation movements across the third world. It combines the roles of motherhood and war, harnessing women for war *without* altering fundamental gender relations. Cynthia Enloe finds in the image an expectation that, after the war ends, mothers will put down the rifles while keeping the babies. She asks: "Where is the picture of the *male* guerrilla holding the rifle and baby?"[51]

The Sandinistas of Nicaragua resemble the other communist revolutionary guerrillas. Women reportedly made up nearly one-third of the Sandinista front's military. After victory, the front's founder praised women for being "in the front line of battle." Women were particularly attracted to the Sandinista front because, as a movement that grew up in a feminist era, the front had a strong women's organization which advocated policies that helped women. Nonetheless, after victory, the "defense of women's role in the military failed. After their victory in July 1979, most women were demobilized, and the rest were placed in all-female battalions." The director of Nicaragua's leading military school explained the "need to train women separately" as being "not because of any limitations the women have. In fact, you might say it's because of failings on the part of some men ... [who] aren't always able to relate to a woman as just another soldier." However, apparently exceptions were made for women of superior military skill, who remained in their male army units. Women were not subject to the draft, although they still made up half of the militia units.[52]

In some ways, the Sandinistas left traditional gender roles firmly in place. Women were mobilized around the image of mothers protecting their children as part of a divine order. One Sandinista official said in 1980, "give every woman a gun with which to defend her children." In fact, however, good mothers were expected to be "Patriotic Wombs" that would provide soldiers for the revolution and happily send them off to die for the cause. The Sandinistas limited abortion and sterilization, among other measures to produce high birth rates, since a small nation at war needed more people. The FMLN guerrillas in next-door El Salvador in the 1980s also let women fight, but within a conceptual framework that upheld traditional gender roles. Cynthia Enloe highlights the story of a woman FMLN guerrilla in El Salvador who, with the end

[50] Turner 1998.
[51] Enloe 1983, 166; Bayard de Volo 1998, 246.
[52] Jones 1997, founder 103; Randall 1981, director 138–39, 147; Seitz, Lobao, and Treadway 1993, 175.

of the war there, is having her IUD removed – a transition from soldier to mother.[53]

In Africa, women guerrillas also have fought and then been pushed aside. For example, Joice Nhongo was the "most famous" guerrilla in the ZANLA forces that overthrew white rule in Rhodesia (Zimbabwe). She was known as "Mrs. Spill-blood Nhongo," and gave birth to a daughter at the camp she commanded, two days after an air raid against it. After ZANLA took power, she became Minister of Community Development and Women's Affairs – safely removed from military affairs. (Reportedly, 4,000 women combatants made up 6 percent of ZANLA forces.[54])

In South Africa in the 1980s, the armed wing of the African National Congress included women guerrillas. Thandi Modise was called the "knitting needles guerrilla" because she carried a handbag with a protruding pair of knitting needles while traveling incognito. She reports that in training camps, the women (under 10 percent of the trainees) received the same uniforms and training, and were treated respectfully, as equals, by the men. She sees no contradiction in being a guerrilla and a mother, and argues that "Marriage and children are necessities, not luxuries." Modise does, however, say that "As a woman I tried to avoid killing people." Although male and female guerrillas received the same training, side by side, and women sometimes outdid men in discipline, sharpshooting, and running, women were excluded from traditional combat roles. As a male guerrilla put it, "Yes, a woman can be a soldier. Many women fight better than men. But I wouldn't deploy women in the front line ... Men go to war to defend their women and children." Manliness played an important role for South African black male guerrillas, and even Nelson Mandela once said that the "experience of military training made me a man."[55]

It is not only in communist revolutionary movements, such as in Yugoslavia, Vietnam, and Nicaragua, that women participate in local militias. This phenomenon is widespread, because militias often constitute a last line of defense of home and family against external attack. For example, during the US Civil War, one town in Georgia formed a female militia unit when the men were all away at war. They drilled, practiced shooting, and in an "apocryphal story" supposedly faced down Sherman's cavalry which had planned to burn the town.[56]

---

[53] Bayard de Volo 1998, give–wombs 246–48; cf. Mora 1998, 170; Luttwak 1997.
[54] Uglow ed. 1989, 400–1; Cock 1991, numbers 182–83; Sylvester 1989, 108; cf. Kenya: Kanogo 1987, 94.
[55] Cock 1991, knitting 149, equals 162–65, luxuries–killing 152–53, 150, defend 165, man 168; Morris 1993.
[56] Hall 1993, apocryphal 104–5; Fellman 1992.

In Sri Lanka currently, women apparently constitute about one-third of the rebel Tamil Tigers' force of 15,000 fighters, and participate fully in both suicide bombings and massacres of civilians. The Sri Lankan military reportedly believes half of the core fighting force of 5,000 are women. (A claim that women are two-thirds of the force appears to be overstated.)[57]

In Iraq in the late 1990s, one of the main guerrilla groups operating against next-door Iran – with 30,000 soldiers, Iraqi backing, and $2 billion worth of weapons – is led by a 43-year-old Iranian woman and her husband. She is the "symbol of the struggle" and their candidate for transitional President of Iran if they should ever seize power. Reportedly, the group is led by mainly female officers, and includes women among its fighters – although how many women is unclear. Members live in gender-segregated quarters and married couples suspend marriages to function as "sisters and brothers" in the group. The force engaged in combat in 1988, and 1991, and reportedly performed well.[58]

The greater fluidity of gender roles in guerrilla as compared with conventional war is illustrated by the Republic of Congo war in 1997. Guerrilla militias included women fighters and commanders. Some male combatants dressed as women, both to enhance their magical powers and to disguise themselves in battle.[59]

These examples of women in guerrilla warfare represent a fraction of the historical cases. In guerrilla war, by contrast with conventional war, women's participation is not rare. One often finds combat units with a nontrivial minority of women in the ranks. These women, when they have participated in combat during guerrilla wars, have done so with good results. They have added to the military strength of their units, and sometimes fought with greater skill and bravery than their male comrades. Yet whenever their forces have seized power and become regular armies, women have been excluded from combat. Evidently, this exclusion is not based on any lack of ability shown by the women soldiers when they participated in the guerrilla phase of war.[60]

Present-day state armies

More than a dozen states – mostly industrialized countries that are US allies – currently allow women into official combat positions. The exact

[57] Filkins 2000, third; Ganguly 2000, half; De Pauw 1998, two-thirds 292; De Alwis 1998; Bennett, Bexley, and Warnock 1995, 135–56, 228–41.

[58] Jehl 1996.

[59] Wallis 1997.

[60] Enloe 1983, 160–72; Tetreault 1992; Boulding 1992/II, 288–92; De Pauw 1998, 290–91.

number depends on how exactly one defines combat. A 1993 list includes Canada, Belgium, Netherlands, Denmark, Norway, and Britain. A 1997 work also includes Spain and Australia, but not Britain. By 1999, in addition, France, Japan, South Africa, Sri Lanka, Taiwan, Israel, and Russia had at least one woman fighter-jet pilot, and women served in navies in Portugal, South Africa, and others. In 2000, an Israeli law and a German court ruling promised to integrate women into more military jobs, though implementation is unclear and ground combat will likely remain off-limits.[61]

Eritrea and South Africa had women in the infantry, owing to the recent integration of former guerrilla forces into state armies there. Eritrean women combatants have seen extensive combat – uniquely among present-day state armies – owing to the highly lethal ground war with Ethiopia in the late 1990s. Some reports put women at one-third of Eritrean combat forces. Eritrea, however, has existed as a state for only a few years, and is still led by former guerrilla commanders, even though fighting a conventional, not guerrilla, war.[62]

Women's status in NATO militaries is evolving year by year, with the policies and numbers shifting continually towards greater women's participation. The different countries are generally moving along a common path in integrating women, though at different speeds – from combat aviation, to combat ships, to submarines, to ground combat. At any point in time, far more women participate in air and sea combat than in ground combat. Women in all these positions total only a few thousand (out of millions of combat soldiers today), but they provide further data points to assess the performance of women in combat. Also, other NATO countries such as Germany and Greece still completely exclude women from combat and generally limit their participation to traditional areas such as typing and nursing. Overall, women's participation has been recent and the units in which they serve have seen little if any combat since being integrated. Women aviators did, however, participate in NATO's 1999 air campaign against Serbia.[63]

Canada is furthest along the spectrum of NATO countries. Canada's military has opened all positions to women, in theory. Furthermore, the military is actively recruiting women interested in serving in ground combat positions. New submarines are being built to accommodate women. Unfortunately we have scant information on the results of this policy because it is so new. Canadian units have not seen combat since women

---

[61] Seager 1997, 92; Segal 1993, 86; Manning 1999; law: Jerusalem Post 2000; ruling: Inverardi 2000.

[62] Fisher 1999; De Pauw 1998, 292.

[63] Lory Manning, personal communication 1998; Enloe 1982, 127–31; NATO 1994.

joined them, although they have deployed on at least ten peacekeeping missions around the world. In the Gulf War, women served on a Canadian supply ship, but only 3 percent of Canadian forces participating in that war were women, compared with over 10 percent in the Canadian military overall at that time. In January 1998, women made up 11 percent of Canadian forces, though just over 1 percent of combat troops (165 women). Sexual harassment and rape are serious problems in the gender-integrated Canadian military, and female soldiers "are often little more than game for sexual predators," according to one recent exposé. An official army study in 1998 "said women in combat units commonly were referred to in coarse sexual terms."[64]

Denmark, Norway, and France are nearly as gender-integrated as Canada. Danish women serve in tank crews, including those that were deployed for peacekeeping in Bosnia. (Although peacekeeping is not usually "combat," Danish tanks had earlier battled Bosnian Serb forces.) Denmark's decision to include women in all military roles resulted from extensive trials in the mid-1980s to find out how women performed in various land and sea combat roles. "The trials proved very satisfactory, and today all functions are open to women...The trial results [show]...that women can do the work just as well as their male colleagues."[65]

France allows women in air, sea, and ground combat, and plans to subject women to the draft starting in 2001. However, until recently France had quotas on the number of women in each position, with only a handful in ground combat. Women are still not allowed in the Foreign Legion, commando positions, or flying naval airplanes, although they no longer face quotas in other positions including flying combat aircraft. As recently as 1994, NATO summarized France's policies on women in combat thus: "A woman's role is to give life and not death. For this reason alone it is not desirable for mothers to take direct part in battle."[66]

In Norway, women serve on submarines, including one as a captain. They are in infantry, artillery, tanks, and all kinds of aircraft. Two served as officers in the UN peacekeeping force in the former Yugoslavia. None of the integrated units has seen combat. Belgium, the Netherlands, and Spain allow women in almost any position in theory, but only a few women serve in practice, especially in ground combat. In the Netherlands, women can serve anywhere except in combat positions in the Marine

[64] NATO 1994, 4; Enloe 1994, 81; O'Hara 1998, 23, 14; Associated Press 1998a; Weinstein and White 1997.
[65] NATO 1994, 6, 8.
[66] NATO 1994, 16.

Corps. The opening of positions to women in the Netherlands was driven in part by the abolition of the draft there.[67]

Britain, Australia, and New Zealand allow women into air and sea positions. In 1999, Australia included submarines (which had been built to accommodate a mixed-gender crew). Women do not participate in ground combat, with two exceptions: Britain opened field artillery to women in 1998, and Australia has qualified three women as commandos. These forces have not yet participated in combat. The British found in the 1982 Falklands War that it was hard to distinguish "combat" from "noncombat" ships, and this may explain why Britain has opened all surface ships to women (about 700 women serve on British ships currently).[68]

The Israeli experience   In Israel, the persistent myth that Israeli women participate in combat is false. Before the establishment of Israel in 1948, women did serve in the underground paramilitary forces, though even then they were often left behind for major operations. A few women also fought before the 1948 war, when isolated settlements came under attack. With independence and the creation of a regular army, however, women were immediately and permanently excluded from all combat roles. Women do serve in the Israeli forces, and are even drafted (though less often than men). Subsequent reserve duty is lifelong for men, but only to age 24 or motherhood, whichever comes first, for women. Over half of female draftees serve in secretarial and clerical jobs. A women's corps (its initials spell "charm") administers the policies concerning Israeli women soldiers, including training them, overseeing their work in various units, and operating some of its own units. A 1980 women's corps brochure states: "Today's Israeli female soldiers are trim girls, clothed in uniforms which bring out their youthful femininity." These women serve as "sister-figure" or "mother-figure" in a unit. Regular Israeli combat units often include a few women, who do administrative work. These assignments are "highly sought after" by women. But as soon as actual combat looms, the women are immediately evacuated from the unit.[69]

In the late 1970s, after the shock of the 1973 Yom Kippur War, and under great manpower pressures, the IDF opened up new nontraditional specialties to women, including instructing men on the use of arms. The 1980 brochure states that women serving as platoon sergeants in all-male basic training "have succeeded outstandingly." The brochure continues:

[67] Manning 1999; NATO 1994, 25.

[68] Manning 1999; NATO 1994.

[69] Van Creveld 1993, 6–9; Gal 1986, 46–57, 32–33, 48–49, brochure 47, sister–sought 52; Bloom 1982; Enloe 1983, 156.

"New recruits do not dare complain of muscle aches and pains or drop out of a long-distance run when it is being led by a female sergeant." Women's success as arms instructors shows that some women can wield weapons effectively – for example, driving tanks, firing guns, and deploying armed groups tactically.[70]

The reasons given for the exclusion of women from combat in Israel revolve around their effects on male soldiers rather than their own combat abilities. For example, men in mixed units supposedly showed excessive concern for the well-being of the women at the expense of the mission. The actual evidence of such effects is very sketchy, however.[71]

The US experience

The US military in recent years has compiled the most extensive experience in integrating women into regular military units – though generally not "combat" units. As of 1999, nearly 200,000 women serve in the US military (14 percent of the total force), over 1 million are veterans, and thousands have operated in combat zones in several wars. (Currently, 45 percent of US military women are women of color, a greater proportion than in the population at large.) US women participate in combat support roles, ranging from the traditional (nursing, typing) to the nontraditional (mechanics, arms training). Sometimes the lines between combat and support blur so that women soldiers have found themselves in a combat zone or engaged in fighting.[72]

Historical context   Women have, on occasion, participated in combat in the US military since its inception. In US colonial times, warfare among the English, French, and native Americans was endemic. "For their own survival, colonial women learned to threaten force and to kill in self-defense. Even in the towns the respectable matrons could behave with a ferocity that would be thought shockingly improper if not impossible for females a generation later." In several historically documented cases, in the countryside women killed American Indians and in towns mobs of women carried out lynchings. During the Revolution, in addition to their roles as camp followers and as soldiers disguised as men, American women fought in militias in the countryside.[73]

In the Revolutionary War, "Molly Pitcher" is a legendary woman who accompanied her husband in the field – a common practice in armies

---

[70] Gal 1986, 50, succeeded–recruits 49–50, 52–53; Van Creveld 1993, 8–9; Jerusalem Post 2000.

[71] De Pauw 1998, 281–86.

[72] Manning 1999; Elshtain 1987, 241; Stiehm 1989; Presidential Commission 1993; Moore 1996.

[73] De Pauw 1975, 174–93, later 174–75; De Pauw 1998, 110–15.

of the time (see pp. 381–83). She used to nurse wounded troops and carry water (hence her nickname). When her husband was killed in the Battle of Monmouth, she took over firing his cannon – to the admiration of her fellow soldiers – and in a dubious epilogue is said to have met George Washington. ("Molly Pitcher" seems to be a composite of three real women who fought in the war.) In the Civil War, women fought on both sides, most of them disguised as men.[74]

In World War I, 13,000 women enlisted in the US Navy, mostly doing clerical work – "the first [women in US history] . . . to be admitted to full military rank and status." The Army hired women nurses and telephone operators to work overseas, but as civilian employees (although in uniform). Plans for women's auxiliary corps – to perform mostly clerical, supply, and communications work – were shot down by the War Department. So were plans for commissioning women doctors in the Medical Corps. The end of the war brought an end to proposals to enlist women in the Army.[75]

In the interwar years, the Army created a Director of Women's Relations to explain to women, now that they could vote, that pacifism was a bad idea. The embattled Director in the 1920s, Anita Phipps, developed a plan for a women's corps which would be part of the Army itself, not an Auxiliary, and would incorporate 170,000 women in wartime. This plan was not approved, however. The Army favored keeping any future women workers in an Auxiliary. Even the auxiliary role was approved only because, as an official memo put it in 1941, "it will tend to avert the pressure to admit women to actual membership in the Army." The same memo declared that the War Department would develop the idea slowly and not rush into it on a large scale.[76]

The realities of World War II, however, quickly changed this approach. With the United States more deeply mobilized for war (and over a longer period) than in World War I, women's participation in the military increased dramatically, to about 3 percent of US forces at the peak. The experience of World War II provides the largest amount of information on women soldiers up until the 1980s and 1990s.[77]

The Women's Army Auxiliary Corps (WAAC) was formed early in 1942, soon after Pearl Harbor. In mid-1943 it became a regular part of the Army, as the Women's Army Corps (WAC). Within the US Army, the incorporation of so many women was an unprecedented development. The WAC encountered serious obstacles in recruiting American women

[74] De Pauw 1998, 115–31.
[75] Treadwell 1954, 6–10, status 10; De Pauw 1998, 225–29; Hewitt 1974.
[76] Treadwell 1954, 18.
[77] Campbell 1990, 107; De Pauw 1998, 247–58; Larson 1995.

(discussed shortly), and it faced continual bureaucratic attacks from the War Department, the Surgeon General, and others. Mattie Treadwell's 1954 history tells the story in detail. The WACs were never assigned to combat and rarely got near it. But their large-scale mobilization into the US Army some 65 years ago gives us valuable information about how women perform as soldiers, on *some* of the dimensions necessary for a functional combat soldier. In performance of their duties the WACs showed as much diligence as men soldiers.

Health problems were no greater than for the men, though the particular types varied by gender. The WACs lost less hospital time than men, and rates of accidents and nonbattle injuries were nearly identical across gender. But men were far more likely to be injured in motor vehicle accidents, whereas women more often fell down in situations unrelated to their jobs – partly because suitable military shoes were not provided. Towards the end of the war, fatigue became a serious problem for WACs, but its character was opposite to the combat fatigue endured by men – for women, it was unrelieved sedentary work with little visible connection to the war effort. Combined with Army food, the sendentary work of WACs led to a "widespread condition of overweight."[78]

The WAC found that menstruation presented only minor problems for efficiency, with most of those being caused by Army regulations that, for example, sent women to the hospital for two days if their cramps made them stop work even just long enough for aspirin to take effect. In the Army Air Forces, women who ferried planes were not supposed to fly for several days around their periods, but male commanders found this rule unenforceable since many women did not cooperate with it, said nothing, and just kept flying. (In the event of pregnancy, a WAC was immediately discharged and left to her own resources.)[79]

In the area of discipline, most of the problems resulted from the novelty of the situation – enforcement varied greatly from one locale to another – and from the men's problems in dealing with women, such as having "great difficulty in punishing a woman for anything." Gender differences in discipline may have resulted from the exclusion of WACs from combat as well. As a 1946 Army field manual states, "the necessity for discipline is never fully comprehended by the soldier until he has undergone the experience of battle." However, overall, morale and discipline were high among the women.[80]

With regard to their ability to function in a hierarchy (see pp. 206–8), WACs differed from their male counterparts. Curiously, the main

[78] Treadwell 1954, 611, 626, overweight 627.
[79] Treadwell 1954, rule 612–14, pregnancy 507–9.
[80] Treadwell 1954, 503–7, punishing 503, battle 676; Campbell 1990, morale 112.

difference is opposite to the emphasis on male autonomy and female connectedness discussed earlier (see pp. 46–47). The WAC Director specifically noted that "women need to remain individuals." This high value on individuality, combined with a lack of experience with loyalty to organizations, made women tend to treat each other as separate individuals, contrary to the military style of hierarchy. If inspired by a WAC leader who set an example of loyalty to the Army, however, WACs' "natural idealism was apt to produce group loyalty and *esprit* of an unexcelled intensity."[81]

The WACs resented the "caste system" separating officers from enlisted personnel, since it restricted enlisted women's contact with close friends or family members who were male officers. Within the WAC itself, however, few of the problems experienced in male–male relations across ranks developed. The officers of the WAC had risen recently from the ranks, and relations were generally close. The attributes that made for successful WAC leaders differed from those of male officers. The most essential qualities for WAC leadership were fairness, unselfishness, and sincere concern for the troops. Selfish ambition, accepted in male officers, was "absolutely disqualifying" when leading WACs. Appearance and technical competence, emphasized in training male officers, did not matter for WAC officers. In terms of fitting the WAC into the larger male-dominated Army of which it was a part, few serious problems developed. Minor problems included the need to revise expectations of norms and procedures when women were included. For example, a male officer invited newly arrived WAAC officers to his hotel room for drinks – an action that would have been quite appropriate for newly arrived male officers. The one serious problem in local Army–WAC relations arose in those few cases where a male commander allowed romantic impulses – especially "immoral" ones – to affect military decisions (such as securing special privileges for one WAC). Such cases were viewed as "complete betrayal" by the rest of the WAC unit, and the unit's effectiveness plummeted.[82]

WACs were often better than men at communications and clerical work, especially in listening to Morse code for long hours. On the other hand, WACs in the Pacific (where they needed armed escorts to protect them from sex-starved GIs) "became demoralized" by their mail censorship duties which required reading sexually explicit letters home to wives and girlfriends.[83]

US women also served in the Air Force and Navy during World War II. The Women's Airforce Service Pilots (WASPs) worked in ferrying planes

---

[81] Treadwell 1954, 675.
[82] Treadwell 1954, caste 511–14, drinks 681–82, immoral 678, betrayal 682, 669–83.
[83] Costello 1985, 49, 52.

Figure 2.4 US WASP pilots after flight in B-17. [US National Archives, 342-FH-4A5344-160449ac.]

and as test pilots. About 1,000 women took part, and 38 died in the line of duty (see Figure 2.4). The Navy WAVES (Women Accepted for Volunteer Emergency Service) participated in air traffic control, naval air navigation, and communications, starting in 1942. There was a Marine Corps Women's Reserve in both World Wars; 18 died in World War II. They became a permanent component of the Marines, and their successors decades later are described as "even more gung ho than many of the males."[84]

At its peak in 1945, the WAC had 100,000 members (at its inception the Army had hoped for 600,000). In all, during World War II, about 150,000 women served in the WAC, nearly 90,000 in the WAVES, about 25,000 in Marine reserves and Coast Guard SPARS, and 75,000 as officer-nurses. Total fatalities appear to be in the range of 200–300 women in all, but apparently few of these were by hostile fire.[85]

Although soldiers and officers who worked with US military women in World War II adjusted to them and came to value their contributions, public opinion lagged behind. The WAC's biggest problem was in

[84] Soderbergh 1992, xv, gung xvii.
[85] Soderbergh 1992, 146–47.

recruiting, especially after a "slander campaign" against it in 1943. The campaign promoted the idea that WACs were really prostitutes, or women with low morals. Leaders had to spend great energy trying to counteract this campaign both through public advertising and through attention to the women's appearance (feminine uniforms) and their actual morals, which were generally upstanding. (In the British Army in World War I, officials omitted a breast pocket on women's uniforms for fear of drawing attention to female anatomy.) Despite efforts to counteract the slander campaign, a survey of Army men in 1945 found that about half thought it was bad for a girl's reputation to be a WAC. Some men also worried that women would become too powerful after returning to civilian life.[86]

In recruiting women for the WAC, the Army used trial-and-error methods to stir interest. A major recruiting theme, "Release a Man for Combat," was abandoned – but could never be fully suppressed in the public mind – when women responded poorly to the notion that their participation could send an American man to his death. Later cheery themes, such as "I'm Having the Time of My Life," were also unsuccessful. An all-out advertising and canvassing campaign in Cleveland in summer 1943 proved a total failure: personal contact with 73,000 families identified 8,000 eligible women, but brought only 168 recruits. At that rate the 100,000 new WACs needed immediately would require contacting 44 million families, more than the total US population. Waiving the requirement of high school graduation also produced few recruits. As a result of this failure to recruit an additional half-million WACs in 1943, the draft was extended to fathers of young families, even though a March 1944 US poll found that three-quarters of the public would rather draft young single women (for noncombat positions) than young fathers.[87]

Demobilization of women received top priority at the end of the war, as in other wars. When the war ended, one Navy commander declared, "I want all the women off this base by noon." After World War II the number of women in the US military dropped drastically, but never back to zero. The World War II experience remained a valuable benchmark of women's potentials as soldiers, which informed the later integration of women in the US military. In the Korean and Vietnam wars, women's service as nurses was notable. Recently, a memorial to women veterans has been completed at Arlington National Cemetery, and the history of US women soldiers is becoming better known.[88]

---

[86] Treadwell 1954, 191–218; Campbell 1990, 115–17, survey 116; Meyer 1996, 33–35, uniforms 154; De Pauw 1998, 251–58; Costello 1985, 47; Enloe 1983, pocket 119, 141.

[87] Treadwell 1954, release 184, failure 189; Costello 1985, cheery–draft 47–48; Bourke 1999, poll 303.

[88] Francke 1997, noon 22.

Recent decades   The large-scale integration of women into the peacetime US military began in the early 1970s, coinciding with the end of conscription after the Vietnam War and the switch to an all-volunteer army. The number of women in the armed forces grew rapidly from under 3 percent to over 8 percent in 1972–80, then more slowly but steadily, reaching 14 percent by 1999. (These levels compare with a peak of 3 percent in World War II and below 1.5 percent from 1945 to 1968.) Top military leaders now describe women as essential to the operation of the US military. Given the ongoing integration of women into previously closed positions, such as flying combat jets or commanding warships (the first took her frigate to the Persian Gulf in 2000), the data here for the late 1990s will change over time.[89]

The current US expansion of women in the military comes in peacetime and has continued in a period of shrinkage of the US military (in the 1990s). Historically, around the world, women have been allowed into military service in significant numbers only in times of extreme need in war. The current US integration reflects the professionalization and technical bureaucracy of the US military, in which being a soldier is "a job" and cost-conscious organizational managers realize that women's labor is cheaper than men's labor of equivalent quality. (Women are now paid the same as men in specific jobs, but women in the all-volunteer force bring with them higher average levels of education.) The expansion also reflects the greater acceptance of liberal feminism in the country's cultural and political norms – women and men should have similar rights in the workplace, and women can do "men's" jobs.[90]

In theory the expanded use of women in the US military maintains women's exclusion from combat. In practice, the lines between combat and support are not so clear-cut. A 1982 Army review noted:

Currently, women are assigned to duty positions and MOS [jobs] that require them to engage routinely in direct combat. Women may be found in every battlefield sector including forward of, alongside of, or interspersed with direct combat units . . . [T]he modern battlefield [is] an extremely fluid environment where many soldiers, assigned to units located in rear areas, are required to perform duties in forward combat areas.

For example, of the nearly 4,000 women then in the US Fifth Corps in Europe, 900 would be located in combat areas if the Corps participated in combat. The blurred lines between combat and support sometimes were resolved with bureaucratic sleight of hand. For example, air tanker

---

[89] Manning and Griffith 1998, number 9; Marlowe 1983; US Army 1982, 2, 1.2, 1.4; Quester 1977, 85; Nabors 1982; Thompson 2000.
[90] Rustad 1982, 46; Enloe 1983, 7; Dyer 1985, 122–25.

missions that had previously been defined as combat (with appropriate medals afterwards) were redefined as noncombat in the 1986 air strikes against Libya because women were participating.[91]

In the 1989 Panama invasion – at that time the largest US military action since Vietnam – women soldiers gained a new visibility. Almost 800 participated, constituting about 4 percent of the total force. At least 150 were in combat areas, some coming under enemy fire and some returning fire. The female captain of a US military police unit, Linda Bray, became a celebrity after leading her unit in capturing a military dog kennel in a half-hour firefight. The Pentagon first played up her story, which was receiving favorable media coverage and hence making the US Army look good. However, when her story threatened to unleash political forces they did not want to face – pressures to lift the combat exclusion law for women – Pentagon officials reportedly leaked disinformation to undermine her account (which some media reports had in fact exaggerated). Bray faced persistent harassment after the episode, and left the Army in 1991.[92]

In the Gulf War, nearly 40,000 US women participated – 6 percent of the US forces deployed (i.e., about half the proportion of women as the overall military had). About a dozen women soldiers died, of whom five were killed by hostile forces. Despite Pentagon fears of a bad public reaction – there had been no women casualties in Panama – the deaths of women soldiers were taken in stride by the American public.[93]

The issue that most worried top military officials – the capturing of US female POWs – also fizzled. Two US women soldiers were taken prisoner by Iraqi forces and returned after the war – a truck driver who stumbled into Iraqi lines in an early battle and a flight surgeon shot down on a helicopter trying to rescue a downed US pilot. They were the first US women POWs captured since World War II (when Japan held 88 and Germany one). The military leadership's fears, in addition to the potentially explosive public reaction which could undermine support for the war effort, were that male POWs might be induced to disclose information if women POWs with them were subjected to sexual abuse. These fears seem exaggerated, both because POWs have usually been (and were in Iraq) questioned and tortured in isolation to maximize psychological pressure, and because women pilots were already making sure men understood that rape was no different from any other torture and that if men caved in when women were abused they would put the women at greater risk of future abuse. Survival schools, which train pilots for their possible capture, had begun desensitizing men to rape, and

---

[91] Corps: US Army 1982, 4.4–4.5; tanker: Francke 1997, 228–29.
[92] Francke 1997, 46–72.
[93] Francke 1997, 76.

preparing women for sexual abuse as they did men for torture. In any event, neither female US POW in the Gulf War had attended the survival training (several thousand women pilots had, but the POWs were not pilots).[94]

In this case, Iraqi authorities made no attempt to exploit the US women's gender. (The 1949 Geneva Conventions mandate treating women POWs "with all the regard due their sex.") Once in custody of the government, the women were generally well treated whereas the men were tortured. Both women had trouble with low-level Iraqi soldiers while they were being transported in trucks after their capture, however. The doctor (whose arms were broken) was molested by one soldier and says she would have been raped if he had been able to get her flight suit off during the ride. The truck driver slapped away a soldier who touched her breast. Neither case destroyed the morale of the POWs, male or female. Opponents of women in combat later used the episodes, nonetheless, to underscore the dangers to women soldiers.

Even more than earlier wars, the Gulf War made it hard for the US military to maintain the distinction between combat and noncombat. In the Gulf War, more than half the 375 US soldiers killed were support personnel, not "combat" troops. The Pentagon followed the rule (as in Panama) that if a soldier was female she must not have been in combat and could not receive combat medals (which are highly valued in military culture). For example, the female doctor POW (Rhonda Cornum; see p. 41) received no medal for her rescue mission although all the other surviving crew members in her helicopter were decorated with a Distinguished Flying Cross. Similarly, the Pentagon would not designate the US truck driver a POW when she was captured, and listed her simply as "missing." They persisted even though her truck had been last seen stuck off the road with Iraqi soldiers running up to it, and later was found without the two drivers, and even though US pilots over Baghdad later spotted her in a prison compound. When she was released after the war and appeared on TV wearing a yellow uniform stamped "PW," her father called a Pentagon official at 3 a.m. and said, "Now, you asshole, will you declare her a prisoner of war?"[95]

Overall, the Gulf War was a big victory for liberal feminism. Women participated in large numbers, and performed capably, and the public proved willing to accept women soldiers as casualties and POWs. The Pentagon's fears proved inflated, and its efforts to manage public perceptions (such as by silencing information about sexual assaults in the

[94] Francke 1997, 73–103; survival 80–82, 87–91; Enloe 1993, 222; WWII: Manning 1999.
[95] Francke 1997, 82, doctor 102, asshole 97; Cornum 1996; Sciolino 1992.

ranks) proved easier than expected. The main problems that arose from the women casualties and POWs were that they generated huge media interest which sometimes caused resentment among male colleagues and sometimes also was unwelcome to the women and their families. These problems arose mostly because of the novelty of the situation.[96]

Current issues   In the 1990s, some problems in US military gender integration persisted, in basic training, military academies, and "sex scandals." Both military academies and basic training socialize new soldiers (officers and enlisted, respectively). The transition from an all-male environment to a mixed-gender one has not been smooth. Sexist elements in military culture have been slow to change, and harassment of women is widespread. Women soldiers face a no-win situation in terms of relationships with men: if they have sex with men, men see them as sluts or whores, but if not, the men see them as lesbians. In a 1992 Pentagon survey, about one-third of women soldiers reported experiencing some form of verbal or physical sexual harassment or abuse. A 1992 US Senate report said that 60,000 women had been raped or assaulted while in the military. (Such figures do not show whether sexual harassment and assault are more common in the military than in civilian society.)[97]

Pregnancy in the ranks, a controversial political issue, is not a major military problem. A retired admiral compares the pregnancy rate of about 10 percent with the "much higher disciplinary problem with the men, unauthorized absenteeism, absence in the brig for more serious offenses. Pregnancy is a wash."[98]

In US military academies – West Point for the Army, Annapolis for the Navy, and the US Air Force Academy in Colorado, alongside various other private and public military academies – women have been integrated since 1976. The academies graduate about 600 women a year, who enter with records as distinguished as their male peers, perform equally in the academies, and go on to successful military careers. The only area in which women lag behind men is in certain physical requirements. Although many women keep up with the men on rigorous marches at West Point, other women (in disproportionate numbers) fall behind or need men's help lightening the load. The average disparities in physical strength are a persistent source of gender conflict, as many men resent the different standard for women than men on certain physical fitness

---

[96] Enloe 1994, 99; Enloe 1993, 201–27; Francke 1997, 96.
[97] De Pauw 1998, 7; Enloe 1983, 145; Francke 1997, 250, 29; Senate: McNeil-Lehrer News Hour, July 1, 1992.
[98] Francke 1997, wash 251.

tests. (In the case of greatest difference, men must do ten pull-ups but women only three.)[99]

In surveys of graduating West Point seniors in the 1980s, fewer than a third of women cadets felt "totally accepted" by other cadets, compared to over half of men. As one male cadet put it, "I would never openly harass women, [but] I hope they understand they are not welcome here." Women cadets dropped out of West Point at twice the men's rate after the second summer which emphasizes combat training (which women would not be allowed to put to use). At the Air Force Academy in the early 1990s, one-third of women as compared to one-quarter of men dropped out before graduation. In the 1990s, incidents of sexual harassment apparently increased at the academies. Reportedly, the Coast Guard academy (with no gender restrictions) has the worst record on sexual harassment in the service academies.[100]

The rough transition is perhaps to be expected; cultures change slowly. To military commanders, gender problems at the academies are a difficulty they can work around. As one West Point officer put it, "This is not an experiment. This is an operational reality." Men's and women's feelings notwithstanding, the military is getting the officers it needs – which must include women in order to meet the needed quality and quantity. Furthermore, despite the sexist culture, most women are getting through the academies with records equal to those of the men. In the words of one woman officer formerly at West Point, "In a nonnurturing environment, they are kicking ass. And that is the bottom line "[101]

In basic training, the problem of unfair treatment (lax or harsh) revolves around the relationship of drill sergeants and company commanders with their troops. By tradition, harsh treatment in boot camp helps socialize new troops into discipline and hierarchy. The drill sergeant – typically male – has unparalleled power over his troops. If some troops are female, this power can be used for sexual domination. In the mid-1990s several abuse-of-authority cases came to light, most visibly at the Army's Aberdeen Proving Grounds where NCOs were accused of a widespread pattern of rape and sexual abuse. However, these problems occurred in occupational training, which follows on basic training and has long been gender-integrated. Congress in 1998 debated mandating the separation of genders during basic training, a move suggested by a commission but opposed by the Pentagon as impractical (since men and women go on

---

[99] Francke 1997, 183–219.

[100] Francke 1997, welcome 205, data 200–7; Moskos 1994, coast 61; Stiehm 1981; Mitchell 1996; Burke 1996.

[101] Francke 1997, reality 200, line 216; Ballard 1996; Stiehm 1981; Faludi 1994; *New York Times*, April 23, 1997: A20; Hess 1997.

to serve together). Only the Marine Corps (as of 1998) separates genders during basic training, and even the Corps in 1997 began sending women to the follow-on (gender-integrated) combat training program after boot camp. As one male trainee said, "Men or women, that doesn't matter...All we see is another Marine." The Navy's boot camp, with about 15 percent women, uses mostly all-male divisions with the rest having equal numbers of men and women (to avoid problems that arise when a few women are scattered in a heavily male group).[102]

Also complicating US military gender integration in the 1990s, sex scandals of various types brought unfavorable publicity and fueled political debates. The first woman to pilot a B-52 bomber with nuclear weapons (a symbolically important role) was forced to resign after she was accused of having an adulterous affair and then lying about it. Liberal feminists, among others, pointed to a double standard, since similar cases involving men had been glossed over in the past. In the wake of the public controversy, a male nominee for Chair of the Joint Chiefs of Staff was passed over because of an affair decades earlier. Military sex scandals moved out of the news, at least temporarily, when journalists' focus switched to the White House in 1997.[103]

New combat positions   While these general issues of gender integration swirled around the US military, the actual focus of women in combat shifted to combat aircraft and ships – the positions most often open to women in the NATO countries discussed earlier. In considering military jobs related to combat in which women might be included, the US military reproduces roughly the same spectrum of tasks discussed earlier under NATO countries. For example, a 1993 survey of retired high-ranking officers regarding women in combat showed, in addition to greater support among those more recently retired, greater support for women in warplanes (29% yes), attack helicopters (24%) and combat ships (24%) than in artillery (22%) and combat engineering (17%), with least support for women in armor (12%) and infantry (10%).[104]

In 1990, an Air Force officer testified to Congress that women – then barred from only 3 percent of jobs in the Air Force, namely aircraft actually engaged in combat missions – "can fly fighters, they can pull Gs. They are physically capable and, I think, emotionally capable." After the Gulf War, a Presidential Commission on women in combat

[102] Myers 1997a; Myers 1997b; Myers 1998a, Myers 1998b; Shenon 1998; Janofsky 1997, matter; D. Johnson 1997, Navy.

[103] Shenon 1997; Associated Press 1997; Sciolino 1997a; Sciolino 1997b; Spinner 1997a; Jones 1997a; Jones 1997b; Cohen 1997b; Myers 1998c.

[104] Presidential Commission 1993, D-9.

recommended by a split vote to keep the status quo, but the Administration lifted the combat exclusion for women on almost all airplanes and ships (except submarines and Navy commandoes). Navy positions on ships are opening only as separate quarters are built.[105]

Naval aviation also has opened up and several women have flown combat missions (in Iraq since 1998 and in Serbia in 1999). Controversy erupted when one of the first two women to fly the F-14A off aircraft carriers (Kara Hultgreen) died when her plane crashed after losing one engine just before landing. Opponents of women in combat aviation – including many of the Navy's male pilots – seized on the accident and claimed that the pilot had substandard flight skills which were tolerated only because of her gender. It appears that Hultgreen's inexperience, rather than substandard skills, caused an equipment failure to spiral to disaster when an experienced pilot *might* have prevented the crash. Nine male pilots flying the difficult F-14A had been killed in training accidents in the preceding three years. Eight out of nine male F-14A pilots who reenacted Hultgreen's landing sequence in a flight simulator also crashed.[106]

The Army and Marine Corps have been more resistant to women in combat. Nonetheless, in 1994 the Army opened combat support positions to women, allowing them into 20,000 previously prohibited jobs at brigade headquarters (closer to the front line). Three years later, however, fewer than 1,400 women had been assigned to those jobs, most doing traditionally women's work (administration, health care, supply) in the newly opened units.

Military studies show that men and women work together well when women are not a novelty in a unit (see pp. 199–203). With the opening of new positions closer to combat, women became a novelty in those units (just as they still seem to be for each entering class at the academies, and in basic training). The Army makes no attempt to avoid assigning one or two women alone to a unit of several hundred soldiers, nor does it train male soldiers effectively to work with women better. As a unit works together, however, and especially if it deploys in the field, unit bonding appears to overcome gender divisions to a great extent.

Women soldiers who made up 10 percent of US forces in Bosnia in 1997 reportedly had "easygoing and untroubled" relations with the men. For one thing, with US peacekeeping troops there wearing protective gear almost all the time, gender was less visible – it took one infantry colonel a week to realize that some of the MPs protecting him in the field were

---

[105] Francke 1997, capable 221.
[106] Manning 1999, several; Francke 1997, 256–58; Spears 1998.

female. In peacekeeping operations, women MPs are generally closer to the "front lines" than are the all-male infantry and armored units. Lines are further blurred by the Army practice of ignoring regulations and using females in supposedly off-limits jobs when practical considerations make it the best way to get the job done. Among the US forces in Bosnia, women blended in by adopting stereotypically "macho" attitudes and behaviors, including swearing, smoking cigars, and getting a thrill from firing guns. Most importantly, they adopted a "warrior spirit." As one female US Lt. Colonel who commanded a Military Police battalion in Bosnia put it, "If a woman thinks like a warrior, believes she's a warrior, then she'll do what it takes. Most women don't think they have it in them, but once you let that spirit loose you find that aggressiveness."[107]

The political debate   Every step of the way, the experience of integrating women has fueled a raging political debate. The two sides tend to draw on two kinds of moral arguments. One concerns *fairness* – whether it is proper, desirable, or just to allow women to participate in combat if they so choose, or even to assign women soldiers to combat on the same basis as men. The second category deals with the *effectiveness* of the military and whether the participation of women in combat would reduce or increase (or neither) its readiness, fighting ability, and morale.[108]

Those who favor allowing women in combat rely on the fairness argument, and think the effects on military performance would be minimal. Women should be allowed any job opportunities for which they are individually qualified, not barred because of their gender alone. This view extends the logic applied to other occupations from which females were traditionally excluded, from police and firefighters to corporate managers, political leaders, and so on. Especially in today's large and bureaucratic US military, being a soldier can be a career path. Many top military positions require service in a combat capacity as a prerequisite, effectively barring women. Congresswoman Pat Schroeder said of the combat exclusion laws that "the only thing they protect women from is promotion." A focal point of women's efforts to increase gender fairness in the military is the Defense Advisory Committee on Women in the Services (DACOWITS). It was created by Defense Secretary George C. Marshall

---

[107] Priest 1997a; Priest 1997b; Priest 1997c; Moskos 1998.
[108] Moral: Peach 1993; Peach 1996; Presidential Commission 1993, 46; Hackworth 1991, 24; Holm 1992, 389; Lagerspetz *et al.* 1988; debate: McNeil 1991; Stiehm 1981; Rustad 1982; Goldman ed. 1982; Mitchell 1989; Blacksmith ed. 1992; Howes and Stevenson eds. 1993; Addis, Russo, and Sebesta eds. 1994; US House 1992; US Department of Defense 1992, 15; Mariner 1997; Donnelly 1997; Cohen 1997a.

in 1951 to help bring more women into military service during the Korean War. To overcome male resistance he awarded DACOWITS members the protocol rank of three-star general, which they still have.[109]

Those who oppose women in combat rely on the effectiveness argument – that the military needs to put priority on its main mission of winning wars, not on social-change experiments. For example, retired General Norman Schwarzkopf said: "Decisions on what roles women should play in war must be based on military standards, not women's rights." However, some opponents of women in combat also rely on a "fairness" argument. They see protection for women as men's end of a gendered division of labor: "Good men respect and defend women." A widely reported exchange between Senator William Cohen and Air Force General Merrill McPeak took place soon after the Gulf War:[110]

Cohen: "Suppose you had a woman pilot . . . of superior intelligence, great physical conditioning, in every way she was superior to a male counterpart vying for a combat position. Would . . . [you personally] because you would not want to see the risk to her life increased . . . pick the male over the female under those circumstances?"

McPeak: "That is correct."

Cohen: "So in other words you would have a militarily less effective situation because of a personal view."

McPeak: "Well, I admit it doesn't make much sense, but that's the way I feel about it."

The two sides interpret the same set of episodes from the late 1980s and early 1990s differently. As in the movie *Rashomon*, contradictory versions of the same episode seem credible and coherent, with the "truth" being difficult to pin down. Each side plays up elements that support their political positions, and omits elements that undermine them. Each side accuses the other of manufacturing false information – to slander military women (with the collusion of male military officials), or to cover up military women's failings (with the collusion of liberal media and politicians), depending which side you take.

Pro-feminist Linda Francke and anti-feminist William Breuer, for example, tell contradictory stories about Linda Bray's experiences at the Panamanian military kennel (see p. 94). According to Francke, Captain Bray arrived at the kennel – which turned out to be a base and

---

[109] Van Creveld 1993, 8; Bendekgey 1992, 19, 23; DeFleur 1992, 25; Fuentes 1992, 35; Katzenstein 1998, 45–103; Summers 1992, promotion 131.

[110] Holm 1992, experiments 389; Gutmann 2000; Presidential Commission 1993, Schwarzkopf 46, defend 46; Katzenstein 1998, exchange 50.

weapons cache for Special Operations troops – ten minutes into a fierce half-hour gun battle in which the unit she led was outnumbered by Panamanian defenders firing from the surrounding woods. She took cover in a ditch, fired her pistol at the enemy once, and rode in the armored vehicle that crashed through the front gate. A few days later, three Panamanian soldiers' bodies were found in the woods, probable casualties of the Bray-led attack. According to Breuer, however, the kennel was militarily insignificant, there was only some sporadic fire and Bray was not even there at the time. She did not crash through the gates or lead her men in combat. Breuer focuses on exaggerated media reports of a long firefight with many dead Panamanians strewn about (one report refers to "a three-hour-long infantry-type battle"). Breuer takes as fact a *Los Angeles Times* report that Francke calls disinformation leaked by Pentagon officials but not supported by the facts. Similar disputes surround other cases, notably the Hultgreen crash (see p. 99).[111]

Women's work   Despite the creeping proximity of women to combat, the gender structure of labor in the US military continues to place women primarily in traditionally feminine areas. The large-scale gender integration creates more of the rare cases of women in and near combat, but these "newsworthy" cases should not blind us to the general pattern of gendered labor.

In the first plans for a women's corps drawn up in the 1930s, the US Army conceived of women as "a menial type of corps of low-grade personnel." Nearly half would be used as clerks and stenographers, with the rest divided between domestic services (cooking, sewing, laundry, and cleaning), driving, labor, and other unskilled occupations. A few would be skilled workers such as telephone operators.[112]

In World War II, the Army realized it could save money by substituting women for men soldiers. Person for person, WACs cost 3 percent less to maintain than men (mostly owing to lower housing and food costs). More importantly, although women replaced men at a one-to-one ratio in driving and mechanical jobs, one woman could do the work of two men in traditional women's jobs such as clerical work. From this experience came the idea decades later – in the all-volunteer force where labor was a commodity to be bought, not conscripted – that budgets could be best utilized by drawing on either men or women according to individual ability for a particular job.[113]

---

[111] Bray: Francke 1997, 46–72; Breuer 1997, 139–40; Dever and Dever 1995, infantry 127; Hultgreen: Francke 1997, 256–58; Breuer 1997, 206–12.

[112] Treadwell 1954, 12.

[113] Treadwell 1954, chapter 37.

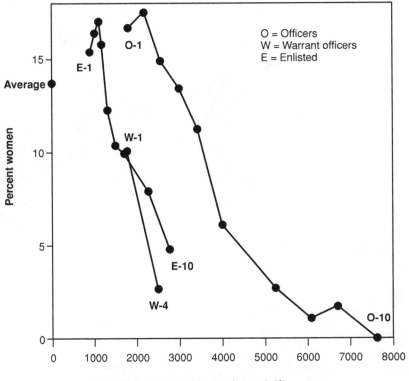

O = Officers
W = Warrant officers
E = Enlisted

Minimum monthly pay for rank ($)

Minimum monthly pay as of January 1, 1997.
Grades E8, E9 and Chief Warrant Officer 3–5 minimum pay reflects time in
   service needed to obtain rank. Salary unavailable for W2, W3, W5.
Average is percent of women in US military across all ranks.
Data source: US Department of Defense, *Active Duty Military Personnel*
   and *Female Military Personnel*, March 31, 1997; as listed at http://www.
   gendergap.com/military/Glasceil.htm.

Figure 2.5 Percent women at each pay rank, US military, 1997.

Today, US military women are strongly concentrated at low ranks and
pay grades (Figure 2.5). Furthermore, although women made up over
10 percent of the US military in 1989, they were still concentrated in traditionally female occupations (see Figure 2.6). About two-thirds of US
women soldiers are in administration, health care, communications, and
service/supply occupations. They are the successors to the historical secretaries, nurses, telephone operators, and "camp followers" (who once

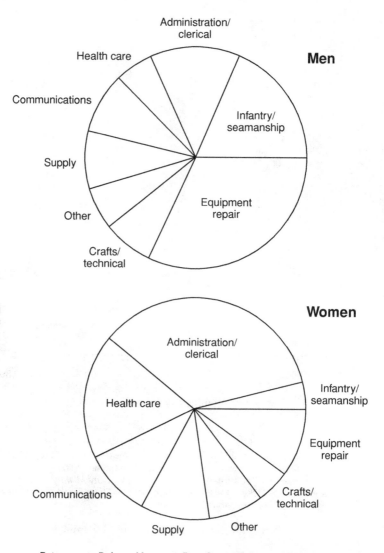

Data source: Defense Manpower Data Center (Arlington, VA), April 1998.

Figure 2.6 Occupations in US military (enlisted) by gender, 1998.

did the cooking, sewing, laundry, cleaning, and supply roles). The main area of change, in terms of women in nontraditional roles, is in equipment repair. Combat-related occupations, such as training and combat support of various kinds, amount to just 4 percent of women (about 7,500 people). Women make up about one-quarter of health care and administration personnel, about 10 percent of service, communications, and technical personnel, and just 2.5 percent of combat-related personnel. These data understate women's combat exposure in the Navy, where 15 percent of women serve on ships and women in traditional *occupations* may serve in combat *positions* (e.g., nurses on combat ships). The opposite applies for the Army, where women in nontraditional occupations are banned completely from combat positions, including infantry, armor, and most artillery units. Although women helicopter pilots received public attention during the Gulf War, in 1991 women pilots represented under 5 percent for each branch – Army, Navy, and Air Force – fewer than 1,000 pilots in all (not counting women navigators and aircrew).[114]

In the US Army in 1997 – after the opening of some combat-support occupations and positions to women but while most women were in occupations chosen before that opening – women troops were still concentrated in administration (one-third), health care (one-sixth), and service and supply (one-sixth). For men, fully 32 percent were in infantry, gun crews, and seamanship. Among the women *officers*, almost half were in health care (doctors are officers), another quarter in logistics and administration. For male officers, by contrast, almost half were in tactical operations. These differences are gradually eroding from year to year, however.[115]

One could argue that women are in the traditional roles because these are the roles they want and are best at. Indeed, most women soldiers do not want combat assignments – but then neither do most men. In a 1992 US survey, 12 percent of enlisted women and 14 percent of officers said they would volunteer for the combat arms if allowed to do so. Another 18 and 15 percent, respectively, said they might do so. (About 75 percent of women soldiers thought that women *should* be allowed to volunteer for combat.) These numbers translate into a pool of nearly 25,000 current soldiers, and possibly twice that number, ready to volunteer for combat.[116]

Overall, the results of the US experience indicate a broad, deep, and well-rounded capability of women to participate in the kinds of actions and operations required for combat, and to hold their own in combat itself when drawn into it. Most of the problems revolve around men's difficulties in adjusting to the presence of women in their midst, and even those problems are most acute when women are a novelty and much less so after men work together with women soldiers. The US experience is

[114] Aviators: Francke 1997, 226; Katzenstein 1998, 79; Navy–all: Manning 1999.
[115] Priest 1997b.
[116] Presidential Commission 1993, D5; Astrachan 1986, 63–65.

significant because it is occurring on a very large scale – the largest such effort ever in peacetime.

C. INDIVIDUAL WOMEN FIGHTERS

The most widespread involvement of women in combat has been neither in all-female nor in gender-integrated units, but rather as individuals scattered through the ranks. Such women combatants are found in many cultures around the world, and in many historical periods, although generally in extremely small numbers compared to male combatants. Put together, these thousands of cases add up to a strong endorsement of the conclusion that individual women can hold their own in combat when circumstances permit (or force) them to do so.

Cross-dressers

Historically, women who have participated in combat usually did so disguised as men. An Englishman joked in 1762 that "so many disguised women were serving in the army that they ought to have their own regiments." This presents a real problem for assessing the evidence: we cannot know how many women have successfully participated in this manner – surviving (or being buried) without detection. We can only know those whose gender came to light, which most often occurred after a serious injury requiring prolonged medical care. Historically, most armies have not provided such care in the way we take for granted today, and wounded women may have left the ranks without discovery. Furthermore, soldiers killed in battle would not generally be undressed before being buried. Thus, we do not know how many women lie in soldiers' graves. Nonetheless, scholars have documented enough cases of cross-dressing women warriors, discovered before or after death, to draw some inferences.[117]

Women soldiers in men's clothes are found in most regions of the world. In the old Chinese story of Mulan, a young woman dresses as a man, serves in the army in place of her sickly father, earns distinction, has her gender discovered after the fact, and ultimately returns home to a feminine role. Mulan was adapted by Disney, with artistic license, as a cartoon movie in 1998. Although probably a fictitious or composite figure even before Disney got hold of her – scholars disagree about when and where she lived, and even her family name – she is probably based on real cases. This basic story recurs in various cultures, including

---

[117] Wheelwright 1989; De Pauw 1998, regiments 105; Enloe 1983, 119–23.

several true stories (perhaps exaggerated for commercial reasons) that spurred popular books, articles, and speaking tours. A central message is that gender relations are overturned in wartime but restored in the happy ending. For example, Franziska Scanagatta reportedly graduated from the Austrian military academy in 1797, during the French Revolutionary Wars. She served in the campaigns of 1797 and 1799, and was promoted to lieutenant in 1800. However, her gender was discovered the next year and she left the army, marrying another lieutenant and having four children. In the US Revolutionary War, Deborah Samson (sometimes spelled Sampson) apparently did serve in male disguise, although her later autobiography and lecture tour were fictionalized. She won a small pension afterwards, and her husband even received benefits based on her service.[118]

The Civil War   Among the best documented cases is the US Civil War. It took place in a transitional era when the military was organized enough to maintain records on individual soldiers but not organized enough to provide all entering soldiers with detailed physical exams. Women participated on both sides. Most women serving at the front in the Civil War did so as nurses (Clara Barton being the most famous), and others served as "daughter of the regiment" – a morale booster and support person (similar to the Israeli role mentioned earlier). These nurses and "daughters" stayed just behind the lines, in theory, but in fact were sometimes caught up in battle. Other women accompanied the troops until combat became imminent, as wives and girlfriends, cooks and laundresses.[119]

In several dozen documented cases, women dressed as men and fought in the ranks. For example, "Frank Mayne" (Frances Day) disguised herself to follow her lover into the Union Army, stayed on after he died from disease a few weeks later, and was promoted to sergeant. Her secret was discovered when she was mortally wounded in battle. Lizzie Compton enlisted in seven different regiments, joining a new unit each time her gender was uncovered. "Frank Martin" (Frances Hook) fought in Tennessee in 1862 but was mustered out, against her pleas, when her gender was discovered after she was seriously wounded in battle. She reenlisted in a Michigan regiment in Kentucky, was found out again, and reportedly served later in an Illinois regiment. Hook was, according to the Michigan regiment records, "quite small, a beautiful figure . . . large blue eyes beaming . . . exceedingly pretty and very amiable." By contrast, another

---

[118] Mulan: Raven and Weir 1981, 32; Ayscough 1937, 214–27; Scanagatta: *Wish Stream* 1964; Samson: De Pauw 1998, 126; Wheelwright 1989, 132–35.
[119] Hall 1993, xi, daughter xiii, 4.

woman soldier wounded in the same Tennessee battle (in a Minnesota regiment), Frances Clayton, was described as very tall and masculine looking. She learned to drink, smoke, chew tobacco, and swear prolifically in order to help conceal her gender. Clayton had enlisted to be with her husband. Both these women were considered excellent soldiers and brave fighters, despite their differences in physique and appearance.[120]

"Albert Cashier" (Jennie Hodgers) served for three years with the Union and was in combat forty times, notably in the brutal 1863 battle for Vicksburg, Mississippi, where Cashier's name is inscribed on the battlefield monument. Cashier was considered dependable, healthy, and fearless by her commanders – the equal of anyone in "his" company, despite a lack of size and brawn. She continued to pose as a man after the war, her story coming to light only in 1913 at age 70, shortly after Hodgers was sent to a hospital for the insane. The story caused a minor sensation. Hodgers's former sergeant visited and reported her "broken" because "she was compelled to put on skirts." She told him: "The country needed men, and I wanted excitement."[121]

On the Confederate side, generally fewer women served near the front than on the Union side, although some women served in support roles usually called "mother" of the troops. Some Confederate women did serve while disguised as men. "Richard Anderson" (Amy Clarke) enlisted in the Confederate army with her husband, stayed after he was killed, and was captured by the Union and released in a dress after her gender was discovered. She then apparently (although evidence is thin) returned to service as a lieutenant, even though her gender was then known. Lucy Matilda Thompson – tall, masculine, and an expert shot – also enlisted in the Confederate army with her husband, and was discovered only after serious injury.[122]

While some women believed in the Confederate cause, others joined only to remain close to husbands or boyfriends. Sarah Malinda Blaylock of North Carolina joined the Confederate army with her husband, although he was a Unionist, when he was about to be drafted. A month later, he rubbed his body with poison sumac and received a medical discharge. She immediately revealed her identity and was discharged as well. They went on to become Unionist partisans, and led raiding parties from the Tennessee mountains.[123]

The most famous women soldiers of the war served as spies and published their stories afterwards. "Franklin Thompson" (Sarah Emma

[120] Hall 1993, 177, 20, 161, Hook 26–28.
[121] Hall 1993, 20–26.
[122] Hall 1993, 98–101.
[123] Hall 1993, 101–3.

Figure 2.7 Sarah Emma Edmonds as "Franklin Thompson," US Civil War. [Courtesy of State Archives of Michigan.]

Edmonds) adopted a male identity before the war and worked in the Union army as a "male" nurse and mail carrier who was recruited to the secret service and slipped behind Confederate lines on numerous occasions to bring back vital military information (Figure 2.7). On these forays, Edmonds adopted disguise-within-a-disguise, as an African

American man, or an Irish woman peddler. She lived through many battles, deserted the army when her identity appeared to be in jeopardy, and published a best-selling book in 1864, *Nurse and Spy*, about her escapades, told as though she were a female nurse who sometimes adopted male disguise. She was the only woman ever accepted into the veterans' group, Grand Army of the Republic, in 1898. (Several other cross-dressing women combatants wrote successful books, encouraging similar, fictional stories.)[124]

Edmonds's counterpart in the Confederacy was "Lieutenant Harry T. Buford" (Loreta Janeta Velazquez). With the help of a fake moustache and beard, Velazquez fought with the Confederate army as an independent lieutenant (floating from one unit to another as needed) in 1861, and at least twice temporarily took charge of a company that had lost its officers. She served under her fiancé without being recognized by him, worked as a spy switching in and out of male and female attire, and was arrested by both the North and the South numerous times on charges of spying or (in the South) being a woman, only to get away each time and carry on. After revealing herself to her fiancé (when both were recovering in a hospital) and marrying him, only to have him die weeks later, Velazquez gave up male disguise and turned to spying full-time, as a woman. She became one of the South's most effective secret agents, working as double (and once triple) agent under the North's secret service, counterfeiting large sums in the US Treasury to finance the Confederacy, blockade-running through Cuba, and making a clean getaway at the end of the war. She published her controversial memoirs in 1876.[125]

Many women were discovered quickly and discharged – often victims of their "feminine" mannerisms, such as how they put on stockings or wrung out dishcloths. Two soldiers were found out when officers threw apples to them, which they tried to catch with their aprons (they were not wearing aprons). Another, according to an 1862 newspaper account, was found out after "trying to put her pants on over her head." Several women were discovered after giving birth, including a Union sergeant whose delivery was "in violation of all military law" according to an outraged superior officer, and a Confederate officer who gave birth after being taken prisoner by the North. Many women, however, were discovered only after injury or death, and an unknown number either were buried on the battlefield or survived the war undiscovered.

---

[124] Hall 1993, 46–97; De Pauw 1998, fictional 106.

[125] Hall 1993, 107–53, temporarily 108, 120; De Pauw 1998, 153; Wheelwright 1989, 139–41.

Figure 2.8 British seaman's wife helps a wounded seaman in battle, 1830. [From Matthew Henry Barker, *The Log Book*. London: J. & W. Robins, 1830.]

Of course, while hundreds of women soldiers may have fought in the Civil War, hundreds of thousands of men did. The participation of women was limited in that they almost always had to pretend to be men in order to fight, and they were summarily dismissed or punished when discovered.[126]

Women at sea   Women have participated in naval warfare and as pirates on a number of occasions, in a variety of roles – disguised as men, working in support jobs on ships, and in rare cases as openly female combatants. In the sailing ships of the British Navy in the eighteenth and nineteenth centuries, it was common for women to accompany men to sea, both as wives and as service workers (prostitutes, cooks). As Figure 2.8 illustrates, in time of battle women participated under fire, facing many of the same dangers as the men. They traditionally helped nurse the wounded and carry gunpowder to the cannons. The

[126] Hall 1993, 155–56, pants 156–57, birth 159–60.

latter was an especially difficult and dangerous task, since heavy car-
tridges had to be carried from the (spark-free) powder room up lad-
ders to the slippery and smoke-filled gun deck, over and over. It was
"not unusual" for the noise, vibration, and stress of battle to induce
labor in a pregnant woman, who gave birth with little assistance from
others.[127]

These combat support roles for women at sea are supplemented by
quite a few cases of women who adopted male dress and joined the Navy
as regular sailors – usually motivated by economic and social restrictions faced by women on land (and by pure adventurousness). Of three
biographies of eighteenth-century women who went to sea with the Royal
Navy, one turns out to be accurate, one is embellished with fiction, and
the third entirely fictitious. The public showed both tolerance of, and
amusement at, the story of a woman dressing as a man and taking to
sea, especially if she went in search of a lost love (which few real women
did) and returned to normal gender roles at the end of the story. It was
surprisingly easy to pass as a man in the eighteenth century, when men
were routinely press-ganged into naval service to fill labor shortages in
the war-prone British Navy. As with all cross-dressing female soldiers, it
is hard to estimate numbers of real historical cases behind the popular
ballads.[128]

Openly female fighters

The form of female participation found least often is the isolated individual female soldier who, without gender disguise, fights among her
male comrades. Cultures tend to treat these as exceptional cases, decoupled from any idea of women's systematic participation. For example,
the Russian Naval Academy's first female cadet, admitted in 1997, is being treated as an exception – admitted by special decision of the Defense
Minister. To quote an officer at the academy, "One girl alone cannot ruin
the navy." Many stories describe individual, remarkable women who simply went to war as women, their strong abilities usually convincing males
to accept them despite their gender. Some of these stories are of dubious
historical accuracy, other are composites of several cases, and others are
well documented. The phenomenon of individual, openly female warriors
is widespread and yet, in most times and places, rare.[129]

---

[127] Stark 1996, 82–122, battle 71–72; De Pauw 1982; Stanley ed. 1995; Creighton and
Norling eds. 1996; Druett 2000.
[128] Stark 1996, motivated 92, biographies 102, easy 88–90.
[129] Stanley 1998, A4.

Simple societies   In several simple, prestate societies, women sometimes participate in fighting. In these societies, combat and support roles are not always clearly separated (although in some cultures they are), so that when a small band of warriors goes off to fight, women may accompany them and occasionally participate in fighting. I have mentioned the case of women of the Eurasian steppes in the early Iron Age (see pp. 13–14). Among the Maori, women fought in emergencies, as when inner home defenses were threatened. This was unusual, however. As the Maori proverb says, "Fighting with men and childbirth with women." Several other cases illustrate women's participation, although in none of them do women play a role equal to men in combat.

Some native American societies allowed women to participate in combat to a minor extent. Among the southern Apaches, some women accompanied war parties and a few "also fought and were known for their bravery and expert marksmanship." Reports are somewhat contradictory, however. Cremony reported in 1868:

Many of the women delight to participate in predatory excursions, urging on the men, and actually taking part in conflicts. They ride like centaurs and handle their rifles with deadly skill... [T]he fighting women... are numerous, well trained, and desperate, often exhibiting more real courage than the men.

However, a 1941 report states that Apache raiding parties were "made up of men only. Women never go on raids." Nonetheless, prisoners taken in battle were often taken back to camp for the women (especially those who had lost loved ones in battle) to torture and kill. Apache girls and young women received much physical training including riding and using knife, bow, and rifle – and were expected to guard camp while males were away. Adult women occasionally joined a raiding or war party, usually to help with cooking, cleaning, and nursing.[130]

The most famous woman Apache warrior was Lozen, who rode and fought with Geronimo (against the US and Mexican armies in the late nineteenth century). Lozen was unusual because she was not married. A witness who, as a child, rode with Geronimo's band recalls: "Lozen... was called The Woman Warrior; and though she may not have had as much strength as one of the men she was as good a shot as any of them." This witness mentions that "no unmarried woman was permitted to go" with a war party. "Lozen? No, she was not married... But to us she was as a Holy Woman... And she was brave!" Lozen, the sister of Chief Victorio, reputedly used her powers as medicine woman to detect the enemy's presence and help the Apache warriors elude capture on many

[130] Griffen 1988, also 12; Cremony 1868, 142; Opler 1941, raids 333, 350–51; Stockel 1991, xii, 17, 46, 30.

occasions. After her brother's death, Lozen rode with Chief Nana, who – with a force of 15 to 40 warriors – eluded a US force of over 1,000 soldiers and won eight battles against them. Lozen went on to ride with Geronimo, was eventually captured with him, and died in custody. Clearly, however, Lozen was the exception. Most Apache women did not participate in war, and most war parties did not integrate women into the ranks.[131]

On the long war expeditions of the extremely aggressive Mundurucú (Brazil), warriors were joined by their wives and "a number of unmarried girls. Their tasks were to carry cooking utensils and all of the equipment of the men, except for their arms... They also cooked, fetched water and firewood and performed other female services. Contrary to [an 1831 report]... that the women helped on the battlefield... the women were always left at a safe distance" during fighting.[132]

Cheyenne Indian women also occasionally, though rarely, went with war parties, and showed courage equal to the men. When the chief's horse was killed in a battle in 1876, his sister charged in among the white troops and rode away with him to safety. According to some reports, Cheyenne women who had been in wars formed a small guild and held meetings. Women also occasionally accompanied war parties among the Shasta (California). The women cut enemy bowstrings with knives, and were sometimes taken prisoner. They also cooked and carried supplies. The Gabrielino society (California) – wrongly characterized by nineteenth-century writers as "timid and peaceful" – used women and children to accompany war parties, carrying the food and supplies, as did the Hidatsa, Choctaw, and Guiana Amerindians. Possibly, Klamath (Oregon) women fought other women in war. The Konkow sometimes allowed women to participate in torturing captured male enemies.[133]

Women's participation in torturing and killing prisoners is found elsewhere as well, scattered across the anthropological record of cross-cultural research on simple societies. For example, among the Tupinamba of Brazil, women enthusiastically helped torture prisoners of war to death and then dismember and eat them. Similarly, Kiwai women of Oceania had the special job of "mangling" enemy wounded and then killing them with knives or digging sticks. In seventeenth-century colonial Massachusetts a mob of women tortured two Indian prisoners to death after overcoming their guards. Afghan women in the nineteenth

---

[131] Stockel 1991, 29–51, 41; Ball 1980, witness 103–4.
[132] Murphy 1957, distance 1022–23; Goldschmidt 1989, 23.
[133] Grinnell 1923, Cheyenne 44–47; Heizer ed. 1978, Shasta 218–19, Gabrielino 546–47, Konkow 380; Turney-High 1971, Shasta–others, 154; Klamath: Gatschet 1890; Barrett 1964; Stern 1965; Cressman 1956; Spier 1930, 31; Goldschmidt 1989, 23.

century tortured enemy survivors of battle. In 1993 a mob of Somali women tore apart four foreign journalists.[134]

It is possible, incidentally, for a culture to mobilize women into combat support without taking away their noncombatant protected status. In Papuan warfare, women "collect stray arrows for their husbands" and scout enemy movements, enjoying immunity from attack. Kapauku warfare (New Guinea) extends total immunity to women who function as support troops in the middle of the battle. "The Kapauku consider it highly immoral for a man to shoot at a female during a battle. Even an accidental injury brings . . . derision and loss of prestige." These cases highlight the distinction between combat and combat-support categories.[135]

In Celtic traditions, women warriors are a recurrent theme. Beyond the historical cases, warrior queens of dubious historical basis also figure prominently in legends and myths of many cultures. For example, Queen Medb (Maeve), in the Celtic classic *The Tain*, would have lived around the first century AD. In the legend, the goddess-warrior Medb commanded 1,500 soldiers but was most fearsome as a single warrior. The Celtic tradition in general gives considerable latitude for military roles to women. In Celtic myth, "again and again it is the magic intervention in the course of battle of a female, goddess, queen or a combination of the two, which provides the focus or climax of the story." Legends refer frequently to warlike queens and goddesses, but little hard evidence indicates actual women fighters. Even the goddesses of war generally do not engage in battle, but use magic to influence battle outcomes, or sometimes train men in the art of war. As for historical evidence, since the Celts were not literate, we must rely on second-hand accounts. A Roman historian claimed that if a Celt called in his wife, foreigners would be hard pressed, since she was stronger than him and could rain blows and kicks of amazing strength on the foreigners. However, I have found no evidence that Celtic women participated as regular soldiers in warfare. If they did so, they left little trace.[136]

Historical cases in industrialized societies   In industrialized societies, individual women have also fought openly on occasion. In the French Revolutionary Wars, which first mobilized a whole national population for war service on a mass scale, several hundred women

[134] Brazil: M. Harris 1989, 321; Kiwai: Turney-High 1971, mangling 162, 7; Massachusetts: De Pauw 1998, 113–14; Somali: Ehrenreich 1997a, 128–29.
[135] Pospisil 1963, 59.
[136] Fraser 1989, story 14–17; Boulding 1992/I, 276–82; Matthews 1989, 76–77; Stone 1979, 47, 49–52, 68–69; Larrington ed. 1992, 123–25; Green 1993, 27–28; Mac Cana 1970, 86; Green 1993, 24; Chadwick 1970, 134–35; Ritchie and Ritchie 1985, 14; Dillon and Chadwick 1972, 25, 146; Hill 1986; Ellis 1996, 77–98.

proposed forming a women's militia. A proposal for a women's battalion was considered, but rejected, in 1793. However, Renée Bordereau served openly in the royalist cavalry, fighting with "unbelievable courage," evidently out of rage at the murder of 42 of her relatives (including her father before her eyes). Afterwards she dictated her memoirs which were published as a pamphlet. In the French siege of Saragossa, Spain, in 1808, a Spanish woman named Agostina served with hundreds of women bringing drink to the 200 defending soldiers and water to swab the cannons. When the French broke through and killed all the artillerymen, Agostina began firing a cannon, and other women joined in, forcing a French retreat. After the war, she continued as an artillery captain, in uniform with standard pay and pension, despite being openly female. A French woman, wearing male clothing but known by all to be female, fought competently in Corsica in 1792–99, and retired as a sergeant major after being wounded. Another woman served openly in the French army in 1793–1815, was wounded six times, and dictated her memoirs afterwards. No attempt was made to discharge her, because she fought well.[137]

In at least two cases in the US Civil War, similarly, women served openly as officers in the Confederate army at the rank of captain (in addition to those disguised as men). During World War I, a number of women participated individually in several armies. One of the most famous, Englishwoman Flora Sandes, fought with the Serbian army on the same terms as the men, and took an Austrian speaking tour in 1920.[138]

D. WOMEN MILITARY LEADERS

Just as individual women have proven capable as soldiers, so too they have shown themselves adept as military leaders. Male soldiers and officers will follow the commands and exhortations of a female leader – and not just one whose gender is disguised – when that leader is deemed to possess proper authority.

Joan of Arc   The most famous case – although it is atypical – is Joan of Arc. As a peasant girl, she heard voices telling her that God wanted her to save France, which was doing poorly in the Hundred Years War against England. The English, with the collusion of some French forces, occupied much of France including Paris and the cathedral of Reims where French kings were crowned, and were besieging Orléans. At

---

[137] Pierson 1987, militia 208–10; De Pauw 1998, 135–39.
[138] Civil: Hall 1993, 104–5, 163–64, 154; WWI: Hirschfeld 1934, 111–15; Wheelwright 1989, 29–36, Sandes 14–16, 147; De Pauw 1998, 212, 207–30; Bourke 1999, 294–97, 299–333.

age 16, Joan somehow convinced the French ruler to provide her some troops and send her to Orléans, where (in 1429) she rallied the demoralized army trying to relieve the siege. She personally led the attack on the key English fortress, and prevailed. Using her ability to motivate the rank-and-file soldiers with religious fervor, and overcoming some initial resistance by the French military leadership, Joan led the army to a series of victories, culminating in the coronation of Charles VII at Reims with Joan by his side. These successes turned the tide of the Hundred Years War. The next year, Joan was captured by Burgundy and sold to the English, who condemned her both for idolatry and for wearing men's clothing, and burned her at the stake.[139]

Joan's main strength as a military leader was her ability to inspire troops to follow her. Leadership is critical in overcoming the paralyzing terror and confusion of soldiers on the battlefield (see pp. 253–58). Joan provided the necessary strong leadership, in a manner not unlike that of the captains of mercenary units at that time. The mercenaries would risk their lives for their captain and were rewarded with plunder, whereas Joan's troops were rewarded with spiritual ecstasy. The French soldiers believed that Joan was a holy presence. They loved her, and rushed to touch her, or her horse. Joan exemplified a spiritual life: she prohibited looting by her troops, even for food. She was charitable to all. She chased away prostitutes (who follow armies; see pp. 342–48). She prayed frequently and heard mass daily. In battle, she refused to shed blood personally, preferring to carry her standard instead of using her sword. Reportedly she could not stand the sight of blood. Her soldiers – the same ones those prostitutes had been serving – claimed they were not sexually aroused around her, even when they saw her breasts or bare legs (when she was dressing, or wounded). Instead, the soldiers "relished the spirituality of their own existence when with her." In addition to these qualities, Joan appears to have had a knack for military tactics. She was especially adept at riding a horse while wielding a lance, at setting up artillery (which was fairly new), and at organizing armies for battle. Her contemporaries described her as a simple, innocent, and ignorant girl *except* in the art of war, where she acted as though she had 30 years' experience.[140]

Warrior queens

Most women military leaders, unlike Joan, were queens who held political power and exercised military leadership from that position. Antonia

---

[139] DeVries 1996; Wheeler and Wood eds. 1996; Enloe 1983, 118–19; Fraioli 1996, 189; Wood 1996, 19; Schibanoff 1996.
[140] DeVries 1996, 5–12, relished 9.

Fraser reviews the record of a dozen such historical "warrior queens." Different stories treat such figures differently – for example, some emphasizing their chastity and others their sexual voracity.[141]

The documented historical cases include Semiramis (Sammu-ramat), who ruled Assyria in 811–806 BC after her husband's death and before her son came of age. Not much is known about her, but Greek writers built her up into a legendary adventuress, conqueror, and voracious lover – a story further embellished, centuries later, in a Voltaire play and a Rossini opera.[142]

The forces of Tomyris, queen and general of the Massagetae in today's eastern Iran, defeated the Persian ruler Cyrus in the sixth century BC, according to the fifth-century Greek historian Herodotus (who here, unlike the Amazon case, is reporting fairly recent history). When Cyrus tried to conquer her territory, using trickery and capturing her son, Tomyris' army crushed the Persians in an extremely violent battle and killed Cyrus. Fifty years later, the Persian king Xerxes battled the Greeks at Salamis, with a warrior queen at his side – Artemisia of Halicarnassus (again, according to Herodotus, who praises her "manly courage"). Although she advised against the unwise naval encounter with the Greeks, Artemisia fought more bravely than Xerxes' male commanders: he is supposed to have said, "My men have turned into women, my women into men." The Greeks, who resented a woman warring against them, had offered a large reward for Artemisia's capture, but she managed to escape the battle alive with some clever tactics. (Tactics included ramming and sinking a friendly vessel, convincing a pursuer that she was on his side, while Xerxes assumed she had sunk an enemy vessel.)[143]

The legendary and historical British queen Boudica (Boadicea or Boudicca) led a rebellion against the Romans around 60 AD (17 years after their invasion). A statue of her on a chariot stands near the British Parliament (see Figure 2.9). Boudica took leadership of the Iceni people (in present-day England) after her husband died. Her Iron Age society was of Celtic heritage (see p. 115) – warlike, reckless, horse-loving, robust and strong, prone to fighting naked accompanied by loud noise and frequent drinking. Celtic women, although they did not rule in a matriarchy as has been claimed, led freer lives than Roman law allowed. Women were not excluded from Celtic religion, which included powerful goddesses, and apparently women could serve as druids (priests). The historian Tacitus said of the Britons (in contrast to the Romans), "they make no distinction of sex in their appointment of commanders." At the

---

[141] Fraser 1989, 11–13.
[142] Fraser 1989, 28–30.
[143] Fraser 1989, 30–34; Lefkowitz and Fant 1977, 11–12.

Figure 2.9 Statue of Boudica, London. [By Thomas Thornycroft. Photo © by Sue Lanzon.]

time Boudica took power, another queen, Cartimandua, presided over the Brigantian territories to the north, as a client of Rome (which had come to her aid when her rule was threatened).[144]

Boudica's own history is sketchy, although the main outlines seem clear. Upon the death of Boudica's husband, the Romans seized his estate, dispossessed the Iceni nobles, flogged the new queen, Boudica, and raped her two daughters. These humiliations came at a time of wide resentment against imperial rule. Drawing on spiritual and political symbols, Boudica

[144] Fraser 1989, 43–106, naked 47–48, Tacitus, 53–55; De Pauw 1998, 70–74.

mobilized her people to rebel, and led an army of possibly 100,000 which overran, burned, and sacked a Roman colonial settlement. Joined by other tribes, the army ambushed the Roman reinforcements and moved on the trading city of London, which the Romans abandoned and the rebels burned, as they did a third city, populated by Britons friendly to Rome. In the course of these attacks, tens of thousands of people died and many atrocities occurred. The Romans regrouped, attacked Boudica's army, and – with superior experience and equipment – routed them and killed tens of thousands of soldiers along with their families who had come to see the battle. Boudica reportedly killed herself afterwards. Rome inflicted vengeance on the Britons, and went on to rule for 400 years. Queen Cartimandua had not joined the rebellion, and remained in power.[145]

Two hundred years after Boudica's rebellion, Queen Zenobia of Palmyra led a similar revolt against the Roman empire, in modern-day Syria. Around 260 AD, Zenobia's husband Odainat, ruler of the Roman colony Palmyra, went to war against Persia and won. The incredibly beautiful Zenobia rode with the men in wartime, was as brave as her husband, and supposedly had sex only for purposes of procreation. When her husband and his heir from an earlier marriage were assassinated, Zenobia took power as regent for her own son. She quickly turned to an ambitious campaign of military conquest, and within a few years ruled a large territory from Egypt to the Bosphorus, then declared independence from Rome. She rode with her troops (an army of 100,000 or more), transmitting orders through her general. Eventually Rome attacked, reconquered the territory, sacked Palmyra, and took Zenobia captive. Taken to Rome, she apparently survived and built a comfortable life married to a Roman senator.[146]

Matilda of Tuscany was an important ally of Pope Gregory VII in his eleventh-century power struggle with the Emperor Henry IV. Pious and largely chaste, she led her army on the battlefield, exhorting her troops and plunging into the battle with sword in hand. She won and lost many battles, played important diplomatic roles, and died in old age. Her body was reburied in St. Peter's (Rome) in the seventeenth century, with the inscription: "This warrior-woman disposed her troops as the Amazonian Penthesilea [of Greek myth] ..."[147]

In the twelfth century, Maud – daughter of King Henry I of England and husband of Emperor Henry V – became heiress to the English throne after her brother and then her husband both died. In the long succession

---

[145] Fraser 1989, 58–101.
[146] Fraser 1989, 107–28; De Pauw 1998, 75–77.
[147] Matilda: Fraser 1989, 131–50; Europe: Boulding 1992/II, 33; De Pauw 1998, 82–87.

Figure 2.10 Trung sisters drive Chinese from Vietnam in 39 AD. [From Fraser 1989, 96f.]

struggle with her (male) cousin following her father's death, Maud both led and defended against various military attacks and sieges.[148]

Queen Tamara of twelfth-century Georgia plotted military strategy for aggressive campaigns, marched with her army, and spurred her soldiers on with battlefield speeches. The voraciously sexual Tamara of Georgian legend contrasts with the real Tamara, "more of a matriarch than an erotic heroine," who was later canonized by the church.[149]

These European queens – to whom we may add Queen Isabella of Spain and Queen Elizabeth of England – are joined by others far from Europe. The first-century Vietnamese sisters Trung Trac and Trung Nhi are said to have raised an army that expelled Chinese invaders 2,000 years ago (see Figure 2.10). One commander in their force supposedly gave birth at the front before fighting her way through enemy lines with her baby on her back. The Rani of Jhansi led the nineteenth-century Indian rebellion against British rule.[150]

Queen Nzinga (or Nzingha, N'Zinga, Jinga, or Mbande Zinga) of seventeenth-century Angola took power when her brother (the king) died. A cannibal who personally beheaded and drank the blood of prisoners,

[148] Fraser 1989, 151–66.
[149] Fraser 1989, 167–81, matriarch 168.
[150] Trung: De Pauw 1998, 269; Rani: Fraser 1989, 272–96.

her economic base was the slave trade. Nzinga ruled first Ndongo and then – never having fully overcome sexist traditions there – neighboring Matamba which had some history of female rulers. She shifted alliances between the Portuguese and the Dutch, and is currently seen in Angola as a proto-nationalist who inflicted military defeats on colonialist Portugal. (Some writers claim that Nzinga's army included many female soldiers, but this seems to have no basis.)[151]

Historical warrior queens sometimes tried to link themselves symbolically (for practical reasons) with well-known goddesses of war – Semiramis (ninth-century BC Babylon) with the goddess Astarte, Cleopatra (first-century BC Egypt) with Isis, and Boudica (first-century AD England) with Celtic warrior goddesses. In other cases, warrior queen figures are symbolic of the nation and removed from military strategy. Queen Louise of Prussia led the fight against Napoleon – as a national symbol dressed in military attire, but not a military strategist or fighter (she suffered disastrous defeat).[152]

Other women in more recent centuries have shown leadership in battle. During the conquest of Paraguay by its neighbors in 1864–70, the dictator's mistress, Elisa (Ella) Lynch, played an important role and held the rank of colonel. In one critical battle in 1868, as a town was being overrun, she rode to the women's camp, organized thousands of women into an "army" carrying hoes and brooms, and marched back over the hill to town, where Argentinian infantry panicked and ran at the rumor of thousands of Paraguayan reinforcements arriving. This seems to have been an isolated incident, although Paraguayans of all ages and both genders participated in home defense in several other desperate battles during that war.[153]

Castle defenders   In feudal times, in both Europe and Asia, it was not unusual for women to take over defense of their castle when their men were away, held prisoner, or killed. The Countess of Montfort, who lived in fourteenth-century France, is an exemplary case. When her husband was taken prisoner by an archrival – a man given to atrocities in war – the Countess organized military affairs including morale, finance, tactics, and diplomacy. When besieged by the rival, she led the defense, dressed in armor, from horseback in the streets, mobilizing women to throw down stones and boiling tar on the enemy. She used a secret gate to

---

[151] Boxer 1952, 227–28, 242, 261, 264–69, 274, 286; Miller 1975; Miller 1976, 203–21; Birmingham 1966, 6, 92–116; Vansina 1966, 134–44; Beachey 1976, 88–90; Alpern 1998, 2; claim: De Pauw 1998, 180–81; Salmonson 1991, 198; Brown 1998.

[152] Fraser 1989, 17.

[153] Barrett 1938, 263.

sneak out with some knights during a lull, then destroyed half the enemy in an attack from behind, breaking the siege. (Although victorious, the Countess ultimately went mad and lived her last 30 years in isolation in a castle.)[154]

Modern political leaders in wartime

Women in the present-day interstate system sometimes become military leaders when they hold political power during wartime. For example, Margaret Thatcher, Golda Meir, and Indira Gandhi led their countries in war. (Thatcher is the only woman to lead a "great power" this century.) Benazir Bhutto of Pakistan and Corazon Aquino of the Philippines both struggled to control their own military forces in the late 1980s (Aquino survived seven coup attempts). Turkey's Tansu Ciller prosecuted a harsh war to suppress Kurdish rebels in the mid-1990s. President Chandrika Bandaranaike Kumaratunga of Sri Lanka (and the prime minister, her mother) practiced war against Tamil separatists after her peace initiatives failed. Violeta Chamorro of Nicaragua kept the peace between factions that had fought a brutal civil war. Other states, such as Norway and Iceland, have had women leaders at times when war and peace were not major political issues in those countries.[155]

Female national leaders use both "masculine" and "feminine" styles in military and diplomatic matters. Aquino's modest femininity was a great asset in diplomacy. On a 1986 US visit, according to a State Department official, Aquino "had hard-bitten politicians eating out of the palm of her hand." However, this femininity made it harder for her to gain loyalty and obedience from her military. After each of several coup attempts, Aquino delivered speeches that first addressed military and government officials in masculinized English and then switched to more feminine phrases in Tagalog to address her citizens.[156]

In sum, overall, women like men seem capable of leading in war or in peace. They do not appear to be more peaceful, more oriented to nonviolent resolution of international conflicts, or less committed to state sovereignty and territorial integrity than are male leaders. We still lack enough data, however. Women national leaders, from World War II through 1993, number 28 individuals (excluding hereditary heads of state) – a small fraction of the total.[157]

[154] Fraser 1989, 158–59; Montfort: Tuchman 1979, 74–75.
[155] Fraser 1989, 307–22; Richardson and Howes 1993; Carras 1995; Harris 1995; Nelson and Chowdhury eds. 1994; Genovese ed. 1993; Norris 1997; Williams 1995; cf. Victoria: Monypenny and Buckle 1912, 1089.
[156] Boudreau 1995, 75, 78–79.
[157] Number: D'Amico 1995, 24–25; McGlen and Sarkees 1993.

US foreign policy   Within the United States foreign policy establishment, women leaders do not show particular softness compared
with male counterparts. Both Secretary of State Madeleine Albright and
UN Ambassador Jeane Kirkpatrick were hard-liners within their admin-
istrations. (Kirkpatrick, incidentally, remarked of the White House Situation Room that "I don't think there had ever been a woman in that
room before.") In the US Congress, it is hard to compare men's and
women's voting records on foreign policy issues because there have been
so few women. The US Senate was 98–99 percent male until 1992, when
it dropped to only 94 percent male. Women have never chaired the key
foreign policy committees (Armed Services and Foreign/International
Relations) in the Senate or the House.[158]

In the US State Department in 1989, women held fewer than 7 percent
of the senior foreign service positions (up from 2 percent in 1970), but
79 percent of the lowest-rank civil service positions (from 72 percent in
1970). Thus, men more often make the policies while women type the
memos. A "glass ceiling" holds women down in the State Department
hierarchy. In the Department of Defense, similarly, women are concentrated at low levels and have trouble moving up the hierarchy either as
service members or as civilians.[159]

A 1993 study of foreign policy insiders found that *career* women in the
State Department were less hard-line and less prone to recommend force
than men. However, for women *political appointees* at State and for both
career and political women in Defense, no such gender gap existed. In
fact, "in the few instances in which they differed from their male counterparts, [women] seemed to be more hard line and conservative." Regarding
the foreign policy process, there were no statistically significant gender
differences. Nearly 90 percent of men and women at both State and
Defense, excluding career women at Defense who split evenly, thought
that having more women in the Department would not affect foreign
policy or process. Overall, little evidence shows that women foreign policy insiders hold a "women's perspective" on international issues or the
policy process.[160]

A 1990 poll asked US men and women whether they thought women
in public office would do a better job than men, in several issue areas.
Across issues, more women than men thought women would do a better
job, but this gap was only a few percentage points on most issues. Both

[158] Burwell and Sarkees 1993, 111, 115; Jeffreys-Jones 1995, room 175; Morin 1995, 274;
McGlen and Sarkees 1993, 2–3; DuBois 1995.
[159] McGlen and Sarkees 1993, 76, glass 83, 87; Burwell and Sarkees 1993, 117–31.
[160] McGlen and Sarkees 1993, 196–215, differed 211, process 254, affect 283, overall 302.

genders on average thought women would do a better job in improving education, assisting the poor, protecting the environment, governing honestly, and working for world peace. Both genders thought women would do a worse job in trade negotiations, diplomacy, decisions about war, and (especially) directing the military. The main societal factors creating difficulty for female US foreign policy insiders were the stereotypes of foreign policy as a male preserve and of women as unknowledgeable about foreign affairs. Among the poll respondents, almost all women and nearly three-quarters of men said the public sees women as knowing less than men about foreign affairs, although only 22 percent of women and 11 percent of men said they personally believed that idea.[161]

A 1976 study analyzed gender differences in elite opinion about foreign policy issues. Of the women, 42 percent were educators or media leaders (occupations that tend to be "dovish"), whereas 38 of the men were military officers or business executives ("hawkish" occupations). The women were also somewhat younger on average, and more likely to be Democrats and self-described liberals; 73 percent of men and 11 percent of women had military service records. Multivariate statistical analysis controlled for some of these variables. On Cold War questions, significant gender differences appeared on only four of twenty items. Of the nine questions in this cluster relating to the use of force, only one showed a significant gender gap. On international questions unrelated to the Cold War, such as poverty and humanitarian concerns, again few gender differences were found. Only on questions regarding "isolationism" did a consistent and significant gender gap appear, with women more isolationist. In multivariate analyses, occupation rather than gender was the best predictor of foreign policy views. This study suggests that US women in leadership positions in the 1970s did not share the tendency of the general population of women to be somewhat more peaceful on foreign policy questions (see pp. 329–30). This could be because women achieved leadership positions by emulating, or being selected for, "masculine" qualities.[162]

Diplomacy   Women's military leadership abilities might overlap with their more general political and diplomatic capacities. US women ambassadors, beginning with the first in 1933, show "striking similarities" as high-energy risk takers, patriotic, courageous, tall, physically fit women who loved their jobs. As girls, they were curious about the world,

[161] McGlen and Sarkees 1993, 37, 46, 47.
[162] Holsti and Rosenau 1981; selected: Cantor and Bernay 1992.

were called tomboys, were voracious readers, and received special attention from parents and teachers. Only 17 of 44 were married while serving as ambassador. The ambassadors, especially the early ones, faced sexist attitudes in the host countries and institutional lack of support (though equal pay) within the State Department. Most "accepted the fact of discrimination as a condition of the times and carried on without too much grumbling." Men, in describing these ambassadors, referred frequently to their "femininity." The women used this to advantage: since they were not considered threatening, they could speak bluntly to male officials without the latter worrying about losing face. However, the first US woman appointed as ambassador to a Middle Eastern country, April Glaspie, was blamed by Congressional critics for supposedly giving Saddam Hussein the "green light" to invade Kuwait. One senior male State Department official reportedly said: "We have some lessons to learn. The first is don't send women as Ambassadors."[163]

Fortunately, Hapsburg emperor Charles V did not obey that logic in 1529, when the Paix des Dames ("Ladies' Peace") ended a destructive war with France. The peace resulted from the initiatives of Marguerite of Austria – the emperor's aunt and regent of the Hapsburg-controlled Netherlands – and Louise of Savoy, who was the French king's mother and Marguerite's sister-in-law. The negotiations grew out of a feeler to Marguerite's ambassador at a party given by Louise in Paris. Both sides were under pressure owing to the complexity of shifting alliances. By negotiating through his mother, the French king kept his allies out of the talks and retained the ability to reject the result if he did not like it. The treaty demonstrated Western Europe's common interests and allowed efforts to be redirected against Turkey. Marguerite is generally credited as the central player and Charles as the main beneficiary of the treaty.[164]

Five centuries later, however, in the emerging international civil service of the United Nations staff, women's potentials remain underutilized. The UN staff is nearly half female at the lowest levels, but women are only about 10 percent of the top staff, just over 5 percent of Assistant Secretaries General, and zero percent of Undersecretaries General (1992 data). All seven Secretaries General have been male. Despite a commitment in the UN Charter that women be eligible to participate equally in any capacity (gained by the activism of Eleanor Roosevelt and a few others in 1945), in reality women have faced persistent discrimination at the UN.[165]

---

[163] Morin 1995, striking 264, 266, 270, 272; McGlen and Sarkees 1993, send 300.
[164] Von Habsburg 1969, 123–24; Knecht 1982, 219; Brandi 1939, 279–80.
[165] Timothy 1995, 86; Galey 1994.

CONCLUSION

The evidence – from large-scale organized female participation through various types of gender integration through the participation of individual women – supports Hypothesis 2. When women have found their way into combat, they have generally performed about as well as most men have. Women in combat support roles, furthermore, have had little trouble fitting into military organizations, and have held their own when circumstances occasionally placed them in combat (especially in guerrilla wars). They can fight; they can kill. Yet exceptional individual women who wanted to go to war had either to overcome stubborn resistance from men or to adopt male disguise.

Overall, the war system works to push women away from killing roles except in the most dire emergencies such as when defending their homes and children. This does not necessarily protect women participants from harm. Women have faced great danger on the battlefield, whether as nurses in front-line trenches, as powder-carriers aboard ships and in artillery units, or as helicopter pilots ferrying male troops around. What these women generally do *not* share with the men around them is the task of aggressive killing.

Most striking are the very rare historical cases in which larger numbers of women were mobilized into combat – a substantial number of the healthy, strong young women in a population. In the nineteenth-century Dahomey Kingdom and the Soviet Union of World War II, women made up a nontrivial minority of the military, and clearly contributed to the war effort. They were a military asset which, when mobilized, increased the effectiveness of the military in combat, in a few cases even turning the tide of battle.

Women's physical strength, while less than men's on average, has been adequate to many combat situations – from piloting to sniping to firing machine-guns. One recurring argument of those opposed to women in combat – that the women would be unable to drag wounded comrades from the battlefield under fire – is refuted by the record of women nurses' doing so. Women's supposedly lower levels of aggressiveness, and their nurturing nature, have been, historically, no obstacle to many women's participation in combat. Furthermore, contrary to the idea that women are too soft-hearted to kill, not only did Soviet snipers coolly shoot down dozens of German soldiers, but in various cases women took the lead in cruelty and torture, especially of prisoners. The next chapter explores men's and women's bodies to see how these historical patterns square with claimed biological gender differences in such areas as strength and aggression.

3   Bodies: the biology of individual gender

> **Hypothesis 3.** Gender differences in anatomy and physiology:
>
> A. Genetics
> B. Testosterone levels
> C. Size and strength
> D. Brains and cognition
> E. Female sex hormones

INTRODUCTION

This chapter considers whether gendered war roles result from differences in men's and women's individual bodies. Moving from the most categorical types of gender difference to the subtler ones, possible explanations might be found in genetics (e.g., a "gene for war" on the Y chromosome), circulating testosterone levels, size and strength, brain "wiring" (cognitive processes), or the pacifying effects of female hormones. I will review each of these in turn, but first consider the larger, controversial issues that surround these topics in public discourse.

The nature–nurture feedback loop

Both war and gender individually, as well as their possible connection, have served as battlegrounds (to use a war analogy), or "contested sites," in the debate over the roles of biology and culture in shaping human social behaviors. The decades-old "nature versus nurture" debate still emphasizes two polar extremes (nature *or* nurture). On one side, genetics explains everything and people are just like other animals. Males and females are made of different stuff – boys of "snips and snails and puppy dog tails" and girls of "sugar and spice and everything nice" – because God or evolution designed us that way. On the other side, any concession that biology has any role in gender or war brings accusations of "essential-ism" and declarations that "biology is not destiny!" The terms of debate still assume a dichotomy. For example, a 1998 *Washington Post* poll used the following phrasing: "What do you think is the main reason for any differences there might be between men and women? Is it mainly because of the way men and women are brought up, or are the differences part of their biological makeup?" Just over 10 percent of both women and men *volunteered* the answer, "both." (Of the rest, incidentally, men split evenly while women split almost 2-to-1 on the "upbringing" side.)[1]

Life magazine's recent cover story, "Were You BORN That Way?" states that "a wealth of new research has tipped the scales overwhelmingly toward nature" in the nature–nurture debate. The actual research results mentioned later in the article, however, show that "the heritability of most personality traits is about 50 percent." (This has long been the consensus in psychology.) Yet the article goes on to conclude that a "child will develop along paths set out by his genes," because people seek out experiences and environments from birth onwards that resonate with their genetic makeup. Science's increasing ability to control genetics, the article concludes, may someday let us "end war by getting rid of aggressive genes."[2]

Two-way causality and feedback loops   "Both" is an obvious answer to "nature or nurture," especially when research finds outcomes to depend about equally on each. But this answer is not good enough. The relationship between biology and social behavior is not just additive – $\frac{1}{2}$ cup nature, $\frac{1}{2}$ cup nurture, mix well. Rather, it is a system of reciprocal causality through multiple "feedback loops" – a complex two-way causality between biology and culture.[3]

Cichlid fish illustrate the feedback between biology and social relationships. The males are hierarchical; 10 percent of them control the feeding territory and do all the mating. These "dominant" males (see pp. 204–6) are larger and more brightly colored than the other males or the females, they are territorial, and they behave aggressively. If a dominant male is removed, other males fight to fill the vacant position in the hierarchy, and a new male becomes dominant in the territory. Then, as a result of this change in *social* relationships, that male's brain changes: certain cells in the hypothalamus grow larger and produce more of a certain hormone, stimulating the pituitary. As a result, the testes become enlarged, more sperm are produced, and the size and coloring of the fish change, as

[1] Evolution: Daly and Wilson 1983; Wilson 1978, 105; Draper 1985; Klama 1988, 3; poll: Morin and Rosenfeld 1998: A17.
[2] Colt and Hollister 1998, 40–42, 44, 48; cf. Begley 2000.
[3] Forrester 1971; Giddens 1984.

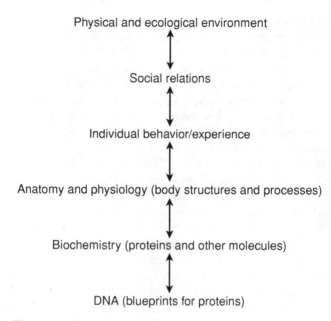

Figure 3.1 Two-way causality across levels of analysis.

does its behavioral pattern of aggression. If a stronger fish later displaces this male from its dominant position, the relevant cells in the displaced male's hypothalamus shrink, and all the other effects reverse themselves in sequence.[4]

Among wrasse fish (and apparently unique to them), if a dominant male dies and another male does not quickly take over the territory, the dominant *female* (among several females that occupied subterritories of the dominant male) develops within a day "into a complete and functional male." Even among orangutans – one of the four animal species closest to humans – males come in two versions, and may switch from one to the other far into adulthood (a kind of long-delayed puberty) depending in part on social relationships. All these examples show that sexual anatomy and physiology can be pliable under social and environmental influences.[5]

Two-directional causality across multiple levels of analysis is illustrated in Figure 3.1. The feedback down to the level of DNA occurs not only in a slow evolutionary sense with the sifting of the gene pool over generations. Higher levels also directly control DNA through the

[4] Fernald 1993; Francis, Soma, and Fernald 1993.
[5] Wrasse: Caspari 1978, 104; orangutans: Wrangham and Peterson 1996, 134–36; physiology: Silver 1992, 401.

process of gene *expression* – the activation of a particular genetic sequence so that a protein is made. (DNA folds up in three dimensions with only some parts of the code activated by being exposed at a given time. Special molecules and systems regulate gene expression according to the needs of the organism.) Indeed, sex hormones such as testosterone have their effects on the body precisely by regulating the expression of certain genes. Those (and other) hormones in turn respond to moods, perceptions, and social relationships, minute by minute, as we shall see. So, the world of culture (nurture) feeds back to the deepest level of biology (nature), and this happens in all of us, every day. The interactions among hormones, brains, and behaviors are "incredibly complex."[6]

A striking example of the influence of human culture on biology is that adolescents are now going through puberty younger than a few generations ago – perhaps as the result of exposure to "grown-up" influences in teenage culture, or possibly because of higher stress. However, this trend is nothing new. It follows a long-term and almost linear decrease in age of puberty over more than a century in European countries. The average age of a woman's first menstrual period dropped from almost 17 in the mid-nineteenth century to about 13 by 1960 (see Figure 3.2). This change may result from urbanization, since in Poland during this time period the average age was about two years younger for city dwellers than country folk.[7]

Another problem in the nature–nurture debate is the common assumption that biology is an immutable force, whereas culture is more controllable. Critics of sociobiology argue that war is "just" a cultural invention, and not "set in stone" like genetics are. In truth, however, scientists understand, control, and change biology (e.g., controlling diseases) much more easily – albeit with real limits – than social scientists or politicians understand and control culture and social relationships, including gender and war. We would be lucky to find that war and sexism were biologically determined, 100 percent. We could find the hormone or neurotransmitter that inhibits these unfortunate behaviors, then add it to the water supply like fluoride. (Instant peace. Just add water.) Unfortunately, real biology is a lot more complicated and less deterministic.[8]

To the extent that biology *is* destiny, that destiny is diversity. As this and the next chapter will show, biological systems are extremely

---

[6] Angier 1994c; Blakeslee 1997; Moyer 1987, incredibly 20.

[7] Herman-Giddens *et al.* 1997; *Newsweek*, October 18, 1999 [cover]; trend: Silver 1992, 402–3.

[8] Mead 1940; D. Jones 1994.

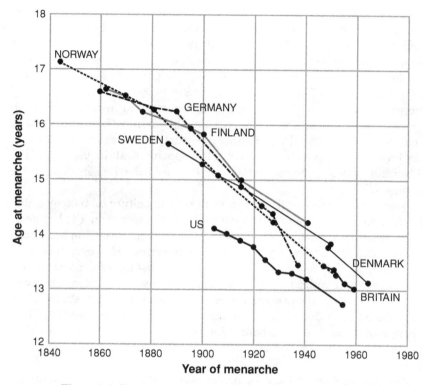

Figure 3.2 Decline in age of puberty for girls, 1845–1965. [From J. M. Tanner, "Earlier Maturation in Man." Copyright © January 1968 by *Scientific American, Inc.* All rights reserved.]

complex, flexible, and varied. Biology and feminism both value and celebrate diversity, both mistrust simplistic theoretical models for that reason, and both struggle against religious fundamentalism – common grounds sometimes overlooked in the heated debates over sociobiology (see pp. 51–52).

Overlapping curves   Real biological gender differences, as opposed to stereotyped ones, are not categorical. Men vary within their gender group, as do women. As we shall see, most psychological measures and behaviors relevant to war-fighting do not show a sharp separation of genders into two non-overlapping categories. Rather, individual characteristics tend to be distributed, within each gender, in a "bell-curve" distribution. Many people cluster in the middle and fewer people

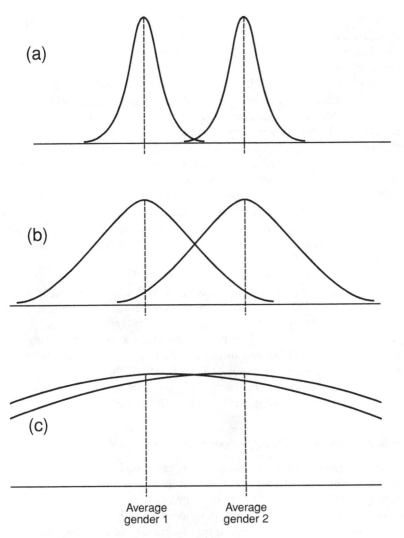

(a)

(b)

(c)

Average   Average
gender 1   gender 2

Figure 3.3 Bell-curve distributions.

are very high or low on a given dimension of ability or style. (Relevant dimensions might include, for example, violent tendencies or physical strength.)

The key issue for the puzzle of gendered war roles is how much the male and female bell-curves overlap. Figure 3.3 illustrates three patterns of overlapping bell-curves, each with the same *average* difference between men and women on some variable. The horizontal axis at the bottom shows a range of scores on some ability; the vertical axis shows how many individuals have a particular score. (Difference feminists emphasize that one bell-curve is shifted from the other, while liberal feminists emphasize the overlapping range of abilities; see pp. 39–49).

In Figure 3.3a, the two bell-curves are almost entirely separate. Virtually all members of one gender score higher than all members of the other on some variable (e.g., testosterone levels). In 3.3b, the two curves show some overlap, so that a minority of the lower gender scores higher than a minority of the higher gender (data on height, for example, show this amount of overlap). In 3.3c, the variation within each gender is much greater than the average difference, so the two curves mostly overlap (differences in cognitive abilities typically follow such a distribution). Knowing a person's gender tells little about an individual's score on such a variable. Discussing average gender differences without taking into account variation within each gender creates a "tyranny of averages" in which individuals are judged by group attributes.[9]

In a population following Figure 3.3c, most individual women are well within the male curve and can perform as well as most men. Indeed, even in the case of Figure 3.3b, women in nontraditional gender roles will probably perform as well as their male counterparts, because presumably women who self-select into such roles (such as by joining the military) are near the high end of the female bell-curve for relevant abilities, whereas the men are closer to the middle of the male curve since more of them participate. Only a variable resembling Figure 3.3a could adequately explain the categorical gender roles found in war.

Gender differences in aggression

Among the most central variables to be examined in this way is "aggression." From one perspective, war is merely a large-scale extension of a more general phenomenon – male aggression – found outside of war from domestic violence and rape to schoolyard bullying and (for some writers) even sports and power-hunger in corporate and governmental life. Measuring "aggression" in both people and animals is important but problematical.

Defining aggression   The concept of aggression is both ambiguous and contested. Defining behavior as aggression depends on controversial definitions on several dimensions – intent (hostile, aimed at harm), behavior (injurious), and emotional state (angry versus

---

[9] Tyranny: James 1997, 221; Thorne 1993, 57–58; Eagly 1995; Maccoby 1998, 79.

instrumental aggression). In one common usage, "aggression" refers to unprovoked hostility towards others, that is, initiating an attack or fight. The idea of aggression as a male quality has drawn on claims that men are violent and competitive.[10]

Early theories of aggression, including those of Freud and of Lorenz, treated it as a "hydraulic" system or "drive" – something that built up inside until it found an outlet. These views have long been in disfavor, however. Among other problems, they would predict relatively constant aggression across societies and through time, in contrast to the great variability in aggression actually found. An alternative – "social learning" – sees aggression not as an inner drive or response to frustrations, but as behavior learned by reinforcement (rewards or punishments) and by observation of role models, especially parents (same-gender parents, according to some), siblings and peers. Social learning theorists emphasize the symbolic mental representations of social events, including "scripts." The 1986 Seville Statement on Violence by aggression researchers – critics of deterministic biology – declares that humans have no innate tendencies towards aggression, violence, and war. The statement was adopted by UNESCO in 1989 and endorsed by the American Psychological Association in 1987 with the caveat that it was not a scientific finding but a social statement aimed at countering unfounded stereotypes about the inevitability of war.[11]

Stimulation of certain regions of the brain can evoke or suppress aggressive behaviors in various species. For example, one type of electrical stimulation to a monkey's brain (via remote control) caused it to attack another, whereas stimulation of a different region caused a dominant monkey to reduce aggressive actions – and no longer receive submission from other monkeys in the group. When the remote control button for this latter region was placed inside the cage, one of the submissive monkeys learned to push it when the dominant monkey made threatening

[10] Van Der Dennen and Falger eds. 1990, 9–10; Baron and Richardson 1994, 6–13; Wilson 1978, 101; Wilson 1975, 248, 242–43; Van Hooff 1990, 28–32; Moyer 1976; Siegel and Demetrikopoulos 1993; Archer and Browne 1989, 4–12, 17; Zahn-Waxler, Cummings, and Iannotti 1986, 7; Weisfeld 1994, 42; Campbell 1993, 7–14; Campbell and Muncer 1994; Berkowitz 1962; Berkowitz 1981, 4; Berkowitz 1989; Berkowitz 1990; Montagu 1976, 8–12; Davies 1987; Blanchard and Blanchard 1989; Klama 1988, 2–10; Foster 1986, 71; Holloway 1967; McGuinness ed. 1987; Geen 1998; Brain and Benton eds. 1981; Turner 1994, 234–35; Archer 1994a; Archer 1994b, 127–35.

[11] Freud 1930; Lorenz 1963; Klama 1988, 106; Berkowitz 1962; Eibl-Eibesfeldt 1979, 4–6, 10–11, 52, 108, 116, 165; Stevenson 1987, 123–31; Van Der Dennen and Falger eds. 1990, 15; Sagan and Druyan 1992, 200; Neuman 1987; Loewald 1988; Tiger and Robinson 1991, xviii–xix; Fox 1991; Keegan 1993, 85–86; learning: Bandura 1973; Geen 1998, 324–26; Ruble and Martin 1998, 976–82; P. Smith 1989, 81–82; Seville: Groebel and Hinde eds. 1989, xvi; Beroldi 1994; Scott and Ginsburg 1994.

gestures. José Delgado once placed an electrode in a Spanish fighting bull's brain, then went into the bull ring and stopped the bull's charge by pushing a button. What these electrical currents really do in the brain we do not know, since any of various effects could produce a halting of aggressive behavior.[12]

Gender differences   Among various types of behavior studied by psychologists, aggression has shown the most consistent gender differences. Eleanor Maccoby and Carol Jacklin's 1974 review of hundreds of studies on gender sorts out gender stereotypes that are supported by the weight of empirical evidence, or are contradicted by it, or where the evidence is ambiguous. Along with several types of cognitive difference, they find a "fairly well established" gender difference in aggression, "observed in all cultures in which the relevant behavior has been observed. Boys are more aggressive both physically and verbally," and have more play-fighting and aggressive fantasies. The gender difference in aggression starts "as early as social play begins – at age 2 or $2^1/_2$. Although the aggressiveness of both sexes declines with age, boys and men remain more aggressive through the college years." Males' primary victims from an early age are other males. Whiting and Whiting's 1975 study of six widely differing cultures worldwide found that overall, "[g]irls are more nurturant and boys more aggressive."[13]

Several recent studies of aggression find significant gender differences in physical aggression, but fewer gender differences – even a slight female edge at certain ages – in verbal or social aggression, such as excluding someone from a group (which can devastate the victim). Some researchers find that "relational" aggression occurs significantly more often among girls than boys, both in preschool and primary years. Girls and boys appear to follow similar developmental paths, in which aggression decreases from childhood to adulthood, and direct physical aggression gives way to indirect aggression based on social relationships, such as ostracism. (During elementary school, children's aggression decreases and becomes more limited to a few individuals. The previous "nonsocial, instrumental nature of aggression" gives way increasingly to "person-oriented and hostile" aggression elicited by "threats and derogations to one's ego.") However, boys lag behind girls at each developmental stage,

---

[12] Moyer 1987, 18; Andy and Stephan 1974, 327; Sagan and Druyan 1992, 193; Delgado: *The New York Times*, May 17, 1965.

[13] Feshbach 1989, 87; Weisfeld 1994, 53; Coie and Dodge 1998, 789–92; Cummings *et al.* 1986, 179; Ahmad and Smith 1994; Maffitt *et al.* 2001; review: Maccoby and Jacklin 1974, 349–53, college 352; Block 1976; Archer and Lloyd 1985, 124–59; Geen 1998, 330; Whiting and Whiting 1975, 148–49, nurturant 167.

especially in adolescence when boys' aggression remains as direct as ever (and more physically injurious) whereas girls' aggression has become mainly indirect. Aggression decreases with age for girl–girl and mixed-gender interactions, but remains high through early adolescence for boy–boy aggression. Despite these average gender differences, many women commit violence against men (how many is contested).[14]

Social psychologists Alice Eagly and Valerie Steffen trace gender differences in adult aggression to different beliefs about the consequences of aggression, using meta-analysis to combine results of fifty previous quantitative studies seeking to explain aggressive behavior. (The method of meta-analysis combines a number of past studies' results in a statistically appropriate manner.) "In general, this meta-analysis shows that men are more aggressive than women and that this sex difference is more pronounced for physical than psychological aggression." However, the sizes of gender effects vary and are often quite small. Women's aggression is reduced when the expected effect would harm the victim, endanger themselves, or provoke intense guilt or anxiety. Similarly, Hyde's meta-analysis of 143 studies also finds significant gender differences for "all types of aggression, all methods of measurement, and all designs, although effect sizes were generally small to moderate" (the distribution curves for males and females overlap a lot).[15]

Many animal species show gender differences in aggression. Even though females can be as aggressive as males, notably when their young are threatened, nonetheless behavior patterns regarding violence often differ for males and females of a given species. Primatologist Meredith Small finds overlap in the distributions of aggressiveness in male and female primate populations. Males are more aggressive and females more social on average, yet females can be aggressive when called for and males care about social interactions.[16]

Altruism   The opposite of aggression, so to speak, is "prosocial" behavior – various kinds of sharing and helping. Armies require great prosocial behavior internally, in service of aggressive behavior directed externally. Altruism and sacrifice are central aspects of war-fighting. Yet,

---

[14] Crick, Casas, and Ku 1999, preschool; Crick and Grotpeter 1995, primary; Maccoby 1998, 40–41, 57–58; Cairns and Cairns 1994, 56–67; Cairns 1986, 77; Coie and Dodge 1998, ego 791; Geen 1998, 331–32; Eagly 1987, 70; Feshbach and Feshbach 1986, 212; Zuger 1998a; Blum 1997, xiv; Pearson 1997, commit 1–32.

[15] Eagly and Steffen 1986, 325; Konner 1988; Geen 1998, 331; Eagly 1987, 70–95; Jacklin ed. 1992, 265–440; Hyde and Linn eds. 1986; Hyde 1986, moderate 51, 63; Eagly 1995, 150–54; Archer 1996; Eagly 1996; Eagly and Wood 1991; Archer and Lloyd 1985, 127; O'Leary, Unger, and Wallston eds. 1985; Tetlock 1998; Deaux and LaFrance 1998; Frodi, Macauley, and Thome 1977.

[16] Klama 1988, 74; Small 1993, 27–28, 57; Ghiglieri 1999.

caring and helping are stereotypically feminine behaviors. More frequent helpfulness and support-giving by girls than boys is found cross-culturally and appears to increase with age.[17]

The empirical evidence in (mainly Western) psychological studies is "equivocal": social psychologists have found only "highly inconsistent effects" of gender on prosocial behavior. Some studies found that men help more than women, others the opposite, and still others no gender difference. (The only consistency is that women *receive* help more often than men.) A meta-analysis of 172 past studies found "extremely inconsistent" gender differences. Another meta-analysis of research on children likewise found results "inconsistent across studies." Gender differences are also greater for self- and other-reports than for observational data, possibly reflecting expectations of "what boys and girls are *supposed* to be like rather than how they actually behave." The gendered construction of prosocial behaviors is thus complex.[18]

Gender differences in prosocial behaviors may result from different contexts – such as men helping in a dangerous emergency and women giving emotional support to friends with relationship troubles. Gender roles may foster heroic and chivalrous helping by males, and nurturant, caring helping by females. Psychological studies of altruism have focused on short-term helping by strangers (as in a famous wallet-left-on-street experiment) – a focus that excludes female-role helping behaviors found mainly in "long-term, close relationships."[19]

Nonetheless a small difference remains even in observational studies, with girls using more prosocial behaviors. Gender differences in empathy and sympathy also vary depending on study method. "One cannot simplistically . . . conclude that one gender is more empathic than the other." Moral reasoning does not differ by gender in young children, but from late middle childhood on girls use certain "sophisticated types of prosocial moral reasoning" more than boys do. Although girls appear to use prosocial behavior somewhat more than boys, the question is unresolved. The widespread view of girls as more prosocial than boys may rest largely on the girls' lower use of physical aggression.[20]

Overall, then, researchers find modest but persistent gender differences in aggression. Of course, we do not know whether these are an effect or a cause of men's roles as potential and actual warriors.

---

[17] Shaw and Wong 1989; Eisenberg and Fabes 1998, 752.

[18] Eisenberg and Fabes 1998, equivocal 752, across 753, behave 754; Batson 1998, highly 289–90, receive 289; Eagly and Crowley 1986, extremely 283.

[19] Eagly and Crowley 1986, 283; Radke-Yarrow, Zahn-Waxler, and Chapman 1983, 509.

[20] Eisenberg and Fabes 1998, remains 754, moral–physical 752–55; Saarni, Mumme, and Campos 1998, conclude 275; empathy: Angier 1995b.

Five lines of argument try to root gendered war roles in individual biology. The rest of this chapter turns to each in turn.

A. GENETICS

William James wrote in 1910 that "[o]ur ancestors have bred pugnacity into our bone and marrow and thousands of years of peace won't breed it out of us." Aggression does have a genetic component because it can be bred in animals, by selectively mating aggressive individuals for several generations. This has been done, for example, in some dogs, fighting cocks, and bulls. Both male and female animals carry the "aggressive genes," however. Females given testosterone prenatally and as adults show male-type aggression. Efforts to compare human identical twins (same genes) with nonidentical twins (genetically distinct) have been inconclusive. Among both adults and children, the results seem to depend on the particular questionnaire used to measure aggression. Studies of antisocial behavior and criminality find some "genetic predisposition," but it appears to be stronger for nonviolent crime than violent crime. Thus, the genetic basis of aggression is neither very specific (a "gene for war") nor very closely tied to gender.[21]

The genetics of gender

Humans have something like 100,000 genes in our DNA, each containing codes for assembling various proteins, the basic building blocks of our bodies. Scientists are just completing a map of the entire human genome. This map, however, does not tell us how the proteins work or what they do. Having a complete set of building blocks, every variety needed to assemble a human body, is very useful but far from the answer to all questions.

The system of an X and a Y chromosome which controls biological gender in humans is common to all mammals. An individual inherits an X from its mother and either an X or a Y from its father. (In birds a different system of sex chromosomes is used. In some reptiles gender is determined by the temperature of the incubating eggs. Most invertebrates do not have individuals of one gender.) In mammals, including humans, the X chromosome contains genes for various proteins that *both* males and females produce. Both men and women have X chromosomes, and

---

[21] James 1910, 164; Carneiro 1994, 7; Moyer 1987, 26–28; Sagan and Druyan 1992, 195; Lagerspetz and Lagerspetz 1983; Ebert 1983; Angier 1995d; humans: Turner 1994, 237–39; Baron and Richardson 1994, 246–48; Morell 1993.

the extra X in women appears to have relatively subtle effects (more blueprints for the same building blocks).[22]

Do Y chromosomes contain codes for proteins that tend to promote aggression (genes for war), and perhaps X chromosomes for proteins that tend to inhibit aggression? The answer is no. For starters, this theory predicts that XYY men (born with an extra Y chromosome) would be more aggressive than "normal" XY men. In fact XYY men commit more crimes than average, but usually nonviolent ones, and their criminal tendencies seem to trace to lower intelligence rather than aggressive tendencies. A second implication of the theory is that males with an extra X chromosome – XXY males – should be less aggressive than XY males. Instead, the limited evidence indicates no difference in aggression, and a tendency of XXY males, like XYY males, to suffer higher rates of mental retardation and incarceration. Among females, the theory predicts that those with only one X chromosome (XO females) should be more aggressive than those with two ("normal" females). The evidence indicates that, if anything, XO females are less aggressive, not more. Furthermore, females with three X chromosomes (XXX females) should be less aggressive than the norm, but in fact are no different in aggression though more likely than average to be institutionalized. Thus the theory of X and Y chromosomes containing anti- and pro-aggressive material does not hold up.[23]

In fact, the Y chromosome contains only *one gene* of importance (yet understood). Of the many thousands of proteins our bodies can make, only this one is unique to males. The Y chromosome acts as an oversized switch to turn on this protein, and with it male gender (or, in its absence, by default, female gender). Beyond that role, the "Y chromosome does not seem to do very much."[24]

This protein coded by the Y chromosome gene is called *testis determination factor* (TDF). In developing embryos, only males have it. For more than a month after conception, the embryo develops without gender differentiation. "Indifferent" gonads develop (see Figure 3.4). Absent TDF, the gonads grow into ovaries, and until birth the body produces little testosterone or estrogen. In the presence of TDF, however, the gonads turn into testes, and the testes begin producing testosterone (and estrogen), as well as a hormone called *müllerian regression factor* (MRF). The indifferent gonads have two sets of ducts connected to them. If MRF is absent, one set develops into fallopian tubes for eggs. If MRF is present

---

[22] Breedlove 1992, 40.
[23] Christen 1987, 40; Baron and Richardson 1994, 251–52.
[24] Breedlove 1992, 41.

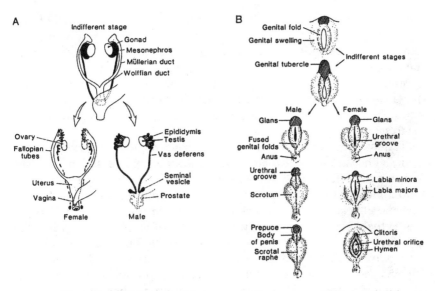

Figure 3.4 Embryonic development of sex organs. [Reprinted with permission from J. D. Wilson, F. W. George, and J. E. Griffin, "The Hormonal Control of Sexual Development," *Science* 211: 1278–84. Copyright 1981, American Association for the Advancement of Science.]

(i.e., in males), the pre-fallopian ducts wither and the other set develops instead, into the vas deferens to carry sperm.

External genitalia also begin undifferentiated. In females a genital tubercle develops into a clitoris, while genital folds develop into a vagina and labia (lips). In the presence of testosterone – and an enzyme that makes testosterone more potent for local applications – the tubercle develops instead into a penis while the folds become the scrotum (the sac of skin holding the testes).

Thus, although we may see male and female sex organs as very different, they are actually very closely related and derive from common genetic blueprints which have the ability to develop in either direction. Men and women have nearly identical genetics, but the male aspects switch on in men. The switch is the single Y chromosome gene that produces the protein that develops the testes that make testosterone.

Sex hormones   The relevant genes that contribute to aggression are latent in both males and females (and hence, can be bred), but are activated differentially by gender. This selective activation is the job of testosterone and other sex hormones – molecules that the body produces, through a series of enzyme-driven reactions, from cholesterol. The "male" sex hormones are called androgens. The most important of these is *testosterone,* and I simplify for convenience by referring only to testosterone, with the understanding that other related molecules are involved, but work similarly. The "female" sex hormones are estrogens and progestins. Again I will simplify by referring only to *estrogen* generically, and *progesterone* (the most important progestin). As its name implies, progesterone is important in pregnancy (gestation), but less important in sex or aggression.[25]

Testosterone, estrogen, and progesterone regulate the expression of genes. They are *steroid hormones* which, after being released, bind to specific *receptors* (molecules into which the hormone molecule fits like a key into a lock). The bound pair of steroid hormone and receptor then has specific effects on DNA, causing the DNA to produce (or not to produce) the specific proteins for which that bit of DNA is a blueprint. This is a very important process, because the 100,000 or so genes in human beings make all kinds of proteins for many purposes. These genes are all over the body, but only certain genes are expressed – producing their designated proteins – in certain places and times. Those proteins in turn are materials for anatomy, physiology, and ultimately behavior. Thus, we all contain both female and male genetics; sex hormones regulate which potentials we realize.

Variations   If any element along the line is missing, the embryo will develop in various mixes of male and female – underscoring the essential *genetic* similarity across gender. For example, occasionally an individual lacks the gene (which is on the X chromosome) that produces the testosterone *receptor,* without which testosterone can be produced but is ineffective. In such a case, females develop normally. Males, however, take a different route. They develop testes (thanks to TDF), which produce MRF, causing the fallopian-tube ducts to wither away. The testes also produce testosterone, but it has no effect because the receptor is absent. Therefore these individuals develop externally as females and "look, act, and think of themselves as females" despite their XY chromosomes.[26]

A different occasional mutation leads to the absence of the enzyme which makes testosterone more potent as the genitals are developing. The result is that males are born with labia containing testes inside, and an enlarged clitoris – superficially female. At the time of puberty, however, the testes produce a surge of testosterone. These individuals grow penises and scrotums, and their bodies develop along "male" lines. The genetic

[25] Hadley 1996.
[26] Breedlove 1992, look 45.

anomaly occurs often in one region of the Dominican Republic. The affected people are usually raised as females, but after puberty begin acting as males.[27]

Occasionally, an individual lacks the gene that produces an enzyme needed in the adrenal cortex. Without it, the hormonal feedback system doesn't work and the adrenal gland ends up producing too much of a hormone that is converted to testosterone. Female embryos with this condition develop masculinized genitalia – an enlarged clitoris and scrotum-like labia. These individuals are often popularly called hermaphrodites although, unlike actual hermaphrodites, they cannot reproduce as males. Until recently, this condition was not "treated" after birth, and the people "experienced a good deal of confusion about their actual gender."[28]

In recent years a movement has developed supporting "intersexuals" of ambiguous biological gender, and opposing "treatment" practices like genital surgery. Intersexual activists call such treatments a form of mutilation, pursued because the rest of society is uncomfortable with intersexuals, not because they themselves are inherently unhappy. Both social taboos and widespread use of surgery and hormones make it difficult to estimate the prevalence of intersexuals in the population (evidently one-tenth of 1 percent by the narrowest definition and perhaps 2 percent by the broadest).[29]

To summarize, men and women are extremely similar genetically, even in the domain of sex itself. Not only is it possible for people to have sex-change operations (activating latent cross-gender blueprints), but wrasse fish do it without even an operation (see p. 130).

All biologically based gender differences relevant to war result from the effects of testosterone. The Y chromosome switch essentially turns on production of testosterone. The most important effect is that testosterone makes people grow larger and stronger after puberty. Before considering this aspect, and other possible subtler effects, I will review the direct behavioral influences of testosterone.

B. TESTOSTERONE LEVELS

Perhaps testosterone causes "aggressive genes" to be expressed. This is plausible in theory, and would provide an excellent possible answer to the puzzle of gendered war roles, because levels of sex hormones show little

[27] Breedlove 1992, 47; M. Harris 1989, 268–69.
[28] Breedlove 1992, 47.
[29] Fausto-Sterling 1993; Fausto-Sterling forthcoming; Maccoby 1998, 1; Harding 1986, 127; Angier 1997a; Angier 1997c; Andersen 1993, 25; Oudshoorn 1994; Feinberg 1996.

overlap between males and females (data are on p. 145). Thus, we could explain a nearly categorical gender distinction (combat roles) with a variable that is also nearly categorical (testosterone levels) instead of one where distributions overlap substantially. This explanation does not hold up empirically, however, any more than genetics does.

How testosterone works

Testosterone and estrogen are called "male" and "female" hormones, respectively, but these labels are actually a bit misleading. Both males and females produce both testosterone and estrogen, in their adrenal glands (above the kidneys). In addition, before birth and again after puberty, testosterone and estrogen are produced in large amounts by the testes and ovaries, respectively. The two molecules are closely connected: a biochemical reaction converts testosterone, which is itself a by-product of progesterone, into an estrogen. In fact, many effects of testosterone in males begin with its conversion into estrogen.[30]

Testosterone levels Do men's testosterone levels cause corresponding levels of aggressive behavior? The answer is mostly no, although testosterone may exert some subtle effects on aggression. Testosterone levels vary greatly – across individuals and through time – and these differences affect both physiology and behavior. Seasonal and menstrual cycles change levels of sex hormones. So do variations over the course of a person's life cycle. Long-term levels vary from one individual to another, and short-term levels fluctuate rapidly within individuals from day to day. The fluctuating production of testosterone (and estrogen) by both the gonads and the adrenal cortex is regulated by other hormones produced in the brain by the pituitary gland, which is in turn regulated by the (adjacent) hypothalamus.[31]

On average, adult men have about 20 times as much testosterone as women, and women have about 3–25 times as much estrogen as men, depending on the menstrual cycle. (Most of men's estrogen comes from converted testosterone, and its role in men is not yet well understood, nor are men's rather high levels of prolactin). In women, about half the testosterone is produced by the andrenal glands and half by the ovaries. The latter source spikes along with estrogen in the ovulatory cycle, so, at the time of ovulation, women whose testosterone levels are normally near the high end of the female range may approach the low end of the male

---

[30] Becker, Breedlove, and Crews eds. 1992; Blum 1997, 159–88.
[31] Fluctuate: Dabbs 1990; Veldhuis et al. 1987.

Table 3.1 *Typical testosterone levels by developmental stage and gender (in nanograms per deciliter of blood)*

	Men		Women	
Developmental stage	Level	Range	Level	Range
Prenatal & first 7 months	60	**15–120**	3	**1–10**
1–7 years old	3	**1–10**	3	**1–10**
8 until puberty	30	5–75	5	1–15
Early puberty	100	20–300	15	3–30
Young adult	**600**	**200–1,000**	50	**15–100**
60 years old	300	30–600	30	3–60

Note: Author's estimates of approximate typical plasma levels in human samples, from several sources. Range shown is two standard deviations in each direction around approximate mean levels (about 95 percent of individuals), where I had such data. This oversimplified schema is meant to illustrate overall trajectories; actual distributions are not normal, and levels vary substantially across samples, individuals, and even times of day.
Data sources: Hines 1982; Wilke and Utley 1987: 1373; Luthold *et al.* 1993: 639; Susman *et al.* 1987: 1120; Nottelmann *et al.* 1987: 251; Brooks-Gunn and Warren 1989: 43.

range. Normal effects of testosterone in girls at puberty include growing pubic and underarm hair, making skin break out, and possibly limiting breast enlargement. In adult women, unusually high testosterone levels can stimulate facial hair, balding, acne, and in severe cases infertility, diabetes, heart disease, and other problems. By one report, 15–30 percent or more of US women may have testosterone-related health problems, but "normal" and "abnormal" levels for women are poorly defined. The point here is that the differences in testosterone levels that separate men and women leave the extremes of those groups close together, even with a bit of overlap – but only a bit.[32]

Table 3.1 summarizes typical testosterone levels in various developmental stages. Before puberty, the gender difference in testosterone production is strongest during the 10th to 24th weeks of gestation, when the physical differences in anatomy take shape. From about age 7 months to 7 years, testosterone levels are low – one-tenth or less of the male level before and just after birth – and *are the same in girls as in boys* (as are estrogen levels). Production comes from the adrenal cortex in both genders, not the testes. Boys' levels of testosterone rise gradually from age 8 to puberty, then shoot up tenfold or more during puberty,

[32] Norman and Litwack 1987, 531, 495–98; Angier 1994a.

and thereafter remain about ten times higher than women's, gradually declining over the decades (by about half by age 60 and then more rapidly).[33]

As shown by the ranges in Table 3.1, individuals differ within each gender. The broad range of adult male testosterone levels is shown in Figure 3.5. Levels also vary somewhat from one population to another. For example, in a group of !Kung men, the average testosterone level was within – but at the low end of – the normal range of European and American men. In both groups, the standard deviation was nearly half of the mean, which implies a wide range of levels across individuals. The top few percent of women have levels near the bottom few percent of men – a pattern rather like (c) on Figure 3.3 above (see p. 133).[34]

To repeat, girls and boys age 1–7 have the same amounts of testosterone (and of estrogen). The mother who calls her Godzilla-like 5-year-old son "testosterone-driven" is wrong. That will come later, when he is a teenager. Hormonally, physiologically, and anatomically (except for sex organs), before puberty boys resemble girls (see pp. 287–93).[35]

Puberty is initiated (nobody knows exactly how) when the brain begins producing more gonad-stimulating hormones, especially in mysterious bursts during sleep. Figure 3.6 shows the daily cycle of testosterone levels in a 14-year-old boy – lingering in the child range, then shooting up more than tenfold to the low end of the adult range (during sleep) and coming down again by mid-morning. Every day, the boy's body tells him, "You're a man for real! Just kidding!" Body changes during puberty are produced by sex hormones. Males after puberty – or females given testosterone – tend to grow beards and more body hair elsewhere as well. Their voices typically drop in pitch. They grow larger and stronger, especially in the upper body. The "steroids" used by body builders and athletes to build muscle and body mass are synthetic versions of testosterone. Female athletes who take steroids may develop "masculine" attributes such as beards.[36]

Not only do testosterone levels vary from one individual to another, they vary substantially from hour to hour (as well as week to week, and seasonally) for a given individual. For both genders, levels drop about 50 percent from the morning to the evening. Thus, in various ways

[33] Estrogen: Watson and Lowrey 1967, 320; Grumbach and Van Wyk 1974, 446; Adams, Montemayor, and Gullotta 1989, 146.

[34] Christiansen 1991, !Kung 40–41; Dabbs 1990, 84; Ellis and Nyborg 1992.

[35] Colt and Hollister 1998, driven 44.

[36] Buchanan, Eccles, and Becker 1992, 64–65; Goodman 1996, 265; Norman and Litwack 1987, 499, 536; Moyer 1987, 23; Constantino et al. 1993, 1218; Brooks-Gunn and Warren 1989, 43–44; Faiman and Winter 1974, 35, 45; Bagatell and Bremner 1996, 707.

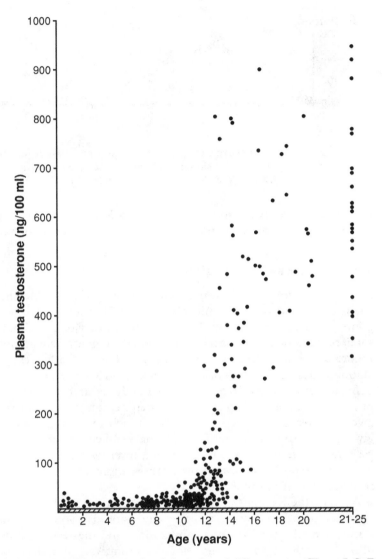

Figure 3.5 Testosterone levels in males of different ages. [From J. S. D. Winter and C. Faiman, "Pituitary-gonadal relations in male children and adolescents." *Pediatric Research* 6: 126–35.]

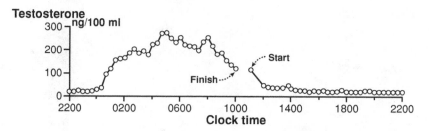

Figure 3.6 Daily cycle of testosterone levels in a 14-year-old boy. [Reproduced with permission from *Journal of Clinical Investigation* 54: 609. By R. M. Boyar, R. S. Rosenfeld, and S. Kapen.]

testosterone levels vary and fluctuate. Behavioral effects including aggression should be dramatic if driven by short-term testosterone levels.

Testosterone and aggression

Do high testosterone levels cause high levels of aggression? Men have high testosterone and men commit most acts of violence, including violent crimes and, of course, war. Furthermore, most violent criminals and soldiers are drawn from the age group with the highest testosterone levels. Figure 3.7 shows arrest rates by gender and age. The highest rates are among males 15–24 years old (peaking at 17–18 years old).[37]

In laboratories, male rats fight regularly. If researchers castrate a male rat, removing the main source of testosterone, it fights much less. If they give it testosterone injections, it fights much more again. Female rats given testosterone injections fight like males. In certain animals, seasonal variations in testosterone correlate with intermale aggression. Thus, it is easy to assume that testosterone causes aggression, and this idea is a recurrent theme of public discourse.[38]

Actually the relationship is more complex. For one thing, the kind of aggression studied most, intermale aggression, is connected most with status hierarchies in breeding competition, and the results do not seem to apply to other forms of aggression, including war. Also, the connection found in rodents does not apply very well to primates, and especially not to humans. Then too, attempts to control aggressive male prisoners by

[37] Monagle 1992.
[38] Sagan and Druyan 1992, 222, 228; Wilson 1975, 251; Konner 1988, 33; Siegel and Demetrikopoulos 1993, 101–7; Rose *et al.* 1974, 287–92; Lisciotto *et al.* 1990; Bernardi *et al.* 1989, 1149; Monaghan and Glickman 1992, 277; Moyer 1987, 21–22; *Newsweek*, July 3, 1995: 61; *The New York Times*, June 20, 1995: A1; *Psychology Today*, June 1993: 12; Dowd 1999.

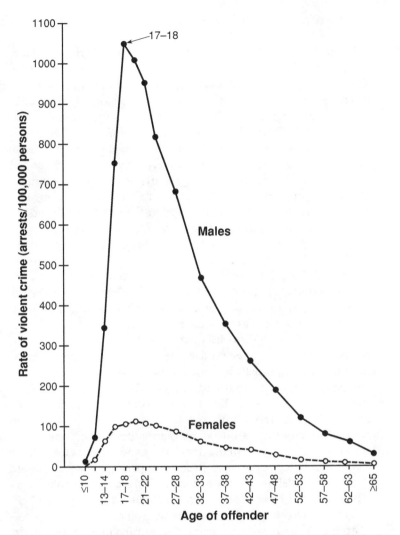

Figure 3.7 Arrest rates for violent crime, by age and gender, United States, 1982. [From Cairns 1986, 80.]

castration have not worked, and eunuchs have led aggressive military campaigns. The relative unimportance of testosterone in causing aggression is seen from the fact that differences in testosterone levels between individuals do not predict subsequent differences in their aggressive behavior – nor do short-term fluctuations in a man's testosterone level predict changes in his levels of aggression. "In humans, if we exclude sexually related actions, it is difficult to see a direct effect of hormones on aggressive behavior."[39]

Robert Sapolsky finds that some relatively small amount of testosterone is necessary for male aggression to occur, but whether it is 20 percent or 200 percent of normal does not affect the frequency of aggression (its presence has a "permissive" effect on aggression). It does affect the intensity of that aggression, however. Testosterone amplifies existing patterns of aggression rather than causing them. For example, in a male rhesus monkey status hierarchy, an individual given very large doses of testosterone behaves more aggressively *only* towards those below him. (Similarly, electrically stimulating the hypothalamus in animals increases intermale aggression without changing its targets.) Elevating testosterone levels does not *cause* bursts of energy in the amygdala, but does increase the frequency of the bursts if they are already occurring.[40]

Much of the human research on testosterone has studied criminals – a problematic sample. Among male prisoners, higher testosterone levels were found in (1) those who had committed violent rather than nonviolent crimes, (2) those rated as "tougher" by their peers (but not as measured by self-reporting on questionnaires), and (3) those displaying chronic aggressive behavior while in prison. Among both male and female "delinquents" (with histories of violent and rebellious behavior), testosterone levels were higher on average than in a control group of college students. Among rapists in a mental hospital, those who had committed more violent rapes were found to have higher testosterone levels. However, these results are difficult to interpret because all the rapists, and some of the prisoners, combined sexual and aggressive behaviors in their crimes. Some of these studies also ignore the fluctuations in testosterone levels during the course of the day, and various studies use different methods of measuring aggression. Studies of prisoners often do not take into account the likelihood that testosterone levels drop sharply as a result of being incarcerated (for reasons explained below, pp. 153–55). Thus, causality is hard to pin down in prison studies.[41]

Studies of men with an extra Y chromosome (XYY syndrome) reveal another difficulty in getting clear answers. Such men – about one-thousandth of the male population – have higher than average testosterone levels, and by some reports have higher than average involvement in

[39] Angier 1995c; Klama 1988, 74–77; Rose *et al.* 1974, 298–99, 292; M. Harris 1989, 264–65; Scott 1974; Benton 1981; Monaghan and Glickman 1992, behavior 283.
[40] Sapolsky 1997, 149–59; Herbert 1989, 67–68.
[41] Dabbs, Jurkovic, and Frady 1991; Siegel and Demetrikopoulos 1993, 109–11; Banks and Dabbs 1996, 54–55; Dabbs *et al.* 1987, 180; Monaghan and Glickman 1992, 282; Turner 1994, 245, 233; Hinde and Groebel 1989.

violent crime. However, more XYY men than average are mentally retarded. Furthermore, the rapid development of boys with XYY syndrome might cause an adult-looking 15-year-old boy's "pranks" to be treated as crimes more than those of a normal 15-year-old.[42]

This raises a general issue in assessing the role of testosterone in causing aggression. Since testosterone increases body size and muscle mass (see pp. 159–62), and gives a more "mature" appearance, how do we know whether any subsequent aggression is really caused by expectations and reactions to the *appearance* of a male with high testosterone levels? Furthermore, the simple *opportunity* for a larger, stronger male to use aggression more effectively could also explain such behavior. None of these would imply a greater *propensity* for aggression in men with high testosterone.

In adult men who are not criminals, some scholars find no correlation of testosterone levels with aggression unconnected to sex. Others find a small but positive correlation. In a sample of 4,500 US military veterans, the top 10 percent of men in terms of testosterone level showed a pattern of "delinquency, substance abuse, and ... excessive behavior," although most of these behaviors were significantly different only among the lower-income men. Because of the large sample size, the differences between high-testosterone men and the others were significant but not very large.[43]

The evidence for a correlation of testosterone with aggression should presumably be strongest for teenagers. Indeed, 15- to 17-year-old high-school boys with higher testosterone are physically and verbally more aggressive when provoked – an effect not found in 10- to 14-year-olds. Again, however, this correlation could result simply from the different appearance of high-testosterone boys. Two studies that followed a hundred boys through three years of puberty found only weak effects of testosterone levels on later self-ratings of aggression or problem behaviors. "Negative affect" – mainly depression, anxiety, and internalizing behavior – does not appear linked to testosterone, during adolescence, nor does testosterone appear to affect "personality" measures that diverge for girls and boys during puberty.[44]

---

[42] Turner 1994, 236; pranks: Monaghan and Glickman 1992, 283; Baron and Richardson 1994, 248–51.

[43] No: Monaghan and Glickman 1992, 283; Baron and Richardson 1994, 255; others: Archer 1991, 14; Siegel and Demetrikopoulos 1993, 109–12; delinquency: Dabbs and Morris 1990; Booth and Osgood 1993; Moyer 1987, 25.

[44] Archer 1994c, 9; Siegel and Demetrikopoulos 1993, 111; Constantino *et al.* 1993; Scerbo and Kolko 1994; Constantino, Scerbo and Kolko 1995; Monaghan and Glickman 1992, appearance 283; two: Halpern *et al.* 1993; Drigotas and Udry 1993; negative: Susman, Dorn, and Chrousos 1991, 167; personality: Udry and Talbert 1988; Buchanan, Eccles, and Becker 1992, 62; Susman *et al.* 1987, 1125–28.

Stereotypes of gay men as less aggressive, or lesbians as more aggressive, than their heterosexual peers appear to be false. Similarly, levels of testosterone do not affect the propensity of heterosexuals or homosexuals to favor men or women as partners. (However, German women's testosterone levels correlate with a "masculinity" scale on a psychological questionnaire.) More testosterone makes gay men more interested in sex – with men. Testosterone given to heterosexual women increases their interest in sex (with men). Heterosexual and gay men have equivalent levels of testosterone (as do heterosexual women and lesbians for estrogen).[45]

Experiments that have attempted to measure the effect of altering testosterone levels in humans have suffered from design problems and small sample sizes, and have produced no compelling evidence of an effect on aggressiveness. One experiment used a "placebo-controlled, double-blind, crossover design" (i.e., a good design). Subjects pushed a button to accumulate points which could be exchanged for money at the end of the study, or another button to subtract points from a (fictitious) opponent. The subjects were provoked by having their own points reduced, supposedly by the "opponent," and their aggression was measured by their pushing the "subtract" button – an odd measure of aggression because it is based on retaliation – as well as by questionnaires. The experiment was repeated for 24 weeks, with testosterone treatment during six of those weeks, and placebo treatment during another six weeks. Each of the six subjects showed higher aggression (and significantly higher self-ratings for having used physical aggression outside the laboratory) after receiving testosterone than after placebo.[46]

We also have a much larger-scale, though less controlled, experiment that alters adult testosterone levels – the use of anabolic steroids by several hundred thousand US men (and tens of thousands of women). In one survey, 7 percent of male US high-school seniors said they had used them. The steroids are typically used in large doses (up to 100 times the clinical replacement dose). Because of the secrecy surrounding performance-enhancing steroids, data are unreliable. About one-third of users report side effects, the most frequent being increased aggressiveness. The reliability of these self-reports has been questioned, however. Recent research shows that steroids do indeed build muscle mass and strength, but the research used low levels – about one-tenth of what athletes sometimes

[45] Gladue 1991; Kozak 1996, masculinity 211; Small 1995, interested 178; Herbert 1989, increases 60; Breedlove 1992, equivalent 64.
[46] Archer 1994c, problems 11–14; experiment: Kouri *et al.* 1995.

use – and did not find any aggression effects. Therefore the results of the steroid experiment in terms of testosterone and aggression are suggestive but inconclusive.[47]

Mazur and Booth conclude that men's high testosterone levels encourage behaviors aimed at dominating other people – behaviors that might or might not play out as aggression (or sometimes as rebellion against authority). Testosterone levels in one study of 13-year-old boys correlated with "social success rather than with physical aggression." James Dabbs argues that testosterone correlates with personality qualities like strength, impulsiveness, and adventurousness, which might or might not manifest as aggression, depending on the social context and opportunities for various actions. For example, he finds that college fraternities whose members had high testosterone levels tended to be more rambunctious than the members of low-testosterone fraternities. The wild and unruly high-testosterone fraternities might or might not actually become antisocial (or the well-behaved ones altruistic), depending on circumstances.[48]

The evidence on the entire question of testosterone and aggression in humans is undermined by problems of measurement, reverse causality, and poor experimental design. The main conclusion is that testosterone seems to influence intensity of aggression in some contexts, but these are not well understood and are not dramatic in magnitude.

Social competition and testosterone levels

The reverse direction of causality – from social aggression to testosterone levels – seems stronger. Men's fluctuating short-term testosterone levels respond to competitive situations, such as a tennis or wrestling match, a chess game, or a competitive task in a psychology laboratory. Levels rise in preparation for the competition, and then go up afterwards in winners, and down in losers. This effect does not depend on direct aggression. It applies to any changes in an individual's perceived status in a social hierarchy. Winning or losing a physical fight often has that effect, but so do other competitions. The testosterone high of competitive victory has been measured in males participating in a ceremony to receive their MD degrees, and even in sports fans when their team wins. (One study of US males in various professions found highest testosterone levels among trial

---

[47] Bagatell and Bremner 1996, survey 711–12; Kouri *et al.* 1995, side 73; find: Bhasin *et al.* 1996.

[48] Mazur and Booth 1998; Schaal *et al.* 1996, success 1322; Dabbs *et al.* 1987, 180; Dabbs, Hargrove, and Heusel 1996; Dabbs 2000.

lawyers and lowest levels among ministers – i.e., among the most, and least, competitive professions.)[49]

The effect on testosterone levels depends on subjective judgments about triumph or defeat, and is strongest when a victory is decisive and results from an individual's own efforts. For example, testosterone changes after professional basketball games correlated not with the game's outcome but the player's assessment of his own contribution to a win or loss and his attribution of the outcome to internal or external causes. Similarly, in judo competitors, post-match testosterone significantly correlated not with the outcome but with the individual's satisfaction with that outcome. Among eight men participating in a New York chess tournament over eight weeks, testosterone levels rose about 10 percent on average in winners of games where the chess ratings of the players were close (the players expected to have to fight hard to win). However, testosterone actually decreased after a win where the ratings showed ahead of time that winning would be easy (down about 10 percent, as with losers). In 17 young male first-offenders in a shock-incarceration ("boot camp") program, testosterone levels dropped dramatically in the first month, but less so in six men who started out with a bad attitude and may have refused to feel defeated. Thus, men's testosterone response to competition depends on "cognitive and emotional aspects rather than ... objective ... outcome or physical exertion."[50]

Outcomes of aggressive interactions affect testosterone levels among animals. When male rodents fight over status and territory, the winner of the fight produces more testosterone and the loser produces less. In rhesus monkeys, researchers studied whether levels of testosterone, prior to the formation of a group from unfamiliar males, would predict the eventual status hierarchy that emerged in that group. They did not. But once that hierarchy was established, the testosterone levels in the top monkey rose dramatically, as much as tenfold. After fighting, defeated males' testosterone levels dropped to 10–15 percent of the prior level. In one study, the top quartile in the dominance hierarchy had significantly higher testosterone levels than the other three-quarters. In long-established and stable hierarchies, however, high-ranking and low-ranking males did not differ in testosterone levels. Thus, testosterone levels appear to reflect *changes* in status – i.e., winning and losing. Similarly, in experiments

[49] Mazur and Booth 1998; Mazur and Lamb 1980; Booth *et al.* 1989; Archer 1991, 17–18; Geen 1998, 321; Blum 1997, 167; Turner 1994, 246; Baron and Richardson 1994, 257; Klama 1988, 77; fans: Bernhardt *et al.* 1998; lawyers: Dabbs, in *Science*, April 26, 1991: 513.

[50] Geen 1998, 321; basketball: Gonzalez-Bono *et al.* 1999; judo: Serrano *et al.* 2000, exertion 440; chess: Mazur, Booth, and Dabbs 1992; boot: Thompson, Dabbs, and Frady 1990.

where male monkeys displayed aggression but did not win or lose an encounter, their testosterone levels were unaffected.[51]

In one pleasant experiment, five men were confined on a sailboat for 14 days and had their testosterone levels monitored. They had similar testosterone levels before and after the trip, but towards the end of the trip the higher-ranking men (in the social hierarchy that emerged during the trip) had more testosterone than the others. These results parallel those in rhesus monkeys. Another experiment found that men's testosterone levels are higher than usual during and immediately after having intercourse, but only slightly higher if at all after masturbation. This suggests that levels of testosterone respond not just to the physiology of sex, but to contextual aspects such as cultural meanings, feelings, or pheramones. Perhaps even sex is subsumed under competition: intercourse, but not masturbation, scores a win.[52]

Since winning social conflicts increases testosterone levels, winners are presumably more sexually motivated than losers. In some species, high-status males who win conflicts (and, sometimes, control territory) do most of the breeding. This may be the original evolutionary reason for testosterone to rise in winners – a higher status in the social hierarchy implying more sexual opportunities. The lingering effects on our physiology could help explain both Henry Kissinger's claim that "power is the great aphrodisiac," and the expansive sexual proclivities of many male political leaders. However, the status hierarchy as regulator of sexual access (rather than just access to food and resources) does not seem to apply well to humans and closely related species (see pp. 204–5). Nonetheless, the competition-testosterone effect may dampen or augment soldiers' sexuality, since their testosterone levels must move *en masse* – downward during both basic training and extended combat (especially for a losing army), but upward before battle and (especially) after a victory.[53]

Does the testosterone response to competition occur in women as well as in men? Evidence is scant, but suggests it does not. Testosterone levels rose before a male–male competition in a video game, but not before a female–female competition. (Neither gender showed a post-outcome response in this experiment, however.) "Apparently T [testosterone] works differently in competition between men than between women." Similarly, when elite women athletes played volleyball and handball, their androgen levels did not change. Testosterone effects in male–female

---

[51] Monaghan and Glickman 1992, rhesus 281–82; quartile: Rose *et al.* 1974, 296–98; Moyer 1987, 22.

[52] Sailboat: Cacioppo, Berntson, and Crites 1996, 74; sex: Silver 1992, 406.

[53] Kissinger in Smith 1971, 12.

competition or dominance "have yet to be addressed in research with humans."[54]

Biochemical pathways The biochemistry by which individual biology carries out these testosterone effects is fairly well understood. In short, subjective judgments about a person's social rank drive a frontal lobe–amygdala–hypothalamus–pituitary–gonad axis, modulating testosterone production and thus regulating the expression of certain genes.

Direct connections link part of the brain's frontal lobes – very large in humans, and central to complex social behaviors including aggression – to the amygdala (which also receives sensory information from the cortex). Nerve bundles in turn link the amygdala to the hypothalamus, generating hormones appropriate to motivated behaviors. The electrical activity of the amygdala "increases during social aggression in monkeys." Damage to the amygdala reduces aggressive behavior in animals and makes monkeys lose social rank. Similarly, damage to the hypothalamus reduces both aggressive and sexual behaviors in male rats, whereas implanting testosterone there restores these behaviors in castrated males.[55]

Thus, sex hormones play an important role in translating social contexts and events – via the frontal lobes, amygdala, hypothalamus, and gonads – into social behaviors such as intermale aggression. The "hypothalamic–pituitary–gonadal axis" described by biologists – illustrated on the *right* side of Figure 3.8 – is embedded in a feedback loop mediated by social relationships on the left side of the figure. Higher testosterone makes individual males stronger and more aggressive towards those already targeted for aggression (those at lower levels in a status hierarchy), though testosterone levels do not directly affect the status hierarchy itself, as we have seen. The right-hand feedback loop, internal to the body, is a self-regulating (negative feedback) loop typical of biological organisms. The left-hand loop, however, tends to be a positive loop (though strongly influenced by external forces) because males who rise in status by winning fights have higher testosterone levels, which make them both stronger and more aggressive towards underlings, in turn making them win fights and boost testosterone.[56]

Testosterone is, however, only a minor influence on changes in status hierarchy, as compared with "social context." This context includes the formation and shifting membership of coalitions (especially important

[54] Allan Mazur, personal communication 2000; video: Mazur, Susman, and Edelbrock 1997; volleyball: Filaire *et al.* 1999; yet: de Catanzaro and Spironello 1998.
[55] Bagatell and Bremner 1996; Herbert 1989, 66–68; Sapolsky 1997, 149–59.
[56] Kemper 1990.

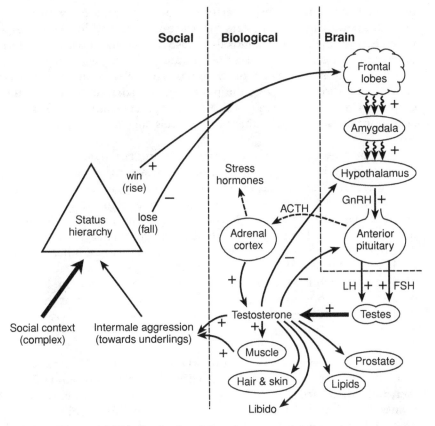

Figure 3.8 Feedback of social environment and testosterone.

near the top of the hierarchy where an "alpha male" often needs allies to stay in power), individual deaths and comings of age, individual intelligence and learning, scarcity or abundance of resources, and other complex elements that affect hierarchical social relationships.

Stress hormones

The stress-response hormones, which are important in war, are quite distinct from the sex hormones. They are not gendered. Basically the body produces these hormones in response to stressful situations, ranging from combat to nervousness before giving a speech. To simplify a complex system of different hormones and pathways, which respond somewhat differently to various types of stressful situations, basically two things happen. The hypothalamus releases a hormone (within seconds) that stimulates the pituitary to release another (within 15 seconds), which acts on the adrenal glands to release *cortisol* (hydrocortisone) and other glucocorticoids (within a few minutes) that regulate metabolism and blood pressure, among other things. At the same time, the nervous system directly triggers the middle of the adrenal gland (not the cortex) to produce *adrenaline* (also called epinephrine), as well as related hormones and some other biochemicals such as endorphins to kill pain.[57]

The outcome of these rapid responses is an "adrenaline rush" from the immediate increase of sugar in the bloodstream, along with faster breathing, rapid heart beat, higher blood pressure, and related changes. These effects make maximum energy available to muscles as quickly as possible. The stress response is costly in the long run. It shuts down the reproductive physiology, inhibits the storage of energy, slows down digestion, diverts blood flow to muscles at the expense of other parts of the body, and turns off the immune system along with the inflammation of injuries (which helps them heal) and the perception of pain. Soldiers occasionally do not even notice pain from grievous injuries at the time. If one is fighting (or running) for one's life, none of these aspects of well-being, which matter greatly over a period of months and years, is important at the moment.[58]

Thus, stress hormones are very important in combat. A soldier charged up in the heat of battle is charged with adrenaline, not testosterone. However, individual variations in levels of stress hormones, and in stress response, including variations caused by exposure to different biochemicals prenatally, are apparently related neither to gender nor to the menstrual cycle. (A forthcoming study claims to find gender differences in stress response, with women supposedly becoming more sociable under the calming influence of the hormone oxytocin, but this is far from clear.) In the video-game and volleyball experiments mentioned above (see p. 155), women's cortisol levels responded similarly to men's, even though their testosterone responses differed.[59]

Overall, the evidence for Hypothesis 3B is suggestive but far from adequate to explain gendered war roles. The evidence connects testosterone with aggression, but as part of a feedback loop in which the stronger causal links run from social behaviors to hormone levels, not the other way around.

---

[57] Sapolsky 1992, 288–95.

[58] Sapolsky 1992, 294.

[59] Sapolsky 1992, 319–21; Maccoby 1998, 103–4; Turner 1994, 243; Dabbs, Jurkovic, and Frady 1991; Turner 1994, 246; Scerbo and Kolko 1994; forthcoming: Suplee 2000.

C. SIZE AND STRENGTH

Opponents of women in combat often describe women as simply not large and strong enough to "hack it" in ground combat, where participants must travel and fight under grueling conditions carrying very heavy packs, and be able to drag their wounded comrades off the battlefield. One retired colonel writes:

I do know from eight years of ground combat that few women could endure its savagery for long... Ground war is not dead. The line doggies will still engage the enemy eyeball to eyeball, belly to belly. And in that setting women are disadvantaged. Brawn will count for more than computer smarts for a while yet. A 110-pound woman with the heart of a lion can't pack out a wounded 200-pound comrade.

Similarly, women's lesser strength is the central argument of a 1999 *Reader's Digest* article on why women should not be allowed into combat. And US soldiers after World War II felt that the best preparation for combat was to improve stamina and strength.[60]

Body size and strength

Assessing data on gender differences in size and strength is problematical because observed differences are not entirely "natural." Size and strength, and the extent of gender differences regarding them, differ considerably from one society to another. Even within a single country, size and strength vary considerably. These variations are strongly affected by culture. For example, weight in various populations is influenced by how people eat, and in many cultures males and females eat differently.[61]

Height Even height, though less than weight, reflects culture. Big differences in height are observed between prosperous and poor areas of a single country, and between one generation and the next. The height of the average Norwegian military conscript has increased by 12 percent in the last 200 years. Furthermore, upper-class 15-year-old British boys were over 10 percent taller than their working-class counterparts on average, in the nineteenth century, and remained about 4 percent taller in the mid-twentieth century. Such class differences in height can be generalized to other parts of the world as well. These cultural influences on height mainly relate to nutrition. In most of the world's populations, boys

[60] Hackworth 1991, wounded 25; Aspy 1999; Ambrose 1997, 288.
[61] Peterson and Runyan 1993, 35; Caspari 1978, 106–7.

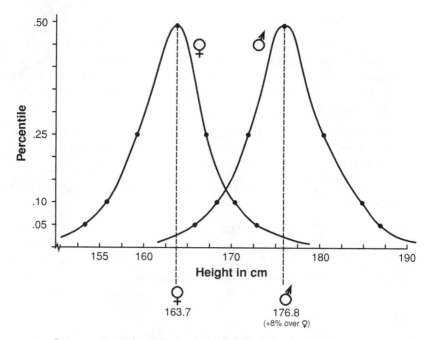

Data source: National Center for Health Statistics (Lentner ed. 1984: 300).

Figure 3.9 Height by gender in US 18-year-olds.

receive preferential nutrition. In the United States in recent decades, girls arguably receive nutrition closer to that of boys, but many girls still eat to get thin while boys eat to get strong.[62]

On average, 18-year-old US men are *8 percent taller* than women. (Note: percentage differences are a bit smaller if expressed inversely; e.g., women are *7 percent shorter* than men.) That difference is well within the range of the cross-national and cross-time height variations just described. Nonetheless that difference is real, and could be crucial in certain combat scenarios.[63]

These average differences tell only part of the story, however. The other half is in the distributions of male and female populations around those average height levels. Figure 3.9 shows the data for US 18-year-olds: two overlapping bell-curves closer to Figure 3.3b above than to 3.3a or 3.3c (see p. 133). About 15 percent of women are taller than the shortest 15 percent of men.

---

[62] Floud, Wachter, and Gregory 1990, 2, 5–6, 23, 26, 185, 226.
[63] Lentner ed. 1984, 300.

Strength   Strength is clearly more influenced by culture than is height. Most US 18-year-old boys have spent far more time than girls in rough-and-tumble play, vigorous sports, and other activities which use and stimulate the development of strength. Their female counterparts have had much less strength-promoting activity, and this was more true of the sample of US 18-year-olds measured in 1982 (see below) than it is today, thanks to girls' sports.

Furthermore, different kinds of physical strength show different gender patterns. Women are *constitutionally* stronger than men – they live longer and are more resilient against fatigue, illness, famine, childbirth (!), and so forth. "Anyone who has observed women of Africa on lengthy treks carrying heavy loads of firewood and water cannot help seeing how arbitrary our indicators of strength are."[64]

Data on strength are available from the US military – not an ideal sample, but similar to the general population in height. A 1982 report rates five areas of strength and gives male soldiers' strength relative to females as follows: upper-body, 72 percent higher; leg extensor, 54 percent; trunk flexor, 47 percent; lean body mass, 33 percent; and aerobic capacity, 28 percent. Upper-body strength, the area of greatest gender difference, is emphasized in military training. Field exercises in which troops march sustained distances carrying heavy packs seem to be a key point at which men rate women as inferior. One West Point colonel said, "The women just drop." On the other hand, sometimes women can use their bodies in different ways than men to achieve the same result.[65]

Lifting capacity shows the greatest gender disparity – probably in part because far more young men than women in US culture in 1982 engaged in weight training. The 1982 data indicate an average lifting capacity for women soldiers of 66 pounds, versus 119 for men (80 percent higher). The difference in lifting capacity is especially critical at around 100–120 pounds. An Air Force test for lifting 110 pounds was passed by 68 percent of men and 1 percent of women. I do not know how important lifting capacity is in the range of capabilities that enhance combat effectiveness, but it does resonate with the clincher line of the retired colonel's argument quoted above (p. 159), that a weakling woman would be unable to save her wounded comrade's life in battle by dragging him away. Thus, the 80 percent difference here seems far more likely than the 8 percent difference in height to explain why so few women participate in combat.[66]

[64] Peterson and Runyan 1993, 35.
[65] US Army 1982, 2.15; Wrangham and Peterson 1996, 181; Francke 1997, drop 248; Lorber 1994, result 53.
[66] US Army 1982, 2.15; Presidential Commission 1993, passed C-74.

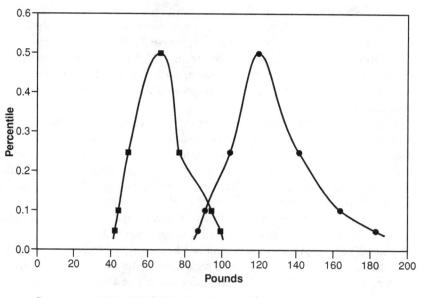

Data source: US Army 1982, 2.15.

Figure 3.10 Lifting capacity by gender, US soldiers, 1982.

Actually, however, the key question is not the difference in gender averages, but rather how much the bell-curves overlap. Figure 3.10 shows the data on lifting capability from the US military data. The curves indeed overlap less than for height, but not much less – still more than 10 percent of the military women have greater lifting capacity than the lowest 10 percent of men. Recall that these data are not biological givens but reflect the influence of a culture where men try to grow up big and strong, girls thin and pretty (back in 1982). Remember, too, that lifting capacity (part of upper-body strength) is the area of *greatest* gender difference among all the kinds of strength that go into combat (running, enduring fatigue, etc.). Thus, even the most pronounced gender differences regarding height and strength alike appear to show a nontrivial overlap of bell-curves, albeit nowhere near gender equality.

Speed and endurance   In addition to being large and strong, combat soldiers travel long distances on foot, sometimes at high speed. This requires running speed and endurance. It is an especially significant capability because of claims that it was important in our evolutionary past. (Some scholars see the human body as especially adapted to running over open terrain, in the context of long-distance hunting

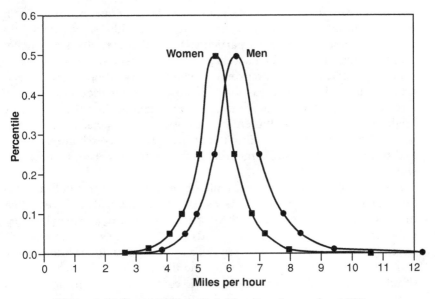

Figure 3.11 Speed in New York Marathon by gender, 1997.

on the African plains. This capability would thus be quite primordial in the evolution of war. Evidence on this question is disputed, however.)[67]

In speed, as in size or strength, men score above women on average but men's and women's bell-curves overlap. I calculated the curves for the 1997 New York Marathon, which had posted on the Internet the rank and time of each of 30,427 people to finish the race (nearly three-quarters of them male). Figure 3.11 shows average speed over the 26.2 mile race. As the figure shows, although the median woman ran 11 percent slower than the median man, the great majority of men finish well behind the fastest women, and the great majority of women finish well ahead of the slowest men. The sample represented here is *not* typical of the general population. The bulk of the curve represents the most motivated and skilled long-distance runners from the New York area – less than 1 percent of the population. The right-hand end of the curve is even less representative since many of the fastest runners in the *world* compete in the New York Marathon. For example, none of the first 13 finishers were Americans. They came from Kenya, Italy, Mexico, and other countries. Presumably this elite sample would exaggerate gender difference, representing as it does the tails of the two bell-curves.[68]

[67] M. Harris 1989, 195.
[68] http://www.nyrrc.org/m9700.htm; cf. Snyder 1998.

Implications   These data on overlapping curves imply that if armies included just the largest, strongest, fastest soldiers, then we should find many cases of women's participation in combat, albeit in smaller numbers than for men. The actual gender composition of such an army would be determined by the extent to which a population was mobilized into the army. If being a warrior were an elite occupation practiced by a select few, say 5 or 10 percent of the population, then the best army might contain virtually all men. If, however, a society needed to induct half of the entire population into the army, it would score highest on size and strength by including something like 85 percent men and 15 percent women.[69]

Perhaps the virtually all-male armies found historically result from warfare's being just an occupation of a small elite. This makes sense in that most people most of the time in the world are not at war, and in many wars only a minority of the population needs be mobilized as combat soldiers. In reality, however, the extent of mobilization of populations into warfare varies greatly from culture to culture and through time. These variations should be reflected, if Hypothesis 3C is correct (and given the data on overlapping bell-curves), in patterns of women's participation in combat. We may frame this as a corollary to Hypothesis 3C – that is, a testable statement that should be true if the hypothesis is true: *the participation of women in combat increases where mobilization for war is more extensive.*

This corollary, however, receives very weak empirical support at best. True, in those few cases where nontrivial numbers of women participated in combat historically, extreme warfare forced extreme mobilization of a population (see pp. 60–70). However, these particular cases are a small minority of the cases in which societies centered around war or faced dire war crises. In the great majority of such cases, even when most of the male population lived by war most of the time, virtually no women participated in combat (see pp. 10–21). These cases include preindustrial warrior societies such as the Sambia of New Guinea and the Yanomamö of Brazil, as well as industrialized societies engaged in "total war" such as the World Wars. So the corollary would lead us to expect far more women in combat and far more fluctuation over time in numbers of women in combat than we actually find.[70]

The problems are compounded by a second corollary: *the introduction of firearms to warfare, both locally and in a global-historic sense, should increase the participation of women in combat (by making size-strength differences less decisive).* The problem is that this hardly ever happened. Furthermore,

---

[69] M. Harris 1989, 278–84, 195; Harris 1974, 77; Harris 1977, 63–64; Casey 1991, 17; Astrachan 1986, 61.
[70] Ambrose 1997, 321; Moon 1998, 91.

this point can be extended to all kinds of forms of industrialized warfare in which machines rather than human bodies alone provide size and strength – tank warfare, air combat, and so forth. The point is not that strength does not matter at all in these occupations, but rather that the introduction of such forms of warfare shifts the importance of body strength in combat forces relative to other combat skills of various kinds. Yet the historical mechanization of war produced little change in the gender ratio of combat forces over the past century – a problem for Hypothesis 3C.[71]

To consider an even more basic corollary: *most wars should be won by the side with the larger, stronger soldiers.* If size and strength are so critical to military effectiveness, they must frequently determine battle outcomes. But in fact this is not true. Military historians emphasize the importance of such factors as strategy, discipline, fighting spirit, accurate intelligence, and (especially) the quality of weaponry, in determining the outcome of battles – more than the importance of one side's physical strength. Indeed, the one war that America has lost, Vietnam, was to an army whose members were substantially shorter and less strong than Americans.[72]

The evolutionary implications of this corollary also run into trouble, since size and strength apparently have not been "selected for" in humans. Compared with species closely related to humans, notably the other great apes, humans have a relatively small gender difference in size. Gorilla and orangutan adult males, for example, are typically almost twice as large as females. Larger size exacts an evolutionary cost, mainly in higher food requirements, which would be worth it only if size and strength mattered greatly in fighting. Apparently for humans they did not. Men were probably about 35 percent heavier than women several million years ago, but only about 15 percent larger starting before Neanderthals several hundred thousand years ago, remaining around 15 percent heavier in modern humans. Furthermore, modern humans totally displaced the substantially stronger and larger Neanderthals about 30,000 years ago.[73]

Finally, if gender differences in size underlay gender differences in participation in war, then we should find among primates that species with large gender differences in body weight should also have low female participation in intergroup fighting. In fact, however, across 21 primate species, these two variables are uncorrelated.[74]

Overall, then, the data on size and strength give limited support at best to Hypothesis 3C. The major problem is that in the context of overlapping

---

[71] M. Harris 1989, 285; Ehrenreich 1997a, 229.

[72] Harris 1974, 84; Dyer 1985, 124; Mead 1949, 133.

[73] Hall 1985, 134–39; Wilford 1997b; Suplee 1997; Wrangham and Peterson 1996, 175, 178; Wilson 1978, 126–28.

[74] Manson and Wrangham 1991, 373.

bell-curves, the considerable variations across time and space – in mobilization of a population for war, in size and strength, and in the importance of size and strength to war – do not produce the variations predicted by Hypothesis 3C in terms of gender composition of war-fighting forces.

Does brain or brawn win wars?

While size gives definite advantages in fighting, the most important advantage for humans – as with all our activities – must come from intelligence: brain more than brawn. (I admit to a bias on this issue, as a professor.) In the US Army in Europe in late 1944, replacements who were rushed to the front with little training or experience suffered staggering casualties in their first battle, often 50 percent or more. They were drastically less effective than "old-timers" who had been at the front a week or more. The new soldiers were strong, but not smart enough about how to survive in combat. One 19-year-old veteran quoted by historian Stephen Ambrose called the newcomers "all good boys with the strength of a mule and the ignorance of old maids ... In the first battle they usually died in heaps."[75]

The extremes of what can be achieved by brain rather than brawn – admittedly a rare case – is shown by the success of one inexperienced US lieutenant in late 1944 who, when told to capture a farmhouse, simply walked up and knocked on the door, then exchanged some words in German with the German sergeant who answered the door in his undershirt. The sergeant systematically called out a hundred German soldiers from their positions and brought them to the village square with the Americans. The two armies frisked each other, then lined up across a road from each other at attention, and the Germans formally surrendered. The US officer who had ordered the lieutenant to "take" the farmhouse watched the whole thing in amazement: "no one got hurt ... That's the way to fight a war."[76]

Another example of substituting brains for brawn, although not a combat case, comes from the US war industry in World War II. Two WAVES assigned to a warehouse were charged by the men to stow truck tires up in a loft. The men went off gleefully, knowing the women lacked the strength to do the job, and were surprised to find the tires in the loft on their return. "We rigged a pulley, of course."[77]

Historically, the outcome of fights between humans have been determined by weapons more than body size and strength. For example, when

[75] Ambrose 1997, 273–89, heaps 277.
[76] Colby 1991, 391–94, way 394; Ambrose 1997, 284–85.
[77] Campbell 1990, 113.

armies with iron swords first appeared in a given region, they swept away all other armies in their path – including those with larger, stronger warriors who had bronze swords. And David's skill with weaponry defeated a larger Goliath.

A striking, and historically important, example of the importance of technology rather than muscle power is found in Pizarro's victory over the Inca emperor Atahuallpa in 1532. Pizarro had 62 soldiers mounted on horses and 106 on foot, yet they overwhelmed and routed 80,000 Inca soldiers, killing thousands without losing any of their own. Pizarro repeated the rout in four subsequent battles, even as the surprise and bewilderment of the initial encounter diminished. The Spanish military advantage lay in "steel swords and other weapons, steel armor, guns, and horses," with the horse proving especially critical. Obviously the physical brawn of the losing army was far greater than the winning army, but irrelevant.[78]

Warfare, of course, no longer consists mainly of hand-to-hand combat without firearms, so brute strength and running speed are less and less relevant as one moves through history. Females, in fact, have physical abilities that are becoming more and more relevant to modern warfare. Women "typically show greater speed and agility at fine motor skills." A particular type of skill showing this gender difference is the rapid completion of a sequence of small movements, such as assembling small components in a certain order. On these tests, women show significantly higher scores, apparently due to both brain differences and smaller fingers.[79]

Modern warfare with its emphasis on the speed and mobility of mechanized vehicles (tanks, fighter aircraft, etc.), differs from ancient hand-to-hand combat. Success and survival now depend much more on the ability to execute rapid sequences of small motions, and much less on upper-body strength. Furthermore, with a trend towards miniaturization in weaponry, smaller bodies become more adaptive. Figure 3.12 shows the size range for which US cockpits are being designed. The large pilots are the problem: "Contractors prefer to design cockpits for the smaller pilot. An increase to the upper limits decreases aerodynamic efficiency, decreases the number of weapon systems in the cockpit... and increases cost," according to a US governmental report. Furthermore, a 1991 Air Force study found that in terms of a pilot's ability to tolerate "G stress," women's smaller size is an advantage since hearts are closer to brains. In Navy tests on potential astronauts in 1961, several women

---

[78] Diamond 1997, 68–77.
[79] Hampson and Kimura 1992, 362–63.

Figure 3.12 Smallest and largest pilot accommodated in US jet cockpit design, early 1990s. [Photo © Martin-Baker.]

outperformed men on tests of stress, lung power, vertigo, and enduring isolation.[80]

---

[80] Presidential Commission 1993, cockpits C-91; Weber 1997; Richman-Loo and Weber 1996, 151; Francke 1997, tolerate 236, Navy 225–26; Gray 1997, 99, 188, 246.

To summarize, Hypothesis 3C (size and strength) has some truth in it. Men on average are larger and stronger, which does contribute to combat capability. This hypothesis alone would provide a sufficient explanation for the observation that warfare is *primarily* a male occupation. But so would other hypotheses. Our puzzle is why warfare is virtually an all-male occupation. Here the size and strength hypothesis falls short.

D. BRAINS AND COGNITION

Testosterone exerts a third effect, in addition to its role in the status-hierarchy feedback loop and its effects on size and strength. It causes subtle changes in brain development prenatally and soon after birth. Perhaps men are "wired" for war and therefore become soldiers later.

This hypothesis is difficult to test, because brains are not well understood. Biologists have identified regions and structures in the brain associated with certain behaviors or activities or thought-processes. Medical scans of people's brains show that these areas "turn on" when the brain engages in a particular kind of task. Biologists also understand a fair amount about how neurotransmitters work. These are specific chemicals that mediate the passage of electrical signals along networks of brain cells, so that certain pathways are active in the presence of these chemicals. Despite these impressive achievements, however, nobody knows how the fundamental processes of the brain such as memory and thought work, much less how a brain achieves consciousness. The early developmental stages in which the brain first grows to its full size are even less well understood.

Brain development

In rodents, the presence of testosterone and estrogen in the first few days after birth – apparently a critical period when certain brain structures develop – normally leads to different anatomy in the brain for males and females, which in turn affects lifelong physiological and behavioral traits such as the ability to ovulate or to copulate successfully. These effects were first observed in the 1930s through the late 1950s, and have since been extended to a range of species and behaviors.

Female rats that receive a single injection of testosterone in the first week of life are unable to ovulate for life. If researchers castrate male rats at birth (removing the main source of testosterone), and surgically implant them with ovaries, they will ovulate after puberty. But without castration, male rats with implanted ovaries do not ovulate. These differences turn out to result from changes in the brain's hypothalamus in the first week after birth. If exposed to testosterone at that critical time, the rat hypothalamus does not, later in adulthood, release the hormone to trigger ovulation. Similar effects occur for sexual behaviors such as ability to copulate, and for aggressive intermale competition for females. In particular, female rodents normally assume a particular position, necessary for copulation, during the appropriate phase of the ovulatory cycle. A female without ovaries will do the same if given a sequence of estrogen and progesterone injections that mimic the ovulatory cycle. But those injections of the adult rodent will not have this effect if she was exposed to testosterone before birth. The brains of rodents are permanently altered, before or just after birth, by the presence or absence of testosterone. Effects triggered later in life depend on the original exposure to testosterone during a specific period of brain development. (The actual gendered biochemistry is more complex than presence-of-testosterone, but that is the main point.) Biologists call these early brain-wiring effects "organizational," and the later effects of hormones in triggering behavior "activation" effects (contingent on earlier organizational effects).[81]

Several of these effects are not the same in primates as in rodents. Furthermore, unlike rodents, uncastrated male monkeys with implanted ovaries *can* ovulate – their brains respond to estrogen, so they were not programmed prenatally in the same way as rodents. It is unclear whether these differences mean that primates follow the same general pattern of gender differentiation in brain development, but with different particular mechanisms, or instead that primate brains are generally less gender differentiated during development than are rodent brains.[82]

Gendered brain anatomy   Since the 1970s, biologists have reported a large and growing number of specific gender differences in observable *structures* of the brain. These anatomical gender differences are prominent in the *preoptic area* (POA) of the hypothalamus, which is involved in sexual behavior in many species. In humans, at least one cluster of brain cells in the POA is larger in males than females, but the difference is less dramatic than in rats, and it is unclear what the cluster does functionally. In 1991, biologist Simon LeVay reported that a region of the human POA is larger in heterosexual men than in gay men.[83]

Differences in brain structures in adults do not *all* trace to permanent changes very early in life of the type we have been discussing. The example of cichlid fish discussed earlier shows that gender differences in the

[81] Breedlove 1992, 50; Davies 1987.
[82] Breedlove 1992, 49, 52.
[83] Fishman and Breedlove 1988; Breedlove 1992, 54, 63; Hampson and Kimura 1992, 369–70; Kimura 1992, 120; LeVay 1991.

structure of the hypothalamus do not necessarily derive from the early and permanent changes described in newborn rodents' brains, but rather from social relationships in adulthood. By implication, the differences in the brains of LeVay's gay and heterosexual men might be effects, rather than (or in addition to) causes of, their sexual orientation. Indeed, cichlid fish themselves readily switch their equivalent of sexual orientation, and the relevant brain differences are reversible and responsive to social conditions. The point here is not whether a tendency towards homosexuality has some genetic component – current evidence suggests it does – but rather that any observed gender differences in brain anatomy might not reflect organizational effects of sex hormones. Furthermore, because research on the human brain is difficult, no definitive answer exists regarding which differences are permanent/developmental and which are part of shorter-term feedback loops with the social environment.[84]

These kinds of brain differences between men and women – and others I will review shortly – are important because they go beyond the hypothalamus and beyond behaviors and physiology directly connected with sex. It is not so surprising that males, for example, might lack brain "circuitry" to control ovulation. What is much more provocative is the idea that men and women "think differently" in more fundamental ways – that they are differentially adapted for different kinds of tasks, and interpret the world in different ways. This idea bears directly on some theories of why men fight wars (see pp. 42–47). Unfortunately, the current state of knowledge offers few satisfactory answers, and only partial glimpses.

Cognitive abilities

One point is easy to confirm. Neither men nor women are more intelligent than the other – including their scores on standardized IQ tests. Men's brains are somewhat larger (so are their bodies), but women apparently have about 10 percent more brain cells. Anyway, neither attribute is correlated with intelligence. In one rhyming task, men used the brain's left side more, and women both sides equally, but neither gender performed the task better. Thus, men and women have similar overall cognitive ability despite sometimes using different cognitive tools to solve problems.[85]

Gender differences   Such differences as exist cut in both directions. Women are slightly better at some tasks, men at others. Women

---

[84] Breedlove 1992, effects 65; Fernald 1993; Francis, Soma, and Fernald 1993; Hamer *et al.* 1993; Barinaga 1991; Burr 1993.

[85] Hampson and Kimura 1992, 358; McCormick and Witelson 1994; correlated: McGuinness 1985, 57.

tend to score higher on verbal abilities, men on spatial abilities. Women tend to score higher on speed and accuracy of perception, men on quantitative abilities. Across the board, gender differences in cognitive abilities are relatively modest, and gender distributions mostly overlap.[86]

The strongest and most consistent gender differences in these areas are found in spatial abilities, such as imagining an object rotated in space or moved, reading maps, solving mazes, and recognizing shapes embedded in complex patterns. Males have done better on these tasks in studies of both Western and non-Western cultures and (to the extent comparable) other species. The strongest of these differences are found on mental rotation tasks. The gender difference in spatial ability appears fully only after puberty, implying that activational effects of testosterone are involved. Gender differences in spatial ability do not appear to be a result of differential dependence on the right side of the brain (which is most responsible for spatial tasks), so the anatomical basis for the gender difference is not well understood. Of course, it is also very hard to segregate out the effects of culture on spatial ability of males and females. People with high scores on a "male sex-role inventory" – who tend to participate in stereotypically male play and activity – score high on spatial ability. Nobody really understands the connections among biology, gender-role concepts, gendered behaviors, and cognitive abilities.[87]

For verbal abilities, in contrast to spatial ones, women consistently score higher than men do, although on most measures the gender difference is somewhat smaller than for spatial abilities. These verbal abilities include learning language as children, comprehension, spelling, grammar, and rapidly producing words in response to a query. In tests of speed and accuracy of perception – both of verbal and nonverbal symbols – women tend to score higher than men. In mathematical reasoning, however, men tend to score higher – this apparently is related to spatial skills – but in arithmetical calculation women score higher. These differences in quantitative abilities have received less attention than spatial and verbal abilities, especially regarding any effect of sex hormones.[88]

Some human gender differences have been reported in the relationship of the two sides of the brain, which biologists call *lateralization*. In processing language, men apparently tend to rely more heavily on the left side of the brain whereas women use both sides in a more equal way. Until recently, lateralization effects, which are somewhat subtle, have been difficult to verify. However, MRI imaging has recently provided much

---

[86] Hampson and Kimura 1992, 359; McGuinness 1985, 93–110.
[87] Hampson and Kimura 1992, 361; Voyer, Voyer, and Bryden 1995, 260–61; Kimura 1992, 119, 124; Signorella, Jamison, and Krupa 1989, 94; Linn and Petersen 1986.
[88] Hampson and Kimura 1992, 361; Fausto-Sterling 1985, 26–33.

stronger evidence. In one study, while evaluating whether two nonsense words rhymed, most men activated mainly the left sides of their brains, while women generally activated both sides. (The effect was not found for two other categories of language tasks.) In an earlier study of a similar question, women who had been exposed before birth to DES (a form of estrogen that caused some testosterone-like prenatal effects) resembled men in their use of the left side primarily, as compared to unexposed women. This suggests (but does not prove) that early presence of testosterone may be responsible for permanent gender differences in brain development regarding the relative roles of the two sides of the brain in language processing.[89]

Differences in navigational methods have been found in various studies. Women score higher than men on ability to recall objects and their locations (and to replace them in exact locations) in a confined space such as a tabletop or room. Whereas men tend to navigate by the use of vectors (general direction and distance) – drawing on spatial/mapping abilities – women tend to navigate by the use of landmarks. (Female rats also appear to use landmarks in navigation more than males do.) Sexual orientation may – apparently only in men – correlate with spatial ability.[90]

Since the conduct of war draws on spatial and long-distance navigational skills extensively, the male edge in these areas could support the view of men as adapted for war. However, the gender differences on such cognitive abilities are far too subtle to be a major factor in gendered war roles. Figure 3.13 is an idealized curve based on "several cognitive abilities [which] do in fact show sex differences of approximately this size" – for instance, women scoring higher on verbal and perceptual ability, men higher on spatial and quantitative ability. Although the average on the right-hand curve is about 25 percent higher than the left – a greater difference than for height or speed, for example – the curves overlap much more. For typical differences in spatial abilities, about one-quarter to one-third of the "low" gender scores higher than the average for the "high" gender. For verbal ability, the difference is even smaller, about half as great.[91]

Psychological measures of personality traits show a similar pattern to scores on cognitive tasks, as Figure 3.14 illustrates. Even for "harm

---

[89] Iaccino 1993; Springer and Deutsch 1993; Breedlove 1992, 65; Benderly 1987, 241–43; Kagan 1998; Kimura 1992, 124–25; Shaywitz et al. 1995; Breedlove 1992, 66–68; Gur et al. 1995.

[90] Kimura 1992, rats 119, 121; orientation: McCormick and Witelson 1994; Gladue et al. 1990.

[91] Levy 1978, war; Iaccino 1993, 140; Springer and Deutsch 1993, 213; Kimura 1992, 125; Hampson and Kimura 1992, typical 359–62.

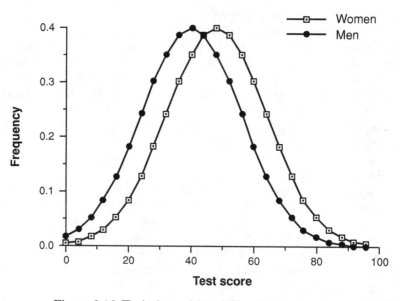

Figure 3.13 Typical cognitive ability distributions by gender. [From Hampson and Kimura 1992, 359. In Jill B. Becker, S. Marc Breedlove, and David Crews (eds.), *Behavioral Endocrinology*. © The MIT Press.]

avoidance" – a measure showing a relatively large average gender difference (women 19 percent higher than men) – the curves overlap greatly, and this is typical of such personality variables. Thus, overall, gender differences in cognitive abilities and related constructs are relatively minor, and not very useful for explaining gendered war roles.[92]

Hormonal effects on cognitive abilities   Some of the gender differences in brain structure and activity relating to spatial and verbal abilities appear to be influenced by sex hormones. Rats given testosterone right after birth learned spatial tasks differently later in life. However, in humans anyway, only large changes in the amount of sex hormones matter. Variations in prenatal exposure within the normal range do not correlate with later spatial abilities.[93]

Such effects in humans are difficult to measure. Some evidence can be found, however. Adult men whose mothers had taken DES during pregnancy – which apparently has "feminizing" organizational effects on the male fetus – scored similarly to women (in contrast to a control group

---

[92] Masters 1989b, 5, 9–10.
[93] Williams, Barnett, and Meck 1990; Kimura 1992, 121; Bucci, Chiba, and Gallagher 1995; Sharps, Price, and Williams 1994.

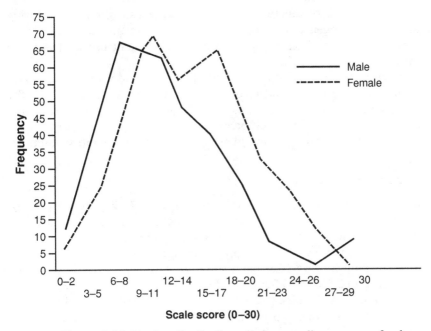

Figure 3.14 Gender distributions on personality measure for harm avoidance, United States, 1987. [From Masters 1989b, 9.]

of men) on a test for identifying shapes by feel with left and right hands. In another study, girls with a genetic condition causing production of high levels of testosterone during fetal life performed better than unaffected girls on spatial tests. Girls with that condition also showed greater preference, when tested at ages 3 and 8, for playing with "boys'" toys over "girls'" toys as compared with their unaffected female relatives. However, girls with this condition, whose masculinized genitals usually had been surgically altered at birth, may not have early childhood experiences comparable to unaffected girls.[94]

Seasonal, inter-individual, and possibly day-to-day fluctuations in testosterone levels – not just organizational effects at birth – may possibly influence men's spatial abilities. Other studies, however, find no correlation of testosterone with cognitive abilities, across individuals. During the menstrual cycle, women's verbal abilities tend to be high, and spatial abilities low, when estrogen levels are high. Fine-motor

[94] Springer and Deutsch 1993, spatial 214–15; Berenbaum and Hines 1992, toys 204–5; Hines 1982.

skills and speech articulation also improve when estrogen is high: during their peak-estrogen phase, women cut 18 percent off the average time required to say "a box of mixed biscuits in a biscuit mixer" five times without error.[95]

In summary, cognitive abilities do differ by gender on average, and in the direction that would favor men over women as warriors, but the men's and women's distributions on such measures overlap greatly. Men and women do not "think differently" in a profound way, but they have modestly different tendencies on average in terms of cognitive abilities.

Wired for aggression?

In some species, early exposure to testosterone (or lack thereof) before or shortly after birth appears to have organizational effects that alter propensities for certain kinds of aggression as adults. However, the evidence for such an effect in humans and other primates is weak. Male mice castrated within 30 days after birth show lowered aggression later in life, but if castrated 50 days after birth they show normal levels of aggression later in life. Female mice treated with testosterone at birth behave more aggressively later than do female mice given testosterone as adults. In comparing female mice from the same litter (whose hormone levels after birth were controlled), researchers found that females positioned in the uterus between two males – and therefore exposed to some testosterone prenatally from their brothers – became more aggressive as adults than females positioned between other females (or without siblings). Similarly, female mice whose mothers were given testosterone while pregnant grew up to be unusually aggressive as adults.[96]

Spotted hyenas provide a fascinating natural experiment in the effects of prenatal testosterone. They are a social, hunting species, related to cats, that inhabit the African plains. Females are larger and more aggressive than males, and dominate the males in feeding and other aspects of social life. Spotted hyenas are typically born as twins (with eyes open and teeth fully functional), and if both are female (or both male) one often kills the other immediately after birth. Instead of rooting around for her mother's nipple after birth, like most mammals do, a female spotted hyena roots around for her younger sister's neck. This extraordinary lifelong female aggression results from prenatal testosterone, produced by the mother's placenta and fed to the developing embryo through the umbilical cord. As a result, female spotted hyenas develop "masculinized" genitals – a

---

[95] Kimura 1992, 122–25; Kampen and Sherwin 1996, other 616; Blakeslee 1991; biscuit: Weiss 1988.

[96] Monaghan and Glickman 1992, 279; Siegel and Demetrikopoulos 1993, 107–8.

closed-up vagina whose labia fuse into an empty "scrotum," and an enlarged clitoris (the size of a penis and fully erectile) through which the
females urinate, have intercourse, and give birth.[97]

Although spotted hyenas are an extreme case, in many other mammals
females are larger than males (about one-quarter of all mammal species)
and act as aggressively as males. Hamster females dominate males in
some situations, and among dogs and wolves it is as common for females
to fight females as for males to fight males (although mixed-gender fighting is uncommon). Most laboratory research has focused on species in
which males are larger and more aggressive, such as mice, rats, and rhesus
monkeys. Less is known about species in which females are larger.[98]

The organizational effects of testosterone on aggression occur at a different stage than the effects in developing genitals. In rhesus monkeys,
genitals are masculinized if a female fetus is exposed to testosterone during days 40–64 of pregnancy. However, if the testosterone treatment takes
place later, during days 115–39, the female monkeys are born with fully
female appearance, but engage in the rough-and-tumble play characteristic of male rhesus monkeys. Obviously, then, such behavior does not
depend merely on a female's looking like or being treated as a male. However, rough-and-tumble play is motivationally different from aggression,
and overall the evidence for organizational effects on adult aggression is
controversial when it comes to primates. For humans, the evidence for
organizational effects of prenatal hormones on later aggression is very
thin and fraught with methodological problems.[99]

Rough-and-tumble   The strongest evidence is for rough-and-
tumble play, which characterizes males much more than females in humans and various mammals, and plausibly serves as training for later aggression. The rough-and-tumble play among young mammals exposed
prenatally to testosterone is a far more robust effect than is any direct
influence of testosterone on aggression itself. Furthermore, among human children in a wide variety of cultures, the most distinctive quality
distinguishing play styles of boys' and girls' groups is the boys' greater
frequency of rough-and-tumble play. Boys engage in more "rough-
housing" or "horseplay" including wrestling and play-fighting (or mock-
fighting).[100]

---

[97] Frank, Glickman, and Licht 1991, 703; Monaghan and Glickman 1992, 264–65; Siegel
and Demetrikopoulos 1993, 108–9; Angier 1992.

[98] Monaghan and Glickman 1992, 263–66.

[99] Monaghan and Glickman 1992, 280; Archer 1991, 4–5; Ruble and Martin 1998, 968;
Stevens 1994, 293; Turner 1994, 244; Harris 1999.

[100] Boulton 1994, 23–30, 35–39; Maccoby 1998, 34, 111–14; Green 1987, 31–32; Hartup
1983, 110; Lee 1983a, 86–88.

Rough-and-tumble is hard to define exactly (Eleanor Maccoby calls the concept "elusive"). It does not refer to high levels of activity in general, but to the quality of interactions as "rougher." Boys' play is more "physical" than girls' play. For example, in one study, 6-year-old boys riding tricycles were more likely than girls to deliberately ram each other. Girls, on the rare occasions when they got to ride the tricycles, carefully avoided hitting each other.[101]

Rough-and-tumble play "basically includes fighting and chasing action patterns that are playfully motivated and delivered." Smiling, laughing, and play-faces distinguish rough-and-tumble from real aggression which is accompanied by frowns, bared teeth, fixed gazes, or crying. Rough-and-tumble play differs from aggressive behavior both in specific acts or postures (e.g., play-face versus stare), in social contexts (e.g., staying together afterwards versus separating), and in affect (e.g., liking versus disliking the other person). Up to about 10 years old, rough-and-tumble and aggression are distinct behaviors. In and after adolescence, the relationship is poorly understood.[102]

Before adolescence, although most rough-and-tumble play occurs between boys, some episodes involve both boys and girls. These mixed-gender encounters are less likely to be preceded and followed by the two individuals' playing together. They may provide a chance for boys to make physical contact with girls briefly without risking self-esteem or ridicule from other boys. Or, they may develop cognitive scripts, in a minority of boys, that play out in later sexual violence against women (many mixed-gender encounters involve boys approaching girls and restraining or playfully assaulting them before being driven off by girls' female friends).[103]

Real physical aggression occurs more frequently in boys' than in girls' groups, but it makes up a much smaller fraction of interactions than does play-fighting. Nonetheless, since an accident or miscue can turn a play-fight into real fighting, "boys' play more frequently puts them on the edge of aggression." This edge of aggression is a zone in which boys learn and practice social and physical skills that will serve them later in social competitions, and of course in war. Boys develop control of aggression by playing near the dangerous edge that sometimes leads to real fighting and injury.[104]

Despite the dangers, most rough-and-tumble play is good spirited, not very competitive, and far from aggressive:

[101] Maccoby 1998, elusive–rougher 290, physical–tricycles 33, 62–63.
[102] Boulton 1994, delivered 23; Smith 1989, 78–80.
[103] Boulton 1994, 35–39.
[104] Maccoby 1998, edge 35.

Among 4-year-olds, boys have a boisterous heyday in their numerous same-sex contacts in rough-and-tumble play, positive teasing, and foolish word play. They wrestle, bump into and fall on one another ... They make machine-gun sounds, and chase one another around with space guns and spray bottles. They are convulsed with laughter as they pretend to make toy horses sneeze and fall down. Boys put clay in one another's hair, play puppet fighting, tickle and pretend to shoot one another, fall dead and roll on the floor.[105]

To summarize, then, prenatal testosterone does have brain "wiring" effects that make men better than women on average at certain cognitive skills relevant to war – notably spatial ability and a propensity for rough-and-tumble play – and worse at other skills. However, the evidence that testosterone wires the male human brain for aggression is weak. If brain wiring were categorically different in males – different enough to account for war's being a virtually all-male occupation – the answers here should be much stronger and clearer.

E. FEMALE SEX HORMONES

The flip side of the proposition that men are warlike is that women are peaceful, based on an ethic of care. Women's peaceful nature could be sufficient, in theory, to explain gendered war roles: if no women show up, war will be all-male. But are women built for caregiving in a way that makes them unsuitable for combat – either because of prenatal brain wiring or because they respond to high levels of estrogen and progesterone as adults? In mammals, maternal and not paternal behaviors seem to be influenced by sex hormones. (In many nonmammalian species, especially birds, fathers play key roles in caring for young offspring. In mammals, however, newborns are nourished primarily by suckling mothers.)[106]

Nursing is closely tied to hormones. A suckling baby creates nerve messages in the mother, from breast to brain, that trigger the release of prolactin and oxytocin, in turn causing the production and release of milk (lactation). In nursing mothers, nontactile stimuli (such as hearing or seeing the baby cry) can trigger milk release without sensory input from the breasts. However, stimulation of the nipples alone can also cause production and release of milk in women who have not been pregnant, and even, in rare cases, in men. If men are capable of producing milk, it seems unlikely to me that the hormones associated with nursing are central to any innate female care-ethic relevant to war and peace.[107]

---

[105] Pitcher and Schulz, in Maccoby 1998, 34.
[106] Becker, Breedlove and Crews eds. 1992, 217.
[107] Rosenblatt 1992, 240–43; Silver 1992, men 407.

Maternal behaviors go far beyond nursing, however. In rats, maternal behaviors include nestbuilding, licking, nursing, and retrieving pups to the nest. These behaviors normally are triggered by hormonal shifts at the end of pregnancy. If pregnancies are terminated early, and pups are then presented to a female rat, it will display the maternal behaviors. If its ovaries are removed, however – reducing production of estrogen – maternal behavior will be delayed. This effect can be reversed with estrogen injections. Maternal behaviors can be evoked by estrogen in rats that were never pregnant, and that have had their ovaries and uteruses removed. External stimuli alone – such as being exposed to pups or to adult males – also can increase the concentration of estrogen receptors in the brain. Thus, estrogen appears to be the main and necessary ingredient in maternal care, although prolactin also seems necessary for maternal behaviors.[108]

Maternal aggression – attacking intruders when nursing pups are in the nest – generally goes along with other maternal behaviors. (This suggests a problem with the maternal ethic of care as leading to peace; see p. 46.) The bits of available evidence indicate that maternal aggression is a distinct behavior with its own characteristic biology independent of sex hormones, although related to other forms of maternal care. The behavioral effects of estrogen generally are poorly understood, however.[109]

Maternal behaviors triggered by hormones operate only in the early stages of parenthood, such as the first weeks when a rat is nursing pups – another reason to doubt their applicability to a peaceful-women explanation of gendered war roles. After weaning, and for most of the duration of parenthood – all of it for males – caregiving behaviors continue but under control of the brain and external stimuli, without a direct hormonal role. Overall, then, maternal behaviors seem to have a biological basis in estrogen, but only within a narrow postpartum and nursing period. These behaviors do not generalize to a lifelong peacefulness; indeed, they include aggressiveness.[110]

Social contexts influence women's sex hormone levels – notably the timing of hormonal changes that produce the menstrual cycle – just as they affect men's testosterone levels. In a group of American women college students living together in a dormitory, menstrual periods were randomly distributed through time at the start of the semester, but

---

[108] Sagan and Druyan 1992, 226; Eibl-Eibesfeldt 1979, 51; Rosenblatt 1992, stimuli 234–38; Chodorow 1978, 24.
[109] Monaghan and Glickman 1992, 275–79; Herbert 1989, 62; Siegel and Demetrikopoulos 1993, 102, 115–16; Rosenblatt 1992, distinct 235–37; Wilson 1975, 253; Korach 1994.
[110] Rosenblatt 1992, 259.

became more synchronized as the semester proceeded. Apparently, female baboons living together also synchronize their ovulation cycles. More strikingly, in one experiment a group of women was exposed daily to recent sweat from a certain woman (mixed with alcohol and applied to the upper lip, with a control group getting alcohol alone). After four months the menstrual periods of the group (but not the control group) had become much more closely synchronized with the cycle of the woman whose sweat was used. The responsible pheramones were identified recently.[111]

Sexual behaviors   The varied and flexible effects of sex hormones on social behaviors extend even to sexuality itself. For example, although some minimal amount of testosterone seems necessary for men to show interest and ability in sex, testosterone levels correlate only weakly with sexual activity. Castration (removal of testes) has been used to try to control sexual behavior – as in eunuchs who guarded harems – but not always with success. Despite very low levels of testosterone, castrated men can sustain sexual activity (including erections and orgasms) for years and decades, although usually at lower frequencies. Apparently the small amounts of testosterone produced by the adrenal cortex, perhaps supplemented by testosterone stored in fat, are sufficient. Similarly, men in their 80s with low testosterone levels can have active sex lives, although some decline in frequency is typical. In other words, testosterone levels are correlated, but only roughly, with sexual behavior.[112]

Male "sexual behavior" is multifaceted and connected with different hormones and brain processes. For example, even when damage to the brain's POA region eliminates consummatory behaviors, sexual motivation can persist. Male rhesus monkeys with damaged POAs were unable to copulate, but were observed masturbating to ejaculation while watching nearby females. Similarly, when male rats had learned to press a lever ten times to gain access to a female rat, damage to the males' POAs made them unable to copulate with the females, yet they kept pressing the lever as much as before. Conversely, damage to a different brain region reduced male rats' motivation but not their ability to consummate. Thus, different aspects of sexual behavior draw on different areas of the brain and different hormones.[113]

Some evidence suggests that testosterone organizes the brain early in development for "masculine" sexual behaviors – and lack of testosterone organizes it for "feminine" behaviors. Female ferrets given testosterone

[111] Silver 1992, 403–4; Angier 1994d.
[112] C. Carter 1992, active 131–34.
[113] Baum 1992, 109–12, 129.

before and after birth showed a preference for estrous females (i.e., acted "male"), whereas females treated only 5 to 20 days after birth did not develop such preferences. For humans, evidence is emerging, but still ambiguous, regarding the controversial idea that prenatal testosterone affects adult sexual orientation.[114]

CONCLUSION

The evidence in this chapter shows that the simple assumptions of difference feminism (regarding gender differences in propensity for war) play out in biology along very complex pathways, including feedback loops connecting culture and biology. The interpretations of evidence are nuanced, and our understanding of biology is incomplete. Nonetheless, when gender differences appear to have a solid biological foundation, those differences almost always are in the direction that would make men more capable or willing to engage in war.

The problem is that none of the gender differences arising from biology is sufficient to explain the puzzle of gendered war roles. Biology provides a partial explanation by showing why war would tend to involve mostly men. It does not, however, provide a sufficient explanation to the puzzle of why war is virtually all-male.

Specifically, the five hypotheses explored in this chapter fared differently depending on the weight of evidence. The idea of a distinctly male genetic code as the basis for warlikeness (Hypothesis 3A) did not hold up at all. Some support was found for the idea that size and strength explain gendered war roles (Hypothesis 3C) and a bit for the idea that brain "wiring" creates gender differences in cognitive abilities relevant to war (Hypothesis 3D). In both cases, the relevant gender differences proved real, but were not nearly strong enough to account for the consistency of gendered war roles. Rather, the gender differences on these dimensions explain only why men *on average* would have greater propensity for war. Hypotheses 3B and 3E do not suffer from this problem of inadequate distinction of gendered abilities: testosterone and estrogen are two variables for which the bell-curves of adult men and women have very little overlap. However, the actual evidence on testosterone implicated it only in a vague way in a feedback loop involving social conflicts. The direct effect of short-term testosterone levels on aggression remains nebulous – present in some form, but not strong enough to make finding it easy – and therefore not strong enough to explain much about gendered war roles.

---

[114] Konner 1988; Baum 1992, ferrets 125; orientation: Hampson and Kimura 1992, 371–73; Meyer-Bahlburg *et al.* 1995.

4 Groups: bonding, hierarchy, and social identity

Hypothesis 4. Innate gender differences in group dynamics:

A. Male bonding
B. Ability to work in hierarchies
C. In-group/out-group psychology
D. Childhood gender segregation

INTRODUCTION

This chapter continues to explore biological explanations of gendered war roles, but at the level of group dynamics instead of individual bodies. War depends on various complex social interactions between and within groups. Perhaps biology adapts men for those interactions. At the group level, biology becomes more elusive than at the individual level (chapter 3). But we know that genes somehow code certain scripted social behaviors in some species – for example, the dance that honeybees use to communicate about food sources.

A number of proposed explanations of gendered war roles draw on the idea of biologically rooted group dynamics. Some writers argue that women cannot take part in "male bonding," which is necessary for military units to fight successfully. Others say that men are innately more hierarchical in orientation – better at giving and taking orders in a chain of command – and therefore better suited for armies. A third variant holds that men adhere more strongly to an in-group versus out-group psychology, allowing them to kill enemies without qualms. Fourth, combat might be gender-segregated because children grow up in gender-segregated settings, and do not learn to work well together in mixed groups.

To infer biologically scripted group dynamics, I will look for consistency in a behavioral pattern (male bonding, gender segregation, etc.) both across human cultures and in the animal species most closely related to humans. Thus, I will assess each hypothesis with regard to evidence from both humans and primates. However, the study of animal behavior – ethology – is controversial. We can observe animal behaviors, but the only interpretations we can put on those behaviors must be drawn from somewhere in our own *human* experience. (Western and indigenous cultures alike are awash in anthropomorphic talking animals.)[1]

The evidence in this chapter shows tremendous diversity across, and even within, species regarding such group dynamics. Beyond one basic structure – dominance hierarchies – few patterns emerge that could help explain gendered war roles. Animal species are so diverse that one or another species can be found to back up almost *any* conclusion. Thus, information about any one species says nothing about humans. Only comparison across many species shows what is common and what is exceptional for a given behavior pattern or setting, and even then we do not know if humans follow the norm or are the exception in that behavior.[2]

Close relations   As Figure 4.1 illustrates, humanity's closest relatives are first the other great apes – bonobos, chimpanzees, orangutans and gorillas – and then other primates (gibbons, monkeys, and prosimians). All mammals are still similar in some ways, but relevance to humans decreases beyond mammals (birds, insects, etc.). Throughout these circles of relatedness the patterns of gender relations and of violence show great diversity.

Humans, chimpanzees, and bonobos

Chimpanzees are one of our two closest relatives. Several decades ago, chimpanzee social organization became an important model for those who considered male domination "natural." Chimpanzee males tend to be power-oriented, violent, and promiscuous. They engage in male bonding and can systematically attack neighboring groups to take over their territories.[3]

Bonobos, however, are equally closely related to humans, though much less studied than chimpanzees. In terms of individual bodies (chapter 3), bonobos and chimpanzees are very similar, especially as regards gender differences. Scientists long disagreed about whether chimpanzees and bonobos (sometimes called "pygmy chimpanzees") were even separate species. Overall, humans share over 99 percent of their DNA with

---

[1] Susman ed. 1984, xix.
[2] Hrdy 1981, 59; de Waal 1989, 168.
[3] Goodall 1986; Zihlman and Tanner 1978, 167–70.

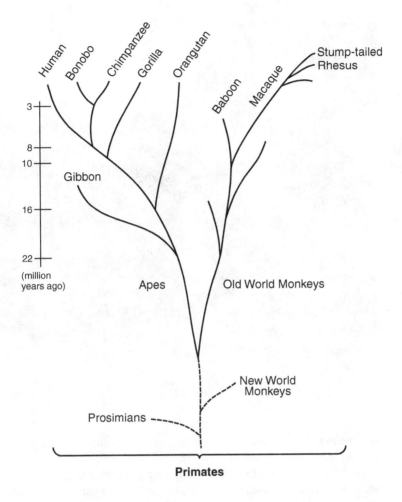

Source: Adapted from de Waal 1989, 173.

Figure 4.1 Human family tree.

chimpanzees and bonobos, which are even more closely related to each other than either is to humans.[4]

Bonobos differ dramatically from chimpanzees in terms of gendered social behaviors, despite the similarity of individual biology. Bonobo males and females are much more integrated, less hierarchical, and more peaceful. Whereas male chimpanzees often threaten and attack females for no

[4] De Waal and Lanting 1997; de Waal 1995; Susman ed. 1984; Zihlman 1984, 180; Jungers and Susman 1984, 143; Sagan and Druyan 1992, 277, 343.

Figure 4.2 Female bonobos having sex. [Courtesy of the Zoological Society of San Diego. Reprinted from de Waal 1996, 200f.]

apparent reason, bonobo males treat females much more respectfully. Bonobos are also especially playful.[5]

Bonobos are radically promiscuous, and bisexual in the case of females and some males, using frequent sexual contact to smooth conflicts within the group, such as over division of food (see Figure 4.2). Bonobos are anatomically adapted for these uses of sex. Bonobo clitorises are larger than any other primate's (including humans), are further forward than in chimpanzees, and become engorged (erect) during sex. Relative to body size, bonobo penises are longer than those of other apes (humans run a close second).[6]

In both chimpanzees and bonobos, females leave their group to live with neighboring groups (i.e., these species are patrilocal). With paternity in doubt, especially among bonobos, this arrangement leaves two

---

[5] Wrangham and Peterson 1996, hierarchical 211; Small 1993, attack 174; Wilson 1975, 166–67; de Waal 1989, playful 193–98, 85.

[6] Small 1993, 175; Kuroda 1984, 317–19, smooth 305; Wrangham and Peterson 1996, 210; penises: Dixson 1998, 255; M. Harris 1989, 177.

lasting connections of known relatedness: brother with brother and mother with son. In chimpanzees, the brotherly connection comes to the fore, and related males dominate the females. In bonobos, by contrast, the mother–son bond predominates. Adult males tend to follow their mothers in the forest. Coalitions of bonobo males are not found. The oldest females are at the center of society, and often determine the social standing of the males. Thus, in chimpanzees, male bonding predominates and females tend to avoid each other; in bonobos, female bonds are central and males tend to stay away from other males. Thus, despite their great similarity in individual biology, the gender patterns of social relationships are quite different in bonobos and chimpanzees.[7]

Warlike chimpanzees   Chimpanzees engage in lethal intergroup violence – "war" by my definition (p. 3). At Jane Goodall's study site in Gombe, Tanzania, and at a number of other locations, primatologists have observed wild chimpanzees using lethal raiding systematically to conquer a neighboring group's territory, kill its males and some females, and incorporate the remaining females. Chimpanzee intergroup aggression shares several features with human warfare, including aggressive coalitions and strategic planning of attacks. The aggression seems driven by "balance of power" in that a group can attack an immobilized individual without restraint at a very low cost. Male chimpanzee aggressors were never observed to be wounded in an attack, and victims were always solitary individuals or male–female pairs, attacked by at least three males. For safety, therefore, chimpanzees travel in larger groups when in border zones than when well within their own territory, but food scarcity sometimes forces chimpanzees to spread out over a larger area, reducing group size and leaving individuals vulnerable to attack.[8]

The Taï National Forest (Ivory Coast) contains the world's largest wild population of chimpanzees. The males engage in territorial activities such as patrols and raids at least every other week. Direct attacks mostly involve five or six males; patrols along or within neighboring territories almost always include four or more males. To communicate group-size, nearby groups sometimes drum at each other while out of visual range, and females join in to make the group seem as large as possible. In direct attacks, which move quickly from "attack calls" to inflicting wounds (or running away screaming), "females with and without infant may join, but they tend to avoid direct physical contact." Intergroup interactions

---

[7] Knauft 1991, 396–97; Kuroda 1984, 311; de Waal and Lanting 1997, 66–67, 86–87; de Waal 1989, 212.

[8] Goodall 1986, 522–34; Goodall 1999, 111–34; Pusey 2001, 8–12; de Waal 1989, 71; Manson and Wrangham 1991, 369–71; Wrangham and Peterson 1996, 5; Van Hooff 1990, 41; Boesch and Boesch-Achermann 2000, 12–15, 32–49, power 30–31.

differ between the Taï and Gombe sites, and others, because of terrain and other contextual factors. For example, visibility is greatly restricted at Taï, making it much harder to monitor the number and gender of individuals in a location. Attacks are thus riskier (and therefore less common) and females' ability to vocalize and drum is more useful.[9]

Chimpanzee raiding parties are primarily but not exclusively male. In the first lethal intergroup attack observed at Gombe, for example, a half dozen of the strongest males were joined by a female – one without children who was relatively fast and strong – and an adolescent male. When the isolated male was being fatally beaten, however, each of the males took turns beating and assaulting him but the female only "screamed and circled around the attack." In the second attack observed, however, the same female after beginning in the same way eventually joined in the attack as well. In the Taï forest, females are constantly and centrally involved in territorial encounters although they tend to lag behind at the point of physical contact. Clearly a strong gender element characterizes these raids, but it is not rigid or categorical.[10]

Peaceful bonobos   Bonobos have rarely been observed in violent intergroup interactions. Intergroup conflicts appear to happen more spontaneously – as when two groups happen to intersect at a rich food resource – and lack the premeditated and organized quality of chimpanzee raids. One violent encounter which caused several serious injuries has been observed in the wild. Intergroup interactions that were *not* violent have also been observed, however. For example, two groups of bonobos happened to arrive at the same time at a site that had been provisioned with sugar cane, in an area where their territories overlapped. They sat facing each other but not mingling for 30 minutes, looking at each other and vocalizing. Then an important female from one side crossed over and had sex with an important female on the other side (possibly a childhood friend, since bonobos are patrilocal). After that, others had sex and they shared the sugar cane. Richard Wrangham, a veteran observer of East African *chimpanzees*, was amazed to see a movie of the encounter, in which bonobo males in one group nonchalantly watched as females from their group went to have sex with males from the other group. Similar peaceful meetings occurred 30 times over the next two months.[11]

---

[9] Boesch and Boesch-Achermann 2000, 32, 44–49, territorial 11, attacks 14, contact 20, 24–25, 20–21, 30–31, 42.

[10] Manson and Wrangham 1991, 371–74; Wrangham and Peterson 1996, screamed 5–6; Boesch and Boesch-Achermann 2000, Taï 38.

[11] Wrangham and Peterson 1996, 214–15; Richard Wrangham, personal communication 2000.

Despite the observed potential for intergroup cooperation, however, bonobos do also have potential for violent intergroup conflict, and do show gender differences in aggression (though less than chimpanzees). Even in the peaceful intergroup meeting just described, older males largely stayed within their own group's space while others crossed over. The sparse data on bonobo intergroup relations in the wild leave many questions. Bonobo males, twice as often as females, show a relatively high rate of injuries to the extremities consistent with violent intergroup conflict. There has been a tendency, since bonobos are much more peaceful and egalitarian than chimpanzees, to idealize bonobos as a pristine vision of ourselves as we wish we were – a variant on the peaceful origins myth. The reality is probably more mixed. Nonetheless, bonobos are still far more peaceful and gender-egalitarian than are chimpanzees: "Chimps are from Mars. Bonobos are from Venus."[12]

Chimpanzee diversity   Actually, it turns out that not even all chimps are from Mars. Some chimpanzee communities diverge from the "standard model" I have just described. The male-bonded patriarchal chimpanzees of East Africa differ from those in the Taï forest in West Africa. To give one example, the bonobo cross-group sex during a border encounter (just described) would be unthinkable among Uganda chimpanzees. But Taï chimpanzees found it thinkable, albeit on a smaller scale: in two observed back-and-forth attacks, as opponents calmed down, facing and threatening each other, "[y]oung oestrus females quietly crossed the lines to join the other males, mated with 1 or 2 of them and returned calmly back to their respective community."[13]

A recent review of the seven longest-term chimpanzee field studies (totaling 151 years of observation) found "significant cultural variation ... far more extensive than ... previously documented for any animal species except humans." *Hunting* by Taï chimpanzees is more sophisticated and social than at Gombe, and follows different gender rules. In one observation, Taï chimpanzees hunted together in a group of three males and one female. The female killed the prey and the top-ranking male shared choice parts of the meat with her. *Mating* patterns also vary modestly. One DNA-based study of paternity patterns claimed that female Taï chimpanzees – who emigrate from their birth group to live and mate in another group – sneak off often to mate with males from outside their current group. Of 14 infants in the group of 55 chimpanzees, in-group paternity was clear for only half. However, methodological

---

[12] Wrangham and Peterson 1996, meeting 215; de Waal 1989, sparse 221, 220; de Waal and Lanting 1997, 84–85; Venus: Angier 1997b.

[13] Boesch and Boesch-Achermann 2000, oestrus 21.

disputes cast this number in doubt. At Gombe, in-group paternity may be 85 percent or higher. In any case, mating is an area in which chimpanzees differ greatly from humans. Chimpanzees show other differences as well. *Tool use* has been observed in more than 32 populations but varies from one location to another, from sophisticated nut-cracking technologies at Taï (almost entirely the domain of females, by the way) to no tool use at all in Uganda. *Mothers* tend to cluster together in Uganda but not in Tanzania. *Male coalitions*, so important in Gombe, are rare in Uganda.[14]

Comparison with humans   In some ways, humans resemble chimpanzees. Historically and cross-culturally, human cultures have been patriarchal – ruled primarily by males – and are thus closer to chimpanzees on this dimension. Simple human societies are prone to frequent warfare (see pp. 24–26), apparently more like chimpanzees than bonobos. Wrangham finds in humans' chimp-like origins (from which he thinks bonobos separately diverged) a streak of murderous male aggression (towards both females and other males) that he calls "demonic." (He sees bonobos' evolutionary path as driven by food sources that let bonobos stay in larger, safer groups.)[15]

In other ways, however, bonobos seem the closer relative to humans. Even Wrangham says that human *females* are more like bonobos than chimpanzees. Several primatologists and photographers have found themselves surprised at bonobos' resemblance to humans in appearance, expressions, and mannerisms. According to primatologist Frans de Waal, bonobos stand and walk on two legs more easily than other apes (although they walk upright only about 10 percent of the time in the wild). Their body proportions are closer to early hominids than are the other great apes. Also like humans, bonobos love water – standing upright in streams, apparently catching fish, splashing and diving under water in pools, all in marked contrast to chimpanzees who can panic and drown in knee-deep water.[16]

In terms of *sexuality*, humans have moved in the same evolutionary direction as bonobos (albeit not as far). Chimpanzee females have visible swellings to denote fertile times; neither bonobos nor humans advertise their fertile times (bonobo females have constant swellings, humans have none). It has been argued (controversially) that the distinctive feature of

---

[14] Whiten *et al.* 1999, cultural 682; hunting: Boesch and Boesch 1989; mating: Gagneux, Woodruff, and Boesch 1997; doubt: Pusey 2001, 28, 30; Anne Pusey, personal communication 2000; other: Gibbons 1992, 287.

[15] Wrangham and Peterson 1996; Ghiglieri 1999.

[16] Wrangham and Peterson 1996, 25–26; de Waal and Lanting 1997, surprised 68; de Waal 1989, 181–86; water: Morgan 1972; Hardy 1960.

early humans was adaptation for sex – so much smooth skin, prominent sex organs, and so forth.[17]

Food sharing among unrelated adults occurs in limited form in bonobo and chimpanzee societies, but humans have taken it much further. Food sharing may be a defining human trait, the basis of a "sharing ethic" in simple human societies. "In all ethnographically known simple societies, cooperative sharing of provisions is extended to mates, offspring, and many others . . . well outside the range of immediate kin." Food sharing is an important basis of social relationships, helping develop social bonding and reciprocity, which are advantages of the human species. Among humans, food sharing is so developed as to be voluntary. Among bonobos, by contrast, sharing consists of allowing others to take one's food when they either attempt to do so or "beg." (Chimpanzees apparently are somewhat more tolerant.) Among gorillas and orangutans, even this level of sharing is largely absent.[18]

Neither chimpanzees nor bonobos are the "true" model of humanity. Where they differ, we cannot say which one's behavior would be more "natural" for us. Moreover, where they converge, we cannot say that humans also converge with them. Some characteristics may be shared by humans and bonobos, some by humans and chimpanzees, some by chimpanzees and bonobos (but not humans), and some by all three species. The important conclusion that comes from the comparison of chimpanzees, bonobos, and humans is not that humans are naturally any particular way, but that what is "natural" for humans apparently covers a broad array of possible social arrangements and behaviors, especially with regard to gender, sex, and violence. Once again, biology is diversity.[19]

Primate diversity

This pattern of inter-species diversity continues in the larger circle of related species. The two other great apes, gorillas and orangutans, differ from humans, chimpanzees, and bonobos. Beyond the great apes, the pattern of diversity continues as we move out through gibbons, Old World monkeys (including baboons and macaques such as rhesus monkeys), New World monkeys, and prosimians. Primate diversity cuts across species and across populations and individuals within a species.[20]

First, gendered differences in body size vary greatly among species. The dramatic size difference in male and female gorillas is unique among

---

[17] M. Harris 1989, 188; Small 1993, 195–98, 128–29.

[18] Knauft 1991, kin 393–95; chimpanzees: Jane Goodall, personal communication 1999; Frans de Waal, personal communication 1999.

[19] De Waal 1989, 227.

[20] Schubert 1991a, baboon 16; Dolhinow 1991, 141; Rodseth *et al.* 1991; Boulding 1992/I, 33; de Waal 1989, 146, 168.

the great apes. So is the orangutan pattern in which some males remain developmentally frozen in a kind of adolescent state (apparently held there by the presence of a big male), get sex by raping females (who prefer the big males), and then change into big males themselves under certain circumstances.[21]

Second, patterns of violence also vary. The other great apes do not share chimpanzees' (and humans') propensity for organized lethal raids on neighboring groups. Among other primate species, levels of violence differ greatly. Some species are remarkably peaceful. Gorillas are notorious for infanticide. A male gorilla in the course of mating with a new female – after defeating her previous mate, or after he dies – routinely kills her existing infants. This has been explained as a way to concentrate resources on his own offspring and to get the female to ovulate sooner. (Other species show a similar pattern of recurrent, though not common, infanticide.) Males dominate females in most, but not all, mammal species. The gender of participants in violent conflicts varies across species. For example, baboon females rarely participate in intergroup encounters. But in a number of monkey species, as well as most prosimians, females participate in fighting, receive injuries, and sometimes even dominate males. (Five mammal species in addition to humans have routine rape, defined as copulation against the victim's best efforts to resist. Three are great apes – orangutans, chimpanzees, and gorillas.)[22]

Among rhesus monkeys, aggressive violence enforces an upper–lower class system, which controls access to food and water in a colony. Groups of rhesus monkeys average more than one aggressive act per hour per individual. (The closely related stump-tail macaque monkeys, by contrast, settle such issues less violently and with better conflict-resolution mechanisms.) Rhesus females, ruled over by a dominating matriarch, commit at least a third of aggressive acts.[23]

Third, in terms of social groupings (see Figure 4.3), orangutans are solitary animals for whom social gatherings are not very important. Gorillas by contrast live in groups centering on a top-status "silverback" male (whose back coloration again shows that individual biology responds to social status), surrounded by females, with solitary males further out. (The absence of such a group seems to be what makes orangutan females vulnerable to rape.) Neither of these social patterns matches the arrangements of chimpanzees or bonobos.

[21] Wrangham and Peterson 1996, 138–46.
[22] Van Der Dennen 1990a, 159; Cheney 1983a, 236–37; Itani 1982; Carpenter 1967; peaceful: Angier 1994d; de Waal 1996, 201; infanticide: Hrdy 1981, 81–94; Small 1993, 177; Goodall 1986, 523–25; de Waal and Lanting 1997, 139; Wrangham and Peterson 1996, 157, 159; Gilbert 1998; baboon: Van Hooff 1990, 39; rape: Wrangham and Peterson 1996, 138–46.
[23] De Waal 1989, 91–97, 109.

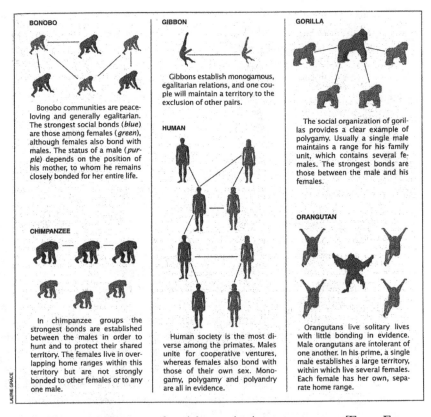

Figure 4.3 Patterns of social organization among apes. [From Frans B. M. de Waal, "Bonobo sex and society," *Scientific American*, March 1995: 85. © Courtesy of Laurie Grace.]

Fourth, in terms of sexuality, orangutans like humans have no visible genital swellings. Gorillas have only subtle signs of ovulation, invisible except under intimate scrutiny. Thus, chimpanzees are the exception among great apes in advertising their fertility. The large pink swellings typical of chimpanzees are found in only 22 of about 200 primate species, mostly in baboons and macaque monkeys.[24]

Fifth, the patrilocality of chimpanzee and bonobo societies does not extend to other great apes or beyond. In most primate species, females stay with their birth group and female–female relationships are more important. Indeed, for most monkey species, "society is given its shape by the relationships between overlapping generations of related females."

[24] Small 1993, 127–28.

In many species, females control and inherit territories, and pass along the local knowledge needed for survival. Except for humans and a few others, "breeding among primates is initiated by the female." Despite these central female roles in primate societies, females usually lose direct confrontations with males, but even here exceptions exist.[25]

Feminist critics note that primatologists impose gender expectations from their own human society onto the animals they study. (Donna Haraway points out a subtext of woman-as-nature, for example, in *National Geographic*'s recurrent story of white women primatologists who connect the reader with nature by coaxing apes to approach and touch.) Among other problems, male scientists' gender biases lead them to study primarily male animals. In 1875, Antoinette Blackwell noted that in an otherwise thorough study, Darwin's *Descent of Man* (published four years earlier) traced the development of masculine characteristics in males but "seems never to have thought of looking to see whether or not the females had developed equivalent feminine characters." For decades primatologists focused on all-male dominance hierarchies and assumed preferential access to mating opportunities for those at the top of the hierarchy, as though females were a passive resource waiting around for males to decide who would get to mate them. Recent studies, including many by women primatologists, focus on female primates' active reproductive choices. Female primates seek out male mates with qualities often different from those that propel males to the top of their hierarchy. Female primate power extends beyond reproduction into other areas of social life as well. Females participate in intergroup encounters, actively maintain hierarchies, and often determine a group's movements.[26]

To summarize, then, primate species, including those most closely related to humans, show great diversity in gender relations and social organization. This overall pattern casts doubt on Hypothesis 4 overall. Any of the four explanations of gendered war roles (covered by hypotheses 4A–D) would have to show a regularity across species and cultures that contrasts with this general diversity.

A. MALE BONDING

A male-bonding hypothesis explicitly underlies the US military's current policies excluding women from combat. The 1994 US decision to keep Army combat units closed to women was justified in terms of the "unique bonds" necessary for mortal combat, which "are best developed in a single

---

[25] Small 1993, 57, 106; Hrdy 1981, shape 17–20, breeding 24, 100; Wilson 1975, 218.
[26] Harding 1986, 92–100; Haraway 1989, touch 147–49; Blackwell 1875 in Hrdy 1981, 12; Small 1993, biases 131, 172, 57; Small ed. 1984.

gender all male environment." The US Army Chief of Staff said in 1993 that "cohesion is enhanced by uniformity, by adherence to a common sense of values and behaviors." The idea that "male bonding" is central to war offers a possible explanation to the puzzle of universally gendered war roles. If males in a group share a special bond that females cannot enter, or (worse yet) that females' presence disrupts, then women could hardly play much part in combat. As this section will show, however, the male-bonding hypothesis finds little empirical support.[27]

Men in groups   Lionel Tiger's 1969 *Men in Groups* proposes that "male bonding" is a biologically based behavior that plays a key role in human society. Tiger distinguishes male bonding from the mere aggregation of all males in a unit. Bonding occurs in a smaller and more select group. Males "reaffirm their solidarity partly by degrading the male–female bond" (e.g., in prenuptial stag parties), which explains both why groups of men are often misogynistic and why it is hard for women to participate in all-male settings, including war. Tiger argues that bonding among males in some species draws on the same sorts of mechanisms that operate in two more widely recognized forms of social bonding – mother–infant and mating (consort) bonds. (The mother–infant bond was a focus of Lorenz's work on imprinting, and central to studies of attachment in developmental psychology.) However, parental and mating bonds manifest in scripted, instinctual behaviors, for which male bonding produces no analogous behavioral scripts.[28]

Based on this theory, Tiger predicted in 1969 that women would not be able to participate in combat, become regular, armed police officers, or become political leaders in significant numbers. Yet, since 1969, female participation in policing and in politics has increased dramatically, while female participation in combat has lagged – a problem for Tiger's theory.[29]

Bonding in combat

Male bonding nonetheless deserves a closer look. Small-group bonding is very important to combat effectiveness, because it provides a central motivation for soldiers to participate in battle. Combat veterans frequently

[27] Ghiglieri 1999, 181–90; Kier 1998, uniformity 6, 9–13, 22–25; MacCoun 1996, 160–63, 167; Stiehm 1994, 157; unique: Priest 1997c.

[28] Tiger 1969, 27–29, 32, 34–47, 78–118; Tiger and Fox 1971, 85–117, degrading 93, mechanisms 95; Morgan 1972, 190–207; Jeffords 1989, 90–91; Wrangham and Peterson 1996, 24–25, 168; Hrdy 1981, 27.

[29] Tiger and Fox 1971, 101; Tiger 1969, 90–91; Kier 1998, 29.

say that they fought not for patriotism primarily but for their close buddies. The bonds of a small group let soldiers keep fighting under fire (see pp. 253–57). I will examine this small-group bonding overall and then ask what role gender plays in it.[30]

The "lowest common denominator of comradeship" is the small group of about five to ten soldiers – the infantry squad (or "section") or alternatively the "weapon group built around a crew-served weapon, such as a mortar or artillery piece." Such groups bond strongly. "A corporal and six men in a trench were like shipwrecked sailors on a raft, completely committed to their social grouping." "In battle the unit will become the only important thing in the infantryman's universe; nothing outside it matters, and no sacrifice for the other men in it is too great." Psychologist Judith Herman, an expert on combat trauma, writes that "[i]n fighting men, the sense of safety is invested in the small combat group. Clinging together under prolonged conditions of danger, the combat group develops a shared fantasy that their mutual loyalty and devotion can protect them from harm. They come to fear separation from one another more than they fear death."[31]

Comradeship within this unit provides a key motivation for fighting, notwithstanding other motivations for participating in the first place, such as patriotism, professionalism, employment, or conscription. A combat veteran says that "among men who fight together there is an intense love. You are closer to those men than to anyone except your immediate family when you were young." As a fourteenth-century knight put it, "You love your comrade so much in war... And then you are prepared to go and die or live with him... [and are] afraid of nothing." In World War II, as in many wars, US soldiers went "AWOL from the field hospital and made their way back" to their unit at the front where conditions were horrific. In World War I, the famous pacifist dissent of the combat-traumatized soldier Siegfried Sassoon (see pp. 270–71) ended when he returned to his unit out of loyalty to his comrades. The sense of obligation to the other members of one's group helps soldiers to overcome natural resistance both to courting danger and to killing other people.[32]

Military psychologist S. L. A. Marshall found after World War II that US infantrymen had seldom fired their weapons, even during intense

[30] Holmes 1985, 24–28; Shalit 1988; Grossman 1995, 5–10; Kellett 1990, 224; Simons 1997.
[31] Holmes 1985, lowest 294, raft [Charles Carrington] 295; Dyer 1985, great 127; Herman 1992, 62.
[32] Holmes 1985, 108, 291, 294–97; Kellett 1990, 225; Dyer 1985, intense 127, 104, 106; Keegan and Holmes 1985, 53, knight 19; Ambrose 1997, AWOL 153; Herman 1992, Sassoon 22; Jeffords 1989, 54–86; Broyles 1984; Seifert 1994, 61; Astrachan 1986, 55–56.

combat. A small percentage of the men did most of the killing. By contrast, crew-served weapons such as artillery or machine-guns were fired frequently and had most effect. This has been attributed to the group cohesion in such units, which have a common focus for their efforts (the weapon), are kept on track by the demands of the task, and can kill more easily because the group diffuses responsibility.[33]

One unplanned experiment in unit cohesion was carried out when the US Army in Europe during World War II fed troops to the front for replacement and reinforcement with little attention to primary unit cohesion. In late 1944, perhaps 80 percent of US infantry troops at the front were new to combat, the product of a replacement system that supplied nearly a million men to the European theater at maximum speed. A new recruit received basic training, was shipped to a camp in France where he knew no one, spent between two days and a week receiving a rifle and possibly a bit of training, and then went to a Replacement Depot ("Repple Depple") and was sent almost immediately to a forward battalion, on to a company, and out to a foxhole. One 19-year-old inexperienced farm boy, "was led to his one-man foxhole and told to get in and watch for Germans. [He] didn't catch the sergeant's name. He couldn't see the men to his right and left. He didn't know what squad, platoon, company, or battalion he was in." The failures of this system led, after the war, to a greater emphasis on primary unit cohesion.[34]

A similar "experiment" involving German soldiers on the eastern front towards the end of World War II, however, suggests opposite conclusions. The disintegration of German forces led to the total disappearance of primary groups (which had been the "backbone of the German army" until then). Yet the soldiers, isolated and not knowing each other, continued to fight with "remarkable cohesion and battle performance." Possibly their primary group loyalty was displaced successfully onto a larger and more abstract group identity.[35]

Cohesion in primary groups is a two-edged sword for military commanders. Loyalty to the primary unit can easily decouple soldiers from the larger army. They may disobey orders together, hunker down together without fighting, or fail to coordinate actions with other units. A US World War II veteran recalls this example:

[T]wo army officers from another unit came up on the line. They were rather bossy and arrogant, and they wanted to know where the front was, and the sergeant

---

[33] Marshall 1947; Holmes 1985, 281, 284, 299; Keegan and Holmes 1985, 42; Dyer 1985, 118–19; Grossman 1995, 3–4, 11, 151–54.

[34] Ambrose 1997, 275–77, battalion 229.

[35] Bartov 1991, backbone–performance 5–6, 29–58; Kier 1998, 14; Fritz 1996; Shils and Janowitz 1948.

said to them, "You go right down there," and they did and they were instantly cut to pieces [by Japanese machine-guns]. Civilians have a great deal of trouble handling that, but the veteran understands it perfectly. You don't love anybody who is not yours.

In addition to these extremes, small-group bonding can also encourage a drug subculture, anti-war activities, and collective indiscipline. It can encourage desertion, if soldiers receive at least tacit support from comrades. In the second half of the US Civil War, Confederate desertion rates were highest in companies recruited on a local basis, which had highest homogeneity and cohesion. Primary group cohesion is also problematic because it depends on social and situational factors that may change, and because personnel replacements may cause frictions. Furthermore, "groupthink" can lead small, isolated groups to make mistakes in combat.[36]

To mitigate some of the negative effects of primary unit cohesion, military hierarchies promote cohesion at a larger-unit level – prototypically the regiment (especially in the British Army historically), which contains several thousand soldiers. "Esprit de corps" based on upholding the group's honor and history serves this purpose.[37]

Military historian William McNeill argues that close-order drill underlies regimental cohesion by creating "muscular bonding" among participants. "Words are inadequate to describe the emotion aroused by the prolonged movement in unison that drilling involved." The art of "keeping together in time" may precede the development of language, and was first expressed through dance, including war dances in simple societies. Although McNeill attributes to close-order drill the superiority of modern European armies, such drill is a historical "oddity," so it would not help explain why gendered war roles are ubiquitous across cultures.[38]

Anyway, muscular bonding is not limited to men. The first US women in the WAAC in 1942 "surprised their male instructors – just as the British ATS had done – by their aptitude and affection for precision drill routines." US women in uniform in World War II "loved to drill," and often practiced during their breaks. At a training base for WAVE officers, the building superintendent had to request the women to break step upon entering the old buildings, which could not take the marching. In the nineteenth-century Dahomey Kingdom (see pp. 60–64),

---

[36] Dyer 1985, veteran 127; Kier 1998, indiscipline 16; Kellett 1990, factors 217, 222; MacCoun 1996, groupthink 161.

[37] Holmes 1985, regiment 293; Kellett 1990, esprit 217, 219.

[38] McNeill 1995, 2–4, dance 102–4, oddity 31; Keegan and Holmes 1985, 44; Ehrenreich 1997a, 180–81, 21–31, 98, 64–65, 4, 3, 64–65.

women warriors built *esprit de corps* with dancing, singing, and music-making.[39]

Social and task cohesion   Scholars distinguish two types of small-group cohesion. *Social* cohesion refers to group members' liking each other, whereas *task* cohesion means that they work together smoothly in a small unit. Experiences from racial integration and the debates about openly gay people in military units suggest that social cohesion, but not task cohesion, decreases when units have members who are dissimilar from each other. The members may not like each other as much if they feel they do not have values and experiences in common, but they still work together well because of discipline and leadership within a military organization. Today, although US black and white soldiers often socialize separately, they usually work together effectively. In the last months of World War II in Europe, the US Army sent 53 all-black platoons forward to serve with previously all-white companies. Cohesion did not suffer, according to postwar surveys of participating troops. One segregationist white sergeant said: "After that first day when we saw how they fought, I changed my mind. They're just like any of the other boys to us." A company commander who had been forced by attrition to assign a white squad to a black platoon reported: "You might think that wouldn't work well, but it did. The white squad didn't want to leave the platoon. I've never seen anything like it." Causality seems to run from effectiveness (especially, facing combat together) to social cohesion more than vice versa. Indeed, too much social cohesion can undermine task cohesion, as when a unit spends too much time socializing on the job.[40]

Is bonding gendered?

Since gendered war roles are pervasive, the causal relationship of gender with small-group bonding is ambiguous. This bonding might appear "male" simply because it occurs in a context that is typically all-male, rather than because the bonding is inherently connected with gender, or accessible only to men. The evidence will show that small-group bonding does not depend on gender.

In primates, small-group bonding is not particularly oriented to male–male bonds, except for chimpanzees. I have noted already the weakness of male bonding in bonobos, and the differing importance, from site to site, of female bonding in chimpanzees. Taï chimpanzees, in contrast to

[39] Costello 1985, surprised 45; Campbell 1990, loved 110, buildings 111; Alpern 1998, Dahomey 106–21.
[40] Kier 1998, 25.

Tanzanian ones, hunt and share meat in cooperative groups that sometimes include both males and females. Among other great apes and primates generally, male bonding is uncommon, even in aggressive species.
Figure 4.3 above shows the variety of bonding patterns among apes
(the five great apes and gibbons), with no strong or general tendency
towards male bonding (see p. 193).[41]

In humans, military organizations have carried out various experiments in gender integration, including in combat-support units, to assess whether unit cohesion suffers. For example, Rhonda Cornum's Gulf
War POW experiences (see p. 41) illustrate that bonding in war can apply
to women. The connection she felt with fellow (mostly male) soldiers is
a recurring theme: "I liked doing things as a group"; "I could never
have even considered letting [friends in a deploying unit] down"; "It
was the feeling of being part of something bigger than oneself." When
the POWs were released to Red Cross custody, each had a separate
hotel room, which was "the last thing in the world that anybody wanted"
after solitary confinement, so "we created a big slumber party." Cornum's
motivation as a soldier was enhanced by this bonding, which appears to
operate about the same in her as in her male comrades.[42]

The US Army in 1993–94 studied the gender integration of basic
combat training at the squad level, for combat-support soldiers. Phase
I compared companies with various gender compositions – all-male, all-
female, 75–25 percent male–female, and 50–50 percent male–female.
Phase II studied four companies integrated with 75 percent males and
25 percent females. The soldiers received little advance information or
special instructions, but participated in planning the training in Phase II.
The study found attitudes towards combat training most positive in all-
male companies and lowest in all-female companies. Women in integrated
companies "were challenged more and pushed themselves harder than females in single-gender companies." More males than females perceived
a double standard in expectations, and males felt more negatively about
women in the Army – a feeling that increased during the basic combat
training.[43]

These negative feelings did not, however, translate into worse performance in integrated companies than segregated ones. On the three
tests soldiers must pass to graduate from the training – physical fitness,
individual proficiency, and marksmanship – there were "no significant
performance differences" between the segregated and integrated settings,

---

[41] Kuroda 1984, 321–22; Gibbons 1992, 288; Boesch and Boesch 1989; Badrian and
Badrian 1984, 342–43; Morgan 1972, 193.
[42] Cornum 1996, 4, 9–12, 18.
[43] US Army 1995.

although the performances of males differed from females in both settings. In a 1995 follow-up study of ten companies, the US Army found
that the gender-integrated environment "improved the physical training
performance [sit-ups, push-ups, running] . . . of female soldiers in all three
events and male soldiers in two of three events." The keys to success were
training drill sergeants to work with female soldiers and providing support
through the chain of command.[44]

The US Navy in the early 1990s experimented with gender-integrated
companies in basic training, comparing nine all-male companies with
four all-female ones and nine integrated ones. The integrated companies'
members perceived their own unit cohesion to be higher than in the segregated companies. In the US Army, gender-integrated basic training in
three battalions produced "no significant trends" according to a report of
the Army Research Institute. In a larger follow-on program, both women
and men in integrated units showed as great or greater socialization than
women and men in gender-segregated units. A 1996 General Accounting
Office study found that gender-integrated basic training "does not negatively affect the performance of trainees." In extended field exercises as
well, the US Army has found that women's presence did not disrupt unit
cohesion – "it is the commonality of experience of the soldiers involved,
rather than their gender, that produces cohesion."[45]

A RAND study found that "gender integration is perceived to have a
relatively small effect on readiness, cohesion, and morale" in US military
forces. The influences of leadership and training were seen as "far more
influential" on these outcomes than was gender integration. A majority of
both genders preferred integrated basic training (75 percent of women,
61 percent of men). These studies thus support the idea that integrating
people of diverse backgrounds in a military unit leads to a decrease in
social cohesion but no loss of task cohesion. Performance is not reduced.
In US gender-integrated units, "the women worked harder to gain male
approval and the men worked harder not to be outdone by the women."
Similarly, among gender-integrated rebel guerrilla units in El Salvador,
according to one woman participant, the presence of women enhanced
men's effectiveness: "When a man was retreating from the front lines and
saw a woman holding her position, he would think if she is going ahead,
then I have to."[46]

In Britain, by contrast, the introduction of all-women platoons
in basic training in 1998 sharply improved pass rates and reduced

[44] US Army 1995; US Army 1996.
[45] Kier 1998, Navy–trends 27–28, GAO 29; commonality: David Segal in Kier 1998, 28;
    Priest 1997c.
[46] RAND: Harrell and Miller 1997, xvii, 97–101; Salvador: in Francke 1997:247.

injuries – apparently because the women concentrated on meeting the standard rather than trying to keep up with the men. The 24 women in the experiment preferred training separately: "The men never treat us as equals anyway." Regarding bonding in these all-female units, one recruit reported, "basically we all love each other to bits." Similarly, the Soviet women pilots in World War II had no trouble bonding. On the contrary, a male commander who led first a men's and then a women's regiment found the women "easier for me to command" because "[t]hey had the strong spirit of a collective unit."[47]

Individual women in male units appear quite able to bond with male comrades, just as women in all-female units do with women comrades. Maria Botchkareva, who fought in Russia (see pp. 72–76), refers to "the true comradeship that made the three years in the trenches the happiest of my life." Similarly, Englishwoman Flora Sandes, who fought with the Serbian army in World War I (see p. 116), was deeply attached to her comrades. As a female US officer put it, "being a woman does not prevent that kind of bond with men. It may enhance it . . . Women understand feelings . . ." The presence of women may enhance familial-type bonds in integrated primary units.[48]

In the Gulf War, sexual relationships formed in, and between, a substantial number of integrated US units. Strong majorities of respondents in one survey indicated that these sexual relationships had little or no effect on readiness or morale. However, in another survey, nearly half of "those who were in mixed-gender units reported that 'sexual activity had a negative impact' on unit morale." The evidence from this case is therefore contradictory.[49]

In the Sandinista guerrilla army in Nicaragua, where women participated in front-line units along with men, "[a]ll of us – men and women – were very close. We thought of each other as brothers and sisters." Women, like men, experienced small-group bonds so strong that wounded soldiers would sneak back to their units: "They took me to a hospital but I wouldn't stay . . . I knew they needed every last one of us on the line."[50]

The evidence on small-group bonding from nonmilitary settings is ambiguous. In mixed-gender groups, men usually dominate the interaction. (Women have no significant influence on group processes if they compose fewer than 15 percent of the members.) Women in the United States

[47] Evans 1999; Noggle 1994, commander 105.
[48] Botchkareva 1919, 319; Sandes: Wheelwright 1989, 14–16, 34–36, 147; feelings: Astrachan 1986, 53; familial: Francke 1997, 247–49.
[49] Francke 1997, 249–50; Moskos 1994, negative 60.
[50] Randall 1981, 149; Randall and Yanz 1995.

are concentrated in administrative-clerical and service occupations, and even in traditionally male occupations where women have begun to enter in substantial numbers, most women remain low in hierarchies of pay and authority (as in the US military data in Figures 2.5 and 2.6 above; see pp. 103–4). These women have developed work cultures that differ in some ways – more conformist, less aggressive towards management, more "familial" – from those of males in low-level occupations. All-female groups tend to differ from all-male ones – more relationship-oriented, cooperative, and trusting. Thus, women's group dynamics may differ from men's in certain ways, but the gender integration of groups does not apparently disrupt small-group bonding. In sum, then, male bonding provides a poor explanation of gendered war roles.[51]

B. ABILITY TO WORK IN HIERARCHIES

Beyond unit bonding, a second type of group dynamic in warfare is the hierarchical organization of participants. Military organizations are especially well-defined hierarchies. Armies mobilize and coordinate masses of people to undertake large-scale tasks. The subordination of the individual to the group is crucial to military success. Effective command in battle, which is both difficult and crucial, requires soldiers' obedience. In the confusion of the battlefield – filled with noise, smoke, patterns of movement that make no intuitive sense, scenes of carnage, raging stress hormones, fear – the effective operation of the group depends on the ability of individuals to automatically obey commands, to follow directives without question. A central purpose of basic training is to instill this instinct to obey orders (see p. 253).[52]

Then again, sometimes a less hierarchical organization motivates individuals better and allows innovation and flexibility in adapting to changing conditions. For instance, one source of US military success in World War II was the ability of people at the bottom levels to innovate, bypass established channels, and get jobs done without waiting for orders from above – in contrast to German and Japanese military styles.[53]

Hierarchical social structures, found widely among animal species, use a layered system of dominant–subordinate status ranks – sometimes a strict linear ranking from top to bottom, sometimes a more flexible and dynamic one – in which those nearer the top receive preferential access to scarce resources such as food. Despite some empirical

[51] Bystydzienski 1993, 39–42, familial 42; Eagly and Karau 1991; Levine and Moreland 1998, 442–43; Eagly and Johnson 1990.
[52] Kellett 1990, 224; Van Creveld 1985.
[53] Ambrose 1997, 65.

complexity not captured by this simple model, nonetheless dominance hierarchies occur in many species including almost all primates. If these hierarchies were innately gendered, so that females could not operate effectively in a male hierarchy, that would help explain gendered war roles.

Dominance

The "dominance" hierarchies mentioned earlier (see pp. 153–57) are an important yet somewhat ill-defined concept. Primatologist Sarah Hrdy's definition of dominance closely resembles what political scientists call power – "the ability of one individual to influence or coerce the behavior of others, usually by threatening to inflict damage but also by promising to give (or withhold) rewards." She describes as dominant the "animal that usually wins in a one-on-one encounter, the animal that typically can approach, threaten, and displace another." She notes, however, that "[n]o one is particularly satisfied with the concept of dominance... [which] is difficult to assess and highly dependent on context" and can differ from one sphere of activity to another.[54]

In animal and human societies, the importance of hierarchy generally correlates with the amount of aggression and violence in that society. Less aggressive ape and monkey species, such as bonobos and stump-tail monkeys, have flatter and more flexible hierarchies than their more aggressive relatives, the chimpanzees and rhesus monkeys respectively. Although this could suggest that hierarchy causes violence, the opposite causality seems more likely (see pp. 213–14).[55]

In an evolutionary perspective, dominance hierarchies can give a reproductive advantage to higher-ranking individuals, in two ways. First, in some species the top-ranking "alpha male" in a group does all or most of the breeding, selectively passing along his particular combination of genes. This is true of the cichlid fish discussed earlier, for example. Presumably, this possibility connects with the response of testosterone levels to status-rank changes, although testosterone also functions to physically strengthen high-ranking individuals, whether or not they breed more (see pp. 159–62). In nonhuman primates, however, any such breeding differential is relatively unconnected with dominance rank. Among chimpanzees, male rank shows little correlation with breeding success. Bonobo promiscuity makes any sexual monopoly impossible. Orangutan subordinate males beat the dominance system by raping

[54] Hrdy 1981, 3–4; Sagan and Druyan 1992, 201–17; de Waal 1996, 98–99; Angier 1995a; Weisfeld 1994, 45; Eibl-Eibesfeldt 1979, 89.
[55] De Waal 1989, 159.

females. Only gorillas among the great apes closely connect alpha-male status with breeding access.[56]

Human cultures occasionally produce a ruler with a huge harem who fathers hundreds of children, and many cultures allow men multiple wives. However, these arrangements have hardly been a central factor in human reproductive advantage – harems account for only a tiny percentage of human breeding, and polygynous arrangements are far from universal (suggesting they are not biologically rooted). In fact, present-day human societies systematically reverse the relationship between status rank and birth rate, with lower-ranking individuals and populations consistently having more children. (In a number of multi-ethnic societies today, such as Kosovo or Lebanon, birth rate differentials aggravate political-constitutional conflicts.)

The second and far more important way that dominance hierarchies affect reproductive success is by regulating access to food and other scarce resources. High-ranking individuals are more likely to survive periods of scarcity. The resource allocation function of hierarchies is found in all great apes including bonobos. High-ranking individuals (usually male) take possession of food most often, and where food sharing occurs it is usually from higher- to lower-ranking individuals. New evidence shows that female chimpanzees' reproductive success depends on dominance rank: "high-ranking females...have significantly higher infant survival, faster maturing daughters, and more rapid production of young," all because of access to good foraging areas. Among humans as well – cross-culturally, historically, and in present-day societies – an individual's rank usually correlates with material well-being (wealth) much more than with sexual promiscuity. The male CEO of a large company may earn 100 times more than a factory worker, but is unlikely to have 100 times as many wives and mistresses.[57]

Among human cultures, hierarchy varies in importance. Status rivalry characterizes complex societies more than simple ones. Many gathering-hunting cultures guard against arrogance or a feeling of superiority, and downplay social status. Physical strength is relatively unimportant in relations within such a group, because weapons serve as "equalizers," and this may help explain why hierarchies in simple human societies are flatter than those of other primates.[58]

Human social hierarchies are more complex than any animal society. Yet they appear to share at least superficial signals with nonhuman

[56] Chimpanzees: Pusey, Williams, and Goodall 1997; Pusey 2001, 27.
[57] Young: Pusey, Williams, and Goodall 1997.
[58] Carneiro 1994, 10–11, equalizers 11; Knauft 1991.

Figure 4.4 Bonobo using outstretched hand for reconciliation. [Courtesy of the Zoological Society of San Diego. Reprinted from de Waal 1989, 213.]

primates. The "fear grin" indicates submission, and has some connection with the human smile. The cold stare, especially with mouth open, indicates a threat. The outstretched hand as a submission gesture and signal for reconciliation (in stump-tailed macaques, chimpanzees, and bonobos) finds its place in the human repertoire as the handshake (see Figure 4.4). Both chimpanzees and humans bow and prostrate themselves as a submissive greeting.[59]

Gender and dominance   Are females less hierarchical? Tiger and Fowler's 1978 edited volume finds little consensus. To the extent that some authors claim gender differences in hierarchies, they are in the direction hypothesized by difference feminism (see p. 47) – "the predisposition to form hierarchies . . . may be more uniquely male than female as a trait" and "when females do organize . . . along hierarchical lines, these forms may be more or less distinct from male ones." In Old World monkeys and apes, "male and female hierarchy have very different properties." Male rankings depend mainly on fighting strength and ability to form alliances, whereas female rankings depend primarily on kinship. Chimpanzee and human males may be more hierarchical – oriented towards competition and status – whereas females are more

[59] Eibl-Eibesfeldt 1979, 93; Sagan and Druyan 1992, 193; de Waal 1996, bow 99.

empathic, although with a "great deal of plasticity" in gender roles. Female chimpanzees are "much less dominance oriented" than males, their "hierarchy is rather vague," and "[t]heir coalitions withstand time" in contrast to the frequent shifts in male coalitions.[60]

Overall, among primates, the gendered nature of hierarchies varies widely. In monkeys like the rhesus and stump-tail macaque, which are matrilocal and matrilineal, female hierarchies are central to social life. In rhesus monkeys, ranks are passed from mother to daughter. One female monkey attacked by another has been known to seek out and retaliate against the latter's sister, and mothers encourage their children to play with the children of higher-ranking individuals. Both behaviors show relatively sophisticated knowledge of both status and kinship relations. Among monkeys, then, females seem as capable of playing status-hierarchy games as males are.[61]

This pattern extends to primates generally, albeit more strongly in monkeys than apes. "In all primates studied, the dominance rank of the mother has a great effect on the social standing of her offspring, both male and female." However, other scholars caution that "the existence of well-defined female dominance hierarchies is far from being the rule among nonhuman primates."[62]

In some primate species, such as baboons and chimpanzees, males and females form separate hierarchies with males dominant over females. In others, however, such as macaques and vervets, "males are generally dominant to females but the latter can form effective coalitions against males. In these species, therefore, the male and female hierarchies are not always clearly separated." Bonobos fall in the latter category with mixed-gender hierarchies. In several captive bonobo populations (albeit a minority of cases), a female is the dominant individual in the group. A leading observer of bonobos calls females "almost co-dominant" with males. However, the whole hierarchy is relatively unimportant in bonobo society (which lacks formalized rituals of dominance and submission), especially among females who rarely fight with each other.[63]

Human all-female groups supposedly can "shift from a nonhierarchical to a hierarchical structure when circumstances demand." For example, in one Israeli kibbutz, 11 females in a group operated in hierarchy when

[60] Tiger and Fowler 1978; Tiger 1978, trait–ones 6–7; Caspari 1978, properties 113; de Waal 1996, plasticity 124, 118–24; de Waal 1989, vague 53, 55.
[61] De Waal 1989, sister 109; de Waal 1996, play 101.
[62] Caspari 1978, offspring 101, 104–5; Chapais 1991, rule 199.
[63] Chapais 1991, coalitions 200; de Waal and Lanting 1997, captive 76–78, 72–73; observer [Takayoshi Kano] 60, 53–55; de Waal 1989, 246, 212.

task-oriented (especially in an emergency such as during a war) but non-hierarchically otherwise. Thus, although female hierarchies are characterized by poor discipline, reluctance to accept authority, and strained relations, these attributes can be overcome when necessary (as in an emergency) and thus may not be "problems."[64]

Childhood pecking orders

In groups of human children, more than adults, interactions resemble dominance systems. In US children studied by developmental psychologists, "dominance aggression" emerges around age 3 as competitiveness increases in such forms as races, play-fighting, and height comparisons. Aggression peaks around 4 years old, a time when boys especially value being tough and greatly overrate their own toughness. Partly for this reason, preschool children cannot produce a consensual ranking of "who is the toughest." By kindergarten, however, nearly two-thirds agree about the order of toughness, and by fourth grade nearly three-quarters agree. Agreement on status ranks emerges first for the top and bottom ranks, and by about age 6 children develop a "true dominance hierarchy featuring prerogatives of rank and a stable, consensual hierarchy." Studies of dominance hierarchies in preschool children, based on naturalistic observations of winners and losers in conflicts over possession of objects, have generally found a nearly linear dominance hierarchy – i.e., a single ranking from top to bottom. Studies of "attention structure" – which children other children look at most – have also found a "highly linear and rigid hierarchy."[65]

Typically, each gender forms its own hierarchy, although children of both genders usually agree on all children's ranks. In middle childhood, "[i]ssues of dominance emerge strongly within all-male groups, but are of much less importance among groups of girls." Children's hierarchies are "strikingly stable, at least among boys," often lasting from age 6 through the mid-teens. As the hierarchy stabilizes, aggression decreases and physical aggression is replaced by verbal aggression. Dominance rank affects children's behavior in various ways. Submissive boys "have suffered repeated social rejection and shame" and tend to be withdrawn, anxious, depressed, lonely, and lacking in self-confidence and social skills. Dominant boys take the lead in playing, mediate conflicts, are verbally assertive, tend to be popular, and have high self-esteem. In one study of 9- to 11-year-olds, individuals who intervened to break up dyadic fights (often receiving some aggression themselves, while getting no assistance

---

[64] Tiger 1978, 17.
[65] Hartup 1983, who–kindergarten 150; Weisfeld 1994, true 51–53, 57; Smith 1989, 82–85, rigid 85.

from the person they helped) usually ranked high in the dominance hierarchy.[66]

The traits that contribute to dominance in boys vary across cultures. In the United States, what matters is "toughness, attractiveness, athletic ability, strength and early maturity." In adulthood, less physical traits such as pro-social skills, personality attributes, and wealth become more important. A study of US high schools found that "intelligence bears no significant relation to peer status," except among seniors at an academically elite high school. For Chinese adolescents of both genders, by contrast, the main correlates of high status were intelligence, academic success, and attractiveness, not athletic ability.[67]

Boys in groups are generally more competitive than girls. In one study, fourth- and sixth-grade boys spent 50 percent, but girls only 1 percent, of their time "engaged in direct competition." Large groups of boys played games far more than girls, and their games involved turn-taking far less often. Boys more often use legal debates to resolve disputes, and learn to play with their enemies and compete with their friends according to the rules. "[M]ost of the male intergroup competition is not aggressive," and elementary-age boys tend to discourage individual aggression when engaged in a competitive game between groups. For American boys, the most basic test is "boy-against-boy competition," especially in sports.[68]

Although boys typically dominate girls – in such areas as winning conflicts, greater access to prized objects, and responsiveness or compliance with demands – these cross-gender interactions less often follow a dominance system than do interactions within each gender. This reflects the less-frequent interactions of children across rather than within gender, and the fact that cross-gender interactions occur more often in adult-mediated settings (see pp. 233–40).

In young adolescents studied in camp settings, for both genders "ridicule was the most frequent dominance behavior." Physical aggression was more likely in boys than girls. Over five weeks, boys' dominance interactions decreased, as the hierarchy solidified, whereas girls' dominance hierarchies "fluctuated more on a day-to-day basis and from setting to setting." These patterns are consistent with the hypothesis that males function in hierarchies more easily than females do.[69]

!Kung children show classic dominance-submission behaviors: "When threatening, the child frowns, clenches his teeth, often exposing them at the same time, and stares at the opponent. Sometimes a hand with or without an implement is

[66] Maccoby 1998, issues 299; Weisfeld 1994, strikingly 57, shame 58; Smith 1989, study 85.
[67] Weisfeld 1994, toughness 55, study–Chinese 56.
[68] Maccoby 1998, engaged–aggressive 39; Gerzon 1982, test 160.
[69] Hartup 1983, 150.

raised... Such display can lead to the submission of one. Then the loser lowers his head, tilts it slightly, turns sideways, and pouts. This behavior strongly inhibits further aggression... [and] the aggressor quite often tries to comfort his victim, seeking friendly contact... Another aggression-inhibiting behavior is crying. Both submissive behaviors are found in all cultures I have visited."

!Kung children of both genders are often aggressive – hitting, kicking, biting, hair-pulling, and so forth – towards other children. Aggressive encounters result from quarrels about possession of objects, punishment by older children, demonstrations of power, and unprovoked spontaneous attacks. One 191-minute observation of a group of seven girls and two boys found 96 acts of hitting, 23 of kicking, 8 of throwing sand, and others – two-thirds of such acts being clearly nonplayful and ten of them causing a child to cry loudly.[70]

In adolescence, dominance hierarchies become more salient in many animal species. Dominant adolescent boys are popular with girls both in the United States and in China. Boys at adolescence, cross-culturally, increase the frequency of "[v]erbal repartee contests" which sometimes escalate. At a US summer camp, rank order stabilized within days and remained stable for the duration of several weeks. For both boys and girls, most "dominance contests were characterized by verbal ridicule," but boys' contests involved "more aggression and physical threats" than for girls. Some researchers describe intense dominance competitions between adolescent sons and their mothers, cross-culturally, with the sons generally emerging as dominant after mid-puberty. (Fathers remain dominant over sons, and both parents over daughters.)[71]

Managing conflict within groups

Formal rituals of status give the hierarchy "much in common with a moral contract," according to primatologist Frans de Waal. With a clear "pecking order," animals in a group need not tear each other to pieces and waste valuable energy fighting constantly over resources. Instead, they can establish an overall structure and fight occasionally in specific ways about position in that structure. Thus, the dominance system serves to channel and contain conflicts within the group. All of this increases the survival prospects of the group, albeit at the price of constant low-level conflict (as each level swats down the level below) and recurrent serious conflicts (as power shifts occur).[72]

---

[70] Eibl-Eibesfeldt 1974, 445–50, 455, visited 446.

[71] Weisfeld 1994, 54–55.

[72] De Waal 1996, 52, 97–105, contract 106–7, 245–46; Caspari 1978, pecking 99; Forsberg 1997a, 63; Eibl-Eibesfeldt 1979, 46–47.

Dominance systems use symbolic and scripted behaviors to acknowledge unequal status between two individuals. Dominance and submission gestures are often paired:

Dominance	*Submission*
Stare	Lower eyes, avert gaze, blink
Touch	"Cuddle" to the touch
Interrupt	Stop talking
Crowd another's space	Yield, move away
Frown, look stern	Smile
Point	Move in pointed direction, obey.[73]

To work effectively, the dominance hierarchy must be connected with means for limiting violence within the group. Four mechanisms accomplish the goal of limiting violence within a hierarchical group – programmed inhibitions on lethal violence, gestures of reconciliation to heal relationships weakened by conflicts, the development of cooperation through reciprocity, and shifting coalitions of individuals to check the absolute power of the highest-ranking individual. What is the role of gender, if any, in each of these mechanisms?

Inhibitions on violence   Within dominance–submission hierarchies, aggression is often expressed as ritualized, nonlethal fighting. This kind of fighting is most common in species with powerful weapons like teeth, claws, horns, venom, or the fighting shrimp's tail. The rules of engagement for intragroup fighting – apparently programmed into the brains of members of such species – strictly prohibit use of such weapons. The rules also specify particular *submission gestures* that immediately terminate an attack. For example, a wolf will roll onto its back and expose its soft underbelly. The matter is settled, no grudges. Until a loser submits formally with a recognized signal, the attack will continue. In chimpanzee power shifts (the overthrow of the former top male by a new one), "the critical moment is not the first victory for the challenger, but the first time he elicits submission." Figure 4.5 illustrates a common submission–dominance ritual in stump-tailed monkeys, the outstretched wrist receiving a mock bite (the proverbial "slap on the wrist").[74]

Such submission behaviors – the wolf lying on its back or macaque monkey offering its outstretched wrist – generally make the submissive individual vulnerable, and frequently invoke infantile or sexual patterns

[73] Nancy Henley in Archer and Lloyd 1985, 154.
[74] Lorenz 1963; Wilson 1975, 128; Eibl-Eibesfeldt 1979, 37, 91; de Waal 1996, moment 100.

Figure 4.5 Stump–tailed monkey dominance–submission ritual. [Photo courtesy of Frans de Waal (from de Waal 1989, 158).]

of behavior as part of the script. The wolf's rolling over, for example, exposes its genitals and evokes the behavior of pups. In some primate species, submissive males "present" and are symbolically mounted by dominant males. Stump-tailed macaques have ritualized this signal into a characteristic "bottom hold" by the dominant monkey towards the submissive one (see Figure 6.5, p. 360). These submissive behaviors evidently smooth intragroup conflict and reduce violence. Generally, male primates are more restrained in their aggression against females and youngsters than against other males. In fact, gorilla males sometimes pick up an infant and hold it while approaching a rival, thus rendering an attack less likely.[75]

Konrad Lorenz argued that humans lack these ritual methods of fighting and "turn-off signals" because they do not have lethal *natural* weapons. When humans invented weapons they were thus unable to keep aggression under control. However, many human cultures – especially those with frequent war – do have similar inhibitions. Cultures in which violence is more frequent are likely to develop ritualized channels for its expression. In a Yanomamö club fight (to cite an extremely violent culture), two men take turns exchanging hard blows to the head with clubs until one falls down. Despite their frequent participation in violence, Yanomamö men have strong norms about controlling it, and once expressed "qualms of conscience" after a raid where they killed some women – this in a war-prone and highly misogynistic culture. Similarly, soldiers in various wars have found themselves unable to kill enemy soldiers caught unawares while naked or in some other way vulnerable and humanized. This phenomenon – Walzer calls it the "naked soldier" syndrome – parallels animals' turn-off signals.[76]

By contrast, some relatively peaceful cultures seem to lack inhibitions on lethal violence, are less able to contain it when it occurs, and have a surprisingly high homicide rate. While aggression is relatively infrequent, incidents can easily escalate to lethal violence, in such societies as the Semai, !Kung, Gebusi (lowland New Guinea), and Copper Eskimo. Violence in these decentralized, egalitarian societies tends to be spasmodic, short-lived, and "compartmentalized" away from everyday life (as it was for the Semai of Malaysia mentioned earlier who became "drunk on blood" when colonial wars temporarily intruded on their peaceful life; see p. 29). Margaret Mead found a negative correlation between "experience in childhood with aggressive behavior" and social violence.[77]

These relatively peaceful societies which lack inhibitions on violence show "a general absence of male status hierarchy," in one cross-cultural study, making this "a distinctive class of societies." Yet violence when it occurs is still a male activity: "Lethal violence in all the societies under consideration is initiated almost exclusively by males," and often results from the escalation of "male disputes over women" in the absence of a male status hierarchy. Thus, in both human cultures and primates, inhibitions on violence are connected with status hierarchies. These systems

---

[75] Hinde 1983, 153; de Waal 1989, 211.
[76] Lorenz 1963; Eibl-Eibesfeldt 1979, qualms 191; Walzer 1977, naked 138–43.
[77] Knauft 1987, 461, 464, 476–77; Lee 1979, 381, 397; Fabbro 1978; Mead, in Eibl-Eibesfeldt 1979, 238.

to limit or contain violence develop most extensively in cultures or species with high levels of violence.[78]

Reconciliation   Reconciliation processes after conflicts form a second method (after scripted inhibitions) for limiting violence within groups. De Waal's comparison of rhesus monkeys, stump-tailed macaques, chimpanzees, and bonobos finds that, in all four species, reconciliation strategies for resolving conflicts come into play following aggressive violence. Individuals "seek contact with former adversaries." (Reconciliation requires the ability to distinguish and remember individuals within the group.) De Waal sees reconciliation, like aggression, as a "potential" or "psychological template" that we fill in through our interactions with those around us. Aggression and reconciliation thus go hand in hand within groups.[79]

Primate species vary in their reconciliation abilities. Stump-tailed monkeys show more developed conflict-resolution behaviors than do rhesus monkeys, and have a high-frequency but low-intensity pattern of aggression. Apes display more complex and "rational" interactions regarding aggression and reconciliation, with reconciliation strategies more highly developed, than do monkeys. Bonobos in particular show highly developed peacemaking behaviors.[80]

Contrary to difference feminism (see p. 47), primate reconciliation or "peacemaking" is not predominantly a female behavior. It is more frequent among males than females for both chimpanzees and rhesus monkeys. For example, in one chimpanzee colony, reconciliation occurred after 47 percent of conflicts among adult males but after only 18 percent of conflicts among adult females. In rhesus monkeys, like chimpanzees, "male–male and male–female fights were more often reconciled than fights among females." For stump-tailed monkeys, however, frequency of reconciliation shows no gender difference, and de Waal calls the question "as yet an unsolved puzzle."[81]

Inhibition and reconciliation signals specifically linked with sex can be enacted by animals of either gender. When male monkeys and apes symbolically "mount" each other after a conflict – with the winner in the male role – they are borrowing a script from male–female interaction. In species where males generally dominate females, "sex roles" (i.e., concerning sex itself) provide ready scripts for acting out power and dominance within a group of males (see pp. 356–61).

[78] Knauft 1987, 476, 477, 479.
[79] De Waal 1989, 242–43.
[80] De Waal 1989, 160, 163–64, 180, 220.
[81] De Waal 1989, colony 48, rhesus 119–25, stump 167, puzzle 48, 119, 167.

Reciprocity   Relationships within a group often develop into cooperation based on reciprocity. One individual performs "altruistic" acts for another unrelated individual, and the second later returns the favor. ("I'll scratch your back, and you scratch mine.") Tit-for-tat reciprocity has been found empirically in various disciplines from biology and anthropology to international relations. Many cultures with frequent warfare develop patterns of symbolic or limited war, often called *feuding*, that has some characteristics of using reciprocity to limit violence.[82]

This reciprocity fundamentally concerns equal parties, because it is based on acts freely undertaken rather than coerced. Reciprocity frequently operates, within the context of status hierarchies, among individuals of relatively comparable rank. Developmental psychologists distinguish hierarchical relationships from reciprocal ones as socialization domains, with reciprocity among "functional equals" but hierarchy among "individuals with unequal control or resources." Learning to use reciprocity is an important step in human children's social development. Piaget thought that only peer relationships, not the power-imbalanced relationships between children and adults, could enable the development of moral reasoning in the area of exchange processes between equal-status individuals. However, actually both adult–child and peer interactions contain a "mix between authority-oriented and more status-equal forms of reciprocity." (Among children, many interactions resemble symmetrical exchanges less than "currying favor from a status superior," and many children do what parents want for reasons other than rewards or punishments.)[83]

In many primate species, reciprocity plays an important role in developing cooperation among individuals of similar rank. In one experiment, a male and a female capuchin monkey were separated by a grid. First one and then the other had exclusive access to food. The monkeys shared by passing food through the grid, and the second monkey's extent of sharing was significantly affected by how much the first monkey had shared earlier. Among chimpanzees, individuals who have shared food with others in the past are more likely to receive food from the others in the future. So are individuals who have groomed the food possessor earlier that day. (Food actually changes hands in only half of the attempts.) However, patterns of reciprocity vary among primate species, and the voluntary food-sharing of the capuchin monkeys would be "unthinkable in most other primates." Anyway, reciprocity is not limited to male–male

---

[82] International: Axelrod 1984; Oye ed. 1986; Goldstein and Freeman 1990; feuding: Otterbein 1994, 133–45.

[83] Bugental and Goodnow 1998, equals 401; Piaget 1932; Maccoby and Martin 1983, 85, mix–currying 86, 12, 72.

interactions. It occurs in male–female and female–female relationships as well.[84]

In contexts where males predominate, including war, reciprocity may have a "masculine" quality. In most cultures, and especially contemporary American culture, reciprocity also takes on gendered characteristics because girls and boys tend to play in gender-segregated groups (see pp. 228–49). Among adults raised in such a culture, some gender differences in the use of reciprocity can be found. It is hard to know what biological basis these differences have, if any. In an experiment based on the Prisoner's Dilemma game – in which reciprocity is the key to mutual success in overcoming the dilemma – psychologists had college students play the game repeatedly (with cumulative scoring) against opponents whose identity and gender they did not know. Pairs of men were significantly more successful than pairs of women in eliciting mutual cooperation through reciprocity. In a different experiment, subjects could give each other electric shocks or turn on a blue light instead. After receiving a shock, subjects' blood pressures rose. Among men it dropped again only after retaliating with a shock, but among women it did not drop if they retaliated but only after cooperating (blue light). Overall, the evidence shows modest gender differences in the ability to use reciprocity to elicit mutual cooperation. However, in nonhuman primates the use of reciprocity does not seem to be limited by gender.[85]

Alliances   Does a "masculine style" of forming alliances – more fluid and shorter-lived – have biological roots? Alliance formation is very important to the maintenance of dominance hierarchies in most species. Very often, the dominant individual is not the strongest or most aggressive, but the one best at creating alliances. Alliances among several of the high-ranking individuals are important to the structure of the hierarchy and are crucial in the process of challenging the top position. Male chimpanzees, in particular, use shifting alliances to play "power games" within the dominance hierarchy.[86]

De Waal sees a deep – biologically based, in his view – gender difference in patterns of alliance and cooperation for humans and other primates. "Among males most cooperation seems of a transactional nature; they help one another on a tit-for-tat basis [reciprocity]. Females, in contrast, base their cooperation on kinship and personal preferences . . . The

[84] De Waal 1996, 135–61; Small 1993, 199, 215, 212; Maccoby 1998, 131–34.
[85] Rapoport and Chammah 1969, game 159; Holmes 1985, shocks 101; Ghiglieri 1999, 186–90.
[86] De Waal 1982, games 53; Haraway 1989, 148; Schubert 1991b, 42–44; Chapais 1991, 200; Cheney 1983c, 283, 278.

preferences of females and youngsters are stable, while those of adult males change over the years." Similar gender patterns in human children's friendships have been observed.[87]

The chimpanzees of Gombe – unlike those in captivity, but not necessarily the same as other African populations – show very stable, lasting alliances among adult brothers and between past and present alpha males (although most males are opportunistic). Among captive chimpanzees, females frequently intervene to bring about reconciliation between two males after a conflict, but at Gombe the females steer clear. Furthermore, gender patterns in alliance formation vary across primate species. For example, alliances of females (and juveniles) against males are common among macaques and vervets, but not baboons. In several primate species, the formation of coalitions plays an important role in mediating intragroup violence and reconciling individuals following a violent episode. Such a mediating role is played mainly by females in some, but not all, species (and human cultures). For example, among golden monkeys (langurs), males mediate conflicts among "their" females.[88]

To summarize, then, dominance hierarchies show some gender differences, though with many inconsistencies. The gender differences found empirically are generally in the directions posited by difference feminists, with men, more than women, being oriented to status hierarchies and relatively willing to switch alliance partners in the dynamic competition for rank. These changes taken together, however, are vague tendencies set against a great deal of diversity from one species or culture to another. They hardly add up to an adequate explanation for gendered war roles.

C. IN-GROUP/OUT-GROUP PSYCHOLOGY

Relations *between* groups draw upon different dynamics than those within groups. The various limits to violence within dominance hierarchies do not apply to intergroup relations. For example, on intergroup raids, chimpanzees continue to deliver fatal beatings to their victims – chimpanzees from neighboring groups – even when the latter use submission signals that would stop an intragroup attack in its tracks. Within a group, aggression aims to elicit submission; outside it, aggression aims to kill (or sometimes just to drive the target away). Intergroup violence may

---

[87] De Waal 1989, years 49–50, 55; de Waal 1996, 118, 193–98, 255; children: Chodorow 1978; Lever 1978; Gilligan 1982, 10–11; Hartup 1983, 156.

[88] Goodall, personal communication 1991, 1999; Goodall 1999, captive 144; Cheney 1983c, vervets 283; de Waal 1996, langurs 31–32; de Waal 1984; de Waal, personal communication 2000.

also enhance the cohesion of in-groups and help maintain their borders, although an enemy is not a necessary condition of group unity.[89]

In war, soldiers direct lethal violence towards members of the enemy group. Perhaps males are inherently more hostile towards outsiders, more able to demonize and dehumanize an enemy (for example, owing to a lack of empathy, or suppressed emotions generally), and hence more willing than females to kill members of their own species who belong to a different group. Perhaps for men the lines between in-group and out-group are drawn more sharply than for women, which might help explain gendered war roles. The evidence does not support this hypothesis, however.

Intergroup competition

Conflicts of interest often characterize separate groups within a species when their habitats abut or overlap, mainly because in times of scarcity they compete for the same food or water. Having a conflict does not mean that two groups will not resolve the conflict to mutual satisfaction, nor that they cannot achieve the benefits of cooperation, nor that their conflicts are intractable or permanent.[90]

Territoriality   The area of land that an animal (or group of animals) occupies is called its *home range*. Whatever part of its range an animal defends is its *territory*. Usually, however, the defense is only against members of its own species, while other animals pass through more freely. Patterns of territoriality differ from one species to another (and even within a species from one context to another, as with seasonal changes). Among species that are territorial, some define ranges and/or territories on an individual basis, others on a group basis, and still others on a group basis with individual subterritories. A single species, like rhesus monkeys in India, can show fierce territoriality (with well-defined and defended borders) in one context and loose overlapping home ranges with little violence in another context. Many animal species are not territorial; territoriality is "much less general" among mammals than birds, and is "spotty" among primates.[91]

The importance of territory varies according to context. Territorial conflicts between same-species groups mainly concern control of food

---

[89] Simmel 1955; Murphy 1957; Eibl-Eibesfeldt 1979, 229; Ehrenreich 1997a, 94, 197; Tajfel and Turner 1986; Brewer and Brown 1998; Pruitt 1998; Ridley 1997, 171–94.
[90] Van Hooff 1990, 37; Holloway ed. 1974; Goodall 1986, 527.
[91] Goodall 1986, 525; Lee 1983b, 231; Wilson 1975, 260–61, 50; Van Hooff 1990, India 37; Scott 1974, general 419, spotty 420; Montagu 1976, 231–57, 237; Hediger 1955, 17–19.

sources and other scarce natural resources (water, predator-safe sites, etc.). When animals hunt free-ranging food sources – as modern humans did with large mammals tens of thousands of years ago – fixed territories are relatively unimportant and borders tend to be fluid. When animals rely mainly on vegetation for food, or on any fixed-location natural resource – and this applies strongly to human societies since the invention of agriculture – territory becomes more important. Overlapping boundaries narrow down to small border zones, and animals are more likely to defend resources in their territory. Territoriality serves to stabilize the allocation of resources between groups, somewhat similarly to the function of hierarchies within groups.[92]

Chimpanzees both follow and diverge from "classical territoriality" in different ways. Among chimpanzees, groups expel strangers who wander into their home ranges (except they recruit some females). They monitor borders frequently, and ranges remain stable for years. Chimpanzees appear nervous in the peripheral areas but confident in the core area. When two groups meet at a border, they may make noise and put on aggressive displays, then retreat without conflict, a pattern found in classical territoriality. However, chimpanzees diverge from the classical model in several ways. Encounters between groups are decided by party size, not location. (A larger party will attack a smaller one even within the latter's territory.) Chimpanzee groups' home ranges overlap considerably, in contrast to most territorial species, and chimpanzees go out of their way to encounter members of other groups at the periphery of their range or even well into another group's home range. It is the variable party size that allows a sizable group of chimpanzees to attack and kill individuals found alone or in a small group. The classical behavior of nonviolently driving away others by using loud aggressive displays is reserved, among chimpanzees, for encounters by groups of roughly equal size. When group size differs in an encounter (especially when a group encounters an individual), the resulting power inequality provides the opportunity for lethal violence to ensue – a pattern also found in hyenas and lions. Jane Goodall concludes that chimpanzees should be considered territorial, but in a more aggressive form that contrasts with the "relatively peaceful, ritualized maintenance of territory" typical of most territorial species. For chimpanzees, territorial behaviors include not only expelling intruders but killing them, not only defending a home range but enlarging it by killing off neighbors, and not only protecting the group's females but recruiting new ones aggressively from other groups.[93]

---

[92] Van Der Dennen and Falger eds. 1990, 10; Eibl-Eibesfeldt 1979, 41.
[93] Goodall 1986, 526–28.

Chimpanzee forms of territoriality are rather strongly gendered. Male chimpanzees will attack and even kill other males near territorial boundaries. Older females with dependent offspring are just as vulnerable as single males. In one attack witnessed by Goodall, several adult males surrounded a mother, rebuffed her submission behaviors, then attacked her and killed her infant. By contrast, "adolescent and young adult females are allowed to move across territorial borders, especially when they are in a sexually attractive state." (Recall the Taï females mentioned earlier who crossed battle lines during an intergroup encounter.)[94]

Bonobos are less territorial than chimpanzees. Bonobo groups apparently do engage in violent attacks, but not much is known about them. Wrangham and Peterson attribute the bonobos' relative peacefulness to the lower variation in group size as compared to chimpanzees. They argue that because bonobos do not share their habitat with gorillas, food is more plentiful and thus larger groups can travel together. By contrast, chimpanzees must roam further in search of food, requiring groups to split up into small parties and individuals, which are then vulnerable. Wrangham argues that early humans resembled chimpanzees and not bonobos in having variable party size, and that this explains why human and chimpanzee males are violence-prone ("demonic").[95]

Wrangham's argument regarding humans is problematical, although party size might well explain why bonobos have less violent intergroup conflict than chimpanzees do. For early humans, as anthropologist Robert Carneiro argues, territoriality probably varied from one situation to another, as it does for modern hunters – being less important when humans hunt migratory game animals than when they rely on stationary food resources. Early humans, whose habitats varied from region to region, "may at times have been territorial and at other times not." Furthermore, even among contemporary hunting societies that do recognize territories, violent conflicts rarely arise from trespassing. Only after agriculture did warfare over *territory* become common. Also, the emergence of modern humans 100,000 years ago – highly social, hunting in cooperative groups, and relying more than before on mobile game animals – would have marked a shift away from the chimpanzee pattern of aggressive territoriality.[96]

Territorial behaviors in primates often include gender-specific roles, though these differ across species. Among vervet monkeys, territorial boundaries sometimes are exclusive and sometimes overlap. In the latter case, when a troop approaches the edge of its home range, high-ranking

[94] De Waal 1989, infant 72, attractive 71.

[95] Wrangham and Peterson 1996, 167–70; Wilson 1975, 132–38.

[96] Carneiro 1994, times 12; Wilson 1975, 564–65; Van Der Dennen 1990a, 159; Hopp and Rasa 1990, 133; Eibl-Eibesfeldt 1979, 182–87.

males move ahead and chase away individual trespassers. When another entire troop is encountered, males and females together form a long line and make threatening gestures, with one or more males foraying occasionally into the opposite line. Females cluster around these males after the forays and groom them intensively (and may even chase nonparticipating males).[97]

The gender patterns in intergroup attacks among chimpanzees fit what we might expect from the overlapping bell-curves of size and strength discussed in chapter 3 (see pp. 159–62). A typical raiding (or hunting) party might include suitable females – say, five males and one female. As I showed earlier (see pp. 14, 60–70), such a composition for human military forces is found in those exceedingly rare cases where women in substantial numbers have participated in combat, such as the early nomadic steppes horse-raiders. Gendered territoriality among primates, then, does not explain the puzzle of why human war is nearly universally fought by males.

Hunting and war   The difference between violent social behaviors within a group and those between groups seems to reflect the operation of *predatory* dynamics in the latter case, rather than (or perhaps in addition to) the *dominance* dynamics found within groups. The treatment of out-groups as if they were a separate species has been called "pseudospeciation." Different behaviors towards an individual are appropriate for wanting to eat it, rather than for just competing with it over resources.[98]

War and hunting have some connection. In a cross-cultural sample of gathering-hunting societies, those that depend primarily on hunting have more warfare. Hunting provides weapons suitable for war (spears, bows and arrows, slings, knives, and clubs), involves searching and killing by coordinated quasi-military groups, extends a group's geographic range (and thus contact with neighboring groups), and in some cases leads to the use of horses (extending range further).[99]

Hunting "scripts" may serve as pathways for intergroup violence to bypass dominance inhibitions. In chimpanzee raids, according to Goodall, the "victims are treated more as though they were prey animals." Rather than loudly advertising their presence as a form of aggressive display (as chimpanzee groups of equal size do), raiders move quickly and quietly to surprise a vulnerable individual. They coordinate their attack, with one chimpanzee holding the victim down while others hit, kick, and bite it.

[97] Whitten 1984, vervet 132.
[98] Van Der Dennen 1990a, 182; Eibl-Eibesfeldt 1979, 168–69, 96; Ehrenreich 1997a, 135.
[99] Otterbein and Otterbein 1997.

These attacks continue for 10–20 minutes despite the complete passivity of the victim, until the victim is not just wounded but incapacitated (typically dying within days or weeks). Experienced observers believe that the attackers' intent was to kill their victim. These behaviors resemble what chimpanzees do when hunting large prey such as an adult monkey, which must be immobilized before being eaten.[100]

In war, enemies are often "dehumanized" and are frequently referred to by specific animal names (pseudospeciation). An extensive US propaganda campaign during World War II, for example, portrayed the Japanese as apes. Ironically, some US *anti-war* activists in the 1960s called police "pigs." The Mundurucú of Brazil defined their own group as "people" and saw enemies (meaning any non-Mundurucú group) as "game to be hunted" – using vocabulary reserved for game animals.[101]

One controversial rendition of the hunting–war connection is Desmond Morris's evolutionary argument that warfare arose out of (male) hunting specifically. This theory does not have much support. Male long-distance hunting probably emerged late in the evolutionary process. At first, meat may have come more often from scavenging animals killed by large predators. Later, humans obtained meat in large quantities by encircling herds or driving them off cliffs, before the consequent depopulation of animals led them to begin tracking down individual animals. The entire human group, not just a select party of hunters, would be close at hand for these mass kills. The large quantity of meat could not easily be moved over long distances. Even in long-distance hunting, although nursing mothers may have been ill-suited, mothers of older children could have left them with elders while hunting.[102]

The main problem with the idea that hunting shaped gendered war roles is that hunting is not very gendered (as a biologically based script). Females participate in the mostly male hunting groups among the Taï chimpanzees, for example, although unlike males they do not *have to* participate to share in the meat afterwards. Females made up 15 percent of the Taï hunters and, when present, made 18 percent of the kills in the Taï forest, 23 percent in Gombe, and 29 percent at Mahale (Tanzania). Furthermore, although chimpanzees (especially males) sometimes

[100] Goodall 1986, 529, prey 532; Goodall 1999, 131; de Waal 1989, 71; Wrangham and Peterson 1996, 219; Zihlman and Tanner 1978, 182; Eibl-Eibesfeldt 1979, 171, 74; Huntingford 1976; Sagan and Druyan 1992, 190, 196.

[101] Goodall 1999, 129–34; Keen 1986; Rieber ed. 1991; Zur 1987; Murphy 1957, game 1028; Dower 1986, Japanese.

[102] Morris 1967; Dart 1953; Foley 1995, 44, 191; Keegan 1993, 102; Ehrenreich 1997a, 39, 118–19, 124; Van Der Dennen 1990a, 160–62; Tiger and Fox 1971, 213; de Waal 1996, 138–41; Van Hooff 1990, 32; Mies 1986, 58–62; Taylor 1996, elders 27.

cooperate to hunt, they sometimes hunt alone, and meat sharing is inconsistent.[103]

Chimpanzees do not rely on hunting much anyway. It occupies only about one-tenth of their feeding time, and Gombe chimpanzees eat only about one-tenth as much meat as do !Kung gatherer-hunters. Other apes, including bonobos, do not hunt. All of this stands in sharp contrast to the idea of a deeply biological, and deeply gendered, tendency for males to hunt over distances in segregated groups in order to bring home meat to share with the larger group. Thus, the specific connection of war with hunting does little to explain the puzzle of gendered war roles, though it may explain other things about war.[104]

Intergroup hostility

Although hunting and territorial competition for resources do little to explain gendered war roles, psychological processes might make men more hostile to members of other groups than women are. Across cultures, people show a tendency to form a social identity around an in-group and subsequently display both cognitive and emotional biases with regard to in-group versus out-group individuals. These psychological mechanisms shape our world view, according to the group we belong to, and ultimately manifest themselves as hostility to outsiders and loyalty to insiders. In today's world, these group identity processes are central to both nationalism and "ethnic conflicts" (which are not all ethnic, but involve divisions along some identity markers such as ethnicity, religion, or language).

Are these group identity processes gendered, making men particularly hostile towards (or afraid of) outsiders? Could women have carried out the mass murders of out-group members that men carried out in Bosnia, Rwanda, Chechnya, and Kosovo in the past decade, or the brutal !Kung raid described earlier (see p. 28)?

Xenophobia   Goodall proposes that chimpanzees "have an inherent aversion to strangers." This is her explanation of the puzzle of recurring attacks on "outside" females by chimpanzees. Although the females' infants are often eaten, Goodall finds the attacks to be poorly explained by infanticide as a reproductive strategy (as in gorillas), because the attacked females were not recruited into the group. Rather, the victims are simply unlucky enough to be found in a border zone where the attacking chimpanzees are already nervous (about encountering out-group males) and poised to attack weak or isolated individuals (Goodall

---

[103] Boesch and Boesch 1989, 560–69.
[104] Knauft 1991, 394.

refers to a "heightened level of arousal" which makes the aggression more fierce). Goodall specifically argues that an inherent aversion to strangers is a preadaptation that disposes humans to engage in war.[105]

Hostility to outsiders is common in many human cultures. Even among the peaceful Greenland Eskimos, until recent times a stranger who crossed into another community and could not establish kinship ties risked being killed. Eibl-Eibesfeldt finds "[f]ear and rejection of strangers" in "all cultures." Infants' reactions to strangers changes from smiling at 3 months to freezing and crying at 9 months – an "inborn program" in humans.[106]

Fear of "outsiders" would be more accurate than "strangers," since both chimpanzee and human attackers (as in Bosnia) sometimes know their victims well, having even grown up together as friends. As Goodall notes, "group identity" among chimpanzees is "far more sophisticated than mere xenophobia" but is based on differentiating "individuals who 'belong' and those who do not."[107]

For several reasons, out-group dynamics do not seem innately gendered. Donald Horowitz's conception of ethnicity gives central place to a shared myth of common ancestry – members act as if they were "family." This suggests that gender is not very central to ethnic identity, since we do not treat some families as male and others as female. Barbara Ehrenreich argues that the original prehistoric threat underlying the "defensive solidarity" of human groups – and ultimately fueling modern nationalism – was predators. Human infants very commonly develop fear of monsters as they become toddlers. Predators such as hyenas, wolves, and large cats that "are circumspect when a human adult is around would happily attack a toddler... When the child begins to amble off on its own, it helps for it to know... that there are monsters out there." Attachment behaviors (mentioned earlier) manifest at this age, with children venturing out incrementally from adult attachment figures. Clearly, these basic programs rooted in fear of predators, which probably inflame intergroup hostility including war, are not strongly gendered.[108]

Although xenophobia, like hunting, probably figures in war, little evidence suggests that men are more hostile to outsiders than women are. In the Bosnia war, Serbian women sat down in roads to prevent UN convoys from delivering humanitarian supplies to starving Muslims. Admittedly, the women were orchestrated by male warlords and stirred up

[105] Goodall 1986, 523, 531.
[106] Nuttall 1992, risked 101; Eibl-Eibesfeldt 1979, 104–6.
[107] Goodall 1986, identity 532.
[108] Horowitz 1985; Ehrenreich 1997a, 94; Sagan and Druyan 1992, amble 233.

by male-generated propaganda, but they felt genuine hatred for their enemies. As I noted earlier (see pp. 113–15), in cultures like the Dahomey
and the Apaches, women specialize in torturing and killing prisoners.
German women ran some concentration camps during World War II,
with extreme cruelty. Furthermore, when crowds are whipped up into
hysterical animosity towards outsiders – at Nazi rallies, for example –
women participate and appear to feel the same surge of emotion as do
the men. "[W]omen nearly as strongly as men supported the Nazis during
the years of their spectacular rise to power between 1930 and 1932."[109]

Another reason to suspect that group identities are not strongly gendered is that those identities appear remarkably flexible. (I am blurring
social psychologists' distinction between social identity – a property of the
individual – and group identity.) These identities can be manipulated, as
politicians frequently do, and as psychologists did in one classic experiment at a boys' summer camp. Psychologists have found no "minimum
criterion" for the emergence of in-group and out-group biases in experimental simulations. Even an arbitrary criterion for group formation, such
as a person's preference for circles versus triangles, can trigger in-group
biases in both groups. Psychologists have identified several consistent biases that accompany group membership, but gender plays little role in
them.[110]

Women's suspect loyalties   One line of argument explains the
gendering of war by the divided loyalties of women in intergroup conflicts.
In the majority of cultures, women move to another community and men
stay put (patrilocality). In the event of war between the two communities, women might have mixed loyalties – to their current husbands and to
their birth families. Suspicions about women's loyalties could explain why
many cultures exclude them from war-fighting, planning and access to
weapons. (Similarly, the predominantly male composition of chimpanzee
intergroup raiders has been attributed to the fact that males breed in their
natal groups whereas females move to breed with neighboring communities.) An alternative way to resolve the dilemma is to draw marriage
partners from within one's own community (endogamy). This has the dis-
advantage, however, of leaving marriage partners in communities where
premarital sexual liaisons may create ambiguities in relationships, instead
of cleaning the slate.[111]

---

[109] Koonz 1987, Nazis 4–6.
[110] Sherif and Sherif 1953; Eibl-Eibesfeldt 1979, 82–83; Tajfel and Turner 1986.
[111] Adams 1983, 7, 198–203, 207–10; Meggitt 1977, exclude 98; Manson and Wrangham
1991, chimpanzee 372–74; cf. vervets: Cheney 1983b, 246–47.

This theory predicts that matrilocal societies, in which men switch communities while women stay put, should allow women more access to war. The prediction holds up as a statistical generalization across cultures, although not all cases fit. In a sample of 67 prestate cultures, women participated at least occasionally as warriors in 9 of them, all of them among the 33 cultures characterized by either exclusively external war or exclusive community endogamy. In all 9 cases – mostly North American Indians – women comprise a small minority of warriors and even those are generally treated as unusual. For example, Navaho war parties never had more than two women, Delaware women "seldom" fought, Fox women warriors were unusual, and Comanche women just sometimes sniped from the fringes.[112]

Cultures with at least some "internal" warfare (i.e., where communities fight neighbors who speak the same language) generally have patrilocal marriage patterns in which the bride goes to live with the husband's family. By contrast, cultures with only "external" war (i.e., where communities fight more distant groups not sharing the same language) usually have matrilocal marriage. The patrilocal marriage system, by keeping the men together in kin groups (fathers and brothers stay together), strengthens communities that frequently fight their neighbors. By contrast, matrilocal marriages break up such ties and thus promote unity across neighboring communities, and this is functional when they together face an external threat. Polygyny (multiple wives) occurs most in societies with high male mortality in warfare. Cultures with infrequent war usually lack strict marriage residency rules. (Some cultures are bilocal; either marriage partner may move in with the other). Causality may thus run from war to marriage type, as much as vice versa.[113]

The majority of communities have internal war, and the majority are patrilocal, but as Table 4.1 shows, all combinations of war and marriage occur in at least a few cultures. Cultures with frequent internal war, patrilocal residence, and at least some exogamy – the ones where women's loyalties could explain gendered war roles – are the largest single category but make up fewer than a third of the 115 cultures in the sample. The big problem with women's loyalties as an explanation of gendered war roles is that it does not explain the rareness of women warriors in the other two-thirds of the cultures, where marriage patterns vary.

I wonder anyway about the assumption that women's loyalties are inherently suspect. In the Dahomey Kingdom, women captured from neighboring societies went on in many cases to serve loyally in Dahomey's

---

[112] Adams 1983, 200–2.

[113] Ember and Ember 1971; polygyny: Ember 1974; Ember 1985; infrequent–causality: Adams 1983, 202–3.

Table 4.1 *Cross-cultural relationship of marriage and war in 115 societies*

Numbers in parentheses indicate cultures practicing only exogamy – marriages from other communities – and only endogamy, respectively. The remainder practice mixed exogamy and endogamy.

| | — Marriage Pattern (Exogamy; Endogamy) — | | | |
	Patrilocal	Matrilocal	Bilocal/other	Total
War pattern:				
Some internal war	44 (19; 9)	5 (1; 4)	9 (1; 4)	58
External war exclusively	8 (2; 1)	14 (2; 7)	3 (0; 1)	25
Infrequent war	15 (9; 2)	5 (1; 4)	12 (1; 3)	32
Total	67	24	24	115

Data source: Adams 1983: 199–200, 203.

own army, even sometimes refusing to return home when given a chance (see pp. 60–64). Similarly, for boys, when Mundurucú warriors beheaded the adult men and women of an enemy village and captured the children, some of the captured boys went on to take part in Mundurucú war parties, even against their own native group, with no reported defections. And men themselves are not entirely exempt from conflicts of loyalties when marriages cross what become battle lines. For example, the patrilineal Kapauku of highlands New Guinea often married spouses of traditional enemy confederacies, and thus "'in-law' relatives, blood relatives, and friends met on the battlefield as enemies. To avoid killing one's own [relatives and friends] one fought on the other end of the battlefield" from them.[114]

Large groups   In small communities, such as chimpanzee societies or boys' camps, each member is known individually to each other member, interacting face-to-face. Wars, however, often involve larger groups, in which members identify with a group whose size precludes knowledge of most of its individual members. Benedict Anderson, for example, calls nations "imagined communities," constructed by members who do not know each other yet share a story about their nation. Large groups, up to and including nations, seem to evoke the loyalties and enmities characteristic of small communities.[115]

National or ethnic identity sometimes appears to compete with gender identity, as when women feel pressure to subordinate their feminism to a national liberation struggle or ethnic rights movement. Anthony Smith

[114] Murphy 1957, 1,025; Pospisil 1994, end 122.
[115] Anderson 1983.

argues that "gender identity, which spans the globe, is inevitably more attenuated ... than other kinds of collective identity in the modern world. Geographically separated, divided by class and ethnically fragmented, gender cleavages must ally themselves to other, more cohesive identities if they are to inspire collective consciousness and action."[116]

In sum, little evidence shows that gender influences the formation of group loyalties. Both males and females express group identities similarly. Although intergroup dynamics play key roles in war, they draw on biological potentials – such as hunting, xenophobia, and attachment – that are largely independent of gender.

D. CHILDHOOD GENDER SEGREGATION

Thus far, chapters 3 and 4 have found several biologically rooted tendencies that would favor men over women as warriors. None of them, however, shows the kind of categorical differences (as opposed to average differences or divergent tendencies) that could adequately explain the pervasiveness of gendered war roles. If, however, biology favored gender *segregation*, with separate male and female groups, then this could more adequately explain all-male warrior groups. If fighting were to be done either by men only or by women only, then plausibly every culture would choose men, given the average gender differences discussed above. (Furthermore, if genders naturally segregated, then members of both genders would plausibly experience their own and the opposite gender as their first, prototypical, in- and out-groups.)

Developmental psychologist Eleanor Maccoby makes a well-grounded, detailed case that children grow up in largely separate gendered peer cultures – in boys' and girls' group activities – which have different styles and norms of behavior. Gender segregation is found across different cultures, and is "fairly resistant to change" since intervention effects are temporary. These findings support the possibility that the genders segregate naturally. Gender segregation is not absolute or "monolithic," however, and considerable variation is found across settings and through time. Sociologist Barrie Thorne treats the same topics somewhat differently – more focused on US elementary schools (where she spent many days observing), more attuned to variations in patterns that Maccoby treats as categorical, and more optimistic about potentials for change. The evidence is most convincing where Maccoby and Thorne agree.[117]

On the individual level of analysis, Maccoby argues, boys and girls show relatively minor differences (compared to within-gender variation), not only on such characteristics as IQ, achievement, and personality traits,

---

[116] Smith 1991, action 4, 143; Eagly and Kite 1987, 459–60; Noakes 1998, 6, 16.
[117] Maccoby 1998, 5, 27–29.

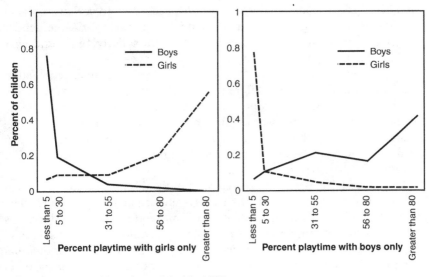

Data source: Maccoby and Jacklin 1987.

Figure 4.6 Maccoby's group-level gender distributions, age 6½. [From Maccoby 1998, 81.]

but even on measures of "masculinity" and "femininity." By contrast, on the group level, boys' and girls' peer groups differ from each other much more than do the individuals considered separately. "The gendered aspect of an individual's behavior is brought into play by the gender of others." The typical overlapping bell-curves of individual gender difference contrast with the very different curves for gender preference in playmates for US first-graders (see Figure 4.6). "By far the most common score for cross-sex play was 0 percent of time."[118]

Extent of gender segregation

Gender segregation in children's peer interaction "appears to be virtually universal in Western and non-Western societies . . . although the extent varies." Even young monkeys and apes "show gender segregation in play." For humans, segregation tends to be more pronounced in cultures with great gender inequality (i.e., male dominance).[119]

Early childhood Children under 2 years old show little gender preference in choosing or interacting with playmates. Thereafter, a preference for same-gender playmates develops in both girls (around age 3)

[118] Maccoby 1998, others 9, time 79; Maccoby 1990.
[119] Ruble and Martin 1998, varies 961; inequality: Hartup 1983, 109; Whiting and Edwards 1988; Maccoby 1998, 28, 79, apes 99.

and boys (more gradually, by ages 4 or 5), according to various research studies. Boys and girls show a substantial preference for same-gender playmates, increasing through early childhood, solidifying around ages 5–8, and peaking in middle childhood around ages 8–11.[120]

Already at preschool age, a "substantial degree" of gender segregation has been found in "many different cultural settings" as well as showing "remarkably consistent results" across a variety of psychology studies. In ten "small societies" worldwide, children choose same-gender playmates (excluding sibling play) about two-thirds of the time by ages 3–6 and three-quarters by ages 6–10 – similar proportions to those found in middle-class American children.[121]

In one US lab experiment, paired 33-month-olds interacted more when placed in same-gender pairs than cross-gender pairs, even though they were dressed in "gender-neutral clothes" and did not know each other's names. Although boys and girls directed equal amounts of social behavior to their partners overall (which is what "sociability" as an individual attribute measures), these interactions were with other-gender partners only about half to two-thirds as often as with same-gender partners.[122]

Gender differentiation occurs primarily in settings that bring together multiple children of similar age, especially with minimal adult structuring of interactions – such as a school playground at recess – and it first develops at the preschool age when parallel play gives way to extended sequences of interactions between children. Children code each other by gender, and react accordingly, whether or not they have met before.[123]

Middle childhood   By middle childhood (elementary school years), "patterns of gender segregation become more firmly entrenched . . . but only in certain settings." In non-Western, nonindustrialized societies, gender segregation is reinforced by the assignment of girls and boys to different tasks, such as herding and child care, which place them in same-gender groupings. In Western contexts, such as US elementary schools, adults more often create gender-integrated social structures (e.g., in classroom seating), so same-gender preferences emerge mostly in contexts not structured by adults (e.g., corridors, playgrounds). The period of middle childhood deserves particular attention as the time when gender segregation solidifies. The elementary school years are "a defining experience" that shapes adolescence and beyond, especially in terms

---

[120] Maccoby 1998, solidifying 169, 18–19, peaking 27–29.
[121] Maccoby 1998, results 21; small: Whiting and Edwards 1988.
[122] Jacklin and Maccoby 1978; Maccoby 1998, 10.
[123] Maccoby 1998, 20–24, 27.

of self-esteem, abstract thinking, self-regulation, and social skills. During middle childhood, pretend play decreases, becoming "almost absent" from interactions with playmates by early adolescence. Rough-and-tumble play also decreases, slowly, and verbal aggression increasingly replaces physical aggression. Children are more concerned with their acceptance in the peer group (including their position in a hierarchy of popularity), and gossip rises with age.[124]

The largest groups, which emerge in middle childhood, are "cliques" of three to nine members, "almost always" of the same gender and race. Cliques have been studied only in children over 10 years old. By age 11, "children report that most of their peer interactions" occur in cliques, and "nearly all children report being a member of one." In one study of cliques in four classrooms (fourth to sixth grades), "not one crossed the line of gender."[125]

Segregation tends to be geographical. The genders claim separate customary play areas, with boys in the "larger, more central spaces." In school lunchrooms, children "usually" establish girls' and boys' tables, and sit next to someone of the other gender only in "very few instances." In one lunchroom, "when the two second-grade tables were filling, a high-status boy walked by the inside table, which had a scattering of both girls and boys. He said loudly, 'Oooo, too many girls,' and headed for a seat at the other, nearly empty, table. The boys at the inside table picked up their trays and moved to join him. After they left, no other boy sat at that table."[126]

Segregation not absolute   Play in mixed-gender dyads and groups does occur in middle childhood, however. In one study of first-graders, about one-quarter (boys) to one-third (girls) of "affiliative activity" was directed to opposite-gender peers. Maccoby reports the ratio of same-gender with *opposite*-gender play (age $6^1/_2$) as 11 to 1, but this omits *mixed*-gender groups (those with at least two boys and two girls), which make up about one-quarter of social play. In a 1993 study, fourth- and sixth-graders during lunch and recess spent 64 percent of time with same-gender groups, 27 percent with mixed-gender groups, and 1 percent with one or more members of the opposite gender and no other members of their own gender. With children spending one-quarter of their unstructured time in mixed-gender groups, the segregation may not be as "overwhelming" as Maccoby claims. However, even mixed-gender

[124] Maccoby 1998, settings–herding 23–24; Hamburg 1992, defining 171, 178–79, 24–25; Rubin, Bukowski, and Parker 1998, absent 639.
[125] Rubin, Bukowski, and Parker 1998, cliques 641, member 642; Thorne 1993, line 47.
[126] Maccoby 1998, central 25, instances 24; Thorne 1993, 33, many 43.

interactions often reinforce gender boundaries, as when boys and girls play on opposite teams, or chase each other. The strong tendency towards segregation, across cultures, is real and important, even "strongly dimorphic," but perhaps not quite "close to being a binary matter." The effect is strong nonetheless – exclusive association within gender two-thirds of the time.[127]

Some specific games seem to be coded as gender-integrated in US playground culture today. In dodgeball and similar games, US school children consistently play in mixed-gender groups. Thorne gives a list of five games: "Girls and boys most often played together in games of kickball, foursquare, dodgeball, handball, and chasing or tag." (Foursquare, chasing and tag, however, usually have two opposing single-gender groups, and thus are not very integrated.) Thorne suggests ease of entry and of play in these games as promoting gender integration. A person joins by entering a line or standing in a group, and no specialized skills or equipment are needed. But a geopolitical explanation seems even more salient: the concrete or asphalt surface where these games take place constitutes an ambiguous intermediate zone between girls' space close to the school buildings and boys' space "out there" in the fields. Games of chase and tag share this quality, being played in the intermediate space between, say, jump-rope and football.[128]

Individual girls with "exceptional athletic skills" can "join otherwise all-male groups," and a high-status boy can occasionally cross into girls' groups without taking abuse from his fellow boys. One class's "unofficial king" – "tall, blonde, athletic, verbally skilled, widely respected, the leader of the largest clique" – could violate gender taboos, such as by participating in dancing or by playing on a girls' team against the boys (to equalize the team sizes), "without being stigmatized," because of his "unquestioned masculinity." By contrast, a fourth-grade boy without such status, who "routinely tried to enter girls' activities as a serious participant" (not a disrupter), did so "essentially as a loner," perhaps labeled by peers as a deviant.[129]

Gender segregation appears stronger at the dyadic level than the group level. Cross-gender *dyads* are especially rare. Such integration as occurs takes place in groups of four or more children. Furthermore, in French-Canadian nursery schools in the 1970s, small groups usually had a "strong focal pair" at the core, which was nearly always same-gender, even when the more marginal group members included both genders. In unstructured play at school during middle childhood – the phase and

[127] Maccoby 1998, affiliative 19, ratio 22, 24, 318, dimorphic 82, binary 80, 293.
[128] Thorne 1993, 34, 44–45, 54–55, 133, 123–24; Maccoby 1998, 25.
[129] Maccoby 1998, skills 65–66; Thorne 1993, cross–king 122–23, 126.

setting of greatest gender segregation – the near-absence of mixed-gender dyads and triads is striking. Children's shunning of these groupings is the core of gender segregation.[130]

Yet when children "of different ages" were asked to name their best friends, about one-quarter included opposite-gender friends. When another study asked older elementary students to name their one "best friend," 23 percent named a cross-gender friend. Another study asked sixth-graders their "close friends" – they named a median of three – and a somewhat smaller minority (18 percent of girls, 9 percent of boys) included anyone of opposite gender. (Maccoby finds even fewer, saying that in middle childhood, "best friends" are "almost exclusively" of the same gender.) Overall, gender seems to be an important influence on choice of friends, though not definitive. Cross-gender friendships may go underground in certain public spaces, especially school. Thorne recalls: "After Jack walked by without even glancing at her, Melanie whispered to me, 'He's one of my best friends . . . [W]e're friends in our neighborhood and at church, but at school we pretend not to know each other so we won't get teased.'"[131]

Even in US elementary schools, "gender separation is rarely total." The study of gendered propensity for same-gender play may suffer from the "tyranny of averages" mentioned in chapter 3 (characterizing individuals by group tendencies; see p. 134). Researchers have paid less attention to mixed-gender groups than same-gender ones, and the two types of interaction have been studied almost entirely in dyads and occasionally triads. Yet by middle childhood most of the cross-gender contact occurs in larger groups, not dyads.[132]

Thus, gender segregation is not absolute. It is strongest in one developmental phase, middle childhood, and even then only in certain settings. Although peers account for 30 percent of social interactions in middle childhood, compared with 10 percent in 2-year-olds, this still leaves 70 percent of interactions that are with siblings, parents, and adults – contexts where gender segregation is far less salient. Of the three "major sites" of contemporary childhood – families, neighborhoods, and schools – schools have by far the least mixing of girls and boys. Since 90 percent of research on children occurs in schools (owing to ease of access), the psychology literature may overemphasize gender segregation.[133]

130 Maccoby 1998, focal 21; Benenson, Apostoleris, and Parnass 1997; Joyce Benenson, personal communication 1999; Hartup 1983, 110, 156; Maccoby 1998, 96, 33; Eleanor Maccoby, personal communication 1999.

131 Thorne 1993, 46, 183, teased 50; Maccoby 1998, 24.

132 Thorne 1993, total 49, tyranny 57–58; Eagly and Chaiken 1998, 281–83; Joyce Benenson, personal communication 1999; triads: Hartup 1983, 156; Maccoby 1998, 95.

133 Rubin, Bukowski, and Parker 1998, 638; Thorne 1993, sites 29, research 46.

Causes and effects of segregation

The fact that gender segregation occurs widely in various cultures does not necessarily imply a biological basis. Maccoby attributes segregation to a combination of biological, socialization, and (less importantly) cognitive-identity components. The biological aspects consist largely in average gender differences (with individual variation) – boys' greater tendency towards rough-and-tumble play, towards using physical aggression, and towards status competitions. These create divergent play styles for boys' and girls' peer groups, so that a child (increasingly through middle childhood) finds himself or herself on unfamiliar ground in the other gender's space. Girls' wariness about being hurt or victimized in boys' rough play, in particular, leads to a "progressive distancing" of the genders. The opposite gender becomes "somewhat alien."[134]

Other potential biological factors do not find empirical support. Boys do not have much "more energy" or a higher "activity level" overall, and the modest differences may reflect, rather than cause, boys' play styles. Nor does evidence show boys to be more excitable or arousable in general. Although girls lead boys in language development, and in learning to inhibit impermissible behavior, they do not mature more quickly overall.[135]

Play styles   In children's gender-segregated groups, "patterns of interaction seen in male and female playgroups" do not differ as starkly as the gender composition of playgroups does. But some consistent differences do emerge. Several particular behaviors are "quite highly differentiated": "[r]ough-and-tumble play, direct aggression, and the themes enacted in pretend play and story-telling." By contrast, "discourse styles . . . are not so robustly different."[136]

Play themes revolve around aggression more for boys than girls, and boys often assume "the role of a heroic character" and act out fantasies with themes of "danger and righteous combat." Appropriate props or costumes will be used but in their absence "children improvise." A 4- to 8-year-old boy "playing alone will also enact heroic or warlike themes by himself," which implies that the script does not depend on the all-boy peer group setting, although it may have been learned or practiced there. Girls' pretend play centers on "cooperative role-taking" around "domestic or school themes." Girls frequently enact family scenes, taking on either

[134] Maccoby 1998, 103–11, 293, 161, 170, 175, distancing–alien 61, 62–64; Ruble and Martin 1998, 943–61, 984–95; Rubin, Bukowski, and Parker 1998, 682.
[135] Maccoby 1998, 100–2.
[136] Maccoby 1998, 80.

the mother or father (the boys seldom play either role). These scenarios revolve around "preparation and serving of food" and, in mother–child roles, other nurturing activities such as feeding baby, putting on Band-Aids, rocking to sleep, or soothing a hurt child.[137]

Enforcement   Gender segregation appears to be reinforced at three levels. First, it is self-reinforcing, both by individual preference and by peer socialization. Maccoby sees girls' dislike of boys' rough play style as a main cause of segregation. She refers to this dislike sometimes as a matter of taste (preferences, affinities) and sometimes in terms of wariness or "fear." This dislike or fear is not based on boys' greater average size or physical strength because they resemble girls in the first ten years. Rather, boys ignore girls, including girls' efforts to negotiate fair shares of valued items. Boys in one study issued more direct demands to playmates as they grew older (from $3^1/_2$ to $5^1/_2$), whereas girls gave more polite suggestions.[138]

Gender segregation is in large part a choice that children themselves make. Various research studies all find that segregation is greater when children are less structured or supervised by adults. Thorne, who is keenly sensitive to the avenues by which adults reinforce sexism and amplify children's tendency to gender segregation, nonetheless concludes that on balance adults in contemporary US elementary schools reduce rather than increase gender segregation. Children act as "full social actors" – agents pursuing their own self-defined interests – in making choices about gender groupings. Peers, even more than parents, transmit gender cultures to new individuals. Gender rules pass from older siblings to younger ones. Children with few or no siblings are "more likely to show gender-egalitarian beliefs," according to "reasonably consistent" results of various research studies.[139]

Second, gender rules are enforced by peers, primarily by teasing. Such teasing can be brutal, and devastating to children who receive it. (To be ostracized for violating social norms is a very serious consequence feared by people worldwide.) "The children who most often violate gender boundaries . . . are especially unpopular with peers." Children also stigmatize cross-gender contact as "romantic or sexual." They tease someone caught across gender lines in a prohibited context for "liking," "loving," or "kissing." Children have to defend themselves by declaring that they "hate" the person. Boys especially risk humiliation as "sissies" if they

---

[137] Maccoby 1998, 41–42.
[138] Maccoby 1998, 290, 62–64.
[139] Thorne 1993, full 3; Maccoby 1998, 294–95, peers 178; Ruble and Martin 1998, consistent 978.

act girlishly by crying or showing emotions, as well as if they associate with girls outside of permitted contexts.[140]

One rendition of the rules governing contact with the opposite gender finds only the following forms of contact permissible: accidental (e.g., bumping into someone by mistake), incidental (e.g., waiting in line next to someone but without talking), instrumental (e.g., "pass the lemonade"), aggressive (e.g., insulting or pushing someone), compelled by an adult, or when accompanied by another member of one's own gender. This last rule provides the covering rule by which integrated group games such as dodgeball and kickball occur on playgrounds.[141]

Thorne refers to children's cross-gender activities that maintain gender separation as "borderwork." It is work because "[g]ender boundaries are episodic and ambiguous." A lot of cross-gender contact occurs in these mildly antagonistic interactions of groups of boys with groups of girls. Such activities include raiding and chasing on playgrounds, especially "chase and kiss." In boy-versus-girl chases, girls often define safety zones in which they take refuge, sometimes close to an adult. "Cooties" (and other "pollution rituals") stigmatize individuals – girls or boys – by treating them as contaminated. Cooties evidently can be transmitted girl–girl, boy–girl, or girl–boy, but not among boys. Often boys see "girls as a group ... as an ultimate source of contamination." "Both sexes understand that when a girl catches and kisses a boy, she has insulted, or ... in some way contaminated him." (In many cultures, beliefs about female pollution relate to menstruation and reproduction, but do not apply to children before puberty.)[142]

Raiding consists mainly of boys raiding girls' games to disrupt them, an activity that a minority of boys "more or less specialize in." Girls chase "to drive the boy out of their space," unlike more playful two-way cross-gender chasing. "Girls may guard their play with informal lookouts ... [and] are often wary about letting boys into their activities." Chasing is a form of play-fighting, with scripted behaviors indicating it is "just in fun" but with heightened emotions and the potential for real conflict. Separation is also reinforced by contests of girls against boys – both those organized by adults, such as classroom competitions, and those organized by the children themselves, especially kickball.[143]

---

[140] Maccoby 1998, unpopular 70, sexual 67, hate 69; Green 1987.

[141] Stroufe, in Maccoby 1998, 71.

[142] Thorne 1993, borderwork 64–88, episodic 84–85, refuge 70, pollution 73–76; Maccoby 1998 66–70, both 67.

[143] Thorne 1993, space–lookouts 77, fun 80, heightened 78, contests 67.

Segregation is enforced by boys more than girls. After age 4, "boys appear to play a more active role in establishing and maintaining the separation of the sexes." Boys seem more intent on excluding girls from groups than vice versa. Girls are more interested in interacting with boys and pursuing masculine activities (notwithstanding many girls' wariness of boys' style) than boys are in girls and feminine activities. Boys' groups, more than girls' groups, "exclude and ignore" the other gender and "vigilantly monitor the boundaries." Boys' groups "achieve more autonomy" and probably more group cohesion despite higher conflict within the group.[144]

Asymmetries skew gender segregation towards male dominance. Boys control as much as ten times the space in school playgrounds as girls do, and more frequently invade and disrupt the remaining girls' spaces. Adults' presence reduces gender separation in part because it "alters the dynamics of power." However, boys' dominance of girls is probably not a universal or "original" source of gender separation. For example, as adult women do in some cultures, girls can turn male fears of female pollution to advantage (e.g., forcing boys to run away for fear of cooties or kisses). Research on children of various ages "reveals great complexity, not unrelenting dominance of boys over girls." Children's power dynamics are "extremely complex."[145]

Parents' effects on segregation   Third, adults promote gender segregation, sometimes more than they think they are doing. Parents, especially fathers, reinforce gender norms, especially with sons. The different treatment of sons and daughters by parents does not have to do with loving one more, nor with giving warmth, responsiveness, or restrictiveness differently. Nor do parents promote independence more in young boys and attachment in girls. Parents are somewhat rougher with boys, but not dramatically so. The major difference, rather, is in promoting specific gender-appropriate behavior, rather narrowly defined, and discouraging cross-gender behavior. Four routes of parent-to-child gender socialization in early childhood are: offering gendered toys, supporting gender-appropriate play themes, playing more roughly with boys than girls, and talking less about feelings with boys.[146]

---

[144] Maccoby 1998, active 29, 52, monitor–autonomy 289.
[145] Thorne 1993, skew 82–84, space 83, alters 56, reveals 58, complex 84, 39; Bugental and Goodnow 1998, 430.
[146] Maccoby 1998, 123–24, 256, 108, routes 124–27, 139–41; Whiting and Edwards 1988; Wilden 1987, 216–20; Archer and Lloyd 1985, 219–21; Block 1973, 517–18.

Maccoby's longitudinal study found "few consistent differences" in how parents treated girls and boys up to age 2. By age 4, however, "[b]oth parents offered masculine toys more to boys, feminine ones more to girls, and... [chose different] play themes that were acted out jointly by the parent–child pair." Providing gender-linked toys may stimulate certain themes and scripts which in turn trigger other gendered patterns of social interaction. Even without parental direction, however, preschool children's toy choices mostly follow gender lines. In one experiment where all toys but a wrong-gender one were removed, "children – especially boys – resisted play with them. One boy threw the baby doll across the room and turned his back on it."[147]

Parents both talk less about feelings with boys, and "actively suppress emotional displays" in them. This may in part derive from boys' greater proneness to "impulsive emotional outbursts" (as girls more quickly develop self-regulation), and their lower compliance to their mothers' demands (found across cultures and age groups). However, parents also find it "especially important for boys not to display the kind of weakness or vulnerability or 'babyishness' that is implied by crying."[148]

Parents also interpret emotions differently based on gender. In one study, psychological subjects tended to perceive a crying infant as angry if it was labeled a boy, but frightened or distressed if the same infant was labeled a girl. Another study found that mothers showed concern in response to boys' anger but expressed anger in response to girls' anger (socializing girls not to express anger). In another study, mothers misinterpreted the anger of their preschool girls more than that of their boys. In lab experiments, adults gave different assessments of videotaped infants and toddlers depending if they thought the child was male or female. A toddler named Chris was rated as "stronger, more assertive, and more aggressive" by adults watching the videotape who thought Chris was a boy than adults told that Chris was a girl. An infant's videotaped reaction to a jack-in-the-box was more often rated as "anger" when the infant was labeled male and "fear" when labeled female.[149]

Parents and teachers reportedly discourage gender segregation more than they enforce it, on balance, although they do promote segregation by arranging same-gender playmates, supplying gendered toys, and giving approval to gender-appropriate activities in single-gender groups. Thorne points to the pervasiveness of gender demarcations in adult "messages" and school scripts. For example, adults mark gender in regularly calling children "boys and girls" (with boys "invariably" mentioned first).

[147] Maccoby 1998, few–pair 124–25, back 173.
[148] Maccoby 1998, suppress–crying 139.
[149] Cummings *et al.* 1986, studies Coie; 185 and Dodge 1998, 790.

Nonetheless, segregation is strongest in the least structured and supervised settings, and extends (less strongly) to structured and supervised settings as well. In elementary classrooms, for example, spontaneous cross-gender helping with schoolwork is "extremely rare."[150]

Teacher interventions   Teacher efforts to increase cross-gender interactions in the classroom "have not usually been effective." In one experiment in the 1970s, teachers of 4-year-olds were asked to "comment approvingly, before the entire class, each time a mixed-sex pair or group of children played together. Over a 2-week period, the rate of mixed-sex play increased by 20%," but it reverted to earlier levels after the experiment stopped. This suggests that gender segregation is relatively resistant to long-term change.[151]

On the other hand, much less same-gender play (40 percent versus 70) was observed at "progressive" or "open" schools (where teachers tried to avoid gender stereotypes) than in traditional ones. Even in traditional third- and fourth-grade classrooms, when given a choice, a "substantial minority" of children were willing to work in mixed-gender groups.[152]

Subtle teacher reinforcement of gender roles is found in a study where two types of "assertive acts" – hitting or pushing, and trying to grab an object – were observed in 13-month infants in playgroups and by the same children 9–11 months later, as toddlers. At first, there were no gender differences in the infants' behavior, nor in peer responses to aggression by boys or girls. However, teachers responded to about 40 percent of aggressive actions by girls and only 10 percent of those by boys (positive and negative responses were about equal). Later, as toddlers, the children showed a gender gap in assertive behaviors, with boys being more assertive especially in grabbing objects, and the teacher response was no longer different for girls and boys.[153]

Adults can intervene to modify, within limits, the nature of children's constructions of gender segregation. Maccoby emphasizes the temporary effects that such interventions have, and finds few good potential "leverage points for social change." Adult interventions have limited effect. Cross-gender interactions (especially in schools) often lead to boys' dominating girls. Yet, empowering girls in separate groups may reinforce segregation and stereotypes (all-male schools or settings being even more dubious in this regard). Finally, increasing male participation in child care runs against both cultural and economic pressures and does not seem to

---

[150] Hartup 1983, promote 109; Thorne 1993, invariably 34; Maccoby 1998, rare 26.
[151] Maccoby 1998, 22–26, effective 26; Hartup 1983, experiment 109.
[152] Maccoby 1998, open 28, minority 25.
[153] Fagot et al. 1985; P. K. Smith 1989, 80–81.

offer "any firm leverage points ... or even a strong social consensus as to what division of labor between parents is most desirable." Thorne is much more optimistic about the possibilities for adults to help children redirect gender relations in ways that take the edge off the enforced segregation that now prevails. She calls "gender separation ... a variable and complicated process, an intricate choreography."[154]

Marketing   Beyond these direct and specific influences, societies induce gender segregation through various other channels, including the ways that companies develop and market children's toys, entertainment programs, and software. In recent years, apparently, US children's marketing has become more segregationist, after two decades of downplaying gendered marketing because of worries that baby-boomer parents would resist gender-typed toys (worries that proved unfounded). A recent redesign of Toys Я Us stores created separate sections: "Boy's World" (a title the store removed in response to consumer complaints) contains "Action figures, Sports collectibles, Radio remote-control cars, Tonka trucks, Boy's role play, [and] Walkie Talkies." The girl's section contains "Barbie, Baby Dolls, Doll houses, Collectible horses, Play kitchens, Housekeeping toys, Girls' dress-up, Jewelry, Cosmetics, [and] Bath and body." In cable television, Fox in 2000 is launching the boyzChannel (e.g., "Spiderman") and the girlzChannel (e.g., "St. Bear's Dolls Hospital") for ages 2–14. Similarly, children's software is increasingly developed for just one gender. Such changes may be one reason that gender-stereotyped behaviors that used to emerge in kindergarten or first grade are now widely found in young preschoolers.[155]

The role of fathers

According to theories of "male gender-identity conflict," distant fathers make for aggressive sons. "In male-dominated cultures where fathers are distant and aloof from their children, frustration develops when young boys, who grow up with especially strong bonds to their mothers, must sever these bonds to meet the societal expectations of adult male behavior." Mothers' ambivalence towards their sons in patrilocal, polygynous societies also contributes to boys' fears of intimacy. Boys with gender-identity confusion act out aggressively as a compensatory mechanism, according to this theory.[156]

[154] Maccoby 1998, 304–11; Thorne 1993, 36, 168–71.
[155] Bannon 2000.
[156] Ross 1993a, 64, aloof 63, 56; Ross 1990; Adorno, Frenkel-Brunswik, and Levinson 1950; Ember 1980; Whiting and Whiting 1975, 45, 147.

Object-relations theorists (see p. 46) consider maternal child care to be a cultural arrangement that could be altered. Margaret Mead argues that if breast feeding were superseded and fathers took equal responsibility for children, the "male drive towards assertion of maleness by differentiation from females" could diminish. "Cultures like the Arapesh show how easily, where parents do not discriminate strongly between the sexes of their children and men take over a nurturing role, this drive in the male may be muted." McBride points out that in North America "the image of grown males caring for infants is so incongruous as to be uproariously funny," as, for example, in the 1987 movie, *Three Men and a Baby*. This may be changing in recent years, however, as US culture modestly promotes men's greater involvement as parents. For example, in 2000 when State Department spokesperson Jamie Rubin quit to stay home for a year with a new baby while spouse Christiane Amanpour worked, he was not treated as crazy. Amanpour called him "incredibly masculine and brave" for doing so, and Secretary of State Albright noted approvingly that Rubin had "figured out a way to rock the baby with one hand and hold the phone with the other."[157]

No biological mandate pushes fathers away from caring for children. Infants form attachments with one or more adults by 6–12 months (see Figure 4.7). Attachment responses to fathers and mothers differ little, compared with responses to a stranger. Among primates, the three species "notorious for paternal aloofness" are gorillas, patas monkeys, and Hanuman langurs. Yet even in these species, "when the occasion arises, these same males play a crucial role in infant survival, even taking on the role of primary caretaker."[158]

As infants and toddlers, "[b]oys do not appear to be more interested in their fathers than girls are, nor are girls more likely than boys to seek closeness to their mothers rather than their fathers." Both genders, rather, tend to look to their mothers for comfort and to their fathers for "fun and games." Typical fathers' games with babies move the babies' limbs in arousing ways; one study found this arousal in 70 percent of father–infant games and only 4 percent of mother–infant ones. Fathers do more bouncing and lifting. As babies become toddlers, fathers use rough-and-tumble play more, whereas mothers offer more toys to initiate interaction. "Both boys and girls . . . enjoy this kind of play with their fathers very much," and neither gender usually finds the father's size and strength threatening. Various other differences in mothers' and fathers' relationships with their children reflect the fact that mothers spend more time with the

---

[157] Mead 1949, muted 149; McBride 1995, funny 205; Rubin: Goldberg 2000.
[158] Archer and Lloyd 1985, little 219; Hrdy 1981, notorious–caretaker 75; Alcorta 1982.

Figure 4.7 Father and son at outdoor worship service, Wrigley Field, Chicago, 1973. [US National Archives, NWDNS-412-DA-13694.]

children. When fathers are present, they participate in teaching and disciplining children. In various cultures such as the !Kung, fathers' presence is strong.[159]

How involved are fathers?   Despite talk of a "new fatherhood," in the United States recently, "male participation in the lives of their children" has probably decreased in recent years, and possibly during the last half-century as well. Women assume most day-to-day childcare responsibility in "all known societies." Whiting and Whiting's 1975 survey of six cultures found that "[f]athers are present considerably less often than mothers." One review of various studies of intact, two-parent families found the ratio of mothers' to fathers' contribution to be 10:1 in responsibility for a child's daily activities, 2:1 in availability, and 3:1 in parent–child interactions.[160]

Even among US couples where both work and they had planned to share child care equally, "the reality usually turns out to be different." Differential earning power – a result of sexism and the average husband's greater age and work experience – becomes a vicious circle after women

---

[159] Maccoby 1998, seek–fun 16, arousal 266, enjoy 267, participate 273–76; Parke 1981; !Kung: Shostak 1981, 45–46, 238–39.

[160] Maccoby 1998, new–societies 256–58, review 259–65; Whiting and Whiting 1975, 45.

interrupt work (however briefly) for childbirth. Mothers reduce work to take care of children, and fathers often increase work hours to fill this gap and make ends meet. Divorce sharpens this differentiation. In those few cases where fathers take a primary role in child care, they risk "scornful or contemptuous reactions from other men... and... are not readily accepted into informal groups of mothers" such as at playgrounds.[161]

Some changes are occurring, however. The number of US single fathers with children rose by one-quarter in 1995–98, to over 2 million, while single mothers remained constant at nearly 10 million. Patterns also differ by age. In England in the mid-1950s, in a major longitudinal study, about six times more children lived with only their mother than only their father at age 7, but only about four times more by age 11.[162]

Effects of fathers' involvement   Children who get more parental attention do better on school achievement tests, and fathers can substantially impact this dimension. The longitudinal National Child Development Study, which tracked all children born in England during one week in 1958, leaves "little doubt... that an actively involved father benefits his children." The child's best situation is "to be one of few siblings or an older child in a family without financial problems in which the father takes an active interest in his children's development." One study found fathers' involvement in child care to be the most important factor correlated with children's development of empathy decades later. Another study found early paternal attachment correlated with individual feelings of patriotism (love of one's country) but not nationalism (desire for that country's superiority).[163]

Recent research on fathers has struggled with methodological problems, and is too young to have developed sophisticated replications and longitudinal studies necessary to reach firmer empirical results. Causality becomes tangled easily. Furthermore, the key in two-parent families may be the parents' relationship – collaborative or conflictual – and the presence of *some* absent fathers (e.g., wife beaters) would not benefit children.[164]

Although fathers' involvement in child care helps children, it also reinforces gender norms. Fathers in contemporary US culture enforce gender identities on young children more than mothers do, and on boys more

---

[161] Maccoby 1998, 256–63.
[162] Number: Associated Press 1998b; England: Archer and Lloyd 1985, 214.
[163] Pollack 1998, 113–44; Gerzon 1982, 157–58; Kindlon and Thompson 1999, 94–100; England: Archer and Lloyd 1985, doubt–best 217; empathy: Koestner, Franz, and Weinberger 1990; patriotism: Feshbach 1987.
[164] Cohen 1998; Archer and Lloyd 1985, 213–14; Bianchi ed. 1998.

than on girls. In one study where toddlers started playing in a room with gender-typed toys and then their parents joined them, mothers intervened to discourage cross-gender play for boys and girls equally, whereas fathers disapproved five times more often of boys' cross-gender play than that of girls. Fathers in a 1983 study interacted differently with their 12-month-old boys and their girls. In their fathers' presence, girls played with dolls about twice as often as boys, while boys touched tempting objects twice as often as girls (these were the two most significant gender differences). In their child's presence, fathers gave dolls two or three times as often to girls as boys, and gave prohibitions two to three times as often to boys as girls (again the two most significant items).[165]

Not only do fathers enforce gender norms more than mothers, they do so more strongly on boys than girls. For "most men . . . an effeminate son is far more worrying than a tomboy daughter. The father places heavy emphasis on the *avoidance* of feminine behaviors, rather than on the active encouragement of masculine ones." Fathers' own "masculinity" influences boys' development in ways that are unclear at best. Overall, the most important variable seems to be fathers' active involvement rather than any particular high rating on some scale of "masculinity." Some empirical studies show that boys with absent fathers develop fewer aggressive behaviors, or more accurately develop them later – part of a pattern of weaker "masculinity" in these boys (contrary to gender-identity conflict theory). Fathers who seek achievement primarily in the world of work and who leave the home to their wives may find their sons do not share their masculine preferences."[166]

In offering gender-appropriate toys and themes, fathers are more active towards sons than mothers towards either gender. (Of course, fathers spend much less time with children than mothers do.) For example, when one toddler boy fell and hurt himself, his mother said, "Come here, honey. I'll kiss it better," while his father said "Oh, toughen up. Quit your bellyaching." In a study of mothers' and fathers' reactions to their preschool children's play, fathers were five times more likely to show a negative reaction to a son playing with feminine materials than to a daughter playing with masculine ones, whereas mothers reacted equally to both sons and daughters. A comparison of 39 studies found a "clear" trend showing that fathers differentiate between sons and daughters more than mothers do, often by being "stricter with boys." Fathers "maintain a stance of male dominance toward their sons, as an older boy might do,"

---

[165] Campbell 1993, enforce–toddlers 20–21; Snow, Jacklin, and Maccoby 1983, dolls 229; Archer and Lloyd 1985, 213–22.

[166] Campbell 1993, strongly 20–21, avoidance 30; Archer and Lloyd 1985, own–preferences 221–22; Green 1987, empirical 56–58, 33; Gerzon 1982, 197–215.

thereby inducting them into the male status hierarchy, despite fathers' sometimes contradictory role as nurturing parent. Fathers' greater role in socializing daughters for gender, if any, is less clear.[167]

There is "extensive evidence that fathers use more imperatives and other forms of power-assertion in talking to children." Mothers by comparison soften demands by using polite language, endearments, and questions. Fathers also use "disparaging remarks and name-calling" more often than mothers, and direct such language more to sons than daughters. Children address "their fathers more deferentially, using questions and polite forms," see them as having more authority, and comply more quickly with their demands than those of mothers. These aspects all add up to a power and status differential between fathers and mothers with respect to their children. However, Maccoby cautions that "average differences between mothers and fathers are not large," and both parents may arrive at similar outcomes (intimacy, influence) by different routes. Although parents may differ in skills and styles, they both *primarily* react to their children as individuals rather than to the child's gender or the gender match of parent and child.[168]

In sum, many developmental psychologists see gender differentiation in children as the outcome of socialization – i.e., motivating children to comply with norms of behavior appropriate in a given culture. Means of socialization include teaching, reinforcement, and modeling, by parents and others. Psychologists reason that cultures differentially socialize children to prepare them for adult gender roles, such as domestic–child workers versus herding–hunting–heavy agriculture (and, I would add, war roles).

Parents' recourse to biological determinism   Outside of academia, more essentialist views of childhood gender are popular. Consider three examples of parents who attribute their child's gender development to biology because they claim to have controlled cultural influences.

Humorist Dave Barry writes that he did not believe males to be naturally more violent "until my son, Robert, was born." Barry and his wife "never bought him violent toys, and . . . [instead of violent cartoons] Robert watched Mister Rogers do educational segments about jute farming." Yet by age $3\frac{1}{2}$, Robert developed a "mad obsession for power. In Robert's mind, the major world figures were, in descending order: God, Superman, Tyrannosaurus Rex, Darth Vader, He-Man, various plant-eating dinosaurs, Batman, and, finally, four-wheel-drive vehicles. . . . And it's not just Robert. It's little boys in general." At Robert's preschool, the

---

[167] Maccoby 1998, 142–43.
[168] Maccoby 1998, 270–78, extensive 270, disparaging 271, large 273.

parents are "nonviolent granola-oriented liberals" and the children have "loving teachers and educational objects such as blocks and books and a rabbit... The little girls use the arts materials to make art. The little boys convert them to atomic laser blasters with which they vaporize each other and, I suspect, the rabbit."[169]

Deborah Blum puts her parenting experience on the first page of her book's introduction. After becoming a parent of two boys, she realized that – unlike what she had learned growing up in a "university-based, liberal-elite famil[y]" – the two genders are like "alien species... [t]otally and mind-bogglingly different." Her $2\frac{1}{2}$-year-old loved only some dinosaurs – "blood-swilling carnivores. Plant-eaters were wimps and losers... I looked down at him one day as he was snarling around my feet and doing his toddler best to gnaw off my right leg, and I thought: This is not a girl thing – this goes deeper than culture."[170]

Anne Campbell similarly summarizes "what mothers have always known": "By the age of three, boys wrestle, hit, kick, tussle, push, and pull far more than girls do." Mothers say defensively, "I don't know where he gets it from – we don't encourage him to fight" and "We never gave him guns. But then he started making them out of old paper-towel rolls." Campbell asserts that boys' aggression develops despite mothers' being "relatively sex-blind when it comes to raising their children." Starting from birth, "the surge of love and protectiveness most mothers experience does seem truly sex-blind... and the day when this small bundle will emerge clearly as a boy or girl seems far off."[171]

Yet none of these three parents have really shielded their children from a gendered culture that is ubiquitous for children growing up in contemporary Western society. For example, Campbell's supposedly genderless "small bundle" is typically wrapped in pink or blue from the moment of birth. Young children pick up gender roles from modeling by parents and other adults, from mass media in all their range and depth, and from peer culture – especially older siblings. The point is not that biology does not matter, but that cultural influences cannot be switched off so easily to reveal biological essences. Infants and children imitate behaviors they observe, and they grow up in settings where gender norms, codings, and incentives are ubiquitous.

By contrast to the above three, a parent who understands the biology of gender especially well, science writer Natalie Angier, criticizes the "categorical distinctions" of gender applied to American children. The pink-and-blue dress code imposed rigidly on babies and toddlers

---

[169] Barry 1984.
[170] Blum 1997, xiii.
[171] Campbell 1993, 19–20.

(whose gender is indistinguishable with a diaper on) amounts to "infant apartheid." Media reinforcement of gender stereotypes is ubiquitous, starting from the hair and dress code on *Barney*, where boys "are close to horror-struck . . . [to] meet a bagpipe player wearing a kilt" – until he reassures them it's "just for special occasions; normally I dress just like you." People too often see gender-stereotypical behaviors as *caused* by gender while behaviors that contradict stereotypes are seen as being caused by individual variation. For example, when an older boy takes away Angier's daughter's cup of milk, the boy's mother attributes the act to his being a boy (rather than an older child, or just an individual with tendencies to thievery). "A moment later, an older girl grabs away my daughter's cup of milk" but nobody attributes this identical act to gender.[172]

Do as I say, not as I do   A 1997 survey of 1,200 US adults found a strong consensus for gender equality in raising girls and boys. Asked whether parents' expectations of their children's educations and careers should be the same or different for girls and boys, nearly 90 percent of both women and men said "the same"; 76 percent of women and 61 percent of men thought the children should be raised with the same "toys and play activities." Based on the data above (see pp. 243–45), however, it is doubtful that 61 percent of fathers actually promote the same toys and activities to girls as to boys.[173]

This disparity of theory and practice becomes sharper when it comes to modeling gender roles for children – an important route of socialization, though not the main one. The same poll found continuing divergence in the parents' involvement with children and the roles they assumed in the family. In a majority of couples, both agreed that the "wife mostly does" tasks involving responsibility for the child's care – arranging for child care or babysitter, staying home from work with sick children, and arranging children's transportation. No more than 6 percent of couples agreed that the husband mostly does any one of these tasks or that both do them equally. (About a third of couples did not agree who "mostly does" a particular task.) The item of strongest equality (26 percent say done by both, and 57 percent disagree who does it more) is disciplining the children. Regarding the role models parents provide, a majority of couples agreed that the "husband does more" of each of these tasks: mowing lawn, shoveling snow, household repairs, working for pay, and taking out trash. The "wife does more" of washing clothes, cleaning, cooking, food shopping, and paying bills. When asked if it would be better overall to return to "the traditional roles . . . in the 1950s," both men and women split

---

[172] Angier 1998a.
[173] Rosenfeld 1998, A17.

three ways between "better," "worse," and "no difference" (a 42 percent plurality of women leaning towards "worse"). Men and women both agreed, by 80 percent to 5 percent, that recent changes in gender roles made it harder for parents to raise children. Nearly 70 percent of both men and women agreed that although women may need to work to support the family, "it would be better if she could stay home and just take care of the house and children." Older respondents held far more traditional views about gender roles than younger ones.[174]

A 1997 survey found substantial change from a 1977 survey in the amount of self-reported time that working men spend with their children – 2.3 hours workdays and 6.4 non-workdays, both up about one-quarter over 20 years. Similarly, for housework, men reported 2.1 hours on workdays, up three-quarters since 1977, and 4.9 hours on non-work days, up one-quarter. These self-reports may exaggerate the actual change, however, because men may simply have learned (over 20 years) the socially expected answer to such a question. In 1997, married working mothers still spent 30 percent more time with children than married working fathers did, and this is the category of child care with the smallest gender difference – simply being "with" the children (including while doing housework, talking on the phone, etc.) rather than being "responsible" for managing the children which is usually the mother's job.[175]

Data from Britain in the 1980s are similar. Primary or sole responsibility for child care fell to women alone in 49 percent, and to men alone in only 1 percent, of the cases (the other half being shared). The respective ratio for housework was 73 percent women alone to 1 percent men, and for household repairs, 83 percent men alone to 6 percent women. About 40 percent of men who were full-time employees worked over 40 hours weekly, compared with about 10 percent of women. Norway introduced affirmative action for men in child care, elementary teaching, and social work in 1998. The Minister of Families and Children said that the policy would help provide male role models to young children and change their views about gender. In other countries, however, such policies are very rare.[176]

Overall, the main problem with the gender segregation hypothesis is that children's gender segregation is much less pervasive and absolute than is gender segregation in war. In addition, in settings where children do operate in mixed groups (e.g., classrooms) they are no less effective as a group. Finally, if gender segregation were the key reason for combat segregation, more armies would take advantage of women's potential

[174] Merida and Vobejda 1998; Morin and Rosenfeld 1998; Grimsley and Melton 1998.
[175] Lewin 1998a.
[176] Edley and Wetherell 1995, 117; Norway: *Washington Post* 1998.

combat contribution by forming segregated women's combat units, as Dahomey did. This is not found, however.

War   Childhood gender segregation is a first step in preparing children for war. All-boy groups in middle childhood develop the social interaction scripts used later in armies. As the military will do at a later age, US elementary schools accomplish "batch processing" of large groups of children by "treating them as members of groups," including gender groups. (US school buildings once had separate entrances engraved "Girls" and "Boys.") In this process, "the unique qualities of individuals (the focus of much family interaction) become subordinated to ways in which they are alike." Indeed, to argue from extremes, Nazi concentration camps organized the intake of inmates with the command, "Men to the left! Women to the right!" Gender segregation began a process intended to "obliterate all signs of individuality." It did not give women any special treatment or lighter labor. The ritual of gender separation was followed even at extermination camps where both groups were to be murdered within a few minutes. Of course, schools are the opposite of concentration camps, dedicated to nurturing and not murdering, but they may nonetheless play a role in preparing children for war.[177]

Childhood gender segregation in different cultures reflects the importance of warfare. The characteristic boys' play styles and themes are very often tied directly to the boys' future roles in wartime (play-fighting, dominance, heroic themes, and specific war scripts). If "boys' culture" is seen as functional in socializing males for adult roles, it surely does so most efficiently with regard to war roles, and somewhat less directly with regard to the work roles – such as heavy agriculture or herding – that Maccoby emphasizes, for example. Preschoolers identified as masculine that which was large, dark, sharp, or rough-textured (including fire, lightning, sharks, and gorillas), and identified as feminine what was smooth, rounded, or pastel-colored (including clouds, ducklings, and soap). Maccoby suggests that these concepts parallel the play materials (guns, swords, monsters, dinosaurs) and themes (danger, struggle) that boys prefer. War seems especially relevant to this list. (I will return to the topic of toughening up boys shortly; see pp. 287–301.)[178]

CONCLUSION

Several hypotheses in chapters 3 and 4 contain some truth but fall short as explanations of gendered war roles. They show a tendency in the direction

---

[177] Koonz 1987, 405–6; Thorne 1993, 31–40.
[178] Maccoby 1998, 167.

of favoring men for combat, but with enough individual variation and gender overlap that one would expect a modest but nontrivial minority of women to be combatants.

Theoretically, the several distinct biological elements *tending* to favor men for combat could, when combined, create an overwhelming mandate for men. These elements, supported by robust empirical evidence, are: (1) men's greater average size and strength; (2) men's subtle brain adaptation for rough-and-tumble play, aggression, and spatial skills; (3) men's somewhat different orientation towards competitive hierarchies; and (4) the tendency to segregate by gender in childhood, reinforcing differences between gendered childhood cultures.

The problem with this multi-causal explanation, however, is that the four elements do not combine additively or multiplicatively so much as they overlap each other. The 10 percent of women who would make the best soldiers are probably the same individuals who are relatively strong, rough, aggressive, spatially adept, and competitive, and as children were "tomboys" who crossed gender lines.

The two hypotheses that would have clearly separated women's suitability for war from men's were the idea that aggression is caused by testosterone levels (on which genders barely overlap at all), or that "aggressive genes" reside on the Y chromosome. These found no empirical support. Gender as an absolute division in war is not explained by the biology of either individuals or groups.

5   Heroes: the making of militarized masculinity

> **Hypothesis 5.** Cultural construction of tough men and tender women:
> A. Test of manhood as a motivation to fight
> B. Feminine reinforcement of soldiers' masculinity
> C. Women's peace activism

INTRODUCTION

This chapter and the next focus primarily on the male soldier's construction of his gender identity – masculinity – in relation to his ability to function as a combatant. Such constructions might explain the exclusion of women from the ranks of male warriors, in any of several ways. Furthermore, masculinity often depends on an "other" constructed as feminine. Feminine roles in the war system are performed by women who support war in myriad ways, voluntarily and involuntarily, in specific nonwarrior roles, such as mothers, nurses, prostitutes, camp followers, rape victims, and even peace activists. Cultures use gender in constructing social roles that enable war. The phrase "cultures use" is shorthand for a more complex process. Cultures do not take actions, but various cultural themes and scripts play functional roles, and are passed on to succeeding generations as cultures evolve. To simplify, however, I will treat cultures as though they were actors.[1]

Culture truncates biology   Cultures do not have complete freedom in constructing war roles, but rather work with a set of biological and psychological elements – building materials, so to speak – that exist across all human cultures. These building materials do not determine the style or functionality of what is made with them, yet common building

---

[1] Shilts 1993, 492 in Thomas and Thomas 1996, 70.

materials mean that a wide variety of structures will have common elements, as we find in gendered war roles. Anthropologist Walter Goldschmidt concludes that with war, as with "all matters cultural, the society shapes natural human capacities and potentialities to its accepted purposes, reinforcing some and suppressing others ... by systematically rewarding and punishing, by indoctrinating youth, creating role models to be emulated, and honoring those who perform well." War as a career draws upon biological capabilities, but the same capabilities could be channeled, in a different culture, into non-warlike practices. Similarly, the functions that war performs in a culture could be filled in other ways.[2]

Clearly, given the discussions in chapters 3 and 4, our innate biological potentials support tremendous diversity. Contrary to the conventional view that biology constrains and culture liberates, it seems to me that culture constrains (channels, harnesses, limits) the diverse potentials of biology. Cultural concepts of masculine and feminine are in many ways more rigid than biological gender. With a few exceptions, cultures create a male–female duality that forces individuals into categories. Certainly this is the case in modern Western cultures, which privilege binary opposition as an organizing device. Not only individuals but whole categories of objects and relationships are sorted into male and female categories.[3]

Thus, where biological gender gives us overlapping bell-curves, cultural gender amputates these curves and gives us squared-off boxes containing all, and only, a certain category of person. Diversity within each category disappears, and with it the overlap of the bell-curves. In this way the modest biological tendencies (discussed in chapters 3 and 4) towards males' higher average war capability become transformed into all-male war. What had been only a potential in biology becomes a mandate in culture. It is possible for an individual and occasionally a group to run against the grain, but it takes some doing.

A. TEST OF MANHOOD AS A MOTIVATION TO FIGHT

Hypothesis 5A proposes that cultures mold males into warriors by attaching to "manhood" or "masculinity" those qualities that make good warriors. War does not come naturally to men (from biology), so warriors require intense socialization and training in order to fight effectively. Gender identity becomes a tool with which societies induce men to fight.

[2] Goldschmidt 1989, well 24; Goldschmidt 1986, career 9, practices 11; Goldschmidt 1990; Groebel and Hinde eds. 1989; functions: Eibl-Eibesfeldt 1979, 231; Vayda 1967; Mead 1967a.
[3] Gilmore 1990, 21.

First consider the problem: with rare exceptions – people who might be considered mentally ill in another context – soldiers who participate in combat find it extremely unnatural and horrible. Any sane person, male or female, who is surrounded by the terrifying and surreal sights and sounds of battle, instinctually wants to run away, or hunker down and freeze up, and certainly not to charge into even greater danger to kill and maim other people. Contrary to the idea that war thrills men, expresses innate masculinity, or gives men a fulfilling occupation, all evidence indicates that war is something that societies impose on men, who most often need to be dragged kicking and screaming into it, constantly brainwashed and disciplined once there, and rewarded and honored afterwards. War is hell.[4]

The difficulty of getting soldiers to fight is underscored by the very common resort to both conscription and harsh discipline in raising and maintaining armies. Even in popular wars, societies generally must rely on conscription to raise armies. Many armies impose the death penalty for desertion, and Roman military units that fought poorly were "decimated" by having one man in ten killed as punishment.[5]

In the most warlike simple societies – the 27 known present-day preliterate societies "in which military activity is salient" – men typically fear war, and have to be coaxed into it by such means as religious beliefs, war dances, and the use of drugs. Boys have to be trained and conditioned for a warrior role. Then after the war, male warriors have to be "rewarded with booty, slaves, women." In only four of the 27 societies is there no material reward for warriors, although in four more the rewards are slight. Even more important are the nonmaterial rewards: honor or prestige, special titles or memberships, political influence or leadership. These various incentives induce boys to grow up as warriors in these warlike societies: "it takes a major effort to make aggressive warriors out of tribal children." Even the most warlike peoples must be "persistently nagged into committing acts of inhumanity." Thus, killing does not come naturally to men.[6]

Fear and functionality in battle

Fear is the emotion that comes "naturally" in combat (recall the stress response in chapter 3; see pp. 157–58). As one US Vietnam veteran

---

[4] McCarthy 1994, 106–7; Keegan 1976, 274–75; Ehrenreich 1997a, occupation 127.
[5] Conscription: Montagu 1976, 265; Ruddick 1989, 152; discipline: Shalit 1988, 120–53; Goldman and Fuller 1983, 136–38; Keegan and Holmes 1985, 39, decimated 55–56.
[6] Goldschmidt 1989, 16–17, children 22–23; Keeley 1996, nagged 146; Hassig 1988, 37–44.

put it, "I learned to function, even though I was scared shitless." Fear poses a severe challenge to soldiers' effectiveness in battle, especially an individual's first battle. In the US Civil War, before a battle "[s]ometimes this fear was so intense that men would fall to the ground paralyzed with terror, bury their face in the grass, grasp at the earth, and refuse to move" despite officers' exhortations and threats. Among wounded US soldiers in 1944, two-thirds said they had been unable to perform adequately in combat because of intense fear, at least once. (Soldiers who started off less self-confident were more likely to become intensely afraid in battle, as were isolated soldiers who lacked a group's moral support.) Fears change over time, as soldiers become less afraid of displaying cowardice and more afraid of being hurt or killed.[7]

In the confusion and terror of the battlefield, noise and surprise paralyze soldiers and reduce their effectiveness more often than direct injury does. "A striking feature of battle is the tendency toward confusion and paralysis which often occurs when a unit first comes under fire, and it is especially difficult to get soldiers to move once they have gone to ground." A central task of officers is to overcome the soldiers' paralysis of fear by demonstrating leadership (since people tend to copy the behavior of others in threatening situations). However, soldiers in various wars tell of officers who ran away or became immobilized at the first experience of combat. One new US lieutenant in Vietnam froze in fear in the open when his platoon came under fire, and lay weeping until a soldier, assuming he was seriously wounded, came out of cover to drag him back to safety.[8]

To capture an enemy machine-gun position, soldiers may need to attack into what amounts to near-certain death for the leading soldiers. Recall the insanely bloody attacks "over the top" from the trenches of World War I. In the 1944 assault on the Normandy beaches, soldiers coming off landing craft were immediately cut down, and subsequent waves of attackers fought across the beach over the bodies of the earlier ones. Similarly, during the Vietnam War, communist forces used "human wave" assaults against fortified French or American positions, as did Iran against Iraq in the 1980s. Chinese communists on the Long March had to attack a fortified position across a river using a single exposed footbridge. Getting soldiers to participate in such attacks is no minor problem.

Rout   The phenomenon of *rout* in warfare shows how serious a problem fear can be. A losing army needs to retreat, in control, in order to minimize losses and regroup for another defense. An orderly pullback of people, weapons, and supplies – destroying what cannot be taken to

---

[7] Turner 1996, scared 17; Dean 1997, paralyzed 54; Kellett 1990, wounded 228–29; Dyer 1985, 118–22; Grossman 1995.

[8] Keegan 1976, 278–84; Kellett 1990, ground 224; Goldman and Fuller 1983, froze 150.

prevent its use by the enemy – presents a great challenge. If the soldiers' self-control begins to "come unglued," as it is never far from doing under the stresses of battle and especially of defeat, panic quickly takes hold. Panic can be "produced by a misunderstood order, the sudden appearance of an unfamiliar enemy weapon, or the sharp jab of a sudden reverse." Individuals and small groups scramble to save themselves, command breaks down, and the army's ability to fight completely disintegrates in a stampede towards the rear. A war correspondent caught up in a panic retreat in North Africa in 1942 described it as "the contagion of bewilderment and fear and ignorance." An enemy taking advantage of such a rout can inflict much greater losses than if the army had held itself together.[9]

Such a panic overcame most of the US front line during the unexpected German offensive of late 1944 (the Bulge), according to historian Stephen Ambrose: "Down the middle of the road came the defeated American troops, fleeing the front in disarray moblike. Many had thrown away their rifles, their coats, all encumbrances. Some were in a panic, staggering, exhausted, shouting, 'Run! Run! They'll murder you! They'll kill you! They've got everything, tanks, machine-guns, air power, everything!'" Among the officers and at rear bases, "[t]here was a breakdown in discipline, compounded by the breakdown of some of the colonels. Among many, fear drove all rational thought out of their mind. Go west as fast as possible was the only thought."[10]

What stopped the German advance and eventually allowed calm to return and reinforcements to reach the front was the willingness of small groups of Americans – a dozen here, a few hundred there – to cling tenaciously to positions at key crossroads and bottlenecks despite staggering losses inflicted by vastly superior German forces. At a critical bridge reached by the lead German forces – the furthest they got in the campaign – a US infantry company (hardly more than 100 soldiers with no heavy weapons) held its positions for hours against the oncoming German armored division (over 10,000 soldiers with tanks and artillery), then pulled back over the bridge and blew it up. Elsewhere, small US units besieged in fortified positions or on isolated hilltops held off German forces for crucial hours or days.[11]

Critical moments   In battles there come critical points where armies collide, where defenses hold or crumble, where attacks break through or fail, where retreats turn into routs. The outcomes of wars can turn on what happens in these times. In several well-documented cases,

---

[9] Kellett 1990, 229; Keegan and Holmes 1985, reverse 42, contagion 42; Watson 1997.

[10] Ambrose 1997, road 205, west 204, 170.

[11] Ambrose 1997, 213–16.

the "fighting spirit" of a few hundred men reversed a large advance and arguably changed the outcome of a major war.

In the battle of Gettysburg, a hill called Little Round Top "lay undefended before the advancing Confederates. Had it fallen, the flank of the Union position ... would have been turned: the battle would be lost, and with it the campaign and even the war." A regiment of 350 soldiers commanded by a college professor arrived just in time but was outnumbered three-to-one. After an hour, with half the men already down and the rest almost out of ammunition, the regiment fixed bayonets and charged, unnerving Confederate forces and breaking their line.[12]

Similarly, in World War I, a German advance in Belgium towards the channel ports in late 1914 threatened to turn the tide of the entire war. The last three British reserve companies – again about 350 men in all – advanced into a blistering battle and, despite high casualties, broke through German lines, sending the unprepared Germans into retreat from a key town and stopping the offensive. The British commander-in-chief said the battalion had "saved the Empire."[13]

The attack against strong defenses, the defense against overwhelming attack, and the controlled retreat – times when soldiers most need to master fear – are one end of a spectrum of battle conditions, with sheer boredom at the other end. Ordinary soldiers can do the job most of the time. Most men in many cultures never end up going to war; usually a minority of men who go to war are at the front; and those men who do participate directly in combat do not usually face the most extreme situations – the ones that get retold in war stories. The problem is that nobody can predict when critical moments in battle will occur. An army thus needs more than just a few soldiers to be tough enough to withstand the extremes. Soldiers in the moment cannot know whether their actions will matter or not, and must be willing to "soldier on" without understanding or consenting to the purpose of their actions. On D-Day, for example, 225 US Rangers were stranded alone after a screw-up in the landing, and took 50 percent casualties in scaling 100-foot-high cliffs under fire in order to destroy German artillery at the top, only to find no artillery there ("wasted gallantry").[14]

Since every society faces the possibility of war, every society has to produce large numbers of potential soldiers who can overcome fear and stay functional in battle. History demonstrates that ordinary people can perform extraordinary acts, including extreme acts of violence and cruelty against other people, if trained and organized to do so. Societies and

[12] Keegan and Holmes 1985, 39.
[13] Keegan and Holmes 1985, 41.
[14] Keegan and Holmes 1985, wasted 255–56.

armies produce brave soldiers in various ways, all of them very imperfect. Some, but not all, of these means involve gender.[15]

Alcohol   Alcohol in many armies has served to suppress soldiers' fears, reward their efforts, overcome their social inhibitions regarding aggressive violence, and help them numb the pain of combat. The British army traditionally has had a "rum ration" each day for soldiers (controlled by officers) and double rations were given before sending soldiers on a particularly risky offensive. In World War II, US soldiers in Europe routinely drank too much – partly because Prohibition meant they had little experience – and acted like "jerks." During the Vietnam War, US soldiers on leave (and sometimes at the front) drowned their troubles in alcohol. After a war, veterans may continue to abuse alcohol. Historical examples of heavy drinking by troops at the front can be found in various wars.[16]

Although alcohol may help overcome fear, however, it also impedes sound decision-making under fire. Heavy drinking took a toll on the British and US armies in World War II, for example. One "quite drunk" British sergeant, not waiting for German soldiers sneaking up on his position to reach a gap in the wall he was covering, jumped out through the gap, rushed the soldiers to capture them, and was shot dead as a result. In the Gulf War, Western forces in Saudi Arabia forwent alcohol in deference to Saudi law, and this may have contributed to their professionalism without unduly sapping morale.[17]

Alcohol is an example of a nongendered solution to the fear problem. The Dahomey women soldiers drank heavily and apparently received a rum ration before battle. Alcohol is not, however, an adequate solution to soldiers' fear.[18]

Religion   Surveys of participants in combat in the twentieth century show that religion is an important force keeping many soldiers going in the trauma of combat. Hundreds of thousands of Iranian teenagers died charging against Iraqi lines in the 1980s, believing that as martyrs they would go directly to heaven. Christian soldiers, similarly, may anticipate heaven if they should die in combat while fighting bravely and nobly. Japanese soldiers in World War II fought fiercely, to the last man, in part because of their belief in reincarnation. Ancient Mayan soldiers transcended the pain of battle by going to war "transformed into their *nahwals*, spiritual companions who were believed to share human souls."

---

[15] Ordinary: Bourke 1999, xvii; Grossman 1995, 141–94; Dyer 1985, 101–30.
[16] De Pauw 1998, 122; Ambrose 1997, jerks 333; Vietnam: Goldman and Fuller 1983, 141; examples: Keegan and Holmes 1985, 53–54.
[17] Fussell 1989, heavy 96–105, drunk 99.
[18] Alpern 1998, rum 129–30.

Good soldiers, however, need to do more than die (or Iran would have defeated Iraq handily). As General Patton said in 1944, wars are won by "making the other poor dumb bastard die for his country." In any case, religion as an important combat motivator is not inherently gendered. It would not preclude women soldiers.[19]

Combat trauma

More gendered responses to the problem of motivating soldiers arise in the context of psychological trauma in combat.

Fatigue   To start with the short-term and simple aspects, in battle, soldiers experience "combat fatigue" as a result of the cumulative effect of the horrors of fighting, sleep deprivation, and extreme psychological stress. Studies of Allied troops in the 1944 Normandy campaign showed that (after one or two weeks of becoming battle-wise, or instant casualties) a soldier's period of maximum efficiency lasts only about a month. Then an extended phase of exhaustion sets in, not noticed initially by the soldier himself. It leaves him first overconfident, then highly reactive, and finally apathetic – ultimately vegetative in most cases (see Figure 5.1). Only 2 percent of soldiers apparently can resist the pressures indefinitely. With these rare exceptions, every soldier is said to have his breaking point, and it comes sooner for soldiers involved in difficult operations like landings and breakthroughs. These stresses and strains of battle are not fundamentally gendered (see pp. 157–58).[20]

In response, armies withdraw soldiers from battle briefly to restore functionality. After heavy fighting in Europe, as many as a quarter of the patients evacuated to US Army medical facilities "were uninjured physically but were babbling, crying, shaking, or stunned, unable to hear or talk ... It was the doctors' job to get as many as possible back to normalcy – and back to the lines – as soon as possible." They did this by keeping them close to the front, giving them a day of rest, hot food, and a change of clothes, and then sending three-quarters of them back to their foxholes. The majority of the rest returned to the front after a three-day treatment regime. This system thus successfully returned 90 percent of broken-down men quickly to duty.[21]

[19] McPherson 1997, 62–76; Dean 1997, 71–72; Goldman and Fuller 1983, 143; Keegan and Holmes 1985, Japanese 51–52; Schele 1991, nahwals 10.
[20] Dinter 1985, 64–67; Gabriel 1988, 2, 31–32; Goldman and Fuller 1983, 143; Bourke 1999, 95–126.
[21] Ambrose 1997, 329–30.

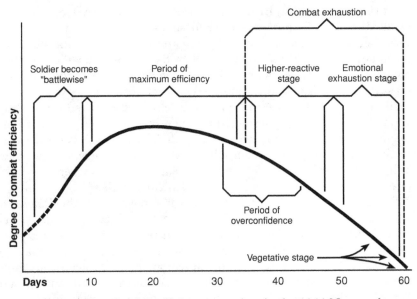

Figure 5.1 Combat efficiency over time in the 1944 Normandy campaign. [From R. L. Swank and W. E. Marchand, "Combat Neurosis: Development of Combat Exhaustion." *Archives of Neurology and Psychiatry* 55, 1946. By permission of the American Medical Association.]

Longer-term effects   Beyond short-term combat fatigue, many soldiers suffer serious and long-lasting psychological damage as a result of combat experience – frequently enough to knock them out of fighting as surely as if they were physically wounded. In World War II, the US Army had to send home nearly 400,000 soldiers for psychiatric problems. In 1973, almost one-third of Israeli and Egyptian casualties were psychiatric. By one estimate, "the number of psychiatric casualties in every war in this century ... have exceeded the number of soldiers killed by hostile fire by 100 percent" (although still less than the number of non-lethal physical casualties). This toll seriously degrades armies' fighting abilities.[22]

These effects have been called, in various wars, "shell shock," "combat neuroses," or "post-traumatic stress disorder" (PTSD) – controversial designations. Symptoms of PTSD have been identified in the accounts of veterans from the US Civil War. Manifestations of combat trauma have been "remarkably constant" through history. The intensified destruction of twentieth-century wars may make combat trauma more pervasive than ever, especially since World War II.[23]

[22] Dinter 1985, home 63; Gabriel 1987, Israeli 4; Gabriel 1988, exceeded 2.
[23] Gabriel 1987, constant 6; intensified 5–6; Civil: Dean 1997; Power 1998.

During World War I, British forces lost 80,000 soldiers – one-seventh of all disability discharges – to shell shock. Military leaders worried that if shell shock became an honorable route to escape from the front, too many soldiers would follow it. A British report after the war thus recommended that pensions be denied to victims of shell shock because no such thing exists. Rather, about 90 percent of such cases were simply total exhaustion, best treated quickly, briefly, and near the front. Only about 10 percent were considered true neuroses – although the outward manifestations looked somewhat similar. In World War II, countries that retained strict diagnostic criteria had a similar psychiatric casualty rate as in World War I (just under 1 percent of all casualties), whereas the US rate quadrupled when it adopted more lenient criteria.[24]

Since the Vietnam War, PTSD has been recognized in the *Diagnostic and Statistical Manual* (DSM) of psychotherapy. (Critics say that PTSD "is not timeless, nor does it possess an intrinsic unity," but is a "historical product" invented and made real in specific times and places.) The DSM-IV defines PTSD as "the development of characteristic symptoms" – persistent reexperiencing, avoidance of associated stimuli, and others – "following exposure to an extreme traumatic stressor involving direct personal experience of ... actual or threatened death or serious injury, or other threat to one's physical integrity." The common denominator of traumatic experiences is a feeling of "intense fear, helplessness, loss of control, and threat of annihilation." Experiences in which a survivor actively participated in killing or committing atrocities are especially traumatic, particularly when such participation cannot be "rationalized in terms of some higher value or meaning."[25]

PTSD results in three main categories of symptoms. "Hyperarousal" reflects a constant expectation of danger. "Intrusion" refers to the lingering imprint of trauma on mental processes. Traumatic memories are separated off from other life memories, and are stored not in verbal and contextual form but as "vivid sensations and images" sometimes reenacted unconsciously in behaviors. "Constriction" refers to the numbing of feelings, a natural response to pain. For example, a World War II veteran recalls seeing what combat soldiers call the thousand-yard stare – "the wide, hollow eyes of a man who no longer cares. I wasn't to that state yet, but the numbness was total. I felt almost as if I hadn't actually been in a battle" (see Figure 5.2).[26]

---

[24] Showalter 1987, lost 63; Leed 1979, worried 166; Dinter 1985, report 64; Ulman and Brothers 1988, 160; Gabriel 1987, criteria 9–10.

[25] American Psychiatric Association 1994, 424–29; Young 1995, timeless 5; Herman 1992, 52–53, intense 33, meaning 54; Davidson *et al.* 1994; Mason *et al.* 1990.

[26] Herman 1992, 35, 38, stare 43.

Figure 5.2 Combat trauma in US Marine in Pacific theater, World War II. [By Tom Lea. Army Art Collection, US Army Center of Military History.]

PTSD typically leads to emotional numbing (and hence to relationship problems), recurrent nightmares, substance abuse (traditionally, alcoholism), and, most frighteningly, delusional outbursts of violence. PTSD usually manifests itself in more subtle symptoms, however. The most immediate psychological symptoms in combat veterans are conditioned reflexes from combat, notably the tendency to "hit the dirt" on hearing a loud noise like a car backfiring. These habits are superficial though, and wear off quickly. The nightmares are long-lasting: a combat veteran sits up in bed, in a deep sleep, shouting "Kill him! Kill him!" or "Get down!" Combat veterans with PTSD may direct their aggression at the very women they depend on for care and connection: "On several occasions, he threw his wife against the wall, mistaking her for an enemy soldier."[27]

Not surprisingly, given the role of stress in weakening the immune system (see pp. 157–58), a recent study of 1,400 US Vietnam veterans showed that those with PTSD – nearly a quarter of the total – were twice as likely to have physical illnesses that included a "broad spectrum of human diseases" such as heart disease. Recent research on psychological trauma victims (from combat and other sources) shows that those with PTSD have a smaller (8 percent in one study) hippocampus, which is associated with memory and learning, in their brains. They scored 40 percent lower on a test of verbal memory than people of the same age and educational background.[28]

At the heart of PTSD is isolation – a feeling of disconnection from peacetime family and friends. "In situations of terror, people spontaneously seek their first source of comfort and protection. Wounded soldiers and raped women cry for their mothers, or for God. When this cry is not answered, the sense of basic trust is shattered. Traumatized people feel utterly abandoned, utterly alone, cast out of the divine systems of care and protection that sustain life. Thereafter a sense of alienation, of disconnection, pervades every relationship."[29]

Traumatized individuals often cannot share traumatic experiences because even if others want to hear horror stories they cannot truly understand them without having been there. "Traumatic events ... breach the attachments of family, friendship, love, and community." As the protagonist of one Vietnam novel hears from her veteran uncle, "women weren't over there ... So they can't really understand." Furthermore, going home from the front breaks a soldier's most important "lifeline" – the bonding with others in a small group. The same nightmare – becoming isolated from one's comrades in battle – comes to both American combat veterans and fierce warriors from two simple societies in New Guinea.[30]

Trauma not gendered   The psychological trauma that results from participation in combat is not innately gendered. Women are as

---

[27] Goldman and Fuller 1983, 13–14, 143; Ulman and Brothers 1988, wall 284.

[28] Study: Boscarino 1997, spectrum 605; brains: Goleman 1995.

[29] Herman 1992, 52.

[30] Ambrose 1997, 162; Herman 1992, breach 51–52; Kinney 1991, novel 40; Keeley 1996, nightmare 146; Ehrenreich 1997a, 156; Costello 1985, 198.

terrified as men during fighting, and as prone to PTSD afterwards. A study of PTSD in US Vietnam veterans found similar patterns for female veterans (mostly nurses) as for males, relative to the level of exposure to war-zone stress (such as exposure to dead and wounded soldiers). Overall, 53 percent of male Vietnam veterans and 48 percent of female ones "have experienced clinically significant stress-reaction symptoms" sometime during their lifetime. Nearly 10 percent of female US military personnel who served in Vietnam were diagnosed with PTSD some 14 to 22 years after their Vietnam service. For those women exposed to high war-zone stress, the current PTSD rate may be as high as 20 percent. For both genders, PTSD rates were higher for veterans who served in Vietnam than those serving elsewhere, and higher still for those in war-zone locations. Consistent with the importance of isolation in exacerbating PTSD, married women have substantially lower rates of PTSD than unmarried ones.[31]

Recently, several scholars have linked PTSD in combat veterans with similar symptoms in women victims of rape or incest. PTSD, in this view, is not specific to men or to combat, but merely one manifestation of a process of trauma and recovery that applies to both men and women. One study of 26 battered US women attending domestic violence clinics found almost half to exhibit PTSD symptoms. Group psychotherapy may help counteract the isolation of PTSD, and the "shattered self" may be reintegrated in the "intersubjective" space of the individual patient–therapist relationship. The restoration of connection with other people is central to treatment of PTSD because only by *telling* trauma stories can survivors overcome an individual and social urge to forget and banish unspeakable memories. "The conflict between the will to deny horrible events and the will to proclaim them aloud is the central dialectic of psychological trauma" for both rape and combat survivors. The stages of recovery also are similar: "establishing safety, reconstructing the trauma story, and restoring the connection between survivors and their community."[32]

Some scholars emphasize killing itself, not subsequent isolation and stigmatization, as the source of PTSD. Other scholars argue that combat trauma is more likely to cause PTSD than are "civilian" traumas including rape, but not because of participation in killing. (Actually, medical personnel in combat theaters are "particularly likely to develop stress-related disorders.") Rather, PTSD results from the soldier's isolation from home and community, the multiple and prolonged traumas, and the uncertainty about the immediate future, in this view.[33]

[31] Study: Kulka et al. 1990, 55, 61, 63; current: Baker, Menard, and Johns 1989, 737.
[32] Ulman and Brothers 1988; Herman 1992, dialectic 1, stages 3; O'Leary and Jacobson 1994, battered 680.
[33] Turner 1996, source 63; Deahl 1997, civilian 136; Bourke 1999, xiii.

Manhood in war

Although combat trauma itself does not depend on gender, cultural *responses* to this problem – tricks to make men keep fighting – depend heavily on gender. In brief, cultural norms force men to endure trauma and master fear, in order to claim the status of "manhood." This is the heart of hypothesis 5A: cultures develop concepts of masculinity that motivate men to fight.

Men are made, not born. Across a broad sweep of cultures, this central theme recurs with stunning regularity, as David Gilmore's cross-cultural study shows. Unlike women, men must take actions, undergo ordeals, or pass tests in order to *become* men. They are told to "be a man" whereas women are not told to "be" women (though certainly women too are socialized into gender roles). In this way, a surprising number of cultures converge in treating masculinity as something that must be created by individual and collective will against the force of instinct or "doing what comes naturally." (Oddly, the term "real men" refers to the aspects of masculinity that are least real biologically.)[34]

Culture after culture features rites of passage from boyhood to manhood. Only select men can achieve "manhood," and it must be won individually. In many cultures' initiation rituals, older males systematically inflict pain and injury on young ones, who must hold up without flinching, or face life-long shame. Men who fail the test become "negative examples ... held up scornfully to inspire conformity." The particulars of these rituals vary by cultural context. In fishing communities, would-be men go on dangerous expeditions into the water. In hunting cultures they risk their lives in hunting exploits. In societies with frequent warfare (the majority of gathering-hunting societies; see p. 24), young males must participate in war – and, for some, kill an enemy – before being called a man. Despite these variations, the passages to manhood are surprisingly similar across cultures in terms of passing harsh tests bravely.[35]

These practices recur in cultures worldwide that "have little else in common," including those with frequent or infrequent war, and simple or complex social organization. In East Africa, boys endure "bloody circumcision rites by which they become true men. They must submit without so much as flinching under the agony of the knife. If a boy cries out while his flesh is being cut, if he so much as blinks an eye or turns his head, he is shamed for life as unworthy of manhood." In an Ethiopian

[34] Gilmore 1990, sweep 11–20; Segal 1990, 111–15; McBride 1995, 189; Mead 1949, 147–48, 180–81; Walsh and Scandalis 1975, 138–39.
[35] Gilmore 1990, conformity 17; Kessler 1976, particulars 79–81; Ulman and Brothers 1988, kill 155.

society where whipping ceremonies are the test, "[a]ny sign of weakness is greeted with taunts and mockery." For the warlike Sambia in New Guinea, boys endure "whipping, flailing, beating... which the boys must endure stoically and silently." For the relatively peaceful !Kung of southwest Africa, before males are considered men and allowed to marry they must "single-handedly track and kill a sizable adult antelope, an act that requires courage and hardiness." Pueblo Indian boys aged 12–15 are "whipped mercilessly ... [and] expected to bear up impassively under the beating to show their fortitude."[36]

Modern industrialized societies continue to enact rites of passage into artificial manhood, albeit in diverse ways. The "heroic image of an achieved manhood" is "deeply ingrained in the American male psyche." Views of manhood have changed in industrialized societies, leading some men to worry, throughout the twentieth century, that nations were going soft, that boys were losing their way on the road to manhood because we now lack the rituals of passage found in simpler societies. The loss of traditional male coming-of-age rituals in contemporary society has been blamed for various ills, including the creation of an "in-between stage" called teenagers or adolescence.[37]

The military provides the main remnant of traditional manhood-making rituals, especially in boot camp and military academies where young men "endure tests of psychological or physical endurance." "The epithets of drill instructors ... – 'faggot,' ... 'pussy,' or simply 'woman' – left no doubt that not becoming a soldier meant not being a man." This method takes advantage of the fluid character of adolescent recruits' psychic structures, "preach[ing] with a fanatical zeal the cult of masculine violence." Drill sergeants draw on "the entire arsenal of patriarchal ideas ... to turn civilian male recruits into 'soldiers.'"[38]

Recruits in the South African army in the 1980s, as in so many other times and places, faced constant ridicule and gay-baiting if they couldn't keep up. Many of those classified on medical grounds as noncombat soldiers "attempted to be reclassified ... because they felt their manhood was threatened. Anything associated with weakness was considered effeminate." Many soldiers interviewed "emphasized that the core of military training was to equate aggression with masculinity."[39]

Since womanhood comes more naturally and does not require passing tests, the process would not work the same way for women. However, if a

---

[36] Gilmore 1990, common 19, bloody–fortitude 13–15; Sambia: Huyghe 1986.
[37] Gilmore 1990, psyche 20; Gerzon 1982, stage 173–75; Segal 1990, 130–33.
[38] Gerzon 1982, endurance 174, epithets 35; Ulman and Brothers 1988, zeal 159; Enloe 1983, arsenal 14; Segal 1990, 98; Levy 1992; Tickner 1992, 40; Watson 1997, 19, 22; Spinner 1997b.
[39] Cock 1991, 59–60.

culture mobilized women for war, it might just borrow the metaphor from men. The Nicaraguan revolutionary song, "Girl of the Sandinist Front," explains that a "simple girl" who takes up a gun for her "own liberation" through "heroic struggles" will find that "girl, you're a woman now." Alternatively, since manhood is an artificial construction anyway, women can just declare, with the women soldiers of Dahomey, that "we are men now," or go to war disguised as men (see pp. 63, 106–11).[40]

Warrior qualities in men   Somewhat contrary to arguments that masculinity is an arbitrary and time-bound social construction, those parts of masculinity that are found most widely across cultures and time are not arbitrary but shaped by the war system. Despite a range of gender variation, across human cultures and historical periods, some common elements recur. What war requires of fighters is not blood-lust or activation of murderous impulses. Rather, war requires men to willingly undergo an extremely painful, unpleasant experience – and to hang in there over time despite every instinct to flee. The basic requirements for being a soldier, furthermore, tend to be the same everywhere. As General Sir John Hackett put it: "Whether he was handling a slingshot weapon on Hadrian's Wall or whether he's in a main battle tank today, he is essentially the same."[41]

Being a warrior is a central component of manhood, forged by male initiation rituals worldwide. "The warrior, foremost among male archetypes ... has been the epitome of masculinity in many societies." A man learns to "deny all that is 'feminine' and soft in himself." Common features of "warrior values" across cultures and time periods are closely linked with concepts of masculinity. Warrior values among young males are widespread in nonstate societies, and underlie the development of an elaborate "warrior caste" holding high status in many complex societies, such as in medieval Europe and Japan, or twentieth-century Nazi Germany.[42]

Several elements recur in various cultures' conceptions of desirable qualities in warriors, notwithstanding some variation from culture to culture:

> *Physical courage:* "The warrior enjoys a fight, is prepared to risk wounds or death, and will if necessary engage superior forces; if death is inevitable he faces it bravely and without flinching."

[40] Randall 1981, song 149.
[41] Construction: Mosse 1996; McLaren 1997, 238; Hackett: Dyer 1985, 4.
[42] Wicks 1996, epitome 29; Keen 1991, 37.

Endurance: "The warrior can withstand extremes of climate, pain, hunger and thirst, and fatigue; he will fight on after defeats and reverses, and is not demoralized ... "

Strength and skill: "The warrior is physically robust, fit, and proficient in the use of his weapons; he is also a shrewd tactician and planner, not merely a berserk thug, although an element of frenzy in the desperate heat of battle is to be expected."

Honour: "The warrior is a 'man of honour'; he keeps his word, is loyal to his leader and to his comrades, and fights honourably ... "

Other values that have sometimes been imputed to a warrior ethos, such as "altruism, sexual potency, generosity, individual ambition, energy and hearty extroversion," are subsumed under these four, or are "peripheral." Except for physical strength, the list of warrior values is surprisingly disconnected from biologically based gender differences discussed in earlier chapters.[43]

Suppressing emotions   Two manly qualities in particular serve warriors' need to remain functional despite great fear – bravery and discipline. The Duke of Wellington had only one requirement for his lieutenants: bravery. Mastering fear is all-important. Too much bravery alone can be counterproductive, however; *some* fear is useful for staying alive amid dangers. Brave fools may die easily but brave heroes need to get the job done.[44]

The necessary discipline (self-control and obedience) to do so requires the suppression of emotions, especially fear and including grief. (Anger is more permissible if it does not cause uncontrollable outbursts.) "The soldier is obliged to conceal his fears lest he cause a panic." If a man is to carry out manly deeds, he cannot be slowed down by taking the time to psychologically heal himself after the terrible things he has witnessed and endured. He must strap down his armor and press on, willing debilitating emotions out of his mind. The battlefield is "a place almost without mercy and utterly without pity, where the emotions which humanity cultivates and admires elsewhere – gentleness, compassion, tolerance, amity – have neither room to operate nor place to exist." To participate requires an "extraordinary reversal of normal psychic and nervous response to danger." This reversal is key to winning battles, and thus wars. In the twentieth century, courage has been seen as "more the management of

---

[43] McCarthy 1994, 105–6.
[44] Keegan and Holmes 1985, 47; Ambrose 1997, lieutenants 159.

fear than the overt display of gallantry and aggression." Some views of courage center on willpower.[45]

Suppression of emotions is taught to soldiers. At West Point, new students are shouted at, "You can't display emotion around here!" One who cried when severely harassed was labeled unsuitable officer material – the reports containing "undertones concerning masculinity and possible homosexuality of a cadet who cried or could not control his emotions." US army life revolves around a "taboo on tenderness," not a celebration of violence (brawls being relatively rare).[46]

The difficulty some veterans have in connecting emotionally with other people reflects a "hardening" of men in combat – an extension of what training in masculinity already has taught boys before they see war. For one Vietnam vet, the war "had hardened him ... It had forced him to master his fears ... It had burned away the boy in him and left a man of tempered steel." The process of "hardening" gives men a tough shell in that they can withstand pain and abuse without losing control. German militarists of the World War I era likened the making of men in battle to a purifying "bath of steel."[47]

Crying seems to be a central taboo for hardened men, notwithstanding some change in this regard in recent years in US culture. In the late nineteenth century, a study of 61 men who became hysterical – not from combat but usually following a physical trauma at the workplace – found that only two ever cried. For a grown man to cry implies "[n]ot only the pain of all he had endured becoming in one moment no longer endurable, but the shattering, at the same moment, of a sheltering, encircling notion of who he was, a strong man, a protector." Women sometimes help enforce the taboo on crying. For example, a US girlfriend of a World War II soldier, upon receiving a letter from him that said he had cried many nights during heavy fighting, "was convinced I had loved a coward. I never wrote to him again." Ashley Montagu bemoans the prohibition on crying. He says that "the feeling of sympathy that elicits weeping" is universal and "deep-seated" in both evolutionary biology and human physiology. The taboo on boys' weeping "in the English-speaking world" makes them repress the desire to cry and eventually lose the ability to do so, manifesting various bodily ailments instead.[48]

---

[45] Fussell 1998, panic C5; Kellett 1990, 229; Gerzon 1982, armor 40–42; Keegan and Holmes 1985, place–reversal 21; Kellett 1990, gallantry 229; Shalit 1988, 97; Brown 1988, 206; Goldman and Fuller 1983, 51; willpower: Mosse 1996, 100.

[46] Gerzon 1982, students 34; Segal 1990, taboo 19–20.

[47] Goldman and Fuller 1983, hardened 176; bath: Theweleit 1987.

[48] Mosse 1996, 85; Griffin 1992, shattering 49; Costello 1985, coward 198; Montagu 1989, 22, 24, 80–81.

Emotional shutting-down comes at a price. Biology endows us with a range of emotional responses because they are useful in a complex language-using social species whose members depend on each other's cooperation. To truncate this range of responses – such as by losing the ability to cry – diminishes a society. It is better for only half of the population to pay this price, especially since the other half has primary responsibility for young children. Apparently this solution is obvious enough that it recurs in many cultures. Men are trained to suppress emotions, in case they have to fight a war. Women pick up the slack in emotional work and relationships. Young men then face a dilemma: pay the price of a warrior mentality – anxiety, PTSD, emotional difficulties in relationships – or pay the price in humiliation and shame that faces the sissy as a failed man.[49]

Shame   Shame is the glue that holds the man-making process together. Males who fail tests of manhood are publicly shamed, are humiliated, and become a negative example for others. The process is reinforced repeatedly as boys grow up and even after they become soldiers. The power of shame should not be underestimated. Goldschmidt argues that prestige in a social group is among the most central motivations of human behavior. Shame centrally punishes failure in masculine war roles in particular – i.e., succumbing to fear in battle and thus proving oneself a coward. (Although many cultures shame as cowards men who do not fight, exceptions exist. Apache culture blamed unwillingness to participate in war on laziness rather than cowardice.)[50]

In World War I, and other cases, shell shock was treated as tantamount to a failure of manliness, i.e., of bravery and discipline. Military doctors in 1917 saw shell shock as an extension of the repressed emotions expected of men in peacetime: "The suppression of fear and other strong emotions is not demanded only of men in the trenches." Shell shock was, as Elaine Showalter puts it, "the body language of masculine complaint, a disguised male protest, not only against the war, but against the concept of manliness itself." Officers suffered from shell shock at four times the rate of enlisted soldiers, and the officers' symptoms were more emotional (nightmares, dizziness, disorientation) than the more physical symptoms of the soldiers (muteness, paralysis, blindness, vomiting). The officers faced greater pressures to uphold a masculine ideal, in order to motivate their men. Not surprisingly, given the label of failed manhood as well as the lowered testosterone levels resulting from defeat,

---

[49] Keen 1991, dilemma 29, 47; Betcher and Pollack 1993, 120–21; Edley and Wetherell 1995, 77–78.
[50] Goldschmidt 1990; Griffin 1992, 39; Opler 1941, Apache 333.

"sexual impotence was widespread" in shell-shocked British men of all ranks.[51]

In World War I cases of shell shock, Britain found that "[n]o longer could [male hysteria] be dismissed as a continental aberration from which stout British manhood was immune." "This parade of emotionally incapacitated men was in itself a shocking contrast to the heroic visions and masculinist fantasies that had preceded it." Similarly, in Australia, shell shock served as a "stark reminder of the fragility of masculinity" since it made men "emotional, dependent and weak – bearing the traits of the feminine." The psychiatric treatment of these men reinforced the feminization of combat trauma victims, in contrast to a masculine ideal of independence and confidence. Men's loss of self-control was feminized by labeling it a form of "hysteria" (a feminine ailment).[52]

Soldiers in World War I were told to pull themselves together and get back to the fight. "Armies on both sides of the line responded to the specter of malingering with a constant barrage of hectoring appeals for men to demonstrate their pluck and manliness." There was a fine line between treatment and punishment. Therapists' goal was not the individual's well-being but rather his willingness to resume his duty to society. To induce him to do so, and to serve as an example for others, disciplinary therapists inflicted electric shocks and cigarette burns, among other methods.[53]

The idea of treating shell-shocked men (primarily officers) with respect and therapy instead of shaming them was a new and largely untried innovation – with the goal of returning men to combat as quickly as possible. It was advocated by British doctor and anthropologist W. H. R. Rivers. His most famous patient was Siegfried Sassoon who wrote in 1917 (while in "treatment" before being discharged back to duty): "I'm back again from hell / With loathesome thoughts to sell; / Secrets of death to tell; / And horrors from the abyss... / For you our battles shine / With triumph half-divine... / But a curse is on my head... / For I have watched them die."[54]

Like soldiers in many wars, those in World War I felt radically disconnected from civilian society – those who had *not* "watched them die." Veterans referred to the Great War as "the Great Unmentionable." Within a few years after World War I, psychological interest in combat trauma

[51] Showalter 1987, suppression 65, complaint 64, impotence 62.
[52] Beveridge 1997, 7, immune 8; Showalter 1987, parade 63; Lake and Damousi 1995, fragility 11–12; hysteria: Pugliese 1995, 168; Showaltar 1985; Herman 1992, 20; Leed 1979, 163; McBride 1995, 177; Mosse 1996, 85; Koonz 1987, 19.
[53] McLaren 1997, pluck 234; Leed 1979, 169, shocks 174–75.
[54] Leed 1979, 190; Herman 1992, 21–23; Barker 1991, poem 25; Young 1995, 43–88; Fussell 1975, 102.

faded, and its victims became "an embarrassment to civilian societies eager to forget." They had been made "strange" because "identities formed in war ... were formed beyond the margins of normal social experience." The changes combatants went through were rooted not in specific horrifying experiences but in "a sense of having lived through incommensurable social worlds – that of peace and that of war." The image of No Man's Land – a grotesque blasted field of mud between entrenched lines – "captured the essence of an experience of having been sent beyond the outer boundaries of social life." It was the "most lasting and disturbing image" of World War I for its veterans. Furthermore, the advent of trench warfare had moved soldiers into a darkened world, intensifying their feeling of invisibility.[55]

A similar sense of isolation plagued US veterans of the Vietnam War. Their PTSD was aggravated by anti-war sentiment at home and the incompetent management of the war by politicians and generals. Veterans felt stigmatized upon their return – facing taunts of "baby killer" from those who opposed the war, and blamed for failure and indiscipline by those who supported it (especially their fathers who had fought in the "good war"). Caught in the middle, returning from "a bullshit war and a bullshit Army," these veterans found it especially hard to reconnect with society or to talk about what they had been through, and thus perhaps suffered longer-lasting and deeper psychological aftershocks from their combat experience. These "returning soldiers often felt traumatized a second time" by this experience. "That year in Vietnam separated me from you" was the inner response of one veteran to a party his family and friends gave for him soon after his return. Some men never regained the ability to feel comfortable in "the mundane world which women also inhabit." Unlike after earlier wars, US society did not successfully sweep veterans' trauma under the carpet, perhaps because civilians also felt traumatized by the war. Australian veterans of Vietnam, who were denied the hero status of earlier veterans, found a "crisis of confidence became a crisis ... of male sexuality."[56]

Men who do not take the manhood bait suffer less emotional damage in war. Soldiers who avoid PTSD despite participating in combat generally have a combination of "stress-resistant" traits found in about 10 percent of the population: they are very sociable, use active coping strategies, and

[55] Herman 1992, unmentionable 70, forget 23; Leed 1979, strange 4, 13–14, outer–lasting 15, invisibility 19; Gilbert 1987; Fussell 1975.
[56] Gerzon 1982, 28–31; Grossman 1995, 281–95; Tripp 1996, fathers; Goldman and Fuller 1983, bullshit 150, year 174, 169–324; Herman 1992, second 71; Ehrenreich 1997a, inhabit 156; Turner 1996, 18, sweep 47; Australian: Gerster 1995, sexuality 225; McHugh 1993.

maintain an internal sense of control. US Vietnam combat veterans with these qualities, who did not develop PTSD, saw the war as a dangerous challenge to meet effectively, "rather than as an opportunity to prove their manhood or a situation of helpless victimization."[57]

Women shaming men into war   Women are often active participants in shaming men to try to goad them into fighting wars. Recall the Russian women in World War I who went "over the top" to try to shame exhausted Russian soldiers into fighting again (see pp. 73–75). In Britain and America during that war, women organized a large-scale campaign to hand out white feathers to able-bodied men found on the streets, to shame the men for failing to serve in combat. Not all women supported it: "Dealer in white feathers / ... Can't you see it isn't decent, / To flout and goad men into doing, / What isn't asked of you?" However, the Women of England's Active Service League pledged never to be seen in public with an able-bodied man not serving in the military, and British recruiting posters told young men their women would reject them if they were "not in khaki" and meanwhile told the young women that men who refused to fight and die for them were not worthy of their affections. (The white feather campaign was briefly resurrected in World War II, and the British government had to issue badges for men exempt on medical grounds.) Some scholars object to blaming women for goading men into World War I. They argue that the poster claiming "Women of Britain Say, 'Go!' " (see Figure 5.3) was propaganda devised by men to affect other men. "[M]any women tried to get their sons out of the army. Others were agitating to prevent conscription."[58]

Women's use of shame to goad men into fighting has been observed in a variety of settings. Before the 1973 military takeover in Chile, for example, right-wing women threw corn at soldiers to taunt them as "chickens." Apache women met successful warriors with "songs and rejoicings" but unsuccessful ones with "jeers and insults. The women turn[ed] away from them with assumed indifference and contempt." Cowardice or incompetence by Zulu warriors, punishable in Shaka's time by death, later earned "humiliation and disgrace ... [W]omen still took it upon themselves to shame a man who was not brave ... sometimes stripping themselves nude in public to mortify a man who had behaved badly." Even warriors who had survived a fierce battle in which the Zulu had fought with incredible

---

[57] Herman 1992, 58–59.

[58] Stites 1978, feathers 281; Tylee 1990, poem 258, agitating 257; Noakes 1998, resurrected 92, 183; Kent 1993, posters 27.

Figure 5.3 "Women of Britain say, 'Go!,'" poster, World War I. [Courtesy of the Imperial War Museum, London.]

bravery, but lost, faced shame. "[W]omen cruelly ridiculed them: 'You! You're no men! You're just women, seeing that you ran away.'"[59]

Once during the Mau Mau rebellion, when a leader was jailed by colonial authorities, a crowd formed and some African male leaders tried to get it to disperse. "The women were enraged by this male compromise, they jeered at the men and taunted them." One woman exposed her genitals to the men, invoking a traditional insult which was in Kikuyu culture "the ultimate recourse of those consumed by feelings of anger, frustration, humiliation or revenge." (!Kung girls also mock men who "deviate from the group's norms" by using "female genital display ... [as] a demonstration of disrespect.") Backed up by ululations from other women in the crowd, she "rebuked the men thus: 'You take my dress and give me your trousers. You men are cowards ... Our leader is in there, let us get him.'" As a result, the crowd lunged forward and the police opened fire, killing 17 men and four women.[60]

Historical examples

Soldiers' gender identity – their idea of proving worthy of "manhood" – has motivated their behavior in battle in many cases. In some premodern cultures that emphasize war, the point is explicit: a man cannot be called a man or marry until he has proven himself in battle. Examples include cases from ancient Greece and Germany, nineteenth-century Africa and Asia, and American Indian cultures. Masculine honor also underlies the code of chivalry in medieval Europe, where women became an "inspirer of male glory" – even though "the code was but a veneer over violence, greed, and sensuality."[61]

In the US Civil War, soldiers on both sides refer frequently, in their own accounts, to the need to show themselves brave, not to behave as cowards, in order to prove their manhood and thus preserve their honor. Most soldiers "wanted to avoid the shame of being known as a coward – and that is what gave them courage." Soldiers considered it a "test of manhood ... Officers especially felt that their manhood was on trial before the rank and file." Some soldiers did run away under fire, or feign illness to avoid battle, and they received the contempt and scorn of the others. The test of manhood as bravery under fire overlapped with other motivations, notably primary group cohesion and belief in the cause.[62]

---

[59] De Pauw 1998, 19; Huyghe 1986, corn 31; Cremony 1868, contempt 216; Zulu: Edgerton 1988, 39, 107.

[60] Mau: Kanogo 1987, recourse 82; Eibl-Eibesfeldt 1974, !Kung 452–53.

[61] Ehrenreich 1997a, premodern 127–28; chivalry: Lynch and Maddern eds. 1995; Tuchman 1979, inspirer 67, veneer 69.

[62] McPherson 1997, avoid–test 77–79, officers 31; Crane 1894.

Married soldiers in the Civil War faced "competing ideals of manhood" – to be responsible husbands and fathers on the one hand and to defend their country on the other (both matters of honor). The latter usually took priority. Even when wives pleaded with them to return, and even when officers could have resigned legally (after what their wives considered adequate service and participation in battles), the men resisted. As one officer wrote his wife: "My manhood is involved in a faithful and fearless sticking to the job until it is finished, or it finishes me" (he died in the war). Soldiers also argued that their own shame would dishonor their families: one father of two wrote home that he "would rather die an honorable Death than to Bring Reproach or Dishonour upon my family or friends."[63]

The Civil War itself has been called a "crisis in gender," especially for defeated Southern men. Confederate newspapers had urged soldiers to "Be a Man." The capture of Jefferson Davis while trying to escape dressed in his wife's clothes symbolized the emasculation of Southern men. They were able to recover their manhood after the war only by returning to the domestic sphere, reasserting control of their own families. Family relationships became the men's "one remaining location of legitimate domination," but the war had "increased ... the autonomy of their women." (Recent psychology experiments, incidentally, show the continuing importance of honor for Southern male students. They, far more than Northern counterparts, responded to unprovoked insults with anger and higher levels of stress and sex hormones.)[64]

In the German wars of liberation of the early nineteenth century, "[i]t is striking how often the word *manliness* was used to designate the seriousness of battle." Manliness meant "courage, strength, hardness, control over the passions" and was embodied in a "so-called manly life ... lived outside the family structure, wholly within a camaraderie of males, the Männerbund ... The desire to pass the test of manliness became a challenge best met in war."[65]

The idea before 1914 that a Great War would be uplifting, cleansing, and invigorating for the participating nations – arguably the single most disastrous idea of the ill-fated twentieth century – is firmly rooted in gender roles. Writings from Germany, Spain, and Ireland before World War I conclude, in parallel, that "the nation which regards [bloodshed] as a final horror has lost its manhood" (Irish version) and "changes ... into a feminine nation" whose honor will be ravished by stronger, more manly nations (Spanish version). Teddy Roosevelt charged Woodrow Wilson

[63] McPherson 1997, 134–40, finishes 137, friends 138.
[64] Whites 1995, 132–38; Nisbett and Cohen 1996, experiments 41–55.
[65] Mosse 1990, 26–27.

with "emasculat[ing] American manhood and weaken[ing] its fiber" by his reluctance to enter World War I. William James argued that war served certain functions, including that of "the great preserver of our ideals of hardihood." (However, although "martial virtues ... are absolute and permanent human goods," they might be realized through other forms of "competitive passion" which might someday become a "moral equivalent of war," according to James.)[66]

Before World War I, by one account, Kaiser Wilhelm II "constantly ... felt the need to parade his power" as a psychic defense against his childlike fear of falling apart. The Kaiser's difficulty in making decisions reflected a "sexual confusion" – the Kaiser displayed public masculinity (self-defined as "remorseless severity" and embodied in heroic portrait poses) to counteract private homosexual desires (probably not acted upon). His closest friend and advisor (evidently in love with the Kaiser, and surrounded by a circle of gay friends) was indicted for homosexuality. "In imperial Germany, with its exaltation of 'manly virtues,' homosexuality was perhaps the most heinous accusation that could be brought against a man." The months-long trial, a sordid scandal, pressured the Kaiser to reaffirm his masculinity. Similar dynamics may have operated in Hitler's case: "In both men, grandiose assertions of power and infallibility served as defenses against feelings of inadequacy and fears of homosexuality."[67]

Even in the mechanized slaughter of World War I, men found in their concept of manhood a serviceable motivation for remaining brave and avoiding the stigma of cowardice. Volunteers sought "proof of manhood" in that war, a proof with which they hoped to energize their lives and countries. A volunteer in 1914 wrote: "I believe that this war is a challenge for our time and for each individual, a test by fire, that we may ripen into manhood, become men able to cope." American soldiers "envisioned the battlefield as a proving ground where they could enact and repossess the manliness that modern American society had baffled." The war accelerated a search in Europe (and especially Germany) for a "new man," a search "focused upon a militant masculinity" which would overcome the decadence of capitalist life. This "concept of manliness" included "physical strength and courage ... combined with the harmonious proportions of the body and purity of the soul." For British men of the World War I generation, manliness was equated with not complaining.[68]

---

[66] Theodore Roszak in Gerzon 1982, parallel 36, 52; Miedzian 1991, 19–39, fiber 21; James 1910, 170–72.

[67] Waite 1990, 144–45, 153, 157.

[68] Mosse 1990, proof 22, cope–militant 60, soul 59; Gerzon 1982, baffled 38; Fussell 1975, complaining 22.

After World War I, the idea of restoring manhood played a central role in the rise of a new militarism, and ultimately fascism, in Germany. A 1925 writer refers to a widespread "upsurge of ... male-manliness." "[T]he stereotype of manliness was strengthened by the war in both England and Germany," but with somewhat different emphases. In the German Free Corps, which fought on against its domestic and foreign enemies in 1919–21, masculinity was an essential and central ingredient in ideology. A strong myth saw Free Corps members as "real men who in their cama-raderie exemplified the best in the nation." In Nazi ideology, grounded in World War I experiences, "manhood was cast in the warrior image." These exemplary images of masculinity filtered down to ordinary men as well, "always linked to the war experience. Even for those who did not take the warrior ideal to its extremes, soldierly comportment mattered – meaning clean-cut appearance, hardness, self-discipline, and courage." Similarly, World War I Australian forces at Gallipoli, despite losing the bloody battle, were widely seen as having passed a collective test of man-hood. They "simultaneously established their masculinity and Australia's worth as a nation." Symbolically, just as boys must break their maternal attachments to become men, Australia had to break from the Mother Country, which it did by fighting independently of Britain in World War II.[69]

During World War II, millions of males in Britain and America un-derwent transformation into soldiers through a "rapid and brutal con-ditioning process." Yet those soldiers did not dwell on upholding manly honor – a concept which seemed empty after the disillusionment of World War I. World War II was "approached by both sexes with much less ideal-ism," and with the advent of total war there was less distinction between the men at the front and the women on the home front. Nonetheless, for US soldiers in Normandy in 1944, "the most important thing a majority of the GIs discovered was that they were not cowards ... [T]hey couldn't be sure until tested. After a few days in combat, most of them ... had neither run away nor collapsed into a pathetic mass of quivering Jell-O (their worst fear...)."[70]

Other US soldiers in World War II, without referring explicitly to man-hood, reflect the sense of Civil War soldiers quoted above, that to give up was shameful. One soldier recalls "the feeling of guilt that seems to come over you whenever you retreat. You don't like to look anyone in the eyes." As the tide of one campaign began to turn, a road had retreating

[69] Corps: Theweleit 1987; Mosse 1990, upsurge 165, both 166, best 168, cast 72, linked 185; Australia: Lake and Damousi 1995, 2.

[70] Costello 1985, brutal 74; Ambrose 1997, empty 14, cowards 46–47; Gubar 1987, idealism 228–29.

troops on one side, watched by civilians who "were silent, their eyes full of reproach," while on the other side advancing troops were cheered on by "young girls waving and laughing." Elsewhere, in Ambrose's accounts of US soldiers taken prisoner by German forces, the word "humiliation" recurs. S. L. A. Marshall's studies of the World Wars convinced him that the most important motivator was to avoid looking like cowards to their comrades. A soldier values "his reputation as a man among other men" more than his life.[71]

After World War II, a "tougher manliness" came into fashion in the United States and Western Europe. Some writers refer to a "John Wayne syndrome" in US men – "hard, tough, unemotional, ruthless, and competitive." In the Vietnam War, even more than World War II, idealistic and patriotic talk was unfashionable. Nonetheless, especially early in the war, the theme of war as a test of manhood recurs. "I needed to prove something – my courage, my toughness, my manhood ... [–] demonstrate to [my parents], and to myself as well, that I was a man after all" (Philip Caputo). "They told us ... that the Marine Corps built men" (Ron Kovic). Becoming a soldier "was the way you proved your manhood" (an army sergeant quoted by Robert Jay Lifton). One US officer saw his presence in the war as "a test of his ego and manhood." One thread of the manhood theme which continues in the Vietnam era is that to lose is shameful. "The veterans of the failed United States mission in Vietnam returned ... to a kind of embarrassed silence, *as if,* one of them thought, *everybody was ashamed of us.*" One veteran's wife notes that most of the veterans felt "just a little bit ashamed" because, fighting in a dirty war, they told themselves "I'll do anything to get out of this alive" even when that meant "they weren't the big hero."[72]

Politicians, in making the decisions that led to the Vietnam War, also sought to prove their manhood. "Manhood was very much in the minds of the architects ... They wanted to show who had bigger balls." President Johnson, by this account, "wanted the respect of men who were tough, real men" because he himself wanted "to be seen as a man." "The thing Johnson feared most was ... that his manhood might be inadequate." Later, Ronald Reagan intervened in Nicaragua because he thought that "America has to show a firmness of manhood."[73]

---

[71] Ambrose 1997, 195, eyes 206, laughing 208, humiliation 358; Marshall: Gerzon 1982, 39; Keegan and Holmes 1985, 52, 56; Marshall 1947.

[72] Mosse 1996, tougher 182; Gerzon 1982, syndrome 34, 45, recurs 32–33; Turner 1996, 21; Segal 1990, 18; Goldman and Fuller 1983, 208, ego 145, silence 7, hero 340.

[73] David Halberstam in Gerzon 1982, balls 93; Halberstam in Miedzian 1991, inadequate 21; Miedzian 1991, firmness 22; Etheredge 1978, 60–62; Lasswell 1930.

The Gulf War created a "new paradigm of manhood" for Americans, according to one view, that negated the loss of manhood in the Vietnam War. The central element of the new manhood was its "slight feminization" through the addition of tenderness to the traditional tough and aggressive version of manhood. Top US war leaders "openly articulated [a] sense of manly vulnerability and human compassion, rather than bravado or stern invincibility," for example, by lavishing attention on their families (Bush and Schwarzkopf) and even weeping in public (Powell). Along with "technowar," which demonstrated the superiority of Western society, the modified model of manhood helped middle-class American men identify with the heroic male warrior role even though they did not physically participate in the fighting. The new visibility of women in the US military rounded out the construction of the new, more family-oriented masculinity. In this view, the triumph of this new masculinity after the challenge of the Vietnam War shows how the concept of legitimate masculinity can expand and adapt to extend masculinity's power.[74]

Representations of manhood in war   The "classic narrative of the war film" has been called the "richest of all texts of masculinity." In short, boy leaves home, faces death (representing fear of castration), wins war, returns to claim bride, and wins acclaim from father-figures. In an alternative post-Freudian interpretation, leaving home to face death represents not a castration fear but a separation from mother-womb to pass a test that establishes autonomous identity.[75]

Representations of the Vietnam War in the United States (in books, films, and TV shows) reinforced "the interests of masculinity and patriarchy" and heralded a broad postwar "remasculinization" of America. *Rambo* films masculinized the independent hero while feminizing the weak-willed political establishment that had prevented the US military from winning the war. Vietnam veterans became emblems of a masculinity unjustly victimized – by "their government, the war, the Vietnamese, American protesters, and the women's movement." The rebirth and purification of American manhood, through rejection of femininity and sexuality, played a central role in the political conservatism of the 1980s, in this view. An alternative view, however, sees these events as the lifting of a "national fog of silence and denial" by which the whole US society dealt with the shared trauma of Vietnam. (For example, the war's Tomb of the Unknown remained empty from 1975 to 1984.)[76]

---

[74] Niva 1998, 118–19.
[75] Simpson 1994, 212–28, classic 213, richest 212.
[76] Jeffords 1989, xi, 116, 186; Turner 1996, denial–tomb 15; Simpson 1994, 238–44.

Gender variation   The common themes connecting war and masculinity in many cultures do not mean that these connections remain uniform, nor that war limits gender to fixed modes of expression. On the contrary, the superficial trappings of masculinity and femininity, such as clothes, hair, ornamentation, and mannerisms, vary wildly from one time and place to another. For example, the portrait of Louis XIV in Figure 5.4 shows a pose considered virile in a Western context 300 years ago, but appearing effeminate today. Scholarship on masculinity – in films, books, diaries, and other media – shows how constructions of masculinity differ across contexts such as age, race, world region, and historical period.[77]

Commonalities across cultures do not prevent individuals from breaking the mold, either. For example, the fluidity of male gender roles around war is illustrated by Chevalier D'Eon in the eighteenth century. He had a successful military and diplomatic career, and then – as a public personality, prominent in the press – hinted and finally confessed that he was a woman in male disguise. She then lived her last three decades in women's clothing – forbidden to cross-dress as a man, by order of the French king. Nonetheless, D'Eon's autopsy found "unquestionably male" genitalia. His decision to live as a woman was "not a compulsion but an intellectual decision ... [made] because he deeply admired the moral character of women and wanted to live as one of them."[78]

Just as relatively peaceful societies hold the latent potential for war (see pp. 28–32), so apparently do cultures that diverge from militarized masculinity hold the potential to resurrect it. The nonmilitaristic norms of Jewish masculinity before the twentieth century gave way, in Zionism, to a new male gender model based on military service. "The New Jew was not supposed to shed tears" (for example, by soldiers at their comrades' funerals). For a tough *sabra* (native-born Israeli), "tears recall the helpless Jews of the ghettos and pogroms, history's victims."[79]

Autonomy and masculinity   Separation from mothers, in some scholars' view, is key to the soldier's ability to commit aggression. The effeminate voices of mothers, teachers, and ministers have trained men not to hurt people, and must be silenced before the soldier can function in combat. Thus, soldiers are terrified of being considered "women" – indeed, of the feminine side of themselves. A soldier's coarse language "symbolically throws off the shackles of the matriarchy in which he grew up" (mothers and old-maid schoolteachers). This view of autonomy as

---

[77] Brittan 1989, 20; Scott 1999; Segal 1990, ix–x, 18; Rotundo 1993, 1, 232–39; Mead 1949, 67, 132–33.
[78] Kates 1995, autopsy xii, one xxiii; De Pauw 1998, 107–9.
[79] Lentin 1996, model 389; Avishai Margalit, in Ferguson 1996, shed 440.

Figure 5.4 Louis XIV in a virile pose. ["Louis XIV, roi de France" by Hyacinthe Rigaud, 1701. Courtesy of the Musée du Louvre, Paris.]

centered on breaking away from mothers resonates with object-relations theory in difference feminism (see p. 46).[80]

One recent manhood type – exemplified by "Rambo" – centers on autonomy. This genre of hero does not capitulate either to an enemy or to a (feminized, wimpy) bureaucrat who tries to restrain him. The "warrior mentality embraces fully the cult of autonomy – the hero must achieve greatness and face his death alone. While he may fight in defense of his kin, the ultimate duty he owes is to personal excellence." This was a theme in the post-Vietnam US culture. The 1986 film *Top Gun* (produced with massive Pentagon assistance) "promoted a new brazen individualism." It laid claim to the collectivist masculinity of World War II (based on teamwork and self-sacrifice) but actually reworked masculinity around "male narcissism" with the hero taking on homoerotic qualities much more overtly than in traditional war films.[81]

Rambo is not, in fact, an ideal man in his hyper-autonomy, however – certainly not for winning wars – since he rejects control and discipline by authorities. Far from being a generic prototype of violent males, Rambo is a complex package – "a peculiarly post-Vietnam, pre-Gulf War type of American militarized male." Contrary to Rambo, the "manly ideal" in most cultures constrains autonomy and restricts individual freedom, as it molds men to the needs of war.[82]

Gilmore's cross-cultural survey of manhood offers another handle on the question of autonomy. Gilmore himself argues that diverse cultures need to create men who can endure pain without flinching, and accomplish feats of courage and strength, because boys need to achieve their gender identities by separating from their mothers, a process fraught with insecurity. Consider, however, the outliers in Gilmore's review: Tahiti and the Semai. In both cases, neither heroic ideas of manhood nor rituals of passage are found. Men consider themselves fairly similar to women. Yet boys separate from mothers in these cultures just as they do in cultures obsessed with proving manhood. The difference, rather, is that the Tahitians and Semai have extremely infrequent war (and this has been true for centuries). They are among the most peaceful societies known. Both cultures go to great lengths to avoid social conflict, to defuse it should it occur, and to encourage people to flee rather than fight. They do not need or want warriors. These are the cultures that lack the man-making rites of endurance found in most cultures. The toughening of

---

[80] Gerzon 1982, voices 40; Costello 1985, shackles 77.
[81] Jeffords 1989, 116; Betcher and Pollack 1993, cult 119–21; Simpson 1994, brazen–overtly 229–52; Segal 1990, 98.
[82] Enloe 1993, type 72–78; Mosse 1996, constrains 8; Keen and Zur 1989.

men to fight wars thus explains common manhood rituals better than mothers and autonomy do.[83]

Summary   To summarize, cultures around the world with few exceptions construct "tough" men who can shut down emotionally in order to endure extreme pain (physical and psychological). The omnipresent potential for war causes cultures to transform males, deliberately and systematically, by damaging their emotional capabilities (which biologically resemble those of females). Thus manhood, an artificial status that must be won individually, is typically constructed around a culture's need for brave and disciplined soldiers.

One approach to masculinity emphasizes that "[m]asculinity...is always local and subject to change." Some scholars tie present-day Western conceptions of masculinity to specific historical phases such as nineteenth-century Europe or the earlier rise of capitalism. These studies, despite their insights about how the parts of masculinity that *do* vary are constructed locally, do not explain well the cross-cultural regularity of gendered war roles documented in this book.[84]

To the extent that cultures employ gender to help motivate fighters, having women in the ranks could disrupt this dynamic. As one US sergeant put it, having females perform masculine soldiering roles "sort of makes the man to feel like – I'm not really the man I thought I was, I've got a female who can do the same job." Proposals to create a women's auxiliary army corps in 1942 provoked this protest from one Congressman: "Think of the humiliation! What has become of the manhood of America?" US General William Westmoreland testified in 1979, after retiring, that "No man with gumption wants a woman to fight his nation's battles." The next year, the US Marine Corps commandant said that women's participation in combat "would be an enormous psychological distraction for the male who wants to think that he's fighting for that woman somewhere behind ... It tramples the male ego. When you get right down to it, you've got to protect the manliness of war."[85]

The men's movement

The shutting down of emotions – a key aspect of molding tough "men" for war – lies at the heart of many of the problems of contemporary masculinity discussed in recent Western writings on men. It bears on men's

[83] Gilmore 1990, 26–29, outliers 201–19.
[84] Brittan 1989, local 3.
[85] Astrachan 1986, job 61; Treadwell 1954, think 25; Francke 1997, 260, gumption 23; Enloe 1983, tramples 153–54.

relations with spouses and children, and thus on the issues of divorce and custody. It bears on the raising of boys (see pp. 287–301), and on alcoholism and other drug abuse. It plays a key role in male violence against women, including domestic violence and rape. Because the culture constructs masculinity to enhance the war-making capabilities of men in general, the damage to men's emotional abilities impacts most men, not just combat veterans.

A few works about men and masculinity do see the centrality of war. Sam Keen writes: "The male psyche is, first and foremost, the warrior psyche. Nothing shapes, informs, and molds us so much as society's demand that we become specialists in the use of power and violence." Although only a minority of (American) men actually serve in the military and even fewer kill anyone, "all men are marked by the warfare system and the military virtues. We all wonder: Am I a man? Could I kill?" Even the gender identities of those who flunk the test of manhood – sissies – are shaped by the test. Keen develops a list of masculine and feminine cultural archetypes that flow from the war context, beginning with "His body and character are hardened to allow him to fight" while "Her body and character are softened to allow her to care." Men are allowed anger but no tears; women are allowed tears but no anger. Keen portrays men's war service as honorable: "manhood has traditionally required selfless generosity even to the point of sacrifice." Until we live in an ideal world, says Keen, someone needs to allow their body to be maimed or destroyed in order to protect their community. We should honor men for doing so, even as we criticize some of the results. Keen's approach, although perhaps oversimplified, brings war to center stage in understanding gender roles.[86]

Warren Farrell also treats war as central, but in an anti-feminist context. Farrell, a former NOW board member who radically changed his views on gender relations, argues that men as a class are victims oppressed by women and feminism – specifically by being made into "war slaves." Men are "disposable" while women are "protected." Men are forced against their will into dangerous and debilitating roles – especially when drafted – and as a result have lower life expectancy (among other indicators) than women. Farrell's argument potentially moves gender discourse forward because it is empirically grounded and points to gaps in feminist thinking about men. Unfortunately, the potential for constructive engagement is lost when Farrell blames and attacks feminists for crimes against men that, if true, long predate modern feminism.[87]

---

[86] Keen 1991, psyche–care 37, 44, sacrifice 47.
[87] Farrell 1993, 123–63; cf. Jones 1996.

Allan Johnson, by contrast, retains a pro-feminist position without losing sight of war. He defines men's war trauma as "massive suffering" but not "oppression," because war is controlled by "patriarchal" systems that do not "oppress men as men" (since women do not "enforce ... and benefit ... from men's suffering"). Also, war "celebrates and affirms ... patriarchal manhood" and benefits men, while most of the victims are women and children. Johnson's argument is undermined by his claims of "nonpatriarchal societies" and peaceful origins, which are empirically unfounded (see pp. 23–26, 396–97).[88]

The evidence in this chapter supports Farrell's empirical cornerstone – that men as men are indeed victims in the war system – but leads to conclusions closer to Johnson's in that men's oppression results from a war system, embedded in patriarchal society, rather than from women as a class. In the war system, men as men are victims, not beneficiaries, but so are women as women (see pp. 396–402).

Most other writers on men and masculinity give little attention to war. This is a shame because a common theme in the men's movement is the need to become less unfeeling and isolated – characteristics connected with men's role as potential warriors. In a 1985 bibliography of hundreds of works in men's studies, only 5 percent concerned war and peace. A current leading anthology of men's studies gives three chapters to war and 54 chapters to such topics as work, family, friendships, sex, and rape. In recent books about men and masculinity, the index entries for such headings as war, military, army, draft, etc. are typically absent altogether, and rarely indicate more than passing reference.[89]

The writings and practices of the "mythopoetic" men's movement – embodied in Robert Bly's 1991 Iron John – deal with war only peripherally. A Jungian archetypal "warrior" image is used, along with a natural and unconstrained "wild man" image, to help men develop assertiveness and self-confidence in their masculinity, which has become insecure in a feminist age. However, the "warrior" feeling of reclaiming power and independence of action is very abstract and distant from the experience of war as described by those who fought one. "[T]he men used their newfound warrior energies ... to be what most people would call mildly assertive."[90]

---

[88] Johnson 1997, 20–21, 45–46, 81–82, 138–42, 272.

[89] Horrocks 1995; Dench 1996; Smith 1996; McLean, Carey, and White eds. 1996; Jesser 1996; Segal 1990; Edley and Wetherell 1995; Bly 1990; Stearns 1990; Hearn and Morgan eds. 1990; Miles 1991; Ehrenreich 1983, 104–6; bibliography: August 1985, 49–56; anthology: Kimmel and Messner eds. 1995, xi.

[90] Bly 1990, 5–8; Schwalbe 1996, assertive 225, 116, 205.

A popular "male identity crisis literature" emerged in the early 1990s. Ronald Levant, drawing on his Reconstructing Masculinity workshops, warns "all American men" that "American manhood is in crisis ... now that the social changes wrought by the feminist movement and the influx of women into the workforce have left our traditional code of masculinity in a state of collapse." In the men he works with, Levant finds "a kind of emptiness; a hollowness; a vague feeling that something is missing. The sense of masculine purpose and pride has gone out of their lives, and they want it back." He argues, however, that Bly's beating-drums-in-the-woods approach leads back into the past. "Traditional masculinity is bad for your health," he warns. What men need instead is "emotional intelligence" to navigate new social contexts.[91]

Although feminists have been suspicious of the men's movement, "some see hope among this new breed of 'sensitive men' – largely white, middle-aged, and middle to upper-class – who ... are willing to talk about and among themselves." However, Arthur Brittan warns that "the current crisis of masculinity" may serve as a "legitimation crisis" in which the old dominant values are defended and rationalized. For example, Stephen Wicks blames men's troubles on women, feminism (a twenty-year "man-bashing crusade"), and a "feminized society" based on women's values and rife with "anti-male sentiment." Wicks cites 1991 US homicide and suicide rates three or four times higher in men than in women for white Americans, and five or six times higher for blacks, to demonstrate the victimization of men. In short, the men's movement encompasses a mix of themes and directions.[92]

Alternative masculinities   Mark Gerzon, among others, proposes themes and scripts that may serve as alternatives to war in shaping masculine identity. To date, however, these themes seem underdeveloped. "[M]any men now repudiate the Soldier" as a masculine ideal, especially because the wars since 1945 "have not bred heroism." In the nuclear age, "the Soldier seems almost obsolete. In nuclear war, aggressiveness is no longer considered a virtue." Antiwar activism during the Vietnam War opened up "a different model of manhood," more accessible to groups that do not "fit the image of the white, able-bodied, successful male." Antiwar demonstrators sought "to disassociate ourselves from a certain kind of manhood ... a masculine identity that breeds" warlike policies.

---

[91] Shweder 1994; Levant 1995, collapse 1, missing 3, past 5, health 211, emotional 23; Kimmel and Messner eds. 1995.

[92] McBride 1995, hope 181; Brittan 1989, 184; Wicks 1996, 42, rates 127; Snodgrass 1979, 271; Kimmel and Messner eds. 1995, 529; Heath 1987; Jardine and Smith 1987; Wetzsteon 1979.

(On the other hand, "antiwar men could be just as sexist" as those supporting the war.)[93]

One alternative masculinity is based on a deeply rooted masculine role as provider. As Mead put it: "In every known human society ... the young male learns that when he grows up ... to be a full member of society ... [he must] provide food for some female and her young." Not only is this role quite distinct from a protector-fighter role, but the two often conflict (as when Civil War officers turned down their wives' pleas to return home and provide for the family; see p. 275). Gerzon suggests building new and diverse masculinities based on emerging masculine roles as healer, companion, mediator, colleague, and nurturer.[94]

Political scientist Craig Murphy summarizes six "masculine roles" in world politics. The masculine virtues of the first role, "good soldier," are privileged and serve to shape the other roles – civilian strategist, military son, good comrade, fashionable pacifist, and "Sisyphean peacemaker." This last peacemaker role expresses masculinity as "determination and good humor" in pursuit of mediation of difficult conflicts. Murphy considers the role a masculine one because it requires "courage, competence, and a deep sense of responsibility" (qualities common to various masculine roles starting with the good soldier).[95]

One list of boys' "impressive qualities" includes "their physical energy, boldness, curiosity, and action orientation" – none of which requires expression as violence or aggression. Similarly, negative "masculine mystique" qualities – "toughness, dominance, repression of empathy, extreme competitiveness" – can be distinguished from men's admirable and attractive qualities such as "unusual courage, curiosity, sense of adventure, and independence from societal pressures." These latter qualities traditionally figure in masculinity, but are compatible with being "gentle, sensitive, caring men."[96]

In sum, the men's movement seems to be going in as many directions as feminist theory, and to pay less attention to war. However, a few promising steps are being taken to recognize the centrality of war to masculinity and to develop alternative expressions of masculine identity.

Toughening up boys

Cultures produce male warriors by toughening up boys from an early age, in addition to the means discussed in the previous sections which

---

[93] Gerzon 1982, heroism 44, model 95, 85–101, breeds 85, sexist 97.
[94] Mead 1949, 189; Gerzon 1982, 235–62.
[95] Murphy 1998, 94–100.
[96] Kindlon and Thompson 1999, orientation 15, xiv; Miedzian 1991, xxi.

apply more to adolescents and young men (at or near the age for war participation). Cultures reproduce – through the socialization of children – adult gender roles suited to the nearly universal need of societies to be prepared for the possibility of war.

Although boys on average are more prone to more rough-and-tumble play, they are not innately "tougher" than girls. They do not have fewer emotions or attachments, or feel less pain. It is obvious from the huge effort that most cultures make to mold "tough" boys that this is not an easy or natural task. When we raise boys within contemporary gender norms, especially when we push boys to toughen up, we pass along authorized forms of masculinity suited to the war system. I will focus mainly on how contemporary US culture does this, because it has received a wave of interest recently. As shown earlier (see pp. 264–65), various cultures use a range of methods to toughen up boys.

Attention to boys   Boys, not girls, are the main issue in the reproduction of gendered war roles. They are the ones who must be made over, at a steep price in emotional capabilities, into something unnatural, a "man." Boys are also the main enforcers of gender segregation in middle childhood. Boys are the recipients of most of the adult efforts to enforce appropriate gendered behaviors as well. Although US girls may now wear pants or dresses, and play with trucks or dolls, boys may not wear dresses or play with dolls. Teachers and parents "seem far less ambivalent about encouraging androgyny in their young daughters than in their sons." In short, boys are the primary focus of gender-molding in children, presumably because boys are the ones who may need to fight wars some day.[97]

In the late 1990s, a wave of interest in boys emerged in both research and popular books. This interest grew out of the work in the 1970s and 1980s on girls, which argued that schools and society were ill-serving girls' needs. Now scholars and activists are applying the same approach to boys, portraying boys as an endangered or victimized group. The portrayal of boys as victims does not sit well with some feminists. Other feminists, however, find it "such a relief" to have gender include males as well as females.[98]

Boys' advocates – the "boys' movement" – point to statistics showing higher male rates of infant mortality, learning disabilities, hyperactivity, school suspensions, arrests, schizophrenia, teen suicide, and both committing and receiving violence. Some trace boys' current troubles to the

[97] Thorne 1993, ambivalent 169.
[98] Kindlon and Thompson 1999; Rosenfeld 1998; Goldberg 1998a, relief A14; Faludi 1999; Sommers 2000.

changing adult social context, in which traditional male skills in dominance and physical strength matter less than understanding emotional depth and complexity.[99]

Psychologist William Pollack argues that many boys experience problems as a result of separating too early from their mothers' care. Although infant boys are actually more fragile than girls, parents think of them as tougher, and pay less attention to them. Pollack also argues that psychologists may overlook boys' depression because it differs from the feminine depression that clinicians focus on. The oppression of boys, in Pollack's view, is the source of their desire to dominate, so "[r]ecognizing boys' pain is the way to change society." Shame is central to the "toughening-up process." Little boys with anxiety about separating from their mothers "are made to feel ashamed of their feelings ... [especially] of weakness, vulnerability, fear, and despair ... The use of shame to 'control' boys is pervasive ... Boys are made to feel shame over and over ... to be disciplined, toughened up ... be independent, keep the emotions in check. A boy is told that 'big boys don't cry.'"[100]

Gender changes in US society may have created a mixed message for boys (a "double standard of masculinity"): they are expected both to fulfill traditional toughness standards, *and* to be adept at handling relationships and feelings. "It's an impossible assignment for any boy." Pollack's "Listening to Boys' Voices" project is studying several hundred young and adolescent boys. He argues that society places boys in a "gender straitjacket" by judging them against nineteenth-century standards of masculinity which "simply have no relevance to today's world." Boys unnecessarily lose connections with family as they mask their emotions and, through shame and fear of vulnerability, become "'hardened,' just as society thinks [they] should be." Pollack wants to "help boys break out of society's gender straitjackets, express a wide range of their true feelings, and function more successfully as confident, open, and caring young men in a difficult world." Adults can try to eliminate their own boy stereotypes, learn to communicate better with boys, and help prepare boys for situations that might trigger vulnerability and fear, such as a doctor visit.[101]

Kindlon and Thompson's *Raising Cain* elaborates in detail the ways that contemporary US "culture conspires to limit and undermine [boys'] emotional life," dooming them to "emotional ignorance and isolation." Boys are "born with the potential for a full range of emotional

---

[99] Goldberg 1998a; Rosenfeld 1998; Lewin 1998b.
[100] Pollack 1998, xxi–xxiii, process 11–12, 20–51; Gerzon 1982, 162; Rosenfeld 1998, pain A17.
[101] Pollack 1998, double 147, impossible 13; Betcher and Pollack 1993.

experience," but toughened up by harsh discipline, rigid expectations, and the threat of rejection. Emotionally illiterate, boys meet adolescence knowing only the "socially acceptable ... 'manly' responses of anger, aggression, and emotional withdrawal." These problems underlie young males' violence (among various other negative outcomes): "boys who turn violent ... lack sufficient psychological resources to control their emotional reactions." Kindlon and Thompson ignore the role of war in society's treatment of boys. In truth, the problems they describe extend far beyond contemporary US culture and connect with a need to produce potential warriors.[102]

Philosopher Christina Hoff Sommers, however, argues that the entire "myth of the emotionally repressed boy" lacks any empirical foundation in research, and wrongly "attribut[es] pathology to normal boys" who actually "do not need to be 'rescued' from their masculinity." Sommers particularly criticizes Pollack's claim that the violent crimes of a few boys reflect a larger pattern affecting all boys. She advocates reversing feminism's "war against boys" (which tries to feminize them), and instead teaching boys traditional "manly virtues" and the "military ethic," which she calls "noble and constructive." In my view, "normal" boys in a world at war do suffer psychological harm, but no more so in the "double standard" America that Pollack decries than in other times and places (indeed probably less so today than historically, as Sommers argues).[103]

Socialization for aggression   Just as adults and peers socialize children into gender norms (see pp. 237–45), so too do they socialize children for aggression, in two main ways – through reinforcement (reward–punishment) and through modeling. Children will imitate adults who punch dolls, especially when the children are angry and the aggression seems justified. "Adults who as children observed hitting between their parents are more likely to be involved in severe marital aggression, even more so than those who were hit as teenagers by their parents." The effect of children's witnessing family violence, on their subsequent aggression as adults, seems to be stronger and more consistent for males than females.[104]

The war system is an important context that shapes socialization of children for aggression, and in turn affects social violence more broadly. One study of a balanced sample of 186 largely preindustrial societies,

---

[102] Kindlon and Thompson 1999, life xv, isolation 3, born 10, harsh 53–57, 14–15, withdrawal 5, reactions 220.

[103] Sommers 2000, myth 137; empirical 140–47; pathology 139, 14; rescued 15; claim 138–57; virtues-noble 136–37; today 135.

[104] Bandura 1973; Hoffmann, Ireland, and Widom 1994, parents 292; Murphy 1998, 105.

"strongly suggest[s] that more homicide and assault is a consequence of socialization for aggression which in turn is a consequence of more war."[105]

Harshness towards children may contribute to their later manifestation of aggression and violence. In one study, hundreds of adults who had been physically or sexually abused or neglected as children were paired with a group matched for age, gender, race, and class. Childhood physical abuse especially, and neglect less strikingly, were strong predictors of later adult criminal violence. This shows that growing up in a violent context – as everyone does to some extent in the war system – increases the likelihood of violence later in life.[106]

By contrast, warmth and affection towards children may facilitate attachment and reduce fears of object loss, reducing hostility in social relationships later in life. Most relatively peaceful societies are marked by permissive child-rearing practices (see Figure 5.5). Adults generally do not force children to engage in undesired activities (e.g., Semai, !Kung). Compliance by children is rarely obtained through physical punishment (Semai, Siriono, !Kung, Eskimo), except by the Mbuti up to age 9. Rather, social control – including control of aggression – is obtained through public opinion or ridicule (among Eskimo children, among Mbuti after age 9, and among Semai, Siriono, and !Kung adults), or by invoking evil spirits (Semai). In a 1978 study of peaceful societies, Montagu found parental affection to be the key. Among seven small-scale societies, all low on internal conflict and aggression, "great affection is frequently directed toward the child... Overt expression of aggression is discouraged, but not through physical punishment. Finally, these societies lack models of highly aggressive persons." Betty Reardon advocates a "paradigm shift ... from a warring society to a parenting or caring society, in which all adults parent the young and care for the vulnerable."[107]

Differential socialization of aggression in boys and girls is hard to study empirically. Maccoby and Jacklin found parents equally permissive of aggression with preschool girls as with boys. A study of 700 mothers of English 4-year-olds found that mothers reported encouraging daughters to fight back as often as sons. A variety of studies have found parents "on average, equally permissive (or nonpermissive) toward aggression in sons and in daughters." A substantial amount of school aggression derives from a "relatively small subset of children," mainly boys, who consistently engage in fighting or bullying. These are not typical or

[105] Ember and Ember 1997.
[106] Widom 1989; Geen 1998, 343–44; Ross 1993a, 60–62; Lakoff 1996, 65–107, 339–43.
[107] Fabbro 1978; Knauft 1987; Montagu: Ross 1990, persons 55–56; Reardon 1989, paradigm 24; Briggs 1998; Jean Briggs, personal communication 2000.

Figure 5.5 Inuit children with permissive mother. [© by Jean L. Briggs.]

ideal-type boys, and gender researchers perhaps focus on these extreme cases too much. The "aggressive" boys tend to come from families in which coercive behavior is high among various family members.[108]

Raising children in war zones   Given these various effects in socializing children for later violence, it is obvious that children traumatized by being in a war zone will likely toughen up and become the next generation of warriors. Political violence may be "more stressful for children than other forms of violence," because it threatens social identity by attacking the child's group. James Garbarino, who has studied thousands of children from war zones, finds deep psychological scars from war experiences. "The sight of a bloodied body attacks the benign myths we quite rightly use to give children a sense their world is secure. It shatters a child's belief that people can be trusted." The problem of children in war zones received growing attention in the 1990s as post-Cold War regional and ethnic conflicts came to the fore. By one estimate, from 1977 to 1987, "armed conflict ... killed 2 million children, disabled 4–5 million, and left 12 million homeless, more than 1 million orphaned or separated ... and some 10 million psychologically traumatized."[109]

According to UN statistics, about 250,000 children under 18 are currently *fighting* in 33 wars worldwide. (Another estimate has 300,000 in 36 conflicts.) In some wars, such as in Angola, a substantial number of boys under 15 are involved. In Sierra Leone, reportedly, 80 percent of rebel soldiers are aged 7–14. Twin brothers aged 12 command a rebel army in Burma. The light-weight and easy-to-use assault rifle makes "girls and boys ... the equals of adults."[110]

TV violence   For US parents, shielding their children from violence in a war zone is, mercifully, not usually a problem – or is it? Children receive massive doses of media violence which, although surely less potent than the real thing, have well-documented effects on aggressive behavior. "[C]onsiderable evidence" shows that "watching such violence is associated with increased aggression in the viewer," both verbal and physical. For boys, the effect is robust in various experimental designs (including a 22-year longitudinal study following children from ages 8 to 30). Exposure to television violence correlates with later adult aggressive behavior

[108] Maccoby 1998, 130–34.
[109] Cairns 1996, stressful 5–8; Garbarino: Goleman 1992; UN Development Program 1998, armed 35.
[110] Walt 1999; Boothby and Knudsen 2000, another 60, Sierra 60, Burma 62; Frankel 1995; rifle: Boutwell and Klare 2000; De Pauw 1998, equals 290.

(as well as with aggressive behavior at the time) in both boys and girls, in a 15-year longitudinal study.[111]

Several studies find that US children watch at least several hours of TV daily, the amount increasing with age. In the 1980s, the number of war-related cartoons on television increased dramatically (part of the post-Vietnam remilitarization of that decade). The popular children's TV show *Transformers* contained an attempted murder every 30 seconds on average. Polls over the last 30 years show that half to three-quarters of the US public thought there was too much violence on TV (excluding news), with women about 10 percentage points higher than men on this question. About one-third favored eliminating all TV programs that show violence.[112]

Television portrayals are "more stereotypic in roles and behaviors than the world children see around them everyday." Enemy images were qualitatively analyzed in 20 episodes of each of "eight of the most highly rated cartoon shows on children's television." As in war films and propaganda, the enemy is a beast or an animal, a barbarian, all-evil, the devil, death, or a torturer. In the shows for younger children, "[l]ions, tigers, panthers, rattlesnakes, and scorpions frequent all the shows. In addition to being dangerous and deadly, their big teeth, their long tails, their black or red coloring, or their ugliness enhance their frightening effects … As a result, fears of the enemy might become associated … with quite primitive, reflexlike fears of predators." In all the series, the enemy is not only evil to the core and authoritarian, but foreign-looking, often with an accent. Cartoon shows have "a characteristic plot" that moves from the heroes' preconflict peaceful activities, to a surprise attack by enemies (motivated solely by greed, malice, or hunger for power), to "a fight or war between heroes and enemies" with intense fighting that miraculously never seems to wound or kill anyone, to a last-minute rescue just when all seems lost, and finally the enemy's escape from complete defeat, leaving the world a dangerous place and the peace a tenuous one. No research has been done specifically on the effect of these enemy images on adults' later views about other national groups.[113]

Video games   US retail sales of video games are estimated around $6 billion per year, nearly as large as movie box-office receipts,

---

[111] Geen 1998, 335–38, viewer 335, robust 336; Zuger 1998a, exposure C5; Ellsworth and Mauro 1998, 687; Hesse and Mack 1991, 145–46; Miedzian 1991, 211–40.

[112] Carlsson-Paige and Levin 1987, hours 14; Hamburg 1992, 177; Carlsson-Paige and Levin 1987, cartoons–murder 13; Smith 1984, polls 395.

[113] Ruble and Martin 1998, more 982; Hesse and Mack 1991, cartoon 133–34, 143–45; Keen 1986; Ehrenreich 1997a.

and growing at 30 percent annually. Some of these games are extremely violent – "As easy as killing babies with axes" to quote one advertising slogan. Unlike TV and movie violence, these games are interactive. In "shooter" games the screen shows what the player would see as he blasts away at realistic people (creating realistic wounds, such as severed heads). A rating system is supposed to keep these "whack-and-hack" games away from young children, but does so imperfectly. Empirical research has not shown compelling evidence that playing violent video games makes children – rather, boys – behave more violently. These games are relatively new, however, so not many studies have analyzed this connection.[114]

Grossman traces a "virus of violence" affecting young US men to three major psychological processes at work in their contemporary culture. First, classical conditioning occurs when adolescents see on TV and film "the detailed, horrible suffering and killing of human beings" and learn "to associate this killing and suffering with ... their favorite soft drink, their favorite candy bar, and the close, intimate contact of their date." Second, operant conditioning trains adolescent males to shoot at pop-up targets, in firing ranges and interactive video games, using the same methods as the military but without "stimulus discriminators" that allow firing only under orders. Third, social learning occurs when children observe and imitate "a whole new realm of ... horrendous, sadistic murderers" in horror movies like *Nightmare on Elm Street*.[115]

Regarding video games in particular, Grossman notes the shift in military training from firing at fixed bull's-eye targets to "man-shaped silhouettes that pop up for brief periods ... inside a designated firing lane." Soldiers who hit the target quickly enough are reinforced by the target's falling down (and, ultimately, "a marksmanship badge and usually a three-day pass"). This method creates "an automatic, conditioned response ... to the appropriate stimulus," just as B. F. Skinner taught rats to press levers. Children in video arcades undergo similar "combat training" but with "no real sanction for firing at the wrong target." Grossman distinguishes, from a wide range of good and bad video games, those "in which you actually hold a weapon in your hand and fire it at human-shaped targets on the screen." Furthermore, the most "violence enabling" games are those with greatest realism, "in which great bloody chunks fly off as you fire at the enemy." As technology advances, "virtual reality" programs offer to replicate realistically, in three dimensions, "all the gore and violence of popular violent movies, except now you are

---

[114] Goldberg 1998b; Berselli 1998.
[115] Grossman 1995, 299–305; Miedzian 1991, 173–80.

the ... killer." Such concerns were heightened after the massacre of high-school students in Littleton, Colorado in 1999 by two students with a reported fondness for violent video games.[116]

War play   Carlsson-Paige and Levin describe a "dilemma" facing peace-loving teachers whose students engage in war play: banning such play may be inappropriate to the developmental needs of the children engaged in it, but allowing it may encourage later real-world violence and legitimize war. Parents complain they cannot "turn on the television, visit other children, or go to a supermarket, toy store, or playground with their children without encountering some reminder of war and weapons play." School peer groups often seem to be the source of children's interests in war play, and "while some girls are attracted to war play, it is most often boys who show a compelling interest."[117]

Compared with a generation ago, war play has changed. The play is more "repetitive" rather than elaborating themes over time. It is based on characters seen on TV, and often on scripted scenarios. "Many children no longer seem to be in full charge of their play." In the previous, long-standing tradition of war play with cap or water guns, children had to create their own play (characters and scripts).[118]

Now, however, US children buy war-related toys based on television shows they watch, creating ready-made and rigid sets of characters. An example of a scripted war toy is the "Rambo 81mm Mortar Thunder-Tube Assault," recommended for ages 5 and up. The box provides a story line ("The S.A.V.A.G.E. Army will stop at nothing in their attempt to control the world ... ," etc.) and factual information about uses of 81mm mortars by US forces. Product tie-ins make TV shows into commercials for such products, generating an industry estimated at $1 billion in sales in the mid-1980s, when it took off during the Reagan Administration and the post-Vietnam cultural adjustment. An "inundation of violent images" – via licensing of copyrighted characters for lunch boxes, toothbrushes, clothes, and so forth – keeps war "images ever present in children's minds." Several studies suggest that images of weapons may "prime" aggressive behavior. US parents recently have begun organizing against violent toys, games, and shows. The Lion and Lamb Project encourages violent-toy trade-in events, and publishes a "dirty dozen" list of toys to avoid – such as a realistic-looking rifle with sound effects, recommended by the manufacturer (Hasbro) for ages 5 and up. The "Peace

[116] Grossman 1995, 312–16; Miedzian 1991, 269–70.
[117] Carlsson-Paige and Levin 1987, 4, turn 9, interest 21, 18; Levin and Carlsson-Paige 1989.
[118] Carlsson-Paige and Levin 1987, 11–13.

Figure 5.6 "National Peace Sculpture," Capital Children's Museum, Washington DC, 2000. [By Paul Gebhardt, Marc Holland, Jessica Klein, Jason Massaro, Laurie Miles, and Rebecca Reetz.]

Sculpture" shown in Figure 5.6 lets children drop notes into a slot to gradually cover the bottom layer of violent toys. The middle layer contains violent toys chopped up into parts, and the top layer has peaceful toys made from the recycled components.[119]

[119] Miedzian 1991, mortar 268; Elshtain 1987, sales 197; Carlsson-Paige and Levin 1987, minds 14; Geen 1998, prime 337–38; www.lionlamb.org/.

Most teachers and parents surveyed by Carlsson-Paige and Levin used one of four approaches to the war-play dilemma: ban it, let it be, allow it with set limits, or actively facilitate it. Banning was the most popular approach with the teachers, while parents either used a *laissez-faire* approach or imposed limits (e.g., not in the house). Carlsson-Paige and Levin argue, however, that the facilitation approach is best for both parents and teachers. It lets adults engage the child in dialogue, share the adult's personal feelings, and model alternatives, while decreasing the salience of TV-based scripts. Among other ideas, they suggest helping girls become involved in war games in nonfeminized roles.[120]

The distinction between "play" and "imitation" – depending whether the child or the outside world controls the content – is critical to how children bring their experiences to bear later in life on political issues like war and peace. Fluid play expands knowledge and gives children developmentally sound foundations for later political concepts, which they can apply in meaningful ways to the political world. They "are certainly learning about war, conflict, and violence" but not necessarily developing "militaristic attitudes." (Miedzian, however, rejects Carlsson-Paige and Levin's arguments, finds war toys an unmitigated negative influence, and recommends banning them by federal government regulation.)[121]

Not only the weaponry has changed in war toys. Psychiatrist Harrison Pope finds in the evolution of G.I. Joe's body since 1964 a trend towards more muscular definition with each redesign, and a similar muscularity in other action-figure dolls. Pope worries that these figures encourage adolescent boys to train with weights excessively and take anabolic steroids (see p. 146).[122]

Carlsson-Paige and Levin argue that part of the appeal of war characters to boys is that they are "clearly defined male models with which to identify." War figures may also offer boys "alternative models to their nurturing mothers" as they master separation. They "offer boys the concrete, powerful models that they are seeking, as well as opportunities to express the possible anger and frustration they are feeling." Boys use war play to "mask ... feelings of helplessness and insecurity ... The boys who are most passionately involved in war play are often those who are most insecure and in need of support in learning to express and act out a range of feelings."[123]

[120] Carlsson-Paige and Levin 1987, 43–51, 66.
[121] Carlsson-Paige and Levin 1987, 33–34; Miedzian 1991, 275–85.
[122] Angier 1998b.
[123] Carlsson-Paige and Levin 1987, identify 21, offer 22, mask 67.

Sports   Many writers have treated present-day boys' competitive sports as training for war. As one US high-school gym teacher told a
boy who cut class, "Son, this class is mighty important. This training you
get here is gonna give you an edge on them gooks in Vietnam." George
Orwell said that "[s]erious sport has nothing to do with fair play. It is
bound up with hatred, jealousy, boastfulness, disregard of all rules and
sadistic pleasure in witnessing violence: in other words it is war minus the
shooting." Competitive team sports have been called a "contemporary
analogue of hunting and tribal warfare." Certainly, choosing up sides on
teams has become a highly regularized dominance ritual for US boys.[124]

For adults, sports teams may serve as identity markers that let fans
"bask in reflected glory ... When your team wins ... you feel good."
From the evidence above (see pp. 153–54), one would suspect that male
fans' testosterone levels rise after their team wins, and in fact this was
true when researchers measured it.[125]

Historian Anthony Rotundo argues that competitive sports took on
"new meaning and heightened importance for Northern [US] men" in
the mid-nineteenth century, as baseball became "a vehicle for expressing
rivalry between towns, neighborhoods, and businesses." Physical culture
shifted focus from strengthening the body to competition, and sports
played an important role in the emergence of the new ideals of manhood
at the turn of the century. Some observers thought sports could promote
some of the "manly traits" developed in war, without the violence, while
others thought sports and militarism complemented each other in this
regard.[126]

Cross-cultural data show a correlation between frequency of war and
importance of combative sports in the culture. Thus, Montagu argues,
sports do not serve as a release valve or alternative channel for an instinctual aggressive drive, but rather "combative sports ... represent the
embodiments of the same theme" as war. But perhaps both sides are
true, as Eibl-Eibesfeldt concludes: "Competitive games can in fact divert
aggression, but at the same time, they train the aggressive system."[127]

Teasing   Boys who become "sissies" by not acting tough enough
face harsh teasing and ridicule (see pp. 235–36). Almost two-thirds

---

[124] Wicks 1996, son 40; McBride 1995, shooting v; Hrdy 1981, tribal 6; Sipes 1975;
    Messner 1992, 67–70; Messner 1990; Messner and Sabo eds. 1990; Pollack 1998,
    282–85; Miedzian 1991, 181–210; Geen 1998, 338; White and Vagi 1990.
[125] Lee Vander Velden in Domenick 1998; testosterone: Bernhardt *et al.* 1998.
[126] Rotundo 1993, 239–44; cf. Kindlon and Thompson 1999, 85–86.
[127] Sipes 1975; Montagu 1976, theme 277; Eibl-Eibesfeldt 1979, system 236.

of 11-year-olds in one study reported having been teased by peers within the previous months. This enforcement becomes the seed of later homophobia, which helps maintain gender norms especially around war and the military (see pp. 374–80).[128]

Cross-gender contacts in middle childhood are interpreted partly in "romantic or sexual terms," and frequently seen by boys as demeaning (e.g., when a girl catches and kisses him). Children who violate norms of gender segregation (which allow only specific kinds of contact) are teased for "liking," loving, or kissing someone of opposite gender. Maccoby states that such "teasing is always about cross-sex attractions ... [N]o observer has yet reported a boy teasing another boy about a specific male–male attraction, as in 'Ha, ha! Johnny likes Jimmy!' The absence of such teasing implies that latent sexuality is interpreted by children exclusively in heterosexual terms."[129]

"[T]omboy girls seldom receive criticism or rejection from other girls" for associating with boys. Thus "girls have considerable freedom to choose how much contact they will have with boys." Cultural tomboy themes contain a "mixed message" – abnormality combined with freedom, neither a "full-fledged insult" nor a compliment – that actually can reinforce gender stereotypes. (Children themselves seldom use the term "tomboy.") Thorne describes a girl of great athletic ability – also the only African American in her class – who participated regularly in boys' games and activities, often sat on the boys' side of the cafeteria, yet maintained close ties with the girls and crossed easily from one gender grouping to the other.[130]

Boys, however, "have less freedom of choice." By contrast with "tomboy," the label "sissy" (applied mostly to gender-deviant boys) has "relentlessly negative connotations." The sissy is someone who appears immature and weak – supposedly feminine qualities ("sissy" derives from "sister"). Applied to boys, the terms also conveys "gender and sexual deviance." "In short, a 'sissy' is a failed male" – synonymous with "girl." Being called a sissy, or its equivalents, constitutes a "stinging insult," and men years later find such memories "painful," in contrast to women who "reminisce quite positively" about being called a tomboy. "Kids target their most severe teasing at boys ... who repeatedly seek access to girls' activities in a respectful and serious rather than hassling or experimenting style."[131]

---

[128] Rubin, Bukowski, and Parker 1998, 642.

[129] Maccoby 1998, 67–69.

[130] Maccoby 1998, criticism 66; Thorne 1993, themes 112–17, athletic 127–30.

[131] Maccoby 1998, choice 66; Thorne 1993, negative–positively 115–17, style 130; Rosenfeld 1998.

Thorne urges adults to "develop more tolerance of different styles of self-expression" including boys' rough-and-tumble play, but to watch the line where "differences of style shade into patterns of harassment or domination." Adults might excuse boys' aggressiveness against girls, and "may even feel quietly reassured that [such] a boy ... is affirming 'normal' masculinity; after all, dominance and control ... are valued in adult men." Parents of quiet or "good" boys, by contrast, may worry that their sons are too feminine, and thus push them into sports or other gender-appropriate activities. In this way, "the specter of 'sissies' ... helps sustain hegemonic masculinity and the structuring of gender as opposition and inequality."[132]

In short, cultures toughen up boys in a variety of ways, from an early age, to produce the kinds of masculine identities in young men that will support potential roles as warriors. More broadly, Hypothesis 5A finds reasonably robust support since so many cultures deploy manhood to help motivate soldiers to fight.

B. FEMININE REINFORCEMENT OF SOLDIERS' MASCULINITY

Hypothesis 5B holds that men's participation in combat requires the psychological construction of a nurturing "feminine" domain – incompatible with women's participation in the men's ranks – to make the trauma of combat tolerable. Women must be kept apart from combat in order to fulfill their feminine roles in the war system, reinforcing soldiers' masculinity.

In the 1922 painting that dominates the stairway of Harvard's main library (Figure 5.7), "Victory" is a voluptuous female who caresses the soul of a dead soldier being carried away by Death. When the war is done, he returns to female company, in this case literally heaven-sent. (Perhaps his army's victory stimulates this soldier's testosterone level even posthumously; see pp. 153–55.)

Male soldiers can better motivate themselves for combat if they can compartmentalize combat in their belief systems and identities. They can endure, and commit terrible acts, because the context is exceptional and temporary. They have a place to return to, or at least to die trying to protect – a place called home or normal or peacetime. In drawing this sharp dichotomy of hellish combat from normal life, cultures find gender categories readily available as an organizing device. Normal life becomes feminized and combat masculinized.

[132] Thorne 1993, 168–69.

Figure 5.7 "Death and Victory," mural, John Singer Sargent, 1922. [Courtesy of the Harvard University Portrait Collection. Anonymous gift to Harvard University.]

Making war abnormal

To participate in fighting, and above all in killing, most people require psychological defenses to overcome both natural and cultural habits and norms. Killing does not come easily. One element of these defenses, for example, is identification with a primary group which absolves the individuals from responsibility (see pp. 195–99). Another element is the well-rooted concept that masculine honor requires a man to do his duty (see pp. 266–78).

License to kill   Yet another psychological defense that soldiers rely on is that war is different from "normal" life. Different rules and obligations apply, and society gives its blessing to the act of killing in war. One cross-cultural study found that "homicide rates tend to increase following a war, whether the nation was defeated or victorious. This result is consistent with the idea that a society or nation legitimizes violence during wartime."[133]

A May 1969 US polling question asked: "Do you feel it is justified or not justified to take the life of another person" in various situations. The following percentages said "justified" for each situation:

	Male	Female
When someone commits cold-blooded murder	51%	38%
When someone commits treason against the US	58	44
In self-defense	82	68
When fighting in a war	82	75

Thus, both genders give war the strongest social approval as a context for killing, with a modest gender gap of 7 points.[134]

In a similar poll in December 1969, 11 percent of men and 20 percent of women said it was "always wrong" to take a life. Yet, when asked about different contexts, the following percentages found taking human life to be justified:

	Male	Female
When executing a cold-blooded murderer	61%	48%
A policeman on duty shooting a criminal	80	73
Killing another person in self-defense	86	82
A soldier in war shooting an enemy	92	86

[133] Ember and Ember 1997.
[134] Smith 1984, 394.

Not only is war again the most approved context for killing, but some of the men and women who said it was "always wrong" to take a life evidently made an exception for war. (This social license does not extend to shooting civilians believed to be helping an enemy in war, however: only 44 percent and 35 percent, of men and women respectively, found such an action justified.)[135]

Armies make the most of the idea that different rules apply in war. Military organizations actively work to break down psychological and social norms in soldiers and remold them to suit military needs. Whether through haircuts or war paint, soldiers move into a social space demarcated as different from "normal" life. The gender-segregated nature of military forces traditionally contributes to the delineation of military from civilian life, but so do many other markers that set off war as a realm where different social norms apply.[136]

Gender as boundary   Gender comes to center stage in another psychological defense used widely by male soldiers – the construction of a feminine "normal" sphere of experience, from which war is separated psychologically. Gender readily structures this division of war and normalcy. Not just the soldier, but the whole society participates in constructing a feminine sphere to be preserved from war, just as Hegel's "beautiful soul" (mentioned on p. 48) protects "the appearance of purity by cultivating innocence" about the harsh world. Women collectively, then, serve as a kind of metaphysical sanctuary for traumatized soldiers, a counterweight to hellish war. In itself this gendering of psychological spheres does not seem sufficient to account for gendered war roles, but it would reinforce other tendencies in that direction, helping force nature's overlapping bell-curves into culture's categorical divisions.[137]

Thinking about home or life after the war appears to be a strong motivator for many soldiers: "all soldiers mention the importance of letters from home... Most soldiers depend on their girlfriends, wives, parents, children, and friends. Keeping in touch with them ... is a second lifeline" after the all-important bond to the primary group in combat. The moral support of family and friends, and most importantly a connection with (often idealized) wives and girlfriends, helps keep soldiers going. A soldier who has just received a "Dear John" letter (from a girlfriend who has dumped him in his absence) is considered a danger to himself and his group. An English postcard from World War I shows a feminine face as "The Star that Shines above the Trenches at Night." Many men keep pictures of their wives or girlfriends with them in combat. Some keep

[135] Smith 1984, 394.
[136] Watson 1997, 21.
[137] Elshtain 1987, Hegel 4.

Figure 5.8 Sarajevo woman and UN peacekeeper, 1994. [Agence France-Presse.]

symbolic objects like the artificial rose, given by his wife, that one US sergeant in Vietnam put on his helmet. "I love you so much," writes a US soldier in Vietnam to his wife. "This has been a nasty 3 day operation . . . but your wonderful letters have cheered me so that all is well."[138]

Some soldiers find motivation to fight in the need to protect women (abstractly if not tangibly). As Vietnam veteran and author Philip Caputo puts it, "war and armies even in peacetime vulgarize and brutalize people. In this century, perhaps the bloodiest in all history, I'd like to think something would not be touched by this brutality and vulgarity. Up to now, it's been women." The UN Protection Force troops pictured in Figure 5.8 embody the division between armed protector man and civilian protected woman. The Geneva Conventions extend specific protections in wartime to women, mothers with small children, and children themselves. Polynesian women were protected by especially strong norms. They could pass freely through enemy lines to take food to their husbands, and even "assisted their husbands in the battle line by parrying spear thrusts," with impunity.[139]

Women's protected status in wartime, however, is not universal, and is often tenuous (see pp. 362–73). Melanesian warriors killed and ate

[138] Dinter 1985, letters 49, 50; Theweleit 1987, star 128; Goldman and Fuller 1983, rose 134, nasty 145, 57.
[139] Caputo, in Astrachan 1986, 53; de Preux 1985, Geneva 292. Turney-High 1971, thrusts 163.

captive women "as gleefully as if they had been men," even though women there did not participate in fighting. The Mundurucú of Brazil killed all adult men and women alike, upon capturing a village (eventually turning their heads into trophies with magical powers to enhance hunting productivity back home). Children of both genders were captured and raised at home. In Fiji's wars, "[w]omen and children were killed ruthlessly and indiscriminately." The "Cauca Valley tribes [of Colombia] also killed women, no matter how young or attractive they might be, and slaughtered children as well." Shaka Zulu sometimes exterminated his enemies – men, women, and children – although in other cases he took women as booty and even incorporated conquered boys to become Zulu warriors.[140]

Because of the feminization of noncombat, the presence of women in combat might upset the male soldiers. When Israeli women took part in combat in 1948, according to some scholars (but disputed by others), "[m]en who might have found the wounding of a male comrade comparatively tolerable were shocked by the injury of a woman, and the mission tended to get forgotten in a general scramble to ensure that she received medical aid." Perhaps, though, men can simply distinguish, as male cadets at West Point do, between their female comrades and "regular" women – the latter category being reserved for "their girlfriends pictured in frilly dresses or bathing suits."[141]

Women's nurturing of men warriors

Women often participate actively as codependants, so to speak, facilitating men's militarized masculinity. Mark Gerzon describes riding a bus decades ago from an Israeli hospital where a minor operation – resulting from a traffic accident in Asia earlier in his trip – had left a bandage on his head. "The women on the bus all stare at me. Whether grandmothers or teenagers, they smile warmly... the sensual, affirming, nurturant beam of old friends, old lovers. 'Why are they looking at me like that?' I ask my friend. 'They think you are a wounded soldier,' she replies."[142]

Witnesses   In various societies, from Germanic tribes of Roman times to American Indians, women have been "the sacred witnesses to male bravery." In medieval Europe, the warrior class devoted itself "full-time to fighting sanctified, in part, through the feminization of

[140] Turney-High 1971, gleefully 163; Brazil: Murphy 1957, 1023; Fiji–Cauca: Carneiro 1990, 199; Zulu: Adam Jones, personal communication 2000.
[141] Holmes 1985, shocked 104; Francke 1997, frilly 209, 211.
[142] Gerzon 1982, 47.

chivalric discourse. Women were witnesses to male bravery and prowess."
British women munitions workers in World War I often enclosed personal
notes in items they produced, to give emotional support to the "Tommy"
who used them. A woman US canteen worker in World War I received
a parcel with a German's buttons, spurs, and insignia and a note from a
US soldier recalling that the woman had "said, 'get me a German.' Here
is all I can mail of him. I'm in hospital myself."[143]

Virginia Woolf wrote that women become "magnifying mirrors" for
men. Whatever a culture expects of women, by conforming to these
norms a woman reflects well on her warrior husband. In South Africa in
the 1980s, for example, the Defence Force Ladies Association instructed
soldiers' wives to reflect well on their men through appearance and behavior. In the Roman army of the sixth century BC, a group of young
officers argued about whose wife was the best. They rode back home to
discover the wives' characters, and the winner was the man whose wife
was found working with her wool (women's traditional occupation) by
lamplight surrounded by her handmaidens, while the others were enjoying a fancy dinner party. But women in ancient Sparta were supposed
to be warriors' mothers and wives, physically fit and competitive, and
to shun feminine decorations (jewelry, cosmetics, colored clothes) and
women's work (wool).[144]

Western societies treat battlefields as "predominantly male preserves"
in which women are occasionally "welcome only in so far as they contribute to a man's warrior ethos." Nurses (see pp. 312–16) and other
women performing feminine roles on the battlefield "improve morale
by enhancing a man's identification of himself as a warrior." In recent
wars, nurses have served this purpose, as mirrors for men to affirm their
masculinity. At Dien Bien Phu, the senior French medical officer called
herself "a witness to men's courage." Vera Brittain writes of nursing during World War I: "Towards the men, I came to feel an almost adoring
gratitude ... for the knowledge of masculine functioning which the care
of them gave me." One US nurse in World War II wrote that she, like other
nurses, "found herself weak with admiration for the wounded men" and
what they had endured. In a published letter to soldiers, she wrote: "We
have learned about our American soldier and the stuff he is made of. The
wounded don't cry ... The patience and determination they show, the
courage and fortitude they have is sometimes awesome to behold. It is
a privilege to receive you and ... see you open your eyes and with that

[143] Elshtain 1987, sacred–prowess 181; Schneider and Schneider 1991, mail 272–73.
[144] Cock 1991, mirrors 120, ladies 119; Sparta: Lefkowitz and Fant 1977, 51–55; Roman:
Evans 1991, 50; wives: Enloe 1983, 46–91.

swell American grin, say, 'Hi-ya, babe.'" (She was killed by a shell the day after writing the letter.)[145]

Part of the power of army nurses comes from the message that, if one is in the presence of women, one is no longer in combat but connected with home. Just the cheery voice and pretty face of a female nurse in an army hospital (or, perhaps, a wife or other female companion during a leave) reminds the soldier that the battlefield is finite and the other world still exists. For wounded Americans in World War II who passed out, the "first sight many of them saw was a nurse ... She was harassed, wearing fatigues, exhausted, and busy. But she was an American girl, she had a marvelous smile, a reassuring attitude, and gentle hands. To the wounded soldier, she looked heaven-sent." As one woman summarized it in World War I, the US soldier's ideal of American womanhood "has stood between him and utter darkness. In this ideal he put all his faith. If he loses it, he loses everything."[146]

Given how quickly men immobilized by combat exhaustion were turned around and sent back to the front, it appears that the mere presence of a female was, along with a chance to eat and sleep briefly, enough to let the men start fighting again. Having heaven-sent girls in nursing positions not far behind the front, therefore, did more than fill "manpower" shortages in support roles. It provided the audience before which men would be most likely to want to prove their manhood by going back on the line – exactly the effect desired by the generals. The nurses were, in effect, witnesses to the men's individual decisions whether to remain helpless or, after one day's rest and a meal, put their pain out of mind and carry on. Three-quarters chose the latter option. Some armies deploy guns behind the lines to shoot at their own troops who flee or retreat. Deploying female nurses behind the lines, perhaps, performs a similar function by other means.

In relationships with women off the battlefield, men seek "positive evidence that, despite the upheavals of military life, one still remains a valuable and valued person." Soldiers care about what women in their home lives will think of them. For example, a US colonel in one story manipulates a hospitalized, shell-shocked marine into returning to battle by telling him that his girlfriend will find out what happened and "never look at you again after this." The trauma of combat, and the isolation it produces, make soldiers "exquisitely sensitive to the degree of support they encounter at home." They crave public recognition, yet most

[145] Holmes 1985, ethos 105, morale 103; Gilbert 1987, adoring 211; Tylee 1990, 47; Dien: Elshtain 1987, 184; Holmes 1985, 100; babe: Ambrose 1997, 326.
[146] Ambrose 1997, heaven 321–22; Schneider and Schneider 1991, loses 266.

public ceremonies fall short emotionally because they create a "sentimental distortion of the truth of combat."[147]

Women, as nurses, mothers, wives, and girlfriends, play a central role in recovery from combat trauma over the longer term. Given that PTSD centers on the breaking of connections with loved ones and community, men traumatized by combat often seek comfort and reconnection (sometimes successfully) in relationships with women. Many US Vietnam veterans found women companions central to the restoration of sanity after the pain and disillusionment of the war. "His girl friend of the moment preserved his sanity, he thought; she would let him rage on and on for a time, 'and then,' he recalled, 'put her arms around me at the end and tell me it was all right.'" "It was Jean who got him through the reentry . . ." If not for his woman, said another veteran, "I'd have been a real mess."[148]

Mothers   For young men in combat, their mothers often epitomize the nurturing feminine sphere that stands in contrast with war. In addition to their actual mothers, soldiers use mother-like figures in similar ways – nurses who care for them, sweethearts who will "mother" them after they return from war and marry them, or wives who already do so (see pp. 310–12). Real mothers seem to matter most.

It is their mothers that dying soldiers most often call out for on the battlefield: "'Mommy!' somebody was crying in the dark. 'Mom – where are you?'" In World War II, a wounded US soldier "thought he was dying. He thought of the mothers of the boys he had mowed down and of his own mother." Another soldier, under an intense German shelling, "thought about my mother and hoped she didn't know where I was or what I was doing." Elsewhere, a soldier recalls that a "wounded man kept crying, 'Mother, Mother! Help me!'"[149]

Just as women participate actively in shaming men, and in serving as mirrors for their masculinity, they also participate as mothers in shaping their sons for war. In theory, since they control infant care, women could change gender norms. They could give nutritional preference to girls, and train girls to be aggressive and boys to be passive. But in fact mothers favor boys over girls in most of the world, and reward boys for being tough and girls for being nice. They raise warriors. The problem is that although women could subdue the males they raise, they cannot control males raised in other communities. "As soon as males for whatever reason

---

[147] Holmes 1985, positive 98; Gerzon 1982, look 43; Herman 1992, exquisitely 70.

[148] Goldman and Fuller 1983, right 172, reentry 176, mess 211.

[149] Goldman and Fuller 1983, dark 53; Ambrose 1997, mowed 195, doing 213, kept 237.

begin to bear the burden of intergroup conflict, women have no choice but to rear large numbers of fierce males of their own."[150]

This motherly support for war can be blunt, as with an early twentieth-century Bulgarian widow who had lost two sons in war: "Don't think I am crying because my two elder sons are dead; I'm crying because my two younger boys are not old enough to go and help drive out the Turks." Such sentiments call into question difference feminism's emphasis on maternal caring as a foundation for peace.[151]

Sweethearts Sweethearts can play the same roles as mothers, in cheering their men off to war and stitching them together on their return. For US soldiers abroad in World War II, "photos of wives and girl friends . . . provided the individual serviceman some romantic escape from the horrors of combat." It hardly mattered if the girl back home was really interested or not, as long as the soldier found in her something to believe in that counterbalanced the trauma of war. "Many soldiers steeled themselves emotionally before combat with the thought of home and the wife or sweetheart in whose memory, or offspring, they would achieve some hope of immortality." This at least was the official construction of the war, as reported by a US senator: "their heads . . . [are] fixed [on] . . . home and the girl they left there." Oddly, as Figure 5.9 illustrates, the same dynamic apparently helped conscientious objectors who were isolated at work camps.[152]

Even transitory love affairs can play the same role for soldiers. They are an escape, a distraction. When the presence of death seems tangible, "the comfort of women takes on great importance." Glenn Gray, a US soldier in Europe in 1943–45, proposes several distinct types of "love" – ranging from the highly physical to the more ethereal – that come into play frequently for soldiers. At the more refined end of the scale, soldiers emote love for people – or even objects such as abandoned pets or "souvenirs" – representing an ideal that contrasts with war. By falling in love with someone they meet, soldiers fulfill a longing "for the gentleness and affection that only women can bring." Soldiers see in ordinary women "angels of beauty and tenderness," qualities of which the soldiers are "starved." The fact that these lovers hardly know each other and often speak different languages allows them to see what they want to see. Love is a refuge, a "counterpoise to the impersonal slaughter around them." Although temporary and based on illusion, such love connections are necessary in "recuperating from the psychical wounds of combat."

[150] Harris 1974, fierce 85–87.
[151] Stobart 1913, sons 36.
[152] Costello 1985, horrors 79, immortality 91, left 79.

Figure 5.9 Conscientious objector, United States, World War II. [Courtesy of Mennonite Central Committee Photograph Collection, Archives of the Mennonite Church, Goshen, IN.]

Gray's own experience of such a love gave him "strength and courage to bear the present and the near future."[153]

A still deeper form of love develops when a foreign soldier and a local woman find a "transcendent" love that simply overrides all demands of war, patriotism, or duty. Soldiers may find themselves deeply in love with "enemy" women. These relationships can be militarily dysfunctional, a source of intelligence leaks or treason (or, more often, just desertion). They are so transcendent that they lift the soldier out of the war psychologically. For that reason, Gray finds this form of love "holy," and was deeply troubled when the French Resistance, in newly liberated towns, publicly shamed (by shaving their heads) local women who had been lovers of German occupiers. Later, in Germany, Gray saw that a German "girl could love an Allied soldier who was fighting and killing her brothers or father."[154]

Western European women held complex views of their relationships with German soldiers of occupation during World War II. The attractions went beyond the practical need to find sources of food and money. A rural Norwegian woman said: "We were used to farm boys who always wanted us doing the laundry. The Germans in their uniforms, my God, they were handsome, we could not believe our eyes. They would open doors for us, push our chairs in at the café, and kiss our hands – they were the big wide world."[155]

Nurses   I mentioned above (pp. 307–8) the roles of female nurses as witnesses to soldiers' masculine bravery and as surrogate mothers. Nurses also carry out a vital function in the war system by nursing injured and sick soldiers. The idea of using female professional nurses in war is little more than a century old, although now widespread. However, for centuries the job of nursing has fallen to wives, camp followers, and other women accompanying military forces (see pp. 380–96 on women's labor). Modern women's military nursing traces from the Crimean War – Florence Nightingale's war and "a turning point in Western military men's thinking about how to organise their forces" by bringing medical care under military control rather than leaving it to camp followers. Women did not enter British military hospitals in large numbers until 1884, however, because military officials thought the idea "violated society's sense of propriety." Military commanders gradually came to see official women nurses as a way to extend military control over medical

---

[153] Costello 1985, comfort 79; Gray 1959, 71–95.
[154] Gray 1959, 76.
[155] Drolshagen 1998 [review translated by Jonathan D. Beard, on H-War@H-Net.msu.edu].

care without diverting scarce manpower from combat, a formula that depended on "keep[ing] women nurses ideologically peripheral to the combat-masculinity core of the military."[156]

Women nurses free up manpower because nursing cannot be neglected in a military campaign. Before the twentieth century, disease caused more casualties in war than injury did – twice as many killed in the Union army, four times as many in the British forces in the Crimean War, and a majority even in World War I.[157]

Military nursing has most often meant very hard work. During the Civil War, Clara Barton, who founded the American Red Cross, performed difficult and dangerous front-line work, without pay or official recognition. She argued that if such work appeared "rough and unseemly for a *woman*, it should be remembered that combat was equally rough and unseemly for *men*."[158]

Similarly, nursing work in World War I, which occupied most of the women who went to the front, was "dirty, dangerous, disgusting, enormously hard and stressful labor," often without remuneration or official support. Two Englishwomen established first-aid stations close to the trenches, to help injured soldiers survive as far as the hospital. They found the upper body strength to get wounded soldiers and their equipment into stretchers and carry them to the aid station. They came under fire several times, and both women were seriously injured in gas attacks. A British woman doctor who in 1914 offered the War Office fully staffed medical units was told "[t]o go home and keep quiet" because the commanders "did not want to be troubled with hysterical women." The women doctors instead provided 14 hospital units for Britain's allies. Mabel Annie Stobart organized a British all-female nursing company that worked at the front for ten weeks in the Balkan–Turkish conflict (before World War I), after the British Red Cross had excluded women from medical teams it dispatched there. She considered nursing "work for which nature has specifically fitted" women, and found in it a way to reconcile her pacifist and feminist views (that war is bad but women should participate in it). Stobart overcame various obstacles, with help from the Bulgarian queen, such as the problem of designing uniforms that were "practical" ("though there is too much skirt") rather than attractive.[159]

US nurses in France in 1944 were terribly overworked and totally task-centered, with little room left for much emotional (much less sexual)

---

[156] Enloe 1983, 92–116, turning 94, propriety 98, core 100.
[157] Keegan and Holmes 1985, 143–44.
[158] Barton: Oates 1994; De Pauw 1998, 156–60, unseemly 160.
[159] De Pauw 1998, 216–18, dirty 218; Tylee 1990, quiet 7; Stobart 1913, excluded 16–17, fitted 3, skirt 64–67.

connection with soldiers, beyond offering a smile. One "typical" evacuation hospital in Normandy in June 1944 had to handle a new arriving casualty every minute on average, around the clock, for its first week. One US nurse reported, "I have never worked so hard in my life. I can't call it nursing. The boys get in, get emergency treatment, penicillin and sulfa, and are out again. It is beyond words." Furthermore, nearly half of the US nurses who volunteered in World War II in Europe had to overcome opposition from close relatives and their closest male friends to do so.[160]

US nurses in Vietnam, like their counterparts in other wars, endured "[l]ong work hours, sexual harassment, and danger," in their work treating "severe trauma cases in often primitive treatment settings." In one sample of 60 survey respondents, about one-quarter had "frequently feared for their physical safety while in Vietnam" and another half occasionally so feared. About one-sixth experienced "flashbacks regarding traumatic events" within two years after a Vietnam tour, and about one-fifth experienced "emotional numbness" in the same period. Despite the hardships, however, a majority of US nurses who served in Vietnam evaluated the experience as positive overall. In one postwar study, 72 percent said their Vietnam service had a positive impact on their lives, and 62 percent expressed willingness to serve again in a similar capacity in the future.[161]

In addition to the manpower aspects, nurses stand in for mothers in the dynamic discussed above. Even the verb, to nurse, means both to care for an injured or sick person and to breast-feed an infant. In Figure 5.10, a British poster from World War I, the casualty on a stretcher is infant-sized, held in the mother's arms in close to a breast-feeding position. Despite the pervasiveness of male fantasies about sexual relations with nurses, requests for the real thing are rare: "When all is said and done, the patient doesn't desire the nurse as a person, but as an incarnation of the caring mother, the nonerotic sister." Similarly, the figure of the nurse in World War I era British literature possesses matriarchal qualities necessary to care for "immobilized and dehumanized" men. A British officer in World War I wrote, "what we need most when our strength is spent [is] women who ... will mother us."[162]

The moral character of nurses has traditionally mattered more to the military than professional ability. Florence Nightingale did not see nursing as a formal profession, arguing that "Nurses can no more be examined and certified than mothers." For the military, fear of disruptive

---

[160] Ambrose 1997, 321–29, words 323, half 322; Fussler 1996.
[161] Baker, Menard, and Johns 1989, 736–39.
[162] Theweleit 1987, nonerotic 126–27; Gilbert 1987, immobilized 211; Holmes 1985, spent 99.

Figure 5.10 "The Greatest Mother in the World," British poster, World War I. [Courtesy of the Imperial War Museum, London.]

sexuality makes it important to construct nurses as nonsexual women. Army nurses, like prostitutes, perform the "physical work of tending to strange men's bodies." (Indeed, Vera Brittain credits the experience around men's bodies with her "early release from ... sex-inhibitions.") Northern women army nurses in the Civil War "confronted impassioned popular condemnation," especially if they were young and single. The War Department appointed Dorothea Dix to oversee nurses. Dix required nurses to be 35–50 years old, healthy, and "matronly" in appearance, with good habits and character. However, surgeons and wounded men wanted young, pretty nurses who would remind them of the "girl next door."[163]

Nurses' work generally does not entail any form of sexuality. Nurses most often position themselves as mothers or sisters (and indeed are sometimes called "sister"). The diaries of Australian nurses in World War I reflect the military's systematic efforts to downplay sexuality, from the initial clothing of nurses' bodies in austere uniforms to the ultimate relegating of women to the margins of war narratives (where any latent sexual disruption from a feminine presence would not interrupt the men's narratives). Images of nurses in the writings of right-wing German militarists after World War I range from cool and motherly to enticing and erotic, but the men's masculinity was better served by the motherly type – "disinfected" of her erotic side. Magnus Hirschfeld's detailed survey of World War I from a Freudian perspective claims that European nurses, especially upper-class volunteers, found their work a "way of sublimating the libido and achieving sexual pleasure." These high-born nurses were ineffective, however, partly because "the patient always had the feeling of insulting [the nurse's] high-born condition ... by requesting the lowly and rather nasty things that he needed," such as help with bedpans.[164]

Other psychological war support roles

In addition to their roles in witnessing, shaming, and mothering male soldiers, women also support war through various other psychological and material contributions. Wars in turn tend to change women's positions in society, but only temporarily.

Simple societies   The role of women in warfare in simple societies varies cross-culturally, but women generally support more than oppose war. No society requires women to participate in war. But often

---

[163] Theweleit 1987, certified 133, 125–26; Lake and Damousi 1995, tending 8; Gilbert 1987, release 212; Leonard 1994, 14, matronly 16, girl 23.

[164] Holmes 1995, diaries; Hirschfeld 1934, pleasure 54, needed 55; Theweleit 1987, disinfected 126.

women are "expected to engage in ceremonial activities ... while their men [a]re away fighting" – dancing, acting out the war, remaining chaste, and so forth. Women sometimes help to drive the men into a war frenzy by dancing, singing, and other activities supportive of a war effort.[165]

Women commonly egged men on to war in Norse legends, among Germans fighting the Roman empire, and among Aryans of India. In the words of a seventh-century Arabian poem addressed to departing soldiers, "Advance / and our embraces / and softest rugs / await you" (but not if you retreat). "Rwala [bedouin] women bared their breasts and urged their men to war." In the Kitwara empire, the Zulu kingdom, and elsewhere in Africa, women stayed at home during a war expedition and followed strict taboos (such as silence in an entire village) to bring magical powers to the war party. Zulu women also ran naked before departing warriors.[166]

Among American Indians, in Arikara culture, during a two-day war-preparation ceremony, women danced in their husbands' clothes and took turns praising their husbands' valor. In the Comanche war preparations, women held up one side of a large drum while men held the other. Teton women wore ornaments indicating their husbands' success as warriors, and Ojibway widows and mothers received the enemy scalps. Among the Chiriguano and Chané (Bolivia), women performed special dances and songs to support the warriors, both before and during battle. Apache women did not sing for the war dance, but did see off the departing warriors. Apache women fulfilled special obligations during the warriors' absence, such as keeping the woodpile neat and behaving "carefully so as not to give bad luck to the man." Thus, women participate in various ways in promoting and rewarding warrior roles for men.[167]

Women in the Civil War The US Civil War disrupted gendered patterns of work and home. Northern "refined" women served as nurses and spies, while Southern women took over responsibilities from absent men. By the end of the war, Southern women increasingly outdid the worn-down men in Confederate patriotism.[168]

In New Orleans, fifty women petitioned the mayor not to surrender the city, after Confederate troops defended it poorly. One woman said, "If the men had half the spunk which the women have, New Orleans

---

[165] Goldschmidt 1989, 24.
[166] Turney-High 1971, egged 163–64, 160, naked 161; Cooper, Munich, and Squier 1989, rugs xiii; Goldschmidt 1989, breasts 23.
[167] Turney-High 1971, valor–scalps 153; Steward ed. 1948, Bolivia 480–81; Opler 1941, sing 338, luck 342–43; Gray 1959, 61–62; Hirschfeld 1934, 146; Wallace 1967.
[168] Clinton and Silber eds. 1992; Ross 1992; Sizer 1992; Rable 1992.

would soon be ours again." Many women defied the occupying troops of General Benjamin Butler, such as by displaying Confederate flags. In response, Butler ordered that "when any female shall, by word, gesture, or movement, insult or show contempt for any officer or soldier of the United States, she shall be regarded and held liable to be treated as" a prostitute. One teenaged girl wrote about her distinctly feminine fantasies towards Butler – to tie him in ropes and have women tug at him; to fry him in a large pan; to make him eat salty food but keep water just out of reach.[169]

Northern women's Civil War roles included as nurses, military support-ers (through sewing circles, benevolent societies, etc.), and professionals – in addition to the "dominant paradigm" of weeping widows. After the war, Northern society downplayed women's war roles, to smooth a tran-sition back to a social equilibrium grounded in traditional gender roles. "[T]he gender system, in the end, demonstrated remarkable rigidity and stability at its core."[170]

Women in the World Wars   Right up to the outbreak of World War I, feminists on both sides pledged themselves to peace, in transna-tional women's solidarity. Within months of the war's outbreak, however, "all the major feminist groups of the belligerents had given a new pledge – to support their respective governments." Suddenly, campaigners for women's suffrage became avid patriots and organizers of women in sup-port of the war effort. Many of these feminists hoped that patriotic sup-port of the war would enhance the prospects for women's suffrage after the war, and this came true in a number of countries. (On women factory workers, see pp. 384–96.)[171]

The more than 25,000 US women who served in Europe in World War I did so on an entrepreneurial basis, especially before 1917. They helped nurse the wounded, provide food and other supplies to the military, serve as telephone operators (the "Hello Girls"), entertain troops, and work as journalists. Many of these "self-selected adventurous women ... found their own work, improvised their own tools ... argued, persuaded, and scrounged for supplies. They created new organizations where none had existed." Despite hardships, the women had "fun" and "were glad they went." Women sent out to "canteen" for the US Army – providing enter-tainment, sewing on buttons, handing out cigarettes and sweets – were "virtuous women" sent to "keep the boys straight." Army efforts to keep

---

[169] Rable 1992, spunk 138, liable 140, fantasies 141.
[170] Leonard 1994, widows xv, downplayed 160, rigidity 199.
[171] Stites 1978, major 281; Woollacott 1994, 189, factory 198; Kent 1993, true 74–96, 113.

women to the rear proved difficult. "Women kept ignoring orders to leave the troops they were looking after, and bobbing up again after they had been sent to the rear." Some of the US women became "horrifyingly bloodthirsty" in response to atrocity stories and exposure to the effects of combat. Looking back, the American women exhibited "contradictory feelings" of sadness about the war, horror at what they had seen, and pride in their own work. Mary Borden, a Baltimore millionaire who set up a hospital unit at the front from 1914 to 1918, wrote: "Just as you send your clothes to the laundry and mend them when they come back, so we send our men to the trenches and mend them when they come back again. You send your socks . . . again and again just as many times as they will stand it. And then you throw them away. And we send our men to the war again and again . . . just until they are dead."[172]

American Elsie Janis performed for British and French troops starting in 1914, and "anticipated Bob Hope in her devotion to entertaining the soldiery." Women entertainers were treated chivalrously by troops, not as sex objects. Doughboys behaved badly towards French women, but put American ones "on a pedestal that grew and grew," as Janis put it. One woman who stayed with 200 doughboys in a canteen near the front said she would feel comfortable leaving a 16-year-old daughter there alone, because "if any man touched her with his finger, these boys would tear him into a thousand pieces." Women entertained troops not only with song and dance but with lectures, dramatic readings, and poetry. "Troops clamored for Ella Wheeler Wilcox's readings of her own sentimental poems" urging sexual purity: "I may lie in the mud of the trenches, / I may reek with blood and mire, / But I will control, by the God in my soul, / The might of my man's desire." A soldier described seeing Sarah Willmer perform (after a 10-mile ride through a storm had, she thought, ruined her dress): "I shall never forget as long as I live the blessed white dress she had on the night she recited to us. We had not seen a white dress . . . in years. There we were with our gas masks at alert, all ready to go into the line, and there she was talking to us just like a girl from home. It sure was a great sight, you bet."[173]

Harriot Stanton Blatch in 1918 (with an endorsement by Teddy Roosevelt) urged American women and the government alike to "mobilize woman-power" for World War I. One reason for US women to support the war effort, she argued, was the character of Prussian culture

---

[172] Schneider and Schneider 1991, served 287–89, hello 177–87, fun 20–21, canteen 118, bobbing 135, bloodthirsty 272, feelings 280–81; Tylee 1990, 19–23; Borden: Tylee 1990, 101.

[173] Schneider and Schneider 1991, devotion 156, pedestal 267, finger 158, poems 161, dress 163.

which glorified brute force, supported men's domination of women, and treated children harshly. To men dubious of women's entry into the labor force, Blatch argued that "[e]very muscle, every brain, must be mobilized if the national aim is to be achieved." Blatch praised women's contributions in Britain, where participating in the war effort had made women "capable... bright-eyed, happy." She described England as "a world of women – women in uniforms; ... nurses ... messengers, porters, elevator hands, tram conductors, bank clerks, bookkeepers, shop attendants ... Even a woman doing ... womanly work ... dusted a room for the good of her country ... They were happy in their work, happy in the thought of rendering service, so happy that the poignancy of individual loss was carried more easily." This happiness seems dubious as a general proposition (see pp. 384–85), but for some individuals it must have been true. One woman wrote that she was "nearly mad with joy" at being sent to Serbia to do war work. Women at the front used very different language than those at home – receiving, in the words of one, "something hidden and secret and supremely urgent. .... [Y]ou are in another world, and ... given new senses and a new soul."[174]

The World Wars shook up gender relations, but only temporarily. Individual British women in the World Wars found new freedoms and opportunities in wartime – "like being let out of a cage," in one woman's words. However, gender changes were short-lived. "[A]ttitudes towards [women's] roles at home and at work remained remarkably consistent over nearly fifty years. Both wars put conventional views about gender roles under strain," but no permanent change occurred in hostility to women in male-dominated jobs, the devaluation of female labor, and the female-only responsibility for home life.[175]

The "reconstruction of gender" in Britain after World War I constrained women's roles and reinvigorated the ideology of motherhood. The feminist movement never regained after the war the status as a mass movement it had held before the war. Where prewar feminists had fought against separate male and female spheres and different constructions of masculinity and femininity, feminists in the interwar period gradually "accepted theories of sexual difference that helped to advance notions of separate spheres." After the "horrific events" of World War I, British society "sought above all to reestablish a sense of peace and security" and this precluded the egalitarian feminism of the prewar years, mandating instead a feminism of separate spheres to avoid "provok[ing] the men to anger."[176]

[174] Blatch 1918, 11–14, 35–59, happy 54, loss 55, 60–85; Kent 1993, mad 51, soul 52.
[175] Braybon and Summerfield 1987, cage ii, strain 2, 6; Tylee 1990, 7; Enloe 1989, 22.
[176] Kent 1993, 4–6.

Several major differences distinguish the two World Wars' effects on women. The first war had more concentrated action, on the Western front and in static trench warfare, leaving civilians relatively safe, whereas the second war was more "total" (drawing in civilians) and more mobile. In Britain, World War I soldiers were "invisible" whereas in World War II the US and British forces were a highly visible presence, the blitz targeted London, and fighter pilots could battle the enemy by day and drink at pubs near air bases by night. The first war was more of a surprise to Britons. Although both wars led to shortages of essential goods, the second war made it much harder for homemakers to compensate. Most importantly, in terms of gender roles, women in the military in the first war were "largely confined to very mundane work like cleaning, cooking, clerical work, waitressing, and some driving ... But in 1939–45 in addition ... women handled anti-aircraft guns, ran the communications network, mended aeroplanes and even flew them from base to base." Nonetheless, gender relations quickly reverted to tradition after World War II as after World War I.[177]

Men in feminine war roles   An omission marks this chapter – and the research literature overall – regarding men's roles in war outside that of combatant. Recent research has given far more attention to women who cross gender lines in war than men who do likewise. In various wars, men have played nearly all the "feminine" roles, from cooking and nursing at the front to providing sex and psychological support behind the lines. Because the nonmale war roles are in effect a residual from the constructed, selective "manhood" roles, men can fill them – both as war boosters and as conscientious objectors, just as women can both support and oppose war – without upsetting the gender coding of war. At least some able-bodied men, in addition to boys and elderly men, usually sit out any particular war. If social order begins to unravel in wartime, more young men may find it easier to gravitate away from the manly war roles (including by draft-evasion and desertion). The question of men in traditionally feminine war roles deserves more attention. Chapter 6 will pick up just one thread of this question, concerning feminization of male enemies.

To summarize the evidence for Hypothesis 5B, women frequently play a wide range of active support roles in war. These roles often draw on feminine constructions that support male soldiers' masculinity, as when women serve as witnesses to male bravery. Wartime disruptions of

[177] Braybon and Summerfield 1987, 2–7, mundane 5; WWII: Bruce 1985; Pierson 1986; Damousi and Lake eds. 1995; Edmond and Milward eds. 1986; Ayers 1988; Fishman 1991; Ås 1982; Shukert and Scibetta 1988; Winfield 1984.

gender norms tend to be temporary (a point I will return to in chapter 6 regarding women factory workers; see pp. 384–96).

C. WOMEN'S PEACE ACTIVISM

A third and final variant of Hypothesis 5 (5C) proposes that women do not participate in combat because their peaceful nature makes them oppose wars. This hypothesis cannot explain gendered war roles, given the evidence, just reviewed, that many women actively support wars. Nonetheless, a sizable number of women in many societies – generally somewhat more women than men, and often women acting in the name of their gender – do oppose wars and work for peace. At the local level, many individual women, such as the Somali woman in Figure 5.11, buffer intermale violence in myriad ways.[178]

In some simple societies, women tend to restrain the men from war or play special roles as mediators in bringing wars to an end. For instance, Andamanese Islands women "tried to settle quarrels and bring fighting to a conclusion." (However, this pattern is not universal. The Ibibio of Nigeria did not permit women to witness peace-making rites lest they upset them.) Among the Kiwai-Papua, after both sides signal a desire for peace, "a number of men accompanied by their wives make their way to the enemy village. The women walk a few paces ahead. It is taken for granted that bringing their wives is a demonstration of peaceful intentions ... During the night, the hosts sleep with the visitors' wives – a practice known as 'putting out the fire.'" After peace is declared, "[g]irls are married to close relatives of the dead, as a means of compensation." This is not women's peace activism, but it does code women with peace. Perhaps some similar idea motivated a Syrian general in 1983 to instruct Lebanese "resistance" forces to direct their attacks at US or British forces but not to hurt any Italian soldiers, because he had a crush on movie star Gina Lollobrigida. In both cases, anyway, women's sexuality seems to cast a protective aura over their menfolk.[179]

History of women's peace movements   In the nineteenth century, a time of relative peace in Europe, women organized both for women's rights and for peace, sometimes connecting the two in the form of women's peace societies. In 1852, *Sisterly Voices* began publication as

[178] Boulding 1995, 408; Pettman 1996a, 107–25; Washburn 1993; McAllister ed. 1982, 416–18; Oldfield 1989; Thompson 1987; Schott 1985; Norris 1928; McLean 1982; McAllister ed. 1982; Gioseffi ed. 1988; Cambridge Women's Peace Collective 1984.
[179] Goldschmidt 1989, quarrels 23–24; Turney-High 1971, witness 161; Kiwai: Eibl-Eibesfeldt 1979, 213; Syrian: Tlas 1998.

Figure 5.11 Woman separates husband and US Marine, Somalia, 1993.
[AP/Wide World Photos.]

a newsletter for these societies. Bertha von Suttner, the author of *Down with Weapons* in 1894, persuaded Alfred Nobel to create the Nobel Peace Prize (which von Suttner won in 1905). The initial 1870 proposal for a "Mother's Day" was to set the day aside for women's advocacy of peace. It did not catch on, and a more generic and commercial version was instituted fifty years later instead.[180]

In the twentieth century, the exemplary women's peace organization is the Women's Peace Party (WPP), founded during World War I and later renamed the Women's International League for Peace and Freedom (WILPF). The WPP grew out of the international women's suffrage movement. It was catalyzed by a US tour in Fall 1914 of a Hungarian woman and a British woman (from enemy sides in the new war). The WPP women "turned a good deal of their energies, in the midst of the suffrage campaign – which they did not abandon – to address the causes and cures of war."[181]

The WPP held an International Conference of Women at the Hague (Netherlands) nine months into World War I in 1915 (three months after the WPP's founding). The conference called for mediation to end the war. Jane Addams chaired the conference, and the WPP. In spite of travel problems and government obstacles, 1,136 voting delegates from 150 organizations in 12 countries attended. The conference brought together women from enemy and neutral countries, a feat that one delegate contrasted with the failure of others: "Science, medicine, reform, labor, religion – not one of these causes has been able as yet to gather its followers from across dividing frontiers." The participants were "a quite extraordinary group of gifted, courageous, and altruistic pioneers." Critics, however, found "conspicuously absent ... representatives of English, French, German, and Russian feminism." Theodore Roosevelt called the meeting "silly and base." Winston Churchill closed the North Sea to shipping, preventing most British delegates from attending. The British Admiralty also detained the US delegation's ship – which the British press called a "shipload of hysterical women" and "feminine busybodies" – until the last minute.[182]

When the United States entered World War I, some feminists remained antiwar activists, but faced difficult challenges as most of their colleagues supported the war effort. The YWCA's work supporting soldiers in World

---

[180] Washburn 1993, day 136–37; Chmielewski 1995.
[181] Degen 1939; Foster 1989; Bussey and Tims 1965, grew 17; Alonso 1996; Adams 1991, 210–13, cures 211; Pois 1995; Washburn 1993, 139–42; Wiltsher 1985.
[182] International Women's Committee of Permanent Peace 1915; Costin 1982; Addams 1922; Bussey and Tims 1965, frontiers 17; Oldfield 1995, gifted 159; Stites 1978, absent 281; Oldfield 1995, busybodies 159.

War I "strained against – and temporarily overwhelmed – its historic pacifism." Addams's efforts to galvanize US opposition to World War I backfired as she "alienated American public opinion by daring to question the 'heroism' of war." She was "instantly accused of besmirching the heroism of men dying for 'home, country, and peace itself.'" She argued, based on visits to military hospitals in Europe, that soldiers were not natural killers and were victims of the sheer horror of mechanized war. Her critics took this to mean she thought men incapable of heroic self-sacrifice. After 1917, Addams "was increasingly isolated" in opposing the war. She admitted moving "from the mire of self-pity to the barren hills of self-righteousness and ... hat[ing] herself equally in both places." After the war, she was branded a traitor, Communist, and anarchist. However, she won the 1931 Nobel Peace Prize.[183]

Addams believed that mothers would be the first to protest the slaughter of their children in war, and that "women of civilization" could help end this senseless killing. However, she did not hold a polarized gender conception of war and peace. In 1915, she dismissed the "belief that a woman is against war simply because she is a woman ... In every country there are women who believe that war is inevitable and righteous; the majority of women as well as men in the nations at war doubtless hold that conviction."[184]

The first woman to serve in the US Congress, Jeannette Rankin, was a pacifist who voted against US participation in both World Wars. The War Resisters League was founded in 1923 by three women. The works of German sculptor Käthe Kollwitz – such as her 1938 *Tower of Mothers* (Figure 5.12) – embody "maternal antimilitaris[m]" based on mothers as protectors of children against violence. Denounced by the Nazi regime, she worked in seclusion from 1933 until her death in 1945.[185]

By contrast, US women who participated in the conscientious objector movement during World War II did so most often in traditional feminine roles, primarily as wives/girlfriends or as workers in CO camps performing traditional feminine work (nurse, dietician). Many called themselves "CO girls." Their participation most often derived from their affiliation with a pacifist religious community (Mennonite especially), rather than from connecting women with peace, unlike the women peace activists of World War I or the Vietnam War.[186]

---

[183] Boulding 1992/II, 225–47; Berkman 1990; Kuhlman 1997; Jeffreys-Jones 1995, 1, 11–64; Schneider and Schneider 1991, strained 139, 139–48; Oldfield 1995, besmirching 161, isolated–places 162, 162–65; Pois 1995.

[184] Oldfield 1995, 165, 167.

[185] Sewall 1915, xi, xv; Albert 1982, founded 139; Kollwitz: Ruddick 1989, 159; Pierson 1987, 217.

[186] Goossen 1997, 41, 129, girls 101–5, 42, pacifist 130.

Figure 5.12 Käthe Kollwitz's "Tower of Mothers," 1938. [Käthe-Kollwitz-Museum, Berlin. © 2001 Artists Rights Society (ARS), New York/VG Bild-Kunst, Bonn.]

The 1962 anti-nuclear movement Women Strike for Peace (WSP) helped achieve the 1963 Limited Test Ban Treaty, according to President Kennedy's science advisor. Although *Newsweek* called the strike participants "perfectly ordinary looking women, with their share of good looks," the right-wing press warned that "the pro-Reds have moved in on our mothers and are using them for their own purposes." WSP members

Figure 5.13 Australian women protest conscription for the Vietnam War. [Union of Australian Women, courtesy of Noel Butlin Archives Centre, Australian National University.]

played up their feminine appearance and demeanor as a tactic when testifying before the House Un-American Activities Committee afterwards, thereby winning the battle for public opinion.[187]

During the Vietnam War, the US group Another Mother for Peace agitated against the war. In Australia, similarly, mothers protested their sons' conscription to fight in Vietnam (see Figure 5.13). Gender-integrated peace organizations, however, although drawing in many women participants, neither embraced feminism nor gave women many leadership roles.

The United Nations Decade for Women began in 1975 with little attention to war and peace, but developed a strong pro-peace theme by 1980. Women played leading roles in the not-especially-feminist antiwar movements of the early 1980s. In this wave of activism, for example, Randall Forsberg authored the nuclear freeze resolution, Women for a Meaningful Summit agitated for US–Soviet cooperation, and Ruth

[187] Swerdlow 1989; Swerdlow 1990, 9, 11.

Sivard compiled data showing the economic burden of military spending on social needs. Helen Caldicott reinvigorated Physicians for Social Responsibility to spearhead a campaign against nuclear weapons. The 1980s also saw new efforts to mobilize women *as* women to seek peace. Caldicott founded Women's Action for Nuclear Disarmament (WAND), and ascribed to war an inherently masculine nature. Among 19 US national women's peace organizations in the 1980s, a wide variety of motivations, strategies, and attitudes prevailed. However, of 27 new international women's networks founded in 1979–87, only three concerned peace issues (fewer than in earlier peace movement traditions). The focus of feminist activism shifted to violence against women, away from "men's wars," even as a subset of women reaffirmed women's peace activism.[188]

The anti-nuclear Greenham Common air base protests in England in the early 1980s, against US cruise missiles, became an exemplar of women's peace organizing, emulated at Seneca Women's Peace Encampment in New York and the Puget Sound Women's Peace Camp. The Greenham women created feminist symbolism designed to contrast with the masculinist war-culture of the air base. For instance, they wove into the base's perimeter fence various objects representing things they would lose in a nuclear war (such as pictures of loved ones). A Greenham newsletter reminded participants that women "are the guardians of life itself and of our future." These creative tactics captured public attention, though they made little impression on military and political officials.[189]

Some Israeli and Palestinian women struggled against the occupation of Palestinian land and the 1982 invasion of Lebanon. Weekly vigils of Jewish "Women in Black" (clothing) called attention to their opposition to war (critics called them "black widows"). In Israel, feminists' solidarity for peace was disrupted by divergent reactions to the Gulf War, however. By the 1990s, right-wing Israeli women in the militant Jewish settlers' movement began imitating tactics of women peace activists from the 1980s. Israeli feminists in 1994 "defended Israeli women for helping their draft-age children face military service proudly and cheerfully."[190]

---

[188] Stephenson 1982; Thompson ed. 1983; Solo 1988; Gioseffi ed. 1988, summit 66–67; Sivard 1996; Caldicott 1986; Jones ed. 1983; Washburn 1993, 142–43; Kelly 1995; McGlen 1987, variety 2; Boulding 1992/II, networks 322–27.

[189] Kirk 1989; Cataldo *et al.* 1987; Krasniewicz 1992; Puget Sound Women 1985; Jones 1987, future 198.

[190] Sharoni 1995; Sharoni 1996a, 1996b; Lentin 1996; Ferguson 1996; Scheper-Hughes 1996, cheerfully 354.

Violent conflicts that followed the collapse of the Soviet Union and former Yugoslavia mobilized women on several occasions to demand peace. In 1989, the Committee of Soldiers' Mothers (renamed "Mother's Heart" a year later) formed in the Soviet Union. In 1991, "250 women from fifty-six towns in Russia held a hunger strike" to demand a say on issues affecting military families. In the former Yugoslavia, Croatian and Serbian women in 1991 "united around their identities as the mothers" of soldiers, and staged protests against the war. However, these protests were quickly put down by authorities, and women were coopted into their nations' war efforts. Nonetheless, in 1999, Serbian women protested against the war in Kosovo. Thus, the women's peace movement worldwide has persevered over decades, with mixed results.[191]

Gender gap in polling Women won the vote in a number of countries after World War I. Many suffrage supporters expected that women would vote for peace, but instead women generally voted like their husbands. Nonetheless, as in the overlapping bell-curves of chapter 3, women have shown a modest propensity to vote for peace more than men do, on average. In the United States, public opinion polling shows that although men's and women's "foreign policy belief systems" apparently resemble each other, "women have consistently shown less support for forceful means of pursuing foreign policy goals."[192]

A review of 285 US polls over four decades shows gender gaps in attitudes towards war, with men supporting "more violent or forceful options" than women in 87 percent of the relevant poll questions. Men favored more peaceful options in 5 percent of the questions, scattered amongst the polls and "in virtually every case of doubtful statistical significance." Men clustered at both extremes (with women more in the middle) for 7 percent of questions, mostly concerning defense spending. Regarding foreign policy questions, the gender gap was about 10 percentage points. The gap was largest for "gray areas" where social norms about violence are ambiguous (for example, the gender gap was larger when public opinion about military interventions was divided). The gender differences "have not appreciably changed since the women's movement was organized in the late sixties, and the gap is the same among profeminist men and women as it is among antifeminists of both sexes,

---

[191] Enloe 1993, heart 12, hunger 13; Yugoslavia: Nikolić-Ristanović 1996, united 359; Gall 1999.
[192] Gallagher 1993, goals 24; Jensen 1987; Silverman and Kumka 1987.

nor do those differences vary by either age or education." Various relevant poll results may be summarized as follows:[193]

Date	Issue	Percent agree Men	Percent agree Women
8/39	Go to war against Germany	19	12
11/40	Take strong measures against Japan	56	42
10/60	Tougher policy towards Russia	60	46
10/61	Fight all-out nuclear war rather than live under Communist rule	87	75
4/68	Describe self as hawk, not dove on Vietnam (step up, not reduce, effort)	50	32
4/75	Wars are necessary to settle differences between nations (not outmoded)	55	38

Survey data from Israel, Egypt, Palestine, and Kuwait find no significant gender difference in any country regarding attitudes towards nonviolent means of resolving the Arab–Israeli conflict. Interestingly, in all four countries, those attitudes correlate significantly with support or opposition to gender equality, rather than with the respondent's own gender. So attitudes to peace and to gender may correlate, but not because women are peaceful.[194]

The dilemma of the women's peace movement   Women's peace activism confronts a serious dilemma. On the one hand, women's peace organizations provide important support for peace movements generally, and sometimes sustain peace activism at low points for peace movements – as during World War I in the United States. The 1980 protesters shown in Figure 1.6 (p. 45) helped sustain the US peace movement after the Vietnam War and lay foundations for the nuclear freeze movement. Also, the fact that *some* women participate in working for peace based on their gender identity means that women's peace organizations are mobilizing participants for peace who otherwise might not join peace movements. Furthermore, women's peace groups contribute creative ideas, and help hold in check the sexism that might otherwise weaken peace movements (e.g., by keeping talented women out of leadership

[193] Smith 1984, options 384, 385–95.
[194] Tessler and Warriner 1997, 274–75.

positions where they can make a difference). In all, the disappearance of women's peace groups would be a major setback for peace activism.

On the other hand, if soldiers are motivated to fight by culturally re-inforced stereotypes of masculinity, then women's peace activism only bolsters this dynamic. As Elshtain argues, women, historically cast as Beautiful Souls, "have served as the collective projection" of a pure and pacifistic Other against which a destructive, beastly male is constructed. Despite women peace activists' fantasies of stopping men's wars, in fact a "nasty historic bargain has been struck here: Beautiful Souls may stay as 'sweet as they are' while 'the boys will be boys.'" Elshtain warns that "total inversions" such as the view that peaceful women will save hu-manity "wind up endorsing – indeed requiring – that which they would oppose."[195]

Making peace feminine, as we have seen, both masculinizes war and draws gender divisions that help soldiers to kill (knowing that they are outside a "normal" world). Furthermore, for those male soldiers who do participate in combat, women's peace activism may heighten their sense of isolation and intensify post-traumatic stress – as the US peace activism of the Vietnam era seemed to do. Thus, whatever its positive aspects in boosting peace movements and perhaps changing national policies, women's peace activism is unlikely to "get through to" male soldiers or to change the gendered nature of the war system.

CONCLUSION

Hypotheses 5A–C concern the abnormality of war fighting. Cultures need to coax and trick soldiers into participating in combat – an extremely difficult challenge – and gender presents a handy means to do so by linking attainment of manhood to performance in battle. In addition, cultures directly mold boys from an early age to suppress emotions in order to function more effectively in battle. This system, supported in various ways by most women, produces men capable of fighting wars, but emotionally impaired. The militarized masculinity of men who fight wars is reinforced by women's symbolic embodiment of "normal" life and by women's witnessing of male bravery. In these ways, gender serves to delineate and separate war from normal life, enabling soldiers both to suspend social norms against killing and to withstand the hell of war. Society's preparation to fight potential wars, however, comes at a high price for all men and women even in times of relative peace.

[195] Elshtain 1990, projection–boys 342, inversions 265.

6 Conquests: sex, rape, and exploitation in wartime

> **Hypothesis 6.** Men's sexual and economic domination of women:
>
> A. Male sexuality as a cause of aggression
> B. Feminization of enemies as symbolic domination
> C. Dependence on exploiting women's labor

INTRODUCTION

This chapter covers three somewhat divergent hypotheses, drawn to-gether by the idea that gendered war roles are nearly universal because men's domination of women is nearly universal. If chapter 5 focused centrally on men as victims, this chapter brings forward *women* victims of war.

The dominance hierarchies discussed in chapter 4 apply not only to men in groups but also to male–female relationships. Men and women in virtually all human cultures occupy dominant and subordinate status ranks. Men often exploit women's work, with and without pay – including sex work, domestic work, child care, nursing, and the array of low-wage jobs in modern industrial economies. Overall, though not everywhere, men enforce women's subordinate condition with widespread threats and uses of "hidden violence . . . [r]ape, battery, and other forms of sexual and domestic violence."[1]

In the context of an exploitive dominance relationship, and especially in wartime when that relationship intensifies, keeping weapons out of the hands of the exploited-subordinate class makes sense. Letting women become warriors could threaten men's dominance over women. There-fore patriarchal cultures (i.e., all cultures) limit women's participation in combat. In this view, the armed male soldier faces both outward to meet dangers and opportunities beyond the border, and inward to maintain

[1] Herman 1992, violence 32; Mies 1986, 153–67.

the gendered hierarchy of domestic society. Some conservative opponents of women in combat today connect war roles with the domestic gender order. According to a 1998 Southern Baptist resolution, the idea of women in combat "rejects gender-based distinctions established by God," negates "the unique gender-based responsibility of men to protect women and children," and implies a "shameful failure of male leadership." For these reasons, it "undermines male headship in the family." Similarly, in South Korea today, universal male conscription helps socialize men for later careers in business and politics, and maintains sharp gender divisions in families – male breadwinners, female housewives.[2]

I will explore three hypotheses sharing the premise that in wartime the exploitation of women intensifies, although this does not apply to every individual or category of woman in every war. First, war (which disrupts social relationships and norms) brings more women into sex work on more exploitive terms (although this sexuality covers a range that includes reciprocity at one end and slavery at the other). Is heightened male sexuality (reflected by women's wartime sex work) necessary for participation in combat? Second, war borrows gender as a code for domination–submission relationships (not just to delimit combat and normal life as in chapter 5). Enemies and subordinates are gendered feminine. As a result, recurrently, victorious soldiers express domination by raping conquered women. Does the tendency of male soldiers to feminize enemies explain the absence of women in their ranks? Third, women's paid and unpaid work (beyond sex work) weighs more heavily on women in wartime than peacetime. In simple societies, furthermore, frequent warfare tends to correlate (imperfectly) with a lower status for women. Do societies direct women away from combat roles in order to exploit their labor more efficiently in wartime?

A. MALE SEXUALITY AS A CAUSE OF AGGRESSION

Hypothesis 6A holds that men's participation in combat harnesses the male sex drive – by the promise of a sexual reward for combat or possibly by aggression-enhancing properties of male sexuality – in ways that would be disrupted by the presence of women combatants.

Sex in wartime

Soldiers show an "almost universal preoccupation with sex" – an "obsession with sex in a community of men . . . deprived of usual social and emotional outlets." A British officer in World War I concluded that

[2] Resolution 3, June 9–11, 1998, Salt Lake City; Korea: Moon 1998.

"[m]ost soldiers were ready to have sexual intercourse with almost any woman whenever they could." As one US soldier in World War II wrote: "army conversation has a beautiful simplicity and directness. It is all on one solid, everlasting subject... Women, Women, Women." Or, another: "Anyone entering military service for the first time can only be astonished by soldiers' concentration upon the subject of women and, more especially, upon the sexual act. The most common word in [their] mouths... does duty as adjective, adverb, verb, noun, and in any other form it can possibly be used."[3]

US and British military culture in World War II promoted this preoccupation with sex. Over 5 million copies of *Life* magazine's 1941 photo of Rita Hayworth (captioned the "Goddess of Love") were sent out to US soldiers. Such "pin-ups" were ubiquitous among US forces. They were published not only in men's magazines but in service publications like *Stars and Stripes* (or for Britain, *Reveille*). The appeal of the "undisputed leader," Betty Grable, "was less erotic than as a wholesome symbol of American womanhood," based on a "carefully groomed exploitation of her good-natured hominess by 20th Century-Fox." Hayworth, however, the "runner-up" to Grable, "exuded the sultry sex appeal of a mature woman" whose "appeal was more erotic than wholesome." Jane Russell's "flamboyant sex appeal made her pin-ups wildly popular with GIs overseas." Her large breasts were shamelessly exploited by movie producers as "the two great reasons for [her] rise to stardom." Moralists at home opposed the pin-up craze. In 1944, the Postmaster General banned *Esquire* with its Vargas Girl fantasies, and Congressional hearings ensued. However, officers decided that pin-ups contributed to soldiers' morale. In Britain, meanwhile, the cartoon heroine "Jane" boosted morale during the Blitz and thereafter by taking her clothes off during periods of bad news. "It was said that the first armored vehicle ashore on D-Day carried a large representation of naked Jane." The comic-strip Jane "finally lost the last vestiges of her modesty during the Normandy campaign" in 1944, and soldiers said, "Jane gives her all."[4]

Disruption of social norms   Whatever other roles male sexuality may play, armies segregate large numbers of post-adolescent males for extended periods, thereby creating a kind of critical mass of pent-up sexual desire. In wartime, social norms are disrupted and soldiers often operate far from home, with new sexual opportunities and motives. The

---

[3] Holmes 1985, almost 93, ready 93; Hicks 1995, outlets 28–29; Costello 1985, subject 78; Gray 1959, 59–70, duty 61.

[4] Griffin 1992, sent 76; Costello 1985, wholesome–vestiges 149–55; Koppes 1995; Parry 1996, vii.

Figure 6.1 US airmen in England, 1944. [AP/Wide World Photos.]

disruption of normal sexual patterns was noted empirically by a New Orleans "madam" whose business increased when America entered World War I: "I've noticed it before, the way the idea of war and dying makes a man raunchy...It wasn't really pleasure at times, but a kind of nervous breakdown that could only be treated with a girl and a set to."[5]

Wars lift social taboos, disrupt relationships, and send large groups of young men far from home. Sociological explanations "fasten upon the uprooting character of war experience...[and the] artificial separation of the sexes." The men see prostitutes, with and without military blessing, and sometimes form relationships with local women (whose relationships may also have been disrupted). Promiscuity increases as people are less focused on the long-term future. A US soldier in France in World War II wrote to his father that he planned to "get my fun where I can get it while I'm still alive. And to hell with tomorrow – it may never come." As Figure 6.1 implies, US airmen in England who beat the odds by

[5] Costello 1985, set 211.

surviving could have sex after a mission (consistent with the testosterone boost produced by a "win"; see pp. 153–55). None of this means that increased sexuality underlies male soldiers' aggressiveness in the war, however. Rather, war may simply disrupt social norms, with sexual changes as a result (another case of reverse causality from war to gender).[6]

The sexless front   The hypothesized link between aggression and sex is weakened by the fact that in wartime the areas of greatest violence – the front lines – have far less sexual activity than the more peaceful areas behind the lines. Soldiers have a lot of sex in at least some wars, but not at the front. Before World War I, popular European writing was full of misconceptions about the effect that a war would have on sexual impulses. War was seen as "a way to erotic liberation and unlimited expression of sensuality" for both soldiers and civilians. In contrast to these "farflung expectations," and the "amorous paradises provided at various military war-stations" for a minority of lucky soldiers, the ordinary soldier found that "[i]n the trenches there was no place for sexual life, at least not for a normal one." This was particularly true of World War I as a mechanized total war that dragged on for years.[7]

According to Hirschfeld, soldiers in the trenches had few outlets for sexual energy and suffered "sex hunger" on a massive scale – an "oppressive sex starvation." Sex hunger was compounded in World War I by the close quarters of men at the front, which often made even masturbation impractical. (In World War II, by contrast, one soldier was more often alone in a foxhole, although a great stigma still attached to masturbation.) Masturbation, "widespread in every army . . . became far more widespread" during World War I. A much-quoted Austrian fighter quipped: "Formerly my wife was my right hand, now my right hand is my wife." Hirschfeld claims that bestiality provided another substitute outlet created by the sexual starvation of the war. A military physician posted with a division of the Austro-Hungarian army on the Italian front reportedly thought that at least 10 percent of the men had sex with animals (usually their horses). Psychological problems after the war often included sexual dysfunction, such as inability to maintain an erection, well after returning to civilian life. Hirschfeld, opposed to masturbation, bestiality, homosexuality, and prostitution alike, argues that the sex hunger of World War I contributed greatly to its dehumanizing effects.[8]

---

[6] Gray 1959, uprooting 62–63; Costello 1985, come 248.

[7] Hartsock 1983, 186–90; Hartsock 1989; Hirschfeld 1934, sensuality–normal 69–70, 31–51, 188–206; Theweleit 1987, 249.

[8] Hirschfeld 1934, 73–77, hunger 81, wife 76, bestiality 86–87, civilian 89–91; Costello 1985, 75, 102; Freud 1915.

In World War II, although soldiers were very lonely, "sexual deprivation and inordinate desire generally did not trouble men on the front line. They were too scared, busy, hungry, tired, and demoralized to think about sex at all. Indeed, the front was the one wartime place that was sexless."[9]

Sex in the rear   Behind the lines, by contrast, sex flourished in World War II. By one calculation, the average US soldier who served in Europe from D-Day through the end of the war had sex with 25 women. The peak was reached after the surrender of Germany in 1945. Condoms had to be rationed at four per man per month and medical officers considered this "entirely inadequate." A 1945 US army survey "revealed that the level of promiscuity among the troops was far higher than officially admitted, and rates rose in direct proportion to the amount of time the men had spent overseas." Over 80 percent of those who had been away over two years admitted to having regular sexual intercourse. In US-occupied Italy, three-quarters of US soldiers had intercourse with Italian women, on average once or twice a month. About three-quarters of these paid with cash and the rest with rationed food, or nothing. The survey showed that fewer than half the US soldiers used condoms.[10]

When German territory fell to the Allies in 1945, a US policy against fraternization with German women was widely flouted, and an "epidemic of promiscuity" ensued. Many German women were openly receptive to relationships with the occupying troops, if only because the latter had food and cigarettes. Thus sex became "a commodity to be traded for the necessities of life." As a US staff sergeant explained, the fraternization policy worked almost like Prohibition except that "a guy could hide a bottle inside his coat for days at a time, but it is hard to keep a German girl quiet in there for more than a couple of hours."[11]

From the soldiers' perspective, the supply of sex never equaled demand, however. Thus, "desire was constantly seeking an outlet it seldom satisfactorily found." Sexual mores of the 1940s (incredibly prudish by today's standards), even under the upheaval of the war, restricted the realm of the imaginable, as did the limited available birth control. Reading ever-so-slightly titillating novels, reciting bawdy verses, sneaking off to masturbate, and "foraging" for local women (prostitutes or otherwise) were the sexual outlets behind the lines.[12]

War stories that focus on the front rarely discuss sex. For example, historian Stephen Ambrose gives detail-oriented accounts of battles, but

---

[9] Fussell 1989, sexless 108.
[10] Holmes 1985, average 97; Costello 1985, peak–survey 97, 262, half 99.
[11] Costello 1985, epidemic 249–52, 95.
[12] Fussell 1989, 105–10.

only a vague mention that Paris after liberation in 1944 "over the next few days had one of the great parties of the war" (see data on VD rates, p. 342). Ambrose mentions that German soldiers in the Battle of the Bulge were motivated by being told that hospitals in Belgium contained "many American nurses," and that US airmen in England had "regular and easy access to a London in which a pack of cigarettes would pay for a woman and a night's worth of booze." When the huge bureaucracy of the US Army's Services of Supply moved to Paris, with access to vast quantities of US supplies arriving in Europe, "taking into account what Paris had to sell, from wine and girls to jewels and perfumes, a black market on a grand scale sprang up ... The supply troops ... got the girls, because they had the money, thanks to the black market." Ambrose can take for granted that "girls" were a commodity in wartime cities. Aside from these occasional references, however, Ambrose bypasses sex, presumably because it does not matter at the front.[13]

Uncoerced sex   Sex in wartime covers a range of contexts, with women's voluntary participation at one end (sometimes becoming "war brides"), their implicit or explicit trading of sex for money or food in the middle, and rape at the other extreme. On this continuum, most war-related sex occurs in the middle, but I will begin at the voluntary end. By some reports, "war aphrodisia" – common among soldiers in many wars – extended into many segments of society during "total war." Thus, among not only soldiers but civilians, "sexual restraint ... [was] suspended for the duration." As one British housewife put it, "We were not really immoral, there was a war on."[14]

The million and a half US soldiers who filled England before D-Day in 1944 had a well-deserved reputation as "wolves in wolves' clothing." They were, in one British phrase of the time, "oversexed, overpaid, and over here." England's men were absent in large numbers, and its women had survived blackout and Blitz. The Americans' "predatory" behavior with English women offended many people but also led to many relationships, only some of which involved either money or marriage. The US soldiers' presence contributed to a shake-up of British sexual mores, already under strain from the war. Race riots broke out among the segregated US forces in England after white British women formed relationships with black US soldiers. In Australia, the influx of US soldiers also altered the gender balance.[15]

---

[13] Keegan and Holmes 1985; Ambrose 1997, parties 106, nurses 190, booze 290, market 337–38; Paris: Costello 1985, 88.
[14] Costello 1985, 3, 7–9.
[15] Costello 1985, wolves 228–32, 240, riots 235; Australia: Lake and Damousi 1995, 9.

Back in the United States, "Victory Girls" gave free sex to soldiers as their "patriotic duty." A 1942 conference of the American Social Hygiene Association concluded that these promiscuous adolescents (most were under 21 and many under 19) practiced "sexual delinquency of a non-commercial character... [seeking] adventure and sociability." An Army doctor blamed these young women for troops' high VD rates: "While mothers are winning the war in the factories, their daughters are losing it on the streets." The ill-defined "'victory girl' was usually assumed to be a woman who pursued sexual relations with servicemen out of a mis-placed patriotism or a desire for excitement. She could also, however, be a girl or woman who, without actually engaging in sexual relations, was testing the perimeters of social freedom in wartime America." A "sur-prising number were young married women." One study of 210 women detained on morals charges in Seattle showed that only one-third were single.[16]

In response to fears of uncontrolled sexuality, a government "social pro-tection" campaign "expanded a health program into a purity campaign dedicated to the search for 'incipient and confirmed sex delinquents' who, not coincidentally, happened always to be women." According to FBI statistics (which tend to undercount local reports), the number of women charged with morals violations doubled in the war years. In Seattle (a "particularly zealous" city), up to 300 women monthly were detained. Although only one-sixth had VD, all had to spend four days in county jail awaiting results of VD tests, whereas their male partners were seldom detained. Detroit banned unescorted women from bars after 8 pm, and in 1945 prosecuted a soldier's wife and the man she was living with.[17]

In Germany too, as social control disintegrated at the end of World War II, civilian gender limits expanded. In the Rhineland in 1945, advancing Allied forces found "Edelweiss gangs" of young men in pink shirts and bobby-sox, who "roamed the rubble hurling insults and stones at the Hitler Youth – when they were not trading sexual favors with willing girls."[18]

Drawbacks of sex   Male soldiers' sexuality creates three par-ticular challenges for commanders. First, prostitutes and lovers can serve as enemy intelligence sources (see Figure 6.2). US soldiers in Vietnam sometimes first learned about their next mission not from their officers but from prostitutes (who presumably also told the Vietcong). British

[16] Costello 1985, sociability–streets 207; Enloe 1983, 29–31; Anderson 1981, perimeters 104, married 110.
[17] Anderson 1981, 104–9.
[18] Costello 1985, 249.

Figure 6.2 British poster warns against intelligence risks of prostitution. [Courtesy of the Imperial War Museum, London.]

troops in North Africa in World War II sang of a legendary seductress working for Germany, who boasted, "The order of the battle, I obtained from last night's rattle." Meanwhile, French prostitutes, whose establishments were taken over intact by occupying German troops, worked with the French Resistance to pass along vital intelligence and to harbor Allied pilots trying to escape occupied France (police generally did not intrude in houses of prostitution frequented by German officers). In occupied French ports where prostitutes might reveal the missions of U-boats, German commanders quarantined their crews for weeks before departure, and brought in German women to staff "rest-camps" with dance halls and hotel-style rooms.[19]

Second, male sexuality that runs amok – especially when it leads to rape – can generate resentments and reactions contrary to the military's mission. For example, the huge US bases in Okinawa, Japan are central to US military operations in East Asia. In 1995, relations with local residents plummeted after US Marines raped a local schoolgirl. This incident, which contributed to a climate where the United States began scaling back the Okinawa bases, clearly worked directly against the effectiveness of the US military. Male soldiers' rambunctious and aggressive sexuality did not contribute to morale, or male bonding, or any military goal, but the opposite. I return to the issue of rape later in this chapter (see pp. 362–71).[20]

The third and most important challenge created by wartime sexuality is the spread of various debilitating sexually transmitted diseases, collectively known as venereal disease (VD), which have taken a serious toll on armies throughout history. (In turn, armies have used VD as a "stalking horse for a far more expansive military misogyny" – an excuse to tighten control on women – as with Britain's 1864 Contagious Diseases Act.) In the present-day AIDS epidemic, the long-standing problem of VD has new salience.[21]

VD apparently spreads more rapidly when an army stays in one position than when it is mobile. Thus, in World War I it was the shift to static warfare after the battles of 1914 that sharply increased VD rates. During the German occupation of part of France in 1870, French prostitutes were urged to deliberately infect masses of German troops. In one German corps during the 1870–71 war with France, an initial 3 percent VD rate increased only to 10 percent during the war but then to 78 percent when the corps had been encamped in France for five months.[22]

---

[19] Goldman and Fuller 1983, Viet 126; Costello 1985, rattle 79, French 218–19.
[20] Pollack 1996; Schmitt 1996.
[21] Enloe 1983, stalking 23–26.
[22] Hirschfeld 1934, 93–94.

During World War I, VD rates rose dramatically in all the participating armies, and only Germany undertook systematic measures to
solve the problem (learning from its 1871 experience). To reduce the
number of infections, Germany and other countries (except England)
distributed literature warning men of the dangers of intercourse, and
of liquor which could lead to risky sex. Military authorities used surprise inspections, and mandatory inspections before leave (to prevent VD from spreading to the homeland). Some military physicians
considered these measures "impracticable for a great army of millions standing in the field." Others disagreed about whether infections
were occurring primarily at the front, in rear stations, or at home.
Hirschfeld concludes that "there was a continual exchange of the germs
of infection between the front and the hinterland." Although British
commanders largely tried to ignore the problem, the Canadian and
New Zealand prime ministers in 1915 ordered the distribution of free
condoms to troops, as did the United States when it entered the
war.[23]

In World War II, "short-arm" (penis) inspections were mandatory once
a year in the British Army and twice a year in the US Army. VD rates
among US forces in Europe increased sixfold in Fall 1944, with two-thirds
of those infected in France citing their time in Paris. VD was not limited
to occupied areas. British national VD rates had increased 70 percent
by mid-1941, fueled by conscription and the corresponding increase in
prostitution around army bases and ports.[24]

Military prostitution

To bring these dangers under control while providing for male soldiers'
morale, military commanders have often encouraged, or directly organized, prostitution to service their armies. The Roman empire operated a system of brothels for its armies. The Spanish army invading the
Netherlands in the late sixteenth century trailed "400 mounted whores
and 800 on foot" who were like "troops" commanded by appointed officers. The word "hooker" comes from US Civil War general Joseph
Hooker, whose Army of the Potomac was accompanied by "Hooker's
girls." In World Wars I and II, French and German armies set up systems of military-supervised brothels. Cynthia Enloe writes that "many
men will not stay in the military if they cannot marry and/or otherwise

---

[23] Hirschfeld 1934, solve 92, field 95, germs 105; Costello 1985, free 211–12.
[24] Costello 1985, 88.

have ready sexual access to women. Women, therefore, must somehow be brought under sufficient military control."[25]

UN peacekeeping troops in Bosnia during the war allegedly used Muslim prostitutes controlled by Serbian forces. After the war, a number of UN police and SFOR troops in Bosnia participated in both local prostitution and trafficking in Eastern European sex slaves. Similarly, international troops in Kosovo in 1999 fueled a prostitution boom. Catherine MacKinnon writes: "Each layer of protection adds a layer of violence against women. Perhaps intervention by a force of armed women should be considered."[26]

A recent study of 500 prostitutes worldwide found that two-thirds had PTSD, a higher percentage than found for combat veterans. The vast majority had suffered repeated physical and sexual assaults. More than 90 percent wanted to get out of prostitution but were unable to do so. In wartime, conditions are even worse.[27]

An extensive system of military brothels was established by both sides in World War I, on both the western and eastern fronts. Germans were the most systematic in attending to the "sexual logistics" of their occupying armies (resulting in a lower VD rate). A first-hand report from July 1917 gives the rate of visitors to a military brothel at Mitau that operated 4–9 pm daily – ranging from about ten customers per prostitute per evening up to a high of 32. After hours, others would sneak in as well. The officers often "went in large groups" to such brothels. The hostesses of the brothels were appointed or recognized by the German occupation army, and German police doctors supervised hygiene, working from nearby huts to examine every soldier admitted. The soldier would have his identity recorded (to follow up on VD cases), then would undergo a genital exam and have his penis treated with protargol and vaseline. On exiting, the soldier would tell which prostitute he had been with, then urinate and get another protargol injection. Since officers were exempt from these exams, VD rates among officers were high.[28]

Although specific elements of the system of military prostitution differed for the eastern and western fronts and for the Allied and German armies, the arrangements were everywhere degrading and mechanistic

---

[25] De Pauw 1998, European 96–100, Civil 165–67, WWI 219–20; Levine 1993; Enloe 1993, 142–60; Hicks 1995, mounted 29; Costello 1985, French 81–82; Enloe 1983, access 4, 6, 18–45; Gray 1959, 65.

[26] Bosnia: Reuters 2000; Kosovo: Agence France-Presse 2000; layer: MacKinnon 1994b, 192.

[27] Zuger 1998b.

[28] Costello 1985, 247–53; Enloe 1993, 145–52; Mitau: Hirschfeld 1934, 149–51.

(like so much else in World War I), for both the men and the women, albeit less so for officers than for soldiers. The French army operated most brothels for Allied soldiers. The static, sedentary nature of trench warfare required an equally static form of "brothelized prostitution." As the war dragged on, the expectation of sexual abstinence by soldiers diminished. Although some field brothels had just a few prostitutes near the front lines, more important were the larger establishments in cities and towns to the rear. Mirroring the pattern of separating ranks in the military, some brothels served only officers and others only common soldiers. They were marked (for Allied armies) by a red or blue lantern, respectively. On several occasions, in Cairo and Sudan, soldiers rioted while waiting in long lines for access to the brothels, and thereafter military guards were placed outside to regulate the crowds.[29]

In World War I, new prostitutes were recruited, after demand outstripped the existing supply, from women "driven by the chronic misery of the occupied districts." In Mitau, the German military issued orders forbidding prostitution except in military-regulated brothels. Secret agents could then coerce any desirable woman into sex, by threatening to report her as an unlicensed prostitute, which would lead the military to put her under its control and send her to a military brothel. Thus, the negative impact of war prostitution extended to women generally and not just women who were already prostitutes.[30]

By World War II, American public opinion forced a less tolerant attitude towards military prostitution than in World War I. British and American commanders in some cases favored setting up licensed brothels on the French model (Eisenhower seriously considered it), but faced strong opposition on moral and religious grounds from organizations back home. In mid-1941, Congress gave military commanders the authority to shut down establishments of prostitution near military bases, to "Blitz the Brothels." Military commanders, however, seldom used such authority, in order not to harm morale. The campaign apparently did result in a sharp reduction in military-related prostitution in the majority of communities affected, but in many cases prostitution merely assumed a more free-lance character.[31]

In Honolulu, organized prostitution near Pearl Harbor was officially tolerated until late in the war. Military commanders felt it boosted morale among sailors, while local residents felt it protected their own women. (An "alchemy of race and sex" made World War II Hawaii a meeting place of American subcultures, a tense and overcrowded zone between home

[29] Hirschfeld 1934, 141–55, brothelized 141.
[30] Hirschfeld 1934, 153.
[31] Costello 1985, less 81–82, blitz–character 213.

and front, with a male–female population ratio of several hundred to one. Soldiers expecting "a hula girl under every palm tree" were sorely disappointed.) In 1942 the Navy administered 600,000 prophylactic treatments in Honolulu. Women with VD received forced hospitalization. When police in 1942 cracked down on the houses of prostitution, which were spreading to new neighborhoods, the prostitutes went on strike and staged street protests, arguing that they were "essential to the welfare of U.S. armed forces." Military police had to control an angry crowd of 185 men waiting to see five strike-breaking prostitutes one afternoon. Within weeks, the police called off their campaign and the prostitutes returned to work.[32]

Meanwhile, "Piccadilly Warriors" sold sex to soldiers in blacked-out London. One Canadian soldier described Piccadilly before D-Day – swarming with prostitutes who provided instant sex in nearby parks and streets – as "a vast battlefield of sex." British sailors' sex life likewise was "crude in the extreme," despite the men's loyalty to wives and girlfriends back home. And in the British Army, "the most popular barrackroom ballads sang the praises of insatiable whores."[33]

Upon the German occupation of Paris in 1940, the military governor immediately took over the best brothels for German officers, and advertised their locations in leaflets with instructions to visit army prophylactic stations afterwards. On the liberation of Paris in 1944, a US army officer toured brothels to allocate them for officers, white enlisted men, and nonwhite enlisted men. Local US military commanders thwarted efforts by Washington to close the brothels to US personnel.[34]

US troops occupying Japan in 1945 used "Special Recreation Centers" set up by Japanese authorities. Price lists were posted on bulletin boards in US army camps with instructions that "MP's will be stationed at the doors to enforce these prices. Trucks will leave here each hour, on the hour ... " (and, be sure to "wear one"!). A US Navy chaplain complained in *Newsweek* about the official brothels for sailors and officers (separate as always), which he had seen generate a line four-abreast and a block long, patrolled by MPs, waiting to pay 10 yen for one of 113 prostitutes on duty that day.[35]

Comfort women   Japan's own army in World War II developed an extensive system of so-called "comfort women." Thousands

[32] Costello 1985, morale 217, treatments–work 216–18; alchemy: Bailey and Farber 1992, 95–132, ratio 43, 35, hula 38.
[33] Costello 1985, warriors 83, crude 80, ballads 79; Fussell 1989, vast 109.
[34] Costello 1985, occupation 211–12, liberation 247.
[35] Costello 1985, 253.

of women in occupied countries were forced into the sexual service of Japanese soldiers under conditions much harsher than those of the European prostitutes just described. It was "a large-scale, officially-organised system of rape by the Imperial Japanese Forces." The women had sex with as many as 30 men per day, working in stations of about 15 women. The total number of women is unknown. Where documented, the ratio of soldiers to women was typically about 50:1. Applying this ratio to all 7 million Japanese soldiers yields a *maximum* size of over 100,000 women in the comfort system. Service near the front was harsh, especially when units in transit passed through a station, or when comfort women were sent with a supply run to service a garrison in a forward pillbox, or when women had to follow military units on marches.[36]

Just as sexual abuse in other contexts leads to secrecy and silence, so did the comfort-women system seemingly disappear from history after the war. In the "huge literature in English on the Pacific War, we could find no mention ... of the comfort women." Just before surrendering in 1945, Japanese forces appointed comfort women as civilian employees (nurses), then destroyed the evidence. A Japanese professor found unpublished documents that forced the Japanese military, after decades of denials, to admit its involvement. Japanese textbooks have omitted the subject, however. "For almost forty years the truth was hidden. Living victims were too intimidated to challenge the might of the Japanese state. All documentary evidence appeared to have been burnt. Then, slowly ... the truth emerged." Hotlines established for a month in 1992 in three Japanese cities collected data on several hundred cases. From these data, it appears that most comfort women were 14–18 years old, and most were Korean.[37]

Asian prostitution since the Vietnam War   During the Vietnam War, US soldiers received R&R leave as a reward. Having sex was often a major component of these leaves. "Married men typically rendezvoused with their wives in Hawaii; the unattached headed for various liberty towns in Southeast Asia ... [including] Bangkok for the sex." Locally, Vietnamese prostitutes and girlfriends were widely visited by US soldiers. US Green Berets had over 25 contacts with prostitutes per man, on average. By 1973, 300,000–500,000 women worked as prostitutes in South Vietnam, the "precise number" being "impossible to calculate because thousands ... worked as cleaners and servants

[36] Hicks 1995, rape 11, 18, ratio 19, marches 73–74; De Pauw 1998, 259–62.
[37] Hicks 1995, mention 7, textbooks 12, truth 8, hotlines 11, Korean 18.

for American troops and thousands more were raped by American soldiers."[38]

Although prostitution has long been institutionalized in Thailand and some other Asian societies, it was during the Vietnam War that Bangkok "first came to prominence as a centre for commercial sex . . . Servicemen on R&R created the tourist infrastructure – the bars, nightclubs and massage parlors – that continue to service the tourist industry." Filipina activist Mary Perpinan describes the role of US military bases in generating the sex industry in Southeast Asia in the late 1960s. In Thailand, "[e]ntertainment centres were established around [US] air bases" and Thai women learned "the art of servicing the foreigner with 'exotic pleasures'" – leading to the establishment of Bangkok as the "sex capital of Asia" within a decade. By the end of the 1970s, as militarized prostitution led to sex tourism, "an estimated 100,000 women in Bangkok were working as prostitutes; 70 percent of them suffered from venereal disease."[39]

In the Philippines, as many as 100,000 women and girls worked in the sex/entertainment industry serving US bases at Subic Bay and Clark, in the Olongapo and Angeles districts. In the 1960s, local businessmen convinced "wary town officials" in Olongapo that "instead of endangering our decent and respectable women to the possibility of rape and other forms of sexual abuse, better provide an outlet for the soldiers' sexual urge and at the same time make money out of it." When US soldiers were based in the Philippines, US commanders supported compulsory medical examinations of local prostitutes and received reports from local authorities with the names of sex workers who had contracted sexually transmitted diseases. Base commanders then ordered pictures of these women "pinned upside down on the public notice board as a warning to the American men." US authorities refused, however, to help pay for treatment of these women. Overall, "the girls [we]re recruited from depressed provinces and given false promises of high pay." They lost their freedom, were mistreated by the men they worked for, and, in the late 1980s, began dying from AIDS. The bases closed in 1992 but the effects linger.[40]

The largest US military presence in Asia is now in Japan and South Korea. The South Korean government worked hard to control and "clean up" (i.e., improve) prostitution around US military bases, in order to help

---

[38] Goldman and Fuller 1983, liberty 141–42; Holmes 1985, contacts 93–94; Enloe 1983, precise 33.

[39] Gerster 1995, first 228; Yayori 1997, 148–52; Chizuko 1997, 294; Perpinan 1994, 149–50; Enloe 1983, estimated 43.

[40] Enloe 1993, industry 149, warning 149–51, linger 149–51; Enloe 1983, money 39–42; Perpinan 1994, pay 149–53.

keep the bases open despite US force reductions in Asia in the 1970s. Despite their strategic value both in "supplying" US bases and acting as "unofficial ambassadors" to the United States, these prostitutes are marginalized in Korean society.[41]

Currently, prostitution in Asia is highly internationalized, but the military plays a less and less central role in it. A thorough recent study sponsored by the International Labor Organization (ILO) concludes that although US military personnel on leave during the Vietnam War era played a role in catalyzing the growth of a foreign-oriented sector of the Thai sex industry, this sector has since been sustained by tourists (especially from Japan and Germany) – notwithstanding periodic visits of US Navy ships. (US Navy ships returning from the Gulf War in 1991 made a sex stop in Thailand.) The transformation of Thailand's economy from agriculture to export-oriented industry (sharpening urban–rural disparities, and providing men more opportunities and women fewer ones) was a "more important influence" in the development of the Thai sex sector than was the foreign military and tourist presence. Although the investment brought in by foreign men helped stimulate the industry, the increasing disposable income of Thai men was more important. "Numerically . . . foreigners are probably only a small proportion of the customers of the commercial sex market . . . Most clients of prostitutes in Thailand are Thai men."[42]

The report estimates that 27,000 prostitutes operate around military bases in South Korea – an impressive presence – but these numbers are dwarfed by nonmilitary prostitution in other countries: several hundred thousand each in Thailand, Indonesia, and the Philippines, and over 2 million in India. Prostitution in Thailand and Japan combined generates annual economic turnover of $50 billion (making up about 5 percent of GDP in Thailand). Many women have been trafficked across international borders in recent years – about 25,000 Burmese women in Thailand, 100,000 Nepalese in India, and 200,000 Bangladeshi women in Pakistan according to ILO estimates. Thus, although military prostitution played a role in the upswing of prostitution in Asia, that role has become peripheral. Globally, war and the military do not appear to shape patterns of prostitution. A new edited volume on global sex workers contains no index entries for war or military aspects. The emphasis is on endogenous structural economic and cultural factors.[43]

---

[41] Moon 1997.
[42] Study: Boonchalaksi and Guest 1998, 133–36, men 137; Lim ed. 1998; Navy: Enloe 1993, 183.
[43] Boonchalaksi and Guest 1998; volume: Kempadoo and Doezema eds. 1998.

Does sex affect aggression?

Thus far, the association of sex with war could plausibly result from war's disruption of social norms. What about the other direction of causality, with sexuality as cause and war as effect? The "conflation of sexuality and violence" is a strong element in popular notions of masculinity. In many animals, "[s]ome of the brain's neural circuitry for aggression seems dangerously cheek by jowl with the neural circuitry for sex." If male sexuality made soldiers aggressive, that could help explain the absence of women in the ranks.[44]

Some soldiers, but apparently a minority, have described combat as sexually gratifying. For them, "the procreative act and the destructive act are inextricably interlinked." One US soldier in Vietnam said, "I was literally turned on when I saw a gook shot." Another said that in combat, like in sex, "the space ... between subject and object ... banged shut in a fast wash of adrenalin." The feeling of a firefight, difficult to recall afterwards, "was the feeling you'd had when you were much, much younger and undressing a girl for the first time." One US Marine captain confessed to disappointment that Iraqi forces in the Gulf War "surrendered too fast to kill a lot of them ... If you've ever got close to a girl hoping to get it and you didn't, it was about the same." (Bourke argues that killing can be "profoundly sexual and an exhilarating experience" for women as well as men.)[45]

Phallic symbolism of weapons   According to some writers, "squeezing the trigger – releasing a hail of bullets – gives enormous pleasure and satisfaction. These are the pleasures of combat ... the primal aggression, the release, and the orgasmic discharge." One US Vietnam veteran said that "[t]o some people carrying a gun was like having a permanent hard-on. It was a pure sexual trip every time you got to pull the trigger." "Many men who have carried and fired a gun – especially a full automatic weapon – must confess in their hearts that the power and pleasure of explosively spewing a stream of bullets is akin to the emotions felt when explosively spewing a stream of semen."[46]

However, phallic imagery hardly requires automatic weapons. Colonel Dave Grossman suggests that "[t]hrusting the sexual appendage (the penis) deep into the body of the victim can be perversely linked to thrusting the killing appendage (a bayonet or knife) deep into the body of the

---

[44] Brittan 1989, conflation 11; Sagan and Druyan 1992, jowl 191; Harris 1974, 106.

[45] Grossman 1995, procreative 134; Keegan and Holmes 1985, shot 267; Michael Herr, in Kinney 1991, wash–undressing 39; McBride 1995, same 58; Costello 1985, 80, 94; Bourke 1999, 302.

[46] Grossman 1995, semen 136.

victim." The phallic character of weapons has seemingly persisted even as technology has evolved – from spears to guns to missiles. The latest nuclear weapon drills deep into the earth before exploding. Each weapon makes sense tactically and aerodynamically, yet the phallic theme still seems surprisingly pervasive.[47]

In US basic training, men chant: "This is my rifle [holding up rifle], this is my gun [pointing to penis]; one's for killing, the other's for fun." In World War II, and the Gulf War, the US military ordered large numbers of condoms to place over gun barrels to keep dirt and sand out (and also as an excuse to distribute them to the men for other uses). A sensible solution to a real problem, this practice nonetheless underscores the gun's phallic nature. Robin Morgan argues that men receive "an orgasmic thrill in violent domination" and that "maleness itself becomes the weapon of destruction." It has been argued that a "man is only a man in so far as he is capable of using his penis as an instrument of power."[48]

Carol Cohn analyzes the gender-laden vocabulary of American "defense intellectuals," whom she worked with and observed for a year. Concepts and terminology employed by those who design and implement weapons policies contained a blatant "sexual subtext." "[L]ectures were filled with discussions of vertical erector launchers, thrust-to-weight ratios, soft lay-downs, deep penetration, and the comparative advantages of protracted versus spasm attacks – . . . 'releasing . . . our megatonnage in one orgasmic whump.' " On a submarine tour, official visitors were given a chance to reach through a hole to "pat the missile" (a nuclear ballistic missile). A lecture mentioned that new nuclear missiles were deployed in Europe "so that our allies can pat them." "What are men doing when they 'pat' these high-tech phalluses? Patting is an assertion of intimacy, sexual possession . . . the proximity of all that phallic power, the possibility of vicariously appropriating it as one's own."[49]

Helen Caldicott reports in *Missile Envy* that Pentagon officials got Congress to approve bigger military budgets during the Cold War by bringing scale models of missiles – red for the Soviets and blue for the Americans – to Congressional hearings. The smaller and more accurate US missiles were superior (US bombs were smaller, relative to explosive power). But the painted scale models carried a subtext: their "great big red missiles" threaten our "small blue missiles." Caldicott notes that the Pentagon always got its money.[50]

---

[47] Grossman 1995, 137; Mosse 1990, 166.
[48] McBride 1995, condoms 56; Morgan 1988, thrill 70, maleness 69; Brittan 1989, instrument 47, 46.
[49] Cohn 1987, 692–93, 695.
[50] Caldicott 1986, 297.

Nuclear weapons carry masculine gender. The bombs dropped on Japan in 1945 were named "little boy" and "fat man." Nuclear weapons scientists referred to bombs as "babies" being born, and expressed hope that their bomb would not be born a girl, i.e., a dud. Edward Teller's coded telegram informing Washington, DC that a test hydrogen bomb had worked said simply, "It's a boy." "The nuclear scientists gave birth to male progeny with the ultimate power of violent domination over female Nature."[51]

Since bombs are male, their containers, vehicles, and targets are female. For example, the plane that dropped the atomic bomb on Hiroshima (the "Enola Gay") was named after the pilot's mother. Ships are always "she," and the first practical British tank built in World War I was named "Mother." The US Army poster from World War II shown in Figure 6.3 tells male soldiers that their military equipment is like a pin-up girl that "won't let you down." During World War II, US soldiers pasted or painted "pin-ups" onto tanks and planes throughout the US military forces, as in naked Jane on D-Day (see p. 334). Commanders also used pin-ups to teach recruits to read grids on maps (Figure 6.4). The "target" was thus explicitly feminized and objectified.[52]

Pilots and ground crews have also often pasted "pin-up" photos of women onto conventional bombs before dropping them. That way the male bomb has a symbolic female target (for orgasmic destruction) when it gets there. The famous pin-up photo of Rita Hayworth was pasted to the first US nuclear weapon exploded over Bikini atoll in 1946, presumably to enhance its potency. Bombing an actual target feminizes it as well. Thus a World War II era *Life* magazine article calls the bombing of German sites "emasculation." The French atom bomb test sites in the South Pacific were all given women's names.[53]

Pornography   Occasional reports suggest that commanders rile up their troops before battle by showing them pornography or lewd entertainment. This would support the idea that male sexuality increases aggressiveness. However, the empirical evidence is scant.

According to one report, pilots on a US aircraft carrier during the Gulf War told a reporter they "had been watching pornographic movies before flying bombing missions." Although this report was picked up by Reuters news wire and then by several newspapers internationally, I cannot verify it. The pilots supposedly made the statement to a reporter from Associated Press, who told a reporter for the *Philadelphia*

---

[51] Easlea 1983, 3; Cohn 1987, progeny 701.
[52] Keegan and Holmes 1985, tank 121.
[53] Griffin 1992, pin-up 76, emasculation 13; Cohn 1987, names 701.

Figure 6.3 "One Pin-Up That Won't Let You Down," US Army poster, World War II. [US National Archives, NWDNS-44-PA-1461.]

Figure 6.4 Poster used for training pilots to read map grids, United States, World War II. [From Gubar 1987, 237. USAAFTC.]

Inquirer about them. She in turn said that military censors deleted the tidbit from her story, and this deletion appeared in a *Washington Post* story about military censorship. Similarly, in 1982 a British women's newspaper reported that British troops on ships bound for the Falklands War were shown pornographic films ranging from "the officially sanctioned soft-porn *Emmanuelle* to the unofficially condoned hard-core pornographic video tapes. Male correspondents aboard the task force ships described some . . . as 'hair-raising.' "[54]

In Serbia, the outbreak of war coincided with the Government's 1991 decision to permit public stations to broadcast hard-core sex films, and was followed by years of rampant gangsterism, hedonism, and pornography in Belgrade, accompanying graphic war pictures of death and mutilation. A local reporter infers that "[t]he war was about the lifting of taboos . . . War and sex became the stimulants" to keep the population from challenging a corrupt and repressive government. Catherine MacKinnon argues that pornography played an important role in the frenzy of Serbian ultranationalism that produced atrocities in Bosnia. Abundant pornography in Serbia primed soldiers for rapes of non-Serbian women, which in turn produced more pornography as films of the actual rapes were sold on Serbian and foreign markets. Completing the cycle, these rape films were aired on Bosnian-Serb TV news with a dubbed sound track to make it appear that the victims were Serbian women being raped by Croatian or Bosniak men – priming the xenophobia that served as the regime's bedrock of power. Thus, "genocide . . . [became] explicitly sexually obsessed."[55]

Psychology experiments in the United States have analyzed the effects of sexual stimulation – exposure to pornographic or "erotic" images – on men's subsequent aggression, defined as retaliation against a male who provoked them. (Again, I consider retaliation a poor measure of aggression; see p. 152). Male subjects were exposed to various stimuli (or none), and then provoked. The *content* of sexual materials determined their effect on men's rate of retaliation. Stimuli perceived as "pleasant but rather nonarousing" reduced the subject's subsequent retaliation, whether the materials were sexual or not (nude female, or adventure film). More explicit sexual materials increased the provoked subjects' retaliatory aggression – more so after arousing than nonarousing materials and more after unpleasant scenes than pleasant ones. However, the same effects resulted from matched stimuli that were not sexual in nature – for example, exciting rock-concert scenes instead of explicit coital scenes, or film of an eye operation instead of scenes of bestiality. The key is whether stimuli are pleasant or disturbing. "The specific sexual theme thus was of little moment other than in producing pronounced excitatory reactions of positive or negative valence . . . Sexual stimulation does not generally facilitate aggressiveness."[56]

[54] Kurtz 1991; Enloe 1983, Falklands 18.
[55] Belgrade: Hedges 1998; MacKinnon 1994a, obsessed 77.
[56] Zillmann 1984, experiments 130–33; Eibl-Eibesfeldt 1979, 92–93.

Misogyny rather than sexual arousal seems to be the key variable in sexual aggression. In psychological experiments, the "relationship between sexual arousal and sexual aggression is... neither simple nor direct." Studies found that men with a high propensity to rape were more aggressive towards women, but not towards men, in laboratory experiments. Male subjects in another experiment reported more likelihood to use sexual coercion after watching a sexually explicit videotape with violence or degradation of women, than an explicit videotape without violence. Another study found a correlation of self-reported sexual aggression with hostility towards women (including wanting to dominate them).[57]

Outside psychology laboratories, too, "very little evidence supports a connection between violence and exposure to sexually explicit material." Sex crimes and violence against women do not show higher rates of incidence where sexually explicit materials are more available, nor do sex offenders use sexually explicit materials more than other offenders. These conclusions are controversial, however.[58]

War and voyeurism   The home consumption of distant bombing in recent wars can be seen as a form of violent and voyeuristic pornography. Judith Butler argues that the Gulf War bombing – consumed euphorically on American TV sets – served to "champion a masculinized Western subject... who determines its world unilaterally." The war conflated "the television screen and the lens of the bomber pilot" through rebroadcasting of images recorded by "smart bombs" as they approached their targets ("a kind of optical phallus"). The viewer is thus constituted as part of the bomber and bomb, identified with the distant action "yet securely wedged in the couch in one's own living room." The kill itself produces no blood since the optical link destroys itself in the process of destroying the target. The viewer thus gains a "radical impermeability," both proximate and distant from the enactment of violence, an embodiment of imperial power. The viewer becomes, like a sniper, "the disembodied killer who can never be killed... securing a fantasy of transcendence... infinitely protected from a reverse-strike through the guarantee of electronic distance." McBride similarly argues that the televised Gulf War "was deeply satisfying to most viewers."[59]

McBride connects war with both battering and male sports (football) in contemporary Western society, arguing that "misogynist violence – either

[57] Geen 1998, direct 342.
[58] Ellsworth and Mauro 1998, very 688.
[59] Butler 1992, 10–12; McBride 1995, 107–9, 112, deeply 60.

figuratively or literally expressed – . . . embod[ies] a culturally constructed psychological need to abuse women for the sake of a male identity . . . Castration anxiety and the imagery of phallic penetration seem to play obsessive compulsive roles in male activities like war and competitive sports." The incidence of woman-battering reportedly increased during both the Gulf War and the Super Bowl. Football, like war, allows males to enter an "adversarial mentality that seeks to dominate, humiliate, and vanquish the foe and restore wholeness." War is exciting to participants and observers alike because it "marks the eruption of ecstatic time into everyday life," a kind of "holy madness" in which desires are "consummated in an ecstatic expulsion of bodily fluids, for example, vomit, urine, semen, blood, and excrement." As for male sexuality itself, however, overall, little evidence suggests that it is a key component of male soldiers' aggressiveness, notwithstanding the temporary dislocation of sexual norms during wartime.[60]

B. FEMINIZATION OF ENEMIES AS SYMBOLIC DOMINATION

A second variant, Hypothesis 6B, proposes that men's participation in combat depends on feminizing the enemy and enacting rape symbolically (and sometimes literally), thereby using gender to symbolize domination. "In war's coding, the inferior and hated enemy is feminine." For example, a US pilot, after shooting down a male Iraqi pilot, reportedly said he "cold smoked the bitch" (not the "bastard"). Men who feminize enemies in this way might be confused by having women warriors in their own ranks.[61]

Male soldiers use gender to represent domination. Psychologically, they assume a masculine and dominant position relative to a feminine and subordinate enemy. Within armies, by the same principle, subordinates are coded as feminine. One US soldier in Vietnam said of his officers that "[w]e are their women." Thus, the feminization not only of enemy troops and civilians, but of subordinates and nonsoldiers, plays into soldiers' militarized masculinity. In war films, the feminine is a "purely symbolic presence" for boys. In an all-male environment, the subordinate males take on feminine gender (as "girls," "pussies," etc.). The absence of actual females frees up the gender category to encode domination. In war films, "the feminine . . . is something to be conquered."[62]

[60] McBride 1995, xvi, xvii, 3, 77–106, eruption 147, 149; Ehrenreich 1997a.
[61] Gray 1997, coding 43, bitch 43.
[62] Gray 1997, women 175; Simpson 1994, presence 217, conquered 234; Trexler 1995, 2, 174; Krauss and Chiu 1998, 70; Jeffords 1989, xi.

Means of feminization

Historian Richard Trexler documents the "inveterate male habit of gendering enemies female or effeminate" throughout the ancient world. Several methods accomplish this regendering of male enemies in ancient and modern cultures.[63]

Gendered massacre The most common pattern in warfare in the ancient Middle East and Greece was to literally feminize a conquered population by executing male captives, raping the women, then taking women and children as slaves. This was the fate of the Melians as told by Thucydides, for example (see p. 55). Kidnapped females have been called the first form of private property. The pattern of gendered massacre recurs even today. In 1995, after conquering the town of Srebrenica in Bosnia (a UN-designated safe haven), Serb forces sorted out the 7,000 men and adolescent boys, executed them all, and buried them in mass graves. The women and younger children they put on busses and deported from Serb-controlled territory, except some young women pulled out, evidently, to be raped. In the Kosovo war, "young men were . . . by far the most targeted" group, and "[m]any were executed on the spot."[64]

Castration Another way to feminize conquered enemies is to castrate prisoners – or to castrate men before or after killing them. The castration of both male prisoners and dead enemies was widespread in the ancient world, practiced by Chinese, Persian, Amalekite, Egyptian, and Norse armies. The type of castration varied by culture, from mere circumcision (symbolic castration, rendering men as boys) to cutting off testicles, to cutting off both testicles and penises.[65]

For enemies killed in battle or executed afterwards, in the ancient world, the method of execution of men, and/or the mutilation of their corpses afterwards, often left no doubt that the ultimate symbolic meaning of the act was to take away their manhood and thus their power. Castration was the most widely practiced of the various means of butchering corpses. "Ancient Egyptian drawings . . . depict mounds of severed genitalia gathered from enemies destroyed in battle . . . [I]n probably every part of the world, such mutilation has been considered the supreme subjugation which the conqueror could bestow on the conquered." Dahomey's

---

[63] Trexler 1995, 1, 12–37.

[64] Ancient: Trexler 1995; Property: Mies 1986, 62; Bosnia: Sudetic 1998; Holbrooke 1998, 70; A. Jones 1994; Kosovo: OSCE 1999, chapter 15; A. Jones 2000.

[65] Trexler 1995, 16–19, 66.

women soldiers brought back male genitalia to the king as war trophies. Two chiefdoms in the Inca empire "cut off an enemy's penis and exhibited it on the road in order to shame the foe." In some cultures, corpses (or soon-to-be-corpses) were mutilated with spears in ways that made the man symbolically a passive-receptive rape victim. The Tumucua warriors reportedly took no male prisoners, but finished off each mutilated corpse of an enemy with an arrow through the anus.[66]

Defeated enemies can be symbolically emasculated *en masse*. The Delaware, after losing to the Iroquois in the eighteenth century, lived within the lands of the Mohawks and under Mohawk protection. They were not allowed to sell land or make war, and had to wear women's clothing and accessories at certain diplomatic events. As the Delaware men reclaimed their manhood a decade later, however, they told the Iroquois to beware "lest we cut off your private parts and make women of you as you have done to us." Meanwhile the Catawba, who had not been defeated by the Iroquois, refused to make peace, declaring that the Iroquois were only women while the Catawba themselves had two penises. The Catawba thus portrayed their enemy as symbolically castrated: "the loser would look like a woman while the winner would sport a double penis."[67]

Such attitudes continue in modern times. President Lyndon Johnson said of the damage inflicted on Vietnamese communists during the 1968 Tet offensive: "I didn't just screw Ho Chi Minh. I cut his pecker off!" McBride sees an "underlying discourse of castration" in the 1991 Gulf War. US General Colin Powell's famous strategy towards the Iraqi Army was to first "cut it off" and then "kill it." Richard Nixon called Saddam Hussein "militarily castrated" by the war, and reporter Sam Donaldson said that Saddam "folded like a banana" under the attack.[68]

In the hyper-masculinized context of war, with manhood on the line, soldiers show widespread castration fear. After World War I, sexual wounds became a common theme of postwar literature, reflecting "symbolic disorders of powerlessness." US pilots in World War II, "[l]ike all men at war . . . feared above all getting hit in the testicles." Ambrose refers obliquely to "the wound that above all others terrified the soldiers" – apparently so scary it should not be named. The theme resurfaced for US soldiers in Vietnam, notably in the best-selling country-western song, *Ruby, Don't Take Your Love to Town*, about a paraplegic veteran who's "not the man I used to be" but still needs his wife's love. Australian

---

[66] Kinsey *et al.* 1953, mounds 739; Alpern 1998, trophies 67; Steward and Faron 1959, foe 209; Trexler 1995, spears 19, arrow 68; cf. Vietnam: Turner 1996, 77–78.

[67] Trexler 1995, 76–78, 72–73.

[68] Kimmel and Messner eds. 1995, pecker xiii; Gulf: McBride 1995, 43–44.

soldiers in Vietnam expressed castration fear more often than warranted by the real dangers of land mines, reflecting a "maimed self-image" among the veterans. (The Vietnam War, for some analysts, represented the failure of a Western "Orientalist fantasy" of sexual conquest in Asia.) During the Cold War, the superpower missile race led some observers to conclude that men in power feared losing phallic weapons. "If disarmament is emasculation, how could any real man even consider it?"[69]

Homosexual rape A third method of feminizing enemy soldiers in the ancient world was anal rape, with the victor in the dominant/active position and the vanquished in the subordinate/passive one. These positions are used symbolically in various animal species to code dominance, as in the hold-bottom ritual of dominance–submission among male stump-tailed macaques (Figure 6.5). Homosexual rape was used in various ancient Middle Eastern and Greek societies to assert dominance relationships (as it is used today in, e.g., US prisons), and this practice was more common in war than in domestic society, although found both places. "[T]he anal rape of male captives . . . [was] notoriously rife in the ancient world." A Greek vase from the fifth century BC (see Figure 6.6) illustrates a fleeing bent-over Persian man pursued by a victorious Greek with erect penis in hand. Warriors of this period "kidnapped boys as well as women." Even in Egypt and other ancient cultures where anal rape was apparently rare in practice, it still played a role in legend and symbol.[70]

The Aztec word for a powerful warrior translates as "I make someone into a passive." Male war prisoners were apparently raped in a variety of Amerindian societies, ranging from the Caribbean and Florida to North America, before the Spanish conquest. In the Old World too, "homosexual rape was used as a military insult." Among the messages inscribed on US bombs in the Gulf War was the theme, "Bend Over, Saddam." Saddam's promised "mother of all battles" would be engaged by American "motherfuckers," and one US Congressman invoked the phrase, "slam, bam, thank you ma'am," substituting Saddam for ma'am. These constructions "were frequently complemented by allusions to both oral and anal violation." The Bosnia and Kosovo wars also saw sexual abuse

---

[69] Showalter 1987, symbolic 62; Ambrose 1997, testicles 47, terrified 143; Ulman and Brothers 1988, 182; Goldman and Fuller 1983, song 10, 78; Gerster 1995, maimed–fantasy 225–28; Cohn 1990, disarmament 35; Ashworth and Swatuk 1998; de Waal 1989, 73–75.

[70] De Waal 1989, ritual 163–65; Sagan and Druyan 1992, 203; Segal 1990, 151; Trexler 1995, 21–29, rife 20, vase 14–15, boys 29, symbol 26–27.

Figure 6.5 Stump-tailed macaques in hold-bottom position of dominance and submission. [Photo courtesy of Frans de Waal (From de
Waal 1989, 164).]

of men (perhaps intensified because Muslim but not Christian men there
were circumcised).[71]

Insults and intimations   Pre-conquest American cultures
used gendered insults between males of opposing armies, accusing each
other of effeminacy. The Aztecs "heaped intimations of homosexual softness" on losers of battle (their own disgraced soldiers or fleeing Spanish
soldiers), and rallied troops by calling them effeminates. In the Inca empire, similarly, a ruler sent women's clothing to his chiefs who had just
lost a crucial battle, and ordered them to wear it when entering the home
city.[72]

Amerindian cultures had a ready category for men who become
women (and thus inferior), which was easily adaptable to humiliating
enemies. The berdache was "a biological male who dressed, gestured,

[71] Trexler 1995, passive 71, prisoners 71, insult 65; Parker *et al.* 1992, bend 6; McBride
1995, mother–violation 56–57; Bosnia: Rieff 1995, 107; Kosovo: A. Jones 2000.
[72] Trexler 1995, 71–72.

Figure 6.6 Greek vase, with erect victorious Greek pursuing bent-over Persian, after 460 BC. [Museum für Kunst und Gewerbe Hamburg.]

and spoke . . . as individual cultures said women did" over the long term. "[T]he berdache served macho males by assuming the female division of labor, often including the sexual servicing of males." Berdaches were tolerated to varying degrees but often treated as inferior or even "odious." According to Zuni myth, the original cross-dressing was forced on the victim of war by their victorious god. In Europe, men might practice homosexuality without transvestitism, or might cross-dress only temporarily, but in the Americas, men who took women's clothes and roles did so for life. The berdache was convenient for Spanish conquerors: because natives practiced the sin of sodomy (unspeakable despite its common presence in the Old World), they could be slaughtered and subjugated with a clear conscience.[73]

Similarly, the 1991 Gulf War was subtly legitimized by the deliberate and repeated mispronunciation of Saddam's name as "sodom," giving him an "onus of illicit sexuality." This feminization, along with the castration imagery described above (pp. 357–59), "effectively transforms the figure of the enemy into a woman" and thus lays the groundwork for rape imagery to intensify the drive towards war. Milder forms of gender insult also exist. For example, one group of US soldiers routinely cut the

[73] Trexler 1995, 64–65, odious 67, 118–40, myth 80, Europe 8, 142, 172, 2; Lorber 1994, 90–93.

belts and buttons off the pants of German POWs to force them to hold up their pants, as a form of humiliation.[74]

Rape in war

As for the rape of women, it is "a 'normal' accompaniment to war." In contexts where war atrocities occur, rape usually is among them. In seventeenth-century Europe, Spanish troops in the Netherlands committed "countless cases of rape, murder, robbery and arson." During the US Civil War, members of the California Volunteers (militia) in Utah perpetrated the Bear River Massacre against Shoshone Indians, and raped surviving women. Massive atrocities including rapes followed the partition of India and Pakistan in 1948. In Central America in the 1980s, brutal guerrilla and counterinsurgency warfare was accompanied by widespread sexual assault.[75]

The association of rape with other atrocities is not universal, however. Wartime rape can occur without other atrocities. For example, in the Kapauku culture, where even accidental injury to women during battle is shameful, unmarried girls near the battlefield are considered "fair game" for rape by warriors. Men claim that the girls "like it anyway." Atrocities can also occur without rape. Recall, for example, that women sometimes help torture male prisoners (see pp. 113–15).[76]

Rape arises from different specific motivations in various wars – revenge for Russian soldiers in Berlin in 1945, frustration for US soldiers in Vietnam, ethnic cleansing in Bosnia. Historically, the main point of rape in war seems to be to humiliate enemy males by despoiling their valued property – "the ultimate humiliation ... the stamp of total conquest." A raped woman "is devalued property, and she signals defeat for the man who fails in his role as protector." Rape is thus "a means of establishing jurisdiction and conquest." "Rape at once pollutes and occupies the territory of the nation, transgresses its boundaries, defeats its protectors." For its victims, rape as a "violent invasion into the interior of one's body represents the most severe attack imaginable upon the intimate self and the dignity of a human being," constituting "severe torture."[77]

---

[74] McBride 1995, onus 57; Ambrose 1997, buttons 352.

[75] Stiglmayer 1994b, normal 84; Keegan and Holmes 1985, 267, arson 280; Shoshone: Madsen 1985, 180–200, 231–38, 233; brutal: Enloe 1993, 121–22.

[76] Kapauku: Pospisil 1963, 59.

[77] Wilden 1987, stamp 179; Mostov 1995, devalued–boundaries 524, 526; Seifert 1994, 55–66, torture 55; Seifert 1996 ; MacKinnon 1994a; Rejali 1996; Copelon 1994, 206–8; Pettman 1996a, 100–4; Reardon 1985, 38–40; Rorty 1993, 112; Warren and Cady 1996, 6–7; Nikolić-Ristanović 1996, 361.

Rape is a crime of domination, and war has everything to do with domination. "[T]he rapist's sexuality is not at the center of his act; it is placed instrumentally at the service of the violent act." Rapes in wartime apparently bear no relationship to the presence of prostitutes or other available women – showing that rape is not driven by sexual desire.[78]

Atrocities in World War I often included rape – "numerous" cases were perpetrated by all the armies. A World War I French poem boldly states, "Germans, we shall possess your daughters." A German soldier describes how Turkish soldiers traveling with the Germans abducted 200 Armenian women and girls, raped them all night, then cut their throats. Hirschfeld credits the military brothel system (see pp. 343–44), "no matter how disgusting," with reducing the incidence of rape in World War I.[79]

In Bosnia, rape was an instrument of ethnic cleansing – used to humiliate and terrorize a population from one ethnic group in order to induce it to abandon desirable territory. The number of women raped (mostly Muslims raped by Serbian forces) has been estimated at 20,000 (by a European Union commission) to 50,000 (by the Bosnian government). "Rape occurs in nearly every war, but in this one . . . degradation and molestation of women was central to the conquest." Some rapes were peculiarly oriented towards forced impregnation as a part of ethnic cleansing. The Bosnia war resulted in the inclusion of rape for the first time in an international tribunal's indictments for war crimes.[80]

The Bosnia case "is not an exceptional case" in magnitude. Systematic mass rape during conquest occurred in the Pakistani war against Bangladesh's independence in 1971 (200,000 women), the Berlin area after World War II (over 100,000), the Japanese "rape of Nanking" [Nanjing] in 1937–38 (over 20,000), and Japan's "comfort women" system (see pp. 345–46). The international women's movement from the late nineteenth century through World War II took steps to organize against rape in wartime. At the 1915 Hague Congress, Jane Addams said: "Worse than death . . . is the defenselessness of women in warfare and their violation by the invading soldier."[81]

Rape as an instrument of territorial control and domination seems to have spread in the 1990s. A "new style of warfare is often aimed specifically at women," using "organized sexual assault as a tactic in terrorizing and humiliating a civilian population." Simultaneously with Bosnia, rape

[78] Seifert 1994, act 56, presence 58; Lorber 1994, 76–78; Wilden 1987, 163–88.
[79] Hirschfeld 1934, 302–5, 314–25, numerous 321, disgusting 319.
[80] Brownmiller 1994; Stiglmayer ed. 1994; Bowery Productions 1996; Enloe 1994; Stiglmayer 1994b, number 85; Gutman 1993, central ix–x; Copelon 1994, 207; Nikolić-Ristanović 1996, 361; Drakulić 1994; tribunal: Socolovsky 2000.
[81] Stiglmayer 1994b, case 85; Bangladesh: Brownmiller 1975, 78–86; Berlin: Seifert 1994, 54; Nanking: Copelon 1994, 197, 205; Addams: Rupp 1996, 345.

played a role in the genocide in Rwanda and in the Haitian military's suppression of resistance. In one town in Mozambique in 1991 (during a little-noticed war that took a million lives), "every woman and girl in the town had been sexually assaulted" while the town was occupied by right-wing guerrillas. In the "ethnic cleansing" of Kosovo by Serb forces in 1999, rapes were again common, though apparently less systematic than in Bosnia. Other recent reports come from Liberia, Sierra Leone, Burundi, Uganda, Algeria, Indonesia, Kashmir, and Burma. At UN refugee camps, workers now regularly provide "morning-after" contraceptive pills to women raped in, or just before arriving at, the camps.[82]

Latin American military governments in the 1980s "developed patterns of punishment specifically designed for women" who opposed the regime. In Central America, governments meted out sexual torture as part of a generalized, day-to-day pattern of violence against villages thought to sympathize with rebels. In Chile, Argentina, and Uruguay, by contrast, individual women were identified by the government as enemies, then jailed and sexually tortured. Gang rape was "the standard torture mechanism." The military sought to break the spirit of these women by arresting them in front of their families and then destroying their sense of self, which was rooted in their identities as mothers, i.e., "morally superior and spiritually stronger than men." Thus, misogynist military states have used female sexual slavery and torture to control women.[83]

Similarly, "women have become central targets" in the Mexican government's counterinsurgency warfare against Zapatista guerrillas. "Rape has become a central tactic" to intimidate women and dominate communities. Furthermore, women are "doubly affected as they often become targets of the frustrations of their husbands and fathers" under the stress of wartime.[84]

Motives and opportunities   Rape in wartime may arise from different motivations than in peacetime. Among other reasons, a male soldier rapes because "war . . . has awakened his aggressiveness, and he directs it at those who play a subordinate role in the world of war." Wartime also offers different opportunities. One US soldier in Vietnam said: "They are in an all-male environment. . . . There are women available. Those

[82] Style: Crossette 1998; Human Rights Watch 1995; Haiti: Human Rights Watch 1994; Mozambique: Nordstrom 1998, 82; Kosovo: Human Rights Watch 2000; Smith 1999; Rohde 1999; Liberia: Human Rights Watch 1997; Sierra Leone: Human Rights Watch 1998b; Farah 2000; Burundi: Human Rights Watch 1998a; Kashmir: Human Rights Watch 1993.

[83] Bunster-Burotto 1994, patterns 156, standard 166, morally 163–64; Davies ed. 1994; Enloe 1993, 60–61.

[84] Mora 1998, 172–73.

women are of another culture, another colour, another society... You've got an M-16. What do you need to pay a lady for? You go down to the village and you take what you want." Some said that having sex and then killing the woman made the soldier a "double veteran."[85]

In one view, raping by soldiers in wartime results from the weakening of social norms – parallel with increased sex, swearing, looting, cruelty, and other such behaviors. Some see a "return to nature" in war. The *US Infantry Journal* in 1943 referred to soldiers as "a society of men, frequently unwashed, who have been dedicated to the rugged task of killing other men, and whose training has emphasized that a certain reversion to the primitive is not undesirable." Romantic or forced sexual conquests reflect "the rapist in every man." "Copulation under such circumstances is an act of aggression; the girl is the victim and her conquest the victor's triumph. Preliminary resistance on her part always increases his satisfaction."[86]

One function of gang rape is to promote cohesion within groups of men soldiers. Men who would not rape individually do so as part of a display within the male group, to avoid becoming an outcast. "There is male bonding in the violence of massive criminal rape – performed in succession, by 3 to 27 men in some cases – against women political prisoners" under Latin American military regimes. Gang rapes may serve to relieve individual men of responsibility, just as groups absolve soldiers in killing (see p. 197). "Rape is obviously not an exclusive preserve of military men. But... aspects of the military institution and ideology" may increase pressure on men to participate in gang rape – to control a chaotic and fearsome external world while proving manhood and toughness to one's buddies within the military "family."[87]

War rapes frequently go unreported, because of backlash against rape victims in traditional societies. The problems of shame associated with being the victim of rape (e.g., in Kosovo) are connected with certain cultural traditions in which family honor is stained by *any* violation of sexual property norms. In Egypt until very recently, a rapist could receive a pardon by agreeing to marry his victim. In some places, adultery or premarital sex are considered the woman's fault by definition, and her male relatives receive taunts impugning their manhood until they kill her to restore family honor (and serve as an example to other women who might

---

[85] Stiglmayer 1994b, awakened 84; Enloe 1983, 32–36, want 321, double 208–9; cf. Turner 1996, 30.

[86] Keegan and Holmes 1985, looting 53; Gray 1959, 63–70, nature 63, rapist 66, triumph 67; Costello 1985, primitive 73.

[87] Jeffords 1989, gang 69–71; Lomnitz 1986, 19; May and Strikwerda 1996; Bunster-Burotto 1994, bonding 168; Enloe 1983, preserve 35.

stray sexually). These "honor killings" apparently accounted for around one-quarter of homicides in Egypt and Jordan in recent years. Killers typically receive light sentences. A Jordanian chief judge explained: "Nobody can really want to kill his wife or daughter or sister. But sometimes circumstances force him to do this." (The United States ruled in 1999 that women who face threats of this nature are not eligible for refugee status.)[88]

Thus, rape in wartime is both a violation of men's cherished property rights, and an extension of everyday misogyny by other means. Susan Brownmiller writes: "Sexual trespass on the enemy's women is one of the satisfactions of conquest... [reflecting] submerged rage against all women who belong to other men."[89]

The rape of Nanking   One horrific case of wartime atrocities accompanied by widespread rape was the so-called "rape of Nanking" (Nanjing), the Chinese nationalist capital, by Japanese forces in 1937–38. Iris Chang provides a detailed account of an array of atrocities, ranging from simple mass executions to torture, mutilation, and rape. The Japanese force of 50,000 soldiers, upon capturing the city which held 90,000 Chinese troops and about 500,000 civilians, proceeded to execute all the Chinese troops and perhaps one-third of the civilians – through systematic mass murders and, over a six-week period, various other means. Chinese men, women, and children were killed for various reasons including bayonet practice, arbitrary summary execution of anyone inconvenient or disliked, murder-for-fun, and murder as the final act of rape. The total number of people killed, by mass execution and by torture-murder, appears to be on the order of 300,000.[90]

The number of women raped has been estimated at from 20,000 to 80,000, although the actual number cannot be known. "[M]ost were killed immediately after rape." The women came from all classes and occupations, and were "systematically" recruited by Japanese soldiers who "searched for them constantly as they looted homes and dragged men off for execution." Sexual torture, "perversion," and invented "games of recreational rape" were reportedly widespread, although Chang does not give statistical estimates.[91]

In addition, "Chinese men were often sodomized or forced to perform a variety of repulsive sexual acts in front of laughing Japanese soldiers." Clearly the aim was to humiliate the vanquished men, as described above

---

[88] Jehl 1999.
[89] Brownmiller in Rejali 1996, 366; Higonnet and Higonnet 1987, 42.
[90] Chang 1997, 42, 99–103.
[91] Chang 1997, number 89, killed 98, dragged 90, games 94.

(p. 359). Cases were reported of castration, and even of selling penises for Japanese men to eat (supposedly to increase their potency).[92]

However, it does not appear, from Chang's account, that sexual assault or sexual mutilation was necessary or central to the overall pattern of atrocities at Nanking. If about 50,000 women were raped and mostly killed, this would be less than 20 percent of the total victims of the assault. The majority of victims apparently were men who were not sexually abused, just executed. Rape seems to be just one among several ways that Japanese forces imposed their domination through extreme cruelty and humiliation. It is impossible to know how central the rapes were to the Japanese soldiers' motivation or capability to participate in the "orgy" of atrocities in Nanking.

Committing atrocities did not come naturally to Japanese soldiers. First, Nanking was not a typical war experience, but an extreme case that historians of Japan have difficulty explaining. Japanese soldiers typically were shocked by the atrocities at first, but became desensitized to them over time through repeated participation and systematic training by commanders. One Japanese commander said of his new troops' shock at seeing hardened veterans torturing civilians to death, "All new recruits are like this, but soon they will be doing the same things themselves." One soldier reported that his first experience watching a killing was "so appalling that I felt I couldn't breathe," but that "[e]veryone became a demon within three months." Afterwards, Japanese veterans consistently "reported honestly that they experienced a complete lack of remorse or sense of wrongdoing, even when torturing helpless civilians."[93]

The rape of Nanking was not militarily useful. On the contrary, it seriously harmed Japan's military conquest of China. If the atrocities were supposed to terrify the Chinese people into submission, they in fact had the opposite effect, galvanizing Chinese patriotism and amplifying resistance to the Japanese occupation. The atrocities also greatly increased opposition to Japanese militarism in foreign countries including the United States – again harming Japan's military interests.[94]

In response to these negative effects of the rape of Nanking, Japanese commanders created the system of "comfort women" discussed earlier. Controlled slave prostitution, spread out across many locations and largely out of public view, would allow Japanese soldiers to rape women without the loss of discipline and the bad publicity that resulted from Nanking. Through the system of comfort women, "the Japanese military hoped to reduce the incidence of random rape of local women" (so as to

---

[92] Chang 1997, 95, 88.
[93] Chang 1997, 54–56, 44, new–civilians 57–59.
[94] Chang 1997, 170–80.

reduce foreign criticism), as well as to control venereal disease and to use sex more efficiently as a reward for soldiers.[95]

Wartime rape in international law   Rape in wartime, including forced prostitution, has long been illegal under international law (the 1949 Geneva Conventions and the 1977 Protocols). However, rape has been treated as a crime against honor, distinct from crimes of violence such as murder, mutilation, and torture. Rape is not mentioned explicitly as a "grave breach" (the most serious war crimes), although it could arguably be subsumed by general grave breaches such as torture and inhumane treatment.[96]

The war-crimes tribunal for the former Yugoslavia included sexual assault among "crimes against humanity," set up a separate unit to prosecute rape, and charged eight suspects in 1996. However, the first case involving only rape (not mixed with other crimes) proved problematical. The defense claimed the memory of the victim (known only as Witness A) was unreliable because she had suffered from post-traumatic stress syndrome.[97]

Notwithstanding such cases as Bosnia and Nanking, most wartime rapes are organized not from above, but by small units and individuals. Commanders' attitudes range, in various wars, from relative tolerance or even encouragement, to relatively strict punishment, of rape. The German army in World War II punished its members who committed rape and plunder on the Western front, but did not discipline such crimes carried out in the East, where enemy civilians and soldiers alike were considered genetically inferior. For German soldiers in Russia, under harsh conditions and strict internal discipline, the ability to exercise total and arbitrary power over civilians served as a psychological "compensation" or "safety valve." Although German commanders executed 15,000 of their own soldiers for indiscipline within the ranks, "the troops went unpunished even when they totally disregarded orders forbidding plunder and indiscriminate shooting." Atrocities, as in other wars, enhanced the army's cohesion by diverting soldiers' pent-up anger and frustration, against defenseless enemies instead of their own superiors. The brutality of Germany's invasion of Russia also reflected the aims of the war, which were to exploit land and food for an expanding Germany (as well as for the army itself which could "live off the land"), at the expense of a population of inferior beings. This brutality, however, "left Russia's civilians with little choice but to resist with ever greater tenacity an invader who

---

[95] Chang 1997, local 52–53; Hicks 1995, 45.
[96] Copelon 1994, 200–1.
[97] Anderson 1996; first: Simons 1998.

promised them only suffering and death" – leading to a vicious cycle in which brutality caused resistance which increased the need for internal discipline in the German army, which increased the need to divert frustration outward onto the Russian civilians through brutality. As in Nanking and Okinawa, rapes were militarily counterproductive.[98]

Defending "our" women   Gender plays a role in ethnonationalism. The nation is often gendered female, and the state male. Women in some sense embody the nation, and the political inclusion of women and the masses of men (democratization) seemed to accompany the rise of nationalism in Europe a century ago. "The figure of a woman often acts as a sign in discursive formations" such as the symbolic constructions underlying nationalism in nineteenth-century Bengal. The process of redrawing territorial borders to unite some people and exclude others sometimes uses women's bodies as symbols of the nation, markers of the in-group, and national "property" to be defended and protected by men.[99]

Rape of "our" women sometimes becomes a dominant metaphor of the danger to the nation from enemy males. An ethnic group's perceived "vulnerability or porousness of national boundaries" is embodied in songs and legends about the abduction or seduction of young women by the enemy. These constructions also provide "opportunities for heroism." During the US Civil War and Reconstruction, the symbolism of sex between white Southern women and black men served to mobilize white Southern men. Invasions, such as the German conquest of Poland and France at the outset of World War II or Iraq's conquest of Kuwait, are frequently described as "rape."[100]

Propaganda in the World Wars used the theme of rape to rally patriotism (see Figure 6.7). In World War I, British propaganda played up German gang rapes, so that "the rape and sexual mutilation of women dominated contemporaries' imaginings and representations of the war." Italy dropped leaflets to Austrian soldiers warning that while they were fighting Italy, Russians would occupy their homes and rape their women. In World War II, Japanese forces warned Australian soldiers that Americans were consorting with their women back home. Germany informed British soldiers likewise. German propaganda played up the

[98] Bartov 1991, 6, 70–73.
[99] Pettman 1996a, 45–63, gendered 49; Chatterjee 1993, formations 68, 137, 135–40; Halliday 1991, 165; Peterson 1996b; Stiglmayer 1994a; Gioseffi ed. 1988, 119; Pettman 1996a, 45, 64; Williams and Best 1982, 130; Smith 1991, 44, 4; Kristof 1998; Bloom 1990; Gurr 1993; Gurr and Harff 1994.
[100] Mostov 1995, 516–23, metaphor 523, porousness 517; Seifert 1996; Civil: Hodes 1992; invasions: McBride 1995, 41, 49; Sasson 1991; Parker et al. 1992, 6.

Figure 6.7 "Keep These Hands Off," bond poster, Canada, World War II. [National Archives of Canada, C-090883.]

humiliation implied by French women having sex with black African troops from French colonies, and British women having sex with black US soldiers. In the former Yugoslavia, rape across ethnic lines became an "ethnomarker" and sharpened intergroup boundaries around the propagandistic promotion of images of the other group as rapists to be feared.[101]

These constructions limit all women's (not just rape victims) gender mobility, reinforcing traditional sexism. Croatian women in the 1990s were scolded by the government for having too few babies, and especially for having abortions (since, as the ruling party put it, a "fetus is also Croat"). Meanwhile the Serbian Orthodox Patriarch told women who had lost their only children in the war that they should have had more children. Beyond their reproductive roles, women are keepers of a group's culture, expected to "preserve tradition in the home... [and] reflect the virtue of the nation."

The symbolism of an enemy danger to "our" women can become bizarre. In 1997, the Palestinian Authority claimed that Israeli chewing gum sold in Palestinian areas was spiked with progesterone as a plot to drive Arab women into a sexual frenzy (undermining Islamic morals and, in one version, setting them up to be prostitute-informants), while sterilizing both girls and boys to reduce the Arab birth rate. The story gained wide credence even though the gum was made in Spain, it contained no progesterone according to an independent analysis, and progesterone tends to slightly reduce rather than increase women's sexual desires (nor would the method have worked as a contraceptive).[102]

War and misogyny

If symbolic and actual rape encode domination, then misogyny serves as an important motor of male aggression in war. Rape is "the ultimate metaphor for the war system," according to Betty Reardon. As a symbolic form of rape, armed violence genders the victor as male and the vanquished as female. Symbolic rape is acted out in various ways in different cultures and contexts, but key themes repeat across time and space.[103]

Some argue that misogyny itself is "the mother's milk of militarism" – that is, essential to the war system. Feminists Mary Beard and Virginia Woolf in the 1930s "recognized the misogyny inherent in militaristic discourse on both sides." A sociologist-soldier describes a "swaggering masculinity and revengeful, contemptuous (and defensive) attitude toward

---

[101] British: Kent 1993, 24–26; Italy: Hirschfeld 1934, 321; Japanese: Gubar 1987, 239; Yugoslavia: Rejali 1996, 370.
[102] Gellman 1997.
[103] Reardon 1985, metaphor 40.

women." Posters and poems of World War II reflect "intense hatred of women," notably in the recurrent images of war as a man-destroying prostitute: "O war is a casual mistress/And the world is her double bed./ She has few charms in her mechanised arms/But you wake up and find yourself dead."[104]

Underlying this misogyny seems to be fear. Fearless warriors' rituals often seem to reflect insecurity about women. Men's houses play prominent roles in the social lives of many preindustrial societies. In these houses, usually located in a community's center, men gather to make decisions and enact male ceremonies (using ritual objects stored there). "Women are strictly forbidden to enter," nor must they ever see or touch ritual paraphernalia, sometimes on pain of death or gang-rape. Nor is there any "similar vehicle for women." Men find in these houses "sanctuary . . . from any danger of female intrusion," and avoid "contamination" by females while engaged in their all-male activities. These men's houses may be rooted in the men's distrust of their wives, who often come from other communities (a majority of cultures are patrilocal) – the problem discussed earlier (see pp. 225–27).[105]

Scripts for male dominance may be rooted in "fear, conflict, and strife." In societies where males dominate, creation myths may reflect a belief by males that "there is an uncontrollable force that may strike home at any time." This force, although ill-defined, is often associated with "female sexuality and reproductive functions." "Men attempt to neutralize the power they think is inherent in women by stealing it, nullifying it, or banishing it to invisibility."[106]

For German men of the Freikorps after World War I, "[w]omen who don't conform to any of the 'good woman' images are automatically seen as prostitutes . . . evil and out to castrate." These proto-fascist men apparently were deeply afraid of women, intimacy, and sex. When the threatening possibility of sex or intimacy with women arises in their stories, it is abruptly avoided and redirected towards violence. Indeed, the stories written by these men construct the world on gender-polarized lines: "Down below: wetness, motion, swallowing up. Up on the height: dryness, immobility, security." The Freikorps soldiers felt love not for women but for fatherland, native town, uniform, comrades, weapons, and animals (especially horses). Armed women, prostitutes, or women that the soldiers considered prostitutes were all seen as "castrating" women who induced fear of "total annihilation and dismemberment." Thus, to attack

---

[104] Reardon 1985, milk 52; Higonnet and Higonnet 1987, sides 42; Costello 1985, 89, 78, swaggering 77; Charles Causley poem in Gubar 1987, 250.
[105] Kessler 1976, enter–contamination 77–79; Gerzon 1982, 41–42.
[106] Astrachan 1986, 72.

"a woman who isn't identified with the mother/sister image is essentially self-defense."[107]

Misogyny was central to these men's identities as soldiers. However, they represent an extreme case (the core of the future Nazi party), not typical of soldiers across other cultures and times. Goebbels called Nazism "in its nature a masculine movement," but this does not make it the ideal or norm of masculinity worldwide. The Freikorps may not typify even German Nazis, much less all soldiers or all men, and thus may not be "the tip of the patriarchal iceberg."[108]

Menstrual blood and sexual intercourse are considered dangerous for male warriors in "many, many tribes." Menstrual taboos, which vary considerably across cultures, do not correlate with sexual inequality in those cultures. Rather, the number of taboos correlates with frequent warfare and with the acquisition of wives from hostile groups. Thus, "the bodily danger faced by men is reproduced in small on the female body." Men tend to see sexuality as dangerous or polluting in societies where food supplies are uncertain, a condition that correlates with war-proneness. (To protect themselves from this danger, the Kiwai [Oceania] had a "complicated war magic" concerning their own genitals and those of the enemy, and they followed strict war chastity. On the other hand, Polynesian warriors "demanded chastity of their wives while they were at war but they did not impose it on themselves.")[109]

Is war then "menstruation envy" – men's response to women's ability to bleed? I doubt it. Nonetheless, the nobility of medieval fighting rested on the shedding of blood, more than on death: "Blood is the basic currency of fights and quests." Other cultures also place high value on blood: "A wounded Ibibio [of Nigeria] could not let a woman see his blood flow, for it was his masculine strength. It was nothing if a man saw a woman's blood flow, for she was inferior anyhow." Aranda warriors in Australia prepared on the night before an attack by cutting open a longitudinal circumcision wound with sharp bones and letting blood flow over each other's shoulders.[110]

Although some of these particular connections of war with symbolic rape may not hold up, the examples show that war itself contains an element of metaphorical rape, as part of a broader pattern of feminization of enemies, that goes well beyond the specific incidences of actual rape in wartime.

[107] Theweleit 1987, 171, 50, security 249, 61, castrating 70, total 205, defense 183.
[108] Tiger 1969, nature 90; Segal 1990, 115–23, iceberg 118.
[109] Turney-High 1971, tribes 162, Kiwai-Polynesian 162; Sanday 1981, 91–112, correlate 105.
[110] Lynch 1995, currency 91; Turney-High 1971, anyhow 161; Eibl-Eibesfeldt 1979, shoulders 172–73.

Military homophobia

The widespread homophobia found in modern armies may result from the need to feminize enemies. Gay men are *men* in the important biological aspects discussed in chapters 3 and 4: they have testosterone; they are big and strong. What differs is how gay soldiers encode sex and dominance. Their presence makes ambiguous the construction of male soldiers as dominant sexual actors whose submissive-receptive partners are women external to the military force – back home, in the next brothel or port, or in pin-ups and wallet photos. "Because homosexuality is read as effeminate, the presence of openly homosexual men shatters the homosocial unity . . . needed to successfully carry out aggression against the enemy conceived as less than a man, that is, a woman." In modern armies "homosexuality was perceived as a threat to the essential aggressive 'manliness' of soldiers," as well as to discipline and the rule against fraternizing across ranks. Virility, which men value above all else, is defined as "that which is not queer," that for which homosexuality is "the Other."[111]

The role in war of the Amerindian berdache (see pp. 360–61) constitutes an interesting test in this regard. These men who dressed for life as women and performed women's work (including sexually) were large and strong, yet culturally defined as female. Thus, if participation in combat were driven by biology, the berdaches should be regular warriors. Instead, berdaches were constrained in their participation in war. Typically they accompanied war parties to carry supplies and weapons, and to take away bodies for burial. When berdaches did participate in fighting, as with the seventeenth-century Illinois tribes, they were allowed to use only clubs and not bows and arrows. Recalling the widespread prohibition on women's having access to specialized weapons of war (and hunting), it is clear that the berdaches participated in feminine roles during battle, and not in roles that would have best used their physical potential.[112]

In contemporary US society too, homosexuality is considered effeminate, and hence the opposite of masculinity and incompatible with a warrior spirit. For example, peace demonstrators in 1967, "at virtually every anti-war demonstration," were taunted by male hecklers as "faggots" and "queers," even though nearly half the demonstrators were women and the rest included a mix of "virile, athletic-looking men," "long-haired hippie types" and some men in military garb ready to battle police. Since the

---

[111] Kier 1998; McBride 1995, shatters 68; Costello 1985, threat 102; Simpson 1994, queer 4.
[112] Trexler 1995, 66–67.

demonstrators were against the war, they were constructed as sissies, effeminates, and hence homosexual.[113]

This present-day homophobic model, ruling out gay male soldiers, is not universal, however. The US military's homophobia reflects a "culturally embedded view that homosexuality represents a feminization of men." By contrast, other cultures elsewhere have constructed homosexuality as "having a masculinizing effect in males" and thus an "asset in military mobilization" (on the Sambia, see p. 20).[114]

In the Theban Sacred Band of ancient Greece – a very capable military force – gay relationships among soldiers were openly encouraged. Men were placed in the ranks alongside their lovers on the theory that they would not disgrace themselves by showing cowardice while their beloved was watching. The sexual bonds between male soldiers enhanced cohesion and boosted motivation. Just as heterosexual men describe deep love for their comrades, motivating them to fight for their buddies, so did the Greek soldiers develop this motivation with sexual ties added.[115]

The Theban case is unusual in historical context, though not unique. Armies have varied in the extent to which they tolerated the presence of gay soldiers in the ranks. In the US military in the twentieth century, tolerance towards gay soldiers in wartime (when demand for soldiers is high and supply low) has given way repeatedly to intolerance in peacetime. These shifts parallel the attitudes towards women in the military. In wartime, rules are bent, whereas in peacetime the military tidies up its ranks to fit an ideal model. (The current US all-volunteer force falls somewhere in between because soldiers are relatively scarce but dire need is absent.)[116]

In some cases, intolerance for gay soldiers has taken extreme form, with the death penalty imposed for homosexual behavior. This was the case for German SS officers in 1942–45. In the British navy as well, until the early nineteenth century, officers convicted of sodomy were hanged from the masts. (Winston Churchill reportedly said during World War II, "Don't talk to me about naval tradition. It's nothing but rum, sodomy, and the lash.")[117]

In modern Western wars, ironically, the intense love that men feel for their comrades creates a sentimental bond associated with femininity in modern thought (but here requisitioned for military use). This bond easily shades into sexuality. The love of man for man extolled by World War I poets contained "homoerotic undertones in unexpected places." Robert

---

[113] Gerzon 1982, 46.
[114] Adam 1994, 104.
[115] Flaceliere 1962, 86; Holmes 1985, 107, 294; Costello 1985, 102.
[116] Holmes 1985, varied 107.
[117] Costello 1985, 102–3.

Graves censored (in his autobiography and list of works) his gay history before age 21. In World War I, according to Hirschfeld, homosexuality in military forces was a recurrent concern of commanders, but the actual extent of such activity was quite limited. An "extremely common notion" held that 2 percent of German soldiers were gay. An "unusual number" of German homosexuals joined up enthusiastically to fight in World War I, some of them returning from having gone into exile to escape German homophobia. Hirschfeld implies that these men jumped into military service either to redeem their manhood or to court death after an unhappy life. In World War II, however, the homoerotic literary themes surrounding the British "lads" of World War I were absent.[118]

Present-day policies   The performance of gay soldiers historically and in present-day Western armies shows them equal to heterosexual male soldiers in bravery and fighting ability. In the US military, according to a 1988 Defense Department-sponsored report (and parallel to a 1957 report), "gender orientation is unrelated to job performance." Nonetheless, impassioned arguments continue to be made against gay soldiers on a wide variety of grounds.[119]

Before 1981, the decision to terminate the service of a gay US soldier was "a matter of command discretion rather than mandatory policy." In 1950 the Uniform Code of Military Justice banned military homosexuality (along with other forms of "sodomy"), following a 1920 law. Policies against gay soldiers became progressively more restrictive from 1945 to 1974, and shifted from a treatment-and-retention model to a separation model. Until the 1970s, regulations allowed enough flexibility to accommodate wartime needs (the 1920 and 1950 laws were passed *after* war needs passed) and cases of "heroic service."[120]

The practice of automatic separation, based on a policy that "homosexuality is incompatible with military service," dates from the last week of the Carter administration. In the 1980s, about 1,500 men and women per year were separated for being gay. In 1993 – after a proposal to loosen restrictions on gay soldiers unleashed a storm of political opposition in the first weeks of the Clinton administration – the US military adopted a policy of "don't ask, don't tell" under which recruits are not questioned about their sexual orientation, commanders are not supposed to pursue

---

[118] Segal 1990, feel 142; Theweleit 1987, 54–57, 204–5; Rowse 1977, places 267–70; Hirschfeld 1934, 124–40, notion 126; Fussell 1989, lads 109; Simpson 1994, 212–28.

[119] Shilts 1993; Herek, Jobe, and Carney eds. 1996; Kier 1998, job 32, 5–6; Zuniga 1995; Korb 1994, 223, 224; wide: Wells-Petry 1993, 120–23, 93–98, 110, 113, 3, 51, 132–71, 187.

[120] Korb 1994, discretion 221; Burrelli 1994, 17–19, heroic 18; Scott and Stanley 1994, xi; Berube 1990.

investigations of subordinates' orientations, and military personnel may not engage in homosexual acts or state openly that they are gay or lesbian. Three surveys of US military personnel in the early 1990s found that most respondents opposed lifting the ban on gay and lesbian soldiers, with greatest opposition coming from males, from junior ranks, and from those in combat positions (and more tolerance from African Americans and older service members). One white male soldier stated simply, "if you place one in my room, bunker, tent, or showers, I'd bash his head in." The survey author writes: "The idea of being approached by gays, being perceived as gay, or being overpowered by gays brings out violent reactions in many male soldiers." By contrast, polls of the US public show increasing support – about two-thirds of the total by 1992 – for allowing gay soldiers.[121]

The ultimate test of the arguments about the effects of gay male soldiers on heterosexual ones comes in the fourteen countries that allow gay soldiers to serve openly in military forces. According to a study by the US General Accounting Office, the presence of gay soldiers "has not created problems" in those countries. Although specific policies vary among countries, military restrictions in these countries were generally lifted in concert with, but delayed from, the evolution of views on homosexuality in the society at large.[122]

Among key NATO allies in 1993, policies and practices show limited tolerance of homosexuality. Britain (all-volunteer) rejects gay recruits and discharges homosexuals but does not criminalize them. Germany asks conscripts about their orientation and rejects gays, while France, the Netherlands, and Denmark do not ask, but allow conscripts to avoid military service by declaring themselves homosexual. Italy accepts gay draftees but not volunteers. Most of these countries do not discharge gay soldiers once in service as a matter of policy, but in practice usually do so in Britain, Germany, and Italy. Thus a variety of policies and practices characterize Western European militaries.[123]

The Netherlands lifted restrictions on openly gay soldiers in 1974, and has implemented policies since the mid-1980s to protect gay rights and change attitudes towards gay soldiers among heterosexual ones. A survey in the 1980s found that heterosexual soldiers and officers accepted gay men as colleagues but kept them at a distance psychologically and socially (as they did with lesbians but less strongly). Almost half the survey respondents at least sometimes heard anti-gay statements in their units.

---

[121] Shilts 1993; Burrelli 1994, 19; Scott and Stanley 1994, xi; Egan 1998; surveys: Segal, Gade, and Johnson 1994, 47; Miller 1994, 69, bash 79–80; Moskos 1994, public 63; Stiehm 1994, 150, 66–67.

[122] US General Accounting Office 1993, 3; Kier 1998, problems 30.

[123] Segal, Gade, and Johnson 1994, 36–40; Gade, Segal, and Johnson 1996.

About a third of the men said they would react with hostility or aggression if a colleague turned out to be gay. However, "no clear connection was found between the masculine image of the armed forces... and the attitude toward homosexuals." In Canada, court-ordered integration of openly gay soldiers into the military has gone forward since 1992. An early report found little change, partly because few gay soldiers had declared their orientation.[124]

In Israel, where most young people are routinely drafted for military service, being gay does not bring an exemption. From 1983 to 1993 Israeli policies allowed for the exclusion of gay soldiers from "some combat units that are highly consolidated and perform under high stress," and from other postings under conditions of "prolonged periods of seclusion." Since 1993, Israeli policy prohibits any restrictions on gay soldiers (a policy enacted over opposition from orthodox religious organizations). In practice, Israeli commanders have responded flexibly, sometimes protecting gay soldiers who performed well during the earlier period of restriction, yet continuing to treat homosexuality as deviant in the current period of egalitarian policy. Overall, Israeli military leaders consider the inclusion of gay soldiers effective, particularly since individuals (gay or straight) who appear unlikely to adapt well to military life are screened out at the time of conscription. Israeli integration of gay soldiers may be facilitated by the relative shortage of military manpower in that country, and by the fact that Israeli soldiers usually serve fairly close to home and are not isolated away from home for long periods.[125]

Currently, arguments against gay male US soldiers frequently express concern for "privacy," a concern some writers find laughable: heterosexual male soldiers apparently live in terror of having their penises seen by gay men whose "gaze is so powerful as to virtually paralyze the phallocratic military machine." In response, a "massive voyeuristic system" of state surveillance spies on the sex lives of gay and lesbian soldiers. This fear lies at the heart of the leading argument against gays in the military – that they disrupt "unit cohesion" – despite the evidence reviewed earlier (see p. 199) showing that the presence of "different" individuals need not disrupt task cohesion in small units. African Americans were integrated into many US military units a half century ago without ruining unit cohesion, despite widespread fears that they would do so. To a large extent the same is true of women in recent decades (see pp. 199–202). The difference with gay men is that they make the heterosexual men potential targets of male sexual energy. A 1991 court decision upholding

---

[124] Andersen-Boers and Van Der Meulen 1994, 205, survey 209; Segal, Gade, and Johnson 1994, 41–42, 38; Park 1994.
[125] Gal 1994, 185–88.

the ban on gay soldiers made this connection explicit in stating that only the absence of homosexuals could allow military personnel to "undress, sleep, bathe, and use the bathroom without fear or embarrassment that they are being viewed as sexual objects." The problem, then, is that gay men disrupt the construction of male soldiers as sexual subjects, not objects.[126]

Lesbians   The current debate on gays in the US military centers on gay men rather than lesbians, even though a greater proportion of women than men are discharged for being gay. Lesbian soldiers do not carry the same emotional charge as gay men soldiers do, for their comrades or their commanders (just as tomboys provoke less reaction than sissies; see pp. 244, 288, 300). During World War II, "[h]omosexual activity was not considered the same disgrace when practiced by women in uniform" as for men, and "did not attract the same penalties." WAAC officers in 1943 were officially instructed that "homosexuality is of interest to you . . . only so far as its manifestations undermine the efficiency of the individuals concerned and the stability of the group." Officers were warned against "hunting and speculating" about enlisted women's close attachments. The US Navy's commander of the surface Atlantic fleet is quoted in a recent leaked memo as saying that "lesbians may be among the Navy's 'top' performers."[127]

We do not know the relative proportion of lesbians among military women compared with gay men among military men. Anecdotal evidence and logic suggest the proportion is higher for women, and this may also explain women's higher rate of discharge for homosexuality. Around 1981, women made up only 5 percent of the British armed forces but over one-third of those dismissed for homosexuality.[128]

In a traditionally male environment (the military), women look and act professional by acting like men – for example, by performing physically demanding tasks, controlling emotions, using raw language or a command voice. Yet lesbians receive most criticism for their man-like appearance (whereas gay men are criticized for their sexual acts). This leaves all military women, more than men, open to appearing homosexual. All US military women are subject to sexual advances from male soldiers and officers; if they resist these self-defined manly men, they must be lesbians. Thus, just as military prostitution adversely affects women who are not prostitutes, so homophobia adversely affects women who are not lesbians.[129]

[126] Moskos 1994, 63; Adam 1994, gaze 110; Shawver 1996, undress 226–27.
[127] Costello 1985, disgrace 69, hunting 69; Adam 1994, top 106.
[128] Enloe 1983, 141.
[129] Stiehm 1994, criticism 155–59.

Figure 6.8 French women plowing by hand, World War I. [from Blatch 1918, 67.]

In sum, modern military homophobia, in its various specific aspects, seems oriented towards preserving the gender of male warriors relative to their feminized enemies. That feminization itself seems to play a robust role across various cultures and times (with many channels and variations), in structuring the participation of male soldiers in war.

C. DEPENDENCE ON EXPLOITING WOMEN'S LABOR

Finally, a third variant, Hypothesis 6C, proposes that patriarchy rests on the exploitation of women's labor, with wartime intensifying the need for this exploitation. Women cannot generally become warriors because their work (which is never done!) keeps the war machine running.

Women war workers

In every society at war, women workers help sustain both the war effort and the economy behind it. Most of this work is unpaid, and largely unmeasured. Figure 6.8, for example, shows French women, deprived of their men and horses by World War I, plowing by hand. When women do get paid, they most often provide lowest-level cheap labor, exploited in a variety of ways by wartime leaders. In the Dahomey kingdom, women who did *not* become the famous soldiers "did all the housekeeping and cooking, reared the children, raised, harvested and marketed crops, engaged in petty trade, tended livestock, collected firewood... made pottery, spun cotton, dyed cloth." Overall, their "lot was difficult." Similarly, Mae women in New Guinea "detest" wars because they fear "being left to bring up children relatively unaided... In addition... they have to bear even more of the burden of food production... in exposed gardens. Finally, the women dread... dislocation" if their villages are routed. A Lebanese woman whose father was killed in the recent civil war said: "The real experience of war is not the shelling, those are just moments... War is what happens afterwards, the years of suffering hopelessly with a disabled husband and no money, or struggling to rebuild when all your property has been destroyed."[130]

War's effects in squeezing women are illustrated in the Roman empire's "Oppian law" imposed in 215 BC during the Carthaginian (Second Punic) War (218–201 BC). It restricted women's possession of gold, wearing of purple, or riding in two-wheeled vehicles. The law's repeal six years after the war ended has been portrayed variously as a victory of women's power or just reinstatement of husbands' authority over their wives after wartime modifications. Within Rome's elite, continual wars of conquest – which sent hundreds of thousands of men away – may have undermined patriarchal society and women's subservience. The last two centuries of the Republic, a period of constant war, gave the "relatively few" women in the Roman elite new rights and status, even "sizable fortunes." Italian peasant women "also experienced unprecedented independence in this period" as their men were conscripted, "but in economically more vulnerable circumstances" than the elite. Many women were driven into prostitution or clothing production, both of which offered "a wretched hand-to-mouth existence." Thus, for all but the richest women, "Rome's unending wars of conquest held out only the promise of a bleak present and still more hopeless future."[131]

Camp followers   "Camp followers" have accompanied armies through history. One 40,000-soldier army during the Thirty Years War reportedly had 100,000 camp followers. The camp follower's life resembles "the life of any woman in a male-dominated society: she is financially dependent on men; her labour is used but she does not control it or reap its rewards; she is expected to be nurturing and self-sacrificing; but if she

---

[130] Dahomey: Alpern 1998, 48; Mae: Meggitt 1977, 99; Lebanon: Bennett, Bexley, and Warnock 1995, 267.
[131] Bauman 1992, Oppian 25; Costello 1985, 2; Evans 1991, elite–circumstances 101, driven–future 144.

Figure 6.9 Soldiers and families on march near Dover, England, *c.* 1830. [Courtesy of the Director, National Army Museum, London.]

steps out of line, she can be labelled a 'common whore' and marginalised even further." Punishments meted out to "unruly" camp followers by the British army in the seventeenth century included the "whirligig," which spun the offender around in a wooden cage until she became violently ill and "commonly emptied . . . her body through every aperture."[132]

In Wellington's campaigns against Napoleon in 1808–15, British women "followed the drum" – a "large entourage of wives . . . joined . . . by numerous Spanish and Portuguese girls, some of whom married British soldiers and some of whom followed the army without benefit of clergy." Most soldiers saw the women as "a great asset, not only as cooks, laundry-women and seamstresses, but as companions who humanized the hard life of the camps," notwithstanding some "administrative and disciplinary problems" their presence caused. Figure 6.9 shows British soldiers on the march with their families in 1830.[133]

In nineteenth-century Britain, the army developed laws and regulations to control the sex lives of soldiers who were no longer seen as "helplessly subjected to their irrepressible licentious natures." At this time, the army was becoming more professionalized and the previous flow of women in

[132] Costello 1985, 210; Enloe 1983, 1, further 6, unruly 3.
[133] Page 1986, 2–3.

and out was diminishing, as society itself was increasingly segregating men and women into public and private spheres. This created problems both for married male soldiers (dual loyalties and the distraction of families) and for single ones (loneliness and VD).[134]

Loyalty to the regiment lifted from a male soldier the Victorian-era obligation of a man to maintain his wife and children, a point used to good effect by recruiting officers. A wife left behind when a regiment was posted away from home faced not only "a broken heart . . . [but] the more pressing problem of how she could feed and house herself and her children." Thus, quite a few wives, often more than the official number, traveled with the army.[135]

A community of camp followers surrounded and sustained the Continental Army during the US Revolutionary War. Despite occasional episodes to the contrary, the camp generally did not include prostitutes (they worked outside the camp), but rather women performing various services such as supply, laundry, and cooking (among others) to the soldiers. Although assumed by nineteenth-century historians to be prostitutes, they in fact closely resembled twentieth-century WACs, field nurses, and army wives. They carried the baggage and received half rations. In battle they were "the primary medics." Most of the followers were attached to male soldiers or officers, and thus made their contributions privately, but others were contractors or employees who served the army as a whole. Camp followers included quite a few men.[136]

Most of the female camp followers were lower-class women, with children in tow, who performed menial chores. By contrast, a smaller but distinctive group of "ladies" were wives of officers, who offered companionship and moral support for their husbands in an upper-class setting. Martha Washington accompanied her husband in camp and claimed to have heard the guns of every campaign. Notwithstanding his wife's presence, George Washington in 1777 found "the multitude of women . . . a clog upon every movement," and instructed officers to "get rid of" those not absolutely necessary and stop women from riding in the wagons. The Continental Congress authorized a ratio of 1 woman to 15 men, but the actual ratio went "well over" that, both because the women's work was essential and because their absence might make men desert.[137]

---

[134] Trustram 1984, natures 2, 3, 6, 29–30, 116–37.
[135] Trustram 1984, 10, 50, 85.
[136] Mayer 1996; De Pauw 1975, WACs 179–80, medics 187–88.
[137] De Pauw 1975, clog 183–86.

Women's labor in the world wars

The armies of twentieth-century total war depended on women in new ways, not only within the army (see pp. 64–76, 88–92) but in the civilian workforce (and in addition to the ongoing responsibilities of women for domestic, reproductive, and sexual work). In 1914, feminist Carrie Chapman Catt warned that "[w]ar falls on the women most heavily, and more so now than ever before." Both Britain and the United States mobilized substantial numbers of women into war-related industries, and into the workplace generally – about 2 million British and 9 million US women in World War II – to make male workers available for military use. These arrangements, although effective in boosting the war effort, almost everywhere were cast as temporary. They used, rather than challenged, existing gender stereotypes.[138]

In World War I Britain, about 1 million mostly lower-class women worked in munitions jobs. They were called "munitionettes" or "Tommy's sister." Unlike nurses, the munitions workers could not profess pacifism since their work directly contributed to the fighting. In fact, in 1918, Scottish women working at a shell factory raised money and bought a warplane for the air force. However, the munitionettes' main motivation was financial, contrary to the popular belief that it was patriotic. The women found the wages "at first livable and later lucrative." Compared with domestic work, war work "offered escape from jobs of badly paid drudgery." However, although they earned more than they would have doing women's work, the women received nowhere near the fortunes they had been led to expect when deciding to take war work.[139]

Eric Leed argues that World War I created for women "an enormously expanded range of escape routes from the constraints of the private family" because the war caused "the collapse of those established, traditional distinctions" that had restricted women. A *Punch* cartoon of the time shows a soldier's wife who receives an allowance: "This war is 'eaven – twenty-five shillings a week and no 'usband bothering about!" Costello credits World War I with winning women both the vote and a "new liberation" in fashion and behavior (smoking, bobbed hair, short skirts, and hedonism). But for British women war workers in World War I, "no doubt conditions varied a lot." Conditions worsened over time, making 1917–18 "the hardest year of the war for civilians," especially in the pan-European 1918 influenza epidemic. Some women complained of barracks-like

---

[138] Enloe 1983, 173–206; Koonz 1987, falls 19; Costello 1985, million 156; O'Brien and Parsons eds. 1995; Weatherford 1990; Noakes 1998.

[139] Woollacott 1994, 2, 7, belief 8, lucrative 1, drudgery 4, 10–11; Woollacott 1996; Braybon and Summerfield 1987, fortunes 57–58.

hostels with poor food and little heat, whereas others found accommodations clean, if crowded, and occasionally even comfortable. Most often, though, the woman war worker had "little in her life now except work and sleep." Work shifts of 10–12 hours were "not uncommon." Conditions in factories were, for women, an "alien environment" of deafening noise and depressing grime, encased by blacked-out windows.[140]

Other scholars doubt that World War I was an exhilarating, erotic release for women who took on traditionally male roles. Some women who drove "trucks, cranes, cars, and motorbikes in Britain during the war did find it thrilling," but many others were "killed, injured, and poisoned" in munitions factories. German women in World War I "shoulder[ed] double burdens," working at heavy machinery but still responsible for their domestic duties.[141]

Costello sees liberating effects in the Second World War, as in the First. As one British woman put it: "They were wonderful days, during the war, despite its dangers." In the United States, "war jobs and long periods of separation gave many wartime wives a new sense of independence." Although the seeds of women's liberation were buried after the war when women returned to domestic and feminine roles, they sprouted decades later in ways made possible by the war experience, in Costello's view. During the war, British women too had learned about new possibilities, such as high-wage work, social independence, birth control, and promiscuity.[142]

World War II disrupted British gender employment patterns more than World War I had. Before the war, British women workers – mostly single women under 35 – had been "concentrated in the lowest grades and most poorly paid sectors of teaching and civil service," and excluded from "high-paying 'men's work' in the steel, engineering, and shipbuilding industries." In the first year of the war, the main change was women's entry into the transport industry in force, as bus conductresses ("clippies"). The government found it difficult to get women to work in war industries. In mid-1940, the British government closed down "nonessential" industries such as textiles, which had employed many women. However, this did not bring enough British women into war work, nor did a massive 1941 advertising campaign. Married women continued to consider their "primary duty . . . to husband and home." As the labor crisis grew acute at the end of 1941 the British government encouraged mothers of

---

[140] Leed 1979, expanded 45; Blatch 1918, bothering 56; Costello 1985, bobbed 3–4, little 156, shifts 159, grime 168; Braybon and Summerfield 1987, varied–comfortable 101–2; Woollacott 1994, 4, 8, 50–58.
[141] Woollacott 1994, poisoned 209–11; Blatch 1918, burdens 81.
[142] Costello 1985, days 192, new 200, sprouted 257–74.

children under 14 to enter the workforce. Only then did the issues of child care and school meals receive attention, but they became mired in a bureaucratic dispute. Women "took to the streets and staged what the press dubbed 'Baby Riots' – traffic-stopping demonstrations of women wheeling strollers daubed with protests such as 'We Want War Work – We Want Nurseries.'"[143]

At the end of 1941, with female labor participation one-third below goals, the British government conscripted women into (their choice of) auxiliary services, civil defense, farm labor, or munitions factories. The conscription applied to single women aged 20 or 21. In 1942 and early 1943 the government took overall control of the labor of women aged 20–40. Those with responsibility for a household could apply for exemption. By 1943 the government also suspended recruiting women into military forces, to direct them instead to the chronically labor-short factories. In 1941 the government began training women for engineering jobs, and by 1943 women made up 40 percent of aircraft industry workers. Overall, 80 percent of single women aged 14–59 were in the workforce or the military auxiliary, as were 41 percent of wives and widows and 13 percent of mothers with children under 14 years old.[144]

Women faced resistance to being treated equally in war jobs. In 1940, British women transport workers won the right to be paid at male rates after six months on the job – a right opposed in heavy industry by craft unions afraid that employers were using the war to water down the skilled male workforce. As women flooded into aircraft work, men resisted the "invasion by a rival labor force" – in some cases even tampering with machines to make it harder for women on the next shift to use them. As one male worker put it, "Here's one woman doing it – they'll be getting other women in and then we'll be out of jobs and sent into the army." Women persisted, against male hostility and the "boredom of repetitive factory work," chiefly because of "the chance to earn relatively good pay."[145]

Unlike many of the men working in these factories, the women did not have wives at home to support them and manage the household. Like their counterparts in World War I, married women war workers in Britain found "they were, in effect, doing a double job." Most married women war workers had to do their own household's shopping, with little accommodation in shop hours. Child care for preschoolers outside the home was rare, and most schools did not sell or provide meals for children. One woman who could not finish the housework before rushing off

[143] Costello 1985, industries 157–58, nonessential 159, duty 165, 179, riots 169.
[144] Costello 1985, conscripted 16–17, training 160, old 156; Scott 1986.
[145] Costello 1985, won 159, rival 160, army 160, boredom 163, pay 160.

to the factory told a survey taker, "It's no good...I just can't manage like this." Absenteeism became a chronic problem as women tried, in the words of the Labour Ministry, "to do two full-time jobs." World War II Britain, in one view, was torn between capitalism (facilitating women's entry into the labor force, e.g., through child care centers) and patriarchy. The Labour Ministry and other government agencies were "active brokers" mediating gender relations and production, most often facilitating continuity of prewar attitudes and practices towards women in both paid and domestic work.[146]

The US mobilization of women was less intensive than in Britain. Even in the dark months after December 1941, war conditions never strained US society enough to cause the War Manpower Commission to conscript women. The president instead directed local authorities to institute enrollment drives using advertising, mail, and house-to-house canvassing to recruit women into war work. In the first half of 1942, over 30,000 women joined 2,000 already employed on aircraft assembly lines. After the initial months, however, the entry of women into the labor force slowed down, and male resistance proved resilient. At the wartime peak in 1944, 19 million US women were employed, nearly 50 percent more than in 1940 (with three-quarters of the increase representing married women).[147]

As in Britain, financial opportunity motivated US women who entered the workforce during the war. Their main reasons, according to surveys, were "to help win the war" and "high pay." Soldiers' wives received $28 from the government in addition to their $22 pay. Many women left office jobs for higher-paying factory jobs. One gun-turret factory worker said, "I used to earn $15 a month at college baking biscuits. Then when I got my first pay check here – $32.60 all in one week – I tell you."[148]

American women workers, like their British counterparts, had to juggle jobs with household responsibilities to get through the day. Married women made up nearly a quarter of the total workforce, outnumbering single women. The US government was less sympathetic than Britain's, however, declaring that "absenteeism is sabotage." The government was slow to provide child care centers. Eventually, the federal government subsidized 3,000 child care centers caring for 130,000 children, but this "did not begin to meet the need." Nonetheless, US retailers adapted to working women's needs better than in Britain. Department stores set up branches at war plants to cater to women workers.[149]

---

[146] Costello 1985, double–manage 166, two 168, 165–68; Summerfield 1984, 4–5, brokers 2.

[147] Costello 1985, lines 179; Anderson 1981, peak 4; Gabin 1995, 107.

[148] Costello 1985, win 190, wives 182, biscuits 191.

[149] Costello 1985, quarter 157, sabotage 189; Anderson 1981, need 6.

The US women's work "frequently was exhausting, and...many women could not cope well with the demands of families and enormous workloads at the factory. Reports of the Women's Bureau showed that one-half of married workers bore full responsibility for housework and were in desperate need of increased community services." One Women's Bureau report cited this case: "A 45 year old woman, living on a farm fifteen miles from the plant, gets up at four, packs lunches for herself and two sons in high school, gets the family breakfast, and leaves home at six o'clock... [I]t is after six when she reaches home. Then she has dinner to get, dishes to wash, and the whole round of household work to do... It is eleven p.m. when she retires, allowing only five hours for rest."[150]

Incessant US recruiting campaigns used various tactics to convince women to take on war jobs. The government suggested telling women that war work paid well and was "pleasant and easy as running a sewing machine." This was not true, however. A 1942 US government campaign to recruit women into war work faced the problem that "[i]t is almost impossible under present conditions to make many of these jobs more attractive... These jobs will have to be glorified as a patriotic war service if American women are to be persuaded to take them and stick to them." The government also tried guilt: "This Soldier May Die – Unless You Man This Idle Machine." However, the government worried about a backlash when the women's male relatives and friends died anyway. So this gave way to peer pressure – "the neighbors are going to think it very strange if you are not working" – and accusations of laziness: "Women can stand a lot... It is only in recent years, and mostly in the United States, that women have been allowed to fall into habits of extraordinary leisure... Are you so blinded by 'women's rights' that you have forgotten that nothing but WORK ever earned them?"[151]

Advertising appealed for women's labor participation while retaining images of women as homemakers and sex objects. The appeal to tradition aimed to reassure women that in taking on men's jobs they would not lose their femininity. In recruiting for factory work, "the vast majority of publicity concerning women workers emphasized glamour." Similarly, in recruiting women into military service, an even more difficult task, the US government decided that appeals to patriotism alone would not work, even with cajoling and threats, because women feared that military service would negate their femininity. Advertising directly addressed this fear: "Many service women say they receive more masculine attention – have more dates, a better time – than they ever had in civilian life. Their

---

[150] Honey 1995, exhausting–rest 98.
[151] Rupp 1978, stick 94, neighbors–earned 97; Costello 1985, idle 190.

uniforms have been styled by some of the world's greatest designers to flatter face and figure."[152]

War work required alterations of the women's expressions of feminine appearance. Boeing banned women from wearing tight sweaters (supposedly a hazard around machines but actually a distraction to men). Veronica Lake cut off her "peekaboo" hair style, copied widely by US women, because it reportedly was hazardous around machines (a patriotic act that sent her career into permanent decline). However, the "unique sex appeal" of the "feminine figure in male garb" was soon exploited by the advertising industry in order to add a patriotic slant. Pond's Cold Cream ads showed women doing various war jobs, saying "We like to feel we *look* feminine even if we are doing a man-size job." A rival hand cream instructed women: "hands that do a man's work can still enchant a man." Magazines gave "secret beauty tips" that let war workers keep their "Femininity Quotient" high. Maintaining a "traditional woman" beneath a "begrimed exterior" served to maintain gender continuity and facilitate the return to traditional roles after the war: the woman war worker "was, inside her coveralls, the same prewar woman who cooked, cleaned, and cared for her family."[153]

Appeals to women's patriotism were "personalized," urging them "to work for their men rather than for their country." One poster advised a young woman, clutching letters, that "Longing won't bring him back sooner. GET A WAR JOB!" (see Figure 6.10). Ads aimed at housewives portrayed "war workers as dutiful wives performing the same function in the factory that they had at home." A woman gas-station attendant, in a gasoline ad, is shown "giving your car the same care she used in keeping house." A woman drill-press operator pictured in a Eureka vacuum cleaner ad "works to the rhythm of a little tuneless song...in the war plant's thud and hum...This is bringing Jimmy back...bringing Jimmy back." The "white, middle-class, heterosexual nuclear family...at home, with its noticeably absent breadwinner" served in propaganda campaigns as "the spiritual center of the mobilization campaign." The government ignored poor and working women, presumably because they needed no coaxing to take well-paying jobs.[154]

Women performed well in nontraditional jobs, and seemed especially adept at light industrial work. A Wisconsin student who spent summers filing the outer edges of aircraft reported: "You had only one-one-thousandth of an inch error...Women were particularly careful...and

[152] Rupp 1978, 147, 98.
[153] Costello 1985, peekaboo 188, size 189; Rupp 1978, 150, traditional 151, family 153.
[154] Rupp 1978, personalized 156, sooner 158, coaxing 99; Honey 1995, dutiful 95, hum 94, spiritual 96.

Figure 6.10 "Longing won't bring him back sooner . . . Get a War Job!,"
US poster, World War II. [US National Archives, NWDNS-44-PA-389.]

light-fingered enough ... [not to] go beyond the minimum tolerance." In shipbuilding – heavier industrial work as compared with aircraft production – women grew to one-third of the workforce in some US yards by 1943. The song "Rosie the Riveter" became a popular hit: "Rosie is protecting Charlie [her Marine boyfriend] / Working overtime on a riveting machine." Norman Rockwell's 1943 *Saturday Evening Post* cover "immortalized a muscularly defiant Rosie" (see Figure 6.11).[155]

Such heavy industrial work brought women into all-male bastions where they faced a mix of cooperation, chauvinism, and outright hostility from the men. One US woman said of her first day at a shipyard job: "The battery of men's eyes that turned on my jittery physique ... soon had me thinking 'Maybe I'm wrong ... Maybe I am from Mars.'" Another woman reported of shipyard men that "we have reason to assume that these men were bred by mothers, that they have wives and daughters and sisters and sweethearts. But that's where we evidently are wrong ... They have, in fact, never before seen or heard or touched or spoken to anything remotely resembling a female ... they whistle and hoot at us ... they yell, half in astonishment, and half in derision: 'There's women in the yard!'" The women entered a formerly all-male world of crude sexist jokes, and faced overt sexual harassment such as groping from their male bosses and men on whom they depended to teach them how the machines worked. Women were usually assigned individually to small work groups, and rarely formed all-female groups, because of male resentment. Rumors of illicit affairs going on in "some vaguely identified warehouse" at shipyards, or that some women shipyard workers were working as prostitutes on the side, further raised barriers to the men's acceptance of women co-workers.[156]

The United States and Nazi Germany used surprisingly similar means to mobilize women into the war effort. In both countries, the rapid change from depression to wartime economy made women "the largest available reserve of [industrial] workers," and both countries used propaganda rather than conscription to draw upon this reserve. Propaganda in both cases centered on Aryan/white-middle-class women and adapted public gender images to wartime needs without challenging traditional assumptions about women. Finally, in both countries World War II had "no permanent impact on women's status in society."[157]

The main difference was ideological. Nazi ideology held that women "owed service to the state above all else," but proclaimed "separate

---

[155] Costello 1985, tolerance 160, 183, Rosie 184–85.
[156] Costello 1985, battery–warehouse 185–88; Woollacott 1994, 201.
[157] Rupp 1978, 3–5, status 181.

Figure 6.11 "Rosie the Riveter" by Norman Rockwell, *Saturday Evening Post* cover, 1943. [Printed by permission of the Norman Rockwell Family Trust. © 1943 the Norman Rockwell Family Trust.]

spheres" for men and women that channeled women's service into family duties rather than politics or the workplace. Hitler argued that "no conflict between the sexes can occur as long as each party performs the function prescribed for it by nature." Goebbels said that "[w]oman's proper sphere is the family . . . If we eliminate women from every realm of public life, we do not do it in order to dishonour her, but in order that her honour may be restored to her." He also prescribed: "Man should be trained as a warrior and woman as recreation for the warrior." For peasant women, the domestic sphere included working in the fields and farmyard, cooking, cleaning, and raising many children. The German mobilization of women into war work thus ran counter to the ideal that "[f]irst and foremost, the German woman fulfilled her duty to her people as a mother." As a result, propaganda addressed to women was relegated to the relatively unimportant women's organization (the Frauenschaft). Its leaders urged women to take war work and declared that "men could warm up their food themselves without... anyone impugning their masculinity." However, while working women and a layer of upper-class women responded, "the middle layer sat tight in their middle-class happiness and resisted the call." The Nazi party sponsored only one major campaign to recruit women for the war effort, in 1941.[158]

Because of these limitations, Nazi Germany was far less successful than the United States in mobilizing women into war jobs. Despite German labor needs, the female workforce increased by only 1 percent in 1939–44, compared with a 32 percent increase in the United States. As each country sent 10 million men into the armed forces, the United States maintained its civilian labor force at nearly full strength, whereas Germany saw its civilian labor force drop by 10 million (about one-quarter), a loss only partly compensated by using POWs for slave labor. The US effort was more successful than the German one both because of more effective propaganda and because of structural factors such as "financial incentive [and] the availability of child care."[159]

British and American marriage rates – followed by birth rates – rose when the country went to war. Hasty marriages resulted partly from a desire to clutch at stability in an uncertain era and partly as a means to win draft deferments for US men who became fathers. Some couples shortened engagements to cement their relationships before the man began military service, although the military found this practice bad for morale. Others married to legitimize sexual relationships, including with near-strangers, that formed during soldiers' leaves. However, the strain of World War II also broke up many marriages, new and old. The number of adultery divorce petitions filed in Britain doubled each year after 1942. The disruption of family life also caused an epidemic of juvenile delinquency in Germany, Britain, and America.[160]

---

[158] Rupp 1978, owed 15, restored 17, 46–49, 118, 96–99, 147, middle 107, 105–8; Koonz 1987, nature 91, 399, xxv, xxiii, 389, 392; Seifert 1994, recreation 64.
[159] Rupp 1978, 75–79, 10.
[160] Costello 1985, couples 192–94, broke 199, delinquency 205.

The war thus widened women's opportunities and yet reflected "the persistence of sexist values and discriminatory practices in the economy, the family, and the society in general." "Because most American women remained homemakers during the war, Rosie was not the typical wartime woman." In 1945, recruitment themes in US advertising were dropped, and women in ads (except servicewomen) were shown in traditional female roles. A Monsanto ad promised a day when "the good new things of peacetime will become important to Rosie the Housewife." Meanwhile a *Life* editorial in January 1945 denounced women as slackers whose thin contributions to the war had let the country down.[161]

Although women's participation in the US labor force increased from the prewar to postwar periods, the temporary influx during the war "had no permanent impact on the [upward] trend" of the 1890–1960 period (see Figure 6.12). The entire transformation of women's image and role during wartime was "meant by the government, and understood by the public, to be temporary."[162]

When World War II ended, American and British women war workers were laid off, based on a "last in, first out" principle. As one Boilermakers union official in Puget Sound wrote: "Our hats are off to the women. Yours is a job well done. We have never heard you complain, after going home from your eight-hour shift in the shipyards, about doing your household work and raising your family...Now we are faced with cutbacks in shipbuilding, and you are being taken off the production team...Let the lowly male species do the work...and you see that he provides the American standard of living to which you are entitled." New child-development theories (including Dr. Spock) also "placed women solely and securely in a domestic setting."[163]

The pattern after World War II is not atypical. After wars end, gender constrictions return. "Campaigns celebrating 'patriotic motherhood'...occur most commonly during the *'post-war era'*" in various countries and times, when "society is being reorganised to relieve whatever tensions developed" during wartime. A postwar era is "a time to demobilise many women recruited into 'men's jobs' during the war. It is a time when any relaxation of sexual mores permitted for the sake of male soldiers' 'morale' is likely to be reversed."[164]

Post-World War I literature in particular returned often to the theme of "the wounded, symbolically if not literally emasculated man who

---

[161] Anderson 1981, sexist 3, 8, homemakers 10; Honey 1995, dropped 97, good 98; Rupp 1978, slackers 160.

[162] Rupp 1978, 177–79, 182–88, temporary 138; Anderson 1981, 8.

[163] Costello 1985, last 191; Anderson 1981, hats 168, setting 176, 178.

[164] Enloe 1983, campaigns–reversed 75–76; Enloe 1993, 252–61.

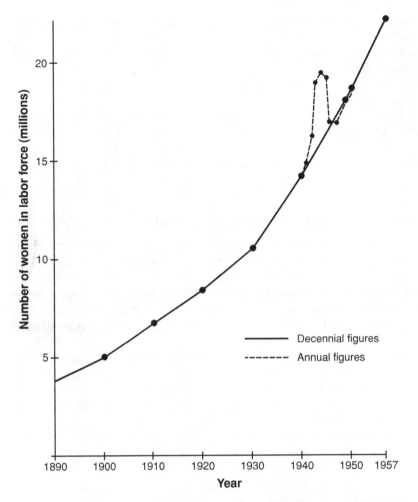

Figure 6.12 US female labor force, 1890–1957. [From Leila J. Rupp, *Mobilizing Women for War: German and American Propaganda, 1939–1945*, p. 178. © 1978 Princeton University Press. Reprinted by permission of Princeton University Press.]

returns from the war to confront women empowered, set free by the social dislocations wrought by the Great War. Male rage against the war turns against the female who apparently reaps its benefits." "[A]s young men became ... increasingly mired in the muck and blood of No Man's Land, women seemed to become ... ever more powerful. As nurses, as mistresses, as munitions workers, bus drivers ... these formerly subservient creatures began to loom malevolently larger." Some scholars also see in "role reversals . . . a release of female libidinal energies, as well as a liberation of female anger, which men usually found anxiety-inducing and women often found exhilarating." (But I doubt nurses ever found it a sexual turn-on to "watch their male patients, one-time oppressors," die; see pp. 312–16).[165]

In sum, women's labor of all kinds is indispensable to military success. Thus, women may be diverted from combat in part because their cheap labor is best used elsewhere. This does not go very far as an explanation of gendered war roles, however. The main connection here seems to be that war sharpens gender disparities (reverse causality again).

Gender inequality and war-proneness cross-culturally

Exploiting women's labor may correlate, across cultures, with waging war, although the answer is clouded somewhat by the difficulty of measuring gender relations (i.e., the relative status of women and men in a society). In a sample of 93 preindustrial societies, status varies – for a given society – across dozens of possible variables in such realms as marriage and divorce, control of property, participation in gatherings, and the gender of gods and spirits.[166]

Gender relations overall range from blatant misogyny to near-equality. At one extreme, the Yanomamö kill each mother's female children until the mother bears her first male. This creates a shortage of women and produces high male possessiveness and abuse towards females. By contrast, the !Kung have been described as "nonexploitative . . . displaying a striking degree of equality." However, "!Kung men . . . do seem to have the upper hand," especially in social influence and authority. For example, in a culture that values meat, "women are prohibited from handling hunting equipment and from participating in the hunt, especially during menstruation." The "male monopoly of the lethal hunting weapons" gives men a decisive advantage.[167]

The only constant is that however small or large the inequality, it always favors men overall. No case of "true matriarchy" has been authenticated. "[I]n the overwhelming majority of societies, women have a lower status than men . . . and their activities are less highly valued." Although occupations defined as "men's" vary from culture to culture, those occupations for a particular culture are considered important. Across most known

---

[165] Kinney 1991, wounded 41; Gilbert 1987, larger 200, role 212, watch 212.
[166] Whyte 1978, 170–72, 140, 153.
[167] Shostak 1981, degree 237, hunt 243–44, 311–13; Lee 1979, monopoly 388; Kessler 1976, 12–18; Stockel 1991, 10.

cultures, "men are the warriors, hunters, and [makers of] weaponry and tools." Cooking and preparation of vegetable foods come close to being all-female domains across cultures. Women are more likely to have economic and political power or authority in simpler societies than in more technologically complex ones.[168]

Beyond these problems of "women's status," confusion arises from the fact that different studies assume different directions of causality. Some treat women's status as the dependent variable (with war among the independent variables), while others treat war as the dependent variable and include gender relations among independent variables. Neither approach actually tests the direction of causality between war-proneness and gender equity (which most likely is bidirectional). Also, the correlation of war with women's status is rather weak, with much variability. For example, knowing that a particular society is especially warlike would not reliably tell us whether women in that society have especially low status (like the Sambia) or relatively high status (like Dahomey) in terms of such elements as property, divorce, political power, labor, violence, and so forth.

Correlation with war   Nonetheless, overall, women's low status correlates somewhat with frequent warfare. A review of a dozen cross-cultural anthropology studies finds that societies with frequent war tend to have wife beating (along with warlike sports, beliefs in malevolent magic, severe criminal punishments, and feuding).[169]

Peggy Reeves Sanday examines female power and male dominance in 150 cultures worldwide. The status of women and their power relative to men vary greatly across cultures. Societies have organized gender relations "in an almost infinite variety of ways." A cross-cultural study of female status, measured on several dimensions, shows that women are subordinate both in societies where they make a low contribution to subsistence and in societies where they make a high contribution. War is modestly correlated with gender inequality: gender relations are very unequal in 33 percent of the societies with "endemic or chronic" war, but in only 17 percent of the others. (Over two-thirds of the societies had endemic war.)[170]

In one study, in cultures with frequent warfare, women's status tends to be lower in terms of joint participation with men but higher in terms of domestic authority and perhaps also (though not with statistical

---

[168] Harris 1974, true 86; Shostak 1981, valued 237; Sanday 1981, tools 77, 128–30, 170.
[169] Ember and Ember 1997.
[170] Sanday 1981, infinite 1, 6–7, endemic 174, 84, 80–81, 35, 135–62; Schlegel 1977, 12–13; Segal 1990, 98; Hrdy 1981, 73.

significance) ritualized female solidarity and value placed on women's lives. Thus, in war-prone societies overall, women if anything have somewhat higher status and are less likely, among other things, to suffer abuse from their husbands. War, however, has only a minor effect on the status of women cross-culturally, in this study.[171]

Other authors found, however, in a sample of 33 gathering-hunting societies, that warfare decreases women's status, although this connection may change in some societies where men are away for extended periods. The authors consider 13 indicators of women's status in coding their sample of societies. They ignore indicators relating to ritual status, which they find to vary independently, and concentrate on indicators of domestic and political status which more often vary together. (Their status variable is a single, ordinal three-point scale in which women are ranked as relatively high on neither, one, or both of the dimensions of domestic and political status.)[172]

A statistical analysis of 90 "small scale, preindustrial societies" connects war frequency with such gender-related measures as the strength of cross-cutting ties between communities within a society (e.g. marriage, trading), the presence of male kin "interest groups" (patrilineality), socioeconomic complexity, harsh child socialization practices, affectionate socialization practices, and "male gender identity conflict" (see p. 240). The study finds that, despite the tremendous diversity in both war practices and gender roles, some differences are usually found between more warlike and more peaceful societies. War seems to be more likely in societies with high gender inequality, harsh child-rearing practices, and the absence of fathers from child-rearing. These characteristics all relate to gender, but only the first bears on gender equality itself.[173]

Low female decision involvement is correlated, in a sample of 82 societies, with low internal conflict (between same-language communities), high external war (with other societies), harsh child socialization, and strong fraternal interest groups. Measures of women's organizations and positions also correlate with external war (and with non-African location, low socioeconomic complexity, and high intercommunity marriage).

Thus, war-proneness correlates somewhat with gender inequality cross-culturally, but only modestly and unevenly. Most often, societies

---

[171] Whyte 1978, 129–31, 156–57, 171.
[172] Hayden *et al.* 1986, 458, 453.
[173] Ross 1990, 55–56, 60; Ross 1986, 848–50; Ross 1993a, 98–102, 118, 126, 148; Fabbro 1978, 7.

with frequent war also have very unequal gender relations – as with the Sambia, Yanomamö, and Mundurucú. At the other extreme, the least war-prone societies – such as the Semai, the Mbuti, Vanatinai islanders, and various Eskimos – more often have relatively egalitarian gender relations (with no known cases of actual full gender equality, however). Arrayed between these two poles are today's states, with perhaps Sweden, the Netherlands and Costa Rica towards the peaceful-egalitarian end, the United States and others somewhere in the middle, and Afghanistan at the warlike-inegalitarian end.

This correlation may help explain the rarity of women in combat. A society would have to be an outlier from the general pattern to have women warriors, because relatively peaceful societies would not need them and highly sexist societies would not tolerate them. The Dahomey kingdom may qualify as a society where women enjoyed a relatively high political status (albeit a very unequal life for most women), yet war was extremely frequent. The Apache bands show some similarities (see pp. 113–14), as do the Iron Age steppes societies (see pp. 13–14). Despite this possible insight, however, the cross-cultural studies of gender inequality seem too inconclusive to explain gendered war roles well. Such correlations as are found more plausibly derive from war's effect on gender relations than the reverse.

Are women or men the main victims of war?

In recent years, some writers argue that civilians, especially women and children, are the main victims of war: "innocents are almost never protected in war, and usually more civilians are killed than combatants. (Wouldn't *you* prefer to shoot at someone who can't shoot back?)" The United Nations Development Program (UNDP) states, with no cited source, that "[c]ivilian fatalities have climbed from 5% of war-related deaths at the turn of the century to more than 90% in the wars of the 1990s." As a result of new weapons and patterns of conflict, "many of the casualties are women and children." A different estimate is that "75 percent of those killed in war are civilians," a figure that "has risen steadily from around 10–15 percent at the beginning of the century." Ratios over 75 percent (civilian to total deaths) have been reported in Angola and Mozambique (particularly destructive civil wars). Clearly war "brings harsh pressures to bear upon women," especially in poor regions and among war refugees. Survivor populations have suffered PTSD at rates of 14–50 percent in various studies in both third world and Western cases. All these undocumented estimates of civilian casualties are, however, "difficult, if not impossible, to substantiate," according to the International Committee of the Red Cross (ICRC).[174]

More reliable data, although sparse, suggest a lower ratio of civilian to military deaths. Of 17,000 people treated by the ICRC for weapons injuries since 1991, only 35 percent were women, children under 16, and men over 50 (although those groups together make up a large majority of the population). A Red Cross study in northwestern Cambodia in 1994–95 found civilians suffered 51 percent of all weapons injuries including from mines and accidents (civilians are, again, a large majority of the population). Another Red Cross study of more than 4,000 deaths in the Croatia war found that civilians were "at most" 64 percent. Presumably, in conventional interstate wars such as between Ethiopia and Eritrea recently, where large armies used heavy weapons across fixed lines on a sparsely populated battlefield, civilian casualties were a much lower percentage. The Sandinista government that took power in Nicaragua in 1979 determined (in awarding compensation to victims' families) that fatalities in the revolution had been 93 percent male. And by one estimate, 70 percent of those killed or "disappeared" in Argentina's "Dirty War" were males as well.[175]

Stephen Wicks argues that men are the main victims of war. Although women are "not immune to the horrors of war . . . far more men have died, often protecting women . . . Although women die in wars, it is usually after many men have perished attempting to keep them out of harm's way." Reportedly, in Belgium and France in 1944, "[i]f a village had been or was the scene of a battle, its civilian population was usually gone." As I have noted, mass executions of men have continued in recent years.[176]

A recent comprehensive worldwide epidemiology survey provided fatality estimates for 1990 that appear much more reliable than any of the figures just mentioned (see Table 6.1). Males were 58 percent of fatalities from war, and 78 percent of other violent deaths. Projections of 650,000 deaths in the year 2000 show a similar gender ratio, as do data on all injuries (not just deaths) from violence. Among 15- to 44-year-olds, war accounted for 5 percent of male deaths and 4 percent of female deaths. These data do not support the idea that women are the main victims of either war or "male violence," but neither do they show women as exempt from those sources of injury and death.

---

[174] Stiehm 1996b, back 285; UN Development Program 1998, 35; Klare 1999, 19; Michael Klare, personal communication 2000; Nordstrom 1998, 80, 85; Bennett, Bexley, and Warnock 1995, risen 1; Clemens and Singer 2000, Mozambique 57; Summerfield 1997, harsh 149, rates 150; ICRC 1999.

[175] ICRC 1999, 4, Cambodia 11, Croatia 4; Mollica 2000; Jones 1996, Nicaragua–Argentina 427.

[176] Wicks 1996, 40–42; Ambrose 1997, gone 235.

Table 6.1 *Fatalities from war and other violence,*
by age and gender, 1990

	From war		From other violence	
Age	*Males*	*Females*	*Males*	*Females*
0–14 years	80,000	70,000	41,000	38,000
15–44	185,000	121,000	325,000	56,000
45 +	25,000	20,000	73,000	29,000
Total	291,000	211,000	439,000	124,000

Source: Murray and Lopez 1996b, Table 244i, Table 238i;
Murray and Lopez 1996a, 182, 163.

Quincy Wright finds that before World War II, civilian losses *directly* from war (excluding epidemics) were much less than service losses, and had been decreasing since the Thirty Years War. However, *epidemics* exacerbated by wartime conditions have caused civilian deaths even more numerous than military deaths. Wright estimates indirect deaths due to war at three times direct deaths in twentieth-century Europe, and even larger elsewhere and earlier. He concludes that "[p]robably at least 10 per cent of deaths in modern civilization can be attributed directly or indirectly to war."[177]

The problem with efforts to quantify and compare civilian with military deaths is that military ones occur directly and within an organized group, whereas most civilian deaths occur indirectly and out of view. The indirect effects of war are important and wide ranging, but hard to quantify. The 1918 influenza epidemic that killed 20 million people worldwide certainly resulted in large part from World War I. The worldwide AIDS epidemic arguably would not have started without warfare in East Africa. On the other hand, penicillin was developed under the pressure of war, as were other technological innovations that saved lives. Should we begin a ledger sheet of lives lost and saved by war? Do we count as saved by World War II those lives that would have been lost to fascism if the allies had not fought Nazi Germany and Japan? Do we count as lost to war those lives of malnourished children around the world who could in theory have been fed with resources that instead sustained the Cold War arms race? Obviously all such counterfactual calculations are problematical.

We should also problematize the category "women and children," which includes boys (even teenaged boys) in a presumed-female concept that consists of well over half the population. For example, one

[177] Wright 1942, 244–46.

author states that "70 to 80 percent of the world's refugees are women and children," which makes it sound as though adult men were off fighting. However, she then adds that half of the refugees are children. Thus, adult women must make up 20 to 30 percent of the total, and the remaining 20 to 30 percent of refugees must be adult men, if these figures are correct. Another author claims that nearly 80 percent of 46 million war refugees worldwide in 1992 were "women and girls." This would imply that men were elsewhere as she claims – "[r]efugee women often serve as their children's sole caretakers." However, counting boys, these numbers could hardly add up even if there were no adult males in the refugee population at all. A similar problem occurs in comparing military with civilian casualties, since the frequent equation of "civilian" with "women" is often empirically untrue. (The related term, "battle-age men," is also problematical since it implies that all men are fighters.)[178]

Whatever the mix of male and female victims in various wars, one thing is clear. Neither men nor women benefit from war at the expense of the other gender. Women do not get a good deal, on balance, when men bear the burden of protecting them, nor do men get a good deal when they run around playing war while women bear the costs. Rather, *both genders lose in war*, although they lose in somewhat different ways.

CONCLUSION

Of the explanations explored in this chapter, Hypothesis 6B finds strongest empirical support because enemies so often are constructed as feminine (using gender to encode domination). Explanations based on sexuality (Hypothesis 6A) are less compelling, because the shifting patterns of sexuality in wartime more likely result from a general disruption of social norms in wartime rather than any specific role of sexuality in triggering aggression. Explanations based on exploiting women's labor (Hypothesis 6C) seem to add only modestly to understanding gendered war roles, because the main regularity – intensified exploitation of women in wartime – does not show why women would have to be so strictly segregated away from combat forces. Hypotheses 5 and 6 taken together provide a reasonably strong explanation for how cultures build on basic – but indeterminate – biological gender propensities in constructing nearly universal gender roles in war.

[178] Enloe 1993, category 166; Nordstrom 1998, 85; Turpin 1998, 4; Bennett, Bexley, and Warnock 1995, 1; battle: Jones 2000, 186.

7   Reflections: the mutuality
of gender and war

This chapter summarizes the empirical evidence from chapters 2–6 regarding the gendering of war, and then briefly speculates on the implications for understanding both war and gender. Several overarching themes emerge from the interdisciplinary evidence. (1) Gender is about men as much as women, especially when it comes to war. (2) War is an extremely complex system in which state-level interactions depend on dynamics at lower levels of analysis, including gender. (3) War is a pervasive potential in the human experience that casts a shadow on everyday life – especially on gender roles – in profound ways. To think into the future beyond the war system requires breaking out of psychological denial regarding the traumatic effects of war on human society. Confronting war in this way may, in turn, reshape gendered relationships.

Sifting the explanations of gendered war roles

Table 7.1 shows the overall level of support for each hypothesis in light of the array of empirical materials reviewed in the preceding chapters. For starters, any explanation of gendered war roles that rests on women's categorical lack of ability to perform in combat must be discarded, given the historical record in chapter 2. Women *can* make good soldiers individually and in both mixed and all-female groups. They can also make excellent commanders of soldiers, and men can follow their leadership in war. These are very strong "possibility proofs," which rule out a whole set of potential explanations based on supposedly insuperable or constitutional barriers to women's effectiveness in combat.

Of the hypotheses engaging biology most directly, two or three find relatively strong empirical support. First (3C), real gender differences exist in average size and strength (after puberty, driven by testosterone), although the overlap of bell curves leaves quite a few large, strong women. Second (4D), a tendency towards childhood gender segregation – marked by boys' rougher group play – works against the later integration of capable women into warfighting groups. This segregation is found widely

Table 7.1 *Status of hypotheses in light of evidence*

The consistency of gender roles in war is explained by:

Hypothesis	Supported?	Comments
1. Gender roles *not* consistent	No	No cases of gender-neutral armed forces; extremely few women fighters overall.
2A–D. Not women's performance	Yes	Those women who have fought under various circumstances performed well.
3A. Genetics	No	Same genetic code, though some parts expressed differentially by testosterone.
3B. Testosterone levels	Slightly	Testosterone does not cause aggression but responds to changes in social status (4B).
3C. Size and strength	Mostly	Genders differ on average but a sizable minority of women should qualify for war.
3D. Brains and cognition	Slightly	Genders differ on spatial and verbal cognitive scores, but genders' curves mostly overlap.
3E. Female sex hormones	No	Maternal behaviors limited to nursing period and include maternal aggression.

4A. Male bonding	No	Social bonding varies among primates; human bonding not inherently gendered.
4B. Ability to work in hierarchies	Slightly	Female hierarchies common but some gender differences; testosterone may play role (3B).
4C. In-/out-group psychology	No	Few gender differences regarding in-group loyalty and out-group hostility.
4D. Childhood gender segregation	Mostly	Segregation common but genders mix as children and adults in many non-war settings.
5A. Test of manhood	Yes	Males toughened for war in most cultures, emotionally shut down to endure trauma.
5B. Feminine reinforcement	Mostly	Women support wars psychologically, including by affirming soldiers' masculinity.
5C. Women's peace activism	No	Only some women oppose wars; would not stop other women from fighting.
6A. Male sexuality and aggression	Slightly	Wartime sex explained by social disruption; combat not sexual for most men.
6B. Feminization of enemies	Mostly	Very common construction cross-culturally; expressed in gendered insults and war rape.
6C. Exploitation of women's labor	Slightly	War intensifies exploitation but this need not stop some women from fighting.

across cultures and perhaps has a biological component, but is far from absolute and may be an effect as much as a cause of gendered war roles. Third (3D), but more weakly and subtly, spatial skills and hierarchical social relations show average gender differences – the differences in hierarchies perhaps connected with the effects of changing social rank on men's testosterone levels (3B). Overall, the main innate average gender differences seem to be in roughness of play before adolescence and size thereafter. The genders overlap somewhat even in these areas. These tendencies are too weak to explain women's nearly universal exclusion from combat.

Of the hypotheses engaging mainly cultural explanations, three receive most support. First, and most strongly (5A), the toughening up of boys is found robustly across cultures, and by linking bravery and discipline in war to manhood – with shame as enforcement – many cultures use gender to motivate participation in combat. Second (5B), women actively reinforce – in various feminine war roles such as mothers, lovers, and nurses – men's tough, brave masculinity. Third (6B), male soldiers use gender to encode domination, feminizing enemies. Connected with this coding, but more elusive empirically, are the possible heightened (or just shaken up) sexuality of male soldiers, and the more intense exploitation of women's labor in wartime. These explanations from chapters 5 and 6 seem to contribute, in a mutually reinforcing way, to the process of turning biological tendencies into historical imperatives – transforming overlapping distributions into non-overlapping gender categories in war.

I would, then, summarize the best explanations of gendered war roles thus:

- small, innate biological gender differences in average size, strength, and roughness of play;
- cultural molding of tough, brave men, who feminize their enemies to encode domination.

Together these solve the puzzle of near-universally gendered war roles, although neither alone would do so.

Falsification   Perhaps as interesting, and often more compelling empirically than the hypotheses that help explain gendered war roles, are the hypotheses that receive little or no empirical support. If Karl Popper was right that knowledge cumulation occurs with the empirical refutation of bold conjectures, then some progress may be found here.

Six cherished myths go down in flames:[1]

1. Claims about *matriarchies* – that matriarchal Amazons once existed and (contradictorily) that matriarchies are (or were) true peaceful societies – do not hold up. No solid empirical evidence points to Amazons, matriarchies, or (with very rare exceptions) peaceful societies.
2. The idea of a separate *genetic code* for men – the genes for war on the Y chromosome – is wrong.
3. The widely held notion that *testosterone* levels cause aggression has weak empirical support. The idea that their higher testosterone levels cause boys to be more aggressive than girls in early childhood is wrong, because boys' and girls' testosterone levels are comparable at ages 1–7.
4. The claim that *female hormones* make women peaceful is not supported either.
5. *Male bonding* turns out to be generic bonding in an all-male setting, and is accessible to women in mixed-gender settings.
6. The evidence also contradicts the idea that most *women oppose wars* and thus choose not to participate in combat. Some women oppose wars (proportionally somewhat more than do men), but most women support wars.

Lessons for scholars of war and peace

The main lesson of this book for war scholars is a simple one: pay attention to gender. (And, of course, this does not mean "pay attention to women.") The heuristics for research proposed by feminist theorists in International Relations (see pp. 53–57) – including recent efforts to problematize masculinity – appear sound. Further research on the nexus of gender, war, and international relations can contribute to scholarship on war far beyond feminist circles. Especially promising is the potential synergy of feminism with traditional liberalism (still largely unrealized) in such research areas as the democratic peace, nationalism, ethnic conflict, international norms, interdependence, nongovernmental organizations, and global telecommunications. (These are all areas of international relations where realist explanations based on state-level rationality are especially inadequate.)[2]

Multiple levels of analysis   Integrating gender in our understanding of war requires using multiple levels of analysis. Like the angels

[1] Popper 1959.
[2] Problematize: Zalewski and Parpart eds. 1998; Zalewski 1998, 1; Ferguson 1993.

on Jacob's ladder, we must carry evidence up and down continually. The different levels of analysis have not been well integrated in scholarship on war, partly because different academic disciplines study them. These disciplinary borders, like international borders, mark shifts in language and culture. Furthermore, levels of analysis are not limited to the range of individuals, states, and interstate systems (as in political science) but extend downward to biochemistry and upward to worldwide trends. As Figure 3.1 showed, causality runs in both directions from ecosystems down to genes and back. The war system cuts across these levels, though political science generally occupies only a layer in the middle.

It has become conventional wisdom in international relations theory, following Kenneth Waltz, that "reductionism" – explanation from lower levels of analysis – is bad. Waltz claims that biologists also oppose reductionism, and he quotes a biologist from 1925 in support of this idea. However, the revolution in biology since the 1950s has demonstrated just the opposite – the spectacular success of reductionism (explaining organisms based on biochemistry generally and DNA specifically). In studying war, I propose, political scientists could learn from biologists. To understand or change the war system we need to understand its constituent elements at lower levels of analysis in a sophisticated way. The cook knows salt, the composer strings, and the gardener soil; the war scholar should know gender.[3]

The interstate system   Sometimes, similar processes recur on different levels of analysis – a kind of fractal effect, so to speak. For example, the physics of spinning masses recurs from subatomic particles through galaxies. The complex feedback loops that keep an organism in balance resemble those that keep an ecosystem in balance. We all think of states as people, and even realist scholars of war extend insights about individual rationality to the state level.

Similarly, it appears that the interstate system reproduces at the level of large groups the biologically based scripts and dynamics found at the level of small groups. The most important principles in the operation of the interstate system – such as hegemony, alliance formation, diplomacy, and reciprocity – draw directly on the small-group dynamics discussed in chapter 4.

What the interstate system does in this way is to transform the politics of very large groups – prone to uncontrolled violence, as in hunting – into the controlled violence of within-group relations based on hierarchies and norms. The individual leaders of states – of great powers in

[3] Waltz 1979, 19.

particular – become the members of a small group of such leaders, in which individuals are well known to each other. The dehumanized "other" group becomes humanized in this process, gaining a face. (In the early modern European system, royal marriages further enhanced this intimacy.)

Thus, the interstate system overlays the dynamics of up–down hierarchies (within-group relations) on the dynamics of in- and out-group relations. Heads of state (and now, in some cases, heads of government) epitomize their states to each other and the world. Citizens participate in the small-group dynamics of interstate relations by experiencing vicariously the actions and statements of their leaders, who are their link to the interstate system.

The interstate system as small-group dynamics also helps explain the enormous psychological impact of behaviors taken straight out of the primate world. The 1993 Arafat–Rabin handshake, for example, was a purely symbolic gesture with no material effect, yet it had a huge impact because the leaders – now operating as individuals *within* a group – enacted the elemental signal of reconciliation among humans, bonobos, and chimpanzees: the outstretched hand (see Figure 4.4, p. 206). The dominance hierarchy was affirmed, as Arafat reached out to Rabin under the paternal gaze of the alpha male (Clinton). The handshake certified acceptance of Palestine as a "person" in the small group represented by the interstate system – and appears to have been a key watershed on the path to Palestinian statehood.

Overall, the international hierarchy resembles a dominance system, fluid international alliances resemble chimpanzee politics, and the tit-for-tat reciprocity studied by international relations researchers resembles the reciprocal behaviors that enable cooperation in small face-to-face groups. This multilevel perspective suggests attention in international relations scholarship to power transition theory, which attributes very large wars to challenges for position in the status hierarchy, especially when a rising power is surpassing (or threatening to surpass) the most powerful state (for example, Germany's rise in the nineteenth century).[4]

This overlaying of intragroup structure on intergroup relations comes at a price. The dominance system, while limiting violence, also sanctions and regularizes it. The European-based modern state system has remained stable but at the cost of recurrent wars. The intragroup dynamics of threats and displays, seldom resulting in serious injury, indeed characterizes the world of diplomats. Their actions, however, set in motion armies that answer to large-group rules – conquest, dehumanization,

---

[4] Organski 1958; Gilpin 1988; Kugler and Lemke eds. 1996.

and lethal violence. Thus the experience of war for soldiers bears little resemblance to the experience of war for diplomats and political leaders.

If the interstate system works like a small group, then perhaps an extended-family model is as apt as a male-status-hierarchy one. Could the interstate system in this way act as a stepping-stone to a global human identity that transcends large-group differences? Eibl-Eibesfeldt writes: "Man has a sense of family, and is in a position by way of symbolic identification to regard humanity as a family" with "[t]he child as unifying symbol." Darwin wrote in 1859 that as "tribes are united into bigger communities," an individual must extend "his sympathies to all men of all nations and races." Currently, global telecommunications are accelerating this process dramatically, with unknown ramifications for the war system.[5]

War as a cause of gender

The persistent strength of "reverse causality" from war to gender pervades this study. The war system influences the socialization of children into *all* their gender roles – a feedback loop that strengthens and stabilizes gendered war roles. War's influence shadows all of our lives. Betty Reardon writes: "Once the actuality or possibility of war becomes the context within which we live, men and women are forced into set roles." Gender serves as a medium or vector, as it were, for war's presence in our most intimate social settings.[6]

Unfortunately, the spot for war on the bookstore's gender shelf is nearly (though not quite) as empty as the spot for gender on the war shelf. For example, British feminist scholar Lynne Segal's book on men and masculinity bypasses war and the military, and treats "male violence" as meaning violence against women, keeping inter-male violence out of view. Mary Roth Walsh's recent edited volume, covering the spectrum of gender topics, also omits war. So do many other works on gender.[7]

Denial may best explain these omissions. Social conventions keep war silent in our everyday lives because it represents trauma. Psychologist Judith Herman emphasizes the gulf between war and daily life: "The war story is closely kept among men of a particular era, disconnected from the broader society that includes two sexes and many generations. Thus the fixation on the trauma – the sense of a moment frozen in time – may be perpetuated by social customs that foster the segregation of warriors from the rest of society." Historian John Keegan calls war "a world

---

[5] Eibl-Eibesfeldt 1979, child 230, races 229.
[6] Reardon 1985, 11; Cock 1991, x; Keen 1991, 37; Goldstein 1995.
[7] Segal 1990; Walsh ed. 1997.

apart" from politics and diplomacy, "a very ancient world, which exists in parallel with the everyday world but does not belong to it." (Jean Elshtain considers this separation a European bourgeois phenomenon, however.)[8]

The single main lesson of this book for those interested in gender is to pay attention to war. To end denial and face war's influence on gender is, I believe, an important step in changing both sexism and the war system.

In particular, I would shine a spotlight on the issue of toughening up boys (see pp. 287–301). In raising boys into men, we can ask ourselves, day in and day out – as fathers, mothers, teachers, and other care-givers – whether we are producing warriors, and if so at what cost to the boy. We may be surprised to see how high the cost is, even if the boy never goes on to fight a war. One big problem with simplistic popular debates about "boys will be boys" is that they lump together a set of complex influences that should be disentangled. Because some gender differences have biological foundations does not mean that all do. We should sort out the aspects of boyhood that have a biological basis – aspects that could be useful in war but need not lead in that direction – from those that cultures impose on boys specifically to prepare them for violence.

Biologically based aspects of boyhood – before puberty – include a propensity for rough-and-tumble play (rambunctiousness and mock aggression), keen attention to competitive status hierarchies, slightly heightened spatial abilities, and slightly reduced verbal and perhaps interpersonal abilities. If you combine these with gendered training for violence against outsiders, you get war. If, however, you combine them with training to adhere to rules, you get sports. Boys' sports may offer a productive point of engagement to change the war system. One can potentially respect and value the abilities and propensities that tend to come easily to boys, without channeling them towards violence and ultimately war through the toughening-up method.

Dilemmas of social change

I began this book hoping to contribute in some way to a deeper understanding of war – an understanding that would improve the chances of someday achieving real peace, by deleting war from our human repertoire. In following the thread of gender running through war, I found the

---

[8] Herman 1992, story 67; Keegan 1993, xvi; Elshtain 1987, 181; Griffin 1992, 16, 32, 38.

deeper understanding I had hoped for – a multidisciplinary and multilevel engagement with the subject. Yet I became somewhat more pessimistic about how quickly or easily war may end. The war system emerges, from the evidence in this book, as relatively ubiquitous and robust. Efforts to change this system must overcome several dilemmas mentioned in this book.

First, peace activists face a dilemma in thinking about causes of war and working for peace. Many peace scholars and activists support the approach, "if you want peace, work for justice." Then, if one believes that sexism contributes to war, one can work for gender justice specifically (perhaps among others) in order to pursue peace. This approach brings strategic allies to the peace movement (women, labor, minorities), but rests on the assumption that injustices cause war. The evidence in this book suggests that causality runs at least as strongly the other way. War is not a product of capitalism, imperialism, gender, innate aggression, or any other single cause, although all of these influence wars' outbreaks and outcomes. Rather, war has in part fueled and sustained these and other injustices.[9]

So, "if you want peace, work for peace." Indeed, if you want justice (gender and others), work for peace. Causality does not run just upward through the levels of analysis, from types of individuals, societies, and governments up to war. It runs downward too. Enloe suggests that changes in attitudes towards war and the military may be the most important way to "reverse women's oppression." The dilemma is that peace work focused on justice brings to the peace movement energy, allies, and moral grounding, yet, in light of this book's evidence, the emphasis on injustice as the main cause of war seems to be empirically inadequate.[10]

Second, women face a dilemma in trying to change the war system (including its sexism). If they join the military and succeed as soldiers – probably the single most gender-dislocating intervention now underway in the gender–war nexus – they contribute to the war system, which reinforces gender roles. As Enloe warns, "gaining equal opportunity for those women ... [used by] the military only *perpetuates* the notion that the military is so central to the entire social order that ... women ... [need it] to fulfil their hopes and aspirations." Women soldiers can bring about only limited changes in the military itself while they remain a small minority of the total force, which they are likely to do well into the future. The success that women combatants have had when tested also suggests that integrating women does not fundamentally alter the military's ability to

[9] Forsberg 1997b.
[10] Enloe 1983, 17.

wage war. If, however, women become peace demonstrators, they also have limited impact on the war system because their actions may feminize peace and thus reinforce militarized masculinity. Finally, if women just try to be good mothers and raise their sons and daughters successfully within their society's norms, they end up mindlessly reproducing gendered war roles in a new generation.[11]

Parents of boys face a third dilemma. If we socialize boys into "masculinity" as understood in our culture, we turn them into warriors and damage their emotional capabilities. However, if we encourage traits and preferences that are considered "feminine" we put boys at risk of being shamed by peers as "sissies" – even becoming social outcasts and scapegoats. Perhaps the "boy movement" will reach some critical mass sufficient to change peer culture and develop a space for alternative (less war-driven) gender identities to develop. However, whole societies would still face an additional dilemma in raising boys: if they raise boys who are not warriors, they could someday be overrun by other societies that keep raising warriors. Again, gender change may depend in part on change in the war system.

Fathers play a problematical part in perpetuating gendered war roles. When fathers are present, they enforce gender norms on boys more strongly than mothers do (and more than fathers do on girls). The best hope for boys' *gender* change, then, might be to get the fathers out of the picture. However, fathers' involvement correlates with other positive outcomes for children (self-esteem, academic success, etc.). The answer must be for fathers to engage more with their sons, but to suggest alternative masculine themes not oriented to war. Movement in this direction has been slow.

In the end, none of us knows the correct direction or doctrine that will end war, equalize gender, or unlink war from gender. One lesson of this book is that the gender–war connection is very complex and that nobody can claim to understand it well or fit it into a simplistic formula. Furthermore, notwithstanding important progress to date, real peace and real gender equity both remain generations away at best.

The good news, nonetheless, is that in a feedback system with multiple causality, leverage at various points affects the whole system. Furthermore, momentum in a dynamic system can be self-sustaining, and recent decades have seen strong momentum, overall, towards both peace and gender equity. The war system is not set in stone, nor driven by any simple formula, but is alive, complex, and changeable. Complex systems hold many possibilities, as biology demonstrates. We can celebrate

[11] Enloe 1983, 17.

this diversity – our birthright as human beings and primates – because it offers many possibilities to choose from. Ultimately, in little ways, we all participate in the war system and we all shape its evolution. To quote an old saying, it is not our duty to finish the work, but neither are we free to neglect it.[12]

[12] Rabbi Tarfon; see Pirké Avot, 2:21.

References

Adam, Barry D. 1994. "Anatomy of a Panic: State Voyeurism, Gender Politics, and the Cult of Americanism." In Scott and Stanley eds.: 103–20.

Adams, Carol J. 1996. "Bringing Peace Home: A Feminist Philosophical Perspective on the Abuse of Women, Children, and Pet Animals." In Warren and Cady eds.: 68–87.

Adams, David B. 1983. "Why There Are So Few Women Warriors." *Behavior Science Research* 18, 3 (Fall): 196–212.

Adams, Gerald R., Raymond Montemayor, and Thomas P. Gullotta, eds. 1989. *Biology of Adolescent Behavior and Development*. Newbury Park, CA: Sage.

Adams, Judith Porter. 1991. *Peacework: Oral Histories of Women Peace Activists*. Boston: Twayne.

Addams, Jane. 1922. *Peace and Bread in Time of War*. New York: Macmillan.

Addis, Elisabetta, Valeria E. Russo, and Lorenza Sebesta, eds. 1994. *Women Soldiers: Images and Realities*. New York: St. Martin's.

Adorno, T. W., Else Frenkel-Brunswik, and Daniel J. Levinson. 1950. *The Authoritarian Personality*. New York: Harper.

Agence France-Presse. 2000. "NATO Forces Spur Kosovo Prostitution Boom." Pristina: AFP, January 5.

Aguilar-San Juan, Delia. 1982. "Feminism and the National Liberation Struggle in the Philippines." *Women's Studies International Forum* 5, 3/4: 253–61.

Ahmad, Yvette and Peter K. Smith. 1994. "Bullying in Schools and the Issue of Sex Differences." In Archer ed.: 70–86.

Ajayi, J., F. Ade, and Robert Smith. 1971. *Yoruba Warfare in the Nineteenth Century*. 2nd edition. Cambridge: Cambridge University Press.

Albert, David. 1982. "Chronology." In McAllister ed.: 416–18.

Albright, Madeleine K. 1997. "Message from the Secretary of State." In Betty Debnam, ed. *The Mini Page* [newspaper column for children]. Universal Press Syndicate, March 16: 4.

Alcoff, Linda. 1988. "Cultural Feminism versus Post-Structuralism: The Identity Crisis in Feminist Theory." *Signs: Journal of Women in Culture and Society* 13, 3: 405–36.

Alcorta, Candace Storey. 1982. "Paternal Behavior and Group Competition." *Behavior Science Research* 17: 3–23.

Alexandre, Laurien. 1989. "Genderizing International Studies: Revisioning Concepts and Curriculum." *International Studies Notes* 14, 1 (Winter): 5–8.

415

Alonso, Harriet Hyman. 1996. "Dissension in the Ranks." *Peace Review* 8, 3: 337–42.

Alonso, Harriet Hyman and John Whiteclay Chambers II, eds. 1995. "Peace and War Issues: Gender, Race, and Ethnicity in Historical Perspective." *Peace & Change* 20, 4 (October): 408–531.

Alpern, Stanley B. 1998. *Amazons of Black Sparta: The Women Warriors of Dahomey.* New York: New York University Press.

Ambrose, Stephen E. 1997. *Citizen Soldiers: The US Army from the Normandy Beaches to the Bulge to the Surrender of Germany June 7, 1944–May 7, 1945.* New York: Simon & Schuster.

American Psychiatric Association. 1994. *Diagnostic and Statistical Manual of Mental Disorders.* 4th edition. Washington, DC: American Psychiatric Association.

Andersen, Margaret L. 1993. *Thinking about Women: Sociological Perspectives on Sex and Gender.* 3rd edition. New York: Macmillan.

Andersen-Boers, Marion and Jan Van Der Meulen. 1994. "Homosexuality and the Armed Forces in the Netherlands." In Scott and Stanley eds.: 205–18.

Anderson, Anne. 1996. "The International Criminal Tribunal for the Former Yugoslavia: Some Psychological Issues Regarding Gender-Specific War Crimes." *International Conflict Resolution Centre Newsletter* 8 (February). University of Melbourne, Australia.

Anderson, Benedict. 1983. *Imagined Communities: Reflections on the Origin and Spread of Nationalism.* New York: Verso.

Anderson, Florence Mary. 1967. *Religious Cults Associated with the Amazons.* New York: AMS.

Anderson, Karen. 1981. *Wartime Women: Sex Roles, Family Relations, and the Status of Women during World War II.* Westport, CT: Greenwood.

Andrew, Barbara. 1996. "The Psychology of Tyranny: Wollstonecraft and Woolf on the Gendered Dimension of War." In Warren and Cady eds.: 118–32.

Andy, Orlando J. and Heinz Stephan. 1974. "Comparative Primate Neuroanatomy of Structures Relating to Aggressive Behavior." In Holloway ed.: 305–30.

Angell, Norman. 1914. *The Foundations of International Polity.* London: William Heinemann.

Angier, Natalie. 1992. "Hyenas' Hormone Flow Puts Females in Charge." *The New York Times,* September 1: C1, C10.

1994a. "Male Hormone Molds Women, Too, in Mind and Body." *The New York Times,* May 3: C1.

1994b. "Feminists and Darwin: Scientists Try Closing the Gap." *The New York Times,* June 21: C1, C13.

1994c. "Keys Emerge to Mystery of 'Junk' DNA." *The New York Times,* June 28: C1.

1994d. "Cotton-Top Tamarins: Cooperative, Pacifist and Close to Extinct." *The New York Times,* September 13: C1.

1995a. "Status Isn't Everything, at Least for Monkeys." *The New York Times,* April 18: C1.

1995b. "Scientists Mull Role of Empathy in Man and Beast." *The New York Times,* May 9: C1, C6.

1995c. "Does Testosterone Equal Aggression? Maybe Not." *The New York Times*, June 20: A1, C3.

1995d. "Gene Defect Tied to Violence in Male Mice." *The New York Times*, November 23: A16.

1997a. "Sexual Identity Not Pliable After All, Report Says." *The New York Times*, March 14: A1.

1997b. "Bonobo Society: Amicable, Amorous and Run by Females." *The New York Times*, April 22: C4.

1997c. "New Debate over Surgery on Genitals." *The New York Times*, May 13: C1, C6.

1998a. "Condemning Our Kids to Life on Mars or Venus." *The New York Times*, November 24: D5.

1998b. "Drugs, Sports, Body Image and G. I. Joe." *The New York Times*, December 22: D1.

Anonymous. 1994. "Olongapo: Exploited by the Army." In Davies ed.: 153–55.

Archer, John. 1991. "The Influence of Testosterone on Human Aggression." *British Journal of Psychology* 82: 1–28.

1994a. "Introduction: Male Violence in Perspective." In Archer ed.: 1–22.

1994b. "Violence between Men." In Archer ed.: 121–42.

1994c. "Testosterone and Aggression." *Journal of Offender Rehabilitation* 21, 3–4: 3–39.

ed. 1994. *Male Violence*. New York: Routledge.

1996. "Comparing Women and Men: What Is Being Compared and Why?" *American Psychologist*, 51, 2 (February): 153–54.

Archer, John and Kevin Browne. 1989. "Concepts and Approaches to the Study of Aggression." In Archer and Browne eds.: 3–24.

eds. 1989. *Human Aggression: Naturalistic Approaches*. New York: Routledge.

Archer, John and Barbara Lloyd. 1985. *Sex and Gender*. Revised North American edition. Cambridge: Cambridge University Press.

Ardrey, Robert. 1966. *The Territorial Imperative*. New York: Atheneum.

Aristophanes. 1987. *Lysistrata*. ed. Jeffrey Henderson. Oxford: Oxford University Press.

Aristotle. 1943. *Politics*. Trans. Benjamin Jowett. New York: The Modern Library.

Aron, Raymond. [1954] 1963. *The Century of Total War*. Boston: Beacon.

Ås, Berit. 1982. "A Materialistic View of Men's and Women's Attitudes towards War." *Women's Studies International Forum* 5, 3/4: 355–64.

Ashworth, Lucian M. and Larry A. Swatuk. 1998. "Masculinity and the Fear of Emasculation in International Relations Theory." In Zalewski and Parpart eds.: 73–92.

Aspy, Catherine L. 1999. "Should Women Go into Combat?" *Reader's Digest*. February.

Associated Press. 1997. "Drill Sergeant Is Found Guilty of Sex Charges." *The New York Times*, May 30: A16.

1998a. "Canada's Army Seeks Women for Combat." *The New York Times*, June 18: A18.

1998b. "Single Fathers with Children Are Up by 25%." *The New York Times*, December 11: A25.

Astrachan, Anthony. 1986. *How Men Feel: Their Response to Women's Demands for Equality and Power*. Garden City, NY: Anchor/Doubleday.

August, Eugene R. 1985. *Men's Studies: A Selected and Annotated Interdisciplinary Bibliography*. Littleton, CO: Libraries Unlimited.

Axelrod, Robert. 1984. *The Evolution of Cooperation*. New York: Basic.

Axelrod, Robert and William D. Hamilton. 1981. "The Evolution of Cooperation." *Science* 211: 1390–96.

Ayers, Pat. 1988. *Women at War: Liverpool Women 1939–45*. Birkenhead, UK: Liver.

Ayscough, Florence. 1937. *Chinese Women Yesterday and To-Day*. Boston: Houghton Mifflin.

Badrian, Alison and Noel Badrian. 1984. "Social Organization of *Pan paniscus* in the Lomako Forest, Zaire." In Susman ed.: 325–46.

Bagatell, Carrie J. and William J. Bremner. 1996. "Androgens in Men – Uses and Abuses." *The New England Journal of Medicine* 334, 11 (March): 707–14.

Bailey, Beth and David Farber. 1992. *The First Strange Place: The Alchemy of Race and Sex in World War II Hawaii*. New York: Free Press.

Baker, Rodney R., Shirley W. Menard, and Lois A. Johns. 1989. "The Military Nurse Experience in Vietnam: Stress and Impact." *Journal of Clinical Psychology* 45, 5: 736–44.

Baldwin, David A., ed. 1993. *Neorealism and Neoliberalism: The Contemporary Debate*. New York: Columbia University Press.

Ball, Eve, with Nora Henn and Lynda Sanchez. 1980. *Indeh: An Apache Odyssey*. Provo, Utah: Brigham Young University Press.

Ballard, Richard F. 1996. "Marching to the Same Drummer." *The Washington Post, Education Review*, July 28: 5.

Bandura, Albert. 1973. *Aggression: A Social Learning Analysis*. Englewood Cliffs, NJ: Prentice-Hall.

Banks, Terry and James M. Dabbs, Jr. 1996. "Salivary Testosterone and Cortisol in a Delinquent and Violent Urban Subculture." *The Journal of Social Psychology* 136, 1: 49–56.

Bannon, Lisa. 2000. "More Kids' Marketers Pitch Number of Single-Sex Products." *Wall Street Journal*, February 14: B1.

Barash, David P. 1977. *Sociobiology and Behavior*. New York: Elsevier.

1979. *The Whisperings Within*. New York: Harper & Row.

Barboza, David. 1998. "Video World Is Smitten by a Gun-Toting, Tomb-Raiding Sex Symbol." *The New York Times*, January 19: D3.

Barfield, Thomas J. 1994. "The Devil's Horsemen: Steppe Nomadic Warfare in Historical Perspective." In Reyna and Downs eds.: 157–84.

Barinaga, Marcia. 1991. "Is Homosexuality Biological?" *Science* 253 (August): 956–57.

Barker, Pat. 1991. *Regeneration*. New York: Dutton.

Baron, Robert A. and Deborah R. Richardson. 1994. *Human Aggression*. 2nd edition. New York: Plenum.

Barrett, S. A. 1964 "The Material Culture of the Klamath Lake and Modoc Indians of Northeastern California and Southern Oregon." *American Archeology and Ethnology* 5, 4: 239–58.

Barrett, William E. 1938. *Woman on Horseback: The Biography of Francisco Lopez and Eliza Lynch*. New York: Frederick A. Stokes.

Barry, Dave. 1984. "Macho Diplomacy: Maybe US Foreign Policy Needs the Feminine Touch." *The Boston Globe*, May 30: 57.

Bartov, Omer. 1991. *Hitler's Army: Soldiers, Nazis, and War in the Third Reich.* Oxford: Oxford University Press.

Batson, C. Daniel. 1998. "Altruism and Prosocial Behavior." In Gilbert, Fiske, and Lindzey eds.: 282–316.

Baum, Michael J. 1992. "Neuroendocrinology of Sexual Behavior in the Male." In Becker, Breedlove, and Crews eds.: 97–130.

Bauman, Richard A. 1992. *Women and Politics in Ancient Rome.* New York: Routledge.

Bayard de Volo, Lorraine. 1998. "Drafting Motherhood: Maternal Imagery and Organizations in the United States and Nicaragua." In Lorentzen and Turpin eds.: 240–53.

Beachey, R. W. 1976. *The Slave Trade of Eastern Africa.* New York: Barnes & Noble.

Becker, Jill B. and S. Marc Breedlove. 1992. "Introduction to Behavioral Endocrinology." In Becker, Breedlove, and Crews eds.: 3–38.

Becker, Jill B., S. Marc Breedlove, and David Crews, eds. 1992. *Behavioral Endocrinology.* Cambridge, MA: MIT Press.

Beckman, Peter R. 1994. "Realism, Women and World Politics." In Beckman and D'Amico eds.: 15–28.

Beckman, Peter R. and Francine D'Amico, eds. 1994. *Women, Gender, and World Politics: Perspectives, Policies, and Prospects.* Westport, CT: Bergin & Garvey.

Beer, Francis. 1981. *Peace against War: The Ecology of International Violence.* San Francisco: Freeman.

Beer, Francis A. and Robert Hariman, eds. 1996. *Post-Realism: The Rhetorical Turn in International Relations.* East Lansing: Michigan State University Press.

Begley, Sharon. 2000. "The Nature of Nurturing: A New Study Finds that How Parents Treat a Child Can Shape Which of His Genes Turn On." *Newsweek*, March 27: 64–65.

Beilstein, Janet. 1998. "The Expanding Role of Women in United Nations Peacekeeping." In Lorentzen and Turpin eds.: 140–47.

Belenky, Mary Field, Blythe McVicker Clinchy, Nancy Rule Goldberger, and Jill Mattuck Tarule. 1986. *Women's Ways of Knowing: The Development of Self, Voice, and Mind.* New York: Basic.

Bem, Sandra Lipsitz. 1993. *The Lenses of Gender: Transforming the Debate on Sexual Identity.* New Haven, CT: Yale University Press.

Bendekgey, Beverly Ann. 1992. "Should Women Be Kept Out of Combat?" In Blacksmith ed.: 17–23 [reprinted from *The G.A.O. Journal* 9 (Summer), 1990: 29–33].

Benderly, Beryl Lieff. 1987. *The Myth of Two Minds: What Gender Means and Doesn't Mean.* New York: Doubleday.

Benenson, Joyce F., Nicholas H. Apostoleris, and Jodi Parnass. 1997. "Age and Sex Differences in Dyadic and Group Interaction." *Developmental Psychology* 33, 3 (May): 538–43.

Bennett, Florence Mary. 1967. *Religious Cults Associated with the Amazons.* New York: AMS.

Bennett, Olivia, Jo Bexley, and Kitty Warnock. 1995. *Arms to Fight – Arms to Protect: Women Speak Out about Conflict*. London: Panos.

Benton, Cynthia J., Anthony C. R. Hernandez, Adeny Schmidt, Mary D. Schmitz, Anna J. Stone, and Bernard Weiner. 1983. "Is Hostility Linked with Affiliation among Males and with Achievement among Females? A Critique of Pollak and Gilligan." *Journal of Personality and Social Psychology* 45, 5: 1167–71.

Benton, D. 1981. "The Extrapolation from Animals to Man: The Examples of Testosterone and Aggression." In Brain and Benton eds.: 401–18.

Berenbaum, Sheri A. and Melissa Hines. 1992. "Early Androgens Are Related to Childhood Sex-Typed Toy Preferences." *Psychological Science* 3, 3: 203–6.

Berkman, Joyce. 1990. "Feminism, War, and Peace Politics: The Case of World War I." In Elshtain and Tobias eds.: 141–60.

Berkowitz, Leonard. 1962. *Aggression: A Social Psychological Analysis*. New York: McGraw-Hill.

    1981. "The Concept of Agression." In Brain and Benton eds.: 3–16.

    1989. "Frustration-Aggression Hypothesis: Examination and Reformulation." *Psychological Bulletin* 106, 1: 59–73.

    1990. "Biological Roots: Are Humans Inherently Violent?" In Glad ed.: 24–40.

Bernardi, Mara, Susanna Genedani, Simonetta Tagliavini, and Alfio Bertolini. 1989. "Effect of Castration and Testosterone in Experimental Models of Depression in Mice." *Behavioral Neuroscience* 103, 5: 1148–50.

Bernhardt, P. C., J. M. Dabbs, J. A. Fielden, and C. D. Lutter. 1998. "Testosterone Changes during Vicarious Experiences of Winning and Losing among Fans at Sporting Events." *Physiology and Behavior* 65, 1 (August): 59–62.

Beroldi, Gerald. 1994. "Critique of the Seville Statement on Violence." *American Psychologist*, 49, 10 (October): 847–48.

Berselli, Beth. 1998. "Girls Tired of Nuking Aliens Get Software to Call Their Own." *The Washington Post*, February 2: A1.

Berube, Allan. 1990. *Coming Out under Fire: The History of Gay Men and Women in World War Two*. New York: Free Press.

Betcher, R. William and William S. Pollack. 1993. *In a Time of Fallen Heroes: The Re-Creation of Masculinity*. New York: Atheneum.

Beveridge, Alan. 1997. "On the Origins of Post-Traumatic Stress Disorder." In Black *et al.* eds.: 3–9.

Bhasin, Shalender, Thomas W. Storer, Nancy Berman, Carlos Callegari, Brenda Clevenger, Jeffrey Phillips, Thomas J. Bunnell, Ray Tricker, Aida Shirazi, and Richard Casaburi. 1996. "The Effects of Supraphysiologic Doses of Testosterone on Muscle Size and Strength in Normal Men." *The New England Journal of Medicine* 335, 1 (July 4): 1–7.

Bianchi, Suzanne M., ed. 1998. "Special Issue: Men in Families." *Demography* 35 (2), May: 133–229.

Birmingham, David. 1966. *Trade and Conflict in Angola: The Mbundu and Their Neighbors under the Influence of the Portuguese 1483–1790*. Oxford: Clarendon.

Black, Dora, Martin Newman, Jean Harris-Hendriks, and Gillian Mezey, eds. 1997. *Psychological Trauma: A Developmental Approach*. London: Gaskell.

Blacksmith, E. A., ed. 1992. *Women in the Military*. New York: H. W. Wilson.

Blackwell, Antoinette Brown. 1875. *The Sexes throughout Nature*. New York: G. P. Putnam.

Blakeslee, Sandra. 1991. "Men's Test Scores Linked to Hormone." *The New York Times*, November 14: B14.

1997. "Some Biologists Ask 'Are Genes Everything?'" *The New York Times*, September 2: C1, C8.

Blalock Jr., Hubert M. 1972. *Social Statistics*. 2nd edition. New York: McGraw-Hill.

Blanchard, Caroline D. and Robert J. Blanchard. 1989. "Experimental Animal Models of Aggression: What Do They Say about Human Behavior?" In Archer and Browne eds.: 94–121.

Blatch, Harriot Stanton. 1918. *Mobilizing Woman-Power*. New York: The Womans Press.

Block, Jeanne Humphrey. 1973. "Conceptions of Sex Role: Some Cross-Cultural and Longitudinal Perspectives." *American Psychologist* 28, 6 (June): 512–26.

1976. "Issues, Problems, and Pitfalls in Assessing Sex Differences: A Critical Review of *The Psychology of Sex Differences*." *Merrill-Palmer Quarterly* 22, 4: 283–308.

Bloom, Anne R. 1982. "Israel: The Longest War." In Goldman ed.: 137–64.

Bloom, William. 1990. *Personal Identity, National Identity, and International Relations*. Cambridge: Cambridge University Press.

Blum, Deborah. 1997. *Sex on the Brain: The Biological Differences between Men and Women*. New York: Viking.

Bly, Robert. 1990. *Iron John: A Book about Men*. Reading, MA: Addison-Wesley.

Boesch, Christophe and Hedwige Boesch. 1989. "Hunting Behavior of Wild Chimpanzees in the Taï National Park." *American Journal of Physical Anthropology* 78: 547–73.

Boesch, Christophe and Hedwige Boesch-Achermann. 2000. *The Chimpanzees of the Taï Forest: Behavioural Ecology and Evolution*. Oxford: Oxford University Press. [Cited page numbers are from chapter 8 in manuscript.]

Boonchalaksi, Wathinee and Philip Guest. 1998. "Prostitution in Thailand." In Lim ed.: 130–69.

Booth, Alan and D. Wayne Osgood. 1993. "The Influence of Testosterone on Deviance in Adulthood: Assessing and Explaining the Relationship." *Criminology* 31, 1: 93–117.

Booth, Alan, Greg Shelley, Allan Mazur, Gerry Tharp, and Roger Kittok. 1989. "Testosterone, and Winning and Losing in Human Competition." *Hormones and Behavior* 23: 556–71.

Boothby, Neil G. and Christine M. Knudsen. 2000. "Children of the Gun." *Scientific American* 282, 6 (June): 60–65.

Bordo, Susan. 1990. "Feminism, Postmodernism, and Gender-Scepticism." In Nicholson ed.: 133–56.

Boscarino, Joseph A. 1997. "Diseases among Men 20 Years after Exposure to Severe Stress: Implications for Clinical Research and Medical Care." *Psychosomatic Medicine* 59: 605–14.

Botchkareva, Maria. 1919. *Yashka: My Life as Peasant, Officer and Exile*. [As set down by Isaac Don Levine.] New York: Frederick A. Stokes.

Boudreau, Vincent G. 1995. "Corazon Aquino: Gender, Class, and the People Power President." In D'Amico and Beckman eds.: 71–84.

Boulding, Elise. 1984. "Focus On: The Gender Gap." *Journal of Peace Research* 21, 1: 1–3.

   1992. *The Underside of History: A View of Women through Time.* Volumes I and II [cited as /I and /II]. Revised edition. Newbury Park, CA: Sage.

   1995. "Feminist Inventions in the Art of Peacemaking: A Century Overview." *Peace & Change* 20, 4 (October): 408–38.

Boulton, Michael J. 1994. "The Relationship between Playful and Aggressive Fighting in Children, Adolescents and Adults." In Archer ed.: 23–41.

Bourke, Joanna. 1999. *An Intimate History of Killing: Face-to-Face Killing in Twentieth-Century Warfare.* New York: Basic.

Boutwell, Jeffrey and Michael T. Klare. 2000. "A Scourge of Small Arms." *Scientific American* 282, 6 (June): 48–53.

Bowen, Kevin and Bruce Weigl, eds. 1997. *Writing between the Lines: An Anthology on War and Its Social Consequences.* Amherst: University of Massachusetts Press.

Bowery Productions. 1996. *Calling the Ghosts* [videorecording]; written and directed by Mandy Jacobson and Karmen Jelinci, in association with Julia Ormond and Indican Productions. New York: [distributed by] Women Make Movies.

Boxer, C. R. 1952. *Salvador de Sá and the Struggle for Brazil and Angola 1602–1686.* London: Athlone Press.

Brady, James. 1997. "In Step with Lucy Lawless." *The Washington Post Parade Magazine,* July 27: 16.

Brain, Paul F. and David Benton, eds. 1981. *Multidisciplinary Approaches to Aggression Research.* New York: Elsevier/North-Holland Biomedical Press.

Brandi, Karl. 1939. *The Emperor Charles V: The Growth and Destiny of a Man and of a World-Empire.* Translated from the German by C. V. Wedgwood. London: Jonathan Cape.

Braybon, Gail and Penny Summerfield. 1987. *Out of the Cage: Women's Experiences in Two World Wars.* London: Pandora.

Breedlove, S. Marc.1992. "Sexual Differentiation of the Brain and Behavior." In Becker, Breedlove, and Crews eds.: 39–70.

Breuer, William B. 1997. *War and American Women: Heroism, Deeds, and Controversy.* Westport, CT: Praeger.

Brewer, Marilynn B. and Rupert J. Brown. 1998. "Intergroup Relations." In Gilbert, Fiske, and Lindzey eds.: 554–94.

Briggs, Jean L. 1982. "Living Dangerously: The Contradictory Foundations of Value in Canadian Inuit Society." In Eleanor Leacock and Richard Lee, eds., *Politics and History in Band Societies.* Cambridge: Cambridge University Press: 109–32.

   1998. *Inuit Morality Play: The Emotional Education of a Three-Year Old.* New Haven: Yale University Press.

Brittan, Arthur. 1989. *Masculinity and Power.* New York: Basil Blackwell.

Brock-Utne, Birgit. 1985. *Educating for Peace: A Feminist Perspective.* New York: Pergamon.

   1989. *Feminist Perspectives on Peace and Peace Education.* New York: Pergamon.

Brooks-Gunn, J. and Michelle P. Warren. 1989. "Biological and Social Contributions to Negative Affect in Young Adolescent Girls." *Child Development* 60: 40–55.

Brown, Marilyn. 1998. World Wide Web site: <http://www.gendergap.com/military/>.

Brown, Seyom. 1994. *The Causes and Prevention of War.* 2nd edition. New York: St. Martin's.

Brown, Wendy. 1988. *Manhood and Politics: A Feminist Reading in Political Theory.* Totowa, NJ: Rowman & Littlefield.

Brownmiller, Susan. 1975. *Against Our Will: Men, Women, and Rape.* New York: Simon & Schuster.

1994. "Making Female Bodies the Battlefield." In Stiglmayer ed.: 180–82 [reprinted from *Newsweek*, January 4, 1993: 37].

Broyles Jr., William 1984. "Why Men Love War." *Esquire* 102 (November): 55–65.

Bruce, Jean. 1985. *Back the Attack! Canadian Women during the Second World War – at Home and Abroad.* Toronto: Macmillan of Canada.

Bryant, Louise. 1918. *Six Red Months in Russia: An Observer's Account of Russia before and during the Proletarian Dictatorship.* New York: George H. Doran.

Bucci, David J., Andrea A. Chiba, and Michela Gallagher. 1995. "Spatial Learning in Male and Female Long-Evans Rats." *Behavioral Neuroscience* 109, 1 (February): 180–83.

Buchanan, Christy Miller, Jacquelynne S. Eccles, and Jill B. Becker. 1992. "Are Adolescents the Victims of Raging Hormones: Evidence for Activational Effects of Hormones on Moods and Behavior at Adolescence." *Psychological Bulletin* 111, 1: 62–107.

Bugental, Daphne Blunt and Jacqueline J. Goodnow. 1998. "Socialization Processes." In Damon and Eisenberg eds.: 389–462.

Bull, Hedley. 1977. *The Anarchical Society: A Study of Order in World Politics.* New York: Columbia University Press.

Bunster-Burotto, Ximena. 1994. "Surviving beyond Fear: Women and Torture in Latin America." In Davies ed.: 156–75.

Burguieres, Mary K. 1990. "Feminist Approaches to Peace: Another Step for Peace Studies." *Millennium: Journal of International Studies* 19, 1: 1–18.

Burke, Carol. 1996. "Pernicious Cohesion." In Stiehm ed.: 205–19.

Burr, Chandler. 1993. "Homosexuality and Biology." *The Atlantic Monthly* (March): 47–65.

Burrelli, David F. 1994. "An Overview of the Debate on Homosexuals in the US Military." In Scott and Stanley eds.: 17–32.

Burwell, Frances G. and Meredith Reid Sarkees. 1993. "Women and National Security Policy." In Howes and Stevenson eds.: 111–34.

Bussey, Gertrude and Margaret Tims. 1965. *Women's International League for Peace and Freedom 1915–1965: A Record of Fifty Years' Work.* London: Allen & Unwin.

Butler, Deborah A. 1990. *American Women Writers on Vietnam: Unheard Voices: A Selected Annotated Bibliography.* New York: Garland.

Butler, Judith. 1990a. *Gender Trouble: Feminism and the Subversion of Identity.* New York: Routledge.

1990b. "Gender Trouble, Feminist Theory, and Psychoanalytic Discourse." In Nicholson ed.: 324–40.

1992. "Contingent Foundations: Feminism and the Question of 'Postmodernism.'" In Butler and Scott eds.: 3–21.

Butler, Judith and Joan W. Scott, eds. 1992. *Feminists Theorize the Political*. New York: Routledge.

Buzan, Barry, Charles Jones, and Richard Little. 1993. *The Logic of Anarchy: Neorealism to Structural Realism*. New York: Columbia University Press.

Bystydzienski, Jill M. 1993. "Women in Groups and Organizations: Implications for the Use of Force." In Howes and Stevenson eds.: 39–52.

Cacioppo, John T., Gary G. Berntson, and Stephen L. Crites, Jr. 1996. "Social Neuroscience: Principles of Psychophysiological Arousal and Response." In E. Tory Higgins and Arie W. Kruglanski, eds., *Social Psychology: Handbook of Basic Principles*. New York: Guilford: 72–101.

Cairns, Ed. 1996. *Children and Political Violence*. Cambridge, MA: Blackwell.

Cairns, Robert B. 1986. "An Evolutionary and Developmental Perspective on Aggressive Patterns." In Zahn-Waxler, Cummings, and Iannotti eds.: 58–87.

Cairns, Robert B. and Beverly D. Cairns. 1994. *Lifelines and Risks: Pathways of Youth in Our Time*. Cambridge: Cambridge University Press.

Caldicott, Helen. 1986. *Missile Envy: The Arms Race and Nuclear War*. Revised edition. New York: Bantam.

Cambridge Women's Peace Collective. 1984. *My Country Is the Whole World: An Anthology of Women's Work on Peace and War*. Boston: Pandora.

Cameron, Mindy. 1991. "The Postwar Challenge for Women." *Seattle Times*, March 3: A18.

Campbell, Anne. 1993. *Men, Women, and Aggression*. New York: Basic.

Campbell, Anne and Steven Muncer. 1994. "Men and the Meaning of Violence." In Archer ed.: 332–51.

Campbell, D'Ann. 1990. "The Regimented Women of the World War II." In Elshtain and Tobias eds.: 107–22.

Cantor, Dorothy W., Toni Bernay, with Jean Stoess. 1992. *Women in Power: The Secrets of Leadership*. Boston: Houghton Mifflin.

Carlsson-Paige, Nancy and Diane E. Levin. 1987. *The War Play Dilemma: Balancing Needs and Values in the Early Childhood Classroom*. New York: Teachers College Press.

Carneiro, Robert L. 1990. "Chiefdom-Level Warfare as Exemplified in Fiji and the Cauca Valley." In Haas ed.: 190–211.

1994. "War and Peace: Alternating Realities in Human History." In Reyna and Downs eds.: 3–28.

Carpenter, C. R. 1967. "The Contribution of Primate Studies to the Understanding of War." In Fried, Harris, and Murphy eds.: 49–58.

Carras, Mary C. 1995. "Indira Gandhi: Gender and Foreign Policy." In D'Amico and Beckman eds.: 45–58.

Carroll, Berenice A. 1987. "Feminism and Pacifism: Historical and Theoretical Connections." In Pierson ed.: 2–28.

Carroll, Berenice and Barbara Welling Hall. 1993. "Feminist Perspectives on Women and the Use of Force." In Howes and Stevenson eds.: 11–22.

Carter, April. 1996. "Should Women Be Soldiers or Pacifists?" *Peace Review* 8, 3: 331–35.

Carter, C. Sue. 1992. "Hormonal Influences on Human Sexual Behavior." In Becker, Breedlove, and Crews eds.: 131–42.

Carter, Susanne. 1992. *War and Peace through Women's Eyes: A Selective Bibliography of Twentieth-Century American Women's Fiction.* New York: Greenwood.

Casey, Geraldine J. 1991. "Eleanor Leacock, Marvin Harris, and the Struggle over Warfare in Anthropology." In Hunter ed.: 1–33.

Casey, Geraldine J. and Ethel Tobach. 1991. "Eleanor Burke Leacock: A Tribute." In Hunter ed.: xiii–xiv.

Caspari, Ernst W. 1978. "The Biological Basis of Female Hierarchies." In Tiger and Fowler eds.: 87–122.

Cataldo, Mima, Ruth Putter, Bryna Fireside, and Elaine Lytel. 1987. *The Women's Encampment for a Future of Peace and Justice: Images and Writings.* Philadelphia: Temple University Press.

Chadwick, Nora. 1970. *The Celts.* Harmondsworth, UK: Penguin.

Chagnon, Napoleon A. 1967. "Yanomamö Social Organization and Warfare." In Fried, Harris, and Murphy eds.: 109–59.

   1990. "Reproductive and Somatic Conflicts of Interest in the Genesis of Violence and Warfare among Tribesmen." In Haas ed.: 77–104.

   1992. *Yanomamö: The Last Days of Eden.* New York: Harcourt Brace Jovanovich.

   1996. *Yanomamö: The Fierce People.* 5th edition. New York: Harcourt Brace.

Chang, Iris. 1997. *The Rape of Nanking: The Forgotten Holocaust of World War II.* New York: Basic.

Chapais, Bernard. 1991. "Primates and the Origins of Aggression, Power, and Politics among Humans." In J. D. Loy and C. B. Peters, eds., *Understanding Behavior: What Primate Studies Tell Us about Human Behavior.* Oxford: Oxford University Press: 190–228.

Chatterjee, Partha. 1993. *The Nation and Its Fragments: Colonial and Postcolonial Histories.* Princeton, NJ: Princeton University Press.

Cheney, Dorothy L. 1983a. "Intergroup Encounters among Old World Monkeys." In Hinde ed.: 233–40.

   1983b. "Proximate and Ultimate Factors Related to the Distribution of Male Migration." In Hinde ed.: 241–49.

   1983c. "Extrafamilial Alliances among Vervet Monkeys." In Hinde ed.: 278–85.

Chesser, Barbara. 1997. Letter to the editor. *Women's Review of Books* 14, 8 (May).

Chizuko, Ueno. 1997. "Are the Japanese Feminine? Some Problems of Japanese Feminism in Its Cultural Context." In Sandra Buckley, ed., *Broken Silence: Voices of Japanese Feminism.* Berkeley: University of California Press: 293–300.

Chmielewski, Wendy E. 1995. " 'Binding Themselves the Closer to Their Own Peculiar Duties': Gender and Women's Work for Peace, 1818–1860." *Peace & Change,* 20, 4 (October): 466–90.

Chodorow, Nancy. 1978. *The Reproduction of Mothering: Psychoanalysis and the Sociology of Gender.* Berkeley: University of California Press.

Christen, Yves. [1987] 1991. *Sex Differences: Modern Biology and the Unisex Fallacy.* [Translated from French.] New Brunswick: Transaction.

Christiansen, Kerrin H. 1991. "Serum and Saliva Sex Hormone Levels in !Kung San Men." *American Journal of Physical Anthropology* 86: 37–44.

Clemens, Walter C., Jr. and J. David Singer. 2000. "The Human Cost of War: Modern Warfare Kills More Civilians than Soldiers." *Scientific American* 282, 6 (June): 56–57.

Clinton, Catherine and Nina Silber, eds. 1992. *Divided Houses: Gender and the Civil War.* Oxford: Oxford University Press.

Cock, Jacklyn. 1989. "Manpower and Militarisation: Women and the SADF." In Jacklyn Cock and Laurie Nathan, eds., *Society at War: The Militarisation of South Africa.* New York: St. Martin's.: 51–66.

1991. *Colonels and Cadres: War and Gender in South Africa.* Oxford: Oxford University Press.

Cohen, J. 1950. "Women in Peace and War." In T. H. Pear, ed., *Psychological Factors of Peace and War.* New York: The Philosophical Library: 93–110.

Cohen, Patricia. 1998. "Daddy Dearest: Do You Really Matter?" *The New York Times,* July 11: A13.

Cohen, Richard. 1997a. "Duty, Gender, Country." *The Washington Post,* April 24: A25.

1997b. "Snooping on Soldiers." *The Washington Post,* May 1: A23.

Cohen, Ronald. 1986. "War and War Proneness in Pre- and Postindustrial States." In Foster and Rubinstein eds.: 253–67.

Cohn, Carol. 1987. "Sex and Death in the Rational World of Defense Intellectuals." *Signs: Journal of Women in Culture and Society* 12, 4: 687–718.

1989. "Emasculating America's Linguistic Deterrent." In Harris and King eds.: 155–70.

1990. "'Clean Bombs' and Clean Language." In Elshtain and Tobias eds.: 33–56.

1993. "Wars, Wimps, and Women: Talking Gender and Thinking War." In Cooke and Woollacott eds.: 227–46.

Coie, John D. and Kenneth A. Dodge. 1998. "Aggression and Antisocial Behavior." In Damon and Eisenberg eds.: 779–862.

Colby, Frank Moore. 1926. "If Women Were Prime Ministers." In *The Colby Essays.* New York: Harper.

Colby, John. 1991. *War from the Ground Up: The 90th Division in WWII.* Austin, TX: Nortex.

Collett, Pamela. 1996. "Afghan Women in the Peace Process." *Peace Review* 8, 3: 397–402.

Colt, George Howe and Anne Hollister. 1998. "Were You Born That Way?" *Life,* April: 39–50.

Condon, Richard G., Julia Ogina, and the Holman Elders. 1996. *The Northern Copper Inuit: A History.* Norman: University of Oklahoma Press.

Constantino, John N., Daniel Grosz, Paul Saenger, Donald W. Chandler, Reena Nandi, and Felton J. Earls. 1993. "Testosterone and Aggression in Children." *Journal of the American Academy of Child and Adolescent Psychiatry* 32, 6: 1217–22.

Constantino, John N., Angela S. Scerbo, and David J. Kolko. 1995. "Testosterone and Aggression – Letters to the Editor." *Journal of American Academic Child Adolescent Psychiatry* 34, 5 (May): 535–36.

Cooke, Miriam. 1987. *War's Other Voices: Women Writers on the Lebanese Civil War*. Cambridge: Cambridge University Press.

1996a. *Women and the War Story*. Berkeley: University of California Press.

1996b. "Subverting the Gender and Military Paradigms." In Stiehm ed.: 235–69.

Cooke, Miriam and Roshni Rustomji-Kerns, eds. 1994. *Blood into Ink: South Asian and Middle Eastern Women Write War*. Boulder, CO: Westview.

Cooke, Miriam and Angela Woollacott, eds. 1993. *Gendering War Talk*. Princeton, NJ: Princeton University Press.

Coole, Diana H. 1988. *Women in Political Theory: From Ancient Misogyny to Contemporary Feminism*. Boulder, CO: Lynne Rienner.

Cooper, Helen M., Adrienne Munich, and Susan Squier. 1989. "Introduction." In Helen M. Cooper, Adrienne Munich, and Susan Squier, eds. *Arms and the Woman: War, Gender, and Literary Representation*. Chapel Hill: University of North Carolina Press: xiii–xx.

Copelon, Rhonda. 1994. "Surfacing Gender: Reconceptualizing Crimes against Women in Time of War." In Stiglmayer ed.: 197–218.

Cornum, Rhonda. 1996. "Soldiering: The Enemy Doesn't Care If You're Female." In Stiehm ed.: 3–23.

Costello, John. 1985. *Virtue under Fire: How World War II Changed Our Social and Sexual Attitudes*. Boston: Little, Brown.

Costin, Lela B. 1982. "Feminism, Pacifism, Internationalism and the 1915 International Congress of Women." *Women's Studies International Forum* 5, 3/4: 301–15.

Cottam, K. Jean. 1983. *Soviet Airwomen in Combat in World War II*. Manhattan, KS: Sunflower University Press.

Crane, Stephen. [1894] 1952. *The Red Badge of Courage*. New York: Appleton-Century.

Creighton, Margaret S. and Lisa Norling, eds. 1996. *Iron Men, Wooden Women: Gender and Seafaring in the Atlantic World, 1700–1920*. Baltimore: Johns Hopkins University Press.

Cremony, John C. [1868] 1969. *Life among the Apaches*. Glorieta, New Mexico: Rio Grande Press.

Cressman, Luther Sheeleigh. 1956. *Klamath Prehistory: The Prehistory of the Culture of the Klamath Lake Area, Oregon*. Philadelphia: American Philosophical Society.

Crick, Nicki R., Juan F. Casas, and Hyon-Chin Ku. 1999. "Relational and Physical Forms of Peer Victimization in Preschool." *Developmental Psychology* 35, 2 (March): 376–85.

Crick, Nicki R. and Jennifer K. Grotpeter. 1995. "Relational Aggression, Gender, and Social-Psychological Adjustment." *Child Development* 66, 3 (June): 710–22.

Crossette, Barbara. 1998. "An Old Scourge of War Becomes Its Latest Crime." *The New York Times*, June 14: D1.

Cummings, E. Mark, Barbara Hollenbeck, Ronald Iannotti, Marian Radke-Yarrow, and Carolyn Zahn-Waxler. 1986. "Early Organization of Altruism and Aggression: Developmental Patterns and Individual Differences." In Zahn-Waxler, Cummings, and Iannotti eds.: 165–88.

Dabbs Jr., James M. 1990. "Salivary Testosterone Measurements: Reliability across Hours, Days, and Weeks." *Physiology and Behavior* 48: 83–86.

2000. *Heroes, Rogues, and Lovers: Testosterone and Behavior*. New York: McGraw-Hill.

Dabbs, Jr., James M., Robert L. Frady, Timothy S. Carr, and Norma F. Besch. 1987. "Saliva Testosterone and Criminal Violence in Young Adult Prison Inmates." *Psychosomatic Medicine* 49, 2 (March/April): 174–82.

Dabbs Jr., James M., Marian F. Hargrove, and Colleen Heusel. 1996. "Testosterone Differences among College Fraternities: Well-Behaved vs. Rambunctious." *Personality and Individidual Differences* 20, 2: 157–61.

Dabbs Jr., James M., Gregory J. Jurkovic, and Robert L. Frady. 1991. "Salivary Testosterone and Cortisol among Late Adolescent Male Offenders." *Journal of Abnormal Child Psychology* 19, 4: 469–78.

Dabbs Jr., James M. and Robin Morris. 1990. "Testosterone, Social Class, and Antisocial Behavior in a Sample of 4,462 Men." *Psychological Science* 1, 3: 209–11.

Daly, Martin and Margo Wilson. 1983. *Sex, Evolution, and Behavior*. 2nd edition. Boston: Willard Grant.

Dalzel, Archibald. 1967. *The History of Dahomy: An Inland Kingdom of Africa*. Compiled from Authentic Memoirs. London: Frank Cass.

D'Amico, Francine. 1994. "Pluralist and Critical Perspectives." In Beckman and D'Amico eds.: 55–74.

1995. "Women National Leaders." In D'Amico and Beckman eds.: 15–30.

1996. "Feminist Perspectives on Women Warriors." *Peace Review* 8, 3: 379–84.

Forthcoming. "Citizen-Soldier: Class, Race, Gender, Sexuality, & the US Military." In S. Jacobs, R. Jacobson, and J. Marchbank, eds., *States of Conflict: International Perspectives on Gender, Violence, and Resistance*. London: Zed.

D'Amico, Francine and Peter R. Beckman. 1994. "Introduction." In Beckman and D'Amico eds.: 1–14.

eds. 1995. *Women in World Politics: An Introduction*. Westport, CT: Bergin & Garvey.

Damon, William and Nancy Eisenberg, eds. 1998. *Handbook of Child Psychology*. 5th edition. *Volume 3: Social, Emotional, and Personality Development*. New York: Wiley.

Damousi, Joy and Marilyn Lake, eds. 1995. *Gender and War: Australians at War in the Twentieth Century*. Cambridge: Cambridge University Press.

Darby, Phillip, ed. 1997. *At the Edge of International Relations: Postcolonialism, Gender and Dependency*. New York: Pinter.

Dart, Raymond A. 1953. "The Predatory Transition from Ape to Man." *International Anthropological and Linguistic Review* 1, 4: 201–18.

Davidson, Jonathan *et al.* [14 coauthors]. 1994. "Posttraumatic Stress Disorder." In Thomas A. Widiger, Allen J. Frances, Harold Alan Pincus, Ruth Ross, Michael B. First, and Wendy Wakefield Davis, eds., *DSM-IV Sourcebook*. Volume II. Washington, DC: American Psychiatric Association: 577–81.

Davie, Maurice R. [1929] 1968. *The Evolution of War: A Study of Its Role in Early Societies*. Port Washington, NY: Kennikat.

Davies, James Chowning. 1987. "Aggression: Some Definition and Some Psychology." *Politics and the Life Sciences* 6, 1: 27–57.

Davies, Miranda, ed. 1994. *Women and Violence*. London: Zed.

Davis-Kimball, Jeannine. 1997. "Warrior Women of the Eurasian Steppes." *Archaeology* 50, 1: 44–48.

Dawkins, Richard. 1976. *The Selfish Gene*. Oxford: Oxford University Press.

De Alwis, Malathi. 1998. "Moral Mothers and Stalwart Sons: Reading Binaries in a Time of War." In Lorentzen and Turpin eds.: 254–71.

De Catanzaro, D. and E. Spironello. 1998. "Of Mice and Men: Androgen Dynamics in Dominance and Reproduction." *Behavioral and Brain Sciences* 21, 3 (June): 371.

DeFleur, Lois B. 1992. "Let Women Fly in Combat." In Blacksmith ed.: 24–26.

De Pauw, Linda Grant. 1975. *Founding Mothers: Women of America in the Revolutionary Era*. Boston: Houghton Mifflin.

1982. *Seafaring Women*. Boston: Houghton Mifflin.

1998. *Battle Cries and Lullabies: Women in War from Prehistory to the Present*. Norman: University of Oklahoma Press.

De Preux, J. 1985. "Special Protection of Women and Children." *International Review of the Red Cross* 248: 292–302.

DeVries, Kelly. 1996. "A Woman as Leader of Men: Joan of Arc's Military Career." In Wheeler and Wood eds.: 3–18.

De Waal, Frans. 1982. *Chimpanzee Politics*. London: Jonathan Cape.

1989. *Peacemaking among Primates*. Cambridge, MA: Harvard University Press.

1991. "Sex Differences in the Formation of Coalitions among Chimpanzees." In Schubert and Masters eds.: 138–60 [reprinted from *Ethology and Sociobiology*, 1984: 239–68].

1995. "Bonobo Sex and Society." *Scientific American* 272, 3: 82–88.

1996. *Good Natured: The Origins of Right and Wrong in Humans and Other Animals*. Cambridge, MA: Harvard University Press.

De Waal, Frans and Frans Lanting. 1997. *Bonobo: The Forgotten Ape*. Berkeley: University of California Press.

Deahl, Martin. 1997. "The Effect of Conflict on Combatants." In Black *et al.* eds.: 134–47.

Dean Jr., Eric T. 1997. *Shook over Hell: Post-Traumatic Stress, Vietnam, and the Civil War*. Cambridge, MA: Harvard University Press.

Deaux, Kay and Marianne LaFrance. 1998. "Gender." In Gilbert, Fiske, and Lindzey eds.: 788–828.

Degen, Marie Louise. [1939] 1974. *The History of the Woman's Peace Party*. New York: Burt Franklin Reprints [Johns Hopkins University Press, 1939].

Demarest, Arthur A. 1993. "The Violent Saga of a Maya Kingdom." *National Geographic* 183, 2: 94–111.

Dench, Geoff. 1996. *Transforming Men: Changing Patterns of Dependency and Dominance in Gender Relations*. New Brunswick, NJ: Transaction.

Dentan, Robert Knox. 1979. *The Semai: A Nonviolent People of Malaya*. New York: Holt, Rinehart and Winston.

Dever, John P. and Marcia C. Dever. 1995. *Women and the Military: Over 100 Notable Contributors, Historic to Contemporary.* Jefferson, NC: McFarland.

Di Leonardo, Micaela. 1985. "Morals, Mothers, and Militarism: Antimilitarism and Feminist Theory"; review essay. *Feminist Studies* 11 (Fall): 599–617.

   ed. 1991. *Gender at the Crossroads of Knowledge: Feminist Anthropology in the Postmodern Era.* Berkeley: University of California Press.

Di Stefano, Christine. 1990. "Dilemmas of Difference: Feminism, Modernity, and Postmodernism." In Nicholson ed.: 63–82.

Diamond, Irene. 1994. *Fertile Ground: Women, Earth, and the Limits of Control.* Boston: Beacon Press.

Diamond, Irene and Gloria Feman Orenstein, eds. 1990. *Reweaving the World: The Emergence of Ecofeminism.* San Francisco: Sierra Club Books.

Diamond, Jared. 1997. *Guns, Germs, and Steel: The Fates of Human Societies.* New York: W. W. Norton.

Diehl, Paul F., ed. 1999. *A Road Map to War: Territorial Dimensions of International Conflict.* Nashville, TN: Vanderbilt University Press.

Dillon, Myles and Nora K. Chadwick. 1972. *The Celtic Realms.* 2nd edition. London: Weidenfeld and Nicolson.

Dinnerstein, Dorothy. 1976. *The Mermaid and the Minotaur: Sexual Arrangements and Human Malaise.* New York: Harper & Row.

Dinter, Elmar. 1985. *Hero or Coward: Pressures Facing the Soldier in Battle.* Totowa, NJ: Frank Cass.

Divale, William Tulio and Marvin Harris. 1976. "Population, Warfare, and the Male Supremacist Complex." *American Anthropologist* 78, 3 (September): 521–38.

Dixson, Alan F. 1998. *Primate Sexuality: Comparative Studies of the Prosimians, Monkeys, Apes, and Human Beings.* Oxford: Oxford University Press.

Dolhinow, Phyllis. 1991. "Tactics of Primate Immaturity." In Robinson and Tiger eds.: 139–58.

Domenick, Jeff. 1998. "FAN-tastic: Sports Mania a Unifying Force." *Pittsburgh Tribune-Review,* July 26.

Donnelly, Elaine. 1997. " . . . But Not Social Engineering." *The Washington Post,* May 1: C7.

Dowd, Maureen. 1999. "No Free War." *The New York Times,* March 31: A29.

Dower, John W. 1986. *War without Mercy: Race and Power in the Pacific War.* New York: Pantheon.

Doyle, Sir Arthur Conan [1892] 1967. "The Adventure of Copper Beeches." In William S. Baring-Gould, ed. *The Annotated Sherlock Holmes.* Volume II. New York: Clarkson Potter.

Doyle, Michael W. 1986. "Liberalism and World Politics." *American Political Science Review* 80, 4: 1151–70.

   1997. *Ways of War and Peace: Realism, Liberalism, and Socialism.* New York: W. W. Norton.

Doyle, Michael W. and G. John Ikenberry, eds. 1997. *New Thinking in International Relations Theory.* Boulder, CO: Westview.

Drakulić, Slavenka. 1994. "The Rape of Women in Bosnia." In Davies ed.: 176–81.

Dransart, Penny. 1987. "Women and Ritual Conflict in Inka Society." In Macdonald, Holden, and Ardener eds.: 62–77.

Draper, Patricia. 1985. "Two Views of Sex Differences in Socialization." In Hall ed.: 5–26.

Drigotas, Stephen M. and J. Richard Udry. 1993. "Biosocial Models of Adolescent Problem Behavior: Extension to Panel Design." *Social Biology* 40, 1–2: 1–7.

Drolshagen, Ebba D. 1998. *Nicht ungeschoren Davonkommen: Die Schicksal der Frauen in den besetzten Laender, die wehrmachtsoldaten Liebten.* Hamburg: Hoffmann und Campe. [Reviewed in *Der Spiegel*, August 17, 1998.]

Druett, Joan. 2000. *She Captains: Heroines and Hellions of the Sea.* New York: Simon & Schuster.

DuBois, Ellen Carol. 1995. "A Peace of Their Own: Is There an Intrinsically Female Approach to Foreign Policy?" *New York Times Book Review*, September 3: 22.

DuBois, Page. 1982. *Centaurs and Amazons: Women and the Pre-History of the Great Chain of Being.* Ann Arbor: University of Michigan Press.

Duchacek, Ivo D. 1970. *Comparative Federalism: The Territorial Dimension of Politics.* New York: Holt, Rinehart and Winston.

Duiker, William J. 1982. "Vietnam: War of Insurgency." In Goldman ed.: 107–22.

Duncan, John. [1847] 1967. *Travels in Western Africa, in 1845 & 1846, Volume 1.* London: Johnson Reprint.

Durbin, E. F. M. and John Bowlby. 1939. *Personal Aggressiveness and War.* New York: Columbia University Press.

Dyer, Gwynne. 1985. *War.* New York: Crown.

Eagly, Alice H. 1987. *Sex Differences in Social Behavior: A Social-Role Interpretation.* Hillsdale, NJ: Lawrence Erlbaum Associates.

1995. "The Science and Politics of Comparing Women and Men." *American Psychologist* 50, 3: 145–58.

1996. "Differences between Women and Men: Their Magnitude, Practical Importance, and Political Meaning." *American Psychologist* 51, 2 (February): 158–59.

Eagly, Alice H. and Shelly Chaiken. 1998. "Attitude Structure and Function." In Gilbert, Fiske, and Lindzey eds.: 269–322.

Eagly, Alice H. and Maureen Crowley. 1986. "Gender and Helping Behavior: A Meta-Analytic Review of the Social Psychological Literature." *Psychological Bulletin* 100, 3: 283–308.

Eagly, Alice H. and Blair T. Johnson. 1990. "Gender and Leadership Style: A Meta-Analysis." *Psychological Bulletin*, 108, 2: 233–56.

Eagly, Alice H. and Steven J. Karau. 1991. "Gender and the Emergence of Leaders: A Meta-Analysis." *Journal of Personality and Social Psychology* 60, 5: 685–710.

Eagly, Alice H. and Mary E. Kite. 1987. "Are Stereotypes of Nationalities Applied to Both Women and Men?" *Journal of Personality and Social Psychology* 53, 3: 451–62.

Eagly, Alice H. and Valerie J. Steffen. 1986. "Gender and Aggressive Behavior: A Meta-Analytic Review of the Social Psychological Literature." *Psychological Bulletin* 100, 3: 309–30.

Eagly, Alice H. and Wendy Wood. 1991. "Explaining Sex Differences in Social Behavior: A Meta-Analytic Perspective." *Personality and Social Psychology Bulletin* 17, 3 (June): 306–15.

Easlea, Brian. 1983. *Fathering the Unthinkable: Masculinity, Scientists and the Nuclear Arms Race*. London: Pluto.

Ebert, Patricia D. 1983. "Selection for Aggression in a Natural Population." In Edward C. Simmel, Martin E. Hahn, and James K. Walters, eds., *Aggressive Behavior: Genetic and Neural Approaches*. Hillsdale, NJ: Lawrence Erlbaum: 103–28.

Edgerton, Robert B. 1988. *Like Lions They Fought: The Zulu War and the Last Black Empire in South Africa*. New York: Free Press.

Edley, Nigel and Margaret Wetherell. 1995. *Men in Perspective: Practice, Power and Identity*. New York: Prentice-Hall.

Edmond, Lauris and Carolyn Milward, eds. 1986. *Women in Wartime: New Zealand Women Tell Their Stories*. Wellington, NZ: Government Printing Office.

Egan, Jennifer. 1998. "Uniforms in the Closet." *The New York Times Magazine*, June 28: 26–31.

Ehrenreich, Barbara. 1983. *The Hearts of Men: American Dreams and the Flight from Commitment*. Garden City, NY: Anchor.

1997a. *Blood Rites: Origins and History of the Passions of War*. New York: Metropolitan.

1997b. "Once Upon a Wartime." *The Nation*, May 12: 21–24.

Ehrenreich, Barbara, Katha Pollitt, R. Brian Ferguson, Lionel Tiger, Jane S. Jaquette. [Separate articles.] 1999. "Fukuyama's Follies: So What if Women Ruled the World?" *Foreign Affairs* 78, 1 (Jan./Feb.): 118–29.

Eibl-Eibesfeldt, Irenäus. 1974. "The Myth of the Aggression-Free Hunter and Gatherer Society." In Holloway ed.: 435–58.

1979. *The Biology of Peace and War: Men, Animals, and Aggression*. New York: Viking.

Eisenberg, Nancy and Richard A. Fabes. 1998. "Prosocial Development." In Damon and Eisenberg eds.: 701–78.

Eisler, Riane. 1987. *The Chalice and the Blade: Our History, Our Future*. San Francisco: Harper & Row.

1990. "The Gaia Tradition and the Partnership Future: An Ecofeminist Manifesto." In Diamond and Orenstein eds.: 23–34.

Eller, Cynthia. 2000. *The Myth of Matriarchal Prehistory: Why an Invented Past Won't Give Women a Future*. Boston: Beacon.

Elliot, Patricia. 1991. *From Mastery to Analysis: Theories of Gender in Psychoanalytic Feminism*. Ithaca, NY: Cornell University Press.

Ellis, L. and H. Nyborg. 1992. "Racial/Ethnic Variations in Male Testosterone Levels: A Probable Contributor to Group Differences in Health." *Steroids* 57: 72–75.

Ellis, Peter Berresford. 1996. *Celtic Women: Women in Celtic Society and Literature*. Grand Rapids, MI: William B. Eerdmans.

Ellsworth, Phoebe C. and Robert Mauro. 1998. "Psychology and Law." In Gilbert, Fiske, and Lindzey eds.: 684–732.

Elshtain, Jean Bethke. 1981. *Public Man, Private Woman: Women in Social and Political Thought.* Princeton, NJ: Princeton University Press.

1982. "On Beautiful Souls, Just Warriors and Feminist Consciousness." *Women's Studies International Forum* 5, 3/4: 341–48.

1985." Reflections on War and Political Discourse: Realism, Just War, and Feminism in a Nuclear Age." *Political Theory* 13, 1: 39–57.

1987. *Women and War.* New York: Basic.

1990. "The Problem with Peace." In Elshtain and Tobias eds.: 255–66.

Elshtain, Jean Bethke and Sheila Tobias. 1990. "Preface." In Elshtain and Tobias eds.: ix–xii.

eds. 1990. *Women, Militarism, and War: Essays in History, Politics, and Social Theory.* Savage, MD: Rowman & Littlefield.

Ember, Carol R. 1978. "Myths about Hunter-Gatherers." *Ethnology* 17, 4: 439–48.

1980. "A Cross-Cultural Perspective on Sex Differences." In Ruth H. Munroe, Robert L. Monroe, and Beatrice B. Whiting, eds. *Handbook of Cross-Cultural Human Development.* New York: Garland STPM: 531–80.

Ember, Carol R. and Melvin Ember. 1990. *Anthropology.* 6th edition. Englewood Cliffs, NJ: Prentice-Hall.

1997. "Violence in the Ethnographic Record: Results of Cross-Cultural Research on War and Aggression." In Martin and Frayer eds.: 1–20.

Ember, Melvin. 1974. "Warfare, Sex Ratio, and Polygyny." *Ethnology* 13: 197–206.

1985. "Alternative Predictors of Polygyny." *Behavior Science Research* 19: 1–23.

Ember, Melvin and Carol R. Ember. 1971. "The Conditions Favoring Matrilocal versus Patrilocal Residence." *American Anthropologist* 73: 571–94.

1994. "Cross-Cultural Studies of War and Peace: Recent Achievements and Future Possibilities." In Reyna and Downs eds.: 185–208.

Emmett, Ayala. 1996. *Our Sisters' Promised Land: Women, Politics, and Israeli–Palestinian Coexistence.* Ann Arbor: University of Michigan Press.

Engels, Friedrich. [1884] 1986. *The Origin of the Family, Private Property, and the State.* New York: Viking.

Enloe, Cynthia H. 1982. "Women in NATO Militaries – A Conference Report." *Women's Studies International Forum* 5, 3/4: 329–34.

1983. *Does Khaki Become You? The Militarization of Women's Lives.* Boston: South End Press.

1989. *Bananas, Beaches and Bases: Making Feminist Sense of International Politics.* Berkeley: University of California Press.

1993. *The Morning After: Sexual Politics at the End of the Cold War.* Berkeley: University of California Press.

1994. "Afterword." In Stiglmayer ed.: 219–30.

2000. *Maneuvers: The International Politics of Militarizing Women's Lives.* Berkeley: University of California Press.

Erlanger, Steven. 1997. "In Afghan Refugee Camp, Albright Hammers Taliban." *The New York Times,* November 19: A14.

Etheredge, Lloyd S. 1978. *A World of Men: The Private Sources of American Foreign Policy.* Cambridge, MA: MIT Press.

Evans, Ivor H. N. 1937. *The Negritos of Malaya*. Cambridge: Cambridge University Press.

Evans, John K. 1991. *War, Women and Children in Ancient Rome*. New York: Routledge.

Evans, Michael. 1999. "Women-Only Platoons Cut Injuries and Increase Pass Rates." *The Times*, February 8: front page.

Fabbro, David. 1978. "Peaceful Societies: An Introduction." *Journal of Peace Research* 15: 67–83.

Fagot, B. I., R. Hagan, M. D. Leinbach, and S. Krosberg. 1985. "Differential Reactions to Assertive and Communicative Acts of Toddler Boys and Girls." *Child Development* 56: 1499–1505.

Faiman, C. and J. S. D. Winter. 1974. "Gonadotropins and Sex Hormone Patterns in Puberty: Clinical Data." In Melvin M. Grumbach, Gilman D. Grave, and Florence E. Mayer, eds., *Control of the Onset of Puberty*. New York: Wiley: 32–55.

Fairbank, John K., ed. 1978. *The Cambridge History of China, Volume 10: Late Ch'ing, 1800–1911, Part I*. Cambridge: Cambridge University Press.

Faludi, Susan. 1994. "The Naked Citadel." *The New Yorker*, September 5: 62–81.
　　1999. *Stiffed: The Betrayal of the American Man*. New York: William Morrow.

Farah, Douglas. 2000. "A War against Women: Sierra Leone Rebels Practiced Systematic Sexual Terror." *The Washington Post*, February 11: A1, A19.

Farrell, Warren. 1993. *The Myth of Male Power: Why Men Are the Disposable Sex*. New York: Simon & Schuster.

Fausto-Sterling, Anne. 1985. *Myths of Gender: Biological Theories about Women and Men*. New York: Basic.
　　1993. "The Five Sexes: Why Male and Female Are Not Enough." *The Sciences* 33, 2: 20–25.
　　1997. "Gender Difference and Sameness: Reading between the Lines." *Journal of Social Issues* 53, 2 (Summer): 233–58.

Feinberg, Leslie. 1996. *Trans-Gender Warriors: Making History from Joan of Arc to Rupaul*. Boston: Beacon.

Fellman, Michael. 1992. "Women and Guerrilla Warfare." In Clinton and Silber eds.: 147–70.

Feminism and Nonviolence Study Group. 1983. *Piecing It Together: Feminism and Nonviolence*. London: The Feminism and Nonviolence Study Group.

Ferguson, Kathy E. 1993. *The Man Question: Visions of Subjectivity in Feminist Theory*. Berkeley: University of California Press.
　　1996. "From a Kibbutz Journal: Reflections on Gender, Race, and Militarism in Israel." In Shapiro and Alker eds.: 435–54.

Ferguson, R. Brian. 1984. "Introduction: Studying War." In Ferguson ed.: 1–82.
　　ed. 1984. *Warfare, Culture, and Environment*. New York: Academic Press.
　　1990. "Explaining War." In Haas ed.: 26–55.
　　1997. "Violence and War in Prehistory." In Martin and Frayer eds.: 321–56.

Ferguson, R. Brian and Neil L. Whitehead, eds. 1992. *War in the Tribal Zone: Expanding States and Indigenous Warfare*. Santa Fe, NM: School of American Research Press.

Fernald, Russell D. 1993. "Cichlids in Love." *The Sciences* 33, 4: 27–31.

Ferrill, Arther. 1985. *The Origins of War: From the Stone Age to Alexander the Great.* London: Thames and Hudson.

Feshbach, Seymour. 1987. "Individual Aggression, National Attachment, and the Search for Peace: Psychological Perspectives." *Aggressive Behavior* 13: 315–25.

—— 1989. "The Bases and Development of Individual Aggression." In Groebel and Hinde eds.: 78–90.

Feshbach, Seymour and Norma Deitch Feshbach. 1986. "Aggression and Altruism: A Personality Perspective." In Zahn-Waxler, Cummings, and Iannotti eds.: 189–217.

Feste, Karen A. 1994. "Behavioral Theories: The Science of International Politics and Women." In Beckman and D'Amico eds.: 41–54.

Filaire, E., C. Le Scanff, F. Duche, and G. Lac. 1999. "The Relationship between Salivary Adrenocortical Hormones Changes and Personality in Elite Female Athletes during Handball and Volleyball Competition." *Research Quarterly for Exercise and Sport* 70, 3 (September): 297–302.

Filkins, Dexter. 2000. "In Sri Lanka, Dying To Be Equals: As Warfare Culls the Tamil Tigers' Ranks, Women Have Become the Rebels' Newest Weapon." *San Francisco Chronicle*, February 21.

Fisher, Ian. 1999. "Like Mother, Like Daughter, Eritrean Women Wage War." *The New York Times*, August 26: A1.

Fishman, R. B. and S. M. Breedlove. 1988. "Sexual Dimorphism in the Developing Nervous System." In E. Meisami and P. Timairas, eds., *Handbook of Human Growth and Developmental Biology*. Boca Raton, FL: CRC Press.

Fishman, Sarah. 1991. *We Will Wait: Wives of French Prisoners of War, 1940–1945.* New Haven, CT: Yale University Press.

Flaceliere, Robert. 1962. *Love in Ancient Greece.* New York: Crown.

Flax, Jane. 1990. *Thinking Fragments: Psychoanalysis, Feminism, and Postmodernism in the Contemporary West.* Berkeley: University of California Press.

Floud, Roderick, Kenneth Wachter, and Annabel Gregory. 1990. *Height, Health and History: Nutritional Status in the United Kingdom, 1750–1980.* Cambridge: Cambridge University Press.

Foley, Robert. 1995. *Humans before Humanity.* Cambridge, MA: Blackwell.

Forbes, Frederick E. [1851] 1966. *Dahomey and the Dahomans*, Volumes I and II [cited as /I and /II]. London: Frank Cass.

Forcey, Linda Rennie. 1989. "Introduction to Peace Studies." In Forcey ed.: 3–14.

—— ed. 1989. *Peace: Meanings, Politics, Strategies.* New York: Praeger.

—— 1991. "Women as Peacemakers: Contested Terrain for Feminist Peace Studies." *Peace and Change* 16, 4: 331–54.

—— 1995. "Women's Studies, Peace Studies, and the Difference Debate." *Women's Studies Quarterly* 23, 3/4: 9–14.

Foreign Affairs. 1997. *The New Shape of World Politics: Contending Paradigms in International Relations.* New York, W. W. Norton.

Forrester, Jay W. 1971. "Counterintuitive Behavior of Social Systems." *Technology Review* 73, 3 (January): 52–68.

Forsberg, Randall Caroline Watson. 1997a. "Toward a Theory of Peace: The Role of Moral Beliefs." Ph.D. dissertation, Department of Political Science, Massachusetts Institute of Technology, June.

  1997b. "Toward the End of War." *Boston Review* 22, 5 (October/November): 4–9.

Foster, Catherine. 1989. *Women for All Seasons: The Story of the Women's International League for Peace and Freedom*. Athens: University of Georgia Press.

Foster, Mary LeCron. 1986. "Is War Necessary?" In Foster and Rubinstein eds.: 71–78.

Foster, Mary LeCron and Robert A. Rubinstein. 1986. "Introduction." In Foster and Rubinstein eds.: xi–xviii.

  eds. 1986. *Peace and War: Cross-Cultural Perspectives*. New Brunswick, NJ: Transaction.

Fox, Robin. 1991. "Aggression: Then and Now." In Robinson and Tiger eds.: 81–93.

Fraioli, Deborah. 1996. "Why Joan of Arc Never Became an Amazon." In Wheeler and Wood eds.: 189–204.

Francis, Richard C., Kiran Soma, and Russell D. Fernald. 1993. "Social Regulation of the Brain–Pituitary–Gonadal Axis." *Proceedings of the National Academy of Sciences* 90 (August): 7794–98.

Francke, Linda Bird. 1997. *Ground Zero: The Gender Wars in the Military*. New York: Simon & Schuster.

Frank, Laurence G., Stephen E. Glickman, and Paul Licht. 1991. "Fatal Sibling Aggression, Precocial Development, and Androgens in Neonatal Spotted Hyenas." *Science* 252 (May): 702–4.

Frankel, Mark. 1995. "Boy Soldiers: Special Report." *Newsweek* August 7: cover, 8–21.

Fraser, Antonia. 1989. *The Warrior Queens*. New York: Knopf.

French, Marilyn. 1994. "Power/Sex." In H. Lorraine Radtke and Henderikus J. Stam, eds., *Power/Gender: Social Relations in Theory and Practice*. Thousand Oaks, CA: Sage: 15–35.

Freud, Sigmund. [1915] 1968. "Thoughts for the Times on War and Death." In John Rickman, ed., *Civilisation, War and Death: Sigmund Freud*. London: Hogarth.

  [1930] 1975. *Civilization and Its Discontents*. Translated by Joan Riviere. Revised and edited by James Strachey. London: Hogarth.

  [1933] 1968. "Why War?" In John Rickman, ed. *Civilisation, War and Death: Sigmund Freud*. London: Hogarth.

Fried, Morton, Marvin Harris, and Robert Murphy, eds. 1967. *War: The Anthropology of Armed Conflict and Aggression*. Garden City, NY: Natural History Press.

Fritz, Stephen G. 1996. "'We are Trying . . . to Change the Face of the World' – Ideology and Motivation in the Wehrmacht on the Eastern Front: The View from Below." *Journal of Military History* 60 (October): 683–710.

Frodi, A., J. Macauley, and P. R. Thome. 1977. "Are Women Always Less Aggressive than Men? A Review of the Experimental Literature." *Psychological Bulletin* 84: 634–60.

Fuentes, Annette. 1992. "Women Warriors? Equality, Yes – Militarism, No." In Blacksmith ed.: 34–40. [Reprinted from *The Nation*, October 28, 1991: 253, 516.]

Fukuyama, Francis. 1998. "Women and the Evolution of World Politics." *Foreign Affairs* 77, 5 (September/October): 24–40.

Fuss, Diana. 1989. *Essentially Speaking: Feminism, Nature and Difference*. New York: Routledge.

Fussell, Paul. 1975. *The Great War and Modern Memory*. Oxford: Oxford University Press.

   1989. *Wartime: Understanding and Behavior in the Second World War*. Oxford: Oxford University Press.

   1998. "The Guts, Not the Glory, of Fighting the 'Good War.'" *The Washington Post*, July 26: C1.

Fussler, Diane Burke. 1996. *No Time for Fear: Voices of American Military Nurses in World War II*. East Lansing: Michigan State University Press.

Gabin, Nancy Felice. 1995. "Women Defense Workers in World War II: Views on Gender Equality in India." In O'Brien and Parsons eds.: 107–18.

Gabriel, Richard A. 1987. *No More Heroes: Madness and Psychiatry in War*. New York: Hill & Wang.

   1988. *The Painful Field: The Psychiatric Dimension of Modern War*. New York: Greenwood.

Gade, Paul A., David R. Segal, and Edgar M. Johnson. 1996. "The Experience of Foreign Militaries." In Herek, Jobe, and Carney eds.: 106–30.

Gagneux, P., D. S. Woodruff, and C. Boesch. 1997. "Furtive Mating in Female Chimpanzees." *Nature* 387, 6631 (May 22): 358–59.

Gal, Reuven. 1986. *A Portrait of the Israeli Soldier*. New York: Greenwood.

   1994. "Gays in the Military: Policy and Practice in the Israeli Defence Forces." In Scott and Stanley eds.: 181–90.

Galey, Margaret E. 1994. "The United Nations and Women's Issues." In Beckman and D'Amico eds.: 131–40.

Gall, Carlotta. 1999. "Women Protest Draftees' Kosovo Duty." *The New York Times*, May 20: A15.

Gallagher, Nance W. 1993. "The Gender Gap in Popular Attitudes towards the Use of Force." In Howes and Stevenson eds.: 23–38.

Ganguly, Dilip. 2000. "Female Fighters Used in Sri Lanka." Associated Press, January 10.

Gatschet, Albert Samuel. 1890. *The Klamath Indians of Southwestern Oregon*. Washington, DC: US Government Printing Office [Department of the Interior].

Geen, Russell G. 1998. "Aggression and Antisocial Behavior." In Gilbert, Fiske, and Lindzey eds.: 317–56.

Gellman, Barton. 1997. "Pop! Went the Tale of the Bubble Gum Spiked with Sex Hormones." *The Washington Post*, July 28: A14.

Genovese, Michael A., ed. 1993. *Women as National Leaders: The Political Performance of Women as Heads of Government*. Thousand Oaks, CA: Sage.

Gerster, Robin. 1995. "A Bit of the Other: Touring Vietnam." In Damousi and Lake eds.: 223–38.

Gerzon, Mark. 1982. *A Choice of Heroes: The Changing Face of American Manhood.* Boston: Houghton Mifflin.

Ghiglieri, Michael P. 1999. *The Dark Side of Man: Tracing the Origins of Male Violence.* Reading, MA: Perseus.

Gibbons, Ann. 1992. "Chimps: More Diverse than a Barrel of Monkeys." *Science* 255 (January): 287–88.

Giddens, Anthony. 1984. *The Constitution of Society: Outline of the Theory of Structuration.* Berkeley: University of California Press.

Gilbert, Daniel T., Susan T. Fiske, and Gardner Lindzey, eds. 1998. *The Handbook of Social Psychology.* 4th edition. Volume II. Boston: McGraw-Hill.

Gilbert, Sandra M. 1987. "Soldier's Heart: Literary Men, Literary Women, and the Great War." In Higonnet *et al.* eds.: 197–226.

Gilbert, Susan. 1998. "Infant Homicide Found To Be Rising in US" *The New York Times,* October 27: D10.

Gilligan, Carol. 1982. *In a Different Voice: Psychological Theory and Women's Development.* Cambridge, MA: Harvard University Press.

Gilman, Charlotte Perkins. [1915] 1979. *Herland.* New York: Pantheon.

Gilmore, David D. 1990. *Manhood in the Making: Cultural Concepts of Masculinity.* New Haven, CT: Yale University Press.

Gilpin, Robert. 1988. "The Theory of Hegemonic War." In Rotberg and Rabb eds.: 15–37.

Gioseffi, Daniela, ed. 1988. *Women on War: Essential Voices for the Nuclear Age.* New York: Simon & Schuster.

Glad, Betty, ed. 1990. *Psychological Dimensions of War.* Newbury Park, CA: Sage.

Gladue, Brian A. 1991. "Aggressive Behavioral Characteristics, Hormones, and Sexual Orientation in Men and Women." *Aggressive Behavior* 17: 313–26.

Gladue, Brian A., William W. Beatty, Jan Larson, and R. Dennis Staton. 1990. "Sexual Orientation and Spatial Ability in Men and Women." *Psychobiology* 18, 1: 101–8.

Goertz, Gary and Paul Diehl. 1992. *Territorial Changes and International Conflict.* New York: Routledge.

Goldberg, Carey. 1998a. "After Girls Get the Attention, Focus Shifts to Boys' Woes." *The New York Times,* April 23: A1.

   1998b. "Children and Violent Video Games: A Warning." *The New York Times,* December 15: A14.

Goldberg, Jeffrey. 2000. "Diaper Diplomacy: Encounter with Jamie Rubin." *The New York Times Magazine,* April 30: 32.

Goldberg, Steven. 1993. *Why Men Rule: A Theory of Male Dominance.* Chicago: Open Court.

Goldberger, Nancy Rule, Jill Mattuck Tarule, Blythe McVicker Clinchy, and Mary Field Belenky, eds. 1996. *Knowledge, Difference, and Power: Essays Inspired by "Women's Ways of Knowing."* New York: Basic.

Goldman, Nancy Loring, ed. 1982. *Female Soldiers – Combatants or Noncombatants? Historical and Contemporary Perspectives.* Westport, CT: Greenwood.

Goldman, Peter and Tony Fuller, with Richard Manning, Stryker McGuire, Wally McNamee, and Vern E. Smith. 1983. *Charlie Company: What Vietnam Did to Us.* New York: William Morrow.

Goldschmidt, Walter. 1986. "Personal Motivation and Institutionalized Conflict." In Foster and Rubinstein eds.: 3–14.

1989. "Inducement to Military Participation in Tribal Societies." In Turner and Pitt eds.: 15–31.

1990. *The Human Career: The Self in the Symbolic World*. Cambridge, MA: Basil Blackwell.

Goldstein, Joshua S. 1987. "The Emperor's New Genes: Sociobiology and War." *International Studies Quarterly* 31 (March): 33–43.

1988. *Long Cycles: Prosperity and War in the Modern Age*. New Haven, CT: Yale University Press.

1995. "International Relations and Everyday Life." In Ruth Zemke and Florence Clark, eds., *Occupational Science: The First Five Years*. Philadelphia: F. A. Davis: 13–22.

2001. *International Relations*. 4th edition. New York: Longman.

Goldstein, Joshua S. and John R. Freeman. 1990. *Three-Way Street: Strategic Reciprocity in World Politics*. Chicago: University of Chicago Press.

Goleman, Daniel. 1992. "Attending to the Children of All the World's War Zones." *The New York Times*, December 6: E7.

1995. "Severe Trauma May Damage the Brain as Well as the Psyche." *The New York Times*, August 1: C3.

Gonzalez-Bono, E., A. Salvador, M. A. Serrano, and J. Ricarte. 1999. "Testosterone, Cortisol, and Mood in a Sports Team Competition." *Hormones and Behavior* 35, 1 (February): 55–62.

Goodall, Jane. 1986. *The Chimpanzees of Gombe: Patterns of Behavior*. Cambridge, MA: Harvard University Press.

Goodall, Jane with Phillip Berman. 1999. *Reason for Hope: A Spiritual Journey*. New York: Warner.

Goodfellow, Kris. 1998. "Sony Comes On Strong in Video-Game War." *The New York Times*, May 25: D5.

Goodman, Ellen. 1984. "Learning the Jargon of War." *The Boston Globe*, June 19: 15.

Goodman, H. Maurice. 1996. *Basic Medical Endocrinology*. 2nd edition. Philadelphia: Lippincott-Raven.

Goossen, Rachael Waltner. 1997. *Women against the Good War: Conscientious Objection and Gender on the American Home Front, 1941–1947*. Chapel Hill: University of North Carolina Press.

Grant, Rebecca. 1991. "The Sources of Gender Bias in International Relations Theory." In Grant and Newland eds.: 8–26.

Grant, Rebecca and Kathleen Newland. 1991. "Introduction." In Grant and Newland eds.: 1–7.

eds. 1991. *Gender and International Relations*. Indianapolis: Indiana University Press.

Gray, Chris Hables. 1997. *Postmodern War: The New Politics of Conflict*. New York: Guilford.

Gray, J. Glenn. 1959. *The Warriors: Reflections of Men in Battle*. New York: Harper & Row.

Gray, John. 1992. *Men Are from Mars, Women Are from Venus: A Practical Guide for Improving Communication and Getting What You Want in Your Relationships*. New York: Harper Collins.

Green, Miranda Jane. 1993. *Celtic Myths: The Legendary Past*. Austin: University of Texas Press.

Green, Richard. 1987. *The "Sissy Boy Syndrome" and the Development of Homosexuality*. New Haven, CT: Yale University Press.

Gregor, Thomas. 1990. "Uneasy Peace: Intertribal Relations in Brazil's Upper Xingu." In Haas ed.: 105–24.

Griesse, Anne Eliot and Richard Stites. 1982. "Russia: Revolution and War." In Goldman ed.: 61–84.

Griffen, William B. 1988. *Apaches at War and Peace: The Janos Presidio 1750–1858*. Albuquerque: University of New Mexico.

Griffin, Susan. 1992. *A Chorus of Stones: The Private Life of War*. New York: Anchor.

Grimble, Sir Arthur. 1953. *A Pattern of Islands*. London: John Murray.

   1972. *Migrations, Myth and Magic from the Gilbert Islands*. Arranged by Rosemary Grimble. London: Routledge & Kegan Paul.

Grimsley, Kirstin Downey and R. H. Melton. 1998. "Full-Time Moms Earn Respect, Poll Says." *The Washington Post*, March 22: A16.

Grinnell, George Bird. 1923. *The Cheyenne Indians: Their History and Ways of Life*. Volume II. New Haven, CT: Yale University Press.

Groebel, Jo and Robert A. Hinde, eds. 1989. *Aggression and War: Their Biological and Social Bases*. Cambridge: Cambridge University Press.

Grossman, Dave. 1995. *On Killing: The Psychological Cost of Learning to Kill in War and Society*. Boston: Little Brown.

Grumbach, Melvin M. and Judson J. Van Wyk. 1974. "Disorders of Sex Differentiation." In Robert H. Williams, ed. *Textbook of Endocrinology*. 5th edition. Philadelphia: W. B. Saunders.

Gubar, Susan. 1987. " 'This Is My Rifle, This Is My Gun': World War II and the Blitz on Women." In Higonnet *et al.* eds.: 227–59.

Gur, Ruben C., Lyn Harper Mozley, P. David Mozley, Susan M. Resnick, Joel S. Karp, Abass Alavi, Steven E. Arnold, and Raquel E. Gur. 1995. "Sex Differences in Regional Cerebral Glucose Metabolism during a Resting State." *Science* 267 (January 27): 528–31.

Gurr, Ted Robert. 1993. *Minorities at Risk: A Global View of Ethnopolitical Conflicts*. Washington, DC: United States Institute of Peace Press.

Gurr, Ted Robert and Barbara Harff. 1994. *Ethnic Conflict in World Politics*. Boulder, CO: Westview.

Gutman, Roy. 1993. *A Witness to Genocide: The 1993 Pulitzer Prize-Winning Dispatches on the "Ethnic Cleansing" of Bosnia*. New York: Macmillan.

Gutmann, Stephanie. 2000. *The Kinder, Gentler Military: Can America's Gender-Neutral Fighting Force Still Win Wars?* New York: Scribner.

Haas, Jonathan, ed. 1990. *The Anthropology of War*. Cambridge: Cambridge University Press.

Hacking, Ian. 1983. *Representing and Intervening: Introductory Topics in the Philosophy of Natural Science*. Cambridge: Cambridge University Press.

Hackworth, David H. 1991. "War and the Second Sex." *Newsweek*, August 5: 24–28.

Hadley, Mac E. 1996. *Endocrinology*. 4th edition. Upper Saddle River, NJ: Prentice-Hall.

Hall, Richard. 1993. *Patriots in Disguise: Women Warriors of the Civil War*. New York: Paragon House.

Hall, Roberta L. 1985. "The Question of Size." In Hall ed.: 127–54.

ed. 1985. *Male–Female Differences: A Bio-Cultural Perspective*. New York: Praeger.

Halliday, Fred. 1991. "Hidden from International Relations: Women and the International Arena." In Grant and Newland eds.: 158–69.

Halpern, Carolyn Tucker, J. Richard Udry, Benjamin Campbell, and Chirayath Suchindran. 1993. "Relationships between Aggression and Pubertal Increases in Testosterone: A Panel Analysis of Adolescent Males." *Social Biology* 40, 1–2: 8–24.

Hamburg, David A. 1992. *Today's Children: Creating a Future for a Generation in Crisis*. New York: Times Books.

Hamer, Dean H., Stella Hu, Victoria L. Magnuson, Nan Hu, and Angela M. L. Pattatucci. 1993. "A Linkage between DNA Markers on the X Chromosome and Male Sexual Orientation." *Science* 261 (July): 321–27.

Hampson, Elizabeth and Doreen Kimura. 1992. "Sex Differences and Hormonal Influences on Cognitive Function in Humans." In Becker, Breedlove, and Crews eds.: 357–400.

Hanley, Lynne. 1991. *Writing War: Fiction, Gender, and Memory*. Amherst: University of Massachusetts Press.

Hansbrough, Henry Clay. 1915. *War and Woman: An Exposition of Man's Failure as a Harmonizer*. New York: Duffield.

Haraway, Donna. 1989. *Primate Visions: Gender, Race, and Nature in the World of Modern Science*. New York: Routledge.

Harding, Sandra G. 1986. *The Science Question in Feminism*. Ithaca, NY: Cornell University Press.

ed. 1987. *Feminism and Methodology: Social Science Issues*. Bloomington: Indiana University Press.

Hardy, Alister. 1960. "Was Man More Aquatic in the Past?" *New Scientist* 7 (April): 642–45.

Harrell, Margaret C. and Laura L. Miller. 1997. *New Opportunities for Military Women: Effects upon Readiness, Cohesion, and Morale*. Washington, DC: National Defense Research Institute, Rand Corporation.

Harrington, Mona. 1992. "What Exactly Is Wrong with the Liberal State as an Agent of Change?" In Peterson ed.: 65–82.

Harris, Adrienne. 1989. "Bringing Artemis to Life: A Plea for Militance and Aggression in Feminist Peace Politics." In Harris and King eds.: 93–114.

Harris, Adrienne and Ynestra King. 1989. "Introduction." In Harris and King eds.: 1–12.

eds. 1989. *Rocking the Ship of State: Toward a Feminist Peace Politics*. Boulder, CO: Westview.

Harris, J. A. 1999. "Review and Methodological Considerations in Research on Testosterone and Aggression." *Aggression and Violent Behavior* 4, 3 (Fall): 273–91.

Harris, Kenneth. 1995. "Prime Minister Margaret Thatcher: The Influence of Her Gender on Her Foreign Policy." In D'Amico and Beckman eds.: 59–70.

Harris, Marvin. 1974. *Cows, Pigs, Wars and Witches: The Riddles of Culture*. New York: Random House.

1977. *Cannibals and Kings: The Origins of Culture*. New York: Vintage.

1984. "A Cultural Materialist Theory of Band and Village Warfare: The Yanomamö Test." In Ferguson ed.: 111–40.

1989. *Our Kind: Who We Are, Where We Came From, Where We Are Going.* New York: Harper.

Harter, Susan. 1998. "The Development of Self-Representations." In Damon and Eisenberg eds.: 553–618.

Hartsock, Nancy C. M. ["Harstock"]. 1982. "The Barracks Community in Western Political Thought: Prologomena to a Feminist Critique of War and Politics." *Women's Studies International Forum* 5, 3/4: 283–87.

1983. *Money, Sex, and Power: Toward a Feminist Historical Materialism.* New York: Longman.

1989. "Masculinity, Heroism, and the Making of War." In Harris and King eds.: 133–52.

Hartup, Willard W. 1983. "Peer Relations." In Mussen ed.: 103–96.

Hassig, Ross. 1988. *Aztec Warfare: Imperial Expansion and Political Control.* Norman: University of Oklahoma Press.

Hayden, Brian, M. Deal, A. Cannon, and J. Casey. 1986. "Ecological Determinants of Women's Status among Hunter/Gatherers." *Human Evolution* 1, 5: 449–74.

Headland, Thomas N., ed. 1992. *The Tasaday Controversy: Assessing the Evidence.* Washington, DC: American Anthropology Association.

Hearn, Jeff and David Morgan, eds. 1990. *Men, Masculinities and Social Theory.* Boston: Unwin Hyman.

Heath, Stephen. 1987. "Male Feminism." In Alice Jardine and Paul Smith, eds., *Men in Feminism.* New York: Methuen: 1–32.

Hedges, Chris. 1998. "Dejected Belgrade Embraces Hedonism, but Still, Life Is No Cabaret." *The New York Times*, January 19: A1.

Hediger, H. 1955. *Studies of the Psychology and Behaviour of Captive Animals in Zoos and Circuses.* London: Butterworths Scientific.

Heizer, Robert F., ed. 1978. "Volume 8 – California." In William C. Sturtevant, ed. *Handbook of North American Indians.* Washington, DC: Smithsonian Institution.

Held, Virginia. 1990. "Mothering versus Contract." In Jane J. Mansbridge, ed., *Beyond Self-Interest.* Chicago: University of Chicago Press: 287–304.

Henderson, James D. and Linda Roddy Henderson. 1978. *Ten Notable Women of Latin America.* Chicago: Nelson-Hall.

Herbert, J. 1989. "The Physiology of Aggression." In Groebel and Hinde eds.: 58–74.

Herdt, Gilbert. 1981. *Guardians of the Flutes: Idioms of Masculinity.* New York: McGraw-Hill.

1987. *The Sambia: Ritual and Gender in New Guinea.* New York: Holt, Rinehart and Winston.

Herek, Gregory M., Jared B. Jobe, and Ralph M. Carney, eds. 1996. *Out in Force: Sexual Orientation and the Military.* Chicago: University of Chicago Press.

Herman, Judith Lewis. 1992. *Trauma and Recovery.* New York: Basic.

Herman-Giddens, Marcia E., Eric J. Slova, Richard Wasserman, Carlos J. Bourdony, Manju V. Bhapkar, Gary Gikoch, and Cynthia M. Hasemeier.

1997. "Secondary Sexual Characteristics and Menopause in Young Girls Seen in Office Practice: A Study from the Pediatric Research in Office Settings Network." *Pediatrics* 99, 4 (April): 505–12.

Herskovits, Melville J. 1938. *Dahomey: An Ancient West African Kingdom.* Volume II. New York: J. J. Augustin.

Hess, Pamela. 1997. "Made to Measure Up." *The Washington Post*, August 24: C2.

Hesse, Petra and John E. Mack. 1991. "The World Is a Dangerous Place: Images of the Enemy on Children's Television." In Rieber ed.: 131–54.

Hewitt, Linda. 1974. *Women Marines in World War I.* Washington, DC: History and Museums Division, Headquarters, US Marine Corps.

Hicks, George. 1995. *The Comfort Women: Japan's Brutal Regime of Enforced Prostitution in the Second World War.* New York: W. W. Norton.

Higonnet, Margaret R. and Patrice L.-R. Higonnet. 1987. "The Double Helix." In Higonnet *et al.* eds.: 31–50.

Higonnet, Margaret Randolph, Jane Jenson, Sonya Michel, and Margaret Collins Weitz, eds. 1987. *Behind the Lines: Gender and the Two World Wars.* New Haven, CT: Yale University Press.

Hill, James Michael. 1986. *Celtic Warfare: 1595–1763.* Atlantic Highlands, NJ: Humanities Press.

Hinde, Robert A. 1983. "Triadic Interactions and Social Sophisticaition." In Hinde ed.: 152–53.

    ed. 1983. *Primate Social Relationships: An Integrated Approach.* Boston: Blackwell Scientific.

Hinde, R. A. and J. Groebel. 1989. "The Problem of Aggression." In Groebel and Hinde eds.: 3–7.

Hines, Melissa. 1982. "Prenatal Gonadal Hormones and Sex Differences in Human Behavior." *Psychological Bulletin* 92, 1: 56–80.

Hirschfeld, Magnus. 1934. *The Sexual History of the World War.* New York: Panurge Press.

Hirschmann, Nancy J. 1989. "Freedom, Recognition, and Obligation: A Feminist Approach to Political Theory." *American Political Science Review* 83, 4: 1227–44.

    1992. *Rethinking Obligation: A Feminist Method for Political Theory.* Ithaca, NY: Cornell University Press.

Hobbs, Margaret. 1987. " 'The Perils of Unbridled Masculinity': Pacifist Elements in the Feminist and Socialist Thought of Charlotte Perkins Gilman." In Pierson ed.: 149–69.

Hodes, Martha. 1992. "Wartime Dialogues on Illicit Sex: White Women and Black Men." In Clinton and Silber eds.: 230–46.

Hoffmann, John P., Timothy O. Ireland, and Cathy Spatz Widom. 1994. "Traditional Socialization Theories of Violence: A Critical Examination." In Archer ed.: 289–309.

Holbrooke, Richard. 1998. *To End a War.* New York: Random House.

Holloway, Ralph L., Jr. 1967. "Human Aggression: The Need for a Species-Specific Framework." In Fried, Harris, and Murphy eds.: 29–48.

    ed., 1974. *Primate Aggression, Territoriality, and Xenophobia: A Comparative Perspective.* New York: Academic Press.

Holm, Jeanne. 1992. *Women in the Military: An Unfinished Revolution.* Revised edition. Novato, CA: Presidio Press.

Holmes, Katie. 1995. "Day Mothers and Night Sisters: World War I Nurses and Sexuality." In Damousi and Lake eds.: 43–59.

Holmes, Richard. 1985. *Acts of War: The Behavior of Men in Battle.* New York: Free Press.

Holsti, Kal. 1985. *The Dividing Discipline: Hegemony and Diversity in International Theory.* London: Allen & Unwin.

Holsti, Ole R. and James N. Rosenau. 1981. "The Foreign Policy Beliefs of Women in Leadership Positions." *Journal of Politics* 43: 326–47.

Honey, Maureen. 1995. "Remembering Rosie: Advertising Images of Women in World War II." In O'Brien and Parsons eds.: 83–106.

Hopp, M. and O. A. E. Rasa. 1990. "Territoriality and Threat Perceptions in Urban Humans." In Van Der Dennen and Falger eds.: 131–46.

Horowitz, Donald L. 1985. *Ethnic Groups in Conflict.* Berkeley: University of California Press.

Horrocks, Roger. 1995. *Male Myths and Icons: Masculinity in Popular Culture.* New York: St. Martin's.

Howard, Michael. 1976. *War in European History.* Oxford: Oxford University Press.

1983. *The Causes of Wars, and Other Essays.* Cambridge, MA: Harvard University Press.

Howes, Ruth H. and Michael R. Stevenson, eds. 1993. *Women and the Use of Military Force.* Boulder, CO: Lynne Rienner.

Hrdy, Sarah Blaffer. 1981. *The Woman That Never Evolved.* Cambridge, MA: Harvard University Press.

Human Rights Watch. 1993. *Rape in Kashmir: A Crime of War* [C509]. New York: Human Rights Watch, May.

1994. *Rape in Haiti: A Weapon of Terror* [B608]. New York: Human Rights Watch, July.

1995. *The Human Rights Watch Global Report on Women's Human Rights* [5469]. New York: Human Rights Watch, August.

1997. *Liberia: Emerging from the Destruction* [A907]. New York: Human Rights Watch, November.

1998a. *Proxy Targets: Civilians in the War in Burundi* [1797]. New York: Human Rights Watch, March.

1998b. *Sowing Terror: Atrocities against Civilians in Sierra Leone* [1003A]. New York: Human Rights Watch, August.

2000. *Kosovo: Rape as a Weapon of "Ethnic Cleansing"* [Yugoslavia, D1203]. New York: Human Rights Watch, March.

Hunt, Swanee. 1997. "Women's Vital Voices." *Foreign Affairs* 76, 4 (July): 6–7.

Hunter, Anne E., ed. 1991. *On Peace, War, and Gender: A Challenge to Genetic Explanations* [*Genes and Gender VI*]. New York: Feminist Press.

Huntingford, Felicity Ann. 1976. "The Relationship between Inter- and Intra-Specific Aggression." *Animal Behavior* 24: 485–97.

Huntington, Samuel P. 1957. *The Soldier and the State: The Theory and Politics of Civil–Military Relations.* New York: Vintage.

Huston, Aletha C. 1983. "Sex-Typing." In Mussen ed.: 387–468.

Huston, Nancy. 1982. "Tales of War and Tears of Women." *Women's Studies International Forum* 5, 3/4: 271–82.

Huth, Paul K. 1996. *Standing Your Ground: Territorial Disputes and International Conflict*. Ann Arbor: University of Michigan Press.

Huyghe, Bernard. 1986. "Toward a Structural Model of Violence: Male Initiation Rituals and Tribal Warfare." In Foster and Rubinstein eds.: 25–48.

Hyde, Janet Shibley. 1986. "Gender Differences in Aggression." In Hyde and Linn eds.: 51–66.

Hyde, Janet Shibley and Marcia C. Linn, eds. 1986. *The Psychology of Gender: Advances through Meta-Analysis*. Baltimore: Johns Hopkins University Press.

Iaccino, James F. 1993. *Left Brain–Right Brain Differences: Inquiries, Evidence, and New Approaches*. Hillsdale, NJ: Lawrence Erlbaum Associates.

ICRC (International Committee of the Red Cross). 1999. *Arms Availability and the Situation of Civilians in Armed Conflict*. Geneva: ICRC, June.

Inglis, Ken. 1987. "Men, Women, and War Memorials: Anzac Australia." *Daedalus* 116, 4 (Fall): 35–59.

International Women's Committee of Permanent Peace. 1915. *International Congress of Women Report*. Amsterdam: International Women's Committee of Permanent Peace.

Inverardi, Matthias. 2000. "EU Court Says German Army Must Open for Women." January 11. Luxembourg: Reuters.

Isaksson, Eva. 1988. "Visions of a Peaceful Future: War and Peace in Feminist Utopias." In Isaksson ed.: 247–59.

 ed. 1988. *Women and the Military System*. New York: St. Martin's.

Itani, Junichiro. 1982. "Intraspecific Killing among Non-Human Primates." *Journal of Social and Biological Structures* 5: 361–68.

Jabri, Vivienne and Elanor O'Gorman, eds. 1999. *Women, Culture, and International Relations*. Boulder, CO: Lynne Rienner.

Jacklin, Carol Nagy, ed. 1992. *The Psychology of Gender*. Volume II. Brookfield, VT: Edward Elgar.

Jacklin, Carol N. and Eleanor E. Maccoby. 1978. "Social Behavior at 33 Months in Same-Sex and Mixed-Sex Dyads." *Child Development* 49: 557–69.

Jaggar, Alison M. 1983. *Feminist Politics and Human Nature*. Totowa, NJ: Rowman & Allanheld.

James, Jacquelyn B. 1997. "What Are the Social Issues Involved in Focusing on Difference in the Study of Gender?" *Journal of Social Issues* 53, 2 (Summer): 213–32.

James, William. [1910] 1982. "The Moral Equivalent of War." In *Essays in Religion and Morality*. Cambridge, MA: Harvard University Press.

Jancar, Barbara. 1982. "Yugoslavia: War of Resistance." In Goldman ed.: 85–105.

Jancar-Webster, Barbara. 1990. *Women and Revolution in Yugoslavia 1941–1945*. Denver, CO: Arden.

Janofsky, Michael. 1997. "Women in the Marines Join the Firing Line." *The New York Times*, April 1: A10.

Jaquette, Jane S. 1997. "Women in Power: From Tokenism to Critical Mass." *Foreign Policy* 108 (Fall): 23–37.

Jardine, Alice and Paul Smith, eds. 1987. *Men in Feminism*. New York: Methuen.

Jason, Philip K., ed. 1991. *Fourteen Landing Zones: Approaches to Vietnam War Literature*. Iowa City: University of Iowa Press.

Jeffords, Susan. 1989. *The Remasculinization of America: Gender and the Vietnam War*. Bloomington: Indiana University Press.

1996. "Telling the War Story." In Stiehm ed.: 220–34.

Jeffreys-Jones, Rhodri. 1995. *Changing Differences: Women and the Shaping of American Foreign Policy, 1917–1994*. New Brunswick, NJ: Rutgers University Press.

Jehl, Douglas. 1996. "Mullahs, Look! Women, Armed and Dangerous." *The New York Times*, December 30: A4.

1999. "Arab Honor's Price: A Woman's Blood." *The New York Times*, June 20: A1.

Jen [Chien] Yu-wen. 1973. *The Taiping Revolutionary Movement*. New Haven, CT: Yale University Press.

Jenness, D. 1970. *The Life of the Copper Eskimos: Part A of Volume XII, A Report of the Canadian Arctic Expedition 1913–1918*. New York: Johnson Reprint Corporation.

Jensen, Mark P. 1987. "Gender, Sex Roles, and Attitudes toward War and Nuclear Weapons." *Sex Roles* 17: 253–67.

Jerusalem Post, Internet edition. 2000. "Peace through Strength." [Opinion article.] January 6.

Jervis, Robert. 1976. *Perception and Misperception in International Politics*. Princeton, NJ: Princeton University Press.

Jesser, Clinton J. 1996. *Fierce and Tender Men: Sociological Aspects of the Men's Movement*. Westport, CT: Praeger.

Johnson, Allan G. 1997. *The Gender Knot: Unraveling Our Patriarchal Legacy*. Philadelphia: Temple University Press.

Johnson, Dirk. 1997. "New Messages Sent at Navy Boot Camp." *The New York Times*, March 17: A10.

Jones, Adam. 1994. "Gender and Ethnic Conflict in ex-Yugoslavia." *Ethnic and Racial Studies* 17, 1: 115–34.

1996. "Does 'Gender' Make the World Go Round? Feminist Critiques of International Relations." *Review of International Studies* 22: 405–29.

2000. "Gendercide and Genocide." *Journal of Genocide Research* 2, 2: 185–211.

Jones, David. 1994. "Sex in the Head." *Nature* 370 (August 4): 332.

Jones, David E. 1997. *Women Warriors: A History*. Washington, DC: Brassey's.

Jones, Kathleen. 1990. "Dividing the Ranks: Women and the Draft." In Elshtain and Tobias eds.: 125–38.

Jones, Lynne. 1987. "Perceptions of 'Peace Women' at Greenham Common." In Macdonald, Holden, and Ardener eds.: 179–204.

ed. 1983. *Keeping the Peace: A Women's Peace Handbook 1*. London: The Women's Press.

Jones, Tamara. 1997a. "US Military Takes Aim at Adultery." *The Washington Post*, April 28: A1, A12.

1997b. "The Pilot's Cloudy Future." *The Washington Post*, April 29: D1, D4.

Jungers, William L. and Randall L. Susman. 1984. "Body Size and Skeletal Allometry in African Apes." In Susman ed.: 131–78.

Kagan, Donald. 1995. *On the Origins of War and the Preservation of Peace.* New York: Doubleday.

Kagan, Jerome. 1998. "Biology and the Child." In Damon and Eisenberg eds.: 177–236.

Kampen, Diane L. and Barbara B. Sherwin. 1996. "Estradiol Is Related to Visual Memory in Healthy Young Men." *Behavioral Neuroscience* 110, 3: 613–17.

Kandiyoti, Deniz, ed. 1996. *Gendering the Middle East: Emerging Perspectives.* Syracuse: Syracuse University Press.

Kanogo, Tabitha. 1987. "Kikuyu Women and the Politics of Protest: Mau Mau." In Macdonald, Holden, and Ardener eds.: 78–99.

Kant, Immanuel. [1795] 1957. *Perpetual Peace.* Lewis White Beck, ed. Indianapolis, IN: Bobbs-Merrill.

Kanter, Emanuel. 1926. *The Amazons: A Marxian Study.* Chicago: Charles H. Kerr.

Kaplan, Laura Duhan. 1996. "Woman as Caretaker: An Archetype that Supports Patriarchal Militarism." In Warren and Cady eds.: 165–74.

Kates, Gary. 1995. *Monsieur d'Eon is a Woman: A Tale of Political Intrigue and Sexual Masquerade.* New York: Basic.

Katzenstein, Mary Fainsod. 1998. *Faithful and Fearless: Moving Feminist Protest inside the Church and Military.* Princeton, NJ: Princeton University Press.

Katzenstein, Peter J., ed. 1996. *The Culture of National Security: Norms and Identity in World Politics.* New York: Columbia University Press.

Keddie, Nikki R. and Beth Baron, eds. 1991. *Women in Middle Eastern History: Shifting Boundaries in Sex and Gender.* New Haven, CT: Yale University Press.

Keegan, John. 1976. *The Illustrated Face of Battle: A Study of Agincourt, Waterloo and the Somme.* New York: Viking.

1993. *A History of Warfare.* New York: Knopf.

Keegan, John and Richard Holmes, with John Gau. 1985. *Soldiers: A History of Men in Battle.* London: Hamish Hamilton.

Keeley, Lawrence H. 1996. *War before Civilization.* Oxford: Oxford University Press.

Keen, Sam. 1986. *Faces of the Enemy: Reflections of the Hostile Imagination.* San Francisco: Harper & Row.

1991. *Fire in the Belly: On Being a Man.* New York: Bantam.

Keen, Sam and Ofer Zur. 1989. "Who Is the New Ideal Man?" *Psychology Today* 23, 11 (November): 54–60. [See "What Makes an Ideal Man?" (A Psychology Today Questionnaire) *Psychology Today* (March): 58–60.]

Keller, Evelyn Fox. 1983. *A Feeling for the Organism: The Life and Work of Barbara McClintock.* New York: Freeman.

1984. "Women and Basic Research: Respecting the Unexpected." *Technology Review* (November/December): 44–47.

1985. *Reflections on Gender and Science.* New Haven, CT: Yale University Press.

Kellett, Anthony. 1990. "The Soldier in Battle: Motivational and Behavioral Aspects of the Combat Experience." In Glad ed.: 215–35.

Kelly, Petra. 1995. "Women and the Global Green Movement." In D'Amico and Beckman eds.: 169–82.

Kelly, Raymond C. 2000. *Warless Societies and the Origin of War*. Ann Arbor: University of Michigan Press.

Kelson, Gregory A. 1999. "State of FEMISA, 1998–1999." Memorandum to Feminist Theory and Gender Studies Section members, International Studies Association, February 10.

Kelson, Gregory A. and Barbara Welling Hall. 1998. "State of FEMISA, 1997–1998." Memorandum to Feminist Theory and Gender Studies Section members, International Studies Association, March 4.

Kempadoo, Kamala and Jo Doezema, eds. 1998. *Global Sex Workers: Rights, Resistance, and Redefinition*. New York: Routledge.

Kemper, Theodore D. 1990. *Social Structure and Testosterone: Explorations of the Socio-Bio-Social Chain*. New Brunswick, NJ: Rutgers University Press.

Kennedy, Paul. 1987. *The Rise and Fall of the Great Powers: Economic Change and Military Conflict from 1500–2000*. New York: Random House.

Kent, Susan Kingsley. 1993. *Making Peace: The Reconstruction of Gender in Interwar Britain*. Princeton, NJ: Princeton University Press.

Keohane, Robert O. 1984. *After Hegemony: Cooperation and Discord in the World Political Economy*. Princeton, NJ: Princeton University Press.

   1986. "Realism, Neorealism and the Study of World Politics." In Keohane ed.: 1–26.

   ed. 1986. *Neorealism and Its Critics*. New York: Columbia University Press.

   1989. "International Relations Theory: Contributions of a Feminist Standpoint." *Millennium: Journal of International Studies* 18, 2: 245–53. [Reprinted in Grant and Newland eds. 1991.]

   1998. "Beyond Dichotomy: Conversations between International Relations and Feminist Theory." *International Studies Quarterly* 42, 1: 193–98.

Kerber, Linda K. 1990. "May All Our Citizens Be Soldiers and All Our Soldiers Citizens: The Ambiguities of Female Citizenship in the New Nation." In Elshtain and Tobias eds.: 89–104.

Kessler, Evelyn S. 1976. *Women: An Anthropological View*. New York: Holt, Rinehart and Winston.

Kier, Elizabeth. 1998. "Homosexuals in the US Military: Open Integration and Combat Effectiveness." *International Security* 23, 2 (Fall): 5–39.

Kimmel, Michael S. and Michael A. Messner, eds. 1995. *Men's Lives*, 3rd edition. Boston: Allyn & Bacon.

Kimura, Doreen. 1992. "Sex Differences in the Brain." *Scientific American* 267, 3: 118–25.

Kindlon, Dan and Michael Thompson with Teresa Barker. 1999. *Raising Cain: Protecting the Emotional Life of Boys*. New York: Ballantine.

King, Ynestra. 1990. "Healing the Wounds: Feminism, Ecology, and the Nature/Culture Dualism." In Diamond and Orenstein eds.: 106–21.

Kinney, Katherine. 1991. " 'Humping the Boonies': Sex, Combat, and the Female in Bobbie Ann Mason's *In Country*." In Jason ed.: 38–48.

Kinsey, Alfred C., Wardell B. Pomeroy, Clyde E. Martin, Paul H. Gebhard *et al*. 1953. *Sexual Behavior in the Human Female*. Philadelphia: W. B. Saunders.

Kirk, Gwyn. 1989. "Our Greenham Common: Feminism and Nonviolence." In Harris and King eds.: 115–30.

Kirk, Ilse. 1987. "Images of Amazons: Marriage and Matriarchy." In Macdonald, Holden, and Ardener eds.: 27–39.

Kitch, Sally L. 1991. "Does War Have Gender?" In Hunter ed.: 92–103.

Klama, John (pseudonym) [John Durant, Peter Klopfer, and Susan Oyama, with others]. 1988. *Aggression: The Myth of the Beast Within.* New York: Wiley.

Klare, Michael. 1999. "The Kalashnikov Age." *The Bulletin of the Atomic Scientists* 55, 1 (January/February): 18.

Klare, Michael T. and Yogesh Chandrani, eds. 1998. *World Security: Challenges for a New Century.* 3rd edition. New York: St. Martin's.

Kleinbaum, Abby Wettan. 1983. *The War against the Amazons.* New York: McGraw-Hill.

Knauft, Bruce M. 1987. "Reconsidering Violence in Simple Human Societies: Homicide among the Gebusi of New Guinea." *Current Anthropology* 28, 4: 457–500.

1991. "Violence and Sociality in Human Evolution." *Current Anthropology* 32, 4: 391–428.

1993. "Inducement to Conflict." *Science* 260 (May): 1184–86.

Knecht, R. J. 1982. *Francis I.* Cambridge: Cambridge University Press.

Koestner, Richard, Carol Franz, and Joel Weinberger. 1990. "The Family Origins of Empathic Concern: A 26-Year Longitudinal Study." *Journal of Personality and Social Psychology* 58, 4: 709–17.

Kohlberg, Lawrence. 1976. "Moral Stages and Moralization: The Cognitive-Developmental Approach." In T. Lickona, ed., *Moral Development and Behavior: Theory, Research and Social Issues.* New York: Holt, Rinehart and Winston.

Konner, Melvin. 1982. *The Tangled Wing: Biological Constraints on the Human Spirit.* New York: Harper.

1988. "The Aggressors." *The New York Times Magazine,* August 14: 33.

Koonz, Claudia. 1987. *Mothers in the Fatherland: Women, the Family, and Nazi Politics.* New York: St. Martin's.

Koppes, Clayton R. 1995. "Hollywood and the Politics of Representation: Women, Workers, and African Americans in World War II Movies." In O'Brien and Parsons eds.: 25–40.

Korach, Kenneth S. 1994. "Insights from the Study of Animals Lacking Functional Estrogen Receptor." *Science* 266 (December 2): 1524–27.

Korb, Lawrence. 1994. "Evolving Perspectives on the Military's Policy on Homosexuals: A Personal Note." In Scott and Stanley eds.: 219–30.

Kouri, Elena M., Scott E. Lukas, Harrison G. Pope, Jr., and Paul S. Oliva. 1995. "Increased Aggressive Responding in Male Volunteers Following the Administration of Gradually Increasing Doses of Testosterone Cypionate." *Drug and Alcohol Dependence* 40: 73–79.

Kozak, D. 1996. "Sex Role Identity and Testosterone Level among Women." *Homo* 46, 3 (March): 211–26.

Krasniewicz, Louise. 1992. *Nuclear Summer: The Clash of Communities at the Seneca Women's Peace Encampment.* Ithaca, NY: Cornell University Press.

Krause, Jill. 1995. "The International Dimension of Gender Inequality and Feminist Politics: A 'New Direction' for International Political Economy?" In MacMillan and Linklater eds.: 107–27.

Krauss, Robert M. and Chi-Yue Chiu. 1998. "Language and Social Behavior." In Gilbert, Fiske, and Lindzey eds.: 41–88.

Kristof, Nicholas D. 1998. "Casanovas, Beware! It's Risky for Non-Koreans." *The New York Times,* February 2: A4.

Krogh, Hilde and Ulrike C. Wasmuht. 1984. "Sexism and Bellism or Women and Peace." *International Peace Research Newsletter* 22, 3: 16–23.

Kugler, Jacek and Douglas Lemke, eds. 1996. *Parity and War: Evaluations and Extensions of the War Ledger.* Ann Arbor: University of Michigan Press.

Kuhlman, Erika A. 1997. *Petticoats and White Feathers: Gender Conformity, Race, the Progressive Peace Movement, and the Debate over War, 1895–1919.* Westport, CT: Greenwood Press.

Kuhn, Thomas S. 1970. *The Structure of Scientific Revolutions.* 2nd edition. Chicago: University of Chicago Press.

Kulka, Richard A., William E. Schlenger, John A. Fairbank, Richard L. Hough, B. Kathleen Jordan, Charles R. Marmar, and Daniel S. Weiss. 1990. *Trauma and the Vietnam War Generation: Report of Findings from the National Vietnam Veterans Readjustment Study.* New York: Brunner/Mazel.

Kuroda, Suehisa. 1984. "Interaction over Food among Pygmy Chimpanzees." In Susman ed.: 301–24.

Kurtz, Howard. 1991. "Correspondents Chafe over Curbs on News; Rules Meant to Protect Troops, Officials Say." *The Washington Post,* January 26: A17.

Kurtz, Lester R., ed. 1999. *Encyclopedia of Violence, Peace, and Conflict.* 3 volumes. San Diego, CA: Academic Press.

Laffin, John. 1967. *Women in Battle.* New York: Abelard-Schuman.

Lagerspetz, Kirsti M., Kaj Bjorkqvist, Helena Bjorkqvist, and Helena Lundman. 1988. "Moral Approval of Aggression and Sex Role Identity in Officer Trainees, Conscientious Objectors to Military Service, and in a Female Reference Group." *Aggressive Behavior* 14: 303–13.

Lagerspetz, Kirsti M. J. and Kari Y. H. Lagerspetz. 1983. "Genes and Aggression." In Edward C. Simmel, Martin E. Hahn, and James K. Walters, eds., *Aggressive Behavior: Genetic and Neural Approaches.* Hillsdale, NJ: Lawrence Erlbaum: 89–102.

Lake, Marilyn and Joy Damousi. 1995. "Introduction: Warfare, History and Gender." In Damousi and Lake eds.: 1–22.

Lakoff, George. 1996. *Moral Politics: What Conservatives Know That Liberals Don't.* Chicago: University of Chicago Press.

Laqueur, Thomas. 1990. *Making Sex: Body and Gender from the Greeks to Freud.* Cambridge, MA: Harvard University Press.

Larrington, Carolyne, ed. 1992. *The Feminist Companion to Mythology.* London: Pandora.

Larson, C. Kay. 1995. *'Til I Come Marching Home: A Brief History of American Women in World War II.* Pasadena, MD: The Minerva Center.

Lasswell, Harold D. [1930] 1960. *Psychopathology and Politics.* New York: Viking.

Leacock, Eleanor Burke. 1981. *Myths of Male Dominance: Collected Articles on Women Cross-Culturally.* New York: Monthly Review Press.

1982. "Relations of Production in Band Societies." In Eleanor Leacock and Richard Lee, eds., *Politics and History in Band Societies.* Cambridge: Cambridge University Press: 159–70.

Leakey, Richard and Roger Lewin. 1992. *Origins Reconsidered: In Search of What Makes Us Human*. New York: Doubleday.

Lee, Phyllis C. 1983a. "Play as a Means for Developing Relationships." In Hinde ed.: 81–88.

1983b. "Home Range, Territory and Intergroup Encounters." In Hinde ed.: 231–32.

Lee, Richard Borshay. 1979. *The !Kung San: Men, Women, and Work in a Foraging Society*. Cambridge: Cambridge University Press.

Leed, Eric J. 1979. *No Man's Land: Combat and Identity in World War I*. Cambridge: Cambridge University Press.

Lefkowitz, Mary R. and Maureen B. Fant. 1977. *Women in Greece and Rome*. Toronto: Samuel-Stevens.

Lentin, Ronit. 1996. "Israeli and Palestinian Women Working for Peace." *Peace Review* 8, 3: 385–90.

Lentner, C., ed. 1984. *Geigy Scientific Tables, Volume III: Physical Chemistry, Composition of Blood, Hematology, Somatometric Data*. 8th edition. Basle: Ciba-Geigy.

Leonard, Elizabeth D. 1994. *Yankee Women: Gender Battles in the Civil War*. New York: W. W. Norton.

Lepowsky, Maria. 1993. *Fruit of the Motherland: Gender in an Egalitarian Society*. New York: Columbia University Press.

Levant, Ronald F. with Gini Kopecky. 1995. *Masculinity Reconstructed: Changing the Rules of Manhood – At Work, in Relationships, and in Family Life*. New York: Dutton.

LeVay, Simon. 1991. "A Difference in Hypothalamic Structure between Heterosexual and Homosexual Men." *Science* 253: 1034–37.

Lever, Janet. 1978. "Sex Differences in the Complexity of Children's Play and Games." *American Sociological Review* 43: 471–83.

Levin, Diane E. and Nancy Carlsson-Paige. 1989. "Piaget, War Play and Peace." *The Genetic Epistemologist* 17, 3: 11–15.

Levin, John M. and Richard L. Moreland. 1998. "Small Groups." In Gilbert, Fiske, and Lindzey eds.: 415–69.

Levine, Philippa. 1993. "Women and Prostitution: Metaphor, Reality, History." *Canadian Journal of History* (December): 479–94.

Levy, Charles J. 1992. "ARVN as Faggots: Inverted Warfare in Vietnam." In Michael S. Kimmel and Michael A. Messner, eds., *Men's Lives*. 2nd edition. New York: Macmillan: 183–98.

Levy, J. 1978. "Lateral Differences in the Human Brain in Cognition and Behavioral Control." In P. Buser and A. Rougeul-Buser, eds., *Cerebral Correlates of Conscious Experience*. New York: North-Holland: 285–98.

Levy, Jack S. 1983. *War in the Modern Great Power System, 1495–1975*. Lexington: University of Kentucky Press.

1985. "Theories of General War." *World Politics* 37, 3: 344–74.

1989. "The Causes of War: A Review of Theories and Evidence," in Philip E. Tetlock *et al.*, eds., *Behavior, Society, and Nuclear War*. Volume I. Oxford: Oxford University Press: 209–333.

Lewin, Tamar. 1998a. "Men Assuming Bigger Share at Home, New Survey Shows." *The New York Times*, April 15: A18.

1998b. "How Boys Lost Out to Girl Power." *The New York Times*, December 12: D3.

Li, Xiaolin. 1995. "Women in the Chinese Military." Ph.D. dissertation, University of Maryland.

Lim, Lin Lean, ed. 1998. *The Sex Sector: The Economic and Social Bases of Prostitution in Southeast Asia*. Geneva: International Labour Office.

Linn, Marcia C. and Anne C. Petersen. 1986. "A Meta-Analysis of Gender Differences in Spatial Ability: Implications for Mathematics and Science Achievement." In Hyde and Linn eds.: 67–101.

Lisciotto, Christine A., Joseph F. DeBold, Margaret Haney, and Klaus A. Miczek. 1990. "Implants of Testosterone into the Septal Forebrain Activate Aggressive Behavior in Male Mice." *Aggressive Behavior* 16: 249–58.

Lisitzky, Gene. 1956. *Four Ways of Being Human: An Introduction to Anthropology*. New York: Viking.

Loewald, Hans W. 1988. *Sublimation: Inquiries into Theoretical Psychoanalysis*. New Haven, CT: Yale University Press.

Lomnitz, Larissa. 1986. "The Uses of Fear: Porro Gangs in Mexico." In Foster and Rubinstein eds.: 15–24.

Lorber, Judith. 1994. *Paradoxes of Gender*. New Haven, CT: Yale University Press.

Lorentzen, Lois Ann and Jennifer Turpin, eds. 1998. *The Women and War Reader*. New York: New York University Press.

Lorenz, Konrad. [1963] 1966. *On Aggression*. New York: Harcourt, Brace.

Luthold, Walter W., Maria F. Borges, Jose A. M. Marcondes, Marina Hakohyama, Bernardo L. Wajchenberg, and Marvin A. Kirschner. 1993. "Serum Testosterone Fractions in Women: Normal and Abnormal Clinical States." *Metabolism* 42, 5: 638–43.

Luttwak, Edward. 1997. "Paradoxes of Conflict." *Boston Review* 22, 5 (October/November): 11–12.

Lynch, Andrew. 1995. " 'The hoote blood ran freyshly upon the erthe': A Combat Theme in Malory, and Its Extensions." In Lynch and Maddern eds.: 88–105.

Lynch, Andrew and Philippa Maddern, eds. 1995. *Venus and Mars: Engendering Love and War in Medieval and Early Modern Europe*. Nedlands, Western Australia: University of Western Australia Press.

Mac Cana, Proinsias. 1970. *Celtic Mythology*. London: Hamlyn.

McAllister, Pam, ed. 1982. *Reweaving the Web of Life: Feminism and Nonviolence*. Philadelphia: New Society.

McBride, James. 1995. *War, Battering, and Other Sports: The Gulf between American Men and Women*. Atlantic Highlands, NJ: Humanities Press.

McCarthy, Barry. 1994. "Warrior Values: A Socio-Historical Survey." In Archer ed.: 105–20.

Maccoby, Eleanor E. 1990. "Gender and Relationships: A Developmental Account." *American Psychologist* 45, 4: 513–20.

1998. *The Two Sexes: Growing Up Apart, Coming Together*. Cambridge, MA: Belknap/Harvard University Press.

Maccoby, Eleanor Emmons and Carol Nagy Jacklin. 1974. *The Psychology of Sex Differences*. Stanford, CA: Stanford University Press.

Maccoby, Eleanor E. and John A. Martin. 1983. "Socialization in the Context of the Family: Parent–Child Interaction." In Mussen ed.: 1–102.

McCormick, Cheryl M. and Sandra F. Witelson. 1994. "Functional Cerebral Asymmetry and Sexual Orientation in Men and Women." *Behavioral Neuroscience* 108, 3: 525–31.

MacCoun, Robert J. 1996. "Sexual Orientation and Military Cohesion: A Critical Review of Evidence." In Herek, Jobe, and Carney eds.: 157–76.

Macdonald, Sharon. 1987a. "Drawing the Lines – Gender, Peace and War: An Introduction." In Macdonald, Holden, and Ardener eds.: 1–26.

1987b. "Boadicea: Warrior, Mother and Myth." In Macdonald, Holden, and Ardener eds.: 40–61.

Macdonald, Sharon, Pat Holden, and Shirley Ardener, eds. 1987. *Images of Women in Peace and War: Cross-Cultural and Historical Perspectives*. London: Macmillan.

McGhee, Robert. 1972. *Copper Eskimo Prehistory*. National Museum of Man Publications in Archeology 2. Published by the National Museums of Canada.

McGlen, Nancy E. 1987. "Gender and Peace: The Attitudes of Women Peace Activists." Presented at the Annual Meeting of the American Political Science Association, Chicago, September 3–6.

McGlen, Nancy E. and Meredith Reid Sarkees. 1993. *Women in Foreign Policy: The Insiders*. New York: Routledge.

McGuinness, Diane. 1985. "Sensorimotor Biases in Cognitive Development." In Hall ed.: 27–56.

ed. 1987. *Dominance, Aggression, and War*. New York: Paragon.

Machiavelli, Niccolò. 1983. *The Discourses*. Translated by Leslie J. Walker S.J. New York: Penguin.

1996. *Discourses on Livy*. Translated by Harvey C. Mansfield and Nathan Tarcov. Chicago: University of Chicago Press.

McHugh, Siobhan. 1993. *Minefields and Miniskirts: Australian Women and the Vietnam War*. Sydney: Doubleday.

MacKinnon, Catherine A. 1989. *Toward a Feminist Theory of the State*. Cambridge, MA: Harvard University Press.

1994a. "Turning Rape into Pornography: Postmodern Genocide." In Stiglmayer ed.: 73–81.

1994b. "Rape, Genocide, and Women's Human Rights." In Stiglmayer ed.: 183–96.

McLaren, Angus. 1997. *The Trials of Masculinity: Policing Sexual Boundaries, 1870–1930*. Chicago: University of Chicago Press.

McLean, Christopher, Maggie Carey, and Cheryl White, eds. 1996. *Men's Ways of Being*. Boulder, CO: Westview.

McLean, Scilla. 1982. "Report on UNESCO's Report: The Role of Women in Peace Movements." *Women's Studies International Forum* 5, 3/4: 317–27.

MacMillan, John and Andrew Linklater, eds. 1995. *Boundaries in Question: New Directions in International Relations*. New York: Pinter.

McNeil, Donald G., Jr. 1991. "Should Women Be Sent into Combat?" *The New York Times*, July 21: E3.

McNeill, William Hardy. 1995. *Keeping Together in Time: Dance and Drill in Human History*. Cambridge, MA: Harvard University Press.

McPherson, James M. 1997. *For Cause and Comrades: Why Men Fought in the Civil War*. Oxford: Oxford University Press.

Madsen, Brigham D. 1985. *The Shoshoni Frontier and the Bear River Massacre*. Salt Lake City: University of Utah Press.

Malcolm, Noel. 1994. *Bosnia: A Short History*. New York: New York University Press.

Manning, Lory. 1999. [Data from Women's Research and Education Institute, Washington, DC.] Personal communication, November 29.

Manning, Lory and Jennifer E. Griffith. 1998. *Women in the Military: Where They Stand*. 2nd edition. Washington, DC: Women's Research and Education Institute.

Manning, Patrick. 1982. *Slavery, Colonialism and Economic Growth in Dahomey, 1640–1960*. Cambridge: Cambridge University Press.

Mansfield, Sue. 1982. *The Gestalts of War: An Inquiry into Its Origins and Meanings as a Social Institution*. New York: Dial.

Manson, Joseph H. and Richard W. Wrangham. 1991. "Intergroup Aggression in Chimpanzees and Humans." *Current Anthropology* 32, 4: 369–90.

Marchand, Marianne H. 1998. "Different Communities/Different Realities/Different Encounters: A Reply to J. Ann Tickner." *International Studies Quarterly* 42, 1: 199–204.

Mariner, Rosemary. 1997. "The Military Needs Women . . . " *The Washington Post*, May 1: C7.

Marlowe, David H. 1983. "The Manning of the Force and the Structure of Battle: Part 2 – Men and Women." In Robert K. Fullinwider, ed., *Conscription and Volunteers: Military Requirements, Social Justice, and the All-Volunteer Force*. Totowa, NJ: Rowman & Allanheld: 189–99.

Marshall, S. L. A. 1947. *Men against Fire: The Problem of Battle Command in Future War*. New York: William Morrow.

Martin, Debra L. and David W. Frayer, eds. 1997. *Troubled Times: Violence and Warfare in the Past*. Langhorne, PA: Gordon & Breach.

Mason, John W., Earl L. Giller, Jr., Thomas R. Kosten, and Victor S. Wahby. 1990. "Serum Testosterone Levels in Post-Traumatic Stress Disorder Inpatients." *Journal of Traumatic Stress* 3, 3: 449–57.

Masters, Roger D. 1989a. *The Nature of Politics*. New Haven, CT: Yale University Press.

1989b. "Gender and Political Cognition: Integrating Evolutionary Biology and Political Science." *Politics and the Life Sciences* 8, 1: 3–39.

1990. "Evolutionary Biology and Political Theory." *The American Political Science Review* 84, 1: 195–210.

Matthews, Caitlin. 1989. *The Elements of the Celtic Tradition*. Shaftesbury, UK: Element Books.

Matthews, Irene. 1993. "Daughtering in War: Two 'Case Studies' from Mexico and Guatemala." In Cooke and Woollacott eds.: 148–76.

May, Larry and Robert Strikwerda. 1996. "Men in Groups: Collective Responsibility for Rape." In Warren and Cady eds.: 175–91.

Mayer, Holly A. 1996. *Belonging to the Army: Camp Followers and Community during the American Revolution*. Columbia: University of South Carolina Press.

Mazur, Allan and Alan Booth. 1998. "Testosterone and Dominance in Men." *Behavioral and Brain Sciences* 21, 3 (June): 353–63.

Mazur, Allan, Alan Booth, and James M. Dabbs, Jr. 1992. "Testosterone and Chess Competition." *Social Psychology Quarterly* 55, 1: 70–77.

Mazur, Allan and T. A. Lamb. 1980. "Testosterone, Status, and Mood in Human Males." *Hormones and Behavior* 41: 236–46.

Mazur, Allan, E. J. Susman, and S. Edelbrock. 1997. "Sex Difference in Testosterone Response to a Video Game Contest." *Evolution and Human Behavior* 18, 5 (September): 317–26.

Mead, Margaret. 1940. "Warfare Is Only an Invention – Not a Biological Necessity." *Asia* 40: 402–5.

1949. *Male and Female: A Study of the Sexes in a Changing World.* New York: William Morrow.

1967a. "Alternatives to War." In Fried, Harris, and Murphy eds.: 215–28.

1967b. "Epilogue." In Fried, Harris, and Murphy eds.: 235–37.

Meggitt, Mervyn. 1977. *Blood Is Their Argument: Warfare among the Mae Enga Tribesmen of the New Guinea Highlands.* Palo Alto, CA: Mayfield.

Merida, Kevin and Barbara Vobejda. 1988. "Battles on the Home Front: Couples in Conflict over Roles." *The Washington Post,* March 24: A1.

Messner, Michael A. 1990. "Boyhood, Organized Sports, and the Construction of Masculinities." *Journal of Contemporary Ethnography* 18, 4 (January): 416–44.

1992. *Power at Play: Sports and the Problem of Masculinity.* Boston: Beacon Press.

Messner, Michael A. and Donald F. Sabo, eds. 1990. *Sport, Men, and the Gender Order: Critical Feminist Perspectives.* Champaign, IL: Human Kinetics Books.

Meyer, Leisa D. 1996. *Creating GI Jane: Sexuality and Power in the Women's Army Corps during World War II.* New York: Columbia University Press.

Meyer, Mary K. and Elisabeth Prügl, eds. 1999. *Gender Politics in Global Governance.* Lanham, MD: Rowman & Littlefield.

Meyer-Bahlburg, Heino F. L., Anke A. Ehrhardt, Laura R. Rosen, Rhoda S. Gruen, Norma P. Veridiano, Felix H. Vann, and Herbert F. Neuwalder. 1995. "Prenatal Estrogens and the Development of Homosexual Orientation." *Developmental Psychology* 31, 1: 12–21.

Michael, Franz. 1966. *The Taiping Rebellion: History and Documents. Volume I: History.* Seattle: University of Washington Press.

Miedzian, Myriam. 1991. *Boys Will Be Boys: Breaking the Link between Masculinity and Violence.* New York: Anchor.

Mies, Maria. 1986. *Patriarchy and Accumulation on a World Scale: Women in the International Division of Labour.* London: Zed.

Miles, Rosalind. 1991. *The Rites of Man: Love, Sex and Death in the Making of the Male.* New York: Grafton.

Miller, Joseph C. 1975. "Nzinga of Matamba in a New Perspective." *Journal of African History* 16, 2: 201–16.

1976. *Kings and Kinsmen: Early Mbundu States in Angola.* Oxford: Clarendon.

Miller, Laura L. 1994. "Fighting for a Just Cause: Soldiers' Views on Gays in the Military." In Scott and Stanley eds.: 69–86.

Mirsky, Jeannette. 1937. "The Eskimo of Greenland." In Margaret Mead, ed., *Cooperation and Competition among Primitive Peoples*. New York: McGraw-Hill: 51–86.

Mitchell, Billie. 1996. "The Creation of Army Officers and the Gender Lie: Betty Grable or Frankenstein?" In Stiehm ed.: 35–59.

Mitchell, Brian. 1989. *Weak Link: The Feminization of the American Military*. Washington, DC: Regnery Gateway.

Moffitt, Terrie E., Avshalom Caspi, Michael Rutter, and Phil A. Silva. 2001. *Sex Differences in Antisocial Behavior: Findings from the First Two Decades of the Dunedin Longitudinal Study*. Cambridge: Cambridge University Press (forthcoming).

Moghadam, Valentine M. 1993. *Modernizing Women: Gender and Social Change in the Middle East*. Boulder, CO: Lynne Rienner.

     ed. 1994. *Identity Politics and Women: Cultural Reassertions and Feminisms in International Perspective*. Boulder, CO: Westview.

Mohanty, Chandra Talpade, Ann Russo, and Lourdes Torres, eds. 1991. *Third World Women and the Politics of Feminism*. Bloomington: Indiana University Press.

Mollica, Richard F. 2000. "Invisible Wounds." *Scientific American* 282, 6 (June): 54–59.

Monaghan, Edward P. and Stephen E. Glickman. 1992. "Hormones and Aggressive Behavior." In Becker, Breedlove, and Crews eds.: 261–86.

Monagle, Katie. 1992. "The Devil's Juice." *Scholastic Update* (Teacher's edition) 124, 16 (May 1): 11–12.

Montagu, Ashley. 1976. *The Nature of Human Aggression*. Oxford: Oxford University Press.

     1989. *Growing Young*. 2nd edition. Granby, MA: Bergin & Garvey.

Montouri, Alfonso and Isabella Conti. 1993. *From Power to Partnership: Creating the Future of Love, Work, and Community*. San Francisco: Harper.

Monypenny, William Flavelle and George Earle Buckle. 1912. *The Life of Benjamin Disraeli, Earl of Beaconsfield*, New and revised edition, Volume II, 1860–1881. New York: Macmillan.

Moon, Katharine H. 1997. *Sex among Allies: Military Prostitution in US–Korea Relations*. New York: Columbia University Press.

Moon, Seungsook. 1998. "Gender, Militarization, and Universal Male Conscription in South Korea." In Lorentzen and Turpin eds.: 90–100.

Moore, Brenda L. 1996. "From Underrepresentation to Overrepresentation: African American Women." In Stiehm ed.: 115–35.

Mora, Mariana. 1998. "Zapatismo: Gender, Power, and Social Transformation." In Lorentzen and Turpin eds.: 164–76.

Morell, Virginia. 1993. "Evidence Found for a Possible 'Aggression Gene.'" *Science* 260 (June):1722–23.

Morgan, Elaine. 1972. *The Descent of Woman*. New York: Stein & Day.

Morgan, Robin. 1988. *The Demon Lover: On the Sexuality of Terrorism*. New York: W. W. Norton. [Pages refer to excerpts in *Ms.*, March 1989].

Morgenthau, Hans. [1948] 1967. *Politics among Nations: The Struggle for Power and Peace*. 4th edition. New York: Knopf.

Morin, Ann Miller. 1995. *Her Excellency: An Oral History of American Women Ambassadors*. New York: Twayne.

Morin, Richard and Megan Rosenfeld. 1998. "With More Equity, More Sweat." *The Washington Post*, March 22: A1.

Morris, Desmond. 1967. *The Naked Ape*. London: Jonathan Cape.

Morris, Patricia. 1993. "Women, Resistance, and the Use of Force in South Africa." In Howes and Stevenson eds.: 185–206.

Mosko, Mark S. 1987. "The Symbols of 'Forest': A Structural Analysis of Mbuti Culture and Social Organization." *American Anthropologist* 89, 4 (December): 896–913.

Moskos, Charles, Jr. 1994. "From Citizens' Army to Social Laboratory." In Scott and Stanley eds.: 53–68.

1998. "The Folly of Comparing Race and Gender in the Army." *The Washington Post*, January 4: C1.

Mosse, George L. 1990. *Fallen Soldiers: Reshaping the Memory of the World Wars*. Oxford University Press.

1996. *The Image of Man: The Creation of Modern Masculinity*. Oxford: Oxford University Press.

Mostov, Julie. 1995. "'Our Women'/'Their Women': Symbolic Boundaries, Territorial Markers, and Violence in the Balkans." *Peace & Change* 20, 4 (October): 515–29.

Moyer, K. E. 1976. *The Psychobiology of Aggression*. New York: Harper & Row.

1987. "The Biological Basis of Dominance and Aggression." In McGuinness ed.: 1–34.

Mulinari, Diana. 1996. "Broken Dreams." *Peace Review* 8, 3: 391–95.

1998. "Broken Dreams in Nicaragua." In Lorentzen and Turpin eds.: 157–63.

Murphy, Craig N. 1996. "Seeing Women, Recognizing Gender, Recasting International Relations." *International Organization* 50, 3 (Summer): 513–38.

1998. "Six Masculine Roles in International Relations and Their Interconnection: A Personal Investigation." In Zalewski and Parpart eds.: 93–108.

Murphy, Robert F. 1957. "Intergroup Hostility and Social Cohesion." *American Anthropologist* 59, 6: 1018–35.

Murphy, Yolanda and Robert F. Murphy. 1985. *Women of the Forest*, 2nd edition. New York: Columbia University Press.

Murray, Christopher J. L. and Alan D. Lopez. 1996a. *The Global Burden of Disease: A Comprehensive Assessment of Mortality and Disability from Diseases, Injuries, and Risk Factors in 1990 and Projected to 2020*. Volume I of "Global Burden of Disease and Injury Series." Cambridge, MA: Harvard School of Public Health on behalf of the World Health Organization and the World Bank [distributed by Harvard University Press].

1996b. *Global Health Statistics: A Compendium of Incidence, Prevalence and Mortality Estimates for Over 200 Conditions*. Volume II of "Global Burden of Disease and Injury Series." See Murray and Lopez 1996a.

Mussen, Paul H., ed. *Handbook of Child Psychology*, 4th edition. *Volume IV: Socialization, Personality, and Social Development*. E. Mavis Hetherington, volume editor. New York: Wiley.

Myers, Steven Lee. 1997a. "Pentagon Is Urged to Separate Sexes." *The New York Times*, December 16: A1.

　　1997b. "To Sex-Segregated Training, Still Semper Fi." *The New York Times*, December 26: A1.

　　1998a. "Army, Navy and Air Force Close Ranks to Oppose Sex Segregation during Training." *The New York Times*, March 11: A18.

　　1998b. "House Votes to Separate Training for Male and Female Recruits." *The New York Times*, May 21: A15.

　　1998c. "Retired General Is Charged with Adultery and Lying." *The New York Times*, December 11: A25.

Myers, William Andrew. 1996. " 'Severed Heads': Susan Griffin's Account of War, Detachment, and Denial." In Warren and Cady eds.: 106–17.

Myles, Bruce. [1981] 1990. *Night Witches: The Untold Story of Soviet Women in Combat*. Novato, CA: Presidio Press.

Nabors, R. L. 1982. "Women in the Army: Do They Measure Up?" *Military Review*, October: 50–61.

NATO, International Military Staff. 1994. *Women in the NATO Forces*. Distributed by the IMS Secretariat, Brussels.

Nelson, Barbara J. and Najma Chowdhury, eds. 1994. *Women and Politics Worldwide*. New Haven, CT: Yale University Press.

Nelson, Keith L. and Spencer C. Olin, Jr. 1979. *Why War? Ideology, Theory, and History*. Berkeley: University of California Press.

Nettleship, Martin A., R. Dale Givens, and Anderson Nettleship, eds. 1975. *War, Its Causes and Correlates*. The Hague: Mouton.

Neuman, Gerard G., ed. 1987. *Origins of Human Aggression: Dynamics and Etiology*. New York: Human Sciences Press.

New York Times. 1997. "Cadets at the Citadel Take Sensitivity Training." *The New York Times*, April 23: A20.

Nicholson, Linda J., ed. 1990. *Feminism/Postmodernism*. New York: Routledge.

Nikolić-Ristanović, Vesna. 1996. "War, Nationalism and Mothers." *Peace Review* 8, 3: 359–64.

Nisbett, Richard E. and Dov Cohen. 1996. *Culture of Honor: The Psychology of Violence in the South*. Boulder, CO: Westview.

Niva, Steve. 1998. "Tough and Tender: New World Order Masculinity and the Gulf War." In Zalewski and Parpart eds.: 109–28.

Noakes, Lucy. 1998. *War and the British: Gender, Memory and National Identity*. New York: I. B. Tauris.

Noggle, Anne. 1994. *A Dance with Death: Soviet Airwomen in World War II*. College Station: Texas A&M University Press.

Nordstrom, Carolyn. 1998. "Girls behind the (Front) Lines." In Lorentzen and Turpin eds.: 80–89.

Norman, Anthony W. and Gerald Litwack. 1987. *Hormones*. Orlando, FL: Academic Press.

Norris, Kathleen. 1928. *What Price Peace? A Handbook of Peace for American Women*. Garden City, NY: Doubleday, Doran.

Norris, Pippa. 1997. "Women Leaders Worldwide: A Splash of Color in the Photo Op." In Pippa Norris, ed., *Women, Media, and Politics*. Oxford: Oxford University Press: 149–65.

North, Robert C. 1990. *War, Peace, Survival*. Boulder, CO: Westview.

Nottelmann, Editha D., Elizabeth J. Susman, Lorah D. Dorn, Gale Inoff-Germain, D. Lynn Loriaux, Gordon B. Cutler, and George P. Chrousos. 1987. "Developmental Processes in Early Adolescence: Relations among Chronologic Age, Pubertal Stage, Height, Weight, and Serum Levels of Gonadotropins, Sex Steroids, and Adrenal Androgens." *Journal of Adolescent Health Care* 8: 246–60.

Nuttall, Mark. 1992. *Arctic Homeland: Kinship, Community and Development in Northwest Greenland*. Buffalo: University of Toronto Press.

Nye, Joseph S., Jr. 1988. "Neorealism and Neoliberalism." *World Politics* 40, 2: 235–51.

O'Brien, Kenneth Paul and Lynn Hudson Parsons. 1995. "Introduction: The Home-Front War." In O'Brien and Parsons eds.: 1–9.

eds. 1995. *The Home-Front War: World War II and American Society*. Westport, CT: Greenwood.

O'Brien, Mary. 1981. *The Politics of Reproduction*. Boston: Routledge & Kegan Paul.

O'Connell, Robert L. 1995. *Ride of the Second Horseman: The Birth and Death of War*. Oxford: Oxford University Press.

O'Hara, Jane. 1998. "Rape in the Military." *Maclean's*, May 25: 14–25.

O'Leary, K. Daniel and Neil S. Jacobson. 1994. "Partner Relational Problems with Physical Abuse." In Thomas A. Widiger, Allen J. Frances, Harold Alan Pincus, Ruth Ross, Michael B. First, and Wendy Davis, eds., *DSM-IV Sourcebook*. Volume III. Washington, DC: American Psychiatric Association.

O'Leary, Virginia E., Rhoda Kesler Unger, and Barbara Strudler Wallston, eds. 1985. *Women, Gender, and Social Psychology*. Hillsdale, NJ: Lawrence Erlbaum Associates.

Oates, Stephen B. 1994. *A Woman of Valor: Clara Barton and the Civil War*. New York: Free Press.

Obichere, Boniface I. 1971. *West African States and European Expansion: The Dahomey–Niger Hinterland, 1885–1898*. New Haven, CT: Yale University Press.

Oldfield, Sybil. 1989. *Women Against the Iron Fist: Alternatives to Militarism 1900–1989*. Cambridge, MA: Basil Blackwell.

1995. "Jane Addams: The Change the World Missed." In D'Amico and Beckman eds.: 155–68.

Opler, Morris Edward. 1941. *An Apache Life-Way: The Economic, Social, and Religious Institutions of the Chiricahua Indians*. University of Chicago Press.

Organski, A. F. K. 1958. *World Politics*. New York: Knopf.

OSCE [Organization for Security and Co-operation in Europe]. 1999. *Kosovo/Kosova As Seen, As Told*. Vienna: OSCE.

Otterbein, Keith Frederick. 1989. "Socialization for War: A Study of the Influence of Hunting upon Welfare." Presented at the American Anthropological Association Meeting, Washington, DC, November 19.

1994. *Feuding and Warfare: Selected Works of Keith F. Otterbein*. Langhorne, PA: Gordon & Breach.

Otterbein, Keith F. and Charlotte Swanson Otterbein. 1997. "The Influence of Hunting upon the Frequency of Warfare among Hunter-Gatherers." State

University of New York at Buffalo. [Unpublished, undated manuscript, received March 1997.]

Oudshoorn, Nelly. 1994. *Beyond the Natural Body: An Archeology of Sex Hormones.* New York: Routledge.

Oyama, Susan. 1991. "Essentialism, Women, and War: Protesting Too Much, Protesting Too Little." In Hunter ed.: 64–76.

Oye, Kenneth A., ed. 1986. *Cooperation under Anarchy.* Princeton, NJ: Princeton University Press.

Page, Brigadier F. C. G. 1986. *Following the Drum: Women in Wellington's Wars.* London: André Deutsch.

Park, Rosemary E. 1994. "Opening the Canadian Forces to Gays and Lesbians: An Inevitable Decision but Improbable Reconfiguration." In Scott and Stanley eds.: 165–80.

Parke, Ross D. 1981. *Fathers.* Cambridge, MA: Harvard University Press.

Parker, Andrew, Mary Russo, Doris Sommer, and Patricia Yaeger. 1992. "Introduction." In Andrew Parker, Mary Russo, Doris Sommer, and Patricia Yeager, eds., *Nationalisms and Sexualities.* New York: Routledge: 1–20.

Parry, Sally E. 1996. "So Proudly They Serve: American Women in World War II Films." Presented at the American Political Science Association Annual Meeting, San Francisco, August 29–September 1.

Patton, Cindy. 1996. "Queer Peregrinations." In Shapiro and Alker eds.: 363–82.

Peach, Lucinda Joy. 1993. *Women at War: The Ethics of Women in Combat.* MacArthur Scholar Series Occasional Paper 20. Bloomington: Indiana Center on Global Change and World Peace.

1996. "Gender Ideology in the Ethics of Women in Combat." In Stiehm ed.: 156–94.

Pearson, Patricia. 1997. *When She Was Bad: Violent Women and the Myth of Innocence.* Toronto: Random House of Canada.

Pennington, Reina. 1993. "Wings, Women and War: Soviet Women's Military Aviation Regiments in the Great Patriotic War." Master's thesis, University of South Carolina.

ed. n.d. [In progress.] *Military Women Worldwide: A Biographical Dictionary.* Columbia: Department of History, University of South Carolina.

Peres, Y. and M. Hopp. 1990. "Loyalty and Aggression in Human Groups." In Van Der Dennen and Falger eds.: 123–30.

Perlez, Jane. 1997. "Joining NATO: Central Europe Sees a Cure-All." *The New York Times,* June 11: A1, A14.

Perlman, David. 1997. "New Evidence of Legendary Women Warriors." *The San Francisco Chronicle,* January 28: 1, A5.

Perpinan, Sister Mary Soledad. 1994. "Militarism and the Sex Industry in the Philippines." In Davies ed.: 149–52.

Peterson, V. Spike. 1988. "An Archeology of Domination: Historicizing Gender and Class in Early Western State Formation." Ph.D. dissertation, School of International Service, The American University, Washington, DC. Ann Arbor: University Microfilms.

1992a. "Security and Sovereign States: What Is at Stake in Taking Feminism Seriously?" In Peterson ed.: 31–64.

1992b. "Transgressing Boundaries: Theories of Knowledge, Gender and International Relations." *Journal of International Studies* 21, 2: 183–206.

ed. 1992. *Gendered States: Feminist (Re) Visions of International Relations Theory.* Boulder, CO: Lynne Rienner.

1996a. "The Gender of Rhetoric, Reason, and Realism." In Beer and Hariman eds.: 257–76.

1996b. "Women and Gender in Power/Politics, Nationalism and Revolution." *Journal of Politics* 58, 3 (August): 870–78.

1997a. "Whose Crisis? Early and Post-Modern Masculinism." In Stephen Gill and James H. Mittelman, eds., *Innovation and Transformation in International Studies.* Cambridge: Cambridge University Press: 185–201.

1997b. *FTGS Timeline.* On the World Wide Web site of the Feminist Theory and Gender Studies Section of the International Studies Association: http:csf.colorado.edu/isa/ftgs/.

Peterson, V. Spike and Anne Sisson Runyan. 1993. *Global Gender Issues: Dilemmas in World Politics.* Boulder, CO: Westview. [2nd edition available, 1999.]

Pettman, Jan Jindy. 1996a. *Worlding Women: A Feminist International Politics.* New York: Routledge.

1996b. "Border Crossings/Shifting Identities: Minorities, Gender, and the State in International Perspective." In Shapiro and Alker eds.: 261–84.

Pettman, Ralph. 1994. "'If Men Are the Problem...'" In Beckman and D'Amico eds.: 187–200.

Phillips, Anne. 1991. *Engendering Democracy.* University Park: Pennsylvania State University Press.

Piaget, Jean. [1932] 1965. *The Moral Judgment of the Child.* Translated by Marjorie Gabain. New York: Free Press.

Pierson, Ruth Roach. 1986. *"They're Still Women After All": The Second World War and Canadian Womanhood.* Toronto: McClelland & Stewart.

1987. "'Did Your Mother Wear Army Boots?': Feminist Theory and Women's Relation to War, Peace and Revolution." In Macdonald, Holden, and Ardener eds.: 205–27.

ed. 1987. *Women and Peace: Theoretical, Historical and Practical Perspectives.* New York: Croom Helm.

Pirké Avot. [c. 200] 1997. *Pirké Avot: Wisdom of the Jewish Sages.* [Chaim Stern, ed.] Hoboken, NJ: Ktav.

Pitkin, Hanna F. 1984. *Fortune Is a Woman: Gender and Politics in the Thought of Niccolo Machiavelli.* Berkeley: University of California Press.

Pois, Anne Marie. 1995. "Foreshadowings: Jane Addams, Emily Greene Balch, and the Ecofeminism/Pacifist Feminism of the 1980s." *Peace and Change* 20, 4 (October): 439–65.

Polanyi, Karl with Abraham Rotstein. 1966. *Dahomey and the Slave Trade: An Analysis of an Archaic Economy.* Seattle: University of Washington Press.

Pollack, Andrew. 1996. "In Okinawa, US Bases Remain a Big Issue." *The New York Times,* March 9: A2.

Pollack, William. 1998. *Real Boys: Rescuing Our Sons from the Myths of Boyhood.* New York: Random House.

Pollak, Susan and Carol Gilligan. 1982. "Images of Violence in Thematic Apperception Test Stories." *Journal of Personality and Social Psychology* 42, 1: 159–67.

Popper, Sir Karl Raimund. 1959. *The Logic of Scientific Discovery*. New York: Basic.

Porter, Bruce D. 1994. *War and the Rise of the State: The Military Foundations of Modern Politics*. New York: Free Press.

Pospisil, Leopold. 1963. *The Kapauku Papuans of West New Guinea*. New York: Holt, Rinehart & Winston.

    1994. "I Am Very Sorry I Cannot Kill You Anymore: War and Peace among the Kapauku." In Reyna and Downs eds.: 113–26.

Pourou-Kazantzis, Ninetta. 1998. "Militarism and Cypriot Women." In Lorentzen and Turpin eds.: 111–18.

Power, J. Tracy. 1998. *Lee's Miserables: Life in the Army of Northern Virginia from the Wilderness to Appomattox*. Chapel Hill: University of North Carolina Press.

Presidential Commission on the Assignment of Women in the Armed Forces. 1993. *Women in Combat: Report to the President*. Washington, DC: Brassey's.

Priest, Dana. 1997a. "Engendering a Warrior Spirit." *The Washington Post*, March 3: A1, A14.

    1997b. "A Trench between Women, Jobs." *The Washington Post*, December 28: A1, A14.

    1997c. "In a Crunch, Ban on Women Bends." *The Washington Post*, December 30: A1.

Pruitt, Dean G. 1998. "Social Conflict." In Gilbert, Fiske, and Lindzey eds.: 470–503.

Puget Sound Women's Peace Camp Participants. 1985. *We Are Ordinary Women: A Chronicle of the Puget Sound Women's Peace Camp*. Seattle, WA: Seal Press.

Pugliese, Joseph. 1995. "The Gendered Figuring of the Dysfunctional Serviceman in the Discourses of Military Psychiatry." In Damousi and Lake eds.: 162–77.

Pusey, Anne. 2001. "Of Genes and Apes: Chimpanzee Social Organization and Reproduction." In Frans de Waal, ed., *Tree of Origin: What Primate Behavior Can Tell Us about Human Social Evolution*. Cambridge, MA: Harvard University Press. [Forthcoming; page citations are to manuscript.]

Pusey, A., J. Williams, and J. Goodall. 1997. "The Influences of Dominance Rank on the Reproductive Success of Female Chimpanzees." *Science* 277 (August 8): 828.

Quester, George H. 1977. "Women in Combat." *International Security* 1 (Spring): 80–91.

Rable, George. 1992. "'Missing in Action': Women of the Confederacy." In Clinton and Silber eds.: 134–46.

Radke-Yarrow, Marian, Carolyn Zahn-Waxler, and Michael Chapman. 1983. "Children's Prosocial Dispositions and Behavior." In Mussen ed.: 469–546.

Randall, Margaret. 1981. *Sandino's Daughters: Testimonies of Nicaraguan Women in Struggle*. Vancouver: Star Books.

    1995. "Women in Revolutionary Movements: Cuba and Nicaragua." In D'Amico and Beckman eds.: 183–98.

Randall, Margaret and Lynda Yanz. 1995. *Sandino's Daughters: Testimonies of Nicaraguan Women in Struggle*. New Brunswick, NJ: Rutgers University Press.

Rapoport, Anatol and Albert M. Chammah. 1969. "The Game of Chicken." In Ira R. Buchler and Hugo G. Nutini, eds., *Game Theory in the Behavioral Sciences*. Pittsburgh: University of Pittsburgh Press: 151–75.

Raven, Susan and Alison Weir. 1981. *Women of Achievement: Thirty-Five Centuries of History*. New York: Harmony.

Reardon, Betty A. 1985. *Sexism and the War System*. New York: Teachers College Press.

1989. "Toward a Paradigm of Peace." In Forcey ed.: 15–26.

1993. *Women and Peace: Feminist Visions of Global Security*. Albany: State University of New York Press.

1996. "Women or Weapons?" *Peace Review* 8, 3: 315–21.

Regan, Patrick M. and Michelle A. Barnello. 1998. "Feminism, Social Constructions and the Democratic Peace: Moving from Dialogue to Empirical Research." Typescript, Department of Political Science, Binghamton University.

Rejali, Darius M. 1996. "After Feminist Analysis of Bosnian Violence." *Peace Review* 8, 3: 365–71.

Reuters. 2000. "UN, SFOR Involved in Bosnian Prostitution." Sarajevo: Reuters, May 18.

Reyna, S. P. 1990. *Wars without End: The Political Economy of a Precolonial African State*. Hanover: University Press of New England.

1994. "A Mode of Domination Approach to Organized Violence." In Reyna and Downs eds.: 29–68.

Reyna, S. P. and R. E. Downs, eds. 1994. *Studying War: Anthropological Perspectives*. Langhorne, PA: Gordon & Breach.

Reynolds, Charles. 1989. *The Politics of War: A Study of the Rationality of Violence in Inter-State Relations*. New York: St. Martin's.

Richards, Janet Radcliffe. 1990. "Why the Pursuit of Peace Is No Part of Feminism." In Elshtain and Tobias eds.: 211–26.

Richardson, Jo A. and Ruth H. Howes. 1993. "How Three Female National Leaders Have Used the Military." In Howes and Stevenson eds.: 149–66.

Richman-Loo, Nina and Rachel Weber. 1996. "Gender and Weapons Design." In Stiehm ed.: 136–55.

Ridd, Rosemary and Helen Callaway, eds. 1986. *Caught Up in Conflict: Women's Responses to Political Strife*. London: Macmillan Education.

Ridley, Matt. 1997. *The Origins of Virtue: Human Instincts and the Evolution of Cooperation*. New York: Viking.

Rieber, Robert W., ed. 1991. *The Psychology of War and Peace: The Image of the Enemy*. New York: Plenum.

Rieff, David. 1995. *Slaughterhouse: Bosnia and the Failure of the West*. New York: Simon & Schuster.

Ritchie, W. F. and J. N. G. Ritchie. 1985. *Celtic Warriors*. Aylesbury, UK: Shire Archaeology.

Robarchek, Clayton. 1990. "Motivations and Material Causes: On the Explanation of Conflict and War." In Haas ed.: 56–76.

Robinson, Michael H. and Lionel Tiger, eds. 1991. *Man and Beast Revisited.* Washington, DC: Smithsonian Institution Press.

Rodseth, Lars, Richard W. Wrangham, Alisa M. Harrigan, and Barbara B. Smuts. 1991. "The Human Community as a Primate Society." *Current Anthropology* 32, 3 (June): 221–54.

Rohde, David. 1999. "Albanian Tells How Serbs Chose Her, 'the Most Beautiful One,' for Rape." *The New York Times*, May 1: A8.

Rorty, Richard. 1993. "Human Rights, Rationality, and Sentimentality." In Stephen Shute and Susan Hurley, eds. *On Human Rights: The Oxford Amnesty Lectures.* New York: Basic: 111–34.

Rose, Robert M., Irwin S. Bernstein, Thomas P. Gordon, and Sharon F. Catlin. 1974. "Androgens and Aggression: A Review and Recent Findings in Primates." In Holloway ed.: 275–304.

Rosenblatt, Jay S. 1992. "Hormone–Behavior Relations in the Regulation of Parental Behavior." In Becker, Breedlove, and Crews eds.: 219–60.

Rosenfeld, Megan. 1998. "Little Boys Blue: Reexamining the Plight of Young Males." *The Washington Post*, March 26: A1.

Rosoff, Betty. 1991. "Genes, Hormones, and War." In Hunter ed.: 39–49.

Ross, Kristie. 1992. "Arranging a Doll's House: Refined Women as Union Nurses." In Clinton and Silber eds.: 97–113.

Ross, Marc Howard. 1986. "Female Political Participation: A Cross-Cultural Explanation." *American Anthropologist* 88, 4 (December): 843–58.

1990. "Children and War in Different Cultures." In Francesca M. Cancian and James William Gibson, eds., *Making War/Making Peace: The Social Foundations of Violent Conflict.* Belmont, CA: Wadsworth: 51–63. [Revised from *Political Psychology* 7 (1986): 427–69.]

1993a. *The Culture of Conflict: Interpretations and Interests in Comparative Perspective.* New Haven, CT: Yale University Press.

1993b. *The Management of Conflict: Interpretations and Interests in Comparative Perspective.* New Haven, CT: Yale University Press.

Rotberg, Robert I. and Theodore K. Rabb, eds. 1988. *The Origin and Prevention of Major Wars.* Cambridge: Cambridge University Press.

Rotundo, E. Anthony. 1993. *American Manhood: Transformations in Masculinity from the Revolution to the Modern Era.* New York: Basic.

Rowse, A. L. 1977. *Homosexuals in History: A Study of Ambivalence in Society, Literature and the Arts.* New York: Dorset Press.

Rubin, Kenneth H., William Bukowski, and Jeffrey G. Parker. 1998. "Peer Interactions, Relationships, and Groups." In Damon and Eisenberg eds.: 619–700.

Rubinstein, Robert A. and Mary LeCron Foster, eds. 1988. *The Social Dynamics of Peace and Conflict: Culture in International Security.* Boulder, CO: Westview.

Ruble, Diane N. and Carol Lynn Martin. 1998. "Gender Development." In Damon and Eisenberg eds.: 993–1016.

Ruddick, Sara. 1989. *Maternal Thinking: Towards a Politics of Peace.* London: The Women's Press.

1990. "The Rationality of Care." In Elshtain and Tobias eds.: 229–54.

Ruggie, John Gerard. 1993. "Territoriality and Beyond: Problematizing Modernity in International Relations." *International Organization* 47, 1 (Winter): 139–74.

Runyan, Anne Sisson. 1994. "Radical Feminism: Alternative Futures." In Beckman and D'Amico eds.: 201–16.

Rupp, Leila J. 1978. *Mobilizing Women for War: German and American Propaganda, 1939–1945*. Princeton, NJ: Princeton University Press.

1996. "Wartime Violence against Women and Solidarity." *Peace Review* 8, 3: 343–46.

Russett, Bruce M. 1990. *Controlling the Sword: The Democratic Governance of National Security*. Cambridge, MA: Harvard University Press.

Rustad, Michael. 1982. *Women In Khaki: The American Enlisted Woman*. New York: Praeger.

Saarni, Carolyn, Donna L. Mumme, and Joseph J. Campos. 1998. "Emotional Development: Action, Communication, and Understanding." In Damon and Eisenberg eds.: 237–310.

Sagan, Carl and Ann Druyan. 1992. *Shadows of Forgotten Ancestors: A Search for Who We Are*. New York: Random House.

Salmonson, Jessica Amanda. 1991. *The Encyclopedia of Amazons: Women Warriors from Antiquity to the Modern Era*. New York: Paragon House.

Sampson, Edward E. 1988. "The Debate on Individualism: Indigenous Psychologies of the Individual and Their Role in Personal and Societal Functioning." *American Psychologist* 43, 1: 15–22.

Sánchez-Eppler, Benigno. 1996. "The Displacement of Cuban Homosexuality in the Fiction and Autobiography of Reinaldo Arenas." In Shapiro and Alker eds.: 383–99.

Sanday, Peggy Reeves. 1981. *Female Power and Male Dominance: On the Origins of Sexual Inequality*. Cambridge: Cambridge University Press.

Sapolsky, Robert M. 1992. "Neuroendocrinology of the Stress-Response." In Becker, Breedlove, and Crews eds.: 287–324.

1997. *The Trouble with Testosterone: And Other Essays on the Biology of the Human Predicament*. New York: Scribner.

Sasson, Jean. 1991. *The Rape of Kuwait: The True Story of Iraqi Atrocities against a Civilian Population*. New York: Knightsbridge.

Sawyer, Kathy. 1997. "Amazons: The Ms. behind the Myth?" *The Washington Post*, May 12: A3.

Sayers, Janet. 1986. *Sexual Contradictions: Psychology, Psychoanalysis, and Feminism*. New York: Tavistock.

Saywell, Shelley. 1985. *Women in War*. New York: Viking.

Scerbo, Angela Scarpa and David J. Kolko. 1994. "Salivary Testosterone and Cortisol in Disruptive Children: Relationship to Aggressive, Hyperactive, and Internalizing Behaviors." *Journal of the American Academy of Child and Adolescent Psychiatry* 33, 8 (October): 1174–84.

Schaal, B., R. E. Tremblay, R. Soussignan, and E. J. Susman. 1996. "Male Testosterone Linked to High Social Dominance but Low Physical Aggression in Early Adolescence." *Journal of the American Academy of Child and Adolescent Psychiatry* 35, 10 (October): 1322–30.

Schebesta, Paul. 1933. *Among Congo Pigmies*. London: Hutchinson.

1973. *Among the Forest Dwarfs of Malaya*. Oxford: Oxford University Press.

Schele, Linda. 1991. "The Owl, Shield, and Flint Blade." *Natural History* (November): 6–11.

Scheper-Hughes, Nancy. 1996. "Maternal Thinking and the Politics of War." *Peace Review* 8, 3: 353–58.

Schibanoff, Susan. 1996. "True Lies: Transvestism and Idolatry in the Trial of Joan of Arc." In Wheeler and Wood eds.: 31–60.

Schiebinger, Londa. 1989. *The Mind Has No Sex? Women in the Origins of Modern Science*. Cambridge, MA: Harvard University Press.

1993. *Nature's Body: Gender in the Making of Modern Science*. Boston: Beacon.

Schlegel, Alice. 1977. "Toward a Theory of Sexual Stratification." In Schlegel ed.: 1–40.

ed. 1977. *Sexual Stratification: A Cross-Cultural View*. New York: Columbia University Press.

Schmitt, Eric. 1996. "War Is Hell. So Is Regulating Sex." *The New York Times*, November 26 [Week in Review].

Schneider, Dorothy and Carl J. Schneider. 1991. *Into the Breach: American Women Overseas in World War I*. New York: Viking.

Schoenewolf, Gerald. 1989. *Sexual Animosity between Men and Women*. Northvale, NJ: Jason Aronson.

Schott, Linda Kay. 1985. *Women against War: Pacifism, Feminism, and Social Justice in the United States, 1915–1941*. Ann Arbor, MI: University Microfilms.

Schubert, Glendon. 1991a. "Introduction: Primatology, Feminism, and Political Behavior." In Schubert and Masters eds.: 3–28.

1991b. "Introduction: Primatological Theory." In Schubert and Masters eds.: 29–36.

Schubert, Glendon and Roger D. Masters, eds. 1991. *Primate Politics*. Carbondale: Southern Illinois University Press.

Schwalbe, Michael L. 1996. *Unlocking the Iron Cage: The Men's Movement, Gender Politics, and American Culture*. Oxford: Oxford University Press.

Sciolino, Elaine. 1992. "Women in War: Ex-Captive Tells of Ordeal." *The New York Times*, June 29: A1, A13.

1997a. "Army Rape Trial Witnesses Tell of a Base Out of Control." *The New York Times*, April 15: A14.

1997b. "Sergeant Convicted of 18 Counts of Raping Female Subordinates." *The New York Times*, April 30: A1.

Scott, Janny. 1999. "Hunk, He-Man, Mensch, Milquetoast: The Masks of Masculinity." *The New York Times*, February 13: A19.

Scott, Jean. 1986. *Girls with Grit: Memories of the Australian Women's Land Army*. Boston: Allen & Unwin.

Scott, Joan Wallach. 1988. *Gender and the Politics of History*. New York: Columbia University Press.

Scott, John Paul. 1974. "Agonistic Behavior of Primates: A Comparative Perspective." In Holloway, ed.: 417–34.

Scott, John Paul and Benson E. Ginsburg. 1994. "The Seville Statement on Violence Revisited." *American Psychologist* 49, 10 (October): 849–50.

Scott, Wilbur J. and Sandra Carson Stanley. 1994. "Introduction: Sexual Orientation and Military Service." In Scott and Stanley eds.: xi–xx.

eds. 1994. *Gays and Lesbians in the Military: Issues, Concerns, and Contrasts.* New York: Aldine De Gruyter.

Seager, Joni. 1997. *The State of Women in the World Atlas: An International Atlas.* 2nd edition. New York: Penguin.

Sedghi, Hamideh. 1994. "Third World Feminist Perspectives on World Politics." In Beckman and D'Amico eds.: 89–108.

Segal, David R., Paul A. Gade, and Edgar M. Johnson. 1994. "Social Science Research on Homosexuals in the Military." In Scott and Stanley eds.: 33–52.

Segal, David R. and Mady Wechsler Segal. 1993. *Peacekeepers and Their Wives: American Participation in the Multinational Force and Observers.* Westport, CT: Greenwood.

Segal, Lynne. 1990. *Slow Motion: Changing Masculinities, Changing Men.* New Brunswick, NJ: Rutgers University Press.

Segal, Mady Wechsler. 1993. "Women in the Armed Forces." In Howes and Stevenson eds.: 81–93.

Seifert, Ruth. 1994. "War and Rape: A Preliminary Analysis." In Stiglmayer ed.: 54–72.

1995. "Destruktive Konstruktionen: Ein Beitrag zur Dekonstruktion des Verhaeltnisses von Militaer, Nation und Geschlecht." [Destructive Constructions: A Contribution to the Deconstruction of the Relationship of Military, Nation, and Sex.] In Erika Haas, ed., *Verwirrung der Geschlechter: Dekonstruktion und Feminismus.* Munich: Profil Verlag.

1996. "Der weibliche Koerper als Symbol und Zeichen: Geschlechtsspezifische Gewalt und die Kulturelle Konstruktion des Krieges" [The Female Body as a Symbol and a Sign: Gender-Specific Violence and the Cultural Construction of War.] In Andreas Gestrich, ed., *Gewalt im Krieg.* Münster: Jahrbuch für Historische Friedensforschung.

Seitz, Barbara, Linda Lobao, and Ellen Treadway. 1993. "No Going Back: Women's Participation in the Nicaraguan Revolution and in Postrevolutionary Movements." In Howes and Stevenson eds.: 167–84.

Serrano, M. A., A. Salvador, E. Gonzalez-Bono, C. Sanchis, and F. Suay. 2000. "Hormonal Responses to Competition." *Psicothema* 12, 3 (August): 440–44.

Sewall, May Wright. 1915. *Women, World War and Permanent Peace.* San Francisco: John J. Newbegin.

Seymour, Thomas Day. 1965. *Life in the Homeric Age.* New York: Biblo & Tannen.

Shalit, Ben. 1988. *The Psychology of Conflict and Combat.* New York: Praeger.

Shapiro, Michael J. and Hayward R. Alker, eds. 1996. *Challenging Boundaries: Global Flows, Territorial Identities.* Minneapolis: University of Minnesota Press.

Sharoni, Simona. 1995. *Gender and the Israeli–Palestinian Conflict: The Politics of Women's Resistance.* Syracuse, NY: Syracuse University Press.

1996a. "Israeli Women and the Politics of Peace." *Ms.* (March/April): 12–14.

1996b. "Gender and the Israeli–Palestinian Accord: Feminist Approaches to International Politics." In Kandiyoti ed.: 107–26.

Sharps, Matthew J., Jana L. Price, and John K. Williams. 1994. "Spatial Cognition and Gender." *Psychology of Women Quarterly* 18, 3 (September): 413–25.

Shaw, R. Paul and Yuwa Wong. 1989. *Genetic Seeds of Warfare: Evolution, Nationalism, and Patriotism*. Boston, MA: Unwin Hyman.

Shawver, Lois. 1996. "Sexual Modesty, the Etiquette of Disregard, and the Question of Gays and Lesbians in the Military." In Herek, Jobe, and Carney eds.: 226–46.

Shaywitz, Bennett A., Sally E. Shaywitz, Kenneth R. Pugh, R. Todd Constable, Pawel Skudlarski, Robert K. Fulbright, Richard A. Bronen, Jack M. Fletcher, Donald P. Shankweiler, Leonard Katz, and John C. Gore. 1995. "Sex Differences in the Functional Organization of the Brain for Language." *Nature* 373 (February): 607–9.

Shenon, Philip. 1997. "Army's Leadership Blamed in Report on Sexual Abuses." *The New York Times*, September 12: A1.

1998. "New Findings on Mixing Sexes in Military." *The New York Times*, January 21: A12.

Sherif, Muzafer and Carolyn W. Sherif. 1953. *Groups in Harmony and Tension: An Integration of Studies on Intergroup Relations*. New York: Harper.

Shils, Edward A. and Morris Janowitz. 1948. "Cohesion and Disintegration in the Wehrmacht in World War II." *Public Opinion Quarterly* (Summer): 280–315.

Shilts, Randy. 1993. *Conduct Unbecoming: Lesbians and Gays in the US Military – Vietnam to the Persian Gulf*. New York: St. Martin's.

Shiva, Vandana. 1993. *Monocultures of the Mind: Perspectives on Biodiversity and Biotechnology*. London: Zed.

Shostak, Marjorie. 1981. *Nisa: The Life and Words of a !Kung Woman*. Cambridge, MA: Harvard University Press.

Shoumatoff, Alex. 1986. *In Southern Light: Trekking through Zaire and the Amazon*. New York: Simon & Schuster.

Showalter, Elaine. 1987. "Rivers and Sassoon: The Inscription of Male Gender Anxieties." In Higonnet *et al.* eds.: 61–69.

Shukert, Elfrieda Berthiaume and Barbara Smith Scibetta. 1988. *War Brides of World War II*. New York: Penguin.

Shweder, Richard A. 1994. "What Do Men Want? A Reading List for the Male Identity Crisis." *The New York Times Book Review*, January 9: 3–24.

Siegel, Allan and Melissa K. Demetrikopoulos. 1993. "Hormones and Aggression." In Jay Schulkin, ed., *Hormonally Induced Changes in Mind and Brain*. San Diego, CA: Academic Press: 99–128.

Signorella, Margaret L., Wesley Jamison, and Martha Hansen Krupa. 1989. "Predicting Spatial Performance from Gender Stereotyping in Activity Preferences and in Self-Concept." *Developmental Psychology* 25, 1: 89–95.

Silver, Rae. 1992. "Environmental Factors Influencing Hormone Secretion." In Becker, Breedlove, and Crews eds.: 401–22.

Silverman, Jane M. and Donald S. Kumka. 1987. "Gender Differences in Attitudes toward Nuclear War and Disarmament." *Sex Roles* 16 (February): 189–203.

Simmel, Georg. 1955. *Conflict* [translated by Kurt H. Wolff] and *The Web of Group-Affiliations* [translated by Reinhard Bendix]. Glencoe, IL: Free Press.

Simons, Anna. 1997. "In War, Let Men Be Men." *The New York Times*. April 23: A31.

Simons, Marlise. 1998. "Landmark Bosnia Rape Trial: A Legal Morass." *The New York Times*, July 29: A3.

Simpson, Mark. 1994. *Male Impersonators: Men Performing Masculinity*. New York: Cassell.

Sipes, Richard G. 1975. "War, Combative Sports, and Aggression: A Preliminary Causal Model of Cultural Patterning." In Nettleship, Givens, and Nettleship eds.: 749–63.

Sivard, Ruth Leger. 1996. *World Military and Social Expenditures 1996*. 16th edition. Leesburg, VA: WMSE Publications.

Sizer, Lyde Cullen. 1992. "Acting Her Part: Narratives of Union Women Spies." In Clinton and Silber eds.: 114–33.

Skeat, Walter William and Charles Otto Blagden. [1906] 1966. *Pagan Races of the Malay Peninsula*. Volume I. New York: Barnes & Noble.

Small, Meredith F., ed. 1984. *Female Primates: Studies by Women Primatologists*. New York: Alan R. Liss.

1993. *Female Choices: Sexual Behavior of Female Primates*. Ithaca, NY: Cornell University Press.

1995. *What's Love Got To Do with It? The Evolution of Human Mating*. New York: Anchor Books.

Smith, Anthony D. 1991. *National Identity*. London: Penguin.

Smith, Bruce D. 1989. "Origins of Agriculture in Eastern North America." *Science* 246 (December): 1566–71.

Smith, Hedrick. 1971. "Foreign Policy: Kissinger at Hub." *The New York Times*, January 19: A1.

Smith, Paul. 1996. *Boys: Masculinities in Contemporary Culture*. Boulder, CO: Westview.

Smith, Peter K. 1989. "Ethological Approaches to the Study of Aggression in Children." In Archer and Browne eds.: 65–93.

Smith, R. Jeffrey. 1999. "Rape as a Weapon of War: Refugees Tell of Gang Assaults by Troops." *The Washington Post*, April 13: A1, A17.

Smith, Robert S. 1989. *Warfare and Diplomacy in Pre-Colonial West Africa*. 2nd edition. Madison: University of Wisconsin Press.

Smith, Tom W. 1984. "The Polls: Gender and Attitudes toward Violence." *Public Opinion Quarterly* 48: 384–96.

Snelgrave, William. [1734] 1971. *A New Account of Some Parts of Guinea and the Slave-Trade*. London: Frank Cass.

Snodgrass, Jon. 1979. "A Critique of the Men's Movement." In Evelyn Shapiro and Barry Shapiro, eds., *The Women Say, The Men Say: Women's Liberation and Men's Consciousness*. New York: Dell: 269–72.

Snow, Margaret Ellis, Carol Nagy Jacklin, and Eleanor E. Maccoby. 1983. "Sex-of-Child Differences in Father–Child Interaction at One Year of Age." *Child Development* 54: 227–32.

Snyder, Bonnie. 1998. "Kenya's Tanui Wins 2nd Boston Marathon: Countryman Chebet Is 3 Seconds Back." *The Washington Post*, April 21: E1.

Socolovsky, Jerome. 2000. "War Crimes Panel Examines Sex Case." The Hague: Associated Press, March 19.

Soderbergh, Peter A. 1992. *Women Marines: The World War II Era*. Westport, CT: Praeger.

Solo, Pam. 1988. *From Protest to Policy: Beyond the Freeze to Common Security*. Cambridge, MA: Ballinger.

Sommers, Christina Hoff. 2000. *The War against Boys: How Misguided Feminism Is Harming Our Young Men*. New York: Simon & Schuster.

Spears, Sally. 1998. *Call Sign Revlon: The Life and Death of Navy Fighter Pilot Kara Hultgreen*. Annapolis, MD: Naval Institute Press.

Spence, Jonathan D. 1996. *God's Chinese Son: The Taiping Heavenly Kingdom of Hong Xiuquan*. New York: W. W. Norton.

Spier, Leslie. 1930. *Klamath Ethnography*. Berkeley: University of California Press.

Spinner, Jackie. 1997a. "Pace of Complaints Cools to Army Abuse Hot Line." *The Washington Post*, May 25: A18.

    1997b. "The New Drill Sergeant." *The Washington Post Magazine*, August 24: 11–17, 25–27.

Spretnak, Charlene. 1990. "Ecofeminism: Our Roots and Flowering." In Diamond and Orenstein eds.: 3–14.

Springer, Sally P. and Georg Deutsch. 1993. *Left Brain, Right Brain*. 4th edition. New York: W. H. Freeman.

Stanley, Alessandra. 1998. "Russian Woman Sails Solo in a Sea of Cadets." *The New York Times*, March 27: A1.

Stanley, Jo, ed. 1995. *Bold in Her Breeches: Women Pirates across the Ages*. San Francisco: Pandora.

Stark, Suzanne J. 1996. *Female Tars: Women Aboard Ship in the Age of Sail*. Annapolis, MD: United States Naval Institute.

Steans, Jill. 1998. *Gender and International Relations: An Introduction*. New Brunswick, NJ: Rutgers University Press.

Stearns, Peter N. 1990. *Be a Man! Males in Modern Society*. New York: Holmes & Meier.

Stefansson, Vilhjalmur. [1921] 1943. *The Friendly Arctic: The Story of Five Years in Polar Regions*. New York: Greenwood.

Stephenson, Carolyn M. 1982. "Feminism, Pacifism, Nationalism, and the United Nations Decade for Women." *Women's Studies International Forum* 5, 3/4: 287–300.

Stern, Theodore. 1965. *The Klamath Tribe: A People and Their Reservation*. Seattle: University of Washington Press.

Steuernagel, Gertrude A. and Laurel U. Quinn. 1986. "Is Anyone Listening? Political Science and the Response to the Feminist Challenge." Presented at the American Political Science Association Annual Meeting, August 28–31, Washington, DC.

Stevens, Gwendolyn and Sheldon Gardner. 1994. *Separation Anxiety and the Dread of Abandonment in Adult Males*. Westport, CT: Praeger.

Stevens, Jane Ellen. 1994. "The Biology of Violence." *BioScience* 44, 5: 291–94.

Stevenson, Leslie. 1987. *Seven Theories of Human Nature*. 2nd edition. Oxford: Oxford University Press.

Steward, Julian H. [1938] 1970. *Basin-Plateau Aboriginal Sociopolitical Groups*. Washington, DC: US Government Printing Office. [Reprint. Salt Lake City: University of Utah Press.]

ed. 1948. *Handbook of South American Indians*. Volume III: *The Tropical Forest Tribes*. Washington, DC: US Government Printing Office.

Steward, Julian H. and Louis C. Faron. 1959. *Native Peoples of South America*. New York: McGraw-Hill.

Stiehm, Judith Hicks. 1981. *Bring Me Men and Women: Mandated Change at the US Air Force Academy*. Berkeley: University of California Press.

1982. "The Protected, the Protector, the Defender." *Women's Studies International Forum* 5, 3/4: 367–76.

ed. 1983. *Women and Men's Wars*. New York: Pergamon. [Previously published as a Special Issue of *Women's Studies International Forum* 5, 3 (1982).]

1988. "The Effect of Myths about Military Women on the Waging of War." In Isaksson ed.: 94–105.

1989. *Arms and the Enlisted Woman*. Philadelphia: Temple University Press.

1994. "The Military Ban on Homosexuals and the Cyclops Effect." In Scott and Stanley eds.: 149–64.

1996a. "Just the Facts, Ma'am." In Stiehm ed.: 60–72.

1996b. "The Civilian Mind." In Stiehm ed.: 270–96.

ed. 1996. *It's Our Military, Too!* Philadelphia: Temple University Press.

Stiglmayer, Alexandra. 1994a. "The War in the Former Yugoslavia." In Stiglmayer ed.: 1–34.

1994b. "Rape in Bosnia-Herzegovina." In Stiglmayer ed.: 82–169.

ed. 1994. *Mass Rape: The War against Women in Bosnia-Herzegovina*. Lincoln: University of Nebraska Press.

Stites, Richard. 1978. *The Women's Liberation Movement in Russia: Feminism, Nihilism, and Bolshevism 1860–1930*. Princeton, NJ: Princeton University Press.

Stobart, Mabel Annie (Boulton). 1913. *War and Women: From Experience in the Balkans and Elsewhere*. London: G. Bell.

Stockel, H. Henrietta. 1991. *Women of the Apache Nation: Voices of Truth*. Reno: University of Nevada Press.

Stone, Merlin. [1979] 1984. *Ancient Mirrors of Womanhood: A Treasury of Goddess and Heroine Lore from around the World*. Boston: Beacon.

Strange, Mary Zeiss. 1997. Letter to the editor. *Women's Review of Books* 14, 8 (March).

Sudetic, Chuck. 1998. *Blood and Vengeance: One Family's Story of the War in Bosnia*. New York: W. W. Norton.

Summerfield, Derek. 1997. "The Impact of War and Atrocity on Civilian Populations." In Black *et al.* eds.: 148–55.

Summerfield, Penny. 1984. *Women Workers in the Second World War: Production and Patriarchy in Conflict*. London: Croom Helm.

Summers, Anne. 1992. "Pat Schroeder: Fighting for Military Moms." In Blacksmith ed.: 129–32.

Sun, Marjorie. 1989. "Anthropologists Debate Tasaday Hoax Evidence." *Science* 246 (December): 1113.

Sun Tzu. 1963. *The Art of War*. Translated by Samuel B. Griffith. Oxford: Oxford University Press.

Sunday, Suzanne R. 1991. "Biological Theories of Animal Aggression." In Hunter ed.: 50–63.

Suplee, Curt. 1997. "Paleontology: Sizing up a View on Sexual Dimorphism." *The Washington Post*, August 25: A2.

2000. "Stressed Women Turn to Mother Nurture, Study Says." *The Washington Post*, May 19: A2.

Susman, Elizabeth J., Lorah D. Dorn, and George P. Chrousos. 1991. "Negative Affect and Hormone Levels in Young Adolescents: Concurrent and Predictive Perspectives." *Journal of Youth and Adolescence* 20, 2: 167–90.

Susman, Elizabeth J., Gale Inoff-Germain, Editha D. Nottelmann, D. Lynn Loriaux, Gordon B. Cutler, Jr., and George P. Chrousos. 1987. "Hormones, Emotional Dispositions, and Aggressive Attributes in Young Adolescents." *Child Development* 58: 1114–34.

Susman, Randall L., ed. 1984. *The Pygmy Chimpanzee: Evolutionary Biology and Behavior*. New York: Plenum.

Swerdlow, Amy. 1989. "Pure Milk, Not Poison: Women Strike for Peace and the Test Ban Treaty of 1963." In Harris and King eds.: 225–37.

1990. "Motherhood and the Subversion of the Military State: Women's Strike for Peace Confronts the House Committee on Un-American Activities." In Elshtain and Tobias eds.: 7–28.

Sylvester, Christine. 1989. "Patriarchy, Peace, and Women Warriors." In Forcey ed.: 97–112.

1992. "Feminists and Realists View Autonomy and Obligation in International Relations." In Peterson ed.: 155–78.

ed. 1993. "Feminists Write International Relations." [Special Issue.] *Alternatives* 18, 1 (Winter).

1994. *Feminist Theory and International Relations in a Postmodern Era*. Cambridge: Cambridge University Press.

Tajfel, H. and J. C. Turner. 1986. "The Social Identity Theory of Intergroup Behavior." In S. Worchel and W. Austin, eds., *Psychology of Intergroup Relations*. 2nd edition. Chicago: Nelson-Hall: 7–24.

Tannen, Deborah. 1990. *You Just Don't Understand: Women and Men in Conversation*. New York: Ballantine.

Taylor, Diana. 1993. "Spectacular Bodies: Gender, Terror, and Argentina's 'Dirty War.'" In Cooke and Woollacott eds.: 20–42.

1997. *Disappearing Acts: Spectacles of Gender and Nationalism in Argentina's "Dirty War."* Durham, NC: Duke University Press.

Taylor, Michael. 1976. *Anarchy and Cooperation*. New York: Wiley.

Taylor, Timothy. 1996. *The Prehistory of Sex: Four Million Years of Human Sexual Culture*. New York: Bantam.

Tessler, Mark and Ina Warriner. 1997. "Gender, Feminism, and Attitudes toward International Conflict: Exploring Relationships with Survey Data from the Middle East." *World Politics* 49 (January): 250–81.

Tetlock, Philip E. 1998. "Social Psychology and World Politics." In Gilbert, Fiske, and Lindzey eds.: 868–914.

Tetreault, Mary Ann. 1992. "Women and Revolution: A Framework for Analysis." In Peterson ed.: 99–122.

Thalbitzer, William. 1941. *The Ammassalik Eskimo: Contributions to the Ethnology of the East Greenland Natives*. Second Part. Copenhagen: C. A. Reitzels Forlag.

Theweleit, Klaus. 1987. *Male Fantasies, Volume I: Women, Floods, Bodies, History.* Minneapolis: University of Minnesota Press. [Translated from the German of 1977.]

Thomas, Elizabeth Marshall. 1959. *The Harmless People.* New York: Knopf.

Thomas, Patricia J. and Marie D. Thomas. 1996. "Integration of Women in the Military: Parallels to the Progress of Homosexuals?" In Herek, Jobe, and Carney eds.: 65–85.

Thompson, Carol B. 1982. "Women in the National Liberation Struggle in Zimbabwe: An Interview of Naomi Nhiwatiwa." *Women's Studies International Forum* 5, 3/4: 247–52.

Thompson, Dorothy. 1987. "Women, Peace and History: Notes for an Historical Overview." In Pierson ed.: 29–43.

    ed. 1983. *Over Our Dead Bodies: Women against the Bomb.* London: Virago Press.

Thompson, Leonard. 1969. "Co-operation and Conflict: The Zulu Kingdom and Natal." In Monica Wilson and Leonard Thompson, eds., *The Oxford History of South Africa.* Volume I: *South Africa to 1870.* Oxford: Oxford University Press: 334–90.

Thompson, Mark. 2000. "Aye, Aye, Ma'am: The Navy Makes History as It Sends the First US Warship Ever Commanded by a Woman toward the Troubled Waters of the Persian Gulf." *Time,* March 27: 30.

Thompson, Wendy M., James M. Dabbs, Jr., and Robert L. Frady. 1990. "Changes in Saliva Testosterone Levels during a 90-Day Shock Incarceration Program." *Criminal Justice and Behavior* 17, 2: 246–52.

Thorne, Barrie. 1993. *Gender Play: Girls and Boys in School.* New Brunswick, NJ: Rutgers University Press.

Thucydides. 1972. *History of the Peloponnesian War.* Translated by R. Warner. New York: Penguin.

Tickner, J. Ann. 1991. "Hans Morgenthau's Principles of Political Realism: A Feminist Reformulation." In Grant and Newland eds.: 27–40.

    1992. *Gender in International Relations: Feminist Perspectives on Achieving Global Security.* New York: Columbia University Press.

    1994. "A Feminist Critique of Political Realism." In Beckman and D'Amico eds.: 29–40.

    1997. "You Just Don't Understand: Troubled Engagements between Feminists and IR Theorists." *International Studies Quarterly* 41, 4 (December): 611–32.

    1998. "Continuing the Conversation . . ." *International Studies Quarterly* 42: 205–10.

Tiger, Lionel. 1969. *Men in Groups.* New York: Vintage.

    1978. "Introduction." In Tiger and Fowler eds.: 1–20.

Tiger, Lionel and Heather T. Fowler, eds. 1978. *Female Hierarchies.* Chicago, IL: Beresford Book Service.

Tiger, Lionel and Robin Fox. 1971. *The Imperial Animal.* New York: Holt, Rinehart and Winston.

Tiger, Lionel and Michael H. Robinson. 1991. "Introduction." In Robinson and Tiger eds.: xvii–xxiii.

Timothy, Kristen. 1995. "Women as Insiders: The Glass Ceiling at the United Nations." In D'Amico and Beckman eds.: 85–94.

Tlas, Mustafa. 1998. "World in Brief." *The Washington Post*, January 3: A16.

Tobias, Sheila. 1990. "Shifting Heroisms: The Uses of Military Service in Politics." In Elshtain and Tobias eds.: 163–86.

Tonkinson, Robert. 1978. *The Mardudjara Aborigines: Living the Dream in Australia's Desert.* New York: Holt, Rinehart and Winston.

Trainor, Bernard E. 1989. "Grim Battle Order Set in Campaign to Mold Well-Read Marines." *The New York Times*, August 10: A8.

Treadwell, Mattie E. 1954. *United States Army in World War II, Special Studies: The Women's Army Corps.* Washington, DC: Office of the Chief of Military History, Dept. of the Army.

Trexler, Richard C. 1995. *Sex and Conquest: Gendered Violence, Political Order, and the European Conquest of the Americas.* Ithaca, NY: Cornell University Press.

Trinh, T. Minh-ha. 1989. *Woman, Native, Other: Writing Postcoloniality and Feminism.* Bloomington: Indiana University Press.

Tripp, Nathaniel. 1996. *Father, Soldier, Son: Memoir of a Platoon Leader in Vietnam.* South Royalton, VT: Steerforth Press.

Tronto, Joan C. 1987. "Beyond Gender Difference to a Theory of Care." *Signs: Journal of Women in Culture and Society* 12, 4: 644–63.

Trustram, Myna. 1984. *Women of the Regiment: Marriage and the Victorian Army.* Cambridge: Cambridge University Press.

Tuana, Nancy. 1983. "Re-Fusing Nature/Nurture." *Women's Studies International Forum* 6, 6: 621–32.

Tuchman, Barbara W. 1979. *A Distant Mirror: The Calamitous 14th Century.* New York: Knopf.

    1984. *The March of Folly: From Troy to Vietnam.* New York: Ballantine.

Turiel, Elliot. 1998. "The Development of Morality." In Damon and Eisenberg eds.: 863–932.

Turnbull, Colin M. 1961. *The Forest People.* New York: Simon & Schuster.

    1965. *Wayward Servants: The Two Worlds of the African Pygmies.* Garden City, NY: Natural History Press.

    1983. *The Mbuti Pygmies: Change and Adaptation.* New York: Holt, Rinehart and Winston.

Turner, Angela K. 1994. "Genetic and Hormonal Influences on Male Violence." In Archer ed.: 233–52.

Turner, Fred. 1996 *Echoes of Combat: The Vietnam War in American Memory.* New York: Doubleday.

Turner, Karen Gottschang (with Phan Thanh Hao). 1998. *Even the Women Must Fight: Memories of War from North Vietnam.* New York: Wiley.

Turner, Paul R. and David Pitt, eds. 1989. *The Anthropology of War and Peace: Perspectives on the Nuclear Age.* Granby, MA: Bergin & Garvey.

Turney-High, Harry Holbert. 1971. *Primitive War: Its Practice and Concepts.* 2nd edition. Columbia: University of South Carolina Press.

Turpin, Jennifer. 1998. "Many Faces: Women Confronting War." In Lorentzen and Turpin eds.: 3–18.

Turpin, Jennifer E. and Lester R. Kurtz, eds. 1997. *The Web of Violence: From Interpersonal to Global.* Urbana: University of Illinois Press.

Tuten, Jeff M. 1982. "Germany and the World Wars." In Goldman ed.: 47–60.

Twitchett, Denis and Michael Loewe, eds. 1986. *The Cambridge History of China, Volume I: The Ch'in and Han Empires, 221 B.C.–A.D. 220.* Cambridge: Cambridge University Press.

Tylee, Claire M. 1990. *The Great War and Women's Consciousness: Images of Militarism and Womanhood in Women's Writings, 1914–64.* Iowa City: University of Iowa Press.

Tyrrell, William Blake. 1984. *Amazons: A Study in Athenian Mythmaking.* Baltimore: Johns Hopkins University Press.

Udry, J. Richard and Luther M. Talbert. 1988. "Sex Hormone Effects on Personality at Puberty." *Journal of Personality and Social Psychology* 54, 2: 291–95.

Uglow, Jennifer S., ed. 1989. *The Continuum Dictionary of Women's Biography: New Expanded Edition.* New York: Continuum.

Ulman, Richard B. and Doris Brothers. 1988. *The Shattered Self: A Psychoanalytic Study of Trauma.* Hillsdale, NJ: Analytic Press.

United Nations Development Program. 1998. *Human Development Report.* Oxford: Oxford University Press.

United Nations Division for the Advancement of Women. 1995. "The Role of Women in United Nations Peace-Keeping." *Women 2000* (December): 1–10.

Unterhalter, Elaine. 1987. "Women Soldiers and White Unity in Apartheid South Africa." In Macdonald, Holden, and Ardener eds.: 100–21.

US Army. 1982. *Women in the Army Policy Review.* Washington, DC: Office of the Deputy Chief of Staff for Personnel, Department of the Army, November.

1995. "Gender Integration of Basic Combat Training." [Newsletter.] Summer.

US Army, Research Institute for the Behavioral and Social Sciences. 1996. "Update on Gender-Integrated Basic Combat Training Study." (http://www.ari.army.mil/110504.html.)

US Department of Defense. 1992. *Tailhook 91: Part 1 – Review of the Navy Investigation.* Department of Defense, Office of Inspector General. September.

US General Accounting Office. 1993. *Homosexuals in the Military: Policies and Practices of Foreign Countries.* Washington, DC: GAO, NSIAD-93-215. June.

US House of Representatives, Committee on Armed Services. 1992. *Women in the Military: The Tailhook Affair and the Problem of Sexual Harassment: A Report of the Defense Policy Panel and the Military Personnel and Compensation Subcommittee.* September.

Van Creveld, Martin. 1985. *Command in War.* Cambridge, MA: Harvard University Press.

1991. *The Transformation of War.* New York: The Free Press.

1993. "Why Israel Doesn't Send Women into Combat." *Parameters* 23, 1: 5–9.

Van Der Dennen, J. M. G. 1990a. "Origin and Evolution of 'Primitive' Warfare." In Van Der Dennen and Falger eds.: 149–88.

1990b. "Primitive War and the Ethnological Inventory Project." In Van Der Dennen and Falger eds.: 247–69.

Van Der Dennen, J. and V. Falger. 1990. "Introduction." In Van Der Dennen and Falger eds.: 1–19.

eds. 1990. *Sociobiology and Conflict: Evolutionary Perspectives on Competition, Cooperation, Violence and Warfare.* New York: Chapman & Hall.

Van Hooff, J. A. R. A. M. 1990. "Intergroup Competition and Conflict in Animals and Man." In Van Der Dennen and Falger eds.: 23–54.

Vansant, Jacqueline. 1988. *Against the Horizon: Feminism and Postwar Austrian Women Writers*. New York: Greenwood.

Vansina, Jan. 1966. *Kingdoms of the Savanna*. Madison: University of Wisconsin Press.

Vasquez, John A. 1993. *The War Puzzle*. Cambridge: Cambridge University Press.
    ed. 2000. *What Do We Know about War?* Lanham, MD: Rowman & Littlefield.

Vayda, A. P. 1960. *Maori Warfare*. Melbourne: A. H. & A. W. Reed.
    1967. "Hypotheses about Functions of War." In Fried, Harris, and Murphy eds.: 85–91.

Veldhuis, J. D., J. C. King, R. J. Urban, A. D. Rogol, W. S. Evans, S. A. Kolp, and M. L. Johnson. 1987. "Operating Characteristics of the Male Hypothalamo-Pituitary-Gonadal Axis: Pulsatile Release of Testosterone and Follicle-Stimulating Hormone and Their Temporal Coupling with Luteinizing Hormone. *Journal of Clinical Endocrinology and Metabolism* 65: 929–41.

Vickers, Jeanne. 1993. *Women and War*. London: Zed.

Viotti, Paul R. and Mark V. Kauppi, eds. 1999. *International Relations Theory: Realism, Globalism, and Beyond*. 3rd edition. Needham Heights, MA: Allyn & Bacon.

Von Habsburg, Otto. 1969. *Charles V.* [Translated from the French of 1967 by Michael Ross.] New York: Praeger.

Voyer, Daniel, Susan Voyer, and M. P. Bryden. 1995. "Magnitude of Sex Differences in Spatial Abilities: A Meta-Analysis and Consideration of Critical Variables." *Psychological Bulletin* 117, 2: 250–70.

Waisbrooker, Lois. 1894. *A Sex Revolution*. 2nd edition. Topeka: Independent Publishing.

Waite, Robert G. L. 1990. "Leadership Pathologies: The Kaiser and the Führer and the Decisions for War in 1914 and 1939." In Glad ed.: 143–68.

Walby, Sylvia. 1990. *Theorizing Patriarchy*. Cambridge, MA: Basil Blackwell.

Walker, R. B. J. 1988. *One World, Many Worlds: Struggles for a Just World Peace*. Boulder, CO: Lynne Rienner.
    1992. *Inside/Outside: International Relations as Political Theory*. Cambridge: Cambridge University Press.

Wallace, Anthony F. C. 1967. "Psychological Preparations for War." In Fried, Harris, and Murphy eds.: 173–82.

Wallis, William. 1997. "It's Make War Not Love for Congo's Colorful 'Amazon' Warriors." *Stars and Stripes*, December 1–14: 21.

Walsh, Mary Roth, ed. 1997. *Women, Men, and Gender: Ongoing Debates*. New Haven, CT: Yale University Press.

Walsh, Maurice N. and Barbara G. Scandalis. 1975. "Institutionalized Forms of Intergenerational Male Aggression." In Nettleship, Givens, and Nettleship eds.: 135–55.

Walt, Vivienne. 1999. "Trained to Kill, and Growing in Number." *The Washington Post*, February 28: B3.

Walton, Patty. 1981. "The Culture in our Blood." *Women: A Journal of Liberation* 8, 1: 39–45.

Waltz, Kenneth Neal. 1959. *Man, the State and War: A Theoretical Analysis.* New York: Columbia University Press.

1979. *Theory of International Politics.* Reading, MA: Addison-Wesley.

Walzer, Michael. 1977. *Just and Unjust Wars: A Moral Argument with Historical Illustrations.* New York: Basic.

Ward, Benjamin. 1979. *The Ideal Worlds of Economics: Liberal, Radical and Conservative Economic World Views.* New York: Basic.

Warren, Karen J. and Duane L. Cady. 1996. "Feminism and Peace: Seeing Connections." In Warren and Cady eds.: 1–15.

eds. 1996. *Bringing Peace Home: Feminism, Violence, and Nature.* Bloomington: Indiana University Press.

Washburn, Patricia. 1993. "Women and the Peace Movement." In Howes and Stevenson eds.: 135–48.

Washington Post, The. 1998. "Norway Unveils Men's Equal Rights Program." *The Washington Post,* July 19: A24.

Watkins, T. 1989. "The Beginnings of Warfare." In General Sir John Hackett, ed., *Warfare: In the Ancient World.* New York: Facts on File: 15–35.

Watson, Bruce Allen. 1997. *When Soldiers Quit: Studies in Military Disintegration.* Westport, CT: Praeger.

Watson, Ernest H. and George H. Lowrey. 1967. *Growth and Development of Children.* 5th edition. Chicago: Year Book Medical.

Weatherford, Doris. 1990. *History of Women in America: American Women and World War II.* New York: Facts on File.

Weber, Rachel N. 1997. "Manufacturing Gender in Commercial and Military Cockpit Design." *Science, Technology, and Human Values* 22, 2 (Spring): 235–53.

Weiner, Bernard, Anna J. Stone, Mary D. Schmitz, Adeny Schmidt, Anthony C. R. Hernandez, and Cynthia J. Benton. 1983. "Compounding the Errors: A Reply to Pollak and Gilligan." *Journal of Personality and Social Psychology* 45, 5: 1176–78.

Weinstein, Laurie and Christie White. 1997. *Wives and Warriors: Women and the Military in the United States and Canada.* Westport, CT: Bergin & Garvey.

Weisfeld, Glenn. 1994. "Aggression and Dominance in the Social World of Boys." In Archer ed.: 42–69.

Weiss, R. 1988. "Women's Skills Linked to Estrogen Levels." *Science News* 134, 22 (November 26): 341.

Weitz, Margaret Collins. 1995. *Sisters in the Resistance: How Women Fought to Free France, 1940–1945.* New York: Wiley.

Wells-Petry, Melissa. 1993. *Exclusion: Homosexuals and the Right to Serve.* Washington, DC: Regnery Gateway.

Wetzsteon, Ross. 1979. "A Feminist Man?" In Evelyn Shapiro and Barry Shapiro, eds., *The Women Say, the Men Say: Women's Liberation and Men's Consciousness.* New York: Dell: 25–26.

Weule, Karl. 1916. *Der Krieg in den Tiefen der Menschheit.* Stuttgart.

Wheeler, Bonnie and Charles T. Wood, eds. 1996. *Fresh Verdicts on Joan of Arc.* New York: Garland.

Wheelwright, Julie. 1989. *Amazons and Military Maids: Women Who Dressed as Men in the Pursuit of Life, Liberty and Happiness.* London: Pandora.

White, Christine A. 1994. "An Introduction." In Anne Noggle, *A Dance with Death: Soviet Airwomen in World War II.* College Station: Texas A&M University Press: 3–14.

White, Philip G. and Anne B. Vagi. 1990. "Rugby in the 19th-Century British Boarding-School System: A Feminist Psychoanalytic Perspective." In Messner and Sabo eds.: 67–78.

Whiten, A., J. Goodall, W. C. McGrew, T. Nishida, V. Reynolds, Y. Sugiyama, C. E. G. Tutin, R. W. Wrangham, and C. Boesch. 1999. "Cultures in Chimpanzees." *Nature* 399: 682–85.

Whites, Lee Ann. 1995. *The Civil War as a Crisis in Gender: Augusta, Georgia, 1860–1890.* Athens: University of Georgia Press.

Whiting, Beatrice B. and C. P. Edwards. 1988. *Children of Different Worlds: The Formation of Social Behavior.* Cambridge, MA: Harvard University Press.

Whiting, Beatrice B. and John W. M. Whiting [in collaboration with Richard Longabaugh]. 1975. *Children of Six Cultures: A Psycho-Cultural Analysis.* Cambridge, MA: Harvard University Press.

Whitten, Patricia L. 1984. "Competition among Female Vervet Monkeys." In Small ed.: 127–40.

Whitworth, Sandra. 1994a. *Feminism and International Relations: Towards a Political Economy of Gender in Interstate and Non-Governmental Institutions.* New York: St. Martin's.

  1994b. "Feminist Theories: From Women to Gender and World Politics." In Beckman and D'Amico eds.: 75–88.

Whyte, Martin King. 1978. *The Status of Women in Preindustrial Societies.* Princeton, NJ: Princeton University Press.

Wicks, Stephen. 1996. *Warriors and Wildmen: Men, Masculinity, and Gender.* Westport, CT: Bergin & Garvey.

Widom, C. S. 1989. "The Cycle of Violence." *Science* 224: 160–66.

Wilden, Anthony. 1987. *Man and Woman, War and Peace: The Strategist's Companion.* New York: Routledge & Kegan Paul.

Wilford, John Noble. 1994. "Sexes Equal on South Sea Isle." *The New York Times,* March 29: C1.

  1997a. "Ancient Graves of Armed Women Hint at Amazons." *The New York Times,* February 25: C1, C6.

  1997b. "New Clues to History of Male and Female." *New York Times,* August 26: C1.

Wilhelm, J. H. 1953. "Die !Kung-Buschleute." In *Jahrbuch des Museums für Völkerkunde zu Leipzig.* Berlin: Akademie-Verlag: 110–89.

Wilhelm, Maria de Blasio. 1988. *The Other Italy: Italian Resistance in World War II.* New York: W. W. Norton.

Wilke, Timothy J. and David J. Utley. 1987. "Total Testosterone, Free-Androgen Index, Calculated Free Testosterone, and Free Testosterone by Analog RIA Compared in Hirsute Women and in Otherwise-Normal Women with Altered Binding of Sex-Hormone-Binding Globulin." *Clinical Chemistry* 33, 8: 1372–75.

Williams, Christina L., Allison M. Barnett, and Warren H. Meck. 1990. "Organizational Effects of Early Gonadal Secretions on Sexual Differentiation in Spatial Memory." *Behavioral Neuroscience* 104, 1: 84–97.

Williams, Harvey. 1995. "Violeta Barrios de Chamorro." In D'Amico and Beckman eds.: 31–44.

Williams, John E. and Deborah L. Best. 1982. *Measuring Sex Stereotypes: A Thirty-Nation Study*. Beverly Hills, CA: Sage.

Wilson, Edward O. 1975. *Sociobiology: The New Synthesis*. Cambridge, MA: Harvard University Press.

1978. *On Human Nature*. Cambridge, MA: Harvard University Press.

Wiltsher, Anne. 1985. *Most Dangerous Women: Feminist Peace Campaigners of the Great War*. Boston, MA: Pandora.

Winfield, Pamela, in collaboration with Brenda Wilson Hasty. 1984. *Sentimental Journey: The Story of the GI Brides*. London: Constable.

Winnicott, D. W. 1965. *The Maturational Processes and the Facilitating Environment*. New York: International Universities Press.

Wish Stream, The [By P.W.C.]. 1964. "The Maria Theresa Military Academy Wiener-Neustadt." *The Wish Stream: The Journal of the Royal Military Academy Sandhurst* (Spring.)

Woehrle, Lynne M. 1996. "Silent or Silenced?" *Peace Review* 8, 3: 417–21.

Wood, Charles T. 1996. "Joan of Arc's Mission and the Lost Record of Her Interrogation at Poitiers." In Wheeler and Wood eds.: 19–30.

Woolf, Virginia. 1938. *Three Guineas*. New York: Harcourt, Brace.

Woollacott, Angela. 1994. *On Her Their Lives Depend: Munitions Workers in the Great War*. Berkeley: University of California Press.

1996. "Women Munitions Makers, War and Citizenship." *Peace Review* 8, 3: 373–78.

Wrangham, Richard and Dale Peterson. 1996. *Demonic Males: Apes and the Origins of Human Violence*. New York: Houghton Mifflin.

Wright, Quincy. [1942] 1965. *A Study of War*. Volume I. Chicago: University of Chicago Press.

Wright, Robert. 1994. *The Moral Animal: The New Science of Evolutionary Psychology*. New York: Pantheon.

Yayori, Matsui. 1997. "Asian Migrant Women in Japan." In Sandra Buckley, ed., *Broken Silence: Voices of Japanese Feminism*. Berkeley: University of California Press: 143–54.

York, Jodi. 1996. "The Truth(s) about Women and Peace." *Peace Review* 8, 3: 323–29.

Young, Allan. 1995. *The Harmony of Illusions: Inventing Post-Traumatic Stress Disorder*. Princeton, NJ: Princeton University Press.

Young, Iris Marion. 1990. "The Ideal of Community and the Politics of Difference." In Nicholson ed.: 300–23.

Yu Hui. [forthcoming]. "A Study of Ch'en Chi-chih's *Treaty at the Pien Bridge*." In *Arts of the Sung and Yuan*. Edited by The Art Museum, Princeton University.

Yudkin, Marcia. 1982. "Reflections on Woolf's Three Guineas." *Women's Studies International Forum* 5, 3/4: 263–69.

Zahn-Waxler, Carolyn, E. Mark Cummings, and Ronald Iannotti. 1986. "Introduction: Altruism and Aggression: Problems and Progress in Research." In Zahn-Waxler, Cummings, and Iannotti eds.: 1–18.

eds. 1986. *Altruism and Aggression: Biological and Social Origins*. Cambridge: Cambridge University Press.

Zalewski, Marysia. 1998. "Introduction: From the 'Woman' Question to the 'Man' Question in International Relations." In Zalewski and Parpart eds.: 1–13.

Zalewski, Marysia and Jane Parpart, eds. 1998. *The "Man" Question in International Relations*. Boulder, CO: Westview.

Zihlman, Adrienne L. 1984. "Body Build and Tissue Composition in *Pan paniscus* and *Pan troglodytes*, with Comparisons to Other Hominoids." In Susman ed.: 179–200.

Zihlman, Adrienne and Nancy Tanner. 1978. "Gathering and the Hominid Adaptation." In Tiger and Fowler eds.: 163–94.

Zillmann, Dolf. 1984. *Connections between Sex and Aggression*. Hillsdale, NJ: Lawrence Erlbaum Associates.

Zuger, Abigail. 1998a. "A Fistful of Hostility Is Found in Women." *The New York Times*, July 28: C1.

1998b. "Many Prostitutes Suffer Combat Disorders, Study Finds." *The New York Times*, August 18: C8.

Zuniga, Jose. 1995. *Soldier of the Year: The Story of a Gay American Patriot*. [Tom Miller, ed.] New York: Pocket.

Zur, Ofer. 1987. "The Psychohistory of Warfare: The Co-Evolution of Culture, Psyche and Enemy." *Journal of Peace Research* 24, 2: 125–34.

1989. "War Myths: Exploration of the Dominant Collective Beliefs about Warfare." *Journal of Humanistic Psychology* 29, 3: 297–327.

Zur, Ofer and Andrea Morrison. 1989. "Gender and War: Reexamining Attitudes." *American Journal of Orthopsychiatry* 59, 4: 528–33.

Author index

Adam, Barry D., 375 n. 114, 379 nn. 126, 127
Adams, Carol J., 47 n. 81
Adams, David B., 225 n. 111, 226, 226 nn. 112, 113, 227 Table 4.1
Adams, Gerald R., 146 n. 33
Adams, Judith Porter, 324 n. 181
Addams, Jane, 324 n. 182
Addis, Elisabetta, 40 n. 65, 100 n. 108
Adorno, T. W., 240 n. 156
Agence France-Presse, 343 n. 26
Aguilar-San Juan, Delia, 78 n. 44
Ahmad, Yvette, 136 n. 13
Ajayi, J. F. Ade, 61 n. 4, 64 n. 9
Alavi, Abass, in Gur et al., 173 n. 89
Albert, David, 325 n. 185
Albright, Madeleine K., 19, 19 n. 20, 42 n. 71
Alcoff, Linda, 51 n. 88
Alcorta, Candace Storey, 241 n. 158
Alexandre, Laurien, 38 n. 61
Alker, Hayward R., 36 n. 60, 36 Table 1.2
Alonso, Harriet Hyman, 57 n. 103, 324 n. 181
Alpern, Stanley B., 11 n. 9, 17 n. 19, 61, 61 nn. 3, 4, 63 nn. 6, 7, 64 nn. 9, 10, 77 n. 43, 122 n. 151, 199 n. 39, 257 n. 18, 358 n. 66, 381 n. 130
Ambrose, Stephen E., 159 n. 60, 164 n. 70, 166, 166 nn. 75, 76, 196 n. 32, 197 n. 34, 203 n. 53, 255, 255 nn. 10, 11, 257 n. 16, 258 n. 21, 262 n. 30, 267 n. 44, 277 n. 70, 278, 278 n. 71, 308 nn. 145, 146, 309 n. 149, 314 n. 160, 337, 338, 338 n. 13, 359 n. 69, 362 n. 74, 400 n. 176
American Psychiatric Association, 260 n. 25
Andersen, Margaret L., 143 n. 29
Andersen-Boers, Marion, 378 n. 124
Anderson, Anne, 368 n. 97
Anderson, Benedict, 227, 227 n. 115

Anderson, Florence Mary, 11 n. 9
Anderson, Karen, 339 nn. 16, 17, 387 nn. 147, 149, 394 nn. 161–63
Andrew, Barbara, 44 n. 74
Andy, Orlando J., 136 n. 12
Angell, Norman, 56 n. 99
Angier, Natalie, 53 n. 92, 131 n. 6, 138 n. 20, 139 n. 21, 143 n. 29, 145 n. 32, 150 n. 39, 177 n. 97, 181 n. 111, 189 n. 12, 192 n. 22, 204 n. 54, 246–47, 247 n. 172, 298 n. 122
Apostoleris, Nicholas F., 233 n. 130
Archer, John, 135 n. 10, 136 n. 13, 137 n. 15, 151 nn. 43, 44, 152 n. 46, 154 n. 49, 177 n. 99, 237 n. 146, 241 n. 158, 243 nn. 162–64, 244 nn. 165, 166
Ardrey, Robert, 52 n. 91
Aristophanes, 44, 44 n. 75
Aristotle, 55, 55 n. 98
Arnold, Steven E., in Gur et al., 173 n. 89
Aron, Raymond, 35 n. 56
Ashworth, Lucian M., 359 n. 69
Aspy, Catherine L., 159 n. 60
Associated Press, 85 n. 64, 98 n. 103, 243 n. 162
Astrachan, Anthony, 105 n. 116, 164 n. 69, 196 n. 32, 202 n. 48, 283 n. 85, 305 n. 139, 372 n. 106
Axelrod, Robert, 52 n. 91, 215 n. 82
Ayers, Pat, 321 n. 177
Ayscough, Florence, 107 n. 118

Bacon, Francis, 52
Badrian, Alison, 200 n. 41
Badrian, Noel, 200 n. 41
Bagatell, Carrie J., 146 n. 36, 153 n. 47, 156 n. 55
Bailey, Beth, 345 n. 32
Baker, Rodney R., 263 n. 31, 314 n. 161
Baldwin, David A., 57 n. 102
Ball, Eve, 114 n. 131
Ballard, Richard F., 97 n. 101

481

Subject index

CPSIA information can be obtained
at www.ICGtesting.com
Printed in the USA
LVHW091308140122
708384LV00010B/22